MW01079034

THE OXFORD HANDBOOK OF

MODERN EGYPTIAN HISTORY

THE OXFORD HANDBOOK OF

MODERN EGYPTIAN HISTORY

Edited by

BETH BARON

and

JEFFREY CULANG

OXFORD
UNIVERSITY PRESS

Oxford University Press is a department of the University of Oxford. It furthers
the University's objective of excellence in research, scholarship, and education
by publishing worldwide. Oxford is a registered trade mark of Oxford University
Press in the UK and certain other countries.

Published in the United States of America by Oxford University Press
198 Madison Avenue, New York, NY 10016, United States of America.

© Oxford University Press 2024

All rights reserved. No part of this publication may be reproduced, stored in
a retrieval system, or transmitted, in any form or by any means, without the
prior permission in writing of Oxford University Press, or as expressly permitted
by law, by license, or under terms agreed with the appropriate reproduction
rights organization. Inquiries concerning reproduction outside the scope of the
above should be sent to the Rights Department, Oxford University Press, at the
address above.

You must not circulate this work in any other form
and you must impose this same condition on any acquirer.

Library of Congress Cataloging-in-Publication Data
Names: Baron, Beth, editor. | Culang, Jeffrey, editor.
Title: The Oxford handbook of modern Egyptian history /
[edited by] Beth Baron and Jeffrey Culang.
Description: New York, NY : Oxford University Press, [2024] |
Series: Oxford handbooks series | Collection of essays by Khaled Fahmy and
24 others. | Includes bibliographical references and index.
Identifiers: LCCN 2023033398 (print) | LCCN 2023033399 (ebook) |
ISBN 9780190072742 (hb) | ISBN 9780197675496 (epub) | ISBN 9780190072766
Subjects: LCSH: Egypt—History—1798– | Egypt—Civilization—1798–
Classification: LCC DT100 .O84 2024 (print) | LCC DT100 (ebook) |
DDC 962—dc23/eng/20230927
LC record available at https://lccn.loc.gov/2023033398
LC ebook record available at https://lccn.loc.gov/2023033399

DOI: 10.1093/oxfordhb/9780190072742.001.0001

Printed by Sheridan Books, Inc., United States of America

Contents

PART III. LAW AND SOCIETY

PART IV. TEXTUAL, PERFORMATIVE, AND VISUAL CULTURE

ACKNOWLEDGMENTS

THIS volume would not have been possible without the editorial assistance of Tamara Maatouk, who helped to push the project along at pivotal moments. We are very grateful for her excellent editing, assistance with the art project, and hard work to compile the index. The volume would not have come to fruition without the enthusiasm of the authors, who persisted through the pandemic in finalizing their contributions. We thank them for their trust in us to see this project through to publication.

It is with great sadness that we note that one of the authors, Kathryn Schwartz, did not live to see her chapter in print. We thank Omar Cheta for stepping up to finalize her contribution for publication. We hope that the inclusion of her piece in the handbook will be a testimony to her bright light and brilliance, which are sorely missed by friends and colleagues.

Many of the chapters in this volume went through a blind review process, and we thank the reviewers for generously giving of their time to strengthen them. Robert Tignor reviewed several chapters and the initial book proposal before his passing in 2022. Over the course of his career, he inspired, shaped, and left his imprint on many historians of Egypt, including more than a few contributors to this handbook.

We would like to extend a special thanks to the artist Mohamed Abla for giving his permission to feature his painting, *The Square II* (2022), on the cover of the book. The square depicted, ʿAbd al-Munʿim Riyad, is in Cairo. While no single image reflects all the themes brought out in this volume, we think this painting conveys both everyday life in Egypt and ideas about time, space, motion, and change inherent to historical questions. We are grateful to Alzahraa K. Ahmed for connecting us with the artist and facilitating the permission process. Gallery Misr kindly shared an image of the painting. On behalf of all the contributors to this handbook, we would like to thank all of the archivists, librarians, and books sellers in Egypt and around the world who helped us to access sources.

It has been our pleasure to work as a team once again, recalling our days as collaborators at the *International Journal of Middle East Studies*. This handbook began with an invitation from Alexandra Dauler at Oxford University Press, who handed us off to the team of Nancy Toff and Brent Matheny, who in turn passed us on to the production team of Jayanthi Dineshkumar and Cindy Angelini. We thank all those at Oxford University Press, past and present, who were involved.

Contributors

Zeinab Abul-Magd is a professor in the Department of History and Chair of International Affairs, Oberlin College.

On Barak is a professor in the Department of Middle Eastern and African History, Tel Aviv University.

Beth Baron is a distinguished professor of history at the City College and Graduate Center, City University of New York and Director of the Middle East and Middle Eastern American Center at the Graduate Center.

Soha Bayoumi is a senior lecturer in the Medicine, Science, and the Humanities program, Johns Hopkins University.

Lucia Carminati is an associate professor in the Department of Archaeology, Conservation and History, University of Oslo.

Omar Cheta is an assistant professor in the History Department and Senior Research Associate in the Middle Eastern Studies Program, Syracuse University.

Jeffrey Culang is a historian of modern Egypt and the Middle East.

Kenneth M. Cuno is a professor emeritus in the Department of History, University of Illinois Urbana-Champaign.

Jennifer L. Derr is an associate professor in the Department of History and Founding Director of the Center for the Middle East and North Africa, University of California, Santa Cruz.

Yoav Di-Capua is a professor in the Department of History, University of Texas at Austin.

Khaled Fahmy is the Edward Keller Professor of North Africa and the Middle East in the Department of History, Tufts University.

Israel Gershoni is a professor in the Department of Middle Eastern and African History, Tel Aviv University.

Pascale Ghazaleh is an associate professor in the Department of History, American University in Cairo.

Carmen Gitre is an associate professor in the Department of History, Virginia Tech.

Joel Gordon is a professor in the Department of History and the King Fahd Center for Middle East Studies, University of Arkansas.

Anthony Gorman is a senior lecturer in Modern Middle Eastern History, University of Edinburgh.

Hanan Hammad is a professor in the Department of History and Director of Middle East Studies, Texas Christian University.

Emad Ahmad Helal is a professor in the Department of History, Suez Canal University.

Hanan Kholoussy is an associate professor in the Department of History, American University in Cairo.

Liat Kozma is an associate professor in the Department of Islamic and Middle Eastern Studies, Hebrew University of Jerusalem.

Nancy Y. Reynolds is an associate professor of History, of Women, Gender and Sexuality Studies, and of Jewish, Islamic, and Middle Eastern Studies, Washington University in St. Louis.

Lucie Ryzova is an associate professor of Middle East History in the Department of History, University of Birmingham.

Kathryn A. Schwartz was an assistant professor in the Department of History, University of Massachusetts Amherst.

James Whidden is a professor in the Department of History and Classics, Acadia University.

Hoda A. Yousef is an associate professor in the Department of History, Denison University.

INTRODUCTION

New Directions in Egyptian History

BETH BARON AND JEFFREY CULANG

This book originated with an invitation from Oxford University Press to fill a void in Egyptian history in its Oxford Handbooks series, which offers high-level surveys of the state of the art. Thinking that the time was ripe for such a book on Egypt—it had been two decades since the publication of the two-volume *Cambridge History of Egypt*, edited by Carl F. Petry and M. W. Daly—we accepted the invitation.[1] *The Oxford Handbook of Modern Egyptian History* brings together a dynamic and diverse group of historians of modern Egypt to map the present state of the field. Rather than adopting a synthetic approach, it aims to showcase the most cutting-edge and promising avenues of research among leading scholars in Egyptian history, laying new ground upon which future generations of scholars may build. The handbook is intended for both a general audience and specialists, who will encounter overviews one would expect from a reference work in history and new research that pushes the field forward, with an emphasis on the latter.

Scholars of Egyptian history long understood the modern period to begin with the movement of European people and ideas to Egypt's northern shores sparked by Napoleon's invasion in 1798. From this perspective, modern Egyptian history was animated by the diverse and sometimes contradictory ways in which Egyptians responded over time to colonial power and modern forms of knowledge. Since the mid-twentieth century, scholars have sought to complicate the facile colonizer/colonized and modern/tradition binaries undergirding this view. This volume builds on this effort. We see modern Egyptian history not as a series of reactions, but as a continuous process of translation and adaptation, invention and reinvention, construction and reconstruction that followed the French invasion but was not dependent upon it and that was far from unilinear. What is modern is less mimicry of Europe and more new technologies of governance, urban and rural structures, productions of law and culture, and ways of seeing the body and body politic.

Temporally, then, the volume explores the nineteenth and twentieth centuries, with a few chapters covering the twenty-first century and post-2011 revolutionary and counterrevolutionary forces. Whereas some chapters carve out large arcs of time, a (long) century or even the whole modern era, others focus on particular periods—such as the khedival or interwar years—or take deep dives into specific decades. The questions asked reflect contemporary concerns and debates, including medical sovereignty and bodily autonomy; the management of the environment; the rights and movements of workers; courts and legal struggles; cultural expression, production, and reception; and the relationship between the army, state, and society.

The handbook includes twenty-five chapters organized into five topical clusters: medicine, environment, and disease; technology, mobility, and labor; law and society; literary, performative, and visual culture; and state, politics, and intellectuals. The authors address long-standing themes in the field, though in new ways, and explore new themes reshaping how we understand modern Egyptian history, and thus Middle Eastern, global, and transnational histories. The topics demonstrate the expansion of Egyptian history beyond the traditional staples in social, economic, and political history.

The histories of medicine, environment, and disease are the fastest-growing fields within Middle Eastern history today. We combine them in the first section to highlight their intersections and amplify the various concerns that run across the chapters in this section, notably the mutual constitution of public health and the state. Recent literature on the history of technology has breathed new life into historical materialism. New technologies needed laborers who came through immigration and internal mobilizations, voluntary and involuntary, and included men and women. These technologies also involved nonhumans, transforming their relationship to both humans and the natural environment. The chapters in the second section draw out some of these connections. Recent legal histories of the modern Middle East have sought to rethink the relationship between Islamic law and secular law, the secularization of law, and the role of law broadly in shaping modern subjectivities and societies in the region. The chapters in the third section build on such efforts by examining underanalyzed areas of Egypt's legal system, drawing on new or different kinds of sources, and/or incorporating new analytical frameworks. Egyptian culture has long had an outsized influence on the Arabic-speaking world, and the field of Egyptian cultural history has reflected that dynamism. The authors in the fourth section show the potential value in revisiting and reinterpreting long-standing archives and the possibilities in creating new ones, whether textual, visual, or performative. The final section poses frameworks for understanding how the Egyptian state was constituted over a long durée, theorizes the place of intellectuals during the colonial and postcolonial periods, including in their relationship to the state, and examines the state's production and reproduction of Egyptian history since 2011, in addition to countervailing renderings of the past. Each of the five clusters maintains a loosely chronological order while attempting to juxtapose chapters that are in conversation with one another.

Readers will surely identify topical gaps in the handbook. These, in part, reflect an acknowledgment on our part that no volume can provide a complete history of modern

Egypt, if such a history were possible. But it also reflects our sense that, in the wake of the 2011 uprising and subsequent retrenchment of authoritarianism under President Abdel Fattah El-Sisi, with all the implications these events have had on research and scholarship, the field is at a hinge point, and now is as good a time as any to take stock of where we are and where we are going. We therefore opted to forgo any attempt to represent all subfields of Egyptian history and instead focus on the questions, topics, and trajectories that are animating the field at present and are likely to shape it in the decade or more to come.

As for the gaps, one of the most glaring may be the history of Egypt's largest minority group, the Copts, even as the handbook addresses other minority groups. The omission of this important and influential community may, however, be indicative of the present state of the field of Egyptian and broader Middle Eastern history, which has moved away from a focus on singular groups and an attendant communal framework and toward analyzing minorities to access "larger" stories, as gestured by two chapters in the handbook. Another related omission is the topic of Nubians, Blackness, and slavery, where there is excellent work in progress. These are but two examples of many that could be listed. For the most part, the handbook likewise does not showcase the work of an emerging generation of researchers whose inclusion would have enriched the volume. This omission is mainly the result of a misalignment between the time pressures of early-career publication and the time to publication of handbooks. We would like to acknowledge the very promising scholarship that this new generation has already produced, which has strengthened the field by addressing lacunae.

Our authors adopt a variety of analytical lenses. Gender cuts across many of the chapters in the handbook, with attention to the (re)training of birth workers, women's labor activism and social welfare work, changes in family law, and the ways in which photography shaped new social practices. Class comes to the fore in explorations of medical professionalization, migrant laborers who worked on the Suez Canal, debt and imprisonment, and petition writers, among other topics. While there is some signaling to race here, particularly in discussions on colonialism, there is much more that could be done, and we look forward to seeing more work in the field that combines analyses of race, class, and gender intersectionality moving forward.[2]

One of the most challenging and interesting developments in the recent writing of Egyptian history is the turn away from the Egyptian National Archives, Dar al-Watha'iq al-Qawmiyya, for reconstructing the past. This is in part by choice but also of necessity. While historians recognize the wealth of material in the archives, teeming as it is with petitions, court cases, administrative files, and so on, access to the archives, long difficult for foreign scholars, has become extremely hard for all but a few scholars in a post-2011 world, for reasons that Pascale Ghazaleh explores in her chapter. While a few of the chapters in this volume are based on trips to the archives in earlier decades, most draw on literary, oral, and visual materials found outside the Egyptian National Archives.

Scholars have collected photographs from the historic book market of Cairo, oral histories from doctors, and documents from family and private archives. Aware that the Arabic periodical press has been a mainstay of historical writing, particularly of cultural and intellectual histories, scholars have drawn on some of the most well-known journals but have also turned to administrative, medical, and theatrical journals, among others. Rather than disregard colonial archives, they have employed new methodologies to read colonial archives creatively. They have found new imperial sources from outside Great Britain, sources in underutilized archives outside Egypt, and sources in languages such as Greek and Italian. The internet has facilitated the search for new materials, connecting scholars to one another, to the holders of private and family collections, and to established and emerging digital archives. There is hope that new initiatives such as H-Egypt will disseminate information on the circulation of such materials.[3] In short, calls to decenter the view from the capital, and by necessity to decenter the national archives, have led to the proliferation of new strategies for locating sources materials, which in turn has led to exciting new work in Egyptian history.

Turning to matters more technical in nature, the handbook follows the *International Journal of Middle East Studies* transliteration system for Arabic, though it generally omits all transliteration marks except those for the letters *'ayn* and *hamza*. This approach, which seems to have become the norm among books in modern Middle Eastern history, is meant to preserve consistent spelling while facilitating ease of reading, especially for non-experts. We have preserved spelling inconsistencies that reflect differences of historical interpretation. Readers may notice, for instance, that some of our authors call the Ottoman governor of Egypt and founder of the khedival family Mehmed or Mehmet Ali, reflecting the Ottoman rendering of his name, while others call him Muhammad 'Ali, reflecting the Arabic rendering. This speaks to a debate in the field about the nature of Ottoman rule in Egypt and the nature of the state that the Pasha created. We have likewise preserved meaningful inconsistencies in nomenclature. Whereas some authors refer to the replacement of the monarchy in 1952 by a group of army officers as a revolt, for instance, others refer to it as a revolution. Readers may also notice that there is not necessarily agreement on the periodizing of precolonial, colonial, semi-colonial, and postcolonial Egypt and whether and how the middle two terms might be distinguished from each other. Inconsistencies around cutoffs, turning points, and terminology reflect debates around the impact of the French invasion and the informal nature of the British occupation and its end. They may also reflect the fact that bodies, society, and different parts of the state were colonized and decolonized at different rates.

Finally, this handbook was some time in the making, due in no small part to the pandemic. COVID set back our timetable, not least because some of our scholars had difficulty accessing libraries and archives as well as finding the space and concentration to write. The editors also faced interruptions and challenges. But we are thrilled with the volume that has resulted. We hope that it lives up to expectations to chart new directions for the field and that its voids and holes are seen by a new generation as opportunities to embrace and challenges to be met head on.

NOTES

1. Carl F. Petry and M. W. Daly, eds., *The Cambridge History of Egypt*, 2 Vols. (Cambridge: Cambridge University Press, 1999).
2. See, e.g., the seminar held at the Middle East and Middle Eastern American Center at the Graduate Center of the City University of New York, https://racemena.gc.cuny.edu/.
3. H-Egypt, https://networks.h-net.org/h-egypt.

PART I

MEDICINE, ENVIRONMENT, AND DISEASE

CHAPTER 1

MEDICINE AND PUBLIC HEALTH IN THE NINETEENTH CENTURY

KHALED FAHMY

DURING the middle decades of the nineteenth century, Egypt witnessed a revolution in medicine and public hygiene. Beginning in the early 1820s, Mehmed Ali Pasha, whom the Ottoman sultan had appointed as governor of Egypt in 1805 but who was running the province independently of Istanbul, started paying close attention to health and medical matters. In rapid succession, he launched a vaccination program to combat smallpox, which was ravaging the country; established an impressive medical school to train hundreds of doctors; imposed quarantines to combat devastating epidemics; opened hospitals and clinics in urban centers offering free medical services to the public; and introduced an intricate system of collecting vital statistics culminating in a comprehensive census.

Out of all of Egypt's nineteenth-century reforms, the medical ones were the most lasting and beneficial. Suffice to say that the medical school / teaching hospital that was opened in 1827, Qasr al-'Ayni, is one of only two institutions founded by Mehmed Ali that are still functioning to the present day (the other being the Bulaq Press). These medical reforms resulted in the ability to control epidemics that used to ravage the country and in the provision of basic medical care for large segments of the population. Compared to the economic, intellectual, and military reforms introduced by Mehmed Ali and his successors, and carefully studied a century later by the first generation of Egyptian academic historians,[1] medical reforms were by far more beneficial to most Egyptians.

This chapter explains how these medical reforms were put in place by paying equal attention to their impetus and their impact on the population. It starts with a brief overview of public health conditions at the turn of the nineteenth century and then traces the gradual evolution of what can be described as a public health policy that entailed medical education, provision of medical services, and attention to matters of public hygiene. The chapter analyzes four specific areas that were the cornerstones of the emerging public health system—namely, the collection of vital statistics, the opening of public hospitals, attention to urban sanitation, and smallpox vaccination. The chapter concludes with some critical remarks about the inherent drawbacks of this public hygiene system and the modern Egyptian state that created it.

HEALTH CONDITIONS IN EIGHTEENTH-CENTURY EGYPT

At the turn of the nineteenth century, just before Mehmed Ali rose to power, the health condition of the Egyptian population was appalling. Due to malnourishment, in turn caused by faulty conservation and utilization of food, the population, estimated at 4.5 million,[2] suffered from various gastrointestinal diseases leading to the death of thousands of children between the ages of one and three.[3] Smallpox affected children's health most seriously, killing between fifty and sixty thousand children each year.[4] This high infant mortality led to an increase in the annual aggregate death rate to three to four per thousand.[5]

The plague also had a devastating impact on public health and put the brakes on population growth. This pestilence was so prevalent that many Europeans believed it was endemic in Egypt. Some attributed the high prevalence of illness to the noxious miasmas emanating from the soil in which human corpses were decomposing. Others blamed the quality of the Nile waters.[6] Behind these competing theories was a desperate attempt to make sense of the frequency with which the plague struck Egypt. According to Michael Dols, throughout the long period extending from 1347 to 1894, Egypt was hit by the plague on average once every nine years.[7] In addition to its frequency, the plague was extremely deadly. According to André Raymond, the 1623–26 plague killed 300,000 people. Another 300,000 people, or one-eighth of the entire population of Egypt, died in the 1718 plague.[8] During one of the deadliest outbreaks, that of 1791, chroniclers reported that up to two thousand were dying daily and that one-fifth of Cairo's population perished.[9]

What made these epidemics so deadly was the almost complete absence of a public health policy.[10] There were no preventative measures to deal with the plague, and when it struck, the authorities' response was, tellingly, limited to fiscal matters. For example, the chronicler al-Damurdashi (d. 1755) says that in the wake of the 1695–96 plague, the Ottoman governor was quick to collect the administrative tax paid on title deeds (*hulwan*) from peasants who were keen to get hold of lands made vacant after their owners had died.[11] Following the devastating plague epidemic of 1791, a sultanic firman was sent to the governor in Cairo, ordering him to provide information about which Ottoman officials had fled the country so that the state could seize their property and money.[12] At the same time, and given the panic these epidemics naturally caused, Ottoman governors were keen to preserve the peace after a plague epidemic. Thus, we see Maqsud Pasha, the Ottoman governor in 1643, ordering the officials of *bayt al-mal*, a government body responsible for, among other things, registering the legacies of the deceased, to suspend their normal business during the plague. The chronicler Abu al-Surur al-Bakri (d. 1650) says that in issuing this order, the governor wanted to lift the financial burden off the plague victims' survivors. He adds that in order not to cause any delays in burials, the governor canceled this registration of the legacies of the deceased, referred to as *al-kashf ʿala al-amwat*, and survivors were told to bury their dead without registration.[13]

Apart from the plague years, which it should be remembered, were not infrequent, medical care was very rudimentary. By the end of the eighteenth century, the few existing hospitals in Cairo had significantly deteriorated since their establishment under the Mamluks.[14] During his long sojourn in Egypt in the 1670s, the famous Ottoman traveler Evliya Çelebi waxed lyrical on the condition of the well-known *bimaristan* that had been founded in Cairo by the Mamluk Sultan al-Mansur Qalawun in 683 AH / 1284 CE. The *bimaristan* comes across in Evliya's account as a well-run institution providing good medical care to its patients.[15] By the time the French visited the institution more than two centuries later, however, it had been reduced to a sad state of disrepair, and its poor inmates were left lingering in rundown wards where they survived on meager rations of bread, rice, and lentils and where they received no medicines or medical attention whatsoever,[16] suggesting that the institution had experienced a precipitous decline in the eighteenth century.[17] But even in its heyday, the Qalawun *bimaristan* provided services that "were insufficient for the large number of sick poor and that the burden of health care was being increasingly shouldered by the less conspicuous *sufi* confraternities of the city."[18] ʿAli Mubarak, writing at the end of the nineteenth century, mentions the names of three such hospices (*takiyyas*), which he claims were the only institutions providing medical services that had been built throughout the entire Ottoman period.[19]

In cities as well as in the countryside, basic health services were provided by barber-surgeons (*mizayyins*) who performed such operations as amputation, bloodletting, wound dressing, tooth extraction, circumcision, and anything else deemed part of "external medicine."[20] ʿAli Mubarak mentions that barber-surgeons in Cairo were organized in a guild that in the late nineteenth century had 836 members, making it the eighth-largest guild in Cairo. For "internal medicine," people sought the expertise of herbalists (*ʿattars*) and physicians (*hakims*), who based their practice on as rudimentary an understanding of Avicennian and Galenic medicine as could be gleaned from the few medical manuscripts in circulation.[21] Women sought the services of midwives (*dayas*) for help with pregnancies, deliveries, and venereal diseases. Above all, people turned to practitioners of folk medicine (*tibb al-rukka*) with their prophylactics based on charms, amulets, and "divination bowls" (*tasat al-khadda*).[22]

With Napoleon Bonaparte's expedition in 1798, matters of health and public hygiene assumed crucial importance. We get a glimpse of the importance the French occupation authorities gave to public hygiene matters from the following incident. On 24 March 1799, the French put up placards throughout Cairo with regulations printed by the French military authorities announcing the imposition of quarantines in Cairo. The placards read as follows: "An address to the people of Cairo, Bulaq, Old Cairo, and vicinity. You shall obey, uphold, and observe, without opposition, the orders. Anybody opposing them will encounter abundant vengeance, painful punishment, and severe retribution. They are precautions against the disease of the plague. In the case of anybody whom you know certainly, or believe, imagine, or suspect to be suffering from this illness in any place, house, caravansary, or building, it is your duty and obligation to establish a quarantine, and the place must be closed off. . . . [Anyone violating these regulations will] suffer capital punishment."[23]

These draconian measures taken to implement the quarantine were not the result of any new scientific discovery of the pathogenic agent causing plague or the presentation of new data that showed statistically that quarantines were effective in controlling the epidemic. Rather, they stemmed from the firm belief that the very survival of the army of occupation, and indeed the success of Bonaparte's imperial enterprise in the Orient, necessitated protecting his army and Egypt's population from the ravages of the plague. Being cut off from home after the British Admiral Horatio Nelson had destroyed their fleet in the Battle of the Nile (August 1798), the French saw the outbreak of plague in Egypt as a grave threat that could very well undermine their imperial designs. This fact became painfully clear when, the following year, the plague decimated the army in Palestine and contributed to the defeat of the entire Syrian campaign.[24]

Mehmed Ali, who rose to power soon after the departure of the French in 1801, had frequent recourse to quarantines as a way of managing the numerous plague epidemics. However, it is noteworthy that in the early years of his long reign, specifically from 1805 to 1820, the quarantines he imposed were aimed to protect himself, his immediate entourage, or his large household. For example, in contrast to the quarantine policy that the French had implemented on the entire city of Cairo in 1799, the quarantines the pasha ordered to deal with the plague of 1813 were imposed only on his palace, something that prompted the famous chronicler 'Abd al-Rahman al-Jabarti to remark sardonically that by doing so the pasha was showing his "desire for the life of this world and the fear of the plague."[25]

FOUNDING A CONSCRIPT ARMY

Indeed, for the first fifteen years of his long reign, Mehmed Ali did not evince any real concern with improving the health of Egyptians, increasing their productivity, or improving their well-being. However, all of this would change when the pasha took the momentous decision to conscript Egyptians for his long-desired army; from that moment, Egyptians acquired a heightened significance in Mehmed Ali's mind as they became his "benefactors," to use the term with which he ironically once referred to his subjects, playing on his title as "the benefactor" (*wali al-ni'am*).

The pasha's desire to build an army stemmed from his deep-seated fears that Istanbul could remove him from his prized province at any time. In 1820, he sent two large expeditions to Sudan to capture as many Sudanese as he could and press them into military service. But lacking a medical corps, these expeditions ended in a disastrous failure. The troops of the expedition fell prey to all kinds of diseases.[26] In addition, and due to insufficient attention to logistical transport, thousands of the captured slaves perished on the long march north. More ominously, many of those who survived the long trip ended up dying in the hastily established camps. Out of twenty thousand enslaved men who had reached Egypt by 1824, only three thousand survived.[27]

When the pasha finally decided to conscript native Egyptians for his army in 1822, lack of medical services continued to hamper his efforts. After incurring huge effort and spending large sums of money in rounding up the peasants and securing their transportation to the camps where they were subjected to modern military drills, the pasha saw his efforts evaporate when large numbers of them fell ill and died in the crowded barracks and training camps. Equally important was the fact that the press gangs, lacking even rudimentary demographic information, relied on village shaykhs to round up whomever they could lay their hands on. The result was that those gathered included old, sick, and infirm peasants who were sent back to their villages after being deemed medically unfit—this at a time when the pasha's agricultural demands could ill afford such a waste of manpower.

With these medical needs in mind, the pasha approached the French consul for assistance in securing an expert who could provide his new army with the desperately needed medical service. The French consul obliged and introduced to the pasha a young physician by the name of Antoine Barthélemy Clot, who had received his medical education in Marseille. In a series of meetings in the winter of 1824–25, the young French physician gave the pasha four pieces of advice about how to build a medical corps for his army, all of which the pasha accepted, with fateful results for the future of public hygiene. First, Dr. Clot suggested that while the pasha could employ European doctors to form the nucleus of a military medical corps, doing so would be too costly. It would be more appropriate, Dr. Clot suggested, to rely on local doctors. Second, he noted that these doctors could be trained locally if a modern medical school were to be founded. Third, he advised the Turkish-speaking pasha that education in this proposed medical school had to be conducted in Arabic so the students would be able, upon graduation, to communicate with their patients in their own language. Last, he insisted that instruction in his proposed medical school had to be squarely based on dissecting human cadavers. Only by seeing the internal structure of the human body with their own eyes, he argued, would the students learn the basics of modern medicine. Neither wax models nor the books of the ancients would suffice.

Having received the pasha's backing, Dr. Clot proceeded to work on the mammoth task ahead. He drafted a blueprint for a medical corps for the army and designed the curriculum and organizational structure of his planned school. After securing the services of European doctors and recruiting promising young students from Azhari Quranic schools (*kuttab*), the Egyptian Medical School was finally opened in 1827 in Abu Za'bal, northeast of Cairo. As mentioned previously, this school would prove to be one of the pasha's most successful institutions, one at which European visitors uniformly marveled. Dr. William Wilde, famous playwright Oscar Wilde's father, upon visiting the school a few years after its founding, described it by saying that "a cleaner, better regulated and better conducted medical establishment I never visited."[28] For his part, James A. St. John wrote that the visitor "is sometimes startled at being addressed in French by ill-conditioned fellahin, who are instructed in history, geography, arithmetic, botany, chemistry together with the theory and practice of medicine and surgery. . . . Practical knowledge is acquired by attending the sick, compounding and making up medicines, and the constant use of the dissecting knife."[29]

In 1831, five years after the medical school's establishment, the first class of students graduated, and Dr. Clot selected the top twelve students to go on an educational mission to France, where they spent the following eight years acquiring specialized education in different branches of medicine.[30] Meanwhile, the rest of the graduates were immediately dispatched to the army, where they were given the rank of lieutenant and put under the supervision of European doctors.[31]

Ten years after founding a conscript army, therefore, Mehmed Ali succeeded in establishing a medical corps that he hoped would help him avoid the mistakes of his earlier attempts at building a reliable fighting force. He now embarked on his most daring military adventure, the invasion of Syria, the aim of which was to defend his dominions from a possible Ottoman attack. But just when all preparations for this ambitious campaign had been put in place, disaster hit. Cholera spread with the pilgrims returning from Hijaz at the end of the summer and soon ravaged the entire country. The pasha had to postpone the launch of the Syria campaign while he instructed Dr. Clot to do his best to spare the army and protect the population at large.

The cholera epidemic was devastating. In a few weeks, it carried away between 150,000 and 190,000 people. Cairo lost 15% of its population, estimated at a quarter of a million inhabitants.[32] When news reached Alexandria that hundreds of people were dying daily in Cairo, the port city was paralyzed with fear. In response, Mehmed Ali proposed that the European consuls in Alexandria form a Quarantine Board to stop the epidemic's spread.[33] He even assigned twenty thousand troops to form a cordon sanitaire around the city. These efforts were too little too late, however, and the epidemic soon spread in the port city, prompting the Quarantine Board to disband itself. Meanwhile, Dr. Clot, unlike many of his European colleagues who fled the country altogether and returned home, redoubled his efforts to do his job and concentrated on protecting the army. He imposed strict quarantines around camps, barracks, and military schools, and managed to spare the army the worst of the epidemic. In recognition of his efforts, Mehmed Ali granted him the title of bey, and henceforth he came to be known as Clot Bey.

The attempts to control the cholera epidemic of 1831–32 can be said to mark the true beginning of Egypt's public health system. While these attempts fell far short of putting the public health system on a firm footing, they indicate some general features that would shape the health system in the years to come. Chief among these features is the centrality of the army, something that was reflected in Clot Bey's official title: *hakimbashi al-jihadiyya*, or chief military physician. Indeed, the Qasr al-'Ayni Medical School (which is how the school came to be known after 1837 when it was moved to Qasr al-'Ayni on the eastern shores of the Nile in Cairo) "never lost its character as a service agency for the military establishment."[34] In addition to Qasr al-'Ayni graduates being dispatched immediately upon graduation to the different war fronts (in Syria, Hijaz, Yemen, Crete, Sudan, and Anatolia), the military nature of the entire public health enterprise can be further detected from the fact that quarantines were made possible only due to the availability of thousands of disciplined troops who imposed cordons sanitaires around cities. A second feature of the embryonic public health system was its heavy reliance on quarantines as the prime means to combat epidemics. Mehmed Ali had an unwavering belief in quarantines, in contradistinction to Clot Bey, who had his doubts about their efficacy. The pasha's deep belief in quarantines became evident when Egypt was struck by another devastating epidemic, the plague, in 1834–37. This epidemic was one of the worst the country had ever witnessed. Unofficial reports claimed that 200,000 people died of the plague in the peak months of the summer of 1835, with Cairo losing one-third of its population.[35] In response, Mehmed Ali ordered quarantines to be imposed not only on his own palace and on military establishments, but also on key government establishments and entire cities throughout the country.[36]

In addition to imposing quarantines, the nascent public health system in the late 1820s and early 1830s became increasingly concerned with collecting vital statistics. During the 1834–37 plague, Mehmed Ali received daily updates on mortality figures from his officials and regional governors. The minute he received information that the plague had appeared in Alexandria in the summer of 1834, for example, he ordered that post-mortem examinations be conducted on all dead male bodies to determine the number of those who had died of the epidemic and that he receive daily updates on those post-mortem examinations.[37] When discovering a discrepancy in these daily reports, he ordered the director of his bureau in Alexandria to investigate the matter.[38] And when these daily reports were delayed, he ordered the person responsible to be given five hundred lashes.[39] He was also keen to compare the mortality figures with pre-epidemic ones and asked his officials to do their best to come up with these earlier figures either by checking their registers or relying on their memory.[40]

By the mid-1830s, significant inroads had been made in the two pillars of the emerging public hygiene system: collecting vital statistics and imposing quarantines. However, serious tensions could already be detected in this nascent system. First, as in Europe, the medical establishment was split between the contagionists and the miasmatists, with Clot Bey, crucially, deeply doubting that the plague was contagious and therefore skeptical about the efficacy of quarantines in dealing with the repeated plague epidemics.[41] In many public lectures he delivered in France, and in his own French- and English-language publications, he expressed this skepticism in no uncertain terms, boasting that "the number of contagionists [was] daily decreas[ing], and I trust that the day is not far off when quarantine regulations will be completely reformed, if not altogether abolished."[42] Nevertheless, faced with the stern belief that his patron, Mehmed Ali, had in quarantines, he had to swallow his words and write to his subordinates in the army, urging them to treat the plague as contagious and to impose quarantines with all due diligence.[43]

Second, there were deep tensions between, on the one hand, Clot Bey and the embryonic organization that he was heading to coordinate medical matters, Shura al-Attiba (the Doctors' Council), and, on the other hand, the Quarantine Board, which, as mentioned above, was the body that the European consuls in Alexandria had established in 1831 to deal with the cholera epidemic of that year and that was reconstituted soon after its initial dissolution. While the shura concentrated its efforts on improving the health conditions of the country at large, the consuls were primarily interested in protecting international trade and believed that quarantines imposed in Egypt's main port city were crucial in issuing clean bills of health for ships trading with their respective countries.

Third, despite the pasha's interest in collecting vital statistics, the country lacked any systematic mechanism to collate and update information about births, deaths, and disease, which hampered conscription and, more importantly, smallpox vaccination. Above all, the embryonic public hygiene system suffered from inadequate numbers of doctors. While Qasr al-'Ayni continued to train hundreds of doctors throughout the first decade of its existence, all of these doctors were dispatched to the various war fronts immediately upon graduation, and occasionally even before finishing their education. While these doctors gained invaluable practical experience as army doctors, surgeons, and pharmacists, the civilian population back home was deprived of their precious experience.

Demobilizing the Conscript Army

All of these problems witnessed an important breakthrough in 1841, when the pasha reached an amicable settlement with the Ottoman sultan and his ten-year-old military conflict with his suzerain came to a successful end, leading to the demobilization of the army.[44] This sudden availability of army doctors coincided with the return from France of the first medical education mission, and the returning doctors were immediately given teaching positions in their alma mater, which boosted medical education considerably. With hundreds of military doctors, surgeons, and pharmacists available to him, Clot Bey believed that the time had finally come to create a reliable health service that could cover the entire country. By contrast, the Alexandria Quarantine Board thought that this sudden availability of qualified and trained doctors was an opportunity to expand quarantine services.[45]

Simultaneously, a minor outbreak of plague in Alexandria afforded Clot Bey the pretext that he needed to push for his ambitious proposals. He therefore drafted for the pasha a set of far-reaching health measures that went beyond imposing quarantines, and in August 1841, Mehmed Ali passed a decree titled "General Regulations Concerning the Public Health in Alexandria and the Interior," which can be seen as marking a qualitatively new step in the history of public health provision. In addition to specifying how physicians were to monitor the quality of food sold in the marketplace, the decree included sections about sweeping the streets, checking the dead, and the "Sanitary polic[ing] of the Environs."[46]

The 1841 decree marks an important shift in the evolution of the public health system. Not only does it point to the triumph of Clot Bey and his Shura al-Attiba over the European consuls in Alexandria with their narrow focus on quarantines; it also marks a shift away from focusing on the health of the conscripts and toward raising the health standards of the population at large. This wider attention to the civilian population can best be analyzed by following four areas that witnessed a rapid expansion in the 1840s: the collection of vital statistics, the opening of hospitals and public clinics, urban sanitation, and vaccination against smallpox.

COLLECTION OF VITAL STATISTICS

As Kenneth Cuno and Michael Reimer remark, with the beginning of military conscription in 1822, the "need for an accurate and detailed account of the population . . . [became] more acute."[47] Mehmed Ali developed a keen interest in vital statistics during the cholera and plague epidemics of the 1830s. But it was the steps taken to conduct a national census that had a long-lasting impact on the creation of a modern statistical regime. Based on the registers in the Egyptian National Archives, Cuno and Reimer argue that "the counting of individuals began in some villages as early as 1843."[48] After a couple of false starts, a nationwide census was finally conducted in 1848, which is noteworthy given that Egypt was witnessing a leadership crisis that year, caused by the pasha's illness. Nevertheless, the authorities managed to complete the census, which, unlike Ottoman censuses, was not limited to counting households and managed to count individuals, including women, children, slaves, and Europeans. In assessing the bureaucracy's success in conducting this census, Cuno and Reimer remark that the "returns . . . are remarkable for their thoroughness, and were almost certainly the most complete of any done within Ottoman domains at this time."[49]

As impressive as conducting the census in this crisis year was, it represented but one component of a complex mechanism of collecting vital statistics. The census was simply a database that had to be regularly updated when new births or new deaths occurred. Given that birth certificates had not been introduced yet, the first of these tasks proved more difficult to accomplish than the second. Still, monitoring and recording daily deaths required putting in place an intricate system of making sure that *every* death was reported to the local health office; that a death certificate was issued by the resident doctor, stating the name, age, and cause of death of the deceased; that in instances of suspicious cases (e.g., homicide or epidemics) the body was sent to the nearest hospital for an autopsy; that undertakers did not perform burials except after receiving a death certificate from the family of the deceased; that burials within the city were banned; and that the monthly registers of the undertakers were routinely checked against the monthly registers of the resident doctors to detect any discrepancies. This intricate system of regular postmortem examinations came to be known as *al-kashf 'ala al-amwat* (literally, checking the dead), which, it should be remembered, is the exact phrase that had been used previously to refer to registering the legacies of the deceased. Nothing captures the full implications of the birth of a modern bureaucracy in Egypt by the middle of the nineteenth century more than the transformation in the meaning of this phrase from checking the inheritance records of the dead to checking the bodies of the dead.[50]

The process of recording newborn babies was more difficult than registering the new deaths. As early as 1845, regulations were issued stipulating that the Department of Civil Affairs should gather information about the number of newborn babies and update this information monthly.[51] This recording was to be done in registers that were to be printed especially for that purpose and eventually preserved at the Department of Education.[52] This information was delivered by the neighborhood shaykhs, *mashayikh al-athman*, who in turn were mandated to collect it daily from the traditional midwives, the *dayas*. But there were repeated complaints that the *dayas* were not punctual in reporting the delivery cases they had performed, and despite repeated threats and punishments, the authorities could not easily establish control over the midwives. This problem was partially addressed by ordering the graduates of the School of Midwives (which had been founded in 1832) to oversee the work of the *dayas* and compel them to deliver accurate and timely information about the babies they had delivered.[53] Still, in light of repeated complaints that new births were not recorded accurately,[54] and that occasionally there were more recorded deaths than births, the introduction of birth certificates that would be the basis of all information regarding "inheritance, income, conscription, marriage, etc." was suggested.[55]

Opening Hospitals

The state of public health was also considerably improved by opening hospitals in major urban centers. Official correspondence states that the Qasr al-'Ayni hospital accommodated 500 patients in 1860 and 850 patients in 1863, and remarks that there was a need to have enough beds for 1,000 patients.[56] In addition to Qasr al-'Ayni, Cairo had another important hospital called al-Isbitaliya al-Mulkiyya, the Civilian Hospital, which began operation in 1837 in the central quarter of Azbakiyya. This hospital catered to the poor of the city, both men and women, in addition to functioning as a center for smallpox vaccination and a maternity ward.[57] In Alexandria, the Mahmudiyya Hospital, founded in 1827, had three hundred beds and was intended to serve twenty-six thousand military men and eleven thousand workers in the arsenal, as well as navy personnel.[58] Civilian hospitals were also constructed in the urban centers of Suez, Damietta, and Rosetta, and seventeen other hospitals, with a total of five hundred beds, were opened in the provinces. Children attending schools and workers employed in factories were treated in hospitals opened in these government establishments.[59] Each of these hospitals, whether in a school or a factory, had a resident doctor, a pharmacist, and several orderlies.[60]

These government hospitals were free of charge, and even when, several decades later, Qasr al-'Ayni started to charge fees, paupers could still be admitted freely.[61] Official government rhetoric stressed that granting free admission to the poor and needy was "one of the many acts of mercy of the Benefactor, Mehmed Ali Pasha."[62] Referring to the Civilian Hospital in Azbakiyya, the shura stated that "what prompted the Khedival Person to found and open the hospital was the compassion he felt towards his sick subjects ['abidihi: literally 'his slaves'] who have been afflicted with many diseases and who cannot afford to pay the cost of their treatment. Accordingly, he issued orders to admit and treat anyone who approached the hospital, whether they be from Cairo itself or from outside the city. In undertaking this 'benevolent' act, no regard will be made to nationality or religion (la yandhur al-fi'l al-khayri la li-farq al-milla wa-la al-diyana). All will be accorded the necessary treatment without distinction."[63]

Despite having at their disposal new hospitals that offered free medical services, most Egyptians, according to archival records, avoided hospitals and preferred treatment at home even if doing so cost them money. Four reasons stand out for this aversion to hospitals. First, the military nature of the entire medical establishment meant that hospitals were run like military barracks, often at the expense of patients' well-being. Gustave Flaubert writes that when he visited the venereal diseases ward of Qasr al-'Ayni in 1849, he saw patients subjected to strict military discipline: "Kasr el-'Aini Hospital. Well maintained. The work of Clot Bey—his hand is still to be seen. Pretty cases of syphilis . . . several cases have it in the arse. At a sign from the doctor, they all stood up on their beds (it was like army drill) and opened their anuses with their fingers to show their chancres."[64]

Second, cases of medical malpractice were frequent, given that the young doctors were in the habit of experimenting on patients' bodies with sometimes fatal results. These incidents prompted the intervention of 'Abbas Pasha in person, who issued a ruling banning vivisection and stipulating that dissection operations ('amaliyyat al-tashrih) were to be conducted only on dead bodies. His order went on to stipulate that patients had to give their prior consent to surgery and that operations should not be conducted solely for the "advancement of the [medical] profession" (tahsil al-taqwiyya li-l-sina'a).[65]

Third, the entire health establishment lacked administrative and financial independence, a factor that adversely affected the daily functioning of hospitals. Shura al-Atibba was not an independent government body; rather, it was a subdivision of the War Department (Diwan al-Jihadiyya) and later of the Department of Civil Affairs (Diwan Khidiwi).[66] This lack of financial and administrative independence meant that the simplest procedure required endless paperwork. Hospital admission, for example, required securing a receipt from the head of Cairo's police department (dabit bey) or the head of the neighborhood (shaykh al-thumn). Clot Bey wrote in vain to his superiors, inquiring, "What will happen in the case of a stranger who needs to be admitted quickly to hospital but who doesn't know the dabit bey or the shaykh al-thumn? Or if someone needs to be admitted urgently and doesn't have time to secure such a receipt?"[67] In a subsequent letter, he complained, "This is a surefire way for patients to die, for [when the patient finally secures] the receipt for admission to the hospital, it will be a receipt for admission to the grave."[68]

Fourth, given these bureaucratic problems, it proved extremely difficult to combat the repeated outbreaks of infection within hospitals. Typhus was the most common of these infections, so common that it came to be known as "hospital fever" (*'ufuna maristaniyya*).[69] Dr. Léon Labat, a French physician who worked in the school of medicine while it was still in Abu Za'bal, wrote that the school had been built too close to a large cemetery where the dead were so carelessly buried that the stench in the hospital was terrible, and the patients were kept awake at night by hyenas fighting over human carcasses.[70] Much later, and after the British takeover of the Sanitary Department in 1883, the head of that department complained of the "overpowering smell" emanating from privies that had been built in the walls and its waft through the patient wards, which created a "pervading horror." "Perhaps it is not surprising," he concluded, "that hardly any single soul ever went to the hospital of his own free will."[71]

Urban Sanitation

More important than hospitals for public hygienic purposes were public clinics, *makatib al-sihha*, which were opened in Cairo soon after the demobilization of the army in 1841. Laverne Kuhnke reports that 21,468 outpatients were treated between 1845, when six such clinics were first established, and 1848, when their number was raised to eight: six for Cairo's eight quarters (*thumns*), one for Bulaq, and one for Old Cairo. These clinics treated "common ailments like ophthalmia, scabies, syphilis, and dislocated or broken limbs. . . . [In addition, they offered] free consultation for all the city's inhabitants; emergency aid to victims of drowning or asphyxiation; dressing injuries; free vaccination; dispatching *hakimas* to confinement cases, [and] verifying and certifying causes of death."[72]

In addition, these public clinics performed what can be termed "health policing."[73] Working under the auspices of a department called Diwan Taftish Sihhat al-Mahrusa (Department of Health Inspection of Cairo), the physicians working in these public clinics were required to go on daily tours accompanied by police soldiers to inspect the health conditions of their neighborhoods, including street cleaning, garbage collection, and the filling in of marshes and ponds. All commercial actors who might have a connection to comestibles were closely supervised: greengrocers, bakers, butchers, fishmongers, and druggists.[74] The quality of the water supply to the city was also carefully monitored after complaints that the water smelled terrible and had a greenish color and a nasty taste.[75] Tanneries and slaughterhouses were moved to the fringes of the city, and minute attention was paid to their cleanliness.[76]

SMALLPOX VACCINATION

None of the measures analyzed so far had a more beneficial impact on public hygiene than the smallpox vaccination campaign, which started in earnest in the mid-1830s and managed to bring this terrible disease under control half a century later. Following the stages of this campaign in some detail offers an opportunity to see how the public health establishment evolved over the fifty-year period from 1825 to 1875.[77]

Clot Bey said that when he arrived in Egypt in 1825, smallpox was killing between fifty and sixty thousand children each year,[78] which, according to Daniel Panzac's calculation, meant that "smallpox alone must have been responsible for increasing infant mortality by 40 to 50 per thousand, which works out to an increase in the annual death rate of 3 to 4 per thousand."[79] Clot Bey also claims that the beginning of smallpox immunization in 1827 was his personal accomplishment. But as Kuhnke points out, smallpox vaccination started at an earlier date.[80]

The earliest record to that effect is a letter from Mehmed Ali dated 2 March 1819 appointing a certain Dr. Francesco to vaccinate peasants against smallpox using the vaccine "whose efficacy has been proven through practice."[81] After he had decided to conscript peasants in 1822, the pasha redoubled his efforts to combat smallpox and "authorized a disbursement for Dr. Dussap, a holdover of Bonaparte's expedition, who had been charged with inoculating the troops assembled in Upper Egypt against smallpox."[82] According to another French doctor, writing mid-century, this early attempt to inoculate the conscripts forever associated vaccination with military service.[83] In 1825, the pasha hired three European doctors to introduce inoculation in Middle and Lower Egypt and teach the village barber-surgeons this vital skill.[84] Three years later, in 1828, he decided to inoculate his own children.[85]

Following his appointment as *hakimbashi al-jihadiyya*, Clot Bey concentrated his efforts on vaccinating all men in arms as well as their wives and children who lived with them in military camps.[86] In May 1836, Mehmed Ali ordered the vaccination of all children in government schools,[87] and a few months later, a comprehensive ordinance was issued establishing a nationwide smallpox vaccination program to be managed by Clot Bey's shura. This ordinance stipulated the appointment of a chief doctor in charge of vaccination, who should roam the provinces and teach provincial doctors and village barbers how to perform the vaccination. Barbers were to receive one piaster for each child they vaccinated. Vaccination was also to be extended to Egypt's dependencies in Sennar, Hijaz, Syria, and Crete.[88]

In Cairo, vaccination was to take place in the School of Midwives located within the Civilian Hospital in Azbakiyya.[89] Neighborhood shaykhs were ordered to roam their neighborhoods and act as town criers (*al-ta'kid bi al-munadah fi al-shawari'*), summoning children to the Civilian Hospital for vaccination.[90] In the countryside, when the provincial doctor arrived in any given village, the local police deputy (*al-afadni mu'awin al-khutt*) would summon the children, have them vaccinated by the doctor or the barber-surgeons, and then record their names in a special register.[91]

These early measures, however, were met with fierce resistance from the public, and the authorities struggled to understand the reasons for this opposition and find ways to overcome it. When it was discovered that only fourteen children out of the registered 450 in a certain neighborhood showed up for vaccination, the shura blamed the Egyptian doctors for their laxity.[92] Parents who refused to deliver their children for vaccination were to be punished to deter others from doing the same thing, the shura reasoned.[93] In Europe, they added in a separate letter, families who prevented their children from being vaccinated were punished by having their children denied admission to school. But since Egyptian families "have no desire to send their children to government schools, given that their minds cannot comprehend what is good and beneficial to their children," this punishment will be meaningless. It had earlier been suggested that any father who refused to vaccinate his child and whose child died as a result should be punished with one hundred lashes.[94] But beating, the shura reasoned, might also be ineffective. Instead, they suggested fining each family between twenty-five and hundred piasters.[95]

In the countryside, the resistance was even fiercer given that peasants were not exempt from conscription as Cairenes were, and given that "vaccination appeared patently linked to the detested troop levies by its resemblance to tattooing; among the common folk, in fact, it was called 'tattooing smallpox.' Had not the pasha ordered smallpox tattooed on all the conscripts from the Sudan when they were herded into the training camp at Aswan? And did not all the men drafted into the navy have an anchor tattooed on their hand to prevent their escape?"[96] It was the deep-seated loathing of conscription rather than any misguided understanding of what was beneficial to them, as the authorities argued, that lay behind the initial resistance to vaccination, a resistance that assumed many forms. They bribed the doctors and the barber-surgeons.[97] They beseeched the provincial governors to exempt their children from vaccination.[98] In one incident, they even physically attacked the French doctor in charge of vaccination in Upper Egypt, Charles Cuny, and would have killed him if not for his subterfuge (*muhayala*) and ability to flee their wrath.[99]

In response, the authorities came up with an ingenious solution, a mixture of paperwork and coercion, which would become the telltale tools of the modern Egyptian state. At the beginning of the campaign, parents were given a certificate when they vaccinated their child. But a black market in these certificates soon developed as parents sold the certificates of children who died of other causes. To close this loophole, more details had to be inserted in the certificate: the name of the father, the child's name, their age, their neighborhood, and their house number. In case the child died, the doctor performing the postmortem examination would take the vaccination certificate and send it with his daily list of names of deceased to the Department of Civil Affairs, which was in charge of collating vital statistics.[100]

At the same time, neighborhood shaykhs, rather than parents, were now pressured to present children for vaccination. Those shaykhs in whose neighborhood a child died without a certificate would be severely punished.[101] Moreover, summoning children for vaccination was not done by crying out loud in the middle of the streets. Rather, each neighborhood public clinic had to check its registers and determine which children were due to be vaccinated based on their age. The clinic would then deliver a list of names and addresses to the neighborhood police officer (*mu'awin al-thumn*), who would inform the neighborhood shaykh to gather these children and deliver them to the vaccination center.[102] Eventually, the neighborhood police commissioner (*ma'mur dabtiyyat al-thumn*) oversaw the whole process to ensure that the shaykhs were diligent in gathering the registered children on time.[103]

The suspension of conscription in 1841 meant that parents no longer opposed having their children vaccinated. As a result, smallpox was brought under control initially in the major cities, and later in the country at large. Already by 1848, "about half of all Cairo's newborn infants were . . . being immunized against [smallpox, and this] scourge . . . had either disappeared or [was] about to do so."[104] Clot Bey's claim that the public health system he had helped put in place managed to vaccinate 80,000 children each year for the period from 1827 to 1850 seems plausible when compared to the figure of 130,823 children that the medical journal *Ya'sub al-Tibb* said had been vaccinated in 1866–67.[105] According to Panzac, by the early 1870s, smallpox accounted for only 0.4 and 0.007% of all deaths in Alexandria and Cairo respectively. . . . This was entirely due to the introduction of smallpox vaccination. . . . Between 1870 and 1872, 74% of newborn babies in Alexandria and 85% in Cairo were vaccinated."[106]

A khedival decree regulating vaccination issued on 17 December 1890 provided a fitting end to the story of vaccination in the nineteenth century. In only six terse articles, it stipulated that smallpox vaccination was mandatory for all children born in Egypt and its dependencies. Vaccination was to be conducted freely by the barber-surgeons in the local public clinic. The state would pay the barbers one piaster for each successful vaccination. For those families who preferred to have their children vaccinated at home, the barbers' wage was to be paid by the family.[107]

CONCLUSION

The clear, self-assured tone of the 1890 khedival decree regulating vaccination is indicative of the progress that the Egyptian public health system had achieved over the previous seventy-odd years. By opening hospitals and free clinics in urban centers throughout the country, by imposing quarantines to control the spread of epidemics, by developing a complex bureaucracy that collected vital statistics, and, above all, by introducing a nationwide smallpox vaccination program, the country had managed to create a public health system that had a beneficial impact on the population. The significance of this public health system cannot be overestimated. It brought major epidemics and diseases—cholera, plague, and smallpox—under control, with the result that the population doubled in size in the second half of the nineteenth century, and the "generation of 1840–1860 witness[ed] an important change: the transition from a semi-stagnant to a steady and assured population growth."[108] With its efficient, self-confident bureaucracy at its core, the very nature of the nineteenth-century Egyptian state was itself the result of the steady, incremental effort to lower infant mortality, limit the impact of epidemics, improve urban sanitation, and increase the size of the population. The intricate bureaucracy created to collect vital statistics, vaccinate children against smallpox, impose quarantines, and run the myriad of medical institutions was the backbone of the modern Egyptian state. In many ways, the modern medical establishment and the modern Egyptian state were mutually constitutive, and it is not possible to fully understand one without understanding the other.

As impressive as this public health system was, it was not without problems. Its military origins and its subsequent close association with the army shaped people's reaction to modern medicine and often gave rise to deep revulsion and fierce resistance. This resistance was not informed only by the high level of coercion with which quarantines were imposed, vital statistics gathered, or smallpox vaccination imposed; it was also informed by people's well-founded suspicion of their government and their conviction that even when they benefited from some measures taken by this government, their own well-being was never the prime motivation.

This sense of alienation from the budding health system could have been ameliorated by the doctors who, it must be remembered, had received their medical education in Arabic specifically so they could communicate with their patients in the same language. However, throughout the nineteenth century, Egyptian doctors were primarily public health providers who had not only been educated by the state, but also worked primarily for the state throughout their active careers. As such, and in addition to the lack of administrative and financial independence that characterized the public health establishment in which they served, Qasr al-ʿAyni graduates were primarily public officials, not physicians for the public. Their inability to achieve complete independence was an essential feature of the public health system in the nineteenth century, as it continues to be in the twenty-first century.

NOTES

1. On this historiographic enterprise, see Yoav Di-Capua, *Gatekeepers of the Arab Past: Historians and History Writing in Twentieth-Century Egypt* (Berkeley: University of California Press, 2009), 91–218.
2. Daniel Panzac, "The Population of Egypt in the Nineteenth Century," *Asian and African Studies* 21, no. 1 (1987): 15.
3. M. de Chabrol, "Essai sur le mœurs des habitants modernes de l'Égypte," *Description de l'Égypte, État moderne*, vol. 2 (Paris: Imprimerie impériale, 1822), 382, quoted in Panzac, "The Population of Egypt," 16.
4. A. B. Clot Bey, *Mémoires* (Cairo: Institut Français d'Archéologie Orientale, 1949), 157.
5. Panzac, "The Population of Egypt," 17–18.

6. A. B. Clot Bey, *De la peste observée en Égypte: Recherches et considérations sur cette maladie* (Paris: Fortin, Masson et Cie., 1840), 212–23, 233–34.

7. Michael W. Dolls, "The Second Plague Pandemic and Its Recurrences in the Middle East: 1347–1894," *Journal of the Economic and Social History of the Orient* 22, no. 2 (1979): 167–68.

8. André Raymond, "Les Grandes Épidémies de peste au Caire aux XVIIe et XVIIIe siècles," *Bulletin d'Études Orientales* 25 (1972): 204–5.

9. Alan Mikhail, "The Nature of Plague in Late Eighteenth-Century Egypt," *Bulletin of the History of Medicine* 28, no. 2 (2008): 254–57, 260.

10. Nasir Ibrahim, *al-Azmat al-Ijtima'iyya fi Misr fi al-Qarn al-Sabi' 'Ashr* (Cairo: Dar al-Afaq, 1998), 184.

11. Ahmad al-Damurdashi Katkhuda 'Azaban, *Kitab al-Durra al-Musana fi Akhbar al-Kinana*, ed. 'Abd al-Rahim 'Abd al-Rahman 'Abd al-Rahim (Cairo: IFAO, 1989), 31–33; 'Abd al-Rahman al-Jabarti, *'Aja'ib al-Athar fi al-Tarajim wa-l-Akhbar*, vol. 1 (Cairo: Bulaq, 1880), 99.

12. Alan Mikhail, *Nature and Empire in Ottoman Egypt* (Cambridge: Cambridge University Press, 2011), 224.

13. Muhammad ibn Abi al-Surur al-Bakri, "al-Kawakib al-Sa'ira fi Akhbar Misr al-Qahira," fol. 80, quoted in Ibrahim, *al-Azmat al-Ijtmia'iyya*, 187.

14. For the history of hospitals in Mamluk Egypt, see Ahmed Ragab, *The Medieval Islamic Hospital: Medicine, Religion, and Charity* (Cambridge: Cambridge University Press, 2015).

15. His account is reproduced in Gary Leiser and Michael Dols, "Evliya Chelebi's Description of Medicine in Seventeenth-Century Egypt: Part I: Introduction," *Sudhoffs Archiv* 72, no. 1 (1988): 52–55.

16. *Description de l'Égypte*, 2nd ed., vol. 18, part 2 (Paris, 1822), 322.

17. Ahmad Isa, *Histoire des bimaristans (hopitaux) à l'époque islamique* (Cairo: Impr. Paul Barbey, 1928), 59ff.

18. Leiser and Dols, "Evliya Chelebi's Description of Medicine," 206.

19. 'Ali Mubarak, *al-Khitat al-Tawfiqiyya al-Jadida*, vol. 1 (Cairo: Bulaq, 1304–06/1882–89), 97. The names of the three *takiyyas* are al-Jalshaniyya, al-Habbaniyya, and al-A'jam.

20. 'Imad 'Abd al-Ra'uf al-Rutayl, *al-Tibb wa-l-'Ilaj fi Misr al-'Uthmaniya wa-'Ahd Muhammad 'Ali* (Cairo: Dar al-Jumhuriya li-l-Sahafa, 2014), 149.

21. For a detailed account of the education of an exceptional eighteenth-century Azhari shaykh well versed in medicine, see Ahmed Ragab, *Medicine and Religion in the Life of an Ottoman Sheikh: Al-Damanhuri's "Clear Statement" on Anatomy* (London: Routledge, 2019).

22. On folk medicine, see John Walker, *Folk Medicine in Modern Egypt; Being the Relevant Parts of the Tibb al-Rukka, or Old Wives' Medicine of 'Abd al-Rahman Isma'il* (London: Luzac, 1934).

23. Al-Jabarti, *'Aja'ib*, vol. 3, 52.

24. Al-Jabarti says that during the siege of Acre (March–May 1799), between fifty and sixty soldiers died each day, and he adds that this was one of the reasons why Bonaparte eventually decided to lift the siege, al-Jabarti, *'Aja'ib*, vol. 3, 68.

25. Al-Jabarti, *'Aja'ib*, vol. 4, 176.

26. Frédéric Cailliaud, *Voyage à Méroé, au Fleuve Blanc, au-delà de Fâzoql*, vol. 2 (Paris: L'Imprimerie Royale, 1826), 313, 316.

27. Henry Dodwell, *The Founder of Modern Egypt: A Study of Muhammad 'Ali* (Cambridge: The University Press, 1931), 64–65.

28. William Robert Wilde, *Narrative of a Voyage to Madeira, Teneriffe and along the Shores of the Mediterranean: Including a Visit to Algiers, Egypt, Palestine, Tyre, Rhodes, Telmessus, Cyprus, and Greece* (Dublin: W. Curry, 1844), 234–35.

29. James Augustus St. John, *Egypt and Mohammed Ali*, vol. 2 (London: Longman, 1834), 402.

30. On this education mission, see 'Umar Tusun, *al-Ba'that al-'Ilmiyya fi 'Ahd Muhammad 'Ali Thumma fi 'Ahdayy 'Abbas al-Awal wa Sa'id* (Alexandria: Salah al-Din, 1934), 123–44.

31. Infantry regiments were each given one European and three Egyptian doctors, while cavalry regiments were each given one European doctor and two Egyptian ones: Amin Sami, *Taqwim al-Nil*, vol. 2 (Cairo: Dar al-Kutub, 1928), 278, letter dated 18 Jumada I 1247/25 October 1831.

32. Cairo's mortality rate was three times higher than that of Paris during the same cholera pandemic of 1831–32. See Catherine J. Kudlick, *Cholera in Post-Revolutionary Paris: A Cultural History* (Berkeley: University of California Press, 1996).

33. The Egyptian National Archives (ENA), Ma'iyya Saniyya, Turki, S/1/58/1 (original no. 41), doc. no. 354, 18 Rabi' I 1247 / 27 August 1831; Laverne Kuhnke, *Lives at Risk: Public Health in Nineteenth-Century Egypt* (Berkeley: University of California Press, 1990), 53–54.

34. Kuhnke, *Lives at Risk*, 37.

35. Edward William Lane, *Manners and Customs of the Modern Egyptians* (London: J. M. Dent & Co., 1908), 3, footnote 1; Kinglake, however, who was in Cairo during the peak of the epidemic, says that Cairo lost half its population, Alexander William Kinglake, *Eothen* (London: Ollivier, 1847), 207.

36. For Mehmed Ali's belief in quarantines and how this contrasts with Clot Bey's skepticism about their efficacy, see Khaled Fahmy, *In Quest of Justice: Islamic Law and Forensic Medicine in Modern Egypt* (Oakland: University of California Press, 2018), 53–62.

37. ENA, Ma'iyya Saniyya, Turki, S/1/60/2 (original no. 59), doc. no. 55, p. 17, 7 Rabi' II 1250 / 13 August 1834. Given the lack of female doctors, the examination of female dead bodies could not be done. This became possible with the opening of the School of Midwives in 1832 and the graduation of its first class of female doctors four years later; see Khaled Fahmy, "Women, Medicine, and Power in Nineteenth-Century Egypt," in *Remaking Women: Feminism and Modernity in the Middle East*, ed. Lila Abu-Lughod (Princeton: Princeton University Press, 1998), 35–72.

38. ENA, Ma'iyya Saniyya, Turki, S/1/60/2 (original no. 59), doc. no. 428, p. 135, 17 Dhu al-Qa'da 1250 / 17 March 1835.

39. ENA, Ma'iyya Saniyya, Turki, S/1/52/2 (original no. 57), doc. no. 530, p. 115, 17 Dhu al-Hijja 1250 / 16 April 1835.

40. ENA, Ma'iyya Saniyya, Turki, S/1/52/2 (original no. 57), doc. no. 602, 5 Safar 1251 / 2 June 1835.

41. For a background to the rivalry between miasmatists and contagionists in Europe, see Lois N. Magner, *A History of Infectious Diseases and the Microbial World* (London: Praeger, 2009), 19–48.

42. A. B. Clot Bey, "The Plague and Quarantine Laws," *The Lancet* 31, no. 806 (9 February 1839): 743–44.

43. A. B. Clot Bey, *Tanbih Fima Yakhuss al-Ta'un* (Cairo: Matba'at Diwan al-Jihadiyya, 1250 AH / 1835 CE).

44. For more on the 1841 settlement, see Khaled Fahmy, *Mehmed Ali: From Ottoman Governor to Ruler of Egypt* (Oxford: Oneworld, 2009), 91–98.

45. Kuhnke, *Lives at Risk*, 145–47; Tassos Demetrios Néroutsos, *Aperçu historique de l'organisation de l'intendance générale sanitaire d'Égypte: séant à Alexandrie, depuis sa fondation en 1831 . . . jusqu' . . . en 1879* (Alexandria: Mourès, 1880), 39–42.

46. The decree was issued in Turkish, but no copy of it could be found in the Egyptian National Archives. Luckily, an English translation is preserved in the British National Archives (TNA), and it is this English translation that is consulted here: TNA, FO 78/502, Barnett, 23 December 1842, enclosures, "General Regulations concerning the public health at Alexandria and the interior to be put into execution according to Order of His Highness the Vice Roy, dated 15 Rejeb 1257 (30 August 1841)." For a brief overview of this important decree, see Fahmy, *In Quest of Justice*, 203–4.

47. Kenneth Cuno and Michael Reimer, "The Census Registers of Nineteenth-Century Egypt: A New Source for Social Historians," *British Journal of Middle Eastern Studies* 24, no. 2 (1997): 197.

48. Ibid., 198.

49. Ibid., 202.

50. The references in the ENA to postmortem examinations are too copious to enumerate, but see, in particular: ENA, Muhafazat Misr, L/1/5/1, from Taftish al-Sihha to Dabtiyyat Misr, doc. no. 1, p. 1, on 16 Safar 1276 / 14 September 1859, where it is stated explicitly that undertakers had to check the burial certificate that should have been issued by a physician and that the certificate should state the nature of the illness and the cause of death. In the absence of such a certificate, a new postmortem examination had to be performed. For more details on *al-kashf 'ala al-amwat*, see Fahmy, *In Quest of Justice*, 51, 58, 82, 279–80. See also Panzac, "The Population of Egypt," 22.

51. For background information on the Department of Civil Affairs, Diwan al-Khidiwi, see F. Robert Hunter, *Egypt Under the Khedives: From Household Government to Modern Bureaucracy, 1805–1879* (Pittsburgh: University of Pittsburgh Press, 1984), 19, 44.

52. ENA, Diwan Madaris, M/1/1/3 (original no. 3), doc. no. 199, p. 872, on 18 Muharram 1261 / 27 January 1845.

53. For more on the intricate relationship between the *hakimas* and the *dayas*, see Fahmy, "Women, Medicine, and Power," 50–51.

54. See, e.g., ENA, Diwan al-Dakhiliyya, reg. no. 1316, doc. no. 48, p. 11, 26 Dhu al-Qa'da 1285 / 11 March 1869, where it is stated that the number of new births in 1284 (1867–68) was smaller than that of the previous year and that this decrease was caused by imprecise information collected from the provinces and villages, as opposed to Cairo and Alexandria, whose statistics showed an increase in births from one year to the next.

55. ENA, Dabtiyyat Misr, L/2/31/1, doc. no. 96, p. 119, 30 Shawwal 1296 / 16 October 1879. For a short account of how sophisticated the system of collection of vital statistics had become by the 1870s, see Fahmy, *In Quest of Justice*, 173–77.

56. See ENA, Diwan al-Jihadiyya, reg. no. 450, letter no. 136, p. 19, 16 Shawwal 1276 / 6 May 1860, where it is stated that the hospital had five hundred inmates and fifty-four nurses and servants; ENA, Muhafazat Misr, Sadir Riyasat al-Isbitaliya, reg. L/1/4/1 (old no. 454), letter no. 2, p. 5, 19 Rabi' II 1280 / 3 October 1863, where it is mentioned that the hospital had 850 patients and there was a need to increase the number of beds to one thousand. By relying on Clot Bey's *Mémoires* and accounts by European travelers, Kuhnke states that the Abu Za'bal hospital could accommodate between four hundred and nine hundred patients, and that after its relocation to Qasr al-'Ayni it had an estimated capacity of between twelve hundred and sixteen hundred beds; Kuhnke, *Lives at Risk*, 136.

57. After its closure in 1847, the location of this hospital was taken over by the Cairo Police headquarters (Diwan al-Dabtiyya), and then by the municipal council, the Urnatu: ENA, Mahkamat al-Bab al-'Ali, reg. no. 556 - sijill mubay'at al-Bab al-'Ali, vol. 3 (new no. 1001-001203), case no. 75, pp. 76–84 (relevant information on p. 76).

58. Kuhnke, *Lives at Risk*, 136. See also 'Ali Mubarak, *al-Khitat*, vol. 7, 72, where he says that the Mahmudiyya Hospital also admitted the poor and needy and that it had a school to teach foundlings, who, in 1831, numbered thirty-four.

59. Regulations stated that those afflicted with minor diseases should be treated at the factory hospitals in the provinces; those with more chronic diseases should be sent to the civilian hospital in Cairo, and if the ailment persisted, the patient should be sent to Qasr al-'Ayni: ENA, Diwan al-Jihadiyya, reg. 440, doc. no. 98, p. 165, 21 Jumada II 1264 / 25 May 1848; Diwan al-Jihadiyya, reg. 440, doc. no. 100, p. 165, 27 Jumada 1264 / 31 May 1848.

60. Kuhnke, *Lives at Risk*, 147–52.

61. Mubarak, *al-Khitat*, vol. 1, 96.

62. ENA, Diwan al-Jihadiyya, Sadir Shura al-Atibba, reg. no. 437, doc. no. 9, p. 46, 6 Dhu al-Qa'da 1262 / 26 October 1846.

63. ENA, Diwan al-Jihadiyya, Sadir Shura al-Atibba, reg. no. 440, doc. no. 105, p. 124, 27 Rabi' II 1264 / 2 April 1848.

64. Gustave Flaubert, *Flaubert in Egypt: A Sensibility on Tour*, trans. and ed. Francis Steegmuller (Chicago: Academy Chicago Press, 1979), 65.

65. ENA, Diwan Khidiwi, S/2/18/1 (original no. 654), order no. 1, pp. 140–2, 3 Muharram 1267 / 8 November 1850.

66. ENA, Diwan al-Dakhiliyya, Awamir Karima, reg. no. 1310, order no. 77, p. 25, 25 Sha'ban 1274 / 10 April 1858.

67. ENA, Diwan al-Jihadiyya, Sadir Shura al-Atibba, reg. no. 440, doc. no. 105, p. 124, 27 Rabi' II 1264 / 2 April 1848.

68. ENA, Diwan al-Jihadiyya, Sadir Shura al-Atibba, reg. no. 440, doc. no. 116, p. 128, 6 Jumada I 1264 / 10 April 1848.

69. ENA, Muhafazat Misr, Sadir Riyasat al-Isbitaliya, reg. L/1/4/3 (original no. 457), doc. no. 33, p. 7, 24 Rabi' II 1281 / 26 September 1864; ENA, Muhafazat Misr, Sadir Riyasat al-Isbitaliya, reg. L/1/4/3 (original no. 457). doc. no. 83, p. 15, 11 Jumada I 1281 / 12 October 1864, where the disease is referred to as *tayfus*. It seems that the infection was so strong that a "huge number" (*'adad 'azim*) of the orderlies and nurses died of it: ENA, Muhafazat Misr, Sadir Riyasat al-Isbitaliya, reg. L/1/4/3 (original no. 457), doc. 45, p. 98, 19 Dhu al-Hijja 1281 / 15 May 1865.

70. M. L. Labat, "De l'hôpital d'Abou-Zabel et de son organisation médicale, considérée sous le point de vue de l'application des principes de la médecine physiologique, aux diverses maladies qu'on observe fréquemment en Égypte," *Annales de la médecine physiologique* 24, no. 1833: 147–48.

71. F. M. Sandwith, "The History of Kasr-el-Ainy," *Records of the Egyptian Government School of Medicine*, vol. 1 (Cairo: National Printing Department, 1901), 19.

72. Kuhnke, *Lives at Risk*, 142. Kuhnke's information is all derived from *al-Waqa'i' al-Misriyya*, Mehmed Ali's gazette.

73. For more details about urban sanitation in Cairo, especially with regard to food inspection, see Fahmy, *In Quest of Justice*, 217–22.

74. The records of the Department of Health Inspection of Cairo contain countless examples of petitions presented by such people to open their shops in Cairo. The answers to these

petitions are also recorded. For those concerning butchers, for example, see the petition presented by some butchers to open shops in al-Rumayla Street: ENA, Muhafazat Misr, L/1/5/1 (original no. 183), doc. no. 199, from Taftish al-Sihha to al-Dabtiyya, p. 183, 18 Muharram 1277 / 6 August 1860. The response is in ENA, Muhafazat Misr, L/1/5/1 (original no. 183), doc. no. 206, p. 185, 25 Muharram 1277 / 13 August 1860. When Ibrahim Muhammad al-Jazzar was discovered by the Taftish to have opened his butchery without a permit, the *dabtiyya* was promptly informed to arrest him and have his shop closed: ENA, Muhafazat Misr, L/1/5/2 (original no. 185), doc. no. 130, p. 132, 29 Shawwal 1277 / 10 May 1861. When the meat sold by 'Abd al-Hadi al-Ghayati al-Jazzar in his butchery was inspected and found unsuitable for human consumption, he was sent to the *dabtiyya* for questioning. A sample of the meat was also forwarded by the Taftish: ENA, Muhafazat Misr, L/1/5/2 (original no. 185), doc. no. 169, p. 158, 12 Muharram 1278 / 20 July 1861.

75. ENA, Muhafazat Misr, L/1/5/2 (original no. 185), doc. no. 28, p. 67, 19 Sha'ban 1290 / 13 October 1873.

76. The information on Cairo's slaughterhouses is as fascinating as that on its butcheries; see the interesting order by Khedive Isma'il approving an earlier decree by Majlis al-Khususi to open two slaughterhouses for Cairo, one in the north and the other to the south of the city, where all slaughtering was to be done: ENA, Diwan al-Dakhiliyya, Daftar Qayd al-Awamir al-Karima, reg. no. 1315, order no. 74, p. 21, 4 Safar 1285 / 27 May 1868. For the unhygienic condition of the northern 'Abbasiyya slaughterhouse ten years after its foundation, see ENA, Dabtiyyat Misr, L/2/31/1, letter no. 197, p. 141, 12 Dhu al-Qa'da 1296 / 28 October 1879. For an example of a team of regular health inspectors who discovered five tanneries within Cairo without a permit and who gave their owners sixty days to relocate outside the city, see ENA, Muhafazat Misr, Reg. L/1/5/2 (original no. 185), doc. no. 135, p. 135, 5 Dhu al-Qa'da 1277 / 15 May 1861.

77. For background information on the resistance to vaccination, see 'Azza 'Abd al-Hadi, "Muqawamat al-Ahali li-Tat'im al-Judari fi al-Qarn al-Tasi' 'Ashr," in *al-Rafd wa-l-Ihtijaj fi al-Mujtama' al-Misri fi al-'Asr al-'Uthmani*, ed. Nasir Ibrahim (Cairo: al-Jam'iyya al-Misriyya li-l-Dirasat al-Tarikhiyya, 2004), 303–12. For Clot Bey's manual on how to perform the vaccination, see A. B. Clot Bey, *Mabhath Ta'limi fi Tat'im al-Judari*, trans. Ahmad Hasan al-Rashidi (Cairo: Bulaq, 1259 AH / 1843 CE).

78. Clot Bey, *Mémoires*, 157.

79. Panzac, "The Population of Egypt," 17–18.

80. Kuhnke, *Lives at Risk*, 112.

81. ENA, Ma'iyya Saniyya, Turki, S/1/47/2 (original no. 3), doc. no. 247, 5 Jumada I 1234 / 2 March 1819. It seems that this is the letter that Sami refers to in summary form: Amin Sami, *Taqwim al-Nil*, vol. 2 (Cairo: Dar al-Kutub, 1928), 278. This may have been Francesco Grassi who would later join Ibrahim Pasha as chief surgeon of the army in the Greek Campaign (1824–27). He later became director of the Alexandria Quarantine Board. See Fahmy, *In Quest of Justice*, 48, 57, 276.

82. Kuhnke, *Lives at Risk*, 113–14.

83. Paul Mouriez, *Histoire de Méhémed-Ali, vice-roi d'Égypte*, vol. 2 (Paris: Louis Chappe, 1855–58), 246.

84. ENA, Ma'iyya Saniyya, Turki, S/1/47/8 (original no. 19), docs. no. 216, 27 Muharram 1241 / 11 September 1825, and no. 218, 1 Safar 1241 / 15 September 1825.

85. ENA, Ma'iyya Saniyya, Turki, S/1/50/8 (original no. 31), doc. 206, pp. 121–122, 13 Dhu al-Qa'da 1243 / 27 May 1828.

86. A. B. Clot Bey, *Introduction de la Vaccination en Égypte en 1827: Organisation du service médico-hygiènique des provinces en 1840: instructions et règlements relatifs à ces deux services* (Paris: Victor Masson et Fils, n.d.), 9–10.

87. ENA, Diwan Mulkiyya, reg. no. 4, doc. no. 60, p. 60, 18 Muharram 1252 / 5 May 1836.

88. ENA, Diwan Madaris, Turki, reg. no. 2021, p. 8, session of 19 Dhu al-Qaʻda 1252 / 25 February 1837. A slightly different version of this ordinance is reproduced in Clot Bey, *Introduction*, 19–22.

89. ENA, Diwan Madaris, M/1/1/3, (original no. 3), pt. 3, doc. no. 48, p. 839, 17 Muharram 1261 / 26 January 1845. Children from Old Cairo, however, were to be vaccinated in the medical school in Qasr al-ʻAyni due to its proximity.

90. ENA, Diwan Taftish Sihhat Misr, M/5/1 (original no. 163), doc. no. 5, p. 6, 19 Dhu al-Qaʻda 1266 / 26 September 1850.

91. ENA, Majlis al-Ahkam, S/7/33/1, "Surat al-Laʼiha al-Sadira fi Haqq al-Effendiyya Muʻawini al-Akhtat," p. 55, 29 Muharram 1262 / 27 January 1846.

92. ENA, Diwan al-Jihadiyya, S/3/122/2 (original no. 437), doc. no. 48, p. 75, 11 Muharram 1263 / 30 December 1846.

93. ENA, Diwan al-Jihadiyya, S/3/122/2 (original no. 437), doc. no. 106, p. 119, 28 Rabiʻ I 1263 / 14 May 1847.

94. ENA, Diwan Shura al-Muʻawana, reg. no. 282, doc no. 537, 18 Jumada I 1256 / 18 July 1840.

95. ENA, Diwan al-Jihadiyya, S/3/122/2 (original no. 437), doc. no. 66, p. 87, 4 Safar 1263 / 22 January 1847.

96. Kuhnke, *Lives at Risk*, 116.

97. ENA, Diwan al-Jihadiyya, S/3/122/2 (original no. 437), docs. no. 11–96, pp. 61–63, 26 Jumada I 1263 / 13 May 1847. These are letters concerning eighty-five provincial doctors who were punished for accepting bribes from the villagers.

98. ENA, Diwan al-Jihadiyya, S/3/122/2 (original no. 437), doc. no. 157, p. 194, 4 Rajab 1263 / 19 June 1847.

99. ENA, Diwan al-Jihadiyya, S/3/122/2 (original no. 437), doc. no. 155, p. 194, 1 Rajab 1263 / 15 June 1847. For the same incident, see Charles Cuny, "Mémoire sur les services rendus par M. Cuny en sa qualité continue de médecin, depuis l'année 1837 jusqu'en 1851, qu'il a servile Gouvernment Égyptien," 4, quoted in Luhnke, *Lives at Risk*, 116, footnote 25.

100. ENA, Diwan al-Jihadiyya, S/3/122/4 (original no. 440), doc no. 142, pp. 156, 159, on 15 Jumada II 1264 / 19 May 1848.

101. ENA, Diwan Taftish Sihhat Misr, M/5/1 (original no. 163), doc. no. 107, p. 48, 7 Rabiʻ II 1267/9 February 1851.

102. ENA, Diwan Taftish Sihhat Misr, M/5/11 (original no. 226), doc. 70, pp. 276, 285, 29 Muharram 1291 / 18 March 1874.

103. ENA, Dabtiyyat Misr, L/2/31/1, doc. no. 290, p. 79, 15 Ramadan 1296 / 2 September 1879.

104. Panzac, "The Population of Egypt," 20.

105. *Yaʻsub al-Tibb*, no. 29, 29 Jumada I 1285 / 23 August 1868. This journal was first published in 1865, and its first editor was Ahmad al-Rashidi, one of the doctors sent to France in 1832.

106. Panzac, "The Population of Egypt," 20, 24.

107. Yusuf Asaf, *al-Taʻdilat al-Qanuniya Allati Udkhilat ʻala al-Qanun al-Ahli al-Misri min Sanat 1886 li-Ghayat Marth [sic] Sanat 1895* (Cairo: al-Matbaʻa al-ʻUmumiya, 1895), 7–9.

108. Panzac, "The Population of Egypt," 16.

BIBLIOGRAPHY

Abd al-Hadi, Azza. "Muqawamat al-Ahali li-Tat'im al-Judari fi al-Qarn al-Tasi' 'Ashr." In *al-Rafd wa-l-Ihtijaj fi al-Mujtama' al-Misri fi al-'Asr al-'Uthmani*, edited by Nasir Ibrahim, 303–12. Cairo: al-Jam'iyya al-Misriyya li-l-Dirasat al-Tarikhiyya, 2004.

Abugideiri, Hibba. *Gender and the Making of Modern Medicine in Colonial Egypt*. London: Routledge, 2010.

Clot Bey, Antoine Barthélemy. *Aperçu général sur l'Égypte*. Paris: Masson, 1840.

Cuno, Kenneth M., and Michael J. Reimer. "The Census Registers of Nineteenth-Century Egypt: A New Source for Social Historians." *British Journal of Middle Eastern Studies* 24, no. 2 (November 1997): 193–216.

Fahmy, Khaled. *In Quest of Justice: Islamic Law and Forensic Medicine in Modern Egypt*. Oakland: University of California Press, 2018.

Fahmy, Khaled. "Women, Medicine, and Power in Nineteenth-Century Egypt." In *Remaking Women: Feminism and Modernity in the Middle East*, edited by Lila Abu-Lughod, 35–72. Princeton: Princeton University Press, 1998.

Gallagher, Nancy Elizabeth. *Egypt's Other Wars: Epidemics and the Politics of Public Health*. Syracuse: Syracuse University Press, 2021.

Kuhnke, Laverne. *Lives at Risk: Public Health in Nineteenth-Century Egypt*. Berkeley: University of California Press, 1990.

Panzac, Daniel. "The Population of Egypt in the Nineteenth Century." *Asian and African Studies* 21, no. 1 (1987): 11–32.

Ragab, Ahmed. *Medicine and Religion in the Life of an Ottoman Sheikh: Al-Damanhuri's "Clear Statement" on Anatomy*. London: Routledge, 2019.

Al-Rutayl, 'Imad 'Abd al-Ra'uf. *Al-Tibb wa-l-'Ilaj fi Misr al-'Uthmaniya wa-'Ahd Muhammad 'Ali*. Cairo: Dar al-Jumhuriya li-l-Sahafa, 2014.

Sonbol, Amira El Azhary. *The Creation of a Medical Profession in Egypt: 1800-1922*. Syracuse: Syracuse University Press, 1991.

CHAPTER 2

··

MIDWIVES AND CHILDBIRTH DURING COLONIAL AND SEMI-COLONIAL RULE

··

BETH BARON

A pair of photographs taken in June 1920 in al-Zaqaziq, in the Egyptian Delta, captures a graduating class of *dayas* (midwives) from the local maternity school (Figs. 2.1 and 2.2). The prototype for such schools had been launched by British imperial medical officers in 1913, and those that followed offered a four-month program to train midwives—or retrain them, as many had earlier experience—in modern methods of delivery. The pictures from al-Zaqaziq show a dozen women in their indoor uniform (Fig. 2.1, white aprons over light blouses, with white head covering) and their outdoor uniform (Fig. 2.2, darker shifts/galabiyas with black head covering). The women all stand or sit erect, staring at the camera. In the image in their indoor uniform, the *dayas* have placed the bowls and gas heaters that they use for sterilizing water at the feet of those seated in the first row. In the second image, some of the women balance the bowls and heaters or boxes containing supplies they will need to perform their trade on their heads. In both images, three additional individuals appear: a British matron (their teacher), who wears a black hat and holds a small pet dog on her lap; an Egyptian *bashdaya* (head midwife), who assists the matron and sits to her left in one image and to her right in the other; and a male attendant, who stands in the back.[1] Photographs of graduating classes of *dayas* from the newly founded maternity schools provide a rare glimpse into the world of birth work, which was part of the new racialized and gendered hierarchies established in maternal medicine under British colonial rule.

The new maternity schools for *dayas* came roughly eighty years after the French doctor Antoine Barthélemy Clot, or Clot Bey as he became known, founded the School of Midwifery in Egypt. Although graduates of both programs were often called midwives in English translation, their roles, skills, and status diverged significantly. The School of Midwifery followed a six-year curriculum not unlike that of the Qasr al-ʿAyni School of Medicine, with which it was affiliated, producing an elite class

FIG. 2.1 Photograph of the Zaqaziq Maternity School class of March–June 1920 with the *dayas* wearing their outdoor uniforms. De Courcy Family Papers, Private Collection (DCFP), Zaqaziq Maternity School (6731 front/6732 back).

of literate *hakimas* (women doctors or health officers), who upon graduation took up work in state hospitals and police stations.[2] *Hakimas* not only delivered babies; they also examined prostitutes for syphilis and gonorrhea, testified in court in legal cases, carried out forensic examinations, and were charged with overseeing *dayas*. The centralizing state of Mehmed Ali Pasha thus used the new *hakimas* to rein in the formerly autonomous *dayas*, instructing those deficient in knowledge, stamping the newly introduced certificates needed to practice, and monitoring their reporting of births and deaths. The *dayas* were meant to call in the better-trained *hakimas* in difficult cases and also participated in vaccination campaigns, performed female circumcisions, and supplied contraceptives and drugs for abortions.[3]

Compared to *hakimas*, there has been relatively little written on *dayas* in Egypt and their role in birth work (both the production of birth workers and the process of childbirth), including during the critical period between 1910 and 1940, which marked the shift from colonial to semi-colonial control of public health in Egypt.[4] Relevant sources for this period include works by the pioneering obstetrician-gynecologist Naguib Mahfouz and an Egyptian gynecologist-obstetrician with an interest in birthing chairs, Aly Alaily; Department of Public Health annual reports and the private papers of Mabel Wolff, a nurse-midwife who worked as a matron in maternal and child

FIG. 2.2 Photograph of the Zaqaziq Maternity School class of March–June 1920 with the *dayas* wearing their indoor uniforms. De Courcy Family Papers, Private Collection (DCFP), Zaqaziq Maternity School (6733 front/6734 back).

health in al-Fayum;[5] and most notably, the records that the imperial women doctors Grace de Courcy (née Russell) and Bonté Elgood (née Amos) left behind, which provide unique insight into the lives and careers of imperial women doctors, the birth workers they sought to remake, and the network of maternity schools that spread across Egypt, transforming the birth experiences of peasant and working-class Egyptian women.

One of the first two women from New Zealand to be trained as a doctor, Grace Russell worked in public health in Egypt for nearly two decades, serving nine years on the International Sanitary, Maritime, and Quarantine Board of Egypt in Suez and nine more as inspector in charge of maternity schools and children's dispensaries. Englishwoman Bonté Elgood had an equally long career in public health in Egypt, working first for the Quarantine Board and then as an inspector of girls' schools. Although Elgood and Russell came from opposite sides of the world—the imperial center and its periphery— they had similar upper-class backgrounds, crossing paths as students at the London School of Medicine for Women and then again as medical officers in Cairo. Their parallel and intersecting trajectories speak to the imperial medical networks of women who staffed the empire and ran health and education programs. The policies and programs they authored, influenced, or implemented reflect a two-pronged colonial strategy regarding midwives in Egypt: on the one hand, to scale back the studies, status, and numbers of *hakimas*, transforming them into specialized nurses, and on the other, to professionalize *dayas*, standardizing their training, licensing, and examination.

The undermining of *hakimas* and subsequent training of male doctors in the new fields of obstetrics and gynecology has led scholars to point to the masculinization of childbirth in Egypt under British rule, with masculinization here referring to the replacement of female birth workers with male obstetricians and gynecologists. This process, it is further asserted, led to the replacement of home deliveries with hospital deliveries by the 1920s.[6] Yet it was *dayas*, and not *hakimas* or male doctors, who delivered the bulk of Egypt's babies during the colonial and semi-colonial period, with most babies being delivered at home. Rather than masculinize childbirth, imperial doctors sought to professionalize female birth workers and modernize the birthing process through the introduction of new medical experts, statistical regimes, sterilization practices, and birthing postures. These innovations, which were not by themselves masculine or feminine in nature, worked to scientize or medicalize childbirth. Yet the *dayas* and the parturient women they assisted did not necessarily follow the new protocols; instead, they often sought to preserve their authority and autonomy over one of the most intimate, natural, and painful physical experiences.

The Opening of a Model Maternity School for *Dayas* in Cairo

In 1911, the British-controlled Department of Public Health laid out a preliminary plan for transforming the system of training *dayas* to bring down high rates of infant mortality and, at the same time, lower maternal mortality rates. Before making changes, officials wanted an expert to examine the current program, a two- to three-week basic training course taught by medical officers in provincial hospitals. The department turned to Bonté Elgood to carry out the study. In 1906, Elgood had been lured away from her job in Alexandria as an assistant medical officer with the Quarantine Board to become the health inspector in Egyptian girls' schools. Given her medical training, family connections, and work experience, her views on maternal health and education matters were solicited by colonial administrators and imperial proconsuls such as Lords Cromer and Kitchener.

Elgood toured Upper Egypt in 1913 with the director-general of the Public Health Department to inspect the training and certification of *dayas* within provincial hospitals. She described the training she encountered as mostly theoretical, with the students seeing a couple of maternity cases, if that, after which they were examined perfunctorily and then issued a white certificate that enabled them to practice. Noting that the students ranged in age from twenty to seventy, with one woman "more than half blind," Elgood had little good to say about the group. As she later testified to the 1918 Commission to Advise as Regards the Future Organization and Work of the Department of Public Health Commission, "The present class of dayah is most hopelessly inefficient." In short, "they were a most dirty, disreputable and incapable class of women."[7]

Village midwives bore the brunt of imperial blame for births gone awry and post-partum problems such as puerperal fever, which was the most common cause of maternal mortality. In 1913, the Department of Public Health reported that seventy-four women had died from puerperal fever, making the death rate for the disease 0.103 per 1,000 people or, based on the number of births, a maternal death rate from this cause as 2.34 per 1,000 childbirths. "Judged by these figures," officials argued, the puerperal rate was low, but they had reason to believe "that the number of deaths from puerperal fever and accidents of child-birth may be somewhat higher than the cases actually certified as from such causes."[8] Pointing to puerperal fever became one way to legitimize the new system for training *dayas*, a system staffed and overseen by imperial medical experts. Collecting more accurate statistics was another: the Department of Public Health and officials such as Elgood did not trust the statistics submitted by *dayas* and wanted greater supervision of their training and closer inspection of their practice.

After Elgood returned from her Upper Egypt tour, Kitchener directed her to set up an experimental maternity training school in Cairo. She selected widowed and divorced women aged nineteen and twenty for the program due to their maturity and need for income. Having organized the first maternity home in Cairo "as a type to be copied elsewhere," she recognized the novelty of the experiment to move obstetric training out of the hospital and articulated an imperial presumption that professionalized birth work was transferable from one location to another.[9] For expertise, the maternity school turned to an executive committee made up of Elgood; Dr. Ferguson Lees, the medical officer for Cairo who had more than five hundred *dayas* under his charge; and Dr. Naguib Mahfouz, who, among other tasks, trained *hakimas* at Qasr al-'Ayni and produced teaching material for them.[10] Mahfouz called Elgood "a very capable lady-doctor" and was eager to participate in her new venture, for he was also critical of *dayas*, though less condescending than her, seeing the archetype *daya* as "an illiterate extremely ignorant woman who learned her profession from any practicing midwife in her district."[11] Mahfouz was particularly concerned with *dayas'* inability to handle difficult labors because over the years, he had seen the imprint of difficult or neglected labors on the bodies of Egyptian women in the form of fistulas, ruptured uteruses, and other complications.[12] But he did not doubt that *dayas* could handle uncomplicated births if they were properly instructed.

The Cairo Maternity Home opened in the Citadel quarter, overseen by Elgood and run by a matron named Miss Jackson, "a capable English Midwife," in Mahfouz's estimation.[13] With Jackson and Egyptian *hakimas* giving theoretical lessons, students practiced normal home deliveries under the watchful eye of the matron, and in difficult cases, Jackson persuaded the patient to allow herself to be transported to Qasr al-'Ayni Hospital. The students spent a month at a children's dispensary learning about infant care. Upon completing their four-month training, the student midwives were examined by members of the executive committee. By the end of 1914, Elgood and Mahfouz had certified 118 women, thirty-seven of whom had come from the provinces; those who passed the exam were given a new green certificate, to be distinguished from the white one issued after the shorter course of study in hospitals.[14]

Three weeks after the start of World War I, the Finance Department sent an order to close the Cairo Maternity House. Although the project cost only 600 Egyptian pounds annually and enjoyed popularity among the working-class Cairene women whose babies it delivered, colonial officials considered it an unnecessary expense in wartime.[15] Elgood pushed hard for reopening the school but faced opposition from the assistant director-general of the Department of Public Health, Dr. Goodman, who wanted to open a women's hospital in Cairo rather than an external midwifery unit. Elgood supported the foundation of a new maternity hospital in Cairo but argued that in the interim there were few opportunities to train or retrain *dayas* in modern birthing methods and that there was also great demand for their services. "Not a week passes," Elgood noted, "without a telephone message reaching me either for a doctor or a distracted husband asking me if the home is not re-opened—if help cannot be sent to some woman in labour."[16]

PROVINCIAL MATERNITY SCHOOLS, THE INSPECTOR, AND HER MATRONS

Seeing the early success and promise of the Cairo Maternity House, in 1913 the Department of Public Health launched schools for *dayas* in six provincial towns, two in Upper Egypt—Suhag and al-Minya—and four in the Delta region—Shibin al-Kum, Tanta, Mansoura, and al-Zaqaziq. All were nominally under the direction of the Central Ladies' Committee, which was made up of the wives of pashas and British colonial officials and chaired by Lady Graham, a nurse and wife of the British director-general of the Department of Public Health, and came under the presidency of Khedive 'Abbas Hilmi II's mother, Amina al-Hamy. With funding from provincial councils rather than the central budget controlled by the British, these schools did not face immediate closure as the Cairo prototype did.[17]

In 1914, the Department of Public Health tapped Grace Russell to become inspector of the provincial maternity schools and children's dispensaries.[18] Her mandate was "to visit each school and dispensary in turn, and to exercise a general personal supervision over the work so as to ensure a uniform standard of training of midwives for their diplomas, and to keep the Central Ladies' Committee in full touch with all that is going on."[19] During the war and revolution that followed, many of the schools faced intermittent closures due to staffing, funding, and security issues—the Tanta school, for example, was closed from 1917 to 1921—but new schools opened as well, including ones in Damanhur and al-Fayum.

As Russell's appointment was considered crucial enough not to be cut by war contingencies, she bid farewell to Dr. Marc Armand Ruffer, head of the Quarantine

Board, and moved from Suez to Cairo. There she met with Sir David Semple, director-general of the Department of Public Health; Dr. Goodman, assistant director-general; and her old friend and colleague Bonté Amos, now "Mrs. Elgood."[20] When Russell tried to meet with members of the Central Ladies' Committee, she discovered that none of them were in Egypt due to the summer break or outbreak of war and considered the committee "rather defunct."[21] Russell eventually collected the committee's files—left by Mrs. Richards, an ex-nurse who had gone to the front with her surgeon husband—gaining background on the work of the committee.[22]

As soon as she took up her job, Russell began inspecting the provincial maternity schools, with the goal of replacing the two to three weeks of instruction offered by the hospital medical officers with a standardized four-month course of training "under qualified English matrons."[23] The creation of maternity schools transferred oversight of *dayas* from Egyptian *hakimas* to English matrons and the imperial "lady doctor" who inspected the homes and examined the graduating class. Russell's visits—intended to make sure that there was "a uniform standard of training of midwives for their diplomas"—were also an opportunity to supervise the children's dispensaries, which were often linked to the schools for *dayas*.[24]

In her first round of visits, Russell met the matrons who ran the maternity schools; they came from Great Britain and beyond, ranging in age, language ability, and, in her estimation, intellect. Starting her tour in the Delta town of Mansoura, where the matron was from North Wales, Russell then went to Tanta, where she found the matron "quite a nice quiet person" who had "a slight inclination to the missionary type but more intelligent than the last."[25] At her next stop, Shibin al-Kum, the matron was a "Russian German Swiss—good linguist but only maternity training."[26] After a respite in Cairo, Russell went on to Suhag, where the matron was "Limerick but no trace of Irish accent remains," and noted, "she's about 50 I should think but quite nice, her Arabic very scanty."[27] After a few days Russell warmed to the woman, now describing her as "a brave little Irish woman with an infinity of patience" who, despite her age, "had tackled the language nobly."[28]

In al-Fayum, Russell saw Mabel Wolff and her sister/assistant Gertrude, both of whom had been born in Port Tawfiq, where their father was a clerk in a shipping firm and their grandfather was, as Russell told her mother, "old Captain Walsworth of Suez."[29] Like most of the matrons, the sisters were from the middle class; unlike most, the sisters spoke Arabic fluently. They had gone to train in Britain as nurse-midwives, after which they had returned to Egypt, settling in the oasis town of al-Fayum, where Mabel Wolff managed the dispensary from 1913 and the maternity school from 1917.[30]

Staffing the maternity homes and finding replacements when British matrons fell ill, took a leave, married, or left for other jobs was part of the inspector's responsibilities. At the outset of the war, Russell told her mother that she had "to find a nurse who has trained some midwives to see if I can get one to go [to] the Provinces."[31] The war and the commandeering of foreign nurses to help with the wounded pouring in from Gallipoli in May 1915 presented Russell with severe staffing shortages. Matrons received telegrams like the one sent to Mabel Wolff: "Moudirieh has been officially notified you are required by General Maxwell for military service at once." Russell arranged for the temporary closing of the maternity schools and dispensaries in al-Fayum and elsewhere.[32] By early July 1915, after nurses had flocked to Egypt from distant parts of the British Empire, midwives could return to reopened maternity training schools. "The native papers have been writing about them being closed," Russell noted. Yet she admitted that this press critique may not have changed the minds of British health officials: "I don't think that would have influenced them unless a good number of nurses had arrived from other places so that they can really be spared."[33] For the British, the health of imperial soldiers took priority over that of parturient Egyptian women.

In 1917, Russell searched for a matron for the new school opening in Damanhur; that year, the Egyptian Department of Public Health engaged three new matrons.[34] On a rare trip to England from July to October 1919 with her new husband (whom she had married in February), she recruited and interviewed candidates in London, Birmingham, and Edgbaston.[35] The next year, Russell looked for a replacement for Mabel Wolff, who had agreed to launch a midwifery training school in Umdurman, Sudan. (Her sister Gertrude would head the nursing program at the Umdurman Civil Hospital.) Upon a return trip to England in October 1920, Russell placed advertisements in a Bristol newspaper: "WANTED, fully-trained Nurse, with C.M.B., as MATRON for Provincial Council Training School for Native Midwives, for Fayoum, Egypt. Good salary, furnished quarters, servant, &c. Candidates must be prepared to learn colloquial Arabic."[36] Imperial jobs in Egyptian maternity schools presented unique travel and employment opportunities to British nurse-midwives, who upon arrival were sent on a tour of schools "to gain an insight into the local conditions" before they settled into their new stations.[37] Despite the shortages of foreign nurses during the war, Russell would not consider elevating Egyptian *hakimas* to this role. Like others in the colonial medical service, she saw British nurses as indispensable in imperial medical structures.

RECRUITING, TRAINING, AND TESTING STUDENTS

With a matron hired and a maternity home rented or built, the schools were ready to open their doors to students. Those initially admitted were practicing midwives who had taken the short course of instruction at a provincial hospital that gave them the white certificate and had come to get the new green one. Other *dayas* who could pass competency tests in identifying diseases but needed licenses to practice were also admitted.[38] Matrons then sought to recruit younger students who they believed might be more amenable to modern birthing and sterilizing techniques. However, when the newly graduated *dayas* were blocked by older ones from getting clients, the maternity schools again changed their recruitment policy. This time they attempted to attract younger women from eighteen to thirty who had an older relative practicing midwifery, in the hopes that when these students returned home they would be able to practice. "The successful practice of the pupils after training seems to depend largely on the *daya* inheriting some relative's clientele," public health officials admitted.[39] To boost the literacy levels of incoming students, older *dayas* were incentivized—with gifts of clothing and other items—to send their daughters to village schools. Over time, the method of selecting candidates for the schools improved, with government doctors occasionally recommending suitable candidates, and demand for spots began to outstrip supply. Students in towns and cities where no maternity school existed sought placement, and officials were pleased with the better "quality" of new students.[40]

From wherever they came, the students boarded at the school during the four-month course. Imperial doctors and matrons intended to remake and modernize these provincial women, instructing them in domestic skills such as sewing, washing, ironing, and general housework in addition to midwifery.[41] Like student *dayas* in Sudan, they were probably issued bedding with their new uniforms and food rations. And just as in Sudan, some of the women may have come with a young child in tow.[42]

The schools themselves were sometimes old and crumbling, with reports describing foundations as cracked or flooded during the high season of the Nile. Russell arrived at Mansoura to find "the Maternity Matron moving into a new house—you never saw such a muddle—no water or light in the place and the floors inches thick—I told her she couldn't possibly move herself and the *dayas* in until the water was connected so I hope she'll follow my advice."[43] It seems the matron did follow the inspector's advice, because the school is later described as "specially adapted for the *dayas* . . . in a central position in the town and most convenient." The new school in Suhag—a "commodious house on the river front"—also had a choice location and plenty of space for the students.[44] In some locations—specifically Asyut and Bani Suwayf—sturdy facilities existed, but the provincial councils either did not have the funds to open the schools or did not want to open them. Not wanting to comply with the dictates of the colonial government, or unable to, the councils let the premises stand vacant, forcing those local women who sought to obtain a midwifery license to travel great distances.[45]

In classes containing between six and twelve students, depending on the size of the school, midwifery training consisted of theoretical lessons and clinical practice.[46] Matrons and medical officers from the government hospital delivered lectures on topics such as determining the cause of death, recognizing common infectious diseases, and identifying deaths caused by criminal activity.[47] The *dayas* were expected to be the eyes of the state, recording and reporting births and death, just as they had been from the time of Mehmed Ali Pasha. The new biomedical understanding of disease transmission gave the collection of accurate statistics that could be used to find disease patterns a renewed impetus.

Since almost all the students were illiterate, lectures were accompanied with diagrams and printed charts, and classes were designed so that students could use their senses to memorize material, whether that meant visualizing disease, listening for heartbeats, smelling medications, or touching flesh.[48] The students may also have seen specimens and watched the matron demonstrate on various models, like the ones Mabel Wolff carried with her from Egypt to Sudan—"a deformed fetus preserved in formaldehyde" and a baby doll.[49] The preserved fetus was possibly prepared by Mahfouz, who used specimens for teaching medical and midwifery students and later launched an obstetric and gynecological museum.[50] The doll may have been standard issue for British imperial nurse-midwife educators.[51] Sudanese students later practiced birthing techniques on a model pelvis that came with a fetus and practiced episiotomies on old tires.[52]

The students accompanied the matron on her patient rounds to observe her in action and gain supervised practice in delivering babies, with the goal of getting hands-on experience in twenty cases. This meant that the new matrons had to collect patients for their students: in her first year, the matron from Mansoura had over 250 cases, which signaled to Russell that she was "apparently a success with the native."[53] It also meant that the matrons and student *dayas* had "freedom of access" to the homes of ordinary Egyptians, which thrilled colonial public health officials, for these medical workers could also detect and report infectious diseases.[54]

As part of an effort to standardize and improve care while reinforcing the protocols that they had established, the British kept detailed statistics on the births that the matron and her students attended. Russell saw the collection of data as critical to improving outcomes in maternal and child health, and among the first numbers she collated were the number of cases seen by the matrons and village *dayas* in the maternity schools. Pregnant women came mostly from the fellahin or working classes and received free treatment, which might have proven particularly attractive to women with prior difficult deliveries. The number given for maternity patients seen in 1915, barely two years into the maternity school program, was 1,760, with a total of 22,928 home visits. This translated to an average of thirteen antenatal and postnatal visits for each mother or mother-to-be, which may have seemed high, but it gave the matron an opportunity to instruct both the student *dayas* and the new mothers in hygiene and infant care. The matrons and fifty-four *dayas* in training delivered 1,480 babies, an average of twenty-seven deliveries by each *daya* or less if they were observing the matron deliver the baby or there were multiples. They arrived too late to deliver another 286 babies, who were born before arrival (BBA), probably because most mothers—82%—had given birth previously (only 18% were primipara, or giving birth for the first time) or because the parturient women and their own *dayas* resisted cooperating with the matrons and maternity schools.[55]

Imperial doctors arrived in Egypt with the notion that Eastern women were supposed to have easy labors, a notion that grew out of the belief that Black and brown women did not experience pain in the same ways that "more civilized" white women experienced it.[56] But colonial medical officers found that this was not true. "It is interesting to note that whereas eastern women are supposed to have easy and uncomplicated labours, the experience of the matrons is that the cases are just as difficult as in England," the 1915 Department of Public Health report noted. "Labours are tedious, usually from uterine inertia, which seems to be due to the frequency of pregnancies commencing from an early age in girls who have not yet attained full growth or maturity."[57] That women gave birth frequently in Egypt from an early age was cause for critique. Birth was not only frequent; it was also long, which is what tedious means here.

Imperial doctors saw childbirth as a normal process, albeit a very painful one, which midwives were equipped to handle. Yet the category of abnormal cases began to expand in the 1910s in correlation with the collection of more detailed statistics to include twins and triplets, transverse and other difficult presentations, instrumental deliveries and complications, premature and ill babies, and maternal and infant deaths. Abnormal cases often called for the intervention of doctors rather than midwives. The prevalence of abnormal cases in the maternity schools was measured at 9.4% in 1916 and 9.5% in 1917.[58] In 1919, the rate jumped to 17%, then dropped, then rose again in 1921 to 21%, and then dropped the following year to 4%.[59] These statistics by no means reflected abnormal births in the population at large, only those cases handled by the maternity schools, which attracted more difficult deliveries in any case. Interestingly, there were very low rates of Caesarian sections among cases that the maternity schools reported: 3 out of 4,076 cases in 1920 and 7 out of 4,419 in 1922.[60] Caesarian sections were seen as emergency operations resorted to only in the most extreme cases.

Upon completing the maternity course, the student *dayas* faced an examination committee headed by Russell, who took up this task as soon as she began work as an inspector. "I may have to hold an exam for midwives before I leave here," she wrote to her mother during her first visit to Mansoura. While working for the Quarantine Board, she had mastered a few words of Turkish and could communicate in French, but she did not trust her colloquial Arabic. "I'll make the native doctor do all the talking," she wrote.[61] Demonstrating her higher rank than Egyptian male doctors in the imperial racial hierarchy, she later bristled when it appeared that a British male doctor, one who was not even specialized in obstetrics, would head another examining team, indicating her subordinate place in the imperial gender hierarchy. After her leadership had been confirmed, she expressed pride in her position as the "president of the examining board."[62]

The student *dayas* facing the examining committees had to master the material and overcome possible language barriers, but those who took the longer training course at one of the six new maternity schools had a greater chance of being certified to practice than those studying in the short courses at one of fourteen provincial hospitals. In 1915, 94% of the fifty-four *dayas* trained in the maternity schools passed the exam, while only 77% trained in the hospitals succeeded.[63] Chances of passing remained consistently higher for the former group but were never guaranteed.

Once examined, the midwives posed for graduation photos that marked their completion of the program, copies of which Russell kept as part of the record of her work in Egypt. The images taken in al-Zaqaziq in 1920 discussed at the opening of this chapter stand out among the graduation photos for how they document the two sets of uniforms that graduates were given and their high quality. The two photographs from al-Zaqaziq stand out for another reason: they are the only ones in the set containing a matron with a dog on her lap. While colonial photograph albums are replete with images of dogs— Elgood has multiple photos of her springer spaniel—this graduation photograph captures the image of the dog amid *dayas* who had been schooled about good hygienic practices. For Muslims, dogs are seen as ritually unclean, and the pet's presence thus challenges the matron's own practices and authority.[64]

The Department of Public Health may have gone out of its way to capture the graduating class of 1920 in this Delta town northeast of Cairo, for officials had plans to expand the school. The following year, Sultan (later King) Fu'ad attended the opening of a new in-patient department set up in a building adjoining the school. Consisting of a "large airy ward" with six beds and operating and lecture rooms, this in-patient facility was the first to be connected to a maternity school.[65] Yet only twenty-nine in-patients came in its first year, for peasant women still preferred to give birth at home.[66] Colonial plans for midwives and their patients did not always meet the reception that public health officials anticipated.

INSPECTION, EXPECTATION, AND PRACTICE

After graduation, one of the newly certified *dayas* stayed on at the maternity school as a *bashdaya* (head midwife), supervising the incoming classes of students and assisting the matron, as the rest of the now-certified *dayas* returned home. This did not mean the graduates were free from follow-up visits and inspections by medical officers, a harbinger of a closer inspection regime to come, as the colonial state would no longer be satisfied with issuing licenses and allowing *dayas* to practice without review. With visits beginning in 1914, medical officers regularly examined midwives to ensure that they followed the practices that imperial "lady doctors" and matrons sought to instill. When Russell was welcomed into the home of one of nine midwives in Suhag, she was struck by the proximity of animals and people and noted that the *daya's* "equipment for the work was absolutely nil."[67] This latter observation led to a standardization of the items that *dayas* were supplied for their work. Not included in the stocked box were forceps, which they were not permitted to use.

By her second year, Russell had increased the number of inspections, with more than one hundred women receiving visits in their homes or on their rounds in 1915.[68] "It has really been quite interesting," Russell wrote from al-Minya of the visits, but also seemed disillusioned, stating that it "makes one very hopeless of ever being able to influence the midwifery customs of this country." At the time unmarried and childless, she noted "the swarms and swarms of children" and was struck by women's fertility—"most of them are like rabbits in their fertility—at least here in Upper Egypt."[69] Fertility was high, but so too was infant mortality, meaning many children did not reach adulthood, and this explains, in part, why Upper Egyptian women had so many children. By contrast, birthrates in Australia, where Russell had practiced, were declining, and Russell herself had been instructed by her mother on contraception. Delaying marriage, as both she and Elgood had done, may have been the most effective way of limiting fertility.[70]

The inspector coordinated her village trips with the *ma'mur* (police officer) or *'umda* (mayor), who would escort her to her destination. She usually managed to visit only one village a day because of erratic train service due to the war and troop movements as well as the distances. On one such visit to a village near al-Zaqaziq, a group had driven out to the 'umda's house, then visited a *daya*, "then back to the omdah's house where all the dayas practicing in the village were summoned and harangued."[71] Russell found visiting *dayas* in the towns and the villages enlightening and commented that whenever she could, "I've had the matrons with me and it's been quite an eye opener for them."[72] Getting the matrons into the countryside gave them a sense of the challenges the *dayas* faced when they returned home.

The inspections were not restricted to graduates of the training schools, as other *dayas* received visits from Russell, who was interested in seeing their work. "The *dayas* of the chief towns have been inspected and it is a testimony to the strong constitution of the Egyptian women that any of their patients survive their ministrations," noted the Department of Public Health report for 1916, "though the number of patients applying for treatment for the after troubles caused by bad midwifery is sufficient evidence of their lack of skill."[73] The inspections of colonial medical officers resulted in the withdrawal of certificates from some blind and incapacitated *dayas*. That women who had previously given birth turned to the matrons for help in resolving a range of gynecological issues was seen as further legitimization for founding maternity schools and enforcing their protocols.

By setting up schools in towns where *dayas* were already practicing, the matrons invariably undermined the local practitioner-patient networks. For one thing, the matrons offered their services free of charge, while *dayas* were compensated. (When some middle-class women wanted to pay matrons for their services, they were turned away and directed to graduates of the maternity schools or the School of Midwifery instead.) By waiving fees, the matrons sought to set up partnerships with *dayas*, though clearly the relationships were hierarchical; the *dayas* were supposed to call on the matrons in difficult cases, and the matrons, in turn, called in a doctor if surgical or instrumental intervention was needed. Mahfouz had set up a similar arrangement in his early days of practicing in Cairo, arranging with medical officers to call him in for difficult deliveries. Calling in the matron was presented as a novel development in colonial maternal healthcare, though in the nineteenth century, *dayas* were meant to call in a *hakima* to help. Yet calling in help did not guarantee the survival of mother or child: in 1915, eight women under the care of the new maternity schools died in labor, twenty-eight infants died soon after birth, and seventy-four babies were stillborn.[74] The number of stillborn, which was consistently high, was attributed to widespread syphilis among town and village women as well as disease outbreaks.[75]

Mortality was blamed on the laboring woman or *daya* rather than the matron or doctor, with reports pointing to delays in calling for help as the cause of maternal deaths. *Dayas* in the provinces, who were meant to be a bridge between the community and colonial rule, may have attempted to subvert the authority of the matron by not calling her. When Mabel Wolff first opened the maternity school in al-Fayum, she expressed her uncertainty about her early results to Russell, who tried to assuage her fears: "I think your numbers are splendid for a beginning," she wrote. "Don't worry about the BBA's [born before arrivals;] probably a great many are purposeful." Russell instructed Wolff to get in touch with the trained *daya* in town, and if she was working well, Wolff was to attend only her difficult cases. Russell also told Wolff to let the new mother's own *daya* do most of the follow-up care, going only once herself for a postpartum visit.[76]

According to the perspective of public health officials, things improved: "Though there is still an obstructive element among the town *dayas*," noted the 1918 annual report, "the majority work well with the school, seek the help of the matron in difficult cases, and are gradually learning to recognize when to call in help."[77] Public health officials claimed that villagers and town residents were responding positively to the changes in the training of *dayas*, noting rising expectations about the quality of care and patients increasingly asking for newly trained *dayas* to attend them. Officials reported receiving questions or information about cases of malpractice and lack of qualification as well as appeals for training for women in districts where no training school existed, such as Alexandria, Cairo, and Port Said; they encouraged those with family connections to take the new training courses. Local doctors, in turn, sent in encouraging reports about the cleanliness of the trained *dayas*, whom they employed in special cases.[78]

Despite state efforts to surveil them, many of the newly trained *dayas* did not implement all the practices they had been taught. Repeated calls in the annual Department of Public Health reports for a Midwives Act similar to the one passed by the British Parliament in 1902 showed a desire to bar certain women from practice, "as many of these women openly defy the instructions of the Health Office."[79] The attempt to create a corps of midwives with a certain dress code, designated tools, and set protocols faced opposition in some quarters; upon their return home with their certificates, *dayas* were said by British observers to "come under the influence of the old *dayas* and the superstitions and customs of centuries" and to revert "to the village ways."[80] Colonial medical officers had little regard for rural birth practices and wanted to implement modern techniques; the *dayas* adopted some new practices but discarded those that they did not find useful.

One area where contention existed was over the delivery boxes, which were fitted with the equipment needed for a "normal" birth. Public health reports complain that the *dayas* had either stored their boxes as a souvenir or given away their contents rather than using them.[81] This is clear from correspondence between Russell and Mabel Wolff. The inspector advised the new matron when she started the maternity school in al-Fayum to get in touch with the trained *daya* there, but then wondered, "is she not that awful woman who was ill and had an absolutely empty box?" (The boxes were supposed to be resupplied regularly on visits to the maternity school.) Of another Fayumi *daya*, she wrote, "Nouza is a trial and as we know keeps her box at the bottom of the family chest double locked away but perhaps the effect of good example will make her bring it out."[82] This was more than resisting the protocols of the maternity schools. Midwives like Nouza—one of the few named midwives—saw the box as having greater value as a souvenir than as a toolkit or saw the commercial value of individual items in the box as greater than their medical utility.

Another area in which some village *dayas* sought to hold on to past practices, to the consternation of public health officials, was in the use of the obstetric chair. "The patients who have a few pence use a special chair at the time, the penniless ones dig a hole in the ground of their huts and sit over that," Russell explained to her mother, who had borne seven children, with an eighth stillborn.[83] The Department of Public Health waged war on the chair, holding it accountable for innumerable injuries. "A considerable number of women suffering from pelvic trouble come to the matron for advice," the 1915 report noted. "Most of these cases are suffering from the result of bad midwifery and many from the use of the 'obstetric chair' during delivery."[84] Imperial doctors sought to displace the chair and the position that went with it with the supine position in childbirth, which was practical for the attending medical professional but not necessarily effective from the perspective of the laboring woman. When Russell was planning the equipment and furniture that the maternity schools needed, she ordered beds, observing that patients rarely had one at home. She hoped to get the matron in Suhag and later other schools a few beds for inpatients that could be used for emergencies and confinements of difficult cases.[85]

Yet the chair remained a fixture of Egyptian births. "I'm afraid the use of the chair will die hard," Russell wrote to Mabel Wolff. "You will hardly be able to abolish it completely in your first year [1917] and certainly not the first term."[86] According to Winifred Blackman—an Oxford-trained anthropologist who spent six months per year for six years beginning in the early 1920s in Upper Egypt observing practices of the peasantry— if the midwife was called, she brought with her the "customary confinement chair . . . for women in Egypt give birth in a squatting attitude."[87] She noted that a woman could squat during delivery without the chair as well, resting on a large sieve, a posture that a local woman demonstrated for her. Blackman also observed that whoever attended the parturient woman—whether a midwife, mother, or some other female relative—would cut the umbilical cord and discard the placenta by burying it, throwing it into the Nile or a canal, or in some other way.[88]

Parturient women, rather than imperial doctors, matrons, or Egyptian *dayas*, determined the longevity of the parturition chair, at least in the short term. In testimony to the 1918 Commission on the Organization of the Department of Public Health, Elgood noted that younger *dayas* graduating from the provincial maternity schools found themselves in a difficult situation. This was not just because "the old dayah has, as a rule, all the cases, and she will not give them up," but also because some of the newly trained *dayas* wanted to transform birthing practices. "The mere fact that the newer class of dayah will not use the horrible maternity chair . . . makes her unfashionable."[89] In many cases, then, some of the new *dayas* were boycotted, though whether this was because of the chair or because laboring women did not trust women trained by the colonial state is not certain.

Another way in which *dayas* subverted colonial mandates and showed entrepreneurial initiative was to pass on their certificates, and presumably their clients, to younger family members, who in this way bypassed the training course. Elgood pushed for the annual re-examination of all practicing *dayas*, noting that "in many cases the women are practicing with certificates which were granted to their mothers or grandmothers."[90] There was obviously a battle taking place between *dayas* from families in which the privilege of practicing had been passed down for generations and those newly trained by the state without the same network. Acknowledging that the *dayas'* training schools were doing good work, Elgood called for further controls and renewal of certification or issuance of annual licenses.[91] "Every certificate-holding-daya should be reinspected, and the blind, the old, and otherwise incapable disqualified," she proposed, lamenting that "no inspection or revision of lists is made now [1918]."[92]

On Russell's return trip from England to Egypt with her husband in November 1919, her husband tragically died. Russell returned to England from April to November 1920 to give birth to a son she named for her deceased husband and then returned to Egypt in November 1920 as a new mother herself. The "lady doctor" in charge of overseeing the maternity schools that trained Egyptian midwives to deliver babies took up work again, this time as someone who had gone through childbirth herself and now had an infant in her care, whom she would occasionally take with her on visits to the maternity schools.[93] Egyptian midwives and pregnant women who might initially have been hesitant to take medical instruction from an imperial doctor who had not been through the birth experience may now have been more willing to discuss intimate matters.

In the 1920s, the Department of Public Health increased the number of inspectors, hiring first two and then four English traveling sisters. They examined midwives who had completed training courses at the maternity schools as well as those who had attended short courses at provincial hospitals, which were now being phased out as more maternity schools were built. In 1921, the new inspectors visited 789 midwives in various provinces, cutting from the rolls those found to be unqualified or incapable.[94] Part of the inspectors' job was also to preserve ties with the recent graduates: "The *daya* is encouraged to re-visit the school from time to time to talk over her cases with the matron and to re-stock her equipment box."[95] The new inspectors left an impression, at least on Blackman, who mentioned that the special training centers for midwives in Egypt were inspected regularly "by a most competent Englishwoman."[96]

With Great Britain and Egypt negotiating an end to the protectorate, the future for imperial medical professionals was uncertain. In 1922, provincial councils replaced British matrons who retired or resigned in Tanta, Mansoura, and Shibin al-Kum with graduates from the School of Midwifery in Cairo. These Egyptian nurse-midwives had not been considered for such posts in the past. Looking ahead, the Department of Public Health sent two Egyptian women to England for a course of midwifery so that they, too, would be ready to replace foreign matrons as they left or retired.[97]

The letter of resignation Russell submitted to the high commissioner on 22 September 1922 shows her disillusionment with the new order. "The conditions of my work have changed completely owing to the recent political situation," she wrote. "Even with English Advisors in Cairo and inspectors in the Provinces my unusual position as a woman advisor to Mudirs and Provincial Councils in a Moslem country was a delicate one, now that there is no English support and there is an Egyptian head in the Department, my position has become quite impossible." She was disturbed by the new appointments, protesting that those "which should have been made through me have been filled by unsuitable candidates of local selection for whose work I am supposed to be responsible." The appointments made by provincial councils of medical officers in charge of the dispensaries and schools, she reiterated, "makes my own appointment professionally futile," and she said she could "see no scope for the advancement of my medical career."[98] After nearly a decade of overseeing a network of maternity schools and dispensaries in Egypt, developing a regime for inspecting *dayas*, and establishing a protocol for deliveries, Russell returned to New Zealand with her young son. Like her schoolmate Elgood, who also retired around then, she was nearing fifty and eligible for a generous pension.

Despite the British loss of control of the Department of Public Health and Russell's disillusionment, the work that she and others had initiated continued. More centers opened, including ones in Shubra and Bani Swayf, with the number reaching sixteen by 1929 and increasing after that. To staff these centers, a new medical professional cadre of Egyptian female health visitors responsible for domestic visits emerged. Simultaneously, maternity schools formally merged with child dispensaries to become child welfare centers. In 1928, there were 2,116 *dayas* who had trained in maternity schools and another 8,535 *dayas* who had trained in hospitals. That year the Department of Public Health stopped the training of *dayas* in general hospitals to focus on training in maternity schools. Wherever they had trained, Egypt's 10,700 *dayas* delivered the bulk—roughly 90%—of the babies born. In 1928, of 2,295,866 fecund married women, 634,486 gave birth, mostly at home.[99]

With the Department of Public Health now under Egyptian control, the work of culling the rolls of registered *dayas* continued, with 179 found to be "medically unfit to work" or "ascertained to be inefficient from the technical point of view" in 1930.[100] Two years later, the department canceled the licenses of 108 women, including some who were of "such an old age" that they were unable to carry out their work satisfactorily and those "found suffering from a disabling disease."[101] Whether the withdrawal of the license came at the hands of imperial inspectors or Egyptian medical officers did not make a difference to those who had worked as *dayas* their whole lives and whose identities and livelihoods were now shattered. An older generation of *dayas* was passing on through removal and death, with seventy-one dying in 1931 and ninety-three in 1932.[102]

CONCLUSION

Imperial women doctors were important actors in reshaping public health and reproduction in Egypt, altering the methods of training and certifying thousands of *dayas* in the early decades of the twentieth century, and aligning delivery practices with modern methods. Rather than masculinize childbirth, the imperial doctors strove, through the maternity schools, to modernize a system of women-centered care for delivery of babies within the home. Imperial doctors moved training out of, not into, hospitals; standardized courses and certificates; and regularly inspected practitioners. As foreign medical experts, they stood at the apex of a structure that blocked male Egyptian doctors interested in maternal health from reaching positions of power in the public health system. By instituting new statistical regimes, sterilization practices, and supine postures—none of which are inherently masculine—imperial women doctors and the matrons they oversaw developed a maternal health model that they believed could be exported. And it was, first to the provinces and then to Sudan, where Mabel and Gertrude Wolff would learn that not all birth work was, in fact, transferrable and that it had to be attentive to local cultural customs and environmental concerns.

Yet the statistical regime that imperial doctors introduced might have been part of the undoing of this women-centered model and the increased medicalization and masculinization of childbirth. The categorization of "normal" and "abnormal" births would eventually lead to a shift from conceptualizing childbirth as a natural process, best carried out in the intimacy of the home, to one considered dangerous and thus requiring preemptive hospital care. But this shift to greater surgical and instrumental interventions at the hands of mostly male obstetrician-gynecologists would be decades in the making.

The students who went through the maternity schools found new opportunities and challenges, as they joined a cohort of women who had practiced or sought to practice as midwives and together came under the watchful eye of foreign matrons, who, in turn, came with their own habits, pets, and senses of purpose. Most of the students passed the exams and returned to work to their villages, towns, and city quarters, often inheriting a family member's patients. Although pressured to give up certain practices, some insisted on holding on to older and sometimes ancient customs, such as using a birthing or parturition chair. Amid surveillance, inspections, and formal visits to their homes and on their rounds, they continued to deliver babies. Some, particularly older midwives, were removed from the lists of those eligible to practice and replaced by a younger generation more open to the modern delivery methods being advocated. These women formed the corps of the professionalized midwives who sat together in graduation photographs, reflecting pride in their learning, skills, and new status. They also, it is hoped, delivered good care to those Egyptian women who turned to them for assistance in one of the most intimate, natural, and painful of bodily experiences—giving birth.

Notes

I would like to thank Rebecca Irvine for her research assistance and suggestions; Jeffrey Culang and Tamara Maatouk for their constructive criticism and excellent edits; and Marie Brown, Hratch Kestenian, Liat Kozma, Sara Pursley, and Seçil Yilmaz for their invaluable comments.

1. De Courcy Family Papers, Private Collection (DCFP), Zaqaziq Maternity School, class from March to June 1920 outdoor uniform (6731 front / 6732 back) and indoor uniform (6733 front / 6734 back). I thank Kate de Courcy for sharing these papers with me and taking

the time to answer an infinite number of questions, and Mark de Courcy for information on various points.

2. On the School of Midwifery, see Hibba Abugideiri, *Gender and the Making of Modern Medicine in Colonial Egypt* (Surrey: Ashgate, 2010), 133. See also Amira El-Azhary Sonbol, "Doctors and Midwives: Women and Medicine at the Turn of the Century," *La France et l'Égypte à l'époque des vice-rois, 1808–1882*, ed. Daniel Panzac and André Raymond (Cairo: Institut Français d'Archéologie Orientale, 2002), 135–48; Khaled Fahmy, "Women, Medicine, and Power in Nineteenth-Century Egypt," in *Remaking Women: Feminism and Modernity in the Middle East*, ed. Lila Abu-Lughod (Princeton: Princeton University Press, 1998), 35–71; Nancy Gallagher, "Writing Women Medical Practitioners into the History of Modern Egypt," in *Re-Envisioning Egypt, 1919–1952*, ed. Arthur Goldschmidt, Amy J. Johnson, and Barak A. Salmoni (Cairo: American University in Cairo Press, 2005), 351–70; Mervat F. Hatem, "The Professionalization of Health and the Control of Women's Bodies as Modern Governmentalities in Nineteenth-Century Egypt," in *Women in the Ottoman Empire: Middle Eastern Women in the Early Modern Era*, ed. Madeline C. Zilfi (Leiden: Brill, 1997), 66–80; Liat Kozma, *Policing Egyptian Women: Sex, Law, and Medicine in Khedival Egypt* (Syracuse: Syracuse University Press, 2011); LaVerne Kuhnke, "The 'Doctoress' on a Donkey: Women Health Officers in Nineteenth Century Egypt," *Clio Medica* 9 (1974): 193–205; and Laure Pesquet, "From the Traditional to the Trained Midwife: Becoming a Daya in Colonial and Interwar Egypt (1913–1925)," *Toplumsal Tarih* 352 (2023): 14–17.

3. Fahmy, "Women, Medicine, and Power," 50–55; Kozma, *Policing Egyptian Women*, 23–24; Serge Jagailloux, *La Médicalisation de l'Égypte au XIXe Siècle (1798–1918)* (Paris: Éditions Recherche sur les Civilisations, 1986), 22.

4. See Abugideiri, *Gender and the Making of Modern Medicine*, and Kozma, *Policing Egyptian Women*, for notable exceptions.

5. On Dr. Naguib Mahfouz, see Beth Baron, "Of Fistulas, Sutures, and Silences," in a Roundtable on De-Centering Egyptian History, *International Journal of Middle East Studies* 53:1 (2021): 133–37. On Mabel Wolff, see Heather Bell, *Frontiers of Medicine in the Anglo-Egyptian Sudan, 1899–1940* (New York: Oxford University Press, 1999), chapter 7; Marie Grace Brown, *Khartoum at Night: Fashion and Body Politics in Imperial Sudan* (Stanford: Stanford University Press, 2017), chapter 2; and Heather J. Sharkey, "Two Sudanese Midwives," *Sudanic Africa* 9 (1998): 19–38. On midwives in another Middle East context, see Hibba Abugideiri, "A Labor of Love: Making Space for Midwives in Gulf History," in *Gulf Women*, ed. Amira El-Azhary Sonbol (New York: Bloomsbury Press, 2012), 167–200.

6. See Abugideiri, *Gender and the Making of Modern Medicine*; and Kozma, *Policing Egyptian Women*, 33.

7. Quotes from Wellcome Institute for the History of Medicine (WI), London, Private Papers (PP) / Elgood (ELG) / D3, Bonté Elgood, appendix 11, 3, and WI, PP/ELG/D3, Bonté Elgood's interview with the Commission, 3. See also The National Archive (TNA), Foreign Office (FO) 371/3203/177595, Ministry of Interior, *Report of a Commission to Advise as Regards the Future Organization and Work of the Department of Public Health* (Cairo: Government Press, 1918), appendix 11; and Naguib Bey Mahfouz, *The History of Medical Education in Egypt* (Cairo: Government Press, 1935), 84–85.

8. Ministry of the Interior, Egypt, Department of Public Health (DPH), *Annual Report for 1913* (Cairo: Government Press, 1915), 58.

9. WI, PP/ELG/D3, Elgood's interview with the Commission, 1; appendix 11, 3–5. It was copied not only in Egypt but in imperial settings such as Sudan.

10. WI, PP/ELG/D3, Elgood's interview with the Commission, 1; Naguib Mafhouz, *Fann al-Wilada*, 4th ed. (Cairo: Dar al-Maʿarif, 1957) and *Amrad al-Nisaʾ* (Cairo: Matbaʿat al-Tawfiq, n.d.).

11. Mahfouz also identified Bonté as "the first qualified woman-doctor that practised in Egypt." Technically if one discounts *hakimas*, she was the first woman doctor to work for the state; American women missionary doctors in Tanta from 1896 practiced, but not in the employ of the state, as did the Syrian doctor who de Courcy mentions but does not name. There were likely others as well. Mahfouz, *History of Medical Education*, 84–85, quotes from page 84.

12. Naguib Mahfouz, *Hayat Tabib* (Cairo: Dar al-Maʿarif, 1966; reprinted Cairo: al-Hayʾa al-Misriyya al-ʿAmma li-l-Kitab, 2013); Baron, "Of Fistulas, Sutures, and Silences."

13. Mahfouz, *History of Medical Education*, 85.

14. WI, PP/ELG/D3, Elgood's interview with the Commission, 3; Mahfouz, *History of Medical Education*, 85; DPH, *Annual Report for 1913*, 36; Abugideiri, *Gender and the Making of Modern Medicine*, chapter 5.

15. Mahfouz, *History of Medical Education*, 84–85; WI, PP/ELG/D3, appendix 11, 3.

16. WI, PP/ELG/D3, appendix 11, 3.

17. DPH, *Annual Report for 1913*, 22.

18. DCFP, Cairo, 3 May 1914, Ministry of Interior, Department of Public Health, D. Semple to Monsieur le Président du Conseil Sanitaire, Maritime et Quarantenaire, Alexandrie; Department of Public Health, Departmental Gazette, Cairo, 19 December 1914; Maslahat al-Sihha al-ʿUmumiyya, Cairo, 19 December 1914.

19. DPH, *Annual Statistical Report for 1914* (Cairo: Government Press, 1916), 20.

20. DCFP, Rossmore House, DPH, Grace to Mother, 3 October 1914.

21. DCFP, Shebin El Kom, Grace to Mother, 20 October 1914.

22. DCFP, Mansourah, Grace to Mother, 11 October 1914. The committee later convened at the British residency. DCFP, Diary, Tuesday 13 April 1920.

23. DPH, *Annual Report for 1913*, 22.

24. DPH, *Annual Statistical Report for 1914*, 20.

25. DCFP, Mansourah, Grace to Mother, 8 October 1914; Grace to Mother, 11 October 1914. Quote from Tanta, Grace to Mother, 16 October 1914.

26. DCFP, Shebin El Kom, Grace to Mother, 20 October 1914.

27. DCFP, Sohag, Grace to Mother, 7 November 1914.

28. DCFP, Assiut, Grace to Mother, 11 November 1914.

29. DCFP, Cairo, Grace to Mother, 19 December 1914.

30. Bell, *Frontiers of Medicine in the Anglo-Egyptian Sudan*, chapter 7; Brown, *Khartoum at Night*, chapter 2.

31. DCFP, Cairo, Grace to Mother, 27 November 1914; see DPH, *Annual Report for 1917* (Cairo: Government Press, 1919), 27.

32. Sudan Archives Durham (SAD), 579/2/18, Egyptian State Telegraphs; DCFP, Cairo, Grace to Mother, 5 May 1915.

33. DCFP, Heliopolis, Grace to Mother, 24 June 1915.

34. DPH, *Annual Report for 1918* (Cairo: Government Press, 1920), 29.

35. DCFP, Nevinson William de Courcy's diary for 1919; private correspondence from Kate de Courcy, 1 March 2021; see also Thursday, 28 August 1919; Monday, 8 September 1919; and Tuesday, 9 September 1919.

36. DCFP, "Medical and Nursing," *Western Daily Press* (Bristol), 22, 23, and 25 October 1920.

37. DPH, *Annual Report for 1920* (Cairo: Government Press, 1922), 41.

38. DPH, *Annual Statistical Report for 1914*, 19.

39. DPH, *Annual Report for 1916* (Cairo: Government Press, 1918), 28–32, quote from page 30; *Annual Report for 1921* (Cairo: Government Press, 1923), 42.

40. See DPH reports for these years.

41. DPH, *Annual Report for 1916*, 29.

42. Bell, *Frontiers of Medicine in the Anglo-Egyptian Sudan*, chapter 7; Brown, *Khartoum at Night*, chapter 2. In the photograph of the graduating class at the Fayum Maternity School taken in 1922, a young girl appears seated next to the matron. DCFP, 6719 front / 6720 back.

43. DCFP, Zaqaziq, Grace to Mother, 5 December 1914.

44. DPH, *Annual Report for 1916*, 28.

45. DPH, *Annual Report for 1918*, 29.

46. DPH, *Annual Statistical Report for 1914*, 19.

47. DPH, *Annual Report for 1918*, 29.

48. Brown, *Khartoum at Night*, 56–57; Bell, *Frontiers of Medicine in the Anglo-Egyptian Sudan*, 209.

49. Brown, *Khartoum at Night*, chapter 2, quote from page 43.

50. Mahfouz, *Hayat Tabib*; Baron, "Of Fistulas, Sutures, and Silences"; see https://obgynmuseum.com.

51. Frances Hasso, *Buried in the Red Dirt: Race, Reproduction, and Death in Modern Palestine* (Cambridge: Cambridge University Press, 2022), 47–50.

52. See also Bell, *Frontiers of Medicine in the Anglo-Egyptian Sudan*, 208.

53. DCFP, Mansourah, Grace to Mother, 11 October 1914; see also DPH, *Annual Statistical Report for 1915* (Cairo: Government Press, 1917), 24.

54. DPH, *Annual Report for 1918*, 29.

55. DPH, *Annual Statistical Report for 1915*, 24–25.

56. See Dorothy Roberts, *Killing the Black Body: Race, Reproduction, and the Meaning of Liberty* (New York: Vintage, 1997); Laura Briggs, *Reproducing Empire: Race, Sex, Science, and U.S. Imperialism in Puerto Rico* (Berkeley: University of California Press, 2002); Harriet A. Washington, *Medical Apartheid: The Dark History of Medical Experimentation on Black Americans from Colonial Times to the Present* (New York: Anchor Books, 2006); and Deidre Cooper Owens, *Medical Bondage: Race, Gender, and the Origins of American Gynecology* (Athens: University of Georgia Press, 2017).

57. DPH, *Annual Statistical Report for 1915*, 24.

58. DPH, *Annual Report for 1916*, 29; *Annual Report for 1917*, 27.

59. DPH, *Annual Report for 1919* (Cairo: Government Press, 1921), 39; *Annual Report for 1921*, 4; *Annual Report for 1922* (Cairo: Government Press, 1925), 86.

60. DPH, *Annual Report for 1918*, 43; *Annual Report for 1922*, 86. Egypt now has one of the highest C-Section rates in the world.

61. DCFP, Mansourah, Grace to Mother, 8 October 1914.

62. DCFP, Cairo, Grace to Mother, 19 December 1914.

63. DPH, *Annual Statistical Report for 1915*, 24–25.

64. DCFP, Zaqaziq Maternity School, class from March–June 1920 outdoor uniform (6731 front / 6732 back) and indoor uniform (6733 front / 6734 back).

65. DPH, *Annual Report for 1921*, 3.

66. DPH, *Annual Report for 1922*, 85.

67. DCFP, Assiut, Grace to Mother, 11 November 1914.

68. DPH, *Annual Statistical Report for 1915*, 24.

69. DCFP, Minia, Grace to Mother, 2 February 1915.

70. DCFP, "Medical Career of Dr. Grace de Courcy (Née Russell) 1874–1967"; R. C. J. Stone. "Russell, John Benjamin," *Dictionary of New Zealand Biography*, first published in 1993, Te Ara, The Encyclopedia of New Zealand, accessed 28 October 2021, https://teara.govt. nz/en/biographies/2r33/russell-john-benjamin.

71. DCFP, Cairo, Grace to Mother, 4 March 1915.

72. Ibid.

73. DPH, *Annual Report for 1916*, 30.

74. DPH, *Annual Statistical Report for 1915*, 24–25.

75. DPH, *Annual Report for 1918*, 30.

76. SAD, 579/2/21, G. Russell to M. Wolff, 21 June 1917.

77. DPH, *Annual Report for 1918*, 29; see also, DPH, *Annual Statistical Report for 1915*, 24; *Annual Report for 1916*, 29; *Annual Report for 1920*, 42.

78. See DPH, *Annual Reports* for 1915 through 1920.

79. DPH, *Annual Report for 1917*, 27. See the text of the British Act that served as a guide: "The Midwives Act," *The British Medical Journal* 2, no. 2172 (16 August 1902): 481–83.

80. DPH, *Annual Report for 1915*, 24.

81. DPH, *Annual Statistical Report for 1915*, 24.

82. SAD, 579/2/21, G. Russell to M. Wolff, 21 June 1917.

83. DCFP, Assiut, Grace to Mother, 11 November 1914; private correspondence from Kate de Courcy, 18 October 2021. For a history of the chair and images from Egypt, see Aly Alaily, *The History of the Parturition Chair* (St. Leonards-on-Sea: Rosewell Publishing, 2000), 22–23.

84. DPH, *Annual Statistical Report for 1915*, 24.

85. DCFP, Assiut, Grace to Mother, 11 November 1914.

86. SAD, 579/2/21, G. Russell to M Wolff, 21 June 1917. See Aly Alaily, *Obstetrics and Gynaecology in Ancient and Modern Egypt* (St. Leonards-on-Sea: Rosewell Publishing, 2000); and Alaily, *The History of the Parturition Chair*.

87. Winifred S. Blackman, *The Fellahin of Upper Egypt: Their Religious, Social, and Industrial Life with Special Reference to Survivals from Ancient Times* (1927; reis., London: Frank Cass & Co., 1968), 63.

88. Ibid., 62–64.

89. WI, PP/ELG/D3, Elgood's interview with the Commission, 3.

90. WI, PP/ELG/D3, Elgood's interview with the Commission, 4.

91. WI, PP/ELG/D3, appendix 11, 3.

92. Ibid., appendix 11, 3.

93. DCFP, Diaries, Wednesday, 27 April 1921.

94. DPH, *Annual Report for 1920*, 42; *Annual Report for 1921*, 4.

95. DPH, *Annual Report for 1920*, 42.

96. Blackman, *The Fellahin of Upper Egypt*, 62.

97. DPH, *Annual Report for 1922*, 85.

98. DCFP, Grace de Courcy to the High Commissioner, Cairo, 22 September 1922.

99. DPH, *Annual Report on the Work of the Department of Public Health for 1928* (Cairo: Government Press, 1931), 129.

100. DPH, *Annual Report on the Work of the Department of Public Health for 1930* (Cairo: Government Press, 1932), 13.

101. DPH, *Annual Report on the Work of the Department of Public Health for 1932* (Cairo: Government Press, 1935), 62; for figures from 1932, see Mahfouz, *Medical Education*, 86.
102. DPH, *Annual Report on the Work of the Department of Public Health for 1931* (Cairo: Government Press, 1934), 48; *Annual Report on the Work of the Department of Public Health for 1932*, 62.

BIBLIOGRAPHY

Abugideiri, Hibba. *Gender and the Making of Modern Medicine in Colonial Egypt*. Surrey: Ashgate, 2010.

Abugideiri, Hibba. "A Labor of Love: Making Space for Midwives in Gulf History." In *Gulf Women*, edited by Amira El-Azhary Sonbol, 167–200. New York: Bloomsbury Press, 2012.

Alaily, Aly. *The History of the Parturition Chair*. St. Leonards-on-Sea: Rosewell Publishing UK, 2000.

Alaily, Aly. *Obstetrics and Gynaecology in Ancient and Modern Egypt*. St. Leonards-on-Sea: Rosewell Publishing UK, 2000.

Baron, Beth. "Of Fistulas, Sutures, and Silences." *International Journal of Middle East Studies* 53, no. 1 (February 2021): 133–37.

Bell, Heather. *Frontiers of Medicine in the Anglo-Egyptian Sudan, 1899–1940*. New York: Oxford University Press, 1999.

Blackman, Winifred Susan. *The Fellahin of Upper Egypt: Their Religious, Social, and Industrial Life with Special Reference to Survivals from Ancient Times*. London: Frank Cass & Co., 1968. First published 1927 by George G. Harrap & Co.

Briggs, Laura. *Reproducing Empire: Race, Sex, Science, and U.S. Imperialism in Puerto Rico*. Berkeley: University of California Press, 2002.

Brown, Marie Grace. *Khartoum at Night: Fashion and Body Politics in Imperial Sudan*. Stanford: Stanford University Press, 2017.

Fahmy, Khaled. "Women, Medicine, and Power in Nineteenth-Century Egypt." In *Remaking Women: Feminism and Modernity in the Middle East*, edited by Lila Abu-Lughod, 35–71. Princeton: Princeton University Press, 1998.

Gallagher, Nancy. "Writing Women Medical Practitioners into the History of Modern Egypt." In *Re-Envisioning Egypt, 1919–1952*, edited by Arthur Goldschmidt, Amy J. Johnson, and Barak A. Salmoni, 351–70. Cairo: American University in Cairo, 2005.

Hasso, Frances. *Buried in the Red Dirt: Race, Reproduction, and Death in Modern Palestine*. Cambridge: Cambridge University Press, 2022.

Hatem, Mervat F. "The Professionalization of Health and the Control of Women's Bodies as Modern Governmentalities in Nineteenth-Century Egypt." In *Women in the Ottoman Empire: Middle Eastern Women in the Early Modern Era*, edited by Madeline C. Zilfi, 66–80. Leiden: Brill, 1997.

Jagailloux, Serge. *La Médicalisation de l'Égypte au XIXe Siècle 1798–1918*. Paris: Éditions Recherche sur les Civilisations, 1986.

Kozma, Liat. *Policing Egyptian Women: Sex, Law, and Medicine in Khedival Egypt*. Syracuse: Syracuse University Press, 2011.

Kuhnke, LaVerne. "The 'Doctoress' on a Donkey: Women Health Officers in Nineteenth Century Egypt." *Clio Medica* 9 (1974): 193–205.

Mahfouz, Naguib. *The History of Medical Education in Egypt*. Cairo: Government Press, 1935.

Mahfuz, Najib. *Hayat Tabib*. Cairo: al-Hay'a al-Misriyya al-'Amma li-l-Kitab, 2013. First published 1966 by Dar al-Ma'arif (Cairo).

Owens, Deirdre Cooper. *Medical Bondage: Race, Gender, and the Origins of American Gynecology*. Athens: University of Georgia Press, 2017.

Roberts, Dorothy. *Killing the Black Body: Race, Reproduction, and the Meaning of Liberty*. New York: Vintage, 1997.

Sharkey, Heather J. "Two Sudanese Midwives." *Sudanic Africa* 9 (1998): 19–38.

Sonbol, Amira El-Azhary. "Doctors and Midwives: Women and Medicine at the Turn of the Century." In *La France et l'Égypte à l'époque des vice-rois, 1808–1882*, edited by Daniel Panzac and André Raymond, 135–48. Cairo: Institut Français d'Archéologie Orientale, 2002.

Washington, Harriet A. *Medical Apartheid: The Dark History of Medical Experimentation on Black Americans from Colonial Times to the Present*. New York: Anchor Books, 2006.

CHAPTER 3

···

HEALTH AND NATION

The Egyptian Medical Profession under British Rule

···

LIAT KOZMA

IN the interwar years, the Egyptian medical profession emerged as a leading national middle-class project. Egyptian doctors asserted their professional identity as they competed with foreign doctors who practiced in Egypt, and they struggled to prove themselves as equal members in the international scientific community. Egyptian doctors saw indigenous medical research on specific Egyptian problems as a sign of local competence and intellectual success and, moreover, as professional independence necessary for national independence.[1]

The Egyptian medical profession is particularly interesting because, unlike in other colonial contexts and more than other white-collar professions locally, it had a long pre-colonial history. Whereas West African or North African doctors, for example, had to study medicine in Europe because they had no alternative at home,[2] Egyptian doctors had had a local medical school since 1827, fifty-five years before the British occupation, and its graduates formed the main cadre of the medical profession in Egypt throughout most of the nineteenth century. Moreover, unlike other colonial contexts, in which the medical profession was taken up by local practitioners during the process of decolonization, in the Egyptian case, from the 1920s onward, the decolonization of the medical profession entailed its re-Egyptianization.

A social and intellectual history of the Egyptian medical profession and its Egyptianization both institutionally and scientifically builds on the rich historical scholarship on Egyptian medicine. The writing of this history started with Dr. Naguib Mahfouz Bey's 1935 *The History of Medical Education in Egypt* and continued, from the mid-1980s, with the important works of Serge Jagailloux, Amira Sonbol, Sylvia Chiffoleau, Khaled Fahmy, Hibba Abugideiri, and Jennifer Derr. All ascribed the roots of the medical profession to Mehmet Ali Pasha (1769–1849) and Antoine Barthélemy Clot (1793–1868), who founded the Qasr al-'Ayni Medical School, where generations of Egyptian medical professionals had studied. In the 1890s, a decade after the start of the British occupation, a British administration took over the school, the school's language of instruction became English, and its cohorts were significantly reduced in size. The cohorts began to grow in the 1910s, and the school gradually recovered and returned to Egyptian hands in the 1920s. The foundation by Qasr al-ʿAyni's physicians of a medical journal in 1917 and a medical association in 1920 enabled the decolonization of the profession. The field of parasitology, in particular, enabled Egyptian doctors to present their professional competence locally and internationally, in relation to and in comparison with their British colonizers. Given that parasitic diseases were endemic to Egypt, parasitology was a field in which Egyptians could show their proficiency.[3]

The corrective to this narrative is threefold. First, by concentrating on Qasr al-ʿAyni's decline between 1890 and World War I, historians of the Egyptian medical profession have missed the diverse educational paths taken by Egyptian medical professionals during this period, paths that facilitated the expansion of Egypt's medical profession to several hundred physicians following World War I. Egyptian students attended medical schools in Beirut, Istanbul, London, Paris, Baltimore, and about a dozen other educational centers. Their education abroad brought together multiple forms of influence and enabled multidirectional flows of knowledge and expertise. Second, Egyptian doctors sought to integrate themselves into global scientific conversations and regional networks. Third, an intellectual revival of the Egyptian medical profession and its scientific production occurred during the interwar years. While historians have concentrated mainly on parasitology, Egyptian doctors saw pediatrics, nutrition, venereology, sexology, and drug addiction, among other fields, as areas in which they could offer local research and expertise. Those fields in which Egyptian doctors claimed to have particular expertise stemming from the specificities of their country's social, economic, and ecological makeup are especially important to analyze. In all of these fields, Egyptian doctors presented themselves as capable of offering solutions to Egypt's pressing problems: child mortality, obesity, prostitution, drug addiction, and more. In this context, the re-emergence of the Egyptian medical profession was, for the most part, an effendi male project, designed to cultivate both the self—that is, the effendi male body— and its other, particularly Egyptian women, who were to be educated into modernity by being taught how to best nourish and care for their children, and peasants, who needed to learn how to discipline their own bodies. Egyptian women doctors would be a marginal part of this scientific community until midcentury and are thus marginal to this chapter as well.

Qasr al-ʿAyni's Precolonial History

The Egyptian medical profession has its roots in the late 1820s. Egypt's Ottoman governor, Mehmet Ali Pasha, invited French surgeon Antoine Barthélemy Clot (later known as Clot Bey) to establish a medical school, first in Abu Zaʿbal (1827), and a decade later in its new location Qasr al-ʿAyni in Cairo. This school offered male Egyptian students a medical curriculum modeled after the French one. Its first instructors were

French, but they were gradually replaced by Egyptians trained in France. They taught in Arabic and used Arabic textbooks that were translated from French, Italian, English, and German in Cairo's School of Languages (founded in 1835). Egyptian students had studied medicine in Europe since 1825, and beginning in the 1840s, students were sent to Europe for further specialization—for example, in ophthalmology and dentistry.[4] The school of *hakimas* (literally: female doctors), founded in 1832, trained female medical professionals, mainly for government service.[5] More broadly, during the nineteenth century, new government schools and missions to Europe offered men of humble origins and some women new paths for upward mobility. Certain families who had previously sent their sons to religious schools and then to al-Azhar now opted for government schools and professional education.[6]

Shortly after the British occupation of Egypt, the training of doctors in Egypt was limited to men. The British authorities stopped the training of women as doctors and turned the *hakimas'* school into a training school for nurses, and its students and graduates became government nurses.[7] The medical training offered to men was gradually reduced, and Qasr al-'Ayni Medical School was gradually colonized. Already in the 1880s, the school had started charging tuition, and a high school certificate became a requirement for school admission. In 1890, a British director replaced the Egyptian one, and in the following years, most of the school's Egyptian staff had resigned. The school's new administration shortened the course of study to four years, reducing the level of training. The language of instruction became English. In addition, in 1893, the British government announced that it could not guarantee government posts to all of its graduates. With the demand for private practice in Egyptian society still limited, and due to competition from foreign doctors, this meant significantly reduced employment prospects.

Combined, these processes limited the attractiveness of Qasr al-'Ayni for Egyptian students. Consequently, the number of students dropped from about 150 per cohort on the eve of the British occupation to about a dozen by 1900. Moreover, Lord Cromer suspended student missions to Europe from 1895 to 1907, and those who studied medicine abroad during this period did so at their own expense. As a result of these processes, in 1912 only 40% of physicians licensed to practice in Cairo were Egyptian, and the figures for other Egyptian cities were even lower. Many of the foreigners practicing in Egypt, mostly in private practice, were Syrians trained in Beirut. Some served as medical officers in the Egyptian Army, stationed in either Egypt or Sudan.[8]

This trend started changing during the first decade of the twentieth century. Cromer's successor, Sir Eldon Gorst (1907–11), and the Egyptian Minister of Education, Sa'd Zaghlul, started opening up more government high schools, offered scholarships for middle- and lower-middle-class students, and reintroduced Arabic as the language of instruction in Egyptian high schools. During World War I, British professors at Qasr al-'Ayni joined the war effort, and Egyptian professors replaced them. Some of the latter were permanently hired after the war. This re-Egyptianization of the school staff was followed by increased enrollment of Egyptian students.[9]

Whereas most historians of the Egyptian medical profession focus on the decline of the profession during the period in which Qasr al-'Ayni was administered by the British,

I argue that as a consequence of this decline, alternative educational paths enabled the expansion of Egypt's medical profession, which numbered several hundred men in the aftermath of the war. By 1922, some physicians were Qasr al-'Ayni graduates, others were Egyptian-born students educated abroad, and many were Arab and European doctors who had moved to Egypt.

The inauguration of Beirut's faculties of medicine—the Syrian Protestant College (SPC, renamed the American University of Beirut [AUB] in 1920) in 1867 and St. Joseph University's faculty of medicine in 1883—added a new pool of physicians, who compensated for the declining numbers of Qasr al-'Ayni's graduates. Chantal Verdeil shows that between 1871 and 1914, 7% of the medical students in Beirut were Egyptians, most of them at St. Joseph University's medical school. Yet they were not the only ones to take up employment in Egypt. Upon graduation, 15.5% of Beirut's medical graduates found employment in Egypt, and most of them were non-Egyptian Arabs.[10] The British administration, as mentioned, shortened and demoted Qasr al-'Ayni's training program and reduced school cohorts. It declared, moreover, that it could not guarantee graduates' employment and preferred the employment of foreign doctors, under the pretext that they had specialization that local doctors lacked and that foreign languages were essential for their work. British policies toward the medical school and its graduates, and the subsequent reduction of school cohorts, left ample employment opportunities for physicians educated abroad in government hospitals and the Anglo-Egyptian Army, in private practice, and in the private sector—for example, the railway and the Suez Canal Company. According to Mahmud Minawi, in 1910, eight-one Egyptian medical students were studying abroad—half of them in France and the rest in Germany, the US, England, Switzerland, and Austria. These students, in addition to forty others sent abroad by the Egyptian government in the 1910s, would form the nucleus of the re-Egyptianization process.[11]

Egyptian-born doctors graduated from the SPC (and later, the AUB) only after World War I.[12] St. Joseph University, however, had already begun admitting Egyptian students in the late 1880s. Of the fifty-eight doctors known to have graduated from St. Joseph University by 1920 and later worked in Egypt, twenty-five were born in present-day Lebanon (nineteen of whom were born in Beirut), twenty-one in Egypt, and eight in Syria.[13] What we learn from this breakdown is that Beirut's faculties offered an educational venue for Egyptian students as well as a source for newly trained Syrian doctors for Egypt.

A list of doctors practicing medicine in Egypt in 1922 provides a rich picture of the doctors' places of study, presenting them as a highly diverse and mobile group. About 36% of physicians licensed to practice in Egypt were educated in Cairo, about 6% were Egyptians who had studied in Europe, and about 19% were graduates of medical schools in Istanbul or Beirut. The rest of Egypt's medical community were Europeans. Egyptians staffed the provincial health bureaus, and European doctors staffed the higher positions of the public health administration.[14]

Looking more closely at the list, we can identify the European and American schools in which Arabic-speaking doctors studied.[15] At the top of the list is London—an obvious choice for aspiring doctors in a British-colonized territory. Beginning in the 1890s, Qasr al-'Ayni provided only four years of medical instruction,[16] so some of its graduates probably chose complementary education in London, particularly as they had already been taught in English. Others might have completed their entire course of study there. Below London on the list were universities in Manchester, Durham, and, most prominently, Edinburgh. Beyond the UK, many studied in French universities, particularly in Paris and Montpellier, and dozens chose Geneva and Lausanne, which also meant instruction in French. Among the American destinations, Baltimore was the most popular, with twenty medical students, probably due to the quality and reputation of the Johns Hopkins School of Medicine, which also specialized in tropical medicine. A dozen chose Chicago, eight St. Louis, six Philadelphia, and four Cincinnati. A handful chose German-speaking universities in Berlin, Munich, and Vienna.[17] From this list we can see (1) the diversity of the educational centers; (2) medical students' tendency to choose colonial capitals, particularly Paris and London, in which Egyptian students would meet students from other parts of the colonial world; and (3) students' preference for centers of tropical medicine, mainly London and Baltimore. This list, moreover, enables us to identify several distinct groups of doctors: those who studied in Cairo, mostly Egyptians; those who studied in Beirut; British doctors employed in Egypt; and European doctors, who reflect the diversity of émigré communities in Egypt. These include Greeks (many of whom graduated from the University of Athens), Italians (graduates of universities in Rome, Naples, and Turin), European Jews educated in Geneva, Bern, Berlin, Kiev, Kharkiv, and others. This demographic makeup changed in the following years, following Egypt's semi-independence in 1922 and the subsequent decolonization of Egypt's public health system.

THE RE-EGYPTIANIZATION OF THE PROFESSION IN THE 1920S

The decolonization of the Egyptian medical profession entailed several interrelated processes: the re-Egyptianization of Qasr al-'Ayni, the establishment of a medical association and professional journal, the Egyptianization of government health services, and the Egyptian monopolization of the profession through legislation.

In 1917, some of Qasr al-'Ayni Hospital's doctors founded *al-Majalla al-Tibbiyya al-Misriyya* (the Egyptian Medical Journal) as an Arabic periodical. The Egyptian Medical Association was founded three years later, and the journal became its mouthpiece. The association saw its goal as solidifying the profession's status through legislation and making Arabic the language of instruction in Qasr al-'Ayni. The school did not Arabize, however, since its administrators feared that Arabic would impede Western scientific instruction. In 1928, the journal became bilingual, publishing articles in English as well as Arabic in order to appeal to international non-Arabic readers.[18] That same year, the association had 450 members; by 1936, this figure rose to 675 members, about 38% of whom lived in Cairo. It also sponsored five affiliated associations—four of physicians specializing in pediatrics, nervous and mental disorders, tropical diseases, and dental surgery, and one of medical historians.[19]

In 1925, Qasr al-ʿAyni was merged into the new Egyptian University and became its faculty of medicine. In 1929, ʿAli Pasha Ibrahim became the faculty's first Egyptian dean and also the first Egyptian to head the institution in forty years. Throughout the 1920s, the faculty admitted growing cohorts of students.[20] In the early 1930s, the Cairo Faculty of Medicine produced 90–100 doctors per year, and a total of 100–150 new licenses were issued annually.[21] In the 1938–39 academic year, the number of students at the schools of medicine and pharmacy combined reached 799. In the 1930s, the faculty of medicine started offering medical specialization, reduced school fees, and scholarships. Government missions to Europe were enlarged. The faculty's graduates had to complete several years of compulsory government service, only after which could they open their own practice.[22]

The interwar years also witnessed the graduation of the first Egyptian female doctors since the training of female doctors at the *hakimas'* school was terminated. From 1922 to 1928, the Lord Kitchener Memorial Fund supported six female medical students who trained in London: Helen Sidarus (graduated 1931), Tawhida ʿAbd al-Rahman (1932), Kawkab Hifni Nasif (1933), and later in the 1930s, Anisa Naji, Habiba ʿAwis, and Fathiya Hamid. When the first three returned to Egypt, the Kitchener Memorial Hospital in Cairo (est. 1923) hired them in positions previously occupied by British female doctors. In October 1929, four female students were enrolled in the Egyptian medical school, six in 1930, two in 1931, six in 1932, and seven in 1933.[23]

The re-Egyptianization of the medical profession took place through government service as well, as Egyptian doctors started occupying higher medical positions in the state administration.[24] Already in 1913, the Department of Public Health at the Ministry of Interior founded an advisory committee on endemic diseases, but it accomplished little due to the outbreak of the war. This committee was re-established in December 1920, prioritizing parasitological research. In 1922, the Department of Public Health was transferred to Egyptian hands and founded its own research laboratory and, in 1931, a new institute for parasitological, entomological, chemical, and clinical research. The department's first challenge was to replace the all-foreign senior administrative and professional staff. The number of Egyptian graduates of the medical school was still relatively small and certainly insufficient for the quickly expanding department. To staff its ranks, the department sent a total of eighty-one medical students abroad. The expansion of the department itself included new bacteriological laboratories, small regional hospitals, infant welfare centers, ophthalmic hospitals and clinics, a health museum, a rabies institute, and portable fumigation machines. The department also prided itself on sponsoring the research that led to the discovery of stibophen, an antibilharzial agent, named Fuʾadin in Arabic, after King Fuʾad.[25]

A 1928 law stipulated that the practice of medicine would be legally restricted to graduates of the faculty of medicine or those who passed its final exam. Already a year later, 1,830 of 2,409 doctors in Egypt, or 76%, were Egyptian, as opposed to the 40% pre–World War I figure. The 1928 law, which was designed to restrict the practice of foreign doctors in Egypt, proved to be overextended and to exclude Egyptian doctors educated abroad. In 1932, these doctors were exempted from the exam.[26] In 1936, the status of the Egyptian medical profession was further solidified with the establishment of a dedicated Ministry of Health.[27]

BUILDING A RESEARCH COMMUNITY

The institutional solidification of the Egyptian medical profession was accompanied by professional conferences that raised its regional and global status. In April 1925, the Egyptian Medical Association urged the minister of public instruction, 'Ali Mahir Pasha, to convene the first postwar international tropical medicine conference in Egypt.[28] King Fu'ad agreed to sponsor the conference. The chosen date marked the centennial of the foundation of the Egyptian medical school, although the conference ended up being held in 1928, 101 years after the school's inauguration. The Dutch Medical Association, which had already started preparing a similar initiative, graciously withdrew and allowed their Egyptian colleagues to lead.[29]

The declared goal of the conference was to place the Egyptian medical community on equal footing with European scholars and showcase Egypt as a research center and not merely a laboratory for others' research.[30] The Egyptian medical community thus declared that in this quintessentially colonial realm of knowledge, Egyptians could participate in scientific debates as equals.[31] Participants from the region included both colonial medical officials and local doctors. The conference hosted 2,400 participants, with 400 lectures, 258 of which concentrated on Egypt.[32]

In the following years, the Egyptian medical profession positioned itself as a regional leader by holding its annual meetings outside Egypt. Beginning in 1931, the annual conferences of the Egyptian Medical Association were held, alternately, in Egypt and a neighboring Arab city—in Beirut (1931), Jerusalem (1933), Damascus (1935), and Baghdad (1938). The Baghdad conference was dubbed the first Arab Medical Conference. The 1946 conference in Aleppo was named the eighteenth Arab Medical Conference, thus Arabizing all previous conferences in retrospect. These conferences brought together doctors from the entire region to discuss both scientific and political questions. Political questions included the Arabization of the language of instruction in Egypt and Lebanon and the Arabization of foreign medical terms. On both topics, the Egyptian representatives at the conference were at odds with their Syrian peers. The medical faculty in Damascus used Arabic as its main language of instruction, and the Syrian medical journal (the Journal of the Arab Medical Institute, Majallat al-Maʿhad al-Tibbi al-ʿArabi) opted for transliteration rather than the Arabization of medical terminology. The Syrians accused their Egyptian peers of neglecting the Arabic language and positioned themselves at the forefront of the Arabization of science.[33]

This interest in scientific research extended also to doctors' publications. A 1935 editorial in the *Egyptian Medical Journal* explained that scientific research on tropical diseases conducted by Western scientists is often oblivious to factors relevant to their spread, such as local customs, education, nutrition, and agricultural and weather conditions. A tropical disease research center, argued the editor, would provide Egyptian doctors an opportunity to study "their own" diseases and ways of combating them and then to apply this knowledge in their own country.[34]

The published products of Egyptian doctors during the interwar period featured two interrelated components: public health information and scientific research. On the one hand, Egyptian doctors debated policy and sought to educate the public regarding hygiene and preventive medicine. On the other hand, they saw themselves as scientists committed to promoting local research.

Parasitology and tropical medicine were promising niches to prove professional specialization on par with European colleagues in medical disciplines created and monopolized by European doctors stationed in Europe's colonies. Egyptian doctors endeavored to prove to their colonizers that they had reached medical competence that allowed them to regain control of Egypt's medical education and public health administration. In 1930, a department of tropical medicine was founded within the Cairo Faculty of Medicine and became the first recognized specialization there. An Association of Tropical Medicine followed a few years later.[35]

Articles in the journal of the Egyptian Medical Association urged local doctors to dedicate more of their time to scientific research and pressed the faculty of medicine, the Egyptian government, and private donors to allocate funds for research institutes and grants. Cutting-edge research on Egypt's diseases, one article stated, would place the country on par with leading research institutes of tropical medicine, such as the Rockefeller Institute in New York, the London School of Hygiene and Tropical Medicine, the Institute for Tropical Medicine in Hamburg, and the Calcutta School of Tropical Medicine. Egyptian doctors specializing in tropical medicine in European research institutes and universities were more than capable of building and sustaining such a research center in Egypt, the article argued, stating that familiarity with manners and customs of different strata of Egyptian society, their educational level, and their nutrition, as well as Egyptian agriculture and weather conditions, gave Egyptian doctors an advantage over their European counterparts.[36] Similarly, in a 1938 article, the editors of the *Egyptian Medical Journal* encouraged Egyptian doctors to study children's diseases because, as they stated, scientific principles discovered and applied in Western pediatrics might not be suitable for the Eastern mentality and customs.[37] Ahmad Khalil 'Abd al-Khaliq, for example, devised standard development charts for Egyptian infants based on data collected from infant welfare centers in Cairo.[38]

In their articles and conference presentations, Egyptian doctors reported on research they conducted on their patients. Sulayman 'Azmi, for example, described experiments conducted on gastroptosis patients, whom he had injected with insulin. The result was the relief of their main symptoms: lack of appetite, pain after food consumption, anemia, and weight loss. Four patients with other medical conditions were used as control subjects and were injected with insulin but showed no improvement.[39] 'Ali Hasan al-Ramli experimented with the rehabilitation of people with drug addictions. He reported that following their imprisonment, these individuals' health quickly deteriorated. When he treated them with stimulants and no opium derivatives, they improved gradually and gained weight.[40] 'Abd al-Wahhab Mahmud described rehabilitation methods that included complete withdrawal, stimulants, sedatives, hypnosis, hot baths, and psychological treatment, and reported 93% success. His article included recommendations for stricter narcotics laws and vigorous anti-narcotic propaganda.[41]

CULTIVATING THE SELF AND THE OTHER

Egyptian doctors researched and experimented with what they diagnosed as Egypt's most pressing problems: infant mortality, gastrointestinal diseases,[42] parasitic infections,[43] drug addiction, and prostitution. Their intervention in public health issues was part of a broader effendi project of reforming the self and the other. The self was the effendi male, and the other were peasants, both men and women, as well as middle-class women, who were to be educated into proper modernity.

A reform of the effendi male body included a wide range of daily practices: how men should dress, how they should spend their free time, and how many hours per day they should spend with their wives. From the medical point of view, masturbation, premarital sex, abstinence, and prostitution were central to this debate. Modernizing the male body involved physical exercise and even bodybuilding, switching from the fez to the brimmed hat, and abandoning prostitution, hashish, and alcohol.[44] Conversely, already in the late nineteenth century, Egyptian journals provided women with medical recommendations on motherhood, hygiene, and domestic roles.[45] Finally, as Michael Gasper and Omnia El Shakry have shown, Egyptian peasants were a stumbling block on the way to Egypt's modernity. Their practices, housing, and nutrition had to be restored for the sake of Egypt's modernity.[46] This dual reform project of the self and the other was at the heart of doctors' internal debates and public interventions.

Egyptian pediatrician and University of Montpellier graduate 'Abd al-'Aziz Nazmi Bey, for example, ascribed child mortality in Egypt to the mothers' ignorance of hygiene principles, which led them to give six- and seven-month-old children food and drink such as cow or buffalo milk, melons, and dates, which, in turn, caused gastroenteritis. In addition, mothers used talismans and amulets, and their dwellings were poorly ventilated and dark. Nazmi Bey suggested childcare training for schoolgirls, public hygiene propaganda (including the use of the cinema and health museums), the establishment of dispensaries for sick children and infant welfare stations, and the appointment of nurses to conduct home visits and teach women how to feed and treat their infants.[47]

In a lecture on gastroptosis (an abnormal downward displacement of the stomach) in Egypt, internist and Qasr al-'Ayni graduate Sulayman 'Azmi Bey ascribed the local frequency of diseases of the digestive tract to the dietary preferences of Egyptians—spicy food, fried onions, garlic, and pepper, all of which led to excessive water consumption. Egyptians, 'Azmi Bey noted, do not stick to regular eating hours and tend to consume lupine and peanuts between meals. The hot climate also leads to excessive consumption of cold lemonade, carbonated water, syrups, ice cream, and watermelons, leading to acute gastrointestinal trouble.[48]

The Egyptian diet was also at the center of George Subhi's article on obesity. He wrote that Egyptians believed that a fat man is stronger than a thin one, but they "must understand that the fat man . . . is weak physically and sexually and timorous mentally." Obesity in Egypt, he argued, is caused by a combination of a diet rich in sugar and fats and a corpulent lifestyle. The children of the obese are not only obese themselves, he remarked, but also gourmands and idle. Subhi maintained that scores of Egyptians believe that they live to eat and not eat to live. It is no rarity to meet a man who could devour an entire turkey or a lamb in one meal, he maintained. Pastries of all kinds are consumed on a huge scale. These contain more fat than flour. Obesity, he concluded, becomes a disease of the nouveau-riches and the profiteers—as ugly and vulgar as the means that have enriched them.[49]

Debates regarding human sexuality, another key public health topic in those years, also revolved around the cultivation of the self. Egyptian doctors deliberated, for example, over the permissibility of masturbation, the intensity of the female orgasm, and changes in sexual activity and desire throughout adulthood.[50] They recommended premarital medical examinations, particularly of men, to detect medical defects, but mainly to test for syphilis. Following the Turkish and Iranian examples, some advocated for compulsory premarital certificates, but no such law was passed.[51]

Faraj Fakhri was Egypt's most vocal sexologist, having specialized in this field in Magnus Hirschfeld's Institute of Sexology in Berlin. Fakhri authored several monographs on female sexuality, prostitution, venereal diseases, and sexual deviance. Upon returning from Berlin, he gave public talks on sexology at the American University in Cairo that were published in the Egyptian Medical Association journal. The talks dealt with questions he would later develop in his books, such as the male and female orgasm, sadism, premature ejaculation, and the physiology of erection.[52] Fakhri wrote extensively about "non-normative" sexual practices and marginalized individuals and practices, including homosexuality.[53] He regularly contributed to the popular Cairo monthly *al-Riyyada al-Badaniyya* (Physical Culture), which also featured an advice column. His plan to establish a sexual science institute in Cairo never materialized.[54]

Al-Riyyada al-Badaniyya became an important venue for the popularization of sexology and the medicalization of sexuality. In a 1940 article, chief editor Mukhtar al-Jawahiri explained that men should be better informed on the nuptial night. Brides are normally virgins, undress for the first time in the presence of a stranger, have no idea what to expect, and often find their first sexual experience traumatic, painful, and degrading, he explained. Men, for their part, often have previous sexual experience, usually with prostitutes, and treat their bride like one. Premarital education, he concluded, would prevent marital problems that begin with this first encounter. Men should learn that women also have sexual desires, which are simply slower to satisfy. While women's own experiences were not heard directly in such discussions, their sexual pleasure was considered.[55] Similarly, the journal's editors explained that they did not, by any means, encourage premarital sex or childlessness. Instead, they encouraged birth spacing for an ideal average of three or four children per family to afford a better quality of life for all family members. They also argued that contraception was legitimate for newlyweds who needed an adjustment period or in cases of inherent defects in one of the spouses' families or their older children.[56]

Drug addiction was another major public health issue discussed in medical journals in the 1920s and 1930s, having become a nationwide problem following World War I, when Allied soldiers brought cocaine and heroin with them to Egypt. By 1930, heroin addiction had reached epidemic proportions, leading both the police and medical professionals to wage vigorous campaigns against it. Given that the Egyptian government refused to fund rehabilitation centers, people with drug addictions admitted themselves to prison. Cut off from the drugs long enough, they ceased to crave them.[57] Medical doctors also advertised their ability to cure drug addiction. In January 1930, for example, two doctors opened a clinic in Cairo promising to cure people with addictions in three to five days with no remission and no side effects. They declared that they had already cured two hundred such individuals for free and were now ready to receive paying patients.[58]

Egyptian doctors also took an active part in debates regarding the medical inspection and regulation of prostitution, imposed by the British authorities in 1883, just months after Egypt's occupation. While nationalists, feminists, and Islamic thinkers advocated the abolition of regulated prostitution, the medical community was divided on this question. Doctors debated, for example, the effects of abolition on the spread of venereal diseases and whether they could be contained if prostitutes were no longer supervised. These debates were related to larger questions, such as whether prostitution could be prevented, whether prostitutes could be rehabilitated, and whether men could do without them.[59]

Egyptian doctors who debated regulation in the interwar period were unanimous on one point: regulation did not work. Medical examinations were not universal but were open to bribery and manipulation and thus provided a false guarantee against disease. Medical examinations were superficial and certainly did not detect any disease in its earlier stages; prostitutes also learned how to conceal symptoms during a superficial inspection.[60] More importantly, some authors noted, most disease carriers were never examined because only women were examined; men were not.[61]

Doctors were divided over whether the solution was abolishing licensed houses or reforming the existing system. Advocates of regulated brothels claimed that abolition would lead to social anarchy. They claimed that prostitution was inevitable because men could not do without it. They saw prostitution as a safety valve for the natural sexual urges of unmarried men who might otherwise assault innocent women.[62] Supply would continue "as long as a fallen woman would be able to profit from trading in her honor." Without formal brothels, however, these women would be exploited by unscrupulous pimps.[63]

Abolitionist doctors argued that prostitution entailed a complete denial of personal autonomy and that few, if any, chose this way of life. Prostitutes could not refuse a client, their profit was meager, and they were constantly indebted to the brothel keeper.[64] Regulated brothels, they claimed, seduced young women to a life of prostitution; created demand for traffic in women; created a class of intermediaries, such as pimps and brothel owners; fueled drug and alcohol consumption; and punished women for a crime that had two parties. Registration, moreover, left women with a permanent stigma. It destined them to a life of prostitution from which it was almost impossible to escape.[65] Abolitionists suggested plans for the rehabilitation and reintegration of prostitutes in general society, the provision of free venereal disease clinics, and large-scale sex education.[66]

Several doctors suggested sex education as a long-term investment that was more effective in disease prevention and hopefully also in discouraging men from frequenting prostitutes. While some medical doctors maintained that the sole solution was abstinence, others claimed abstinence was not a realistic goal and advocated sexual education that would restrict, though not eliminate, the spread of venereal diseases.[67] Another measure that some suggested was sex education for schoolboys aged ten to fifteen, including an explanation of the dangers of prostitution and even visual representation of patients with venereal diseases and the effects of these diseases on the human body.[68]

Conclusion

The participation of Egypt's doctors in policy-related debates was the culmination of a decades-long process of the emergence of an Egyptian medical profession. This entailed training, in Egypt and abroad, institutional Egyptianization, and then the formation of platforms that enabled professional and political debates about Egyptian bodies. Doctors were able to express themselves on policy because of the cultural capital they gained through education as well as their integration into existing *effendiyya* debates on the modernity of the personal and national body.

In the context of a social and intellectual history of the Egyptian medical profession, the question of the Egyptianization of the profession can benefit from a global and regional perspective that explains the multiple origins of the profession and the regional and global networks of which these doctors were a part. The centrality of Egypt's parasitology notwithstanding, Egyptian intervention in medical research extended to pediatrics, drug addiction, and other public health issues. Part of medical professionals' work was research oriented, while some of their findings informed public debates and acute public health challenges.

NOTES

1. On other professions, see, e.g., Donald Malcolm Reid, "Cultural Imperialism and Nationalism: The Struggle to Define and Control the Heritage of Arab Art in Egypt," *International Journal of Middle East Studies* 24, no. 1 (1992): 57–76; and Donald Malcolm Reid, "The Rise of Professions and Professional Organizations in Modern Egypt," *Comparative Studies in Society and History* 16, no. 1 (1974): 24–57.

2. Adell Patton, *Physicians, Colonial Racism, and Diaspora in West Africa* (Gainesville: University Press of Florida, 1996); Nancy E. Gallagher, *Medicine and Power in Tunisia, 1780–1900* (Cambridge: Cambridge University Press, 1983); Hannah-Louise Clark, "Doctoring the Bled: Medical Auxiliaries and the Administration of Rural Life in Colonial Algeria, 1904–1954" (PhD diss., Princeton University, 2014).

3. Naguib Mahfouz, *The History of Medical Education in Egypt* (Cairo: Government Press, 1935); Serge Jagailloux, *La Médicalisation de l'Égypte au XIXe Siècle (1798–1918)* (Paris: Éditions Recherche sur les Civilisations, 1986); Amira Sonbol, *The Creation of a Medical Profession in Egypt, 1800–1922* (Syracuse: Syracuse University Press, 1991); Khaled Fahmy, "Medicine and Power: Towards a Social History of Medicine in Nineteenth-Century Egypt," *Cairo Papers in the Social Sciences* 23 (2000): 1–45; Hibba Abugideiri, *Gender and the Making of Modern Medicine in Colonial Egypt* (London: Ashgate, 2010); Jennifer L. Derr, *The Lived Nile: Environment, Disease, and Material Colonial Economy in Egypt* (Stanford: Stanford University Press, 2019).

4. Sami Amin, *Taqwim al-Nil*, vol. 2 (Cairo: al-Matba'a al-Amiriyya, 1936), 606–11.

5. Sonbol, *The Creation of a Medical Profession*, 46–47, 83–84; Khaled Fahmy, "Women, Medicine, and Power in Nineteenth-Century Egypt," in *Remaking Women: Feminism and Modernity in the Middle East*, ed. Lila Abu-Lughod (Princeton: Princeton University Press, 1998), 35–72; Mahfouz, *The History of Medical Education*, 71–76; Mervat F. Hatem, "The Professionalization of Health and the Control of Women's Bodies as Modern Governmentalities in Nineteenth Century Egypt," in *Women in the Ottoman Empire: Middle Eastern Women in the Early Modern Era*, ed. Madeline C. Zilfi (Leiden: Brill, 1997), 66–80; Abugideiri, *Gender and the Making of Modern Medicine*, 115–58.

6. Donald M. Reid, "Arabic Thought in the Liberal Age Twenty Years After," *International Journal of Middle East Studies* 14, no. 4 (1982): 350, 354.

7. Abugideiri, *Gender and the Making of Modern Medicine*, 133.

8. Sonbol, *The Creation of a Medical Profession*, 106–13; Abugideiri, *Gender and the Making of Modern Medicine*, 109–10; Mahmud al-Minawi, *Hukama' Qasr al-'Ayni* (Cairo: Nahdat Misr, 1999), 25–26, 369–70. On Syrian medical officers in Sudan, see Heather Bell, *Frontiers of Medicine in the Anglo-Egyptian Sudan, 1899–1940* (Oxford: Oxford University Press, 1999), 34–49.

9. Minawi, *Hukama' Qasr al-'Ayni*, 358, 369; Sylvia Chiffoleau, *Médecines et médecins en Égypte: Construction d'une identité professionnelle et projet médical* (Paris: L'Harmattan, 1997), 61.

10. Chantal Verdeil, "Naissance d'une nouvelle élite ottomane. Formation et trajectoires de médecins diplômés de Beyrouth à la fin du XIXe siècle," *Revue des mondes musulmans et de la Méditerranée* 121/122 (2008): 217–37.

11. Chiffoleau, *Médecines et médecins en Égypte*, 67–70; al-Minawi, *Hukama' Qasr al-'Ayni*, 26.

12. Alumni Association, *Directory of Alumni, 1870–1952* (Beirut: American University of Beirut, 1953).

13. *Liste officielle de MM. les médecins et pharmaciens diplômés de la faculté française de Beyrouth* (Beirut: Université Saint-Joseph, Faculté française de médecine et de pharmacie, 1922).

14. *Listes officielles des médecins, vétérinaires, dentistes, sages-femmes, pharmaciens et aides-pharmaciens exerçant leurs professions en Égypte au 31 Décembre 1922* (Cairo: Ministry of Interior, Public Health Administration, 1922). See also Chiffoleau, *Médecines et médecins en Égypte*, 67.

15. This list makes no distinction between Egyptian and other Arab doctors—we do not have their place of birth, and this dataset, therefore, cannot help us map doctors' country of origin. This list does not include those doctors who spent their postgraduate studies abroad.

16. Sonbol, *The Creation of a Medical Profession*, 113.

17. *Listes officielles des médecins.*

18. Abugideiri, *Gender and the Making of Modern Medicine*, 112, 172–74; Chiffoleau, *Médecines et médecins en Égypte*, 82.

19. Abugideiri, *Gender and the Making of Modern Medicine*, 172; "Taqrir Majlis Idarat al-Jam'iyya al-Tibbiyya al-Misriyya 'an A'mal al-Jam'iyya wa-Amwaliha fi Sanat 1936," *al-Majalla al-Tibbiyya al-Misriyya (MTM)* 19, no. 2 (1936): 113–19.

20. Minawi, *Hukama' Qasr al-'Ayni*, 28; Sonbol, *The Creation of a Medical Profession*, 122.

21. Chiffoleau, *Médecines et médecins en Égypte*, 71.

22. Many of them retained their government post alongside their private clinic, which led to criticism of the doctors' divided loyalties, Sonbol, *The Creation of a Medical Profession*, 140–41.

23. 'Abd al-Ra'uf Hasan, "Iftitahiyya: al-Tabibat al-Misriyyat wa-Talibat al-Tibb," *MTM* 16, no. 12 (1933): 711–15; Margot Badran, *Feminists, Islam, and Nation: Gender and the Making of Modern Egypt* (Princeton: Princeton University Press, 1995), 179.

24. Abugideiri, *Gender and the Making of Modern Medicine*, 161–62.

25. "Sura wa-Mudhakara: al-A'mal Allati Qamat bi-ha Maslahat al-Sihha al-'Ummumiyya," *MTM* 14, no. 1 (1931): 58–61; "Iftitahiyya: Hawla Ma'ahid al-Abhath al-Tibbiyya fi Misr," *MTM* 16, no. 2 (1933): 57–61.

26. Chiffoleau, *Médecines et médecins en Égypte*, 65; Abugideiri, *Gender and the Making of Modern Medicine*, 168.

27. Chiffoleau, *Médecines et médecins en Égypte*, 59–80.

28. "Introduction," in *Congrés international de médecine tropicale et d'hygiène: Comptes rendus* (Cairo: Imprimerie Nationale, 1929), 1–2. On the prewar tropical medicine conferences, see Deborah J. Neill, *Networks in Tropical Medicine: Internationalism, Colonialism, and the Rise of a Medical Specialty, 1890–1930* (Stanford: Stanford University Press, 2012).

29. "Introduction," 7.

30. Ibid., 4.

31. Abugideiri, *Gender and the Making of Modern Medicine*, 180.

32. *Congrés international de médecine tropicale*; Sonbol, *The Creation of a Medical Profession*, 172; Chiffoleau, *Médecines et médecins en Égypte*, 92.

33. Liat Kozma, "Doctors Crossing Borders: The Formation of a Regional Profession in the Interwar Middle East," in *Middle Eastern and North African Societies in the Interwar Period*, ed. Kate Fleet and Ebru Boyar (Leiden: Brill, 2018), 124–44.

34. "Ahamiyyat al-Bahth al-'Ilmi fi Amradina al-Mutawattina," *MTM* 18 (1935): 142–43.

35. Abugideiri, *Gender and the Making of Modern Medicine*, 170; Chiffoleau, *Médecines et médecins Égypte*, 87.
36. 'Abd al-Ra'uf Hasan, "Iftitahiyya: Hawla al-Bahth al-'Ilmi wa-Wasa'ilihi fi al-Awsat al-Misriyya," *MTM* 15, no. 12 (1932): 829–33; "Iftitahiyya: Hawla Ma'ahid al-Abhath al-Tibbiyya," 57–61.
37. "Tamsir Tibb al-Atfal," *MTM* 21, no. 6 (1938): 330–34.
38. Ahmad Khalil Abdel Khalik, "Standard Development of Egyptian Infants," in *Congrès international de médecine tropicale*, vol. 2, 979–90.
39. Soliman Azmy Bey, "Insulin Therapy as a Fattening Agent with Special Reference to Its Application in Gastroptosis," in *Congrès international de médecine tropicale*, vol. 2, 325–41.
40. Aly Hasan El Ramly, "Heroin Habit in Egypt as Seen in Prisoners," in *Congrès international de médecine tropicale*, vol. 2, 711–16.
41. Abdel Wahab Mahmud, "Investigation of Narcotics in Egypt," in *Congrès international de médecine tropicale*, vol. 2, 979–90.
42. Beth Baron, "Perilous Beginnings: Infant Mortality, Public Health and the State in Egypt," in *Gendering Global Humanitarianism in the Twentieth Century Practice, Politics and the Power of Representation*, ed. Esther Möller, Johannes Paulmann, and Katharina Stornig (London: Palgrave Macmillan, 2020), 197–204; Mine Ener, *Managing Egypt's Poor and the Politics of Benevolence, 1800–1952* (Princeton: Princeton University Press, 2003), 108–13.
43. Derr, *The Lived Nile*, 127–56.
44. Lucie Ryzova, *The Age of the Efendiyya: Passages to Modernity in National-Colonial Egypt* (Oxford: Oxford University Press, 2014), 212–28; Wilson Chacko Jacob, *Working Out Egypt: Effendi Masculinity and Subject Formation in Colonial Modernity, 1870–1940* (Durham, NC: Duke University Press, 2010), 156–85.
45. Hibba Abugideiri, "Egyptian Women and the Science Question: Gender in the Making of Colonized Medicine, 1893–1919," *Arab Studies Journal* 4, no. 2 (1996): 46–78.
46. Michael Gasper, *The Power of Representation: Publics, Peasants, and Islam in Egypt* (Stanford: Stanford University Press, 2008); Omnia El Shakry, *The Great Social Laboratory: Subjects of Knowledge in Colonial and Postcolonial Egypt* (Stanford: Stanford University Press, 2008), 89–144.
47. Abdel Aziz Nazmy Bey, "La grande mortalité infantile en Égypte," *Congrès international de médecine tropicale*, vol. 2, 995–1002. See Ener, *Managing Egypt's Poor*; and Baron, "Perilous Beginnings."
48. Soliman Azmy Bey, "Gastroptosis in Egypt," *Congrès international de médecine tropicale*, vol. 2, 311–23.
49. George Sobhi, "Obesity in Egypt," *Congrès international de médecine tropicale*, vol. 2, 625–47. Quote taken from page 627.
50. Liat Kozma, "'We, the Sexologists . . .': Arabic Medical Writing on Sexuality, 1879–1943," *Journal of the History of Sexuality* 22, no. 3 (2013): 426–45.
51. On voluntary and compulsory gynecological treatment in interwar Iran and Turkey, see Firoozeh Kashani-Sabet, "The Politics of Reproduction: Maternalism and Women's Hygiene in Iran, 1896–1941," *International Journal of Middle East Studies* 38, no. 1 (2006): 14–15, 21; Cyrus Schayegh, *Who Is Knowledgeable, Is Strong: Science, Class, and the Formation of Modern Iranian Society, 1900–1950* (Berkeley: University of California Press, 2009), 125–26, 139–41; and Emine O. Evered and Kyle T. Evered, "Sex and the Capital City: The Political Framing of Syphilis and Prostitution in Early Republican Ankara," *Journal of the History of Medicine and Allied Sciences* 68, no. 2 (2013): 266–99.

52. Faraj Fakhri, "Lidhat al-Jima' al-Kubra," *MTM* 8, no. 3 (1923): 203.

53. Kozma, "We, the Sexologists," 134–74.

54. Fakhri does not explain this failure; he merely mentions it. Faraj Fakhri, *al-Mara wa-Falsafat al-Tanassuliyyat* (Cairo: al-Matba'a al-'Asriyya, 1924), 23.

55. Mukhtar al-Jawahiri, "al-Zawj al-Jahil," *al-Riyyada al-Badaniyya (RB)* 12, no. 365 (1940): 112–14.

56. M. F. J., "Hawl Tahdid al-Nasl Aydan," *RB* 3, no. 10 (1931): 116–63; Muhammad al-Jawahiri, "Hal Nahnu Ibahiyyin?," *RB* 12, no. 405 (1940): 844–47; Mahmud Isma'il, "Kayfa Sasughu al-Ijhad?," *RB* 10, no. 291 (1938): 927–34.

57. Thomas Wentworth Russell, *Egyptian Service, 1902–1946* (London: Murray, 1949), 234.

58. An advertisement for a rehabilitation center, *al-Lata'if al-Musawwara*, 23 June 1930, 22.

59. Emad Ahmad Helal, *al-Baghaya fi Misr: Dirasa Ta'rifiyya wa-Ijtima'iyya, 1834–1949* (Cairo: al-'Arabi li-l-Nashr wa-l-Tawzi', 2001).

60. Muhammad Amin Bey, "Ba'd Mulahazat 'ala al-Amrad al-Sirriyya 'and al-'Ahirat fi Misr," *MTM* 12, no. 6 (1929): 452.

61. Riyad Hilmi, "Nizam al-Bagha' al-Rasmi wa-Limadha Fashila," *RB* 9, no. 257 (1938): 42–48.

62. Dr. S., "Mushkilat al-Bagha'," *RB* 4, no. 8 (1932): 818–26.

63. "Itijar bi-l-Nisa' wa-l-Atfal fi Taqrir Lajnat Mukafahat al-Bagha'," *RB* 7, no. 140 (1935): 1170–71.

64. Ahmadif, "Bi-Munasabat Mashru' al-Hukuma fi Ilgha' al-Bagha': Masir al-Baghaya, Wasa'il Mukafahat al-Bagha' wa-l-Amrad al-Siriyya," *RB* 11, no. 338 (1939): 732–33; Faraj Fakhri, *Kitab al-Amrad al-Tanassuliyya wa-'Ilajuha wa-Turuq al-Wiqaya Minha*, 2nd ed. (Cairo: al-Matba'a al-'Asriyya, 1931), 411–19; Muhammad Farid al-Junaydi, *al-Bagha': Bahth 'Amali wa-'Ilmi* (Cairo: Matba'at al-Nasr, 1934), 112–16; Fakhri, *al-Amrad al-Tanassuliyya*, 414; Riyad Hilmi, "Mushkilat al-Amrad al-Zuhariyya," *Majallat al-Amrad al-Tanassuliyya* 20 (1937): 758–59.

65. Shahin Basha, "al-Bagha' al-Rasmi fi Misr," *RB* 4, no. 7 (1932): 845; Muhammad Shahin, "Bayan Wajiz 'ala al-A'mal allati Qamat bi-ha Maslahat al-Sihha al-'Ummumiyya," *MTM* 14, no. 1 (1931): 63; Muhammad Kamal Barada, "al-Amrad al-Zuhariyya fi al-Hay'a al-Ijtima'iyya al-Misriyya," *MTM* 16, no. 1 (1933): 44–45.

66. Shahin Basha, "al-Bagha' al-Rasmi," 845.

67. "Al-Bagha wa-Mushkilat al-Luqata," *RB* 4, no. 11 (1932): 1186–87.

68. Jamil Bayruti, "al-Khatar al-Zuhari wa-Kayfiyyat al-Qada' 'alayhi fi al-Sharq," *MTM* 22, no. 2 (1939): 107–26.

Bibliography

Abugideiri, Hibba. "Egyptian Women and the Science Question: Gender in the Making of Colonized Medicine, 1893–1919." *Arab Studies Journal* 4, no. 2 (1996): 46–78.

Abugideiri, Hibba. *Gender and the Making of Modern Medicine in Colonial Egypt*. London: Ashgate, 2010.

Baron, Beth. "Perilous Beginnings: Infant Mortality, Public Health and the State in Egypt." In *Gendering Global Humanitarianism in the Twentieth Century Practice, Politics and the Power of Representation*, edited by Esther Möller, Johannes Paulmann, and Katharina Stornig, 197–204. London: Palgrave Macmillan, 2020.

Bell, Heather. *Frontiers of Medicine in the Anglo-Egyptian Sudan, 1899–1940*. Oxford: Oxford University Press, 1999.

Chiffoleau, Sylvia. *Médecines et médecins en Égypte: Construction d'une identité professionnelle et projet médical*. Paris: L'Harmattan, 1997.

Derr, Jennifer L. *The Lived Nile: Environment, Disease, and Material Colonial Economy in Egypt*. Stanford, CA: Stanford University Press, 2019.

Fahmy, Khaled. "Medicine and Power: Towards a Social History of Medicine in Nineteenth-Century Egypt." *Cairo Papers in the Social Sciences* 23 (2000): 1–45.

Fahmy, Khaled. "Women, Medicine, and Power in Nineteenth-Century Egypt." In *Remaking Women: Feminism and Modernity in the Middle East*, edited by Lila Abu-Lughod, 35–72. Princeton, NJ: Princeton University Press, 1998.

Hatem, Mervat F. "The Professionalization of Health and the Control of Women's Bodies as Modern Governmentalities in Nineteenth-Century Egypt." In *Women in the Ottoman Empire: Middle Eastern Women in the Early Modern Era*, edited by Madeline C. Zilfi, 66–80. Leiden: Brill, 1997.

Helal, Emad Ahmad. *Al-Baghaya fi Misr: Dirasa Ta'rifiyya wa-Ijtima'iyya, 1834–1949*. Cairo: al-'Arabi li-l-Nashr wa-l-Tawzi', 2001.

Jacob, Wilson Chacko. *Working Out Egypt: Effendi Masculinity and Subject Formation in Colonial Modernity, 1870–1940*. Durham, NC: Duke University Press, 2010.

Jagailloux, Serge. *La Médicalisation de l'Égypte au XIXe Siècle (1798–1918)*. Paris: Éditions Recherche sur les Civilisations, 1986.

Kozma, Liat. "Doctors Crossing Borders: The Formation of a Regional Profession in the Interwar Middle East." In *Middle Eastern and North African Societies in the Interwar Period*, edited by Kate Fleet and Ebru Boyar, 124–44. Leiden: Brill, 2018.

Mahfouz, Naguib. *The History of Medical Education in Egypt*. Cairo: Government Press, 1935.

Al-Minawi, Mahmud. *Hukama' Qasr al-'Ayni*. Cairo: Nahdat Misr, 1999.

Reid, Donald Malcolm. "Cultural Imperialism and Nationalism: The Struggle to Define and Control the Heritage of Arab Art in Egypt." *International Journal of Middle East Studies* 24, no. 1 (1992): 57–76.

Reid, Donald Malcolm. "The Rise of Professions and Professional Organizations in Modern Egypt." *Comparative Studies in Society and History* 16, no. 1 (1974): 24–57.

Ryzova, Lucie. *The Age of the Efendiyya: Passages to Modernity in National-Colonial Egypt*. Oxford: Oxford University Press, 2014.

Sonbol, Amira. *The Creation of a Medical Profession in Egypt, 1800–1922*. Syracuse, NY: Syracuse University Press, 1991.

Verdeil, Chantal. "Naissance d'une nouvelle élite ottomane. Formation et trajectoires de médecins diplômés de Beyrouth à la fin du XIXe siècle." *Revue des mondes musulmans et de la Méditerranée* 121/122 (2008): 217–37.

CHAPTER 4

··

COLONIZING AND DECOLONIZING EGYPTIAN MEDICINE

··

SOHA BAYOUMI

UNLIKE in other regions of the world with distinct medical bodies of knowledge, the story of modern biomedicine in Egypt was not necessarily a story of "Western" medicine versus local medicine (whether the latter is conceived of as folk medicine, traditional medicine, ethnomedicine, popular forms of religious healing, or literate medical traditions—categories that, in the context of medical history in Egypt, have been permeable and fungible).[1] The fact of the matter is that Galenic-Hippocratic medicine, in its Islamic variant, had dominated medical thought and practice in Egypt, as it did in Europe, well into the mid-nineteenth century.[2]

Colonialism manifested itself in medicine in Egypt in the form of the modern (semi-colonial, colonial, and postcolonial) state's takeover of public health starting in the early to mid-nineteenth century and the mobilization of public health as a tool of biopower and social control (a phenomenon that is not unique to Egypt). However, unlike other colonial contexts where the colonial encounter led to transformations in biomedical paradigms, changes in medical thought and practice in Egypt had more to do with the bureaucratic administration of health, competition over power and control between colonial authorities and local elites, and a dialectic of emulation and resistance. In India, for example, scholars have shown that, in addition to colonial biomedicine serving as a tool of empire, significant transformations of traditional medicines and negotiations between those and colonial biomedicine took place in ways that led to reconfigurations of the former.[3] The changes in Egypt also manifested in political authority taking the form of medical and public health interventionism, such as canceling religious fairs for public health reasons; the establishment of a modern medico-statistical apparatus (registering, counting, and inspecting bodies—from registration of births, mostly for military recruitment, to mandatory medical inspections and mandatory vaccinations);[4] and other forms of medicalized state coercion and surveillance, from quarantines during periods of epidemics[5] to nationally mandated treatment campaigns of hookworm and schistosomiasis in the first half of the twentieth century.[6]

The fact that this transformation started in the shadow of colonialism—beginning with Mehmet Ali's rule and his modernizing project, immediately following Egypt's first encounter with European colonialism via the Napoleonic expedition (1798–1801)—and that it was consolidated under colonial and semi-colonial rule in the late nineteenth century and the first half of the twentieth century makes this a story about the dynamics of colonization and decolonization par excellence. Medicine in that sense is what Wilson Chacko Jacob calls "an assemblage of colonial modernity"—a site that combines colonial, decolonial, and postcolonial anxieties that reflect the tensions between the local and the global, the national and the international, and the particular and the universal.[7] Analyzing a combination of primary and secondary sources and oral history interviews sheds light on some of the most significant sites of contestation in modern Egyptian medicine, from the establishment of the first medical school in Egypt during Mehmet Ali's reign, to the various spaces that medicine needed to navigate and negotiate in postcolonial Egypt, to the role played by medicine in the 2011 Egyptian uprising and its aftermath. It also highlights racial and gender dynamics in the history of these contestations, different sites of resistance both to medical colonization and to the use of medicine as a tool of control, and how medicine, especially in the postcolonial era, has been negotiated as a site for claims-making and resistance to abuses of power by successive Egyptian regimes. Medicine serves as an important lens not only for understanding scientific modernity in Egypt, but also for reading many of the political transformations witnessed by modern Egypt. The colonial and postcolonial trajectory of medicine in Egypt is primarily a story of the rise and collapse of state medicine.

THE RISE OF STATE MEDICINE: FROM MEHMET ALI TO GAMAL ABDEL NASSER

Throughout his work on Mehmet Ali's state-building project, Khaled Fahmy shows how, as in many national contexts, modern biomedicine in Egypt was viewed as a tool in the service of the state's public health apparatus and national interests—starting with the first medical school built in 1827 in Abu Za'bal to cater to the needs of a growing army in service of an emergent regional power.[8] He and others also show that those state interventions, many relying on biomedicine as a tool of surveillance and inspection, were met with episodes of popular resistance and acts of defiance, large and small, from resisting quarantines to vaccine hesitancy.[9] Fahmy argues that the Egyptian state attains its modern form through this nexus of power and resistance, with its various manifestations in the field of medicine.[10] The state's modernizing project in medicine entailed a reconfiguration not only of medical practice and thought (from debates around dissection to germ theory, to the construction of disease categories),[11] or of medical hierarchy and expertise,[12] but also of gender and race relations in the medical establishment. Various scholars, including Khaled Fahmy, Hibba Abugideiri, Liat Kozma, and Sherry Gadelrab, have explored the multifaceted role played by gender and race in the establishment of modern medical hierarchies in Egypt and how gender and sexuality became a contested terrain for modern biomedicine in a colonial and semi-colonial context.[13] These contestations continued throughout the khedival period.

The turn of the twentieth century witnessed constant movement on the question of medicine and medical education. When Sa'd Zaghlul Pasha became the minister of education in 1906, his agenda included the Arabization of curricula in schools and universities. This change was difficult to realize in the School of Medicine, given the dominance of European instructors among its faculty. Zaghlul focused, therefore, on sending Egyptian students to Europe on large-scale educational and training missions and appointing Egyptian doctors to the faculty of the School of Medicine.[14]

During World War I, many British doctors and faculty members enlisted in the British army, which helped to advance the position of Egyptian doctors and faculty members in the School of Medicine, leading its director since 1898, Dr. Henry Keatinge, to give "Egyptian staff a bigger share of the higher posts."[15] Soon after the end of the war, the 1919 Egyptian revolution against British rule lent further momentum to the Egyptian doctors' status and visibility, as many more of them became more vocal in their support of the nationalist movement and started elaborating a national(ist) medical project that grew in parallel with their socio-professional identity. The promise of national independence meant, for many of these doctors, further social and professional mobility. The Egyptian Medical Association (EMA) was founded in April 1920 by 'Ali Ibrahim Pasha (1880–1947), who at the time was a surgeon at the medical school. The founding members of the EMA were staunch nationalist doctors who decided to exclude foreigners from the membership of their nascent association. The EMA started expressing clear political stances supporting the Wafd Party after meeting with its leader, Zaghlul Pasha, in June 1920.[16]

The interwar period, especially the years following Egypt's nominal independence from Great Britain in 1922, witnessed significant developments in the reconfiguration of the medical field, mirroring some of the characteristics of the political upheaval coloring the period and the maturation of the nationalist movement into different political factions with varying attitudes toward Britain's colonial power—ranging from outright antagonism to accommodation to collaboration. Naguib Mahfouz Pasha remarks that, by the early 1920s, the number of Egyptians "appointed to full staff posts" in the School of Medicine equaled that of their English counterparts.[17] By 1925, the School of Medicine was integrated into the Egyptian University under the rectorship of Ahmad Lutfi al-Sayyid (1872–1963), becoming one of the first four faculties of the Egyptian University.[18] In 1929, the school and the Qasr al-'Ayni Hospital were fully entrusted for the first time to an Egyptian, 'Ali Ibrahim Pasha, who was elected to serve as the first Egyptian dean of the Faculty of Medicine and director of the hospital. Ibrahim was the first dean to admit women to the medical school, making it one of the first Egyptian faculties to do so. In 1929, four women were admitted to the School of Medicine, followed by six in 1930, two in 1931, another six in 1933, seven in 1934, and five in 1935, with the first cohort of women graduating in 1934.[19] In 1940, Ibrahim founded the Egyptian Medical Syndicate, and he was also appointed minister of health—a position that he held for only one year before he returned to his academic work and became president of King Fu'ad I University (now Cairo University). Despite Ibrahim's historic contributions to modern Egyptian medicine and to consolidating its independence from the British, he was seen as steadily promoting active connections with European medical bodies. In fact, in his obituary published in *Plarr's Lives of the Fellows*, the Royal College of Surgeons of England's collection of biographies of deceased fellows, Ibrahim is described as "a patriot of broad mind, who believed that the interests of Egyptian educational and scientific progress could best be served by attracting the best men of whatever nationality."[20] It is clear, though, that Ibrahim held his own and ensured the autonomy of his decision-making in the face of powerful British doctors. In his 1946 book, *One Hour of Justice: The Black Book of the Egyptian Hospitals and a Fellaheen Charter*, A. Cecil Alport, who worked as chair of medicine in the Faculty of Medicine at King Fu'ad I University between 1937 and 1943, under the deanship of Ibrahim for the first three years, writes of many instances in which his suggestions to the Egyptian dean about improving medical education and focusing on clinical versus theoretical training were turned down.[21]

The first half of the twentieth century, starting with the interwar years, witnessed another shift in medical thought and practice, namely the shift of the medical focus from epidemics, which were one of the animating anxieties for Mehmet Ali's early efforts to establish modern medicine in Egypt, to a focus on endemic diseases, notably bilharziasis and ankylostomiasis. Sylvia Chiffoleau shows how the focus on these two ailments, respectively affecting an estimated 80% and 50% of the Egyptian population at the time, became a marker of Egyptian medical nationalism and a focus for Egyptian doctors. This shift in medical focus certainly coincided with the colonial interest across the globe in "tropical" diseases. Various scholars, however, have demonstrated that Egyptian doctors and researchers contributed not only to new knowledge production on these diseases, but also to thinking about political solutions to them.[22] However, colonial and semi-colonial interests continued to play a significant role in shaping the politics of medicine and public health in the country. British–American rivalries were exacerbated by the entrance of the Rockefeller Foundation into the country and the oversized role it began to play in the administration of the public health system in the wake of the 1943 cholera epidemic in Egypt. The prominence of American power in the region during and following World War II was perceived by the British as a potential threat to their dominance. Immediately following the war, the US Naval Medical Research Unit 3 (NAMRU-3) was established and was focused on studying "epidemic diseases that could infect US troops stationed in the Near East, Africa, and India."[23]

Meanwhile, Egyptian medicine continued to be a battlefield in the fight for authority between Egyptian and European doctors for the following decade until decolonization. Nasser's decolonial project ushered in a process of nationalization of the medical profession that stripped many European doctors of their privileges, put many restraints on medical practice by foreigners, and heralded a pact between the regime and Egyptian

doctors. This pact came to be known as "the Big Compromise," through which the regime guaranteed the political loyalty of Egyptian doctors by granting them those aforementioned privileges.[24]

In Nasser's Egypt, medicine played a central role in the state-making project. The
regime viewed medicine as an important weapon in its decolonial arsenal. Much
scholarship has focused on medicine as a colonial tool and as a weapon in imperial
arsenals, whether wielded via exercising control over colonized populations or via
the legitimization, justification, and humanization of colonialism and its "civilizing
mission." However, more recent scholarship has started focusing on how anticolonial
forces have also instrumentalized medicine in their nationalist fight.[25] In that sense,
Nasser's decolonial project was not an exception, especially regarding how medicine
was viewed as integral to social engineering. Nasser's regime increased the number of
medical schools in the country, focused on medical education (which was only available to students who received the highest grades in high school), and committed to
providing medical education free of charge to all medical students and hiring all medical graduates in government jobs. Public spending on health significantly increased,
as did the number of hospitals and health units. The health insurance system, which
began in 1936 primarily as a form of insurance against workplace accidents and occupational hazards, was significantly expanded in 1964 to cover all civil servants and public
industry workers.[26] Expanding medical coverage was seen as one of the most important accomplishments of the Nasserist regime, reflecting the brand of state socialism
it championed, which prioritized health and education. It also enabled and reinforced
the state's decolonial rhetoric, which blamed colonialism for allowing the spread of
the dreaded triad of "poverty, ignorance, and disease" (*al-faqr wa-l-jahl wa-l-marad*),
casting the decolonial state as a legitimate caretaker of the population.[27]

At the same time, the regime maintained a solid image of the doctor as a national
hero who not only treated the ills of the uneducated poor but also combated their ignorance and superstition. Nasserist era movies, such as Tawfiq Salih's *Sira' al-Abtal*
(Struggle of the Heroes, 1962) and *al-Mutamarridun* (The Rebels, 1968), featured stories
of physicians fighting on behalf of their underserved patients, fighting inequalities, and
even investigating how medicine had been used in colonial times as a tool of oppression
of the poor. Some doctors started taking control of the narrative themselves by inserting
their voices and their writing into the public discourse and using their experience and
medical expertise as a lens through which to analyze what they saw as society's social and
political ailments and how those were often responsible for physical ailments. Perhaps
most renowned among those doctors was Yusuf Idris, whose novels and short stories
offered a poignant dissection of issues related to health, illness, and poverty, from the
health conditions of railway workers in his novel *al-Bayda'* (The White Woman, written
in 1955 but published as a serial in *al-Jumhuriyya* in 1960 and as a novel in 1970), to
overpopulation and lack of access to contraceptives in his short story collection *Arkhas
Layali* (The Cheapest Nights, 1954), to a critique of the symbolic power and erotic sway
of medicine in his "'Ala Waraq Silufan" (On Cellophane Paper, 1971).[28]

Another famous example of a literary doctor is Nawal El-Saadawi, whose novel *Mudhakkirat Tabiba* (Memoirs of a Woman Doctor, 1958) ushered in her career as one of Egypt's most vocal and founding feminists.[29] In that semiautobiographical book published right after she graduated from the Qasr al-'Ayni medical school, El-Saadawi tells the story of a young Egyptian woman who defies her family to pursue medical studies. In it, she also explores, through that doctor's eyes, what the government saw at the time as taboo subjects, such as female genital cutting and the concept of honor as it relates to sexuality and virginity, topics that led to parts of the book being censored in its first edition. Even in its censored version, the book caused significant uproar from all parties concerned: the political authorities, the religious authorities represented by al-Azhar University, the medical authorities represented by the Ministry of Health and the medical syndicate, and even literary and cultural authorities represented by the Ministry of Culture.[30] El-Saadawi's later publication of *al-Mar'a wa-l-Jins* (Woman and Sex) in 1972 caused an even bigger uproar, which led to her firing from the Ministry of Health.[31]

In all these narratives, as well as in scholarly works, we see that, despite the regime's rhetoric and efforts, widespread inequalities in health persisted. The well-off sought medical care in private hospitals and clinics and had personal doctors, while most of the population sought care in overcrowded public hospitals. Additionally, despite the medical profession opening up, scholarship has noted how (usually male) children of senior doctors ended up inheriting their fathers' prestigious university positions, leading to the concentration of power within the medical profession in the hands of a medical elite composed of some well-known medical dynasties. Pursuing a medical career became the next most prestigious option for many aristocratic families with European-educated children, stripped of their former feudal titles.[32]

NEOLIBERALIZATION, ISLAMIZATION, AND THE COLLAPSE OF STATE MEDICINE

The mid-1970s ushered in a period of economic liberalization, which meant many changes for the medical field. For one thing, the focus on liberalization and privatization spelled the gradual decline of service in public hospitals, accelerating the entrenchment of a two-tiered healthcare system in which the poor sought subquality care in free or quasi-free public hospitals that were understaffed and underequipped, and the rich sought what was meant to be better healthcare in private hospitals. In fact, Anwar al-Sadat's *Infitah* (open-door) policy heralded the new phenomenon of the so-called investment hospitals (*al-mustashfayat al-istithmariyya*)—private hospitals established beginning in the mid-1970s and described as "investment hospitals" in reference to Law No. 43 of 1974 on Arab and foreign investment—and marked the first significant entry of private capital into the healthcare industry. Those liberalization efforts coincided with geopolitical factors: workforce migration to oil-rich Gulf countries and, with it, the first significant wave of health brain drain to the Gulf, which deepened the healthcare crisis in Egypt. The mass migration of both blue-collar and white-collar Egyptians to the Gulf brought, in addition to petrodollars, significant social and cultural changes. One such change is what has been described as the "Islamic awakening," "re-Islamization," or even "wahhabization," of Egyptian society. The so-called Islamist current (*al-tayyar al-Islami*), comprising various Islamist groups and movements, from the Muslim Brothers to various strands of Salafis, began playing a more significant role, not only in the political sphere but also in the social sphere. This manifested primarily in the delivery of various social services, for free or for nominal fees, in areas such as healthcare and education for the lower and low-middle classes in both urban and rural areas. Thus, "Islamic" schools, daycares, and clinics emerged, filling the gap created by the retrenchment of the state and public spending in those areas.[33]

Structural adjustment programs and other economic policies enforced by international financial institutions in Egypt and other countries in the Global South in the mid-1990s valued the privatization of social, health, and education services and a "cost recovery" model for expenses incurred in public healthcare facilities through increased premiums, copays, and service fees. The push was clearly visible in the Egyptian public health sector, which became severely underfunded, underequipped, and understaffed. The government's plan seemed to be the same as that employed in other sectors: cutting funds for the public sector to render its services less efficient and thus less attractive in order to push for privatization as a more efficient, and thus more attractive, alternative. Doctors in the public sector saw their wages stagnate and their working conditions deteriorate due to those developments. The push for privatization also meant establishing new private medical schools that graduated many more doctors, increasing competition in an already tight job market. The regime ceased to see the doctors as an asset and started to see them instead as a burden, considering the large number of medical graduates compared to the diminishing public spending on health, which hampered the regime's ability to guarantee government employment to all medical graduates. These changes coincided with increased competition faced by Egyptian doctors in Gulf countries from other migrant physicians, particularly those of South Asian origin. Gradually, the oil-rich Gulf countries became no longer reliant on Egyptian doctors for staffing their health sectors. Facing increased competition at home and abroad, a renunciation of their role by the state, a deterioration of their working conditions, and an erosion of both their symbolic and economic capital, doctors were finally confronted by the reality of the collapse of "the Big Compromise" brokered by the Nasserist state.

Moreover, Egypt's military regime, which since Nasser's era had placed great importance on the control of professional unions by the state, had put significant limits on unionization and the creation of independent unions. The Egyptian Medical Syndicate, the only recognized doctors' union in Egypt, was monopolized by the regime and ruled by an alliance formed by members of the National Democratic Party (the ruling party between 1978 and 2011) and the Muslim Brothers. No elections at the medical syndicate were held between 1992 and the eruption of the Egyptian uprising of 2011, effectively turning the medical syndicate into a mouthpiece for the regime, while giving the Muslim Brothers—who occupied many seats on the board of the syndicate—space to rally on questions related to the Palestinian cause, as well as pan-Arab and pan-Islamic causes, by coordinating with the Arab Doctors Union and the Islamic Relief committee in the syndicate.[34]

Doctors Taking Charge: Medicine as Resistance

Underpaid and overworked, lacking opportunities for training and continuing education, and deprived of the sympathy of their patients and the support of the political regime, groups of doctors started to form in the mid-2000s to play a significant social and political role and to join in the political momentum Egypt was witnessing. The year 2007 saw several important shifts, particularly the formation of two key groups that played central roles in envisioning healthcare and health demands in Egypt. The first was Atibba' bi-la Huquq (Doctors Without Rights), which was formed by several doctors who were alarmed by the dismal state of their rights and profession. Inspired by the name of the international humanitarian organization Doctors Without Borders, Atibba' bi-la Huquq played on the phonetic similarity between the words borders (hudud) and rights (huquq) in Arabic.[35] The second group was Lajnat al-Difa' 'an al-Haq fi al-Sihha (Committee for Defending Citizens' Right to Health [CDCRH]), which comprised more than twenty civil society organizations active in the fields of health, human rights, and women's rights, among others. The CDCRH was formed in response to the prime ministerial Decree No. 637 in March 2007, which aimed to transform the not-for-profit Health Insurance Organization into a for-profit holding company. The CDCRH viewed the decree as a major step by the Mubarak regime on the "road to full privatization of health insurance in Egypt" and attacked the government's spending priorities. It also blamed the regime for the failure of public health services because of its role in depriving the Ministry of Health of sufficient numbers of qualified physicians and employees due to the low salaries of doctors and other healthcare workers and the "inefficient management" of public hospitals and the public health sector as a whole. The committee condemned the government for trying to turn the right to health into a form of charity provided to the poor after showing "a poverty certificate."[36]

Predating those two groups is another organization offering a clear example of how medicine played a visible role in countering the regime's political interests and the police state's impingement on personal rights: the al-Nadim Center for the Rehabilitation of Victims of Violence. Founded in 1993 as a nonprofit clinic registered with the Ministry of Health and the medical syndicate, al-Nadim was the brainchild of three women doctors, Magda Adly, Suzan Fayad, and Aida Seif Eldawla, who hoped for it to simply offer a clinical setting for addressing the medical and psychiatric/psychological needs of an overlooked population traumatized by various forms of violence. In an interview conducted by the author with Seif Eldawla, she explained how, over the span of a year and a half, the founders realized that the patients they were working with were mostly survivors of state violence and that the issues they were handling were "not primarily intrapsychic issues" but rather proportionate manifestations of the violence to which these patients were subjected.[37] This led al-Nadim to expand its scope from a strictly clinical venue to a human rights organization that provides medical and psychological care, as well as legal assistance to individuals who experienced violence and torture, in addition to engaging in various forms of advocacy, networking, and pressuring the legislative bodies in Egypt to adopt the international definition of torture in Egyptian laws. In 1995, al-Nadim changed its registration to a nongovernmental organization that includes a clinic, among other activities and programs. It continued to play a significant role in documenting cases of torture, political violence, and police brutality and training younger doctors in that line of work—activities that earned the organization the wrath of the regime, which continually harassed al-Nadim's founders and employees by regularly raiding and searching their offices, physically assaulting them,[38] and stripping them of their license to practice.[39] This role played by feminist women doctors is not unique: from El-Saadawi, to al-Nadim's founders, to Mona Mina, founder of the group Atibba' bi-la Huquq and the first woman to serve as the secretary-general of the medical syndicate (she took office in October 2011), women doctors were at the forefront of the battle over medicine's soul and the question of whom medicine served in Egypt.

2011 AND THE RISE OF "REVOLUTIONARY" MEDICINE

The popular uprising in January and February 2011 signaled, at least for a brief period, the emergence of new platforms for the interaction of medicine and politics and for inserting a medical and public health discourse into political debates and public discussions. Physicians played major roles in the various political events that marked the Egyptian revolution, both as perpetrators of state violence (for instance, conducting the so-called virginity tests on female protesters;[40] performing procedures on hospitalized protesters without the use of anesthesia;[41] restraining protesters in their hospital beds or denying them care and pain medication; and fabricating causes of death on death certificates[42]) and as agents of change and resistance to that violence (creating and staffing makeshift field hospitals to tend to injured protesters in moments of political violence; documenting torture, state violence, and police brutality; and agitating for reforming the healthcare system). The opening of the public sphere, ushered in by the revolution, allowed doctors to reinsert themselves into the political and social discourses in novel ways: as defenders of medical ethics and the principle of medical neutrality,[43] as advocates for comprehensive healthcare reform, and as protectors of their patients' dignity in the face of a massive police apparatus and a brutal military regime.[44] In fact, medicine managed to play a role that discredited the regime and its official narrative about the political events of 2011 and its aftermath. Groups of doctors wielded their technical expertise and their spatially and temporally privileged access to bodily suffering and loss of life to undermine the regime's version of political events and offer alternative narratives. Others, especially older generations of doctors, relied on their prestige and cultural capital to lend legitimacy to protesters and their demands.[45] This change in the political scene and the new ways in which groups of doctors were able to reinvent and interject themselves into the public discourse worked to redeem medicine, in the eyes of a wider Egyptian audience, as a potentially liberatory practice and not just as a tool of the regime.

During moments of violent confrontation marking the 2011–13 period, groups of doctors, such as the group Atibba' al-Tahrir (Tahrir Doctors), appealed to the principle of medical neutrality—a principle championed by international humanitarian medical organizations, such as Doctors Without Borders, and enshrined in international humanitarian law as the culmination of many decades of attempts to "civilize" European wars. However, it was the Egyptian doctors' embeddedness as citizens and as doctors *within* borders that lent more credibility to their mobilization, especially at a time when the regime was fomenting mistrust toward everything foreign and blaming the political uprising on foreign agitators and their agents in Egypt who were trying, according to the regime, to sow chaos in the country.[46] In their mobilization, these doctors resorted to a form of patriotism or nationalism that has been described as *immanent*—that is, the notion that the nation is ultimately the people and that there is no guaranteeing the safety of the nation without guaranteeing the safety and happiness of the people. This version of nationalism worked to counter the regime's *transcendent* rhetoric of the nation—one that sees the nation as an abstract entity to defend, sometimes even against the people themselves, who are seen as misguided or untrustworthy.[47]

MEDICAL CHICANERY AND THE AUTHORITARIAN INSTRUMENTALIZATION OF SALVIFIC MEDICINE

The heyday of the mobilization for better health in Egypt was between 2011 and 2014—a period marked by two three-month-long strikes in public hospitals in 2012 and 2014, numerous protests, and various other forms of mobilization. However, this activity was brought to a standstill soon after the military coup of July 2013, the crackdown on dissidents, both Islamist and secular, the passing of the draconian anti-protest law in November 2013, and Abdel Fattah El-Sisi's official takeover in June 2014. El-Sisi's regime signaled an entrenchment of *transcendent* nationalism and an obsession with Egypt's perceived glory. Shortly before El-Sisi took office, the Egyptian armed forces announced two miraculous devices: one that was said to noninvasively detect HIV and hepatitis C in patients through a moving antenna, and another that was reported to be successful in completely curing both HIV and hepatitis C. The doctor who invented and revealed the devices, General Ibrahim ʿAbd al-ʿAti, acquired instant fame when he announced that the curing device, which supposedly worked like a renal dialysis machine, "takes the virus from the patient, turns it into protein and gives that protein back to the patient—so [it's like] I'm taking the AIDS from the patient and giving it back to him as a kofta [ground meat] skewer."[48] The military announced that the curing device would be available within months and would eradicate hepatitis C (a disease of which Egypt had the highest prevalence rate in the world) within a couple of years. Patients were encouraged to sign up through an online portal set up by the military. The miraculous devices turned out to be a hoax, leading to the coining of the term *koftagate* to describe this episode of medical chicanery aimed at consolidating authoritarianism in the hands of the military. However, this scandal raised the hopes of a population ravaged by hepatitis C, a chronic and life-threatening illness that was, according to many analyses, spread, at least in part, through state-enforced iatrogenic means (as a result of the national treatment campaign against schistosomiasis)[49] and unhygienic shaving and personal hygiene practices during the conscription of most of the young male population. The regime, in an attempt to save face and deliver on its promise, had to scramble to provide actual treatment for those whose hopes had been falsely raised. This sent the government in a hectic search for an agreement with multinational pharmaceutical companies that would make some of the more recent antiviral drugs affordable for more Egyptians, leading to unprecedented progress in treating and eliminating the disease.[50] However, the trajectory of hepatitis C in Egypt and the dramatic twists and turns on the road to addressing it remain a clear manifestation of the enmeshment of medical narratives in political maneuverings and yet another example of how medicine has been instrumentalized by different political regimes in Egypt—in this case, by a hypernationalist/militaristic regime.

The continued crackdown on civil and political liberties and the slow progress in achieving higher salaries, better working conditions, and the reforms they had fought for over the past decade led many Egyptian doctors to migrate at even higher rates than previous years in search of more dignified living and working conditions. Some doctors who were imprisoned for a period for their activism ended up seeking asylum or going into forced exile abroad.[51] These circumstances compounded the health brain drain phenomenon affecting Egypt at least since the mid-1970s. No official figures exist, but some estimates put the percentage of Egyptian doctors living and practicing outside the country after receiving their medical education in Egypt at about 60%. In fact, diasporic doctors figure centrally in the collective imagination surrounding medicine in Egypt—from the fictional Ismaʿil in Yahya Haqqi's *Qindil Umm Hashim* (The Lamp of Umm Hashim),[52] who grappled with the notions of tradition and modernity in his practice, to the benevolent Sir Magdi Yacoub, who received his medical education in Egypt before going on to become a renowned cardiothoracic surgeon in England and then later establishing the Magdi Yacoub Heart Foundation in Aswan following his retirement from the National Health Service in the UK. Diasporic doctors, especially those practicing in the Global North, have been self-fashioned and perceived by society in ways that highlight their success abroad and how it enables them to better serve their country, either by being "good ambassadors," by connecting Egypt and Egyptian medicine to global networks of medical knowledge production, or by accumulating enough economic, cultural, and symbolic capital to allow them to found philanthropic medical institutions in their home country.

Conclusion

The history of the colonization and decolonization of medicine in Egypt can be traced in great detail—from the categorization of diseases to medical professionalization, and from the place of race and gender in the medical establishment and medical practice to the political instrumentalization of medicine and the social and political roles of doctors. Some of these areas are manifestations of colonization and decolonization in Egyptian medicine, but new and emerging scholarship continues to deepen our understanding of these intricate stories.

As examined in more detail by existing scholarship, medicine and healthcare in Egypt operated as a site of political contestations in various forms, with the colonial state using both as tools of control. Decolonial battles in medicine manifested both as professional struggles by local medical elites against colonial doctors and medical and bureaucratic authorities and as shifts in medical interests toward new categories of disease that impacted the local population. The decolonial state saw medicine and healthcare as a tool for gaining legitimacy in the eyes of the local population, and doctors were perceived as important agents of the state's postcolonial project. However, the vagaries of postcolonial state power have translated into various changes in how medicine has been instrumentalized and doctors have been perceived, culminating in doctors rising as major agents of resistance to abuses of state power during the 2011 uprising and in its aftermath. The entrenchment of authoritarianism since the 2013 military coup has also manifested in a renewed interest in the legitimizing potential of medicine as a tool of power. Within these different configurations of the nexus of medicine and politics, women doctors have been integral to catalyzing narratives around medicine's role in resisting state hegemony. Medicine has been claimed time and time again by various state and nonstate actors, from the successive political regimes to medical professionals, demonstrating the Janus-faced nature of medicine as both a tool of political repression and a potentially liberatory discourse and practice.

NOTES

1. On imperial medicine, see Pratik Chakrabarti, *Medicine and Empire: 1600–1960* (New York: Palgrave Macmillan, 2013); David Arnold, ed., *Imperial Medicine and Indigenous Societies* (Manchester, UK: Manchester University Press, 1991); and Roy M. MacLeod, ed., *Disease, Medicine, and Empire: Perspectives on Western Medicine and the Experience of European Expansion* (New York: Routledge, 1988).

2. Hormoz Ebrahimnejad, "The Development of Galenico-Islamic Medicine: Assimilation of Greek Sciences into Islam," Wellcome Trust Centre for the History of Medicine at UCL, 2005, 127–40, http://www2.ihp.sinica.edu.tw/file/4748AMUBeZq.pdf.

3. For how this played out in the case of India, see David Arnold, *Colonizing the Body: State Medicine and Epidemic Disease in Nineteenth-Century India* (Berkeley: University of California Press, 1993). On the interactions between Western biomedicine and traditional medicines in India, see, e.g., Projit Bihari Mukharji, *Doctoring Traditions: Ayurveda, Small Technologies, and Braided Sciences* (Chicago: University of Chicago Press, 2016).

4. Timothy Mitchell, *Colonising Egypt* (Berkeley: University of California Press, 1988).

5. LaVerne Kuhnke, *Lives at Risk: Public Health in Nineteenth-Century Egypt* (Berkeley: University of California Press, 1990); Nancy Elizabeth Gallagher, *Egypt's Other Wars: Epidemics and the Politics of Public Health* (Syracuse, NY: Syracuse University Press, 1990).

6. Jennifer L. Derr, *The Lived Nile: Environment, Disease, and Material Colonial Economy in Egypt* (Stanford, CA: Stanford University Press, 2019).

7. Wilson Chacko Jacob, *Working Out Egypt: Effendi Masculinity and Subject Formation in Colonial Modernity, 1870–1940* (Durham, NC: Duke University Press, 2010).

8. Khaled Fahmy, *All the Pasha's Men: Mehmed Ali, His Army, and the Making of Modern Egypt* (Cambridge: Cambridge University Press, 1997).

9. Khaled Fahmy, *In Quest of Justice: Islamic Law and Forensic Medicine in Modern Egypt* (Berkeley: University of California Press, 2018); LaVerne Kuhnke, "Resistance and Response to Modernization: Preventive Medicine and Social Control in Egypt, 1825–1850" (PhD diss., University of Chicago, 1971).

10. Fahmy, *In Quest of Justice*, 281.

11. Anne-Marie Moulin, "The Construction of Disease Transmission in Nineteenth-Century Egypt and the Dialectics of Modernity," in *The Development of Modern Medicine in Non-Western Countries*, ed. Hormoz Ebrahimnejad (New York: Routledge, 2009), 56–72.

12. Amira El Azhary Sonbol, *The Creation of a Medical Profession in Egypt, 1800–1922* (Syracuse, NY: Syracuse University Press, 1991).

13. Khaled Fahmy, "Women, Medicine, and Power in Nineteenth-Century Egypt," in *Remaking Women: Feminism and Modernity in the Middle East*, ed. Lila Abu-Lughod (Princeton, NJ: Princeton University Press, 1998), 35–72; Khaled Fahmy, "Prostitution in Egypt in the Nineteenth Century," in *Outside In: On the Margins of the Modern Middle East*, ed. Eugene Rogan (London: I. B. Tauris, 2002), 77–103; Hibba Abugideiri, *Gender and the Making of Modern Medicine in Colonial Egypt* (Farnham, UK: Ashgate, 2010); Liat Kozma, *Policing Egyptian Women: Sex, Law, and Medicine in Khedival Egypt* (Syracuse, NY: Syracuse University Press, 2011); Sherry Sayed Gadelrab, *Medicine and Morality in Egypt: Gender and Sexuality in the Nineteenth and Early Twentieth Centuries* (London: I. B. Tauris, 2015).

14. In his book on the history of medical education in Egypt, Naguib Pasha Mahfouz (1882–1974) favorably documents this period of rapid change in the School of Medicine. Naguib Mahfouz, *The History of Medical Education in Egypt* (Cairo: Government Press, Bulaq, 1935), 55–56.

15. Ibid., 56.

16. Sylvia Chiffoleau, *Médecines et médecins en Égypte: Construction d'une identité professionnelle et projet médical* (Paris: L'Harmattan, 1997), 61, 76.

17. Mahfouz, *The History of Medical Education in Egypt*, 57.

18. Ibid., 59.

19. Khalid 'Azab and Suzan 'Abid, eds., *'Ali Pasha Ibrahim: Ra'id al-Nahda al-Tibbiyya al-Hudilha* (Alexandria, Egypt: Bibliotheca Alexandrina, 2007), 39.

20. "Ibrahim, Sir Ali (1880–1946)," The Royal College of Surgeons of England, accessed 25 March 2021, https://livesonline.rcseng.ac.uk/client/en_GB/lives/search/detailnonmodal/ent:$002f$002fSD_ASSET$002fo$002fSD_ASSET:376426/one?qu=%22rcs%3A+E00 4243%22&rt=false%7C%7C%7CIDENTIFIER%7C%7C%7CResource+Identifier.

21. Arthur Cecil Alport, *One Hour of Justice: The Black Book of the Egyptian Hospitals and a Fellaheen Charter* (London: Crisp, 1947), 35–36.

22. Chiffoleau, *Médecines et médecins en Égypte*, 59–109; Derr, *The Lived Nile*.

23. Gallagher, *Egypt's Other Wars*, 77–115. NAMRU continued its mission in Egypt until 2019, when an assessment determined the need for security upgrades and relocated NAMRU-3 to the US Naval Air Station Sigonella in Southern Italy: Dean J. Wagner, "NAMRU-3 Moves to Sigonella, Italy," 12 December 2019, https://www.c6f.navy.mil/Press-Room/News/News-Display/Article/2051364/namru-3-moves-to-sigonella-italy/.

24. Alaa Shukrallah and Mohamed Hassan Khalil, "Egypt in Crisis: Politics, Health Care Reform, and Social Mobilization for Health Rights," in *Public Health in the Arab World*, ed. Samer Jabbour, Rita Giacaman, and Marwan Khawaja (Cambridge: Cambridge University Press, 2012); Chiffoleau, *Médecines et médecins en Égypte*.

25. Jennifer Johnson, *The Battle for Algeria: Sovereignty, Health Care, and Humanitarianism* (Philadelphia: University of Pennsylvania Press, 2016).

26. Chiffoleau, *Médecines et médecins en Égypte*, 294.

27. Jennifer Johnson highlights a similar dynamic in the context of Algeria. See Johnson, *The Battle for Algeria*.

28. Yusuf Idris, *al-Bayda': Riwaya*, 2nd ed. (Beirut: Dar al-'Awda, 1979); Yusuf Idris, *Arkhas Layali*, al-Kitab al-Masi (Cairo: al-Dar al-Qawmiyya li-l-Tiba'a wa-l-Nashr, 1954); Idris, "'Ala Waraq Silufan," in *Bayt min Lahm, wa-Qissas Ukhra* (Cairo: 'Alam al-Kutub, 1971).

29. Nawal El-Saadawi, *Mudhakkirat Tabiba* (Cairo: Dar al-Ma'arif, 1965).

30. Nawal El-Saadawi, "Mudhakkirat Tabiba ba'd 63 'Aman min al-Qahr," al-Hiwar al-Mutamaddin, 11 August 2019, http://www.ahewar.org/debat/show.art.asp?aid=646230.

31. Nawal El-Saadawi, *al-Mar'a wa-l-Jins* (Cairo: al-Nashirun al-'Arab, 1972).

32. Shukrallah and Khalil, "Egypt in Crisis."

33. Soheir A. Morsy, "Islamic Clinics in Egypt: The Cultural Elaboration of Biomedical Hegemony," *Medical Anthropology Quarterly* 2, no. 4 (1988): 355–69; Steven Brooke, *Winning Hearts and Votes: Social Services and the Islamist Political Advantage* (Ithaca, NY: Cornell University Press, 2019).

34. Amani Qindil, *al-Dawr al-Siyasi li-Jama'at al-Masalih fi Misr: Dirasat Halat Niqabat al-Atibba', 1984–1995* (Cairo: al-Ahram Center for Political and Strategic Studies, 1996); 'Amr

Shubaki, *Niqabat al-Atibba'*, Silsilat al-Niqabat al-Mihaniyya (Cairo: al-Ahram Center for Political and Strategic Studies, 2004).

35. Sherine F. Hamdy and Soha Bayoumi, "Egypt's Popular Uprising and the Stakes of Medical Neutrality," *Culture, Medicine, and Psychiatry* 40, no. 2 (2015): 1–19.

36. "The Founding Statement for the Defense Committee of Citizen's Right to Health (Against Privatization of Health Insurance)," al-Haq fi al-Sihha, accessed 12 February 2015, https://el7a2felse7a.wordpress.com/the-founding-statement/.

37. Interview by the author with Dr. Aida Seif Eldawla, 12 February 2021.

38. In 2008, Dr. Magda Adly's arm was broken after al-Nadim doctors were chased by the police, causing her a permanent disability in her left shoulder, which ended her medical practice. Interview by the author with Dr. Adly, 3 July 2013.

39. In the latest episode, in January 2021, an Egyptian administrative court vindicated the al-Nadim Center, after four years of litigation, by overturning the Cairo governor's 2016 decision to close down the al-Nadim Center.

40. Sherine Hafez, "The Revolution Shall Not Pass through Women's Bodies: Egypt, Uprising and Gender Politics," *The Journal of North African Studies* 19, no. 2 (2014): 172–85.

41. Patrick Kingsley and Louisa Loveluck, "Egyptian Doctors Ordered to Operate on Protesters without Anaesthetic," *Guardian*, 11 April 2013, http://www.theguardian.com/world/2013/apr/11/egypt-doctors-operate-protesters-anaesthetic.

42. Mohamed El-Fiki and Gail Rosseau, "The 2011 Egyptian Revolution: A Neurosurgical Perspective," *World Neurosurgery* 76, no. 1–2 (2011): 28–32.

43. Hamdy and Bayoumi, "Egypt's Popular Uprising and the Stakes of Medical Neutrality."

44. Soha Bayoumi, "Is Socio-Professional Mobilization Leading the Way Out of Egypt's Political Impasse?," *Citizen*, 18 March 2016, https://www.thecitizen.in/index.php/en/NewsDetail/index/6/7169/Is-Socio-Professional-Mobilization-Leading-The-Way-Out-Of-Egypts-Political-Impasse.

45. Soha Bayoumi and Sherine F. Hamdy. "Nationalism, Authoritarianism, and Medical Mobilization in Post-revolutionary Egypt," in *Culture, Medicine, and Psychiatry* 47 (2022): 37–61, https://doi.org/10.1007/s11013-022-09802-4.

46. Hamdy and Bayoumi, "Egypt's Popular Uprising and the Stakes of Medical Neutrality."

47. Bayoumi and Hamdy, "Nationalism, Authoritarianism, and Medical Mobilization in Post-Revolutionary Egypt."

48. Mohamed Ashraf Abu Emaira and Mohamed Hamama, "From the Kofta Machine to 100 Million Healthy Lives: Egypt's Success in Stemming Hepatitis C," *Mada Masr*, 27 May 2019, https://www.madamasr.com/en/2019/05/27/feature/society/from-the-kofta-machine-to-100-million-health-lives-egypts-success-in-stemming-hepatitis-c/.

49. Derr, *The Lived Nile*.

50. Ted Alcorn, "Why Egypt Is at the Forefront of Hepatitis C Treatment," *Atlantic*, 29 May 2018, https://www.theatlantic.com/health/archive/2018/05/why-egypt-is-at-the-forefront-of-hepatitis-c-treatment/561305/.

51. Examples include Dr. Muhammad Fattuh for his criticism of the military on *koftagate* and Dr. Tahir Mukhtar because of the lawsuit he was facing. Many more doctors were imprisoned in the years following the military takeover in 2013.

52. Yahya Hakki, *The Lamp of Umm Hashim: And Other Stories*, trans. Denys Johnson-Davies (Cairo: American University in Cairo Press, 2006).

BIBLIOGRAPHY

Abugideiri, Hibba. *Gender and the Making of Modern Medicine in Colonial Egypt*. Farnham, UK: Ashgate, 2010.

Bayoumi, Soha, and Sherine Hamdy. "Nationalism, Authoritarianism, and Medical Mobilization in Post-Revolutionary Egypt." *Culture, Medicine, and Psychiatry* 47 (2022): 37–61. https://doi.org/10.1007/s11013-022-09802-4.

Chiffoleau, Sylvia. *Médecines et médecins en Égypte: construction d'une identité professionnelle et projet médical*. Paris: L'Harmattan, 1997.

Derr, Jennifer L. *The Lived Nile: Environment, Disease, and Material Colonial Economy in Egypt*. Stanford, CA: Stanford University Press, 2019.

El-Mehairy, Theresa. *Medical Doctors: A Study of Role Concept and Job Satisfaction: The Egyptian Case*. Vol. 33. Leiden: Brill, 1984.

Fahmy, Khaled. *In Quest of Justice: Islamic Law and Forensic Medicine in Modern Egypt*. Berkeley: University of California Press, 2018.

Fahmy, Khaled. "Women, Medicine, and Power in Nineteenth-Century Egypt." In *Remaking Women*, edited by Lila Abu-Lughod, 35–72. Princeton, NJ: Princeton University Press, 1998.

Gallagher, Nancy Elizabeth. *Egypt's Other Wars: Epidemics and the Politics of Public Health*. Syracuse, NY: Syracuse University Press, 1990.

Hamdy, Sherine. *Lissa: A Story about Medical Promise, Friendship, and Revolution*. Guelph, Ontario: University of Toronto Press, 2017.

Hamdy, Sherine. *Our Bodies Belong to God: Organ Transplants, Islam, and the Struggle for Human Dignity in Egypt*. Berkeley: University of California Press, 2012.

Hamdy, Sherine, and Soha Bayoumi. "Egypt's Popular Uprising and the Stakes of Medical Neutrality." *Culture, Medicine, and Psychiatry* 40, no. 2 (2015): 1–19. https://doi.org/10.1007/s11013-015-9468-1.

Kozma, Liat. *Policing Egyptian Women: Sex, Law, and Medicine in Khedival Egypt*. Syracuse, NY: Syracuse University Press, 2011.

Kuhnke, LaVerne. *Lives at Risk: Public Health in Nineteenth-Century Egypt*. Berkeley: University of California Press, 1990.

Shukrallah, Alaa, and Mohamed Hassan Khalil. "Egypt in Crisis: Politics, Health Care Reform, and Social Mobilization for Health Rights." In *Public Health in the Arab World*, edited by Samer Jabbour, Rita Giacaman, and Marwan Khawaja, 447–88. Cambridge: Cambridge University Press, 2012.

Sonbol, Amira El Azhary. *The Creation of a Medical Profession in Egypt, 1800–1922*. Syracuse, NY: Syracuse University Press, 1991.

CHAPTER 5

....

THE BODY OF THE NILE

Environmental Disease in the Long Twentieth Century

....

JENNIFER L. DERR

In 1924, the Egyptian Department of Public Health published a report on the state of disease among the Egyptian population. The report focused on hookworm and schistosomiasis, both diseases caused by infection with parasites. Physician and researcher Muhammad Khalil 'Abd al-Khaliq, who headed the program devoted to research on schistosomiasis—bilharzia or bilharziasis, as it was more commonly known in Egypt—compiled the report and authored nearly all of its chapters. In its third chapter, which described efforts to control the spread of schistosomiasis among the population, Khalil offered a list of directives for avoiding infection with the parasites that cause the disease. He advised that one should not bathe in, drink from, or allow one's skin to come in contact with the water that filled irrigation canals and drains. He also observed that while those who did not themselves practice agriculture could abide by his recommendations with ease, "As far as the agricultural population are concerned it is not possible to follow these suggestions in such a way as to be effective in combatting the disease. The working class population have [*sic*] to work in the water as long as the methods of cultivation remain as they are."[1]

When Khalil's work was published, hookworm and schistosomiasis topped the list of Egypt's public health challenges. A decade later, the first nationwide surveys of the two diseases were performed. The studies estimated that just under 60% of the population was infected with the parasites that cause schistosomiasis, and just over 40% was infected with hookworm.[2] This epidemic of parasitic disease had begun to make itself known in the last years of the nineteenth century when the number of patients arriving at hospitals to seek relief from the symptoms of these diseases was on the rise. This increase was notable among a population that had historically steered clear of state hospitals.[3] Patients presented with large and debilitating growths on sensitive regions of their bodies. Their abdomens were sometimes visibly distended with fluid. In the psychiatric hospital located in the Cairo neighborhood of 'Abbasiyya, the number of patients admitted with severe dementia was on the rise. These were the signs of severe disease, experiences of which drove patients to travel many miles in the hope of relief or sanctuary. In the countryside, other, less striking symptoms had become typical. Diarrhea and malnutrition were commonplace. Boys began to express blood in their urine when they reached maturity. Severe anemia disqualified many conscripts for military service.[4]

The prevalence of disease was one facet of the material environment that Egypt's colonial economy helped to produce and perpetuate. In the century that stretched from the 1860s, the cultivation of long staple cotton for export dominated this economy. A small class of large landowners controlled the countryside, while many Egyptian peasants lived lives marked by poverty, violence, and—importantly—the pain of disease. That bodily pain was a common experience of colonial economy and was not unique to Egypt. The Central African workers who migrated to South Africa to work in its mines perished from pneumonia at an alarming rate.[5] In the 1870s, many people in drought-stricken regions of India died of famine when grain from other parts of the country was exported to Great Britain rather than kept for local consumption.[6] In Egypt, disease resulted from the change to the agricultural environment that the widespread cultivation of cotton necessitated and from the forms of interaction—labor primary among them—that bound rural communities to these environments. Disease not only loomed large during the century of Egypt's colonial economy; it continued to haunt Egypt, as the environmental changes that had come of age with a colonial economy became central to postcolonial material renderings of the nation.

COLONIAL ECONOMY IN RURAL EGYPT

In 1863, a new ruler took charge of the Ottoman Egyptian state. The rule of Khedive Isma'il began amid a faraway conflict that would help to transform Egyptian agriculture. In April 1861, US President Abraham Lincoln proclaimed a naval blockade of the Confederacy, preventing the export of cotton from the American South to textile mills in the north of England. As a result, the price of cotton rose sharply, and other parts of the globe expanded production. In Egypt, the cultivation of long staple cotton for export had begun four decades earlier under the strong Ottoman governor Mehmed Ali but had declined following his death. Its ascent during the rule of his grandson would prove long-lasting.

The spread of cotton was associated with the coalescence of a distinct set of social relations in the countryside. In the nineteenth century, a class of elite landholders consolidated their control over agricultural land. Mehmed Ali had awarded loyal state officials and members of the royal family plots of land; his successors continued the practice. Their estates became sites of cash crop production, especially cotton. As elites enlarged their holdings, their claims buttressed by the passage of new laws, many Egyptian peasants were dispossessed of the land that they farmed. The nineteenth-century Ottoman Egyptian state conscripted peasants for the military and raised the burden of taxation. The state also altered the nature of the long-standing labor tax, corvée, demanding that peasants travel farther, work under more dangerous conditions, and devote a longer stretch of the year to this labor. Peasants who could not pay taxes or fled the state's demands were stripped of their land, which often enlarged elite holdings.

When the British occupied Egypt in 1882, they prioritized increasing the country's cotton production. The Ottoman Egyptian state had accrued significant debt in the decades of Isma'il's rule, much of it through the state's construction of new infrastructure and urban space. British authorities argued that increasing the cultivation and sale of cotton was the most effective means of resolving this debt. In the four decades of the occupation's first phase, the social relations that had come to define Egypt's colonial economy during Khedive Isma'il's rule only became more pronounced. Cotton remained Egypt's top export, large landholders controlled the countryside, and increasing numbers of landless and land-poor peasants lived lives of poverty, many residing on large estates, 'izab (singular 'izba), where they cultivated cotton crops in exchange for a small plot of land for their own subsistence. When a new regime came to power after World War I, these trends continued. The marks of colonial economy in Egypt only began to be undone in the 1950s and 1960s under the populist authoritarian leadership of President Gamal Abdel Nasser.

COLONIAL ECONOMIC ECOLOGIES

The consolidation of Egypt's colonial economy was linked to an environmental transformation of the countryside. Agriculture depended on the Nile River for irrigation. In the Nile Delta and the larger Nile Valley, crops grew in large basins until the nineteenth century. Each year, after the arrival of the annual flood, cultivators cut the walls of these basins to let in floodwaters that would soak and fertilize the soil. When the basins were filled, some villages existed as islands, only accessible by boat. After farmers evacuated this water, they planted in the soils that had been soaked. The crops they sowed, *shitwi* or winter crops, were harvested in spring. Wheat was the most valuable among them. Other crops, *sayfi* (summer) and *nili* (flood), were planted in late spring, grew when basins were filled during the flood season, and were harvested in fall. This produce grew on the fringes of the agricultural landscape. Cotton was a summer crop, and so were sugarcane and corn, the increased production of which were also hallmarks of Egypt's colonial economy.

As cotton cultivation spread in the second half of the nineteenth century, new irrigation regimes and infrastructure construction transformed agricultural environments. When cotton was first introduced, Mehmed Ali had directed the excavation of deep irrigation canals to replace basins in regions where the crop was planted. Under Isma'il, these canals, which facilitated the practice of perennial irrigation, proliferated. Perennial irrigation enabled year-round agricultural production and the large-scale cultivation of summer crops. Canals changed the shape and experience of the river as its waters, channeled into complex vasculature, no longer engulfed villages during the flood. Larger pieces of infrastructure were also built. The Ibrahimiyya Canal, which stretched north from the central Egyptian town of Asyut, its two branches ending in the regions of Giza and the oasis of al-Fayum, watered the sugarcane that grew in large sections of Isma'il's estates. The Delta Barrage, completed in 1861, was designed to raise the level of the river and better fill canals where cotton was concentrated in the Delta.

Following their 1882 occupation of Egypt, the British engineers appointed to oversee the Public Works Ministry focused their energy on repairing and maintaining existent irrigation infrastructure.[7] In 1898, construction began on the first dam that would be built on the Nile River. The dam signaled the dawn of a new era in which the practice of perennial irrigation would become permanently entrenched in Egypt. Located near the town of Aswan in Egypt's deep south, this dam, Khazan Aswan, was completed in 1902.[8] A definitive regional geography of agriculture and irrigation practice was consolidated in the years that followed its completion. In the Nile Delta and throughout the northern regions of central Egypt—where cotton cultivation was concentrated—perennial irrigation produced new agricultural environments and ecological relationships.[9] Canals replaced basins, and fields were watered year-round. In regions of Egypt further south, most cultivators continued to practice basin agriculture with its single primary agricultural season. The main exception to this differentiated agricultural geography were the regions of Egypt's south, where sugarcane cultivation and processing was concentrated, and which also had access to year-round irrigation. A decade after its completion, the dam was raised to expand the holding capacity of its reservoir. Following the project's completion, 3.3 million of Egypt's 5.3 million cultivable acres were perennially irrigated.[10] In 1933, the dam was raised and its holding capacity expanded a second time.

Infrastructure was not born fully formed, nor did agriculture happen independently of human work. When cotton cultivation first began to spread, state-compelled corvée labor excavated and maintained the new networks of canals that watered it. Each year, the work required to maintain their function included removal—with rudimentary tools and bare hands—of the sediment that threatened to clog them. Corvée laborers also built the Delta Barrage and excavated the Ibrahimiyya Canal. During the British occupation, gangs of wage laborers, organized and paid a pittance by a labor shaykh, maintained irrigation infrastructure for the Public Works Ministry. In regions with access to perennial irrigation, a shift in the agricultural calendar had significant implications for labor. For peasant proprietors, sharecroppers, wage laborers, and, in the nineteenth century, slaves and corvée laborers, the work of farming became year-round as they tended, irrigated, and harvested multiple crops. Some cultivators from the south even migrated north in the late spring and summer, the dry season of basin agriculture, to tend cotton.

The ecological relationships that characterized the agricultural landscape changed with the introduction of perennial irrigation. Two species of moth were especially fond of Egyptian cotton plants. Larvae of the *Earias insulana* species, commonly known as the Egyptian bollworm, tunneled into the buds of cotton plants and fed on their bolls. Those of the *Spodoptera littoralis* species, the Egyptian cotton worm, were somewhat less discriminate, feasting on shoots, leaves, bolls, and buds. The cotton worm was not new to Egypt; it also ate the clover that was plentiful throughout the country.[11] The material changes that resulted from the damming of the Nile also created the conditions for the arrival of new species. During World War II, the *Anopheles gambiae* mosquito, which carries the *Plasmodium falciparum* parasite that causes a malignant form of malaria, appeared in Egypt's south.[12] Among the factors that facilitated the mosquito's arrival were the shifting ecologies of a slowed Nile River, specifically the islands of *Potamogeton crispus*—curly pondweed—that had appeared and floated north along the river.[13]

Parasites also thrived. The extension of perennial irrigation produced a more habitable environment for the organisms that cause hookworm disease. While hookworms of the *Ancylostoma duodenale* species are endemic to Egypt, the higher moisture content of perennially irrigated soils produced an environment more conducive to their survival. Larvae hatch from eggs that pass from the human body in feces and live in the earth, waiting to infect another human host, often through the skin of their feet. With the proper moisture and temperature conditions, larvae can survive in the soil for up to two years by feeding on bacteria and organic material. In late nineteenth- and early twentieth-century rural Egypt, latrines were a rarity. Moreover, the earth in which hookworm larvae lived formed the structures of daily life—houses, irrigation canals, and fields. In the early twentieth century, scientists believed that hookworm had historically been more common in Egypt's south, where the temperature was warmer, but that the spread of perennial irrigation had made the disease more common in the Nile Delta.[14] It especially thrived in central Egypt, with its relatively hotter climate than the Nile Delta, in regions that practiced year-round agriculture.

The parasites that cause schistosomiasis also flourished in the water that filled irrigation canals. So did the snails that were their intermediate hosts, one species of which multiplied in the tangles of the curly pondweed that carried *Anopheles gambiae* mosquitos to Egypt and grew in irrigation canals. The changed irrigation landscape produced an environment conducive to the infection of human bodies with *Schistosoma haematobium* and *Schistosoma mansoni* parasites. The eggs of these parasites exit human bodies in urine and feces. In slow-moving freshwater, they hatch, and the organism that emerges infects tiny freshwater snails that serve as the intermediate hosts for *Schistosoma* parasites. The parasite emerges from the snail transformed in the organismal form that infects human beings. One was most likely to be infected in the early summer when cotton crops needed water, and cultivators who did the work of irrigation were at the highest risk of infection. Rural Egyptians were also exposed to infection through daily tasks. Women washed and fetched water in canals; children swam in them in summer. Although the parasite was present in areas that continued to practice basin irrigation, the infection rate was low.[15]

Diet was another factor in the production of historically specific experiences of embodiment. The spread of perennial irrigation influenced which crops were grown as food. Egyptian peasants had historically relied on a mostly plant-based diet rich in local grains that included sorghum, millet, and wheat. The spread of perennial irrigation reinforced the increasing popularity in the Nile Delta of corn, whose growing season closely mirrored that of cotton. After its introduction to Europe, corn, a New World crop, spread to Egypt and then through sub-Saharan Africa. Many cultivators came to favor the crop because it did not require much labor, grew quickly, produced high yields, and was easy to harvest and store. Among impoverished populations, its popularity often led to poor health. In a diet without the necessary diversity, depending too heavily on corn for nutrition can result in the appearance of the disease pellagra, which is caused by a shortage of niacin in the human body (corn contains a form of niacin that humans cannot digest). Without niacin, the body cannot produce nucleic acids, which are its most important biomolecules, causing a whole host of bodily maladies.

The symptoms of disease were one facet of human experience in the ecologies of colonial economy. It was common for rural Egyptians to suffer some combination of pellagra, hookworm, and schistosomiasis. While each disease produces its own set of symptoms, inhabiting a rural body in the period of Egypt's colonial economy, especially a laboring body, often included those of multiple diseases. Fatigue, fever, aches, cough, diarrhea, abdominal pain, constipation, weight loss, and vomiting were commonplace. These experiences could be accompanied by blood in the urine; cancer of the bladder; high blood pressure through the liver; an enlarged spleen; the buildup of fluid in different parts of the body; swollen areas in the esophagus and digestive tract that could rupture and bleed; severe anemia; stunted growth; difficulty concentrating; impotence; a photosensitive rash; painful growths on the scrotum, vagina, and rectum; and disorders of the nervous system that caused memory loss, depression, and eventually dementia. Under the nineteenth-century Ottoman Egyptian state, some experiences of the body—those associated with military conscription and corvée labor, for example—were shared broadly across the Egyptian peasantry. The forms of embodiment that marked rural experiences of colonial economy were regionally specific, confined to the Nile Delta and areas of central and southern Egypt that had access to perennial irrigation.

Treating the Perennially
Irrigated Body

By the first decade of the twentieth century, it was clear to those who staffed Egypt's hospitals that the countryside was unwell. In the second half of the nineteenth century, European scientists and doctors had begun to migrate to Egypt, some to take up appointments at the medical school at Qasr al-'Ayni in Cairo. Their records serve as powerful evidence of the position of human bodies within the agricultural ecologies of colonial economy. For example, Theodor Bilharz, who lent schistosomiasis one of its alternate names, made note of the quantities of parasites present in autopsied Egyptian bodies.[16] When, in 1897, Lord Cromer, the British agent and consul-general of Egypt, solicited a review of the medical school and the main hospital at Qasr al-'Ayni, one of the primary suggestions was that the institution should develop a specialization in the parasitic diseases that were so prominent in the country. In 1898, the prominent German parasitologist Arthur Looss was appointed to direct research on parasitic disease at Qasr al-'Ayni. It was Looss who first understood that hookworms infect human bodies by penetrating the skin.[17]

In 1914, aided by funds from the International Health Division of the Rockefeller Foundation, the Egyptian Public Health Department began a program to survey and treat rural populations in two regions of northern Egypt, Qalyubiyya and Sharqiyya.[18] Four years earlier, the Rockefeller Sanitary Commission for the Eradication of Hookworm Disease had organized a program in the American south, where the proportion of those infected was comparable to Egypt, to eradicate the disease.[19] The commission's program in Egypt was cut short by World War I but resumed in 1920 under the auspices of the Public Health Department, which also began to treat schistosomiasis. There was no similar endeavor to treat pellagra, which prominent health officials in Egypt at the time believed was caused by mold that grew on corn rather than malnutrition.[20]

During the interwar period, the quasi-independent Egyptian regime paired treatment for parasitic disease with its endeavor to secure and expand the country's access to irrigation water from the Nile. Britain's diminished role in Egypt meant a shift in British priorities along the Nile; Egypt's upstream position on the river left it vulnerable. During the 1920s, Egyptian government officials negotiated hard in order to ensure the country's access to the quantity of Nile water necessary to sustain its agricultural landscape.[21] Egypt's large landowners, the royal family—who played key roles in Egypt's new government—among them, were also aware of the relationship between perennial irrigation and the transmission of parasitic disease. The sharecroppers and wage laborers who worked their estates—planting, tending, and harvesting cotton—were among the sickest workers in the country. Concerned about the productivity of their laborers, the rural elite were enthusiastic advocates of treatment programs that might lessen the impact of disease among the labor force who helped grow their wealth.

Clinics devoted to the treatment of hookworm and schistosomiasis were established in Egypt's major towns and cities and at different sites in the countryside, especially in the Nile Delta, where the prevalence of infection was highest. The most prominent Egyptian physician associated with this effort was Muhammad Khalil 'Abd al-Khaliq. In 1922, he was appointed to head the Bilharzia Research Section of the Ankylostomiasis and Bilharziasis Committee (ankylostomiasis is an alternative term for hookworm). Muhammad Khalil—the name under which he published—was Egypt's leading authority of the period on parasitic disease. In the years after treatment had begun, it became clear that hookworm was relatively easier to eliminate than schistosomiasis, and by 1927, the treatment had been reduced to a single dose of medication.[22] The treatment for schistosomiasis was lengthy and painful, consisting of a month-long series of injections, the side effects of which were considerable.[23] In addition to the physical dis-comfort that came with treatment, a month without wages was a difficult proposition for most rural Egyptians. The numbers of patients attending clinics tended to decrease during the times of the year when the demand for agricultural labor was high.[24] Despite these difficulties, by the middle of the 1940s, approximately 400,000 patients passed through treatment facilities each year.[25]

One of the primary problems with this endeavor was the threat of reinfection. Even if cured, most patients became sick again through patterns of labor and daily life that were inescapable during this period. Recognizing this challenge, physicians and scientists sought other means of reducing the prevalence of disease. In 1927, the Rockefeller Foundation returned to Egypt, this time looking to test the effect that hy-giene measures might have on rates of parasitic infection. Claude Barlow and James Allen Scott, the lead parasitologists assigned to the project, conducted a seven-year ex-periment in which they measured the effect that constructing latrines had on the prev-alence of parasitic disease. Most Egyptian villages lacked latrines, and their residents defecated in the open, their feces one piece in the pathway of disease transmission. When the experiment ended and its results were assessed, Barlow and Scott concluded that while latrines had made for more pleasant villages, they had failed to reduce rates of parasitic infection.[26] With respect to schistosomiasis, one explanation for these results stemmed from the centrality of irrigation canals in daily life. The conditions of agricultural work were such that even where latrines existed, they were distant for farmers working in fields and canals.

Another environmental strategy of reducing rates of schistosomiasis infection targeted the snails that lived in networks of irrigation canals and drains. This approach was rooted in the proposition that if the intermediate hosts for *Schistosoma* parasites were eliminated, parasites would not be able to undergo the organismal changes that allowed them to infect human beings. Experiments using chemical agents to elimi-nate snails began in the 1920s.[27] In 1940, the Egyptian government formed a new sec-tion within the Public Health Ministry (the department had become a ministry in 1936), the Bilharzia Snail Destruction Section, which attempted a combination of techniques to eliminate snails from canals. The methods deployed included the application of the chemical copper sulfate to canals, the continued implementation of a mandatory period in winter when canals were closed, and the use of a special wire net to clear waterways of mollusks and the vegetation in which they lived. Barlow, who left the Rockefeller Foundation to serve as the "expert" appointed to the new section, was especially keen on the new net, which he had designed, believing canal closure and the application of chemical molluscicides to be ineffective.[28] In 1939, the section began a large experiment in al-Fayum Oasis to test the efficacy of an approach that paired the use of copper sul-fate with the clearance of snails and vegetation from canals.[29] Following early promising results, the section expanded its work to other areas of Egypt.[30] To aid their efforts, the state passed Law 29 in 1948, which mandated that landowners clear the streams on their land of snails twice each year or pay the section to do this work.[31]

NEW POLITICS, OLD ECOLOGIES

When a young group of junior army officers seized control of the state in July 1952, the Egyptian government was no closer to solving the problem of parasitic disease. Government officials described schistosomiasis as Egypt's primary health problem while moving forward with a project to build another dam on the Nile, the Aswan High Dam, which would complete the country's conversion to perennial irrigation.[32] Nasser's approach to the economy, however, represented a break from the century before. The industrial sector expanded, with the state playing a primary role in its direction. A set of land reforms—in 1952, 1961, and 1969—sought to redress the dramatically unequal distribution of agricultural land by reducing the acreage that an individual could legally own. The reforms also reflected Nasser's attempt to undermine the social and political power of wealthy landowners in rural areas. The state promoted the establishment of agricultural cooperatives that assumed some of the roles once played by the rural elite, distributing seed, fertilizer, and equipment and purchasing agricultural produce from cultivators at set prices. Egypt continued to grow cotton, but whereas once the crop had served as fodder for British textile mills, under Nasser, an increasing proportion of the commodity was used locally.[33]

As Egypt struggled to move past the colonial legacies of its past, it remained hamstrung by the prevalence of disease among its population and the absence of infrastructure in rural areas. As many villages continued to lack access to freshwater, irrigation canals maintained their centrality in the life of the community and the practice of agriculture. Even as mechanical irrigation pumps—long present in the countryside— became more common, manual labor remained an important part of agricultural work, and the inclusion of more significant numbers in the industrial workforce did not mean a livelihood free of infection. Some industrial workers suffered from schistosomiasis acquired during their childhood; others became infected with the disease as adults in regions that were neither urban nor rural. Many laborers lived in peri-urban areas or in villages that were in the process of being swallowed by cities. These areas were a mix of rural and urban; fields and irrigation canals were scattered within them, and they lacked access to freshwater and other forms of infrastructure. Even before 1952, some factories administered treatment for schistosomiasis, and workers who had been cured of infection were issued certificates attesting to this fact.[34]

Schistosomiasis treatment continued much as it had during the interwar period but under an expanded system. After 1961, initiatives to expand the reach of state-sponsored health services in rural areas intensified as the state turned its attention to rural Egypt. Between 1951 and 1963, the state budget devoted to healthcare nearly quadrupled.[35] The number of rural health care units also increased, from 382 before the coup to 1,525 by 1965.[36] In some towns and villages of the countryside, the state built what were known as combined units.[37] These facilities contained a healthcare center, a social service center, a school, a nursery, and housing for local officials.[38] Schoolchildren were often the subjects of treatment programs as their infection rates were high and their attendance more predictable than that of adults. In 1962, a new institute was established to treat schistosomiasis, the Theodor Bilharz Research Institute, supported in part by the German government.[39] The institute was located in Giza, which bordered Cairo and at the time was still rural. Its setting gave the scientists who worked at the institute the opportunity to treat patients and conduct field experiments in the same setting.[40]

Despite these changes under Nasser, the treatment endeavor remained fraught. The state failed to meet its ambitious targets for establishing health care facilities in the countryside, and fewer facilities were constructed than had been planned.[41] More importantly, the project to treat those infected with schistosomiasis continued to face many of the same challenges that it had during the interwar period. Treatment remained lengthy, painful, and all too easily erased through reinfection. Rates of absenteeism during the regimen were high.[42]

The treatment of the environment in which schistosomiasis was transmitted also persisted under Egypt's new populist authoritarian regime. Many international public health officials were skeptical that the treatment of human patients alone could reduce infection rates.[43] Some scientists argued that while treatment had failed to produce a significant decline in infection, it had reduced the overall prevalence of the disease and its most severe symptoms.[44] To support this point, they marshaled the results of small field surveys conducted in the 1950s that showed a decrease in the prevalence of schistosomiasis. Officials at the World Health Organization, formed in 1948, were somewhat more skeptical. They questioned the broad applicability of these studies, arguing that it was necessary to perform an extensive and nationwide survey to assess what had happened to infection rates since a survey of this scope had last been conducted in the 1930s.[45] International organizations were enthusiastic that new chemical agents might potentially eliminate populations of snails and reduce the prevalence of disease. Many global public health officials believed that identifying a safe, effective, and affordable chemical was necessary to make strides in the battle against schistosomiasis.

The project to eliminate snails from Egypt's irrigation canals and drains was implemented locally and aided by funds from an array of international actors. Where they existed, the combined units were charged with managing the treatment of irrigation canals and the attempted elimination of snail populations.[46] The World Health Organization, the United Nations Children's Fund (UNICEF), and the governments of the United States and West Germany demonstrated a keen interest in the success of these projects. The first project began in 1953 in the Waraq al-'Arab region, a scant ten kilometers northwest of the existent boundaries of Egypt's capital city. The district covered roughly sixteen square kilometers and contained six villages with approximately thirty-three thousand inhabitants. Organized by the Egyptian government in cooperation with the US International Cooperation Administration, the project tested the efficacy of a new chemical compound, sodium pentachlorophenate, against populations of snails. Copper sulfate, the primary compound in use, was expensive, and while it killed snails, it did not kill their eggs. In field tests conducted by the Laboratory of Tropical Diseases at the National Institute of Health in Bethesda, Maryland, sodium pentachlorophenate had shown promise. Four years after the Waraq al-'Arab project had begun, it was reported that no infected snails had been found in the treated area and that among children, the prevalence of infection with *Schistosoma* parasites had decreased.[47]

The Waraq al-'Arab project was only the first in a series of endeavors in which the Egyptian state worked with foreign governments and international organizations to test the use of chemical molluscicides. In 1962, in conjunction with the World Health Organization and UNICEF, the Egyptian government began the UAR-0049 project, which compared the efficacy of different molluscicides, one of which, Bayluscide, was manufactured by Bayer Pharmaceuticals. Bayer was one of a host of chemical and pharmaceutical companies that came to be important players in the field of global public health in the second half of the twentieth century.[48] Despite tremendous enthusiasm during the UAR-0049 trials, the project's final results showed chemical molluscicides had not sustainably reduced rates of infection.[49] The West German government continued to promote the use of Bayluscide, cooperating with the Egyptian government to begin a field test of the compound in al-Fayum Oasis. When Nasser died in 1970, experiments with chemical molluscicides in Egypt were ongoing, despite the failure of past efforts to produce results that might be replicable on a national scale.

In Egypt, chemical molluscicides never became the solution to the problem of schistosomiasis that many had believed they could be. The complexity of the vasculature of the Nile made it nearly impossible to "treat it" with chemicals, as the river existed not only within its banks but in and through complex networks of irrigation canals and drains. Most of these smaller waterways were populated by the snails that facilitated infection with *Schistosoma* parasites. For a postcolonial state with numerous demands on its finances, the purchase of large quantities of chemicals was cost-prohibitive.[50] During the 1950s and 1960s, experimental design was conscious of this financial burden, testing methods through which portions of the Nile and regions of the countryside might be treated rather than pursuing strategies that presumed the whole system would be. Finally, the application of chemicals to the environment on such a large scale was toxic for humans and animals alike, especially workers tasked with carrying out the application.[51] In a recent interview, a prominent Egyptian specialist of internal medicine, someone who had treated many cases of schistosomiasis, raised the issue of toxicity as an impediment to using chemical molluscicides on a nationwide scale.

CONCLUSION

In 1962, Muhammad Salah, Minister of Scientific Research, helped to inaugurate the First International Symposium on Bilharziasis. In his opening speech, he anticipated the global significance that would come to be attached to schistosomiasis: "Bilharzia which is the United-Arab-Republic's [*sic*] first health problem is also an international problem, since statistics estimate that more than 150 million people are affected with the different forms of this disease which is the second most prevalent disease in the world after malaria. It is expected to become the world's foremost health problem now that malaria is under control."[52]

In the years that followed the conference, the construction of large dams, throughout Africa and globally, meant that the disease became significant in new corners of the earth. Its spread continues. While Salah's predictions were prescient, his omissions were also telling. His recounting of the disease's historical arc omits any mention of the role played by the construction of infrastructure on the Nile River or the practice of perennial irrigation in fueling the spread of disease and elevating it to its status as Egypt's "first health problem." The pain experienced by countless Egyptian peasants during the period of Egypt's colonial economy was one price of cotton production. In the postcolonial era, rural Egyptians continued to pay this bodily price as the regime pursued a path forward that perpetuated experiences of a disease for which a solution had not yet been found. Under Nasser, the problem of schistosomiasis—like so many problems—was characterized as a problem of underdevelopment, fueled by a history of colonialism, rather than as a known consequence of a particular agricultural practice and its relationship to the damming of the Nile. What had once been an element of the ecologies and practices that supported colonial economic agriculture was made an integral piece of the national path of modernity in the second half of the twentieth century. This path was a material project, in part actualized through the form and practice of the Nile River.

Notes

1. M. Khalil, "The Control of Bilharziasis in Egypt," in *Reports and Notes of the Public Health Laboratories Cairo: Ankylostomiasis and Bilharziasis in Egypt* (Cairo: Government Press, 1924), 98.
2. James Allen Scott, "The Incidence and Distribution of the Human Schistosomes in Egypt," *American Journal of Epidemiology* 25, no. 3 (1937): 578, 610, cited in Jennifer L. Derr, *The Lived Nile: Environment, Disease, and Material Colonial Economy in Egypt* (Stanford: Stanford University Press, 2019), 105; James Allen Scott, "The Prevalence and Distribution of Hookworm Infection in Egypt," *American Journal of Epidemiology* 26, no. 3 (1937): 493, cited in Derr, *The Lived Nile*, 110.
3. Derr, *The Lived Nile*, 128–29, citing LaVerne Kuhnke, *Lives at Risk: Public Health in Nineteenth-Century Egypt* (Berkeley, CA: University of California Press, 1990), 150–51.
4. Derr, *The Lived Nile*, 99–126.
5. Randall Packard, "The Invention of the 'Tropical Worker:' Medical Research and the Quest for Central African Labor on the South African Gold Mines, 1903–36," *Journal of African History* 34 (1993): 271, citing Alan Jeeves, *Migrant Labor in South Africa's Mining Economy: The Struggle for the Gold Mines' Labour Supply, 1890–1920* (Montreal: McGill-Queen's University Press-MQUP, 1985), 323–33.
6. Mike Davis, *Late Victorian Holocausts: El Niño Famines and the Making of the Third World* (London: Verso Books, 2000), 21–59.
7. Derr, *The Lived Nile*, 35–39.
8. Ibid., 49–53.
9. Ibid., 57–58.

10. Ibid., 61, citing Terje Tvedt, *The River Nile in the Age of the British: Political Ecology and the Quest for Economic Power* (London: I. B. Taurus, 2004), 91.

11. Aaron Jakes, "Bugs, Boom, Bust: Egypt's Ecology of Interest, 1882–1914," *Antipode* 49, no. 4 (2017): 1048.

12. Timothy Mitchell, "Can the Mosquito Speak?," in *Rule of Experts: Egypt, Techno-Politics, Modernity* (Berkeley: University of California Press, 2002), 19–20; Nancy Elizabeth Gallagher, *Egypt's Other Wars: Epidemics and the Politics of Public Health* (Syracuse, NY: Syracuse University Press, 1990), 20–40.

13. Mitchell, "Can the Mosquito Speak?," 24.

14. Derr, *The Lived Nile*, 110.

15. In areas that continued to practice basin irrigation, Scott pegged the rate of infection at 6%. Scott, "Incidence and Distribution," 610, cited in Derr, *The Lived Nile*, 105.

16. Derr, *The Lived Nile*, 116–17.

17. Ibid., 118–19.

18. Ibid., 130. The Rockefeller Foundation was incorporated in 1913 and the International Health Division formed the same year. Barry Goldberg, "The Long Road to the Yellow Fever Vaccine," accessed 19 October 2023, https://resource.rockarch.org/story/the-long-road-to-the-yellow-fever-vaccine/.

19. John Ettling, *The Germ of Laziness: Rockefeller Philanthropy and Public Health in the New South* (Cambridge, MA: Harvard University Press, 1981), 2.

20. Derr, *The Lived Nile*, 120.

21. Tvedt, *The River Nile,* 93–96; Derr, *The Lived Nile,* 61–69, 127–56.

22. Derr, *The Lived Nile*, 133.

23. Ibid., 133, 140–41.

24. Ibid., 140.

25. Ibid., 138.

26. Ibid., 147.

27. Ibid., 147.

28. Ibid., 148–50.

29. *Annual Report for 1943, Ministry of Public Health* (Cairo: Government Press, 1944), 94–95.

30. See, e.g., *Annual Report for 1945, Ministry of Public Health* (Cairo: Government Press, 1946), 93.

31. *Annual Report of the Ministry of Public Health for 1951* (Cairo: Government Press, 1952), 174, 192.

32. Salah al-Din Hidayat, "Speech—May 3, 1962," in *Proceedings of the 1st International Symposium on Bilharziasis* (Cairo: National Information and Documentation Centre, 1962), 9.

33. In 1930–31, just 1% of cotton was consumed locally. That number progressively climbed until 1965 when 45% of the commodity was consumed locally. Roger Owen, "A Long Look at Nearly Two Centuries of Long Staple Cotton," *Proceedings of the British Academy* 96 (1999): 353, citing Bent Hanson and Girguis A. Marzouk, *Development and Economic Policy in the UAR (Egypt)* (Amsterdam: North-Holland Pub. Co., 1965), 97; Robert Tignor, *Egyptian Textiles and British Capital, 1930–1956* (Cairo: American University in Cairo Press, 1989), 45, 49.

34. See, e.g., *Annual Report of the Ministry of Public Health for 1951* (Cairo: Government Press, 1952), 154–55.

35. Raymond William Baker, *Egypt's Uncertain Revolution Under Nasser and Sadat* (Cambridge, MA: Harvard University Press, 1978), 220.
36. Ibid., 219–22.
37. The project to build these centers had begun in 1946. Ibid., 219.
38. James Mayfield, *Rural Politics in Nasser's Egypt: A Quest for Legitimacy* (Austin: University of Texas Press, 2014), 175–76.
39. Al-Din Hidayat, "Speech," 9–10.
40. Dr. Ahmad al-Garem, interview, 3 March 2020.
41. Baker, *Egypt's Uncertain Revolution*, 221–22.
42. Farag Rizk, "The Problem of Schistosomiasis in Egypt," 1956, 8, schisto1-emro-egypt 1955–62, Archives of the Parasitology Collection, World Health Organization.
43. Donald B. McMullen and Marshall B. Rainey, "Report on the Preliminary Survey by the Bilharziasis Advisory Team, Part II Egypt," 20 February 1959, 24, schisto1-emro-egypt 1955–62, Archives of the Parasitology Collection, World Health Organization.
44. Derr, *The Lived Nile*, 155; Rizk, "The Problem of Schistosomiasis," 2, 8.
45. McMullen and Rainey, "Report on the Preliminary Survey," 24.
46. Mayfield, *Rural Politics in Nasser's Egypt*, 201–2.
47. McMullen and Rainey, "Report on the Preliminary Survey," 14–16.
48. In 1964, senior scientific officer at the Tropical Pesticides Research Institute in Arusha, Tanzania, N. O. Crossland reported "considerable activity at the present time on the part of industry and other interested parties in the development of molluscicides." N. O. Crossland, "Some Recent Developments in the Use of Molluscicides at the Bilharziasis Pilot Project in the United Arab Republic 7 March–5 September 1964," 4, schisto1-emro-egypt 1964, Archives of the Parasitology Collection, World Health Organization.
49. H. M. Gilles, "Assignment Report: Independent Evaluation of Project UAR 0049, 15 February–16 March 1971," 3, schisto1-emro-egypt 1970–1971, Archives of the Parasitology Collection, World Health Organization.
50. McMullen and Rainey, "Report on the Preliminary Survey," 13.
51. José Antonio Jove, "Use of Molluscicides in the Control of Bilharziasis in Venezuela: Equipment and Methods of Application," *Bulletin of the World Health Organization* 14, no. 4 (1956): 631; Norman D. Levine, "Integrated Control of Snails," *American Zoologist* 10, no. 4 (1970): 580; Ronald Eisler, *Pentachlorophenol Hazards to Fish, Wildlife, and Invertebrates: A Synoptic Review* (Laurel, MD: Fish and Wildlife Service, US Department of the Interior, 1989), 1; D. M. Blair, "Dangers in Using and Handling Sodium Pentachlorophenate as a Molluscicide," *Bulletin of the World Health Organization* 25, no. 4–5 (1961): 601.
52. Al-Din Hidayat, "Speech," 8.

BIBLIOGRAPHY

Abbas, Ra'uf, and Assem El-Dessouky. *The Large Landowning Class and Peasantry in Egypt, 1837–1952*. Edited by Peter Gran. Translated by Amer Mohsen and Mona Zikri. Cairo: American University in Cairo Press, 2012.

Abul-Magd, Zeinab. *Imagined Empires: A History of Revolt in Egypt*. Berkeley: University of California Press, 2013.

Anderson, Warwick. *Colonial Pathologies: American Tropical Medicine, Race, and Hygiene in the Philippines*. Durham, NC: Duke University Press, 2006.

Aso, Michitake. *Rubber and the Making of Vietnam: An Ecological History, 1897–1975*. Chapel Hill: University of North Carolina Press, 2018.

Derr, Jennifer L. "Labor-Time: Ecological Bodies and Agricultural Labor in 19th and Early 20th Century Egypt." *International Journal of Middle East Studies* 50, no. 2 (2018): 195–212.

Derr, Jennifer L. *The Lived Nile: Environment, Disease, and Material Colonial Economy in Egypt*. Stanford, CA: Stanford University Press, 2019.

El Shakry, Omnia. *The Great Social Laboratory: Subjects of Knowledge in Colonial and Post-Colonial Egypt*. Stanford, CA: Stanford University Press, 2007.

Fahmy, Khaled. *In Quest of Justice: Islamic Law and Forensic Medicine in Modern Egypt*. Berkeley, CA: University of California Press, 2018.

Gallagher, Nancy. *Egypt's Other Wars: Epidemics and the Politics of Public Health*. Syracuse, NY: Syracuse University Press, 1990.

Gratien, Chris. "The Ottoman Quagmire: Malaria, Swamps, and Settlement in the Late Ottoman Mediterranean." *International Journal of Middle East Studies* 49, no. 4 (2017): 583–604.

Gross, Miriam. *Farewell to the God of Plague: Chairman Mao's Campaign to Deworm China*. Berkeley, CA: University of California Press, 2016.

Jakes, Aaron. "Bugs, Boom, Bust: Egypt's Ecology of Interest, 1882–1914." *Antipode* 49, no. 4 (2017): 1035–59.

Kozma, Liat. *Policing Egyptian Women: Sex, Law, and Medicine in Khedival Egypt*. Syracuse, NY: Syracuse University Press, 2011.

Mayfield, James. *Rural Politics in Nasser's Egypt: A Quest for Legitimacy*. Austin: University of Texas Press, 2014.

Mikhail, Alan. *Nature and Empire in Ottoman Egypt*. New York: Cambridge University Press, 2011.

Mosallam, Alia. "'We Are the Ones Who Made This Dam "High"!' A Builders' History of the Aswan High Dam." *Water History* 6, no. 4 (2014): 297–314.

Nash, Linda. *Inescapable Ecologies: A History of Environment, Disease, and Knowledge*. Berkeley: University of California Press, 2006.

Packard, Randall. "The Invention of the 'Tropical Worker:' Medical Research and the Quest for Central African Labor on the South African Gold Mines, 1903–36." *Journal of African History* 34 (1993): 271–92.

Sellers, Christopher. "Thoreau's Body: Toward an Embodied Environmental History." *Environmental History* 4, no. 4 (1999): 486–514.

Tilly, Helen. *Africa as a Living Laboratory: Empire, Development, and the Problem of Scientific Knowledge, 1870–1950*. Chicago: University of Chicago Press, 2011.

PART II

TECHNOLOGY, MOBILITY, AND LABOR

CHAPTER 6

....

COALONIZING EGYPT

Carbonization in the Long Nineteenth Century

....

ON BARAK

HISTORIANS of Egypt will recognize that the title of this chapter pays homage to Timothy Mitchell's 1988 *Colonising Egypt*, a seminal book demonstrating, among other things, that we cannot periodize the country's colonial era as beginning with the 1882 British occupation, but that we must start much earlier, at the beginning of the nineteenth century, with the development of new technologies of governance by Egypt's Ottoman Turko-Circassian ruling elite. Decades before the British bombardment of Alexandria, the country was already part of a London-centered global economy and subjected to the encroachment of European epistemologies.[1] Mitchell's later work attended to the material aspects of such technologies, launching a wave of science and technology studies in Egypt and the region more broadly. In what follows, I draw attention to the hitherto ignored energy source at the heart of these transformations—coal—and its contribution to ushering in a colonialism that was at once European and Ottoman. As we will see, the same *colonizing* Turko-Circassian elite was indispensable for what I call *coalonialism* in Egypt—a connection of energy and empire where materiality was as important as cultural or political affiliation and where fossil fuels had an agency that begs to be acknowledged as a facet that inflects conventional configurations of colonialism in unexpected ways. Today the Middle East is often associated with exported oil, mainly from the Persian Gulf, but in the nineteenth century, the region was shaped by imported British coal, with Egypt as the locomotive driving the process.[2]

   Coal animated almost everything that can be ascribed to Egypt's social, technological, cultural, or political modernity. Even Islamic theology was changed by this fossil fuel. Yet rather than uprooting and replacing older powers, the "age of coal" depended on the survival, repurposing, and often proliferation of the existing powers of human and nonhuman muscle, wind, and water. It also depended on existing cultural dispositions and even on Islamic theological horizons.[3] Nevertheless, and perhaps even due to this continuity, we would be justified in diagnosing a rupture in how existing powers were rearranged under coal and in periodizing the beginning of the modern era with this transformation as its marker.

There was another, more global aspect to the process: if a fossil fuel originating in the British Isles was the key driving force for modernity in Egypt, this latter setting was simultaneously a key junction and an important accelerator for the worldwide advancement of the hydrocarbon economy. Egypt had no known coal of its own in the nineteenth century, though its rulers had a great interest in global and Ottoman carbon politics. Nonetheless, local elites launched extensive geological searches and translations of European geology and stratigraphy literature and reached out to some of the most prominent talents in the British engineering scene.[4] Moreover, absorbing British coal into Egypt changed not only Egypt but also the British and Ottoman empires at large. Indeed, in relative terms, only a tiny portion of the coal mined in the British Isles was exported outside of Europe, and only a small amount of that coal was shipped to the Middle East, with the Egyptian portion being even smaller. Yet the relative perspective of statistics obscures the fact that this amount of coal was sufficient to fuel a revolution of steamboat imperialism and coal-fired cash cropping that eventually helped bring coal mining to life in the Ottoman Empire, as well as in India, China, and elsewhere. Exporting coal and then coal mining connected British industrialization and imperialism. What was Egypt's role in this global carbonization? And what was coal's importance in transforming Egypt?

LIKE COAL AND WATER

Approaching the globalization of coal from the unusual Egyptian angle helps push this decentering further, in a technological sense. We tend to notice mainly one kind of relationship between coal and water, captured by the notion of an "age of steam"—the coal-fired heating of liquid into a gas and the harnessing of the energy generated in this expansion of matter. Yet even the initial function of steam power—to pump out flooded coal mines in the British Isles—reveals other nexuses between coal and water. Steam power soon made other kinds of wheels turn in water, allowing new kinds of oceanic navigation. It provided the mechanical energy to dredge waterways such as the Suez Canal, enabled perennial irrigation with coal-fired pumps, and facilitated water desalination and even ice making, which was indispensable in arid and sweltering environments such as Port Said. In short, beyond (and often via) its gaseous form, coal interacted with water in its other forms of matter. Let us consider the maritime, riverine, agricultural, and potable aspects, respectively.

Egypt was a keystone in a system of regularly spaced British coaling depots that emerged, beginning in the 1830s, in places like Gibraltar, Malta, and Alexandria and then Port Said, Mocha, Aden, and Bombay. Egypt's centrality in this global system had to do with factors such as lack of wood, the country's geographic position, and waves of epizootics that decimated much of its animal muscle power around the turn of the nineteenth century, preparing it for new driving forces.[5] Furthermore, Egypt's central role in global carbonization was informed by the British agenda of perennial transportation, the Egyptian agenda of perennial irrigation and cash cropping (best manifesting in what Jennifer Derr has called "the perennial Nile"[6]), and how the imperial aspirations of both flowed into one another via waterways that were gradually centralized and becoming coal-dependent. Coal initially dumped in Egyptian depots for the benefit of British steamships soon started flowing into the interior and fueling dredgers and steam pumps that facilitated the gradual transition from an agriculture based on the Nile's annual flood to one based on fossil-fueled mechanical irrigation, which was later combined with large-scale damming. Steam navigation and modern irrigation worked in synergy with one another as cash crops that needed regular year-round watering could be transported quickly via rail and steamer lines to be processed into finished goods in Western Europe, again with fossil-fueled machines.

That the 1830s also represent the beginning of British coal's globalization is no coincidence. The Industrial Revolution, based on processing imported raw materials, depended on a revolution of agricultural industrialization in the raw materials' places of origin. Both processes were fired by coal. Foreign settings such as Egypt, new technopolitical arrangements in these places, and steam-enthusiast rulers such as Mehmet Ali Pasha, Ottoman Egypt's governor, allowed the hydrocarbon economy to go global. As Colonel Patrick Campbell, the British consul-general and East India Company (EIC) agent in Egypt, put it in 1838, the Egyptian ruler "gives to the steam communication every and the most cordial aid and assistance in his power[;] indeed without this aid our difficulties from the circumstances which I have already mentioned would be great, and almost insuperable."[7] Campbell referred to technical help in the iron foundries of Cairo, where workers were tasked with repairing broken steamer engine parts; to governmental license to establish coal depots in Cairo, Suez, Alexandria, and the Red Sea islands of Kamaran and al-Qusayr (built, in fact, by the Egyptians for the use of the EIC); and to camels and boats provided to transport coal to these depots.

Moreover, the coal depots of Jeddah and Mocha were under the auspices of the EIC in Egypt. In fact, some of Mehmet Ali's eagerness to enter the age of steam had to be assuaged by the British, for example, when he offered to build, maintain, and guard a coaling depot for the use of British ships at Aden. By the 1830s, it was clear to all actors that the establishment of these stations was an excellent pretext for imperial expansionism, an agenda that was central to both the Egyptians and the British—the latter conquering Aden themselves and establishing such a depot in 1839. During that decade, Egypt had taken control of the entire east coast of the Red Sea, from Suez and Aqaba to the first coal depot of Mocha. Egypt's control also stretched to the north, toward Greater Syria. In this expansion, Mehmet Ali was seeking to augment diminishing wood supplies and declining animal power, expand his empire, and take part in the nascent global carbon politics game, as well as finding effective ways to protect himself from similar centralization policies in Istanbul, which was then beginning to adopt coal power.

Finally, the 1830s marked a watershed in the British textile industry when steam engines took over the older technology of waterwheels, used in this sector up until this time.[8] This coevalness between British and Egyptian coal dependence, and the fact that these dependencies were interlinked, suggests that we must reconsider the received wisdom about the Industrial Revolution, according to which this was a process that started in the British Isles, only later proliferating outward. This narrative is familiar in the history of science and technology as "the diffusional model," and it has been debunked repeatedly.[9] Instead, we might provincialize the steam engine and replace this model with a global history of carbonization in which, for better or (as we now know) mainly for worse, non-European actors played an active and early role, often as enablers of British coalonization.

British steamers themselves depended on foreign settings for their development. The first steamer ever built and used for naval combat was designed to battle an Ottoman fleet in the Mediterranean under Greek flags during the Greek War of Independence. The ship was brought, along with its coal, from England, but in 1826 it was a novelty even there. When a conservative British admiralty finally introduced fighting steamers to the Royal Navy (RN) during the 1840s, a decade and a half had passed since British engineers and soldiers of fortune, as well as colonizing corporations such as the EIC, had begun experimenting with this technology away from the metropole. The construction of this pioneering ship, the *Karteria*, reveals some of the conditions for scientific progress in this inter-imperial environment. The Greeks entrusted the project to the engineer Alexander Galloway. Other actors in Europe's periphery identified this pioneer even earlier, demonstrating how well they had England's technical landscape mapped. The first student mission from the Islamic world knew how to find Galloway in 1815.[10] Egypt's Mehmet Ali was also familiar with him and employed Galloway's son as chief engineer. Mehmet Ali's own son, Ibrahim Pasha, commanded one of the fleets that fought the Greek secessionists for the Ottoman sultan. With the Galloways providing engineering services to both sides of the conflict, Galloway Senior deliberately delayed the completion of the ships for as long as possible. The *Karteria*'s eventual introduction into the arena was a breaking point for all parties involved. Its success, along with the success of British steamers sent to Ottoman Palestine to stop an Egyptian invasion and to China in the following decade and a half, convinced the admirals of the RN that the age of steam had, in fact, begun for them as well.[11]

The multidimensional impact of the development of maritime steam navigation on Egypt is perhaps best revealed by the fact that dredging the Suez Canal during the 1860s required the largest concentration of mechanical energy in human history. As Lucia Carminati has noted, although early photos of the vast dredgers sought to conceal this fact, human muscle power remained indispensable in all canal works well after the introduction of dredging machines. Dredgers could operate only after workers had cut the soil to water level and carried the earth away from the furrow they had dug.[12] Moreover, the Suez Canal was partly modeled on the Mahmudiyya Canal, completed in 1820 but soon thereafter proving too shallow for passage (similarly to the Suez Canal in later years), requiring in the 1840s the adoption of new measures, now aided by steam power, to deepen it.

The Mahmudiyya was one of Mehmet Ali's major engineering projects, meant to connect Alexandria to the Nile, provide summer irrigation to nearby cotton fields, and facilitate the passage of pilgrims to Arabia.[13] The canal provided Alexandria with freshwater and cotton cargos, allowing the city to more than quadruple its size within a few years and become Egypt's key port. The adjacent *khazzan*, a new artificial reservoir feeding the canal, proved wasteful in terms of evaporation and ground absorption, and in 1849 two pumping stations were constructed to feed the canal directly from the river. Until the 1890s, they were periodically enlarged and furnished with new steam pumps, combining a system of pumps and waterwheels connected to "inverted marine steam engines" of the type developed and used in steamships; this reliance on coal-fired technologies nearly doubled their output every decade. By the 1890s, portable steam engines were also the norm for watering the fields of the larger landholders. Usually, an eight-horsepower engine connected to an eight-inch pump was placed on a plot of level ground, and the pump was supported on a wooden trestle or fixed inside a masonry well. In 1899, there were more than thirty-three hundred portable engines in the country, with a total output of about thirty thousand horsepower, mainly burning British coal. Simultaneously, steam power became increasingly important for canal maintenance and dredging. The two main dredging companies, the Behera Company and the Egyptian Dredging Company, employed various kinds of mechanics, such as the Priestman dredger (from the engineering firm that later built the Priestman oil engine, a prototype for the internal combustion engine) and mainly twelve-inch centrifugal sand and mud pumps that required thirty-five- to forty-horsepower engines.[14]

The connection of Alexandria to the Nile via the sweet-water Mahmudiyya Canal enabled the dramatic expansion of this port city. Regular freshwater provision and an effective aqueous driving belt for transport also facilitated the emergence of the Suez Canal city of Port Said as one of the major global coaling stations after the canal's 1869 inauguration. In the city's early years, Nile water was carried to it by boat and on camelback. In the late 1850s, three thousand camels and donkeys were sent regularly from Alexandria to Port Said, and about eight hundred animals carried water from Qalyubiyya. These flows were compounded in the summer of 1859 by two steam condensers (with the addition of a third in 1861), each capable of desalinating five thousand liters daily. This desalination method required one kilogram of coal per liter of water and was three times costlier than getting barreled water.

During the early 1860s, before the Suez Canal was finished, Port Said was connected to Ismailia via pipes through which drinking water was pumped by steam power, and then by the sweet-water Isma'ilia Canal, providing Suez and Port Said with drinking water and facilitating the transportation of materials for the construction of the Suez Canal, food for the workers, and coal for the dredgers. In turn, the Suez Canal required regular mechanical, coal-fueled dredging. From the mid-1860s until the 1890s, the city's water supply developed further with pipes, canals, and distribution facilities. Water provision was a constant bone of contention in Port Said, leading to regular water theft and clashes between residents, as well as attempts at regulating the quantity and price of water, which had to be distributed between private residences, the docking warships, telegraph and government offices, the animal quarantine, and other parties. Generally, foreigners enjoyed larger quantities of water day and night than residents of the Arab quarters, who received water only during the day and in smaller portions. Carbon politics animated hydropolitics and prepared the ground for new social hierarchies in the city.[15]

The historical literature on Egypt is still Cairo-centric, reflecting a similar bias of political elites and intellectuals over the last two hundred years or more.[16] Carbonization was clearly manifest in Cairo, with a railway built in 1852, a tramway inaugurated in 1896, and streetlights, running water, and multiple other infrastructures powered by coal. The rise of the modern interventionist state likewise depended on the fossil-fueled motion between the capital and provinces, which allowed judges, police officers, irrigation and medical inspectors, and other state officials to commute between Cairo and its peripheries. Much of the same can be said about Alexandria, Egypt's second-largest urban center, whose rapid growth owes a great deal to the powers of steam and coal, as we have seen. However, carbonization and its effects are perhaps best demonstrated not only in the country's key commercial and political urban centers or in the cotton-growing rural areas, which underwent a coal-fired industrial revolution in irrigation and agriculture, but also in the new canal cities of Port Said and Isma'ilia, built to service the new steamer traffic and the global carbon economy. Of the two, Port Said was more important and has been better studied.[17] Port Said was a boomtown. In 1859, only 150 people lived there. In 1869, when the canal was opened for navigation, the town's population numbered 10,000, and by the 1882 British occupation, it had reached 17,580. Given the novelty of Port Said, the town throws into sharp relief many of the dynamics that existed in more diluted forms in other places in Egypt. For example, many of the town's new residents were practitioners of a new profession—coal heaving—and organized into a newly established guild in 1870.[18]

The city's nonhuman population was also exploding, making it a truly multispecies boomtown. The steamers that transited the canal had a buoyancy problem inherent in burning their fuel supply that caused them to rise in the water to the verge of capsizing. To compensate for this upsurge, ballast water started being used and was dumped in different ports of call—that is, until the procedure was recognized as a key vector for marine pollution. Moreover, the artificial saltwater passage between the Red Sea and the Mediterranean not only created the first physical connection between these bodies of water and marine ecosystems, but also standardized their salinity and temperature. Ecological barriers that had kept the Mediterranean insulated were now breached, and migration to the eastern Mediterranean of invading species from the Red Sea and the Indian Ocean began en masse. Marine biologists call this shift the Lessepsian Migration after Ferdinand de Lesseps, founder of the Suez Canal Company. This migration increased the number of fish and produced a vibrant fishery. Simultaneously, salt made available by the seawater evaporation and land reclamation processes that created much of Port Said allowed a fish-salting sector to emerge. Together with the installation of coal-burning water-desalination condensers and other engines that solidified this desalted liquid into artificial ice, salted and frozen Port Said fish were increasingly traded throughout Egypt and its coastal neighbors. The town's expanding fisheries and fish-salting industry attracted, in turn, a growing number of water birds that could also be hunted, salted or frozen, and similarly shipped across the region. Coal-burning and meat-eating went hand in hand.

Yet, as Mohandas Gandhi, a celebrity visitor to the town in 1931, repeated frequently, violence toward animals often translated into violence toward and between humans. Such processes soon created a host of problems resulting, for example, from differential fishing and bird hunting permits (foreigners were allowed to shoot from boats, whereas local Egyptians could only use nets). Property rights on land reclaimed from the sea became another bone of contention and were articulated as tensions between "natives" and "foreigners." Intercommunal tensions were also sparked by access to desalinated water. In short, this canal town, which was initially a tabula rasa with no one "native" to it, grew into a dual city split into Arab and European quarters. Many of the most pressing political and social issues can be traced back to the various material infrastructures that were powered by coal or that were built to facilitate its use.[19]

Gandhi also reminds us that coal animated new kinds of diets and new meanings attached to food. Steamer traffic, and especially the introduction of coal-fired transoceanic refrigeration ships in the 1870s and 1880s, globalized meat consumption, expanding access to animal protein in Egypt, where the lower classes seldom ate meat. The process had started with Mehmet Ali's military reorganizations, which for the first time in Ottoman history transformed peasants into soldiers and thus also into carnivores since the state provided them a meat-based diet, and it greatly accelerated with the availability of frozen meat. Yet already in 1888, on his first voyage to England via Egypt, the future Indian reformer experimented with vegetarianism as a form of anti-imperial resistance. In later years, his thought proliferated in Egypt in Arabic translation in the pan-Islamic magazine al-Manar.[20] Again, carbon politics proved both global and intimate, yielding new configurations of power and resistance.

Egypt's geographically central position in the global coal economy and its growing importance as a key junction of carbonization in the British Empire were combined with the growing political marginalization of the country's elites, which allowed outside forces to tighten their grip on Egypt. This combination of centrality and marginality offers another context for internal transformations—such as the deployment of modern transportation and communication infrastructures—that, in turn, further bolstered foreign intervention. Two such infrastructures, in particular, which initially were seen as competitors with one another—the first railway in Africa, built in the early 1850s to connect Cairo, Alexandria, Suez, and Port Said, and the Suez Canal, which connected the Indian Ocean to the Mediterranean and was inaugurated at the end of the following decade—demonstrate the importance of coal in these internal transformations. Put differently, Egypt's carbonization entailed not simply the arrival of British coal at its shores, but also the country's transformation into a global coaling hub. This hub was gradually shaped by coal spatially, but also temporally and culturally, as we will see in the following section.

Coal first arrived in Egypt for the use of British steamers in the Mediterranean and the Indian Ocean. Egyptian oceangoing ships followed suit and became reliant on this energy source. Daniel Stolz retraced the voyages of the Ottoman Egyptian steamer *Samannud*, which circumnavigated Africa in the 1860s, showing that the ideological outlook of Egypt's new military-technical elite who commanded such vessels was similar, in many respects, to the viewpoints of their European counterparts.[21] The aforementioned connection between coal and water and between sailing and pumping similarly informed Egyptian river steamboats, which capitalized on the fact that water-pumping stations and their coal dumps were stationed along the navigable canals and the Nile.[22] As with the Mahmudiyya and other canals, deepening and broadening the Suez Canal continued long after the ceremonial opening and has actually never stopped. The Suez Canal might not have opened the floodgates to the age of the steamship, but it certainly kept expanding the crack, with every enlargement allowing bigger and heavier ships to be designed. Offering a bridge connecting the British Empire to its Indian "jewel in the crown," the Suez Canal significantly shortened travel times and facilitated the flow of British coal to the east, injecting the fuel into economies predicated on more sustainable driving forces.

The constricted waterway of the canal gave shape to the steamship by promoting rear propellers and demoting sidewheelers that bumped against the banks of the narrow channel. Other features of the canal also changed the shape of ships; for example, there were significant price differences for coal east and west of the canal. As long as the canal's depth forced heavy ships, when fully loaded, to replenish their supplies east of the canal, light steamers had the advantage in terms of money and coaling time. The gradual deepening of the canal propelled an increase in the size of steamships, just as the ships' size encouraged the canal's deepening.

Coal, of course, was not only used to move through or desalinate water. After aborted attempts in the 1830s, in the early 1850s a railway system—one of the first outside Western Europe—started to quickly expand in Egypt. The first line connected Cairo and Alexandria, and subsequent lines joined Suez and Port Said to the network. Egyptian State Railways (ESR) was the country's largest coal consumer and was dependent on supplies from the British Isles after coal searches in the region failed. It was also the country's largest employer, making it a key technopolitical hub. Yet ESR kept various affinities to traveling by water even beyond the use of water to generate steam. Importantly, the expansion of rail transport occurred literally alongside the aforementioned waterways. According to William Willcocks, the chief British irrigation engineer in Egypt, canals and railways were designed together.[23] The main branch stretched along the Nile and depended on the river as a water source for steam generation and boiler cooling, and on animals to carry this water. Thus, river-bound steam navigation found itself in direct competition with ESR—a government monopoly—and faced heavy tolls and other governmental obstructions meant to encourage the railway.

Given the involvement of British commodities and engineers in the railway and the reliance of imperial troops en route to India on this route, the British were first opposed to the French-supported Suez Canal, which was seen as a competitor to ESR.

Nevertheless, after the canal's 1869 inauguration, they soon came to embrace the project, pushing for relevant adjustments in the railway. To survive the displacement of India-bound traffic to the canal, ESR had to undergo a dramatic restructuring, including the development of internal lines to attract local passengers and goods. The distribution of most of the Egyptian population along the Nile Valley and main railroad facilitated this transition, and between the mid-1860s—when it became clear that the canal was feasible—and the late 1870s, ESR tripled its size.

This synergy between existing and new waterways and older and newer railways—modes of transportation that first appeared to be at odds with one another—is indicative of a larger trend in the history of coal. The notions of "energy regimes" and "energy transitions" tend to color our perspective of this history. In this framework, new driving forces make old ones obsolete and replace them soon after they are introduced. Coal-fired technologies are seen as replacing reliance on waterpower (hence the steam engine supposedly replaced the waterwheel) and animal and human muscle. Coal-fired engines were, in turn, supposedly replaced by oil-burning devices. Yet the reliance on existing technologies and on animals and human workers only increased as a result of the nineteenth-century introduction of steam engines. The synergy of water and steam powers informed the so-called transition in the 1830s, which was, in fact, an extension and intensification of existing powers. Moreover, as a result of growing traffic and the need to transport more passengers and goods to multiple new locations, there were more sailboats and even rowboats after the arrival of steamers, more camel caravans alongside the railway, and more donkeys in Cairo's streets after the arrival of the coal-fired electric tram.[24] In other words, intensification, rather than transition, is the organizing principle of energy history. This fact has grave consequences for the prospects of transitioning away from fossil fuels in favor of renewable energies in the future.

THE TIME OF COAL

The critique of neat breaks and clear historical transitions between "energy regimes," which the history of coal throws into sharp relief, can be applied on another level to the more quotidian dimensions of temporality and timekeeping that coal informed.[25] A similar hybridization of old and new or local and foreign, and of mechanical and human elements, characterized "softer" domains informed by coal power and shaped it in turn. Indeed, while the proliferation of British coal in Egypt was first manifested in large-scale, durable infrastructures such as coaling depots, canals, and railroads, the reverberations of this process were also felt in less tangible domains. For example, imperialist assumptions about oriental despotism and the lethargy of local workers shaped the form and function of the Egyptian railway. Key among such interfaces between infrastructure and culture were the restructuring of timekeeping and the emergence of an "Egyptian time," as well as the transformation of the Arabic language and the development of new prose styles. Let us examine how the more solid and tangible aspects of coal connected to its softer power.

In 1870, the first timetables were published by ESR, a process that went along with the centralization of coaling in the railway. Examining how coaling informed scheduling arrangements in ESR reveals how the introduction of modern timekeeping into Egypt followed a unique trajectory that helped create a specific "Egyptian time." This trajectory complicates the expectations of nineteenth-century engineers and bureaucrats and twentieth-century modernization theorists about the supposed generic rationalizing and secularizing impacts of modern technologies.

The shift of the British India traffic to the canal pushed ESR directors to look for ways to reduce costs and increase efficiency. One of the first targets was coaling, "the largest item in a railway bill,"[26] especially in a place such as Egypt, where local labor was cheap and fuel was imported at great cost. Until 1870, the different sections of the Egyptian railway operated independently, both technically and administratively. Every station had a coal warehouse and the workforce necessary for coaling. Trains were loaded with only enough fuel to reach the next station, where they would be refueled. Because of these arrangements and a lack of space in the central stations, locomotives were stored at intermediary stations, where they were used for repairs and track work, creating un-expected congestion along the railroad. Coal, too, was stored along the way, exposed to the elements. Such arrangements did not allow a centralized accounting of coal expend-iture or a timetable for the entire railway, due to the congestions that disrupted planning and because human coaling labor was difficult to control and synchronize precisely.

In many respects, this mobility pattern was akin to the horses of the Egyptian postal service or the camels that aided commercial life prior to and alongside steam. Animals were indeed initially growing in numbers and importance as modes of transportation and eventually as fuel or meat as well (especially after coal-fired refrigeration), and steam engines inherited from animals several key features and yardsticks (such as the measure of "horsepower"). However, animalistic and mechanical modes of transport also differed in several important respects. Animals required rest along the way and spent more time in resting stations than moving between them. A locomotive, on the other hand, consumed as much as one-tenth of its daily fuel supply simply heating itself to the point where it could produce enough steam to carry its own weight and therefore combined thrift in time and money: the train that lingered at the stations wasted more money than the train that did not wait. The decision to set fixed times for passenger pickup drew its logic from this nexus of time, fuel, and money.

Yet if the centralization of coaling and the introduction of a unified timetable were interdependent, both of these processes could be articulated in multiple ways, and not only in the forms that were standardized in Western Europe. This was partly because as long as passengers and goods waited for trains rather than the trains waiting for them, it mattered little how long the passengers waited. In both Europe and the Middle East, the interest of the public in "regularity, speed, safety, and economy" often contradicted the objective of the company "to obtain a good return for the capital expended."[27] In 1873, when competitive pressures in British railway companies and the coal industry turned into a global depression, railway companies around the world were forced to cut costs, sometimes prioritizing coal thrift over the public's interests. The global coal crisis struck Egypt just as the cotton boom of the 1860s ended. Loans taken to underwrite large-scale projects, such as completing the canal and dramatically extending the railway, pushed Egypt toward a spiraling indebtedness to European creditors, leading to the gradual sale of the government's shares in the canal beginning in 1875 and to the 1876 formation of the Caisse de la Dette Publique, an international committee securing European financial control. In 1877, debt also brought to Egypt Evelyn Baring, the future Lord Cromer (1841–1917), the British representative in the Caisse and the notorious architect of British colonialism in the country. Under this new regime, ESR was forced to hand over 55% of its annual revenue to the Caisse, leaving only 45% for working expenses. It was also subjected to an international board of three directors—an Egyptian, a Frenchman, and an Englishman—making the company very difficult to manage. This complex management scheme was seen by many as a main cause for the railway's poor performance and frequent delays.[28]

Delays were also related to austerity measures and coal-saving policies. There were economic reasons for keeping a schedule but not necessarily keeping to it. A good example is a policy born in the early 1870s, together with the aforementioned means of economizing spending within ESR. We have already seen how reforms in scheduling were connected to the new need for fuel efficiency. For superintendents and drivers, the easiest way to estimate coal consumption has always been to use the clock. Indeed, "the efficiency of a railway may be judged by reference to statistics of its train delays."[29] But what should be classified as a delay? Looking in the early 1930s at the history of ESR, the company's deputy chief mechanical engineer argued that the answer should be different for a railway whose "employees are drawn from the uncivilized population on which years of training must be devoted before they become competent workmen who realize what efficiency means."[30] In a colonial railway, he maintained, "the company would continue to employ cheap labour and shut its eyes to failures and delays until its passengers clamoured for better service." Punctuality in this model depended on pressure from the public, which became increasingly time-minded. "[I]n the development of a railway, an inducement to eliminate failures is generated, and the incentive: an ever increasing number of fastidious passengers automatically provides the capital necessary for their elimination." Different railways, he added, should have different efficiency goals according to which failures and delays are to be classified as "avoidable" or "unavoidable."[31] If two extremes are compared, a British railway and a colonial one, more delays should be classified as "avoidable" and corrected in the former.

The conceptualization of "colonial punctuality" joined another incentive, at odds with the "inducement to eliminate failures," coal thrift, percolating from the chief mechanical engineer to the shed foremen as policy guidelines for deciding which locomotive to assign to which loads. One of the primary reasons for train delays was the assignment of certain loads to locomotives that could not carry them in the tabulated time. This method was frequently and deliberately used during the 1870s and 1880s to save on "light mileage"—energy wasted on carrying too light a load. During these two decades, all of ESR's five-ton goods wagons were converted into ten-ton wagons to avoid carrying light loads. In 1877, ESR's engine fleet was composed of sixty models purchased from all over the world within almost three decades. In the absence of spare parts, when an engine or a carriage broke down, parts from another vehicle were used to repair it. These hybrid engines had very different capacities and therefore resulted in significant light mileage. Moving to heavier wagons meant reducing light mileage but also a poorer record of keeping on schedule.

The resulting "Egyptian time" created by ESR (and later characterizing parts of the tramway system deployed in Cairo in 1896 and Alexandria in 1897) was at first resisted by Egyptian train passengers, who compared their railway's performance standards to what they were familiar with in Europe or the press. Concern with delays and speed inflected the supposed generic process of "time\space compression" by constant comparisons to elsewhere. In this respect, trains in Egypt could be at once fast and punctual (compared diachronically to standards of the same railway in the past) and slow and tardy (when synchronically compared to trains in Europe or the US). Discussions of train schedules in the Egyptian press tended to exaggerate both the Egyptian tendency to squander time and Western impersonal time thrift: "Time is a fleeting treasure. . . . We all know time is costly, yet spend it deliberately. . . . [W]e value and save dirhams; unfortunately, we are too generous with our time."[32] One of many articles titled "The Value of Time" quoted with approval a British observation that "the Egyptians are the most observant people when it comes to setting their clocks . . . but the most time-wasteful people when it comes to their professional lives."[33] While mechanical time was steadily gaining ground in Egypt with train schedules and timepieces, its advance was accompanied by reprimands and a discourse of hierarchical difference on both the British and Egyptian sides.

Yet this discourse soon sprang local and even traditional roots, which in turn inflected it. In 1907, a Cairo-based weekly magazine dedicated a long article to unpunctuality.[34] The article stressed the immoral dimensions of tardiness and analyzed this phenomenon in the realm of Islamic ethics (*akhlaq*). Not arriving at one's scheduled appointments on time was seen to threaten the bonds most vital to a civilized society: communal reliance and mutual help. Several years later, a translated advice book titled *'Alayka* (Duty) similarly framed timekeeping as promises to be kept: "You must keep your promise (*wa'd*), and a set date (*maw'id*) is a contract or pact between yourself and the other party."[35] Indeed, promise and date are conjugations of the same Arabic root (*wa'ada*), stressing the interpersonal nature of timekeeping. This moralization of punctuality happened through Islamic and Arabic dictums and references. In such texts, newly imported temporal conventions retroactively sprouted authentic roots. Clock time became responsive to a communal subject rather than an individual one in Europe. This gradually gave rise to critiques of monetizing time in general.

Moreover, with time, Egyptians started seeing advantages in the fact that, unlike the alienated, impersonal, and rigid temporal standards in industrial Europe, their time was more attuned to interpersonal relations and laxer, and that a modernist fascination with speed and punctuality was tempered in Egypt by an appreciation of slowness and asynchrony.[36] In a novel from the early 1930s, one of the passengers in a second-class train carriage explains that in Europe, "the poison of 'efficiency' had spread through the souls of Europeans. A dog-eat-dog strife prevailed with emphasis on the personal welfare of the individual. Everyone, both the turbaned and the befezzed, pondered these words and this claim. It seems he had laid bare to them a reality that had previously been concealed under the cloak of that word."[37] Telegraph operator turned public intellectual 'Abd Allah al-Nadim pioneered the critique of efficiency when contrasting Eastern and Western customs. For example, he distinguished Egyptian solidarity from the fate of a poor English worker driven to commit suicide after being fired from his London factory for arriving a few minutes late to work. European objectifying, man-eating efficiency did not stop at death: the corpse of that wretched soul was taken by train to the English Channel to be used as fish bait.[38] Alongside intellectuals, in the name of "Egyptian time" and its difference from other temporalities, railway workers defended their right for a chronometer-free toilet break at al-'Anabir, the railways' central repairs facility in Cairo.[39] Singers transformed waiting into an artistic principle that kindled audiences' excitement, and lovers transformed missing balcony trysts into a calculated way of flaming a suitor's passion.[40]

Such a comparative approach might be exactly what we need today when seeking to situate "Egyptian time" in a broader context. This analytical maneuver can also help explicate what this particular temporality contributes to current conversations about the supposedly generic Anthropocene, the age when undifferentiated humanity has in its entirety become a geological force. As Sebastian Conrad has shown, when European clocks first arrived in Japan in the seventeenth century, they were put to completely different uses than their designers had intended. The clock's first appearance did not bring about precision and regularity: instead of adapting cosmology, Japanese craftsmen began to modify the technology to maintain the varying differences between daytime and nighttime hours and create season-specific clock faces. Two centuries later, the situation had changed. One of the earliest measures of the Meiji government was abolishing the lunisolar system and adopting the Gregorian calendar. Time was severed from cosmology.[41] Very similar stories can be told about the Ottoman Empire, as Avner Wishnitzer has shown for Istanbul.[42] Daniel Stolz has demonstrated that, similarly to what happened in Tokyo and Istanbul, the 'ulama' in Ottoman Cairo shaped the use of mechanical timepieces in the eighteenth and early nineteenth centuries.[43] In all cases there was a shift away from looser local agentive uses of clock time. What accounts for the vastly different outcomes of these episodes of mechanical clock introduction? My answer, as the previous exploration of the ESR timetables reveals, is coal-fired global connectivity, integration, and imperialism. These timetables seem to suggest that Lewis Mumford's famous statement that "the clock, not the steam-engine, is the key machine of the modern industrial age" must be put on its head. Modern timekeeping and its global inflections are, in fact, a result of the worldwide proliferation of fossil fuels and the technologies that combusted them.

Rather than a diffusion from the West to the rest, coal and its rhythms simultaneously informed the British Isles, as the introduction of battle steamships to the RN also revealed. Let us return to the tumultuous decade of the 1830s one last time and situate what is probably the most famous example of modern time discipline in the context of coal and water. Before steam power spread in the British Isles, the protagonists of E. P. Thompson's classic 1967 article "Time, Work-Discipline, and Industrial Capitalism" could assert their agency in the face of clock time in the 1820s and 1830s but far less so under coal.[44] For these laborers, the clock was a means to fight their employers. Yet a shift occurred in the context of the wave of labor unrest among weavers struggling for the Ten Hour Work Day Act. As Andreas Malm demonstrated, tensions resulted from the fluctuation and irregularities of waterpower: when the river was high, workers were forced to stay at waterwheel-powered mills beyond the mandatory twelve-hour workday.[45] Thompson showed how, especially in cotton mills, where clock discipline was most rigorously imposed, the contest over time became most intense. In these mills, his blue-collar protagonists adopted their employers' equation of time and money to better fight them at their own game. Steam engines offered capitalists a crucial advantage: by 1830, these machines were mobile enough to compete with waterpower, which had bound production to riverbanks. Mobile generators and portable fuels allowed mills to be moved to urban centers, where workers were abundant and thus replaceable.

Against the ebbs and flows of water and work time, the regularity of coal and steam power afforded more efficient exploitation of human work. Portable steam engines were now increasingly assembled on steamships plying the longer waterways than those in the British Isles, allowing the exchange of coal for Egyptian or Indian cotton. As Hatice Yıldız has shown for cotton mill workers in colonial Bombay and silk workers in Ottoman Bursa in the following decades, employers in Europe's periphery often chose to ignore the clock in their steam mills, whereas workers, for their part, fought for more regular clock-timed shifts, but often in vain.[46] Steam engines clearly trumped clocks and informed whether and where time discipline would be imposed and, as in Egypt, what mechanical time actually meant in different places.

CONCLUSION

Existing understandings of the age of coal and steam have emphasized synchronization, standardization, and compression, and all these processes are evident also in the Egyptian coal-fired transportation sector and the cultural arrangements its engendered. However, the passage and use of coal in Egypt was also informed by local factors, such as the maritime, riverine, and other liquid realities that inflected a supposedly generic process of carbonization cum modernization. This multiplicity could become a source of inspiration. Coal-fired industrialization (of agriculture, seafaring, locomotion, etc.) happened in fields outside of Western Europe as well. Indeed, following coal rather than cotton presents a different picture of the world system, in which industrialization is not merely the processing of raw materials into finished goods, but also a transformation that involves the cultivation and transportation of the raw materials themselves. The supposed peripheries of the global system may now provide resources to rethink how we might heed Walter Benjamin's understanding of revolution as an attempt to grab the emergency brakes of a locomotive dashing toward climate collapse. These emergency brakes might very well involve the reformation of agriculture, fashion, or meat consumption alongside transportation. Moreover, carbon politics did not replace hydropolitics, just as coal did not replace the powers of water and human and animal muscle. Existing powers in locales like Egypt included the "softer" forces of culture, language, and social relations. If carbonization depended on those powers for its global march, perhaps they might also inform how we try to arrest it.

Notes

1. Timothy Mitchell, *Colonising Egypt* (Berkeley: University of California Press, 1991).
2. Much of the following discussion is explicated more fully in On Barak, *Powering Empire: How Coal Made the Middle East and Sparked Global Carbonization* (Oakland: University of California Press, 2020).
3. Plans for deploying a railway in the country in the 1830s, for example, were promoted by the need to facilitate the pilgrimage to Mecca.
4. See Barak, *Powering Empire*, chapter 6.
5. Alan Mikhail, "Unleashing the Beast: Animals, Energy, and the Economy of Labor in Ottoman Egypt," *The American Historical Review* 118, no. 2 (2013): 317–48.
6. Jennifer L. Derr, *The Lived Nile: Environment, Disease, and Material Colonial Economy in Egypt* (Stanford: Stanford University Press, 2019), chapter 1.
7. John Bowring, *Report on Egypt and Candia: Addressed to the Right Hon. Lord Viscount Palmerston, Her Majesty's Principal Secretary of State for Foreign Affairs, &c. &c. &c.* (London: W. Clowes and Sons for Her Majesty's Stationery Office, 1840), 190.
8. Andreas Malm, *Fossil Capital: The Rise of Steam-Power and the Roots of Global Warming* (London: Verso, 2016).
9. Kapil Raj, "Mapping Knowledge Go-Betweens in Calcutta, 1770–1820," in *The Brokered World: Go-Betweens and Global Intelligence, 1770–1820*, ed. Simon Schaffer, Lissa Roberts, Kapil Raj, and James Delbourgo (Sagamore Beach, MA: Science History Publications, 2009), 105–50.
10. Nile Green, *The Love of Strangers: What Six Muslim Students Learned in Jane Austen's London* (Princeton, NJ: Princeton University Press, 2016).
11. Barak, *Powering Empire*, chapter 4.
12. Lucia Carminati, "Port Said and Ismailia as Desert Marvels: Delusion and Frustration on the Isthmus of Suez, 1859–1869," *Journal of Urban History* 46, no. 3 (2019): 622–47.
13. See Alan Mikhail, *Nature and Empire in Ottoman Egypt: An Environmental History* (Cambridge: Cambridge University Press, 2011).
14. Barak, *Powering Empire*, chapter 1.
15. Ibid.
16. Lucia Carminati and Mohamed Gamal-Eldin, "Decentering Egyptian Historiography: Provincializing Geographies, Methodologies, and Sources," *International Journal of Middle East Studies* 53, no. 1 (2021): 107–11.

17. Zayn al-'Abidin Shams al-Din Najm, *Bur Sa'id: Tarikhuha wa-Tatawwuruha mundhu Nash'atiha 1859 hata 'Amm 1882* (Cairo: al-Hay'a al-'Amma al-Misriyya li-l-Kitab, 1987); Valeska Huber, *Channelling Mobilities: Migration and Globalisation in the Suez Canal Region and Beyond, 1869–1914* (Cambridge: Cambridge University Press, 2013); Lucia Carminati, "Port Said and Ismailia as Desert Marvels."

18. John Chalcraft, "The Coal-Heavers of Port Sa'id: State-Making and Worker Protest, 1869–1914," *International Labor and Working Class History* 60 (2001): 110–24.

19. See Barak, *Powering Empire*, chapter 2.

20. Roy Bar Sadeh, "Debating Gandhi in *al-Manar* During the 1920s and 1930s," *Comparative Studies of South Asia, Africa and the Middle East* 38, no. 3 (2018): 491–507.

21. Daniel. A. Stolz, "The Voyage of the Samannud: Pilgrimage, Cholera, and Empire on an Ottoman-Egyptian Steamship Journey in 1865–66," *International Journal of Turkish Studies* 23, nos. 1–2 (2017): 1–18.

22. Barak, *Powering Empire*, 36.

23. Canay Ozden, "The Pontifex Minimus: William Willcocks and Engineering British Colonialism," *Annals of Science* 71, no. 2 (2014): 183–205.

24. See Barak, *Powering Empire*, chapter 1; and David Edgerton, *The Shock of the Old: Technology and Global History since 1900* (Oxford: Oxford University Press, 2007).

25. Much of the discussion in this section is explicated more fully in On Barak, *On Time: Technology and Temporality in Modern Egypt* (Berkeley: University of California Press, 2013).

26. J. A. Kilby, "Notes on the Economical Operation of Locomotives," *Egyptian State Railways Magazine*, May 1932, 7.

27. UK Parliament, Transport and Communication, *Report from Select Committee on Railway Companies Amalgamation* (London: 1872).

28. Barak, *On Time*, chapter 2.

29. W. D. Knight, "Failures," *Egyptian State Railways Magazine*, May 1932, 7.

30. Ibid.

31. Ibid.

32. *al-Hilal*, 15 January 1895.

33. *Majallat al-Musawwar al-Haditha al-Musawwara*, 11 December 1929.

34. "Wait Just Five Minutes," *al-Sihafa*, 29 December 1907.

35. Samuel Smiles, *'Alayka: Nasa'ih. li-Tabasur al-Shubban bi-Muqtadayat al-'Aysh wa-Asrar al-Najah*, trans. Ibrahim Ramzi (Cairo, 1914), 9.

36. Barak, *On Time*, chapter 2.

37. Tawfiq al-Hakim, *Return of the Spirit: Tawfiq al-Hakim's Classic Novel of the 1919 Revolution*, trans. William M. Hutchins (Washington, DC: Three Continents Press, 1990), 156–57.

38. 'Abd Allah al-Nadim, *al-Tankit wa-l-Tabkit*, 7 August 1881.

39. *al-Ahram*, 18 October 1910.

40. See Barak, *On Time*, 16–18.

41. Sebastian Conrad, "'Nothing Is the Way It Should Be:' Global Transformations of the Time Regime in the Nineteenth Century," *Modern Intellectual History* 15, no. 3 (2018): 821–48.

42. Avner Wishnitzer, *Reading Clocks, Alla Turca: Time and Society in the Late Ottoman Empire* (Chicago: University of Chicago Press, 2015).

43. Daniel A. Stolz, "Positioning the Watch Hand: 'Ulama' and the Practice of Mechanical Timekeeping in Cairo, 1737–1874," *International Journal of Middle East Studies* 47, no. 3 (2015): 489–510.
44. E. P. Thompson, "Time, Work-Discipline, and Industrial Capitalism," *Past & Present* 38, no. 1 (1967): 56–97.
45. Malm, *Fossil Capital*.
46. Hatice Yıldız, "The Politics of Time in Colonial Bombay: Labor Patterns and Protest in Cotton Mills," *Journal of Social History* 54, no. 1 (2020): 206–85.

BIBLIOGRAPHY

Barak, On. *On Time: Technology and Temporality in Modern Egypt*. Berkeley: University of California Press, 2013.

Barak, On. *Powering Empire: How Coal Made the Middle East and Sparked Global Carbonization*. Oakland: University of California Press, 2020.

Bar Sadeh, Roy. "Debating Gandhi in *al-Manar* during the 1920s and 1930s." *Comparative Studies of South Asia, Africa and the Middle East* 38, no. 3 (2018): 491–507.

Carminati, Lucia. "Port Said and Ismailia as Desert Marvels: Delusion and Frustration on the Isthmus of Suez, 1859–1869." *Journal of Urban History* 46, no. 3 (2019): 622–47.

Conrad, Sebastian. "'Nothing Is the Way It Should Be:' Global Transformations of the Time Regime in the Nineteenth Century." *Modern Intellectual History* 15, no. 3 (2018): 821–48.

Derr, Jennifer L. *The Lived Nile: Environment, Disease, and Material Colonial Economy in Egypt*. Stanford, CA: Stanford University Press, 2019.

Edgerton, David. *The Shock of the Old: Technology and Global History since 1900*. Oxford: Oxford University Press, 2007.

Green, Nile. *The Love of Strangers: What Six Muslim Students Learned in Jane Austen's London*. Princeton, NJ: Princeton University Press, 2016.

Huber, Valeska. *Channelling Mobilities: Migration and Globalisation in the Suez Canal Region and Beyond, 1869–1914*. Cambridge: Cambridge University Press, 2013.

Malm, Andreas. *Fossil Capital: The Rise of Steam Power and the Roots of Global Warming*. New York: Verso Books, 2016.

Mikhail, Alan. *Nature and Empire in Ottoman Egypt: An Environmental History*. Cambridge: Cambridge University Press, 2011.

Mitchell, Timothy. *Colonising Egypt*. Berkeley: University of California Press, 1991.

Mitchell, Timothy. *Rule of Experts: Egypt, Techno-Politics, Modernity*. Berkeley: University of California Press, 2002.

Raj, Kapil. "Mapping Knowledge Go-Betweens in Calcutta, 1770–1820." In *The Brokered World: Go-Betweens and Global Intelligence, 1770–1820*, edited by Simon Schaffer, Lissa Roberts, Kapil Raj, and James Delbourgo, 105–50. Sagamore Beach, MA: Science History Publications, 2009.

Shams al-Din Najm, Zayn al-'Abidin. *Bur Sa'id: Tarikhuha wa-Tatawwuruha mundhu Nash'atiha 1859 hata 'Amm 1882*. Cairo: al-Hay'a al-'Amma al-Misriyya li-l-Kitab, 1987.

Stolz, Daniel A. "Positioning the Watch Hand: 'Ulama' and the Practice of Mechanical Timekeeping in Cairo, 1737–1874." *International Journal of Middle East Studies* 47, no. 3 (2015): 489–510.

Stolz, Daniel A. "The Voyage of the Samannud: Pilgrimage, Cholera, and Empire on an Ottoman Egyptian Steamship Journey in 1865–66." *International Journal of Turkish Studies* 23, nos. 1/2 (2017): 1–18.

Thompson, E. P. "Time, Work-Discipline, and Industrial Capitalism," *Past & Present* 38, no. 1 (1967): 56–97.

Wishnitzer, Avner. *Reading Clocks, Alla Turca: Time and Society in the Late Ottoman Empire.* Chicago: University of Chicago Press, 2015.

Yıldız, Hatice. "The Politics of Time in Colonial Bombay: Labor Patterns and Protest in Cotton Mills." *Journal of Social History* 54, no. 1 (2020): 206–85.

CHAPTER 7

....

OF MACHINES AND MEN

Mechanization and Migrant Labor on the Suez Canal,
1859–64

....

LUCIA CARMINATI

In the words of Egyptian engineer, bureaucrat, and technology enthusiast ʿAli Mubarak, a "new and modern city" bearing the name of the then-ruler Saʿid Pasha appeared on Egypt's northern coast in 1859: Bur Saʿid (Port Said). The fledgling center lay in the spot where the north–south excavation of a saltwater channel (*al-khalij al-malih*), to become known as the Suez Canal, was launched to unite the Mediterranean Sea and the Red Sea. The undertaking took off after engineering explorations led to the approval of plans for the course of the brand new canal.[1] ʿAli Mubarak does not dabble on the diplomatic technicalities involved, but the project was born out of agreements made in November 1854 between the Egyptian ruler Saʿid and the French diplomat Ferdinand de Lesseps, who was charged with creating and heading a Compagnie Universelle du Canal Maritime de Suez (Universal Company of the Maritime Canal of Suez; hereafter the Company) with the participation of "capitalists of all nations." The Company was aimed at cutting the Isthmus of Suez, operating a passage suited to great navigation, preparing a Mediterranean entry and a Red Sea entry, and establishing one or two ports.[2] By law, it was an Egyptian joint-stock or incorporated (*anonyme*) company with an intended international character.[3] Yet it soon appeared as an eminently French preserve, to which scholars refer in shorthand as a "French private company."[4]

The Suez Canal "abridged time and space in a way and to an extent that no other enterprise ha[d] ever before done in the history of the world" and required the largest scale of digging ever recorded.[5] Contemporary observers of the canal project mostly drew readers' attention to its technical aspects. They glorified science and technology (approached here both expansively as "achievements in material culture"[6] and specifically in terms of the techniques of dredging and embankment construction emerging in the nineteenth century), while erasing their human enablers. As I discuss in detail elsewhere, while later Egyptian historiography and popular culture have successfully unearthed the history of the forced drafting of Egyptian workers, Western historiography has mostly replicated earlier technophile biases.[7] For example, the canal venture has been described as a project in which "construction by massive manpower, an Egyptian tradition since the first pharaohs, had given way to the biggest concentration of mechanical energy ever assembled,"[8] as if mechanical power had simply swept away a primordial form of human toil. In contrast, laborers were recruited and organized to undertake the excavation of the Suez Canal between 1859 and 1864 and populated the supposedly dehumanized landscape of the canal region. Human toil and mechanical exertion, far from being on the extremes of a spectrum of work arrangements, coexisted with one another, albeit in occasional tension. Together, they redress this predominantly technological historiography. While machines have overshadowed migrant workers in the narrative of the canal undertaking, they always necessitated the drudgery of these workers to function.[9]

The available published and archival historical materials show that contemporary observers of the canal excavation, set in motion in 1859, seemed to be enamored by its technological novelty and unmoved by its human protagonists. However, the Company's demand for labor prompted diplomatic exchanges and disagreements between the Egyptian, British, and Ottoman governments, resulting in a transition toward a regime of forced labor for Egyptians on the canal worksites, officially in place between 1862 and 1864. As the composition of the workforce changed, migrant labor became increasingly central to the diplomatic sketching of the Suez Canal, its actual execution, and the struggle to achieve regional power. The end of coerced recruitment of Egyptians for the canal works in 1864 brought a fatal shortage of manpower, forcing the Company to introduce additional machinery into the isthmus and to lure more foreign workers via international enlistment campaigns while continuing to rely on locally recruited laborers.

OF MACHINES AND MEN

Uninterested in the legal and diplomatic machinations behind the canal, 'Ali Mubarak turned his attention elsewhere. In the passage on Port Said in his topographic encyclopedia, he keenly pointed out that, around 1860, two dredgers began scouring the mud from the bottom of the nearby Lake Manzala so that the dredged-up material could be thrown over hollow areas to fill them up and building surface could be carved from the formerly lacustrine ground. He also noted that "huge workshops" were due to appear. Finally, he took pains to describe the innovative and lengthy process that yielded, in the absence of locally available stones, artificial rocks from the blending of sea sand and lime imported from France. Once deposited on the sea bottom by cranes standing on barges, these man-made rocks would shape the harbor to be. 'Ali Mubarak strove to illustrate the technological and scientific endeavors—what he termed *al-kayfiyyat wa-l-tadbirat al-'ajiba* (marvelous measures)—ushering in the making of Port Said and the

Suez Canal.[10] By contrast, except for a few fleeting references to their presence, he paid no attention to the exertion of all those who manned the dredgers, workshops, steam-operated cranes, barges, and railways.

In his time, 'Ali Mubarak was not alone in emphasizing the canal's artificial and newly built character and the centers sprouting on its banks. Many Western travelers likewise focused on those same features. Dredgers, in particular, became a commonplace representation of the enterprise's technological triumph. They impressed visitors with their round-the-clock drudgery to keep the desert sand from intruding into and blocking the canal.[11] Dredging necessitated a considerable annual outlay: nearly two million cubic yards of material had to be removed in a single year from the bed of the canal in order to maintain the requisite depth.[12] Some observers were so in awe that they likened these devices to cathedrals. Others compared them to ancient war machines aggressively pushing back against the invasive desert sand.[13] Passing artists also immortalized dredgers and other machinery in the conspicuous iconography that resulted from their Suez trips. Western armchair travelers became acquainted with the imagery of the machines stationed in Port Said via, for example, the sundry woodcuts displayed in magazines such as the *Illustrated London News*[14] or in paintings, lithographs, and, later, photographs and postcards (Fig. 7.1). In most of these representations, workers casually appeared as happenstance bystanders or mere sidekicks of the gears chugging on the frontlines. Egyptians, in particular, were relegated to the margins.[15]

FIG. 7.1 Postcards enabled armchair travelers to associate the imagery of machines with the Suez Canal, "Port Said. Courbe de Toussoun" [*sic*], late nineteenth to early twentieth century. American University in Cairo, Rare Books and Special Collections Library, Postc_B1_100_b.

That such emphasis on the role of technology in the isthmus excavation was to be deployed and replicated is not surprising because it served multiple political agendas. For its part, the Egyptian government espoused the grand narrative that, thanks to its sponsorship of the canal, "science together with industry, after having overcome greatest material challenges, would open up a new path for worldwide commerce," as the governmental invitation to the king of Prussia to partake in the 1869 inauguration festivities boasted. Meanwhile, Western governments replied to such invitations by declaiming that "science proved capable of overcoming the physical challenges and succeeded in uniting two oceans that seas of sands used to keep separate."[16] These words, chosen to flatter the Egyptian ruler, suggest that the praise of "science" as a victor over the isthmus's physical elements was popular in both European and Egyptian circles. In fact, French firms had been developing skills in engineering, the organization of public works, mechanics, and forms of innovative entrepreneurship.[17] As Mohamed Gamal-Eldin and I have expounded elsewhere, wresting land away from the desert, sea, and lake posed numerous difficulties. Yet harping on such struggles also conveniently celebrated the eventual success of Westerners' technology and talent.[18] Moreover, with their visually impressive facilities, the canal worksites could showcase the "progress" that was supposed to be implemented shortly in other parts of the country.[19] Change in the canal region promised to hurl Egypt as a whole into the future.

According to a persisting Orientalist trope, Egypt appeared to some as an "old" country, "where fables and statistics, strategy and legend, geopolitics and negotiation came together."[20] By the early nineteenth century, the ancient past of Egypt had already become a subject of curiosity and craving in the West.[21] Therefore, the canal's novelty, even if cloaked in positive terms, still stood out as an oddity in a context that was primarily associated with antiquity. An early twentieth-century visitor, for example, claimed that Port Said was the nemesis of Luxor, a southern Egyptian destination commended for its impressive ancient ruins.[22] Perhaps because of the disorienting feelings that this collision of past and future aroused, Isthmus of Suez visitors often felt the urge to draw comparisons between the canal sites and familiar locations elsewhere: if Suez could become the "Marseille of the Red Sea" or the "Venice of the Red Sea" and Ismailia could turn into the "Venice of the Desert," imagining Port Said as "another Alexandria" or an "Egyptian Calcutta" would not be unreasonable.[23] Whatever the flights of their fancy, contemporary European observers tended to portray these sites as places where the deafening din of machinery drowned out all other voices.

LABOR AS AN IMPERIAL CONCERN

In January 1856, representatives of the Egyptian government and the Suez Canal Company redacted a concession premised on a previous one from November 1854 that had assigned De Lesseps the "exclusive power" to create and lead the Company. The 1856 concession stipulated that at least four-fifths of the labor force employed by the

Company was to be made up of Egyptian workers. It also clarified that the piercing of the isthmus would begin once the Ottoman sultan ratified the latter document.[24] The document did not suggest how its redactors envisioned such a workforce quota be obtained; neither did it clarify who exactly would compose the remaining fifth. It also did not sketch a timeline for when the works would officially commence.

However vague, the 1856 stipulation still accomplished several diplomatic goals. In part, the assurance that four-fifths of the workers would be Egyptian may have hinted at the possibility that the Egyptian government would take responsibility for providing them, thus quelling the Company's anxiety about retrieving the necessary manpower. Incidentally, it saved the Company the costs associated with hiring a mass of free workers. The point about four out of five workers being Egyptian did not constitute a capitulation by the Egyptian government to the Company's whims. In fact, it assuaged concerns about the influx of a copious "European" populace into the country.[25] The Egyptian government feared the invasion of Egypt by a "swarm" of foreign workers "scattering through the country and bringing about disorder and even subversive ideas, which the government would be unable to harness" due to the protection that Egypt's regime of consular jurisdictions afforded foreigners.[26] According to De Lesseps, the Egyptian government had insisted on this disposition in order to "provide to *certain external [sources of] disapproval* some guarantees against the roundup of numerous foreign workers on the isthmus, a gathering that had been loudly denounced as a threat to the independence of the country."[27] Here, De Lesseps seems to suggest that the Egyptian ruler simply caved in to Ottoman pressure. Nonetheless, by committing to provide most of the necessary manpower, the Egyptian government did retain a degree of leverage over the Company. In fact, Egyptian officials later tried to exploit the withdrawal of Egyptian labor as a lever to recuperate the lands they had initially conceded to the Company. By 1863, they would want both Egyptian workers and lands out of the Company's hands.[28]

Whatever the principle behind the four-fifths quota, the Company was theoretically forbidden to recruit abroad and unable to enlist workers locally. From the Company officials' viewpoint, the Egyptian government had a "duty" to step in and provide the labor. To them, the use of coerced labor posed no quandary. Appealing to the fact that the Egyptian government had long relied on it for useful public works in agriculture, navigation, and commerce, they argued that it was now France's turn to enjoy the resources that Egypt had to offer.[29] On 20 July 1856, in the Decree and Regulation for the Fellah, the Egyptian government eventually committed itself to providing the workers for the canal, paying them each 2.5 to 3 piasters per day and feeding them (for an unspecified period of time). Workers under twelve would receive only one piaster per day but full rations of food. Those defined as "skilled workers" (*ouvriers d'art*), such as masons, carpenters, stonemasons, and blacksmiths, were to receive pay in compliance with what the Egyptian government normally paid for such work. The decree also established that the Company would provide all workers with abundant fresh water at its own expense and would accommodate workers in tents, hangars, or other "suitable" lodgings. Moreover, the Company was supposed to erect a hospital for sick workers. The decree established that the Company would pay those workers who were unable to work due to sickness a salary of 1.5 piasters during recovery. Finally, it called for the Company to cover travel expenses so that the workers and their families could get to the worksites.[30]

At least on paper, this regulation promised to better the lot of those Egyptians who were forcibly recruited to work for the government—that is, if we believe those testimonies claiming that, customarily, each government-mandated corvée shift took sixty days, during which men left their fields uncultivated and let their families go hungry. Reportedly, workers were supposed to bring their own provisions and tools: each man was to take his own basket, and each third man a hoe. Exposed to bad weather, they faced the risk of freezing to death. Reportedly, they received neither pay nor food. Those who could afford it could pay for another man to take their corvée shift and pay for the man's foodstuff.[31] There is evidence that the Egyptian state did pay the men it conscripted, even if reluctantly.[32] There is also indication that, in Suez, it was the Company that eventually compensated them.[33] Yet the Company may not have always kept its word: some claimed that the canal workers returned home with no pay and the burden of having had to pay for their food or that, alternatively, they were paid only one-tenth of what had been initially promised.[34]

By establishing the principle that forced labor could be employed on the Suez Canal worksites, the Egyptian government enshrined the Suez Canal project as one among other comparable governmental public works in Egypt. In the mid-nineteenth century, the corvée was still common practice in Egypt. During one single year, as many as 400,000 men could be summoned against their will.[35] The government relied on the corvée to carry out most of the major public works it undertook, including railways, improvements to the irrigation system, and the cleaning of the main canals to ensure they could continue to carry water during the summer, when the Nile was at its lowest. In many cases, men were coerced to work far from home.[36] The massive undertaking of the Mahmudiyya Canal, which connected Alexandria and Cairo (1817–20), stood out as the Suez Canal's infamous predecessor. In order to have it dug, then-ruler Muhammad 'Ali forcibly drafted as many as 315,000 workers. The death toll would be as high as 100,000 due to exhaustion, starvation, disease, dehydration, accident, cold, or heat.[37] According to pro-canal sources, the grandiose "Canal of the Two Seas" now deservedly commanded a similar sacrifice.[38]

To Egyptian administrators in the country's capital, Egyptian workers on the canal embodied the means to attain control over the sparsely inhabited Suez region. As Khaled Fahmy notes in regard to the Mahmudiyya Canal, "the sheer size of the labor force involved as well as the cost and duration of the project testify to the ability of the Pasha's administration in Cairo to tap and control the human and material resources of his province."[39] If, as argued by Alan Mikhail, managing the Mahmudiyya Canal epitomized Egypt's move toward a more centrally controlled bureaucracy, so could the Suez Canal a mere four decades later.[40] But this Franco-Egyptian eastward push irked the Ottoman state, which found Egyptian actions to violate Ottoman territorial sovereignty. The Egyptian viceroy had given explicit assurances that activities on the isthmus ought to involve only preliminary examinations and not the piercing itself. Yet Istanbul found that the operations that had been undertaken were not simply preparatory surveys but "of a more compromising nature."[41]

On 16 March 1859, the Egyptian government forbade the presence of workers in the area of the projected canal's northern opening in Port Said. But that proscription must have proven insufficient because, on 22 July 1859, the government further instructed Ja'far Pasha, the governor in Damietta, to go to the spot where "De Lesseps's workers" (*'ummal wa-shughghala*) could be found, round up all the "Arabs of Egyptian nationality" (*awlad al-'arab al-masri al-jinsiyya*), bring them back to Damietta, and report their total number to Cairo. From that moment, no more Egyptian workers were allowed to participate in the works.[42] Apparently, the governors of Damietta and the neighboring province of al-Daqahliyya received similar directives to stop the influx of workers and monitor those who had already made it to the isthmus. Finally, Ja'far Pasha was also secretly instructed to import no more food or water to the area. By the summer of 1859, it had become clear to foreign consulates in Egypt that the Egyptian government had seemingly entered a state of great embarrassment after the Ottoman sultan had invited the Egyptian viceroy to stop the works right away and wait for a firman (imperial order).[43]

A few months later, in October 1859, the Ottoman delegate Mukhtar Bey landed in Egypt. According to Company representatives, Mukhtar Bey had not originally been dispatched to alter the status quo that the Company and the viceroy had reached and maintained for a few months with the "implicit authorization" of the sultan. They claimed that, after all, Egyptian authorities and Egypt-based consulates had de facto facilitated the circulation of intermediaries (*agents*), the recruitment of European workers, the establishment of duty-free imports (*entrée en franchise*), and the debarkation and transportation of machinery and materials. The Company had done nothing but assert "uncontestably acquired rights" that could not be ended abruptly. As a matter of fact, they could appeal to the 1856 concession pledging that the Egyptian government would exonerate the Company from all custom rights, of entry or otherwise, over all machines and materials that it brought to Egypt from abroad to serve its construction and operational needs. Company representatives blamed the Ottoman intrusion on the British, particularly the British ambassador in Istanbul, Sir Henry Bulwer, who had apparently managed to transform Mukhtar Bey's harmless mission into a troublesome inquiry.[44]

In fact, the British government initially opposed the canal project, both out of fear that it would drive a wedge between Egypt and "Turkey" and due to skepticism that it would ease access to Britain's "Indian possessions."[45] In particular, British authorities opposed the forced labor scheme being deployed on the canal worksites. They did not object in principle to forcibly recruiting Egyptians; in fact, they relied on this method themselves, including in the operation of the British Peninsular and Oriental Company and in the building of the Alexandria–Cairo railroad.[46] Revealing that the pursuit of the abolition of the corvée was not a primary concern of his administration, the British consul-general in Egypt asserted that the *abuse* rather than the *use* of forced labor ought to be lamented. Specifically, British observers condemned the principle that Egyptians could be compulsorily conscripted en masse to serve French interests. They feared the idea that as many as twenty to thirty thousand men would be placed under France's tacit command.[47]

For their part, Company sources concluded that Britain's actual concern was not humanitarian, but rather aimed at destroying the financial enterprise and alarming its shareholders.[48] By claiming that the condition of Egyptian corvée laborers was excellent considering "where [they] had come from" and even better than that of the British workers, they mocked the status of British workers while also demeaning Egyptians as undeserving. They went as far as alleging that the Company was, in any case, a preferable employer to the Egyptian government, which they accused of not paying the workers it drafted for its public works.[49]

THE TRANSITION TO FORCED LABOR

By December 1859, despite Ottoman opposition and Egyptian embarrassment, the presence of thirty so-called Arab workers, often but not necessarily always identifiable as Egyptians, was recorded in Port Said. They had been freely recruited in Damietta, a coastal town to the west, with no apparent opposition from the governor. Other similarly unrestrained engagements had taken place in Cairo around the same time. Later that month, individuals who could speak Arabic and "knew local customs" were dispatched throughout areas of the Nile Delta neighboring the isthmus to recruit fellahin.[50] In early 1861, De Lesseps gave orders to have a notice publicizing job opportunities on the canal worksites translated into Arabic, printed in Cairo, and distributed in both the capital and the main villages of Middle and Lower Egypt, via either Company agents or other trusted individuals. Notices in Arabic were also to be affixed to mosque gates, in railway stations, and at the entrance of police stations. They promised advantages to village heads who sent workers. Recruiting efforts also reached Palestine, where they may have extended as far as Bethlehem: De Lesseps was particularly interested in mustering just enough Syrian Christians, including elderly men, women, and children, to guarantee work progress while Muslims fasted during Ramadan.[51] Workers specifically identified as "Syrians" were present on the Suez worksites as early as 1861. Most of them came from the surroundings of al-ʿArish and Ghazza. Ostensibly, many resided for some time in Port Said, Ismailia, and Suez before moving on to Cairo and Alexandria in their search for better economic opportunities.[52]

Nonetheless, the Company's early efforts to secure a sufficiently large and diversified workforce for the Canal works floundered overall. Twenty-five Maltese who had been engaged in August 1859, for example, fled as soon as they disembarked in Alexandria after having traveled at the Company's expense and received one month's pay in advance.[53] Reportedly, men "from all quarters of Europe" had convened on the isthmus but "were with difficulty held together by the mere hope of gain." Similarly, the so-called Arabs who had joined the works had done so "from imperative necessity" and sought to leave as soon as they had earned a few days' wages. Even if they had been offered unu-sually high compensation, the fact that they were always kept ten days in arrear of their pay showed the Company management's great fear of their absconding and difficulty in retaining them.[54]

By the end of 1860, the number of Egyptian workers still hovered around a mere seventeen hundred. On 25 January 1861, Mougel Bey, an engineer at the service of the Egyptian government, announced he would prepare a deal with some contractors to provide ten to twelve thousand workers (presumably each month).[55] These numbers would soon surge, through De Lesseps's seemingly bold imposition, to twenty thou-sand.[56] Egyptian chronicler Amin Sami increased this figure further by claiming that the Egyptian government eventually pledged to provide as many as twenty-seven thou-sand workers monthly to the Suez undertaking at no charge.[57]

By early 1861, an informal transition to forced labor appears to have been in place. Still, both the Egyptian government and the Company persisted in portraying workers as mere volunteers. The former made open profession of having simply permitted De Lesseps to recruit. The latter backed up this version. Without mentioning coercion, De Lesseps emphasized that the orders released to provincial governors only facilitated the recruitment of fellahin.[58] In actuality, starting in May 1861, the governors of the provinces that neighbored the isthmus began drafting hun-dreds and then thousands of workers to be dispatched to the canal worksites, such as al-Gisr and Qantara, as well as to the sweet-water canal in the making.[59] By June 1861, British sources reported that eyewitnesses had seen men brought up in gangs from their villages and handed over by government officers to the Company's agents. These agents, stationed in several districts, rigorously inspected every batch and carefully picked the necessary men. Although some of the dragooned workers con-trived to escape from the train that carried them, they were recaptured in a matter of days and sent back to their taskmasters.[60] By September 1861, laborers' numbers had increased to 5,771. Nevertheless, Company officials remained dissatisfied with the re-cruitment effort.[61]

In January 1862, the Egyptian administration officially instituted a systematic scheme of corvée on the canal's worksites. A representative of the Egyptian ruler and later a gov-ernor of the isthmus saw to it that a sufficient and stable workforce attended to the needs of the canal undertaking.[62] The first officially drafted contingent, twenty thousand men hailing from Upper Egypt, reached the isthmus in February 1862. By March 1862, the canal worksites brought workers from Upper Egypt and Lower Egypt together. Sources specify that workers from Upper Egypt would eventually be drafted in the Minya, Asyut, Qina, Isna, and Nubia areas. Workers from Lower Egypt departed the central Delta areas of al-Manufiyya and al-Qalyubiyya; al-Buhayra in the western Delta; and al-Daqahliyya (Mansoura in particular) and al-Sharqiyya in the eastern Delta.[63] Depending on the fellahin's level of compliance, their trip could be more or less tough. Virtually enslaved, they were often bound to each other by their neck with ropes or wooden rods; handcuffs were also used. Each of them brought a bundle with tobacco and food, including bread, cheese, and *batrakh* (grey mullet roe), for the road.[64]

Reportedly, at any given time, up to twenty thousand men were on their way to the works, twenty thousand were digging, and twenty thousand were commuting home.[65] These figures were rough estimates, in part because drafted workers occasionally brought their families with them to the sites.[66] In May 1862, De Lesseps spoke of "a peaceful army of 40,000 workers" present on the isthmus.[67] In April 1863, arrivals peaked, with 22,480 forced Egyptians landing at the canal sites.[68] Such a remarkable surge could hardly have gone unnoticed by Ottoman administrators.

At this point, Istanbul took a firmer stance on the issue of Egyptian forced labor, with full British support. On 6 April 1863, the Ottoman government addressed a note to the sultan's representatives in Paris and London expressing regret that the "unauthorized works" on the isthmus were still advancing. The note pointed out that the Porte had never approved the plan for the canal in the first place. Moreover, it reported that the Ottoman ruler was particularly vexed by Egypt's reliance on forced labor.[69] The corvée had, in theory, been abolished throughout the Ottoman Empire since the beginning of the reign of Sultan Abdulmaçit I (1839–61) as part of his Tanzimat reforms. In fact, the corvée may be conceived as an in-kind form of taxation.[70] The *Hatt-i Sharif* of Gulhane of 1839 stated that, henceforth, "every subject of the Ottoman society should be taxed a certain tax quota, determined in reason of his fortune and his means, and that nothing besides that should be exacted from that person."[71] And yet, thirty years later, in 1869, Ottoman authorities surreptitiously reinstated the corvée and continued to exploit it for road building and repairs until 1889, when it was replaced with an equivalent tax levied on villages adjacent to the roads.[72] However, back in 1863, the sultan claimed he was in no position to sanction forced labor in the empire's autonomous yet subordinate Egyptian province. The pursuit of "progress and the civilization in the Orient," the grand vizier wrote at the time to the viceroy of Egypt, was incompatible with a system of labor that had been condemned by all "civilized nations," in whose fold he implicitly included their own.[73]

Even if the Company had shown little respect for the sultan's rights as the "territorial sovereign," the 1863 note continued, he was still willing to show goodwill toward the enterprise. The sultan's government, however, demanded that the Company scrap all "inadmissible clauses" and fulfill some "indispensable guarantees." First, the Ottoman government requested that international stipulations declare the complete neutrality of the canal, as in the case of the Dardanelles and the Bosphorus Straights.[74] Second, forced labor ought to cease on the canal worksites. Istanbul could not accept that every month tens of thousands of men were forced to abandon their jobs and return home at their own expense, and often travel great lengths to do so. Approximately sixty thousand were snatched away monthly from agriculture, industry, and commerce: while twenty thousand toiled, forty thousand more were either on their way or preparing to leave, with "disastrous effects." Finally, the Ottoman government stated, Cairo ought to stop ceding lands to the Company. The Porte feared that the Company would take possession of these lands and that Port Said, Timsa-Ismailia, Suez, and the entire border with the Syrian province would fall into the hands of "a joint-stock company mostly composed by foreigners who responded to the jurisdiction and authority of their own respective countries." The Company, the Porte noted, would thus acquire the power "to create, on this important portion of the territory of the Ottoman Empire, colonies that would be almost independent from [said] Empire." No government "with some sense of independence and duty," the note continued, "would subscribe to a transaction of such scale." Finally, the note emphasized that the Egyptian viceroy was nothing but a "high official" who governed under the sovereignty of his sultan and only with his sanction. Could Paris and London seriously expect the Ottoman government, the note rhetorically asked, to let the Company establish itself on its own imperial territory and claim dubious rights issued by its Egyptian underling?[75]

In January 1863, Isma'il succeeded his uncle Sa'id at the head of the Egyptian government upon the latter's death. Unlike his predecessor, Isma'il endorsed Ottoman directives. He did not look favorably on the fact that large tracts of territory had been assigned by the former ruler to the Company. Moreover, he was hostile to the forced labor scheme and favored its demise.[76] By 1863, the still-raging US Civil War had caused a global shortage in cotton. Isma'il may have viewed the Suez Canal excavation sites as outlets that drained the agricultural manpower the country needed to cultivate that highly demanded staple. The labor previously used by the Company was now to be diverted into the cultivation of cotton. Indeed, by the mid-1860s, 40% of all fertile land in Lower Egypt had been converted into cotton farms, and Egyptian rural cultivators had quintupled their cotton production.[77] However, Isma'il did not relinquish the forced-labor scheme for the Suez Canal right away, suggesting at least some ambivalence on the matter on the part of the Egyptian government. In mid-1863, for example, Nubar Pasha, the director of Egypt's foreign affairs, suggested that the viceroy, rather than dismissing the forced laborers altogether, should reduce their numbers to a mere six thousand per month. According to Nubar, this would have allowed the Egyptian government to keep its leverage with the Company.[78]

On 1 August 1863, Istanbul once again restated the principle that "forced labor ought to be abolished and cease as soon as possible."[79] Dispatched to Istanbul in August 1863, Nubar expressed Egypt's commitment to negotiating the abolition of the corvée on the canal (as well as to buying back, at any cost, the land concessions the previous Egyptian ruler had handed out). De Lesseps prepared to react aggressively. He confided that the prospective changes would not cripple the enterprise but was nonetheless prone to sell the land at the most expensive price possible.[80] In early 1864, the Egyptian viceroy gave in to the demand that his differences with the Company be arbitrated by the French emperor, not minding the fact that the latter had proven sympathetic to De Lesseps's grievances before. In July 1864, Napoleon III announced his unsurprisingly one-sided decision. For the annulment of forced labor, the Egyptian government would disburse to the Company an "indemnity" of 38 million francs. For the retrocession of lands, the Egyptian government would pay 30 million francs.[81] Conventions that were agreed upon in January and February 1866 eventually settled the dispute, with the participation of an Ottoman commissioner and two representatives chosen, respectively, by the Egyptian viceroy and De Lesseps.[82] In June 1866, the Egyptian ruler and De Lesseps agreed to scrap both Article 2 of the 1856 concession prescribing that four-fifths of the labor force be composed of Egyptian fellahin and the regulation of 20 July 1856 concerning the employment of fellahin. The Suez Canal Company was to see to the necessary laborers itself "with no privileges and no obstacles." Incidentally, both parties acknowledged that the Company needed space for depots, workshops, vegetable gardens, and houses for the guards, foremen, and those workers charged with maintenance and administration.[83]

The French public considered the sentence unfavorable to the Company.[84] Along similar lines, Italian diplomats dispatched to Egypt praised the Egyptian ruler for liberating a huge portion of land from Company ownership. They also insinuated that the Company was hardly in a prosperous situation.[85] However, the arbitration sentence, by stipulating that the Company—even if it no longer owned the lands along the canal—could now dispose of land along both the maritime waterway and the sweet water canal (10,264 and 9,600 hectares, respectively) for these channels' "establishment, exploitation, and conservation" still deprived Egypt, the "territorial power," of the possibility to determine itself the size of the lands falling under the Company's purview. Simultaneously, the outcome still infringed on the sultan's rights.[86] On the whole, as David S. Landes argues, these transactions ratified a "confiscation masquerading as equity" that may have been even more vexatious and costly than earlier abuses.[87] By the spring of 1864, the average monthly contingent of forced workers had dwindled to twelve or thirteen thousand men. It kept decreasing until May 1864, when the Egyptian government withdrew all contingents. The corvée system on the canal worksites officially came to an end in mid-1864.[88]

MECHANIZATION: THE ONLY FEASIBLE WAY

The suppression of forced labor on the Suez worksites deprived the Company of thousands of cheap laborers and forced a transition to mechanized labor. Before the corvée system came to a halt, Company officials had decried that each simple earthwork laborer (terrassier) would eventually end up costing up to eight francs (equal to eight times what was initially envisioned per worker per day), given the outlays for tools and lodging and the expected travel and repatriation expenses for those coming from abroad.[89] Such momentous alteration in the composition of the workforce prompted the Company to import machines. Contemporaries agreed that mechanization, after the departure of forced workers, was the only feasible way to continue the enterprise.[90] At this point the bucket-chain dredger, increasingly spotted on the worksites, became "the emblematic machine of the piercing of the canal."[91] In reality, though, machines and men got the job done together (Fig. 7.2).

Rather than choosing innovation of his own volition, De Lesseps was forced to think creatively about how he could substitute machines for men.[92] From 1862 to 1864, when the Company could still rely on forced labor, its leadership had maintained an ambiguous balance between its willingness to mechanize and its reliance on manual work. As early as 1862, Company officials began to realize they could not count on indigenous forces in the

Drague et son personnel.

FIG. 7.2 While technology has overshadowed labor in the narrative of the canal excavation, machines and men worked in tandem. "Dredger and its crew," by the Zangaki brothers, 1869–1885. Archives Nationales du Monde du Travail á Roubaix, France (ANMT), Compagnie Universelle du Canal Maritime de Suez (CUCMS), 1995 060 1488 012, Association du Souvenir de Ferdinand de Lesseps et du Canal de Suez.

long run and hypothesized they would have to find mechanical substitutes.[93] In 1863, De Lesseps claimed that the works were nearing the point where it was possible, indeed advisable, to substitute dredges and other devices for handwork. Indeed, even before being pushed to do so in 1864, the Company experimented with ways of replacing workers with machines (Fig. 7.3). For the lifting and transportation of the excavated soil, for example, it had purchased, at great cost, forty-four dredges. For the piercing of the middle isthmus tract at al-Gisr, the Company had finalized a deal with an entrepreneur who committed his own workers and mechanical excavators. And, in order to obtain similar results at the Serapeum worksite, it strove to actively negotiate with other contractors. But even when the reduction of corvée workers was looming, De Lesseps insisted on the Company's right to rely on the stipulated conventions and the guaranteed supply of Egyptian labor to ensure the prompt achievement of the enterprise.[94]

Première drague montée à Port-Saïd et lancée dans le canal du lac Menzaleh.

FIG. 7.3 Even before 1864, the Company experimented with ways of replacing workers with machines. "First dredger assembled in Port Said and launched in the canal of the Menzaleh [*sic*] lake." Marius Etienne Fontane and Edouard Riou. *Le canal maritime de Suez illustré; histoire du canal et des travaux.* Paris: Aux bureaux de l'Illustration A. Marc et Cie., 1869, 48.

The employment of machines on a large scale, while a necessity, was also a seriously onerous operation.[95] The "indemnity" disbursed by Egypt for the end of the corvée on the canal helped pay for the elaborate dredging equipment that the Company brought to the isthmus, without which the canal could not have been completed.[96] In May 1864, when the Egyptian government put an end to forced labor, the Company readied an avalanche of new and costly equipment to dredge the portion of the canal between Lake Manzala and Lake Balla: twenty dredgers that had cost 230,000 francs each, twenty cranes worth 30,000 francs each, and 120 rowboats valued at 6,000 to 8,000 francs each.[97] Adding to the final bill, some of the earthmoving juggernauts were imported from the Netherlands. At least one of the hopper dredgers (*dragues porteuses*) had been purchased from the company Simons & Co. of the Scottish town of Renfrew. Other machines, such as bucket excavators, came from France.[98] The mechanical workshop of Menpenti, a Marseille neighborhood, produced steam-operated cranes, dredging equipment, and a propulsion system for barges (*chaloupes*) it had patented. Notwithstanding their provenance, most machines and materials began their Mediterranean voyage in Marseille, where an agent of the Company named Auguste Saint-Aude oversaw the uploading of freight, and ended it in Port Said.[99]

Yet the Company still had to rely on manual labor alongside mechanization. Firstly, locomotives, barges, and dredgers left Europe as mere components and had to be assembled once they reached Port Said.[100] Secondly, even if machinery did the work of a large number of workers, it sometimes proved to be insufficient or needed repairs. "The subjugation of nature" around the canal banks, as Valeska Huber notes, "did not proceed without accidents."[101] After functioning for just one year, for example, the dredger *La Puissante*, first tested on the Scottish river Clyde, had to stand still for about eight months after its driveshaft was damaged. Following a stint of normal work, extracting and carrying debris into the sea to the east of Port Said from 4:00 a.m. to 6:00 p.m. daily, new problems with the same mechanism arose again and immobilized the behemoth for six more months. It needed a new frame to be recast at the local Company workshops.[102]

But even when the work was proceeding at top speed, sometimes machines could operate only after workers had suitably prepared the ground for them (Fig. 7.4). For dredgers to be operational, for example, laborers had to cut the soil to water level and transport the earth away from the furrow they had traced.[103] By 1863, workers had dug

FIG. 7.4 Workers advanced ahead of machines, at least in some tracts and moments of the canal undertaking. Photograph by Sartre, 1859–69. Musée Nicéphore Niépce, Ville de Chalon-sur-Saône, MNN.1977.74.2.96.

a narrow channel, just big enough to accommodate mechanical dredgers, most of the way across the isthmus. Even later, the maneuvering techniques of the crews operating the dredgers remained important for the correct functioning of the machines.[104] Finally, the earth in the southern part of the isthmus was discovered to be rocky and had to be treated with more traditional methods involving the use of wheelbarrows, baskets, camels, and mule-drawn wagons. These methods were extended southward to the plain near the town of Suez. All in all, the need for workers remained, even as it varied according to the local terrain and circumstances: while the excavation of the canal itself needed men to prepare its embanking, for instance, the basin for repairs in Suez necessitated more machines than men.[105]

In 1864, after the end of the corvée on the isthmus, the need for workers presented practical and moral obstacles to the momentum on the Company's works. Attempts intensified, both locally and internationally, to recruit the scores of laborers that the canal project still needed to reach completion. The Company dispatched emissaries to the Egyptian Delta, Syria, and the Greek archipelagos, but only a few reinforcements were initially mustered.[106] The thousands of Egyptian fellahin who had been connecting locations in Upper and Lower Egypt to the Isthmus of Suez against their will were no longer forcibly carried to the canal worksites. Yet some apparently chose to relocate there. Reportedly, individuals from Upper as well as Lower Egypt found work in the businesses of coal-heaving and transporting goods.[107] Upper Egyptians were dispro-portionately incentivized to settle in the isthmus. In the second half of the nineteenth century, even as sugar cane cultivation was expanding and an extended railway system allowed easier connections, Southern Egypt was still much less economically developed than the more prosperous and populous north, where the Nile Delta had been converted to perennial irrigation and expanded cotton cultivation.[108] In time, foreign workers also began arriving to the isthmus. There were Georgians and Armenians, Syrians and Druze, Algerians and Moroccans. Immigrants hailed to the canal region from different parts of the Italian peninsula. Prospective workers departed from France as well as the Adriatic, Dalmatia, and the Greek archipelagos. The isthmus attracted English and Scottish workers. Irish, German, Polish, Spanish, Maltese, and "Uniate" Greeks simi-larly felt enticed by job prospects on this strip of land. The death of a carpenter originally from the Ticino area attests to the fact that isthmus-bound workers also left that region of Switzerland.[109]

On the canal worksites, the number of workers did not decrease due to the introduc-tion of machines. Rather, insufficient manual labor spurred the use of new technology. Problems with fluctuating numbers of workers had already arisen, as in May 1863.[110] But this time, the definitive withdrawal of forced labor posed a greater set of challenges: recruiting workers, remunerating them, importing machinery, assembling it, repairing it, and making sure hands and tools worked in unison. Officially, Company represent-atives dismissed the transition from primarily manual to mostly mechanical work as a painless one for the enterprise.[111] They also tried to shrug off the issue of international re-cruitment by declaring that the Company had no responsibility for luring those coming from, among other places, Greece, Italy, and Dalmatia looking for work. They claimed the canal had a naturally "strong force of attraction that radiated in a wide circle and exerted a pull over workers from the whole of the Mediterranean basin."[112] Yet they did not approach the new reliance on machinery lightly. Nor did they succeed in automatically solving all the technical issues they faced or attracting all the labor they needed to finalize the undertaking.

Conclusion

In a novel published in 1896, Joseph Conrad wrote that there had been a time "when the French mind set the Egyptian muscle in motion and produced a dismal but profitable ditch." So unceremoniously described, the Suez Canal must have left him unimpressed in his to-ing and fro-ing between England, India, and beyond. Writing at a time when the advent of steamship navigation was disrupting the maritime world, Conrad cried for the lost beauty and mystery of the sea, which he saw as marred by countless steamboats sending out a great pall of smoke and transformed into a "used-up drudge, wrinkled and defaced by the churned-up wakes of brutal propellers."[113] Clearly unenthusiastic about modern-day contraptions, Conrad drew a line in time between pre– and post–Suez Canal. He also set up a contrast between French fine intellect and Egyptian brute force. Finally, he pitted technological ingenuity against human brawn.

However, the story of the canal worksites featured a more complicated plot than a mind-versus-muscle confrontation and revealed a more ambiguous ploy than the one implied by a clash between French and Egyptian interests. The Egyptian government, threatened with what it saw as unwelcome "swarms" of foreign workers, actively weighed the pros and cons of committing Egyptian forced labor to the canal project. Meanwhile, the Ottomans developed a perspective of their own in the canal affair, especially when it came to the exploitation of forced labor, and felt the urge to intervene. The British also came into the picture but were not this history's propellers, as otherwise suggested by the notion that "British pressure on the Ottoman and Egyptian governments forced a technological revolution upon the canal company."[114] Even if Western triumphalist narratives of the cutting of the isthmus eventually left out workers, the latter were neither absent nor antagonistic to engines. In fact, the introduction of machinery rearranged rather than obliterated muscle power and ushered in a sometimes-uneasy synergy between the two.[115]

Disentangling the constantly changing configuration of mechanical and manual work in the Suez Canal project disrupts the idea that technological determinism alone fueled innovation in the Company's halls of power or among its cadres. Company echelons were not simply driven to mechanize the mode of production on the canal worksites by their mere pursuit of economy.[116] On the one hand, they were persuaded to adopt machines once workers, by dint of political decisions, were no longer cheaper than the engines that would replace them. On the other hand, the Company reluctantly took the path of mechanization while still relying on human toil. Acknowledging this ambiguity denaturalizes and historicizes market mechanisms, modes of calculation, and ways of construing human wealth unique to capitalism.[117] In fact, it questions the assumptions of both liberal and Marxist economic theory, according to which free wage labor in capitalist economies unavoidably replaces all forms of indenture. Forced and free labor continued to coexist, depending on evolving power relationships and means of production.[118]

Moreover, fleshing out the reconfiguration of human toil and mechanical work undermines the notion that the Company, in its self-ascribed civilizing mission, bestowed scientific and technological progress to non-Western technologically primitive peoples.[119] Those very same unsavvy people, by withdrawing their previously free labor as per Ottoman and Egyptian political decisions, pushed the Company into a hole, from which it had to climb out on stilts. Ottoman and Egyptian initiatives, then, deflate the notion that the French or the British, directly or indirectly, forced their scientific and technological skill down the throat of Istanbul and Cairo.

In 1864, the stoppage of forced labor converged with state and imperial politics, budgetary concerns on the part of the Company, and technical exigencies due to the stage of the canal works to precipitate a shift toward mechanization on the canal worksites. Reconfigurations of different forms of labor, as well as of manpower and machinery, ought to be conceived as transitions replete with hiccups and glitches. Historians of other contexts have shown that, after having fleshed out the unequal working conditions and disparate legal statuses of different groups of workers, it is analytically more useful to think of various types of labor on a continuum rather than as sharply delineated opposites.[120] Unduly sharp distinctions between machine and human, voluntary and forced labor regimes obfuscate the actual characters involved, prevent us from seeing the legacy of the corvée past its formal temporal benchmarks, and ultimately whitewash the earlier as well as the later history of large infrastructural undertakings such as the Suez Canal.

NOTES

1. 'Ali Mubarak, *al-Khitat al-Tawfiqiyya al-Jadida li-Misr al-Qahira wa-Muduniha wa-Biladiha al-Qadima wa-l-Shahira*, vol. 10 (Cairo: al-Matba'a al-Kubra al-Amiriyya, 1887), 26.

2. Jules Charles-Roux, *L'Isthme et le canal de Suez: historique, état actuel*, vol. 1 (Paris: Hachette, 1901), 442–44; "Firman de concession de S. A. Mohammed-Said, vice-roi d'Égypte," Cairo, 30 November 1854.

3. Originally, the Egyptian government held 44% of shares, small French shareholders controlled 54%, and only 4% was in the hands of shareholders of other countries. In 1875, when Britain took over the Egyptian shares, Egypt lost all control over the Company. Caroline Piquet, "La compagnie du canal de Suez. Une concession française en Égypte (1858–1956)," *Entreprises et histoire* 52, no. 3 (2008): 68. See also Faruk Bilici, *Le canal de Suez et l'Empire ottoman* (Paris: CNRS Editions, 2019), 258.

4. Nubar Nubarian, *Mémoires de Nubar Pacha*, ed. M. B. Ghali (Beirut: Librairie du Liban, 1983), 232. See Nathalie Montel, *Le chantier du Canal de Suez: 1859–1869. Une histoire des pratiques techniques* (Paris: Presses de l'École nationale des ponts et chaussées, 1999), 39; and Barbara Curli, "Dames Employées at the Suez Canal Company: The 'Egyptianization' of Female Office Workers, 1941–56," *International Journal of Middle East Studies* 46, no. 3 (2014): 555.

5. J. Stephen Jeans, *Waterways and Water Transport in Different Countries: With a Description of the Panama, Suez, Manchester, Nicaraguan, and Other Canals* (London: E. & F. N. Spon, 1890), 257, 254.

6. Michael Adas, *Machines as the Measure of Men: Science, Technology, and Ideologies of Western Dominance* (Ithaca, NY: Cornell University Press, 1989), 3.

7. Lucia Carminati, "Suez: A Hollow Canal in Need of Peopling. Currents and Stoppages in the Historiography, 1859–1956," *History Compass* 19, no. 5 (2021): 1–14.

8. Daniel R. Headrick, *The Tools of Empire: Technology and European Imperialism in the Nineteenth Century* (New York: Oxford University Press, 1981), 155.

9. In turn, the male workers employed on the canal worksites have overshadowed women, children, and others who found employment in fields other than the excavation proper. I have addressed their histories elsewhere. See Lucia Carminati, *Seeking Bread and Fortune in Port Said, 1859–1906: Labor Migration and the Making of the Suez Canal* (Oakland, CA: University of California Press, 2023). I am also aware that this chapter's perspective only tells part of the canal story since people, machines, and other nonhuman actors ought to be conceptualized together. See On Barak, "Three Watersheds in the History of Energy," *Comparative Studies of South Asia, Africa and the Middle East* 34, no. 3 (2014): 440–53; and Alan Mikhail, "Unleashing the Beast: Animals, Energy, and the Economy of Labor in Ottoman Egypt," *American Historical Review* 118, no. 2 (2013): 317–48. On the importance of steam, iron, and steel, see Nathalie Montel, *Le chantier du Canal de Suez*, 288. For hints at other crucial materials, such as the vegetable oil needed to lubricate engines or the explosives intended to break the isthmus rock formations, see Fabien Bartolotti, "Le Chantier du siècle. Les entreprises marseillaises et le creusement du canal de Suez (1859–1869)," *Revue Marseille* 260 (2018): 46–48; and Fabien Bartolotti, "Mobilités d'entrepreneurs et circulations des techniques: les chantiers portuaires de Dussaud frères d'un rivage à l'autre (1848–1869)," *Revue d'histoire du XIXe siècle. Société d'histoire de la révolution de 1848 et des révolutions du XIXe siècle* 51 (2015): 171–85. The history of animal power on the canal worksites remains to be written.

10. Mubarak, *al-Khitat al-Tawfiqiyya*, vol. 10, 26–29. Mubarak must have visited the Isthmus of Suez in person at least a few times. See Zayn al-ʿAbidin Shams al-Din Najm, *Bur Saʿid: Tarikhuha wa-Tatawwuruha, mundhu Nashʾatiha 1859 hatta ʿAmm 1882* (Cairo: al-Hayʾa al-Misriyya al-ʿAmma li-l-Kitab, 1987), 142–43, 265, 281, 416. On ʿAli Mubarak as the expression of concerns of his age with Egypt's urban space, see Timothy Mitchell, *Colonising Egypt* (Berkeley: University of California Press, 1988), 63.

11. Valeska Huber, *Channelling Mobilities. Migration and Globalisation in the Suez Canal Region and Beyond, 1869–1914* (Cambridge: Cambridge University Press, 2013), 46, 111. Fascination with technology on the sites continues to inform contemporary accounts. See, e.g., Sylvia Modelski, *Port Said Revisited* (Washington, DC: FAROS, 2000), 28.

12. Jeans, *Waterways and Water Transport in Different Countries*, 250.

13. Hélène Braeuner, "À la frontière de l'Égypte. Les représentations du canal de Suez," *In Situ. Revue des patrimoines* 38 (2019): 1–14; L. A. Balboni, *Gl'Italiani nella civiltà egiziana del*

secolo XIX; storia-biografie-monografie, vol. 2 (Alexandria: Tipo-litografico v. Penasson, 1906), 141.

14. Richard Allen, *Letters from Egypt, Syria, and Greece* (Dublin: Gunn & Cameron, 1869), 26.

15. Mohamed Gamal-Eldin, "Photography and the Politics of Erasure: A Case Study of the Suez and Ismailia Canals Construction and the Silencing of the Egyptian Laborer" (paper presented at the Annual History Seminar, Department of Arabic and Islamic Civilizations, American University in Cairo, 30–31 March 2018).

16. Dar al-Watha'iq al-Qawmiyya, National Archives, Cairo (DWQ), Qanat al-Suways, Suez Canal (QS), 5009-000219, Invitation to the King of Prussia, n.d.; QS, 5009-000219, Thank you letter, n.d. and no signature.

17. Hubert Bonin, *History of the Suez Canal Company, 1858–1960: Between Controversy and Utility* (Geneva: Droz, 2010), 59.

18. Lucia Carminati, "Port Said and Ismailia as Desert Marvels: Delusion and Frustration on the Isthmus of Suez, 1859–1869," *Journal of Urban History* 46, no. 3 (2019): 622–47. On water management in Port Said and Ismailia, see Mohamed Gamal-Eldin, "Cesspools, Mosquitoes and Fever: An Environmental History of Malaria Prevention in Ismailia and Port Said, 1869–1910," in *Seeds of Power: Explorations in Ottoman Environmental History*, ed. Onur İnal and Yavuz Köse (Winwick, Cambridgeshire: White Horse Press, 2019), 184–207.

19. I am borrowing this idea from Michael J. Reimer, "Urban Regulation and Planning Agencies in Mid-Nineteenth Century Alexandria and Istanbul (with Documentary Appendix)," *Turkish Studies Association Bulletin* 19, no. 1 (1995): 1–2.

20. Bernard Simiot, *Suez: 50 siècles d'histoire* (Paris: Arthaud, 1974), 10.

21. Elliott Colla, *Conflicted Antiquities: Egyptology, Egyptomania, Egyptian Modernity* (Durham, NC: Duke University Press, 2008), 33.

22. Ronald Storrs, *The Memoirs of Sir Ronald Storrs* (New York: G. P. Putnam's Sons, 1937), 223. The entry is dated 26 April 1917.

23. Casimir Leconte, *Promenade dans l'isthme de Suez* (Paris: N. Chaix, 1864), 113; Archivio Storico Diplomatico del Ministero Affari Esteri, Rome (ASDMAE), Archivi Rappresentanze Diplomatiche e Consolari all'Estero (ARDCE), Consolato Cairo (CC), Busta (B) 12, Corrispondenza 1869, Suez, 7 July 1869, Italian Vice-Consul to Italian Consul in Cairo; Zachary Karabell, *Parting the Desert: The Creation of the Suez Canal* (New York: A. A. Knopf, 2003), 241; Ferdinand de Lesseps, *Lettres, journal et documents pour servir à l'histoire du canal de Suez*, vol. 5 (Paris: Didier et cie, 1875), 278; De Lesseps to *The Times* editor, 30 October 1855; D. A. Farnie, *East and West of Suez: The Suez Canal in History, 1854–1956* (Oxford: Clarendon Press, 1969), 43–44.

24. Charles-Roux, *L'Isthme et le Canal de Suez*, vol. 1, 447–52, "Acte de concession et cahier des charges pour la construction et l'exploitation du Canal maritime de Suez et dépendance," Alexandria, 5 January 1856.

25. Olivier Ritt, *Histoire de l'isthme de Suez* (Paris: L. Hachette et cie, 1869), 284–85.

26. Nubarian, *Mémoires de Nubar Pacha*, 226.

27. Ferdinand de Lesseps, *Lettres, journal et documents*, vol. 4, 355. The entry is dated 29 October 1863. Italics are mine.

28. The National Archives, London, Kew (TNA), Foreign Office (FO) 423-1, Constantinople, 27 June 1863, Sir H. Bulwer, to Earl Russell, 210; Nubarian, *Mémoires de Nubar Pacha*, 222, 224.

29. De Lesseps, *Lettres, journal et documents*, 1875, vol. 4, 355, entry dated 29 October 1863; Ritt, *Histoire de l'isthme de Suez*, 284–85; P. Dubois, "Le *Constitutionnel* et l'Égypte," *L'isthme de Suez. Journal de l'union des deux mers*, 10 May 1858, 229.

30. Charles-Roux, *L'Isthme et le Canal de Suez*, vol. 1, 469–70, "Décret et règlement pour les ouvriers fellahs," Alexandria, 20 July 1856.

31. Lucie Duff Gordon, *Letters from Egypt* (New York: McClure, Phillips & Co., 1902), 243, 257. See Kenneth M. Cuno, *The Pasha's Peasants: Land, Society, and Economy in Lower Egypt, 1740–1858* (Cambridge: Cambridge University Press, 1992), 122.

32. Ehud R. Toledano, *State and Society in Mid-Nineteenth-Century Egypt* (Cambridge: Cambridge University Press, 1990), 189.

33. Jules Charles-Roux, *L'Isthme et le canal de Suez: historique, état actuel*, vol. 1 (Paris: Hachette, 1901), 469.

34. Nubarian, *Mémoires de Nubar Pacha*, 227, 230, 232, 236.

35. Toledano, *State and Society*, 188; Charles Philip Issawi, *An Economic History of the Middle East and North Africa* (New York: Columbia University Press, 1982), 104.

36. Roger Owen, *The Middle East in the World Economy, 1800–1914* (London: I. B. Tauris, 2009), 143.

37. On Barak, *Powering Empire: How Coal Made the Middle East and Sparked Global Carbonization* (Oakland: University of California Press, 2020), 38; Alan Mikhail, *Nature and Empire in Ottoman Egypt: An Environmental History* (Cambridge: Cambridge University Press, 2011), 281–82.

38. Dubois, "Le *Constitutionnel* et l'Égypte," 229.

39. Khaled Fahmy, *All the Pasha's Men: Mehmed Ali, His Army, and the Making of Modern Egypt* (Cairo: American University in Cairo Press, 2002), 10.

40. Mikhail, *Nature and Empire in Ottoman Egypt*, 289. On forced labor on the Mahmudiyya Canal, see Mikhail, "Unleashing the Beast," 346; Fahmy, *All the Pasha's Men*, 10; Kenneth M. Cuno, *The Pasha's Peasants: Land, Society, and Economy in Lower Egypt, 1740–1858* (Cambridge: Cambridge University Press, 1992), 121–22; Robert L. Tignor, *Modernization and British Colonial Rule in Egypt, 1882–1914* (Princeton, NJ: Princeton University Press, 1966), 121–22; and Helen Anne B. Rivlin, *The Agricultural Policy of Muhammad 'Ali in Egypt* (Cambridge, MA: Harvard University Press, 1961), 216–21.

41. Istituto per l'Oriente Carlo Nallino, Rome, Italy (IPOCAN), Busta (B) 1956–1961, Letter of the Grand Vizier to the Viceroy of Egypt, 21 Safer 1276/19 September 1859; TNA, FO 423-1, Alexandria, 6 October 1859, Colquhoun, to Sir H. Bulwer.

42. Ordinance to the head of the Khedivial Da'ira, 11 Sha'ban 1275/16 March 1859; Ordinance to Ja'far Pasha, governor of Damietta, 21 Dhu al-Hijja 1275/22 July 1859, in Amin Sami, *Taqwim al-Nil*, vol. 3, part 1 (Cairo: al-Matba'a al-Amiriyya, 1916), 317, 329.

43. Najm, *Bur Sa'id*, 22; IPOCAN, B1956-1961, Vienna, 21 July 1859, Ministry of Foreign Affairs, to Ministry of Commerce. See Faruk Bilici, *Le canal de Suez et l'Empire ottoman* (Paris: CNRS Éditions, 2019), 94–95.

44. IPOCAN, Bundle "1956 al 1961," Folder 1859, Paris, 23 October 1859, Secretary General P. Merruare, Note presented to the Emperor by the delegation of the Board of Directors of the Suez Canal Company. See Charles-Roux, *L'Isthme et le Canal de Suez*, vol. 1, 450, "Acte de concession et cahier des charges pour la construction et l'exploitation du Canal maritime de Suez et dépendance," Alexandria, 5 January 1856.

45. Jeans, *Waterways and Water Transport in Different Countries*, 264–65.

46. For reliance on forced labor by the Peninsular and Oriental Company, see Lesseps, *Lettres, journal et documents*, vol. 4, 207, 218, 230; and Charles W. Hallberg, *The Suez Canal: Its History and Diplomatic Importance* (New York: Columbia University Press; King & Son, 1931), 201. On forced labor for the railway, see Helen Anne B. Rivlin, "The Railway Question in the Ottoman-Egyptian Crisis of 1850–1852," *Middle East Journal* 15, no. 4 (1961): 375–76, 384; David S. Landes, *Bankers and Pashas: International Finance and Economic Imperialism in Egypt* (London: Heinemann, 1958), 180; Ettore Anchieri, *Il Canale di Suez* (Milano: Libreria Lombarda, 1937), 95; and William F. V. Fitzgerald, *The Suez Canal, the Eastern Question, and Abyssinia* (London: Spottiswoode and Co., 1867), 54.

47. TNA, FO 423-1, Alexandria, 24 January 1863, (no. 142), Colquhoun, to Earl Russell; "The Death of Said Pasha," *The Times*, 20 January 1863, 8; IPOCAN, Bundle "1956 al 1961," Folder 1860, Vienna, Ministero Affari Esteri, Canale di Suez, 3 July 1860. On British ambiguities and the later inter-imperial rivalries between Britain and France on the issue of forced labor in Egypt, see Aaron Jakes, *Egypt's Occupation: Colonial Economism and the Crises of Capitalism* (Stanford, CA: Stanford University Press, 2020), 50–52.

48. IPOCAN, Bundle "1956 al 1961," Folder 1859, Paris, 23 October 1859, Secretary General P. Merruare, Note presentee a l'Empereur par la deputation du Conseil d'Administration du Canal de Suez.

49. Ernest Desplaces, "Le Travail Anglais et le Travail Égyptien," *L'isthme de Suez*, 1 August 1861, 264; J. Mane Y. Flaquer, "Presse étrangère," *L'isthme de Suez*, 1 June 1863, 204.

50. Archives Nationales du Monde du Travail à Roubaix, France (ANMT), Compagnie Universelle du Canal Maritime de Suez (CUCMS), 1995 060 1323, n.d., Excerpts of the Reports of the Director General.

51. De Lesseps, *Lettres, journal et documents*, vol. 4, 18, El Guisr, 8 February 1861, to Ruyssenaers, Agent Superior in Alexandria; ibid., 14–15, Cairo, 23 January 1861, to M. Nicolas Portalis, Company Agent in Beirut; Montel, *Le chantier du Canal de Suez*, 1999, 40.

52. TNA, FO 423-1, Alexandria, 17 May 1861, Colquhoun, to Lord J. Russell. Arthur Mangin, "Percement de l'isthme de Suez," *Journal des économistes. Revue scientifique et industrielle* 3, no. 1 (1866): 449. See Najm, *Bur Sa'id*, 56; and Mas'ud Dahir, *Hijrat al-Shawam. Al-Hijra al-Lubnaniyya ila Misr* (Cairo: Dar al-Shuruq, 2009), 104–5.

53. Mangin, "Percement de l'isthme de Suez," 449; Montel, *Le chantier du Canal de Suez*, 40–41.

54. TNA, FO 423-1, Alexandria, 26 April 1860, Robert G. Colquhoun, to Lord J. Russell, Report by J. Coulthard.

55. De Lesseps, *Lettres, journal et documents*, vol. 3, 398. Entry is dated 11 November 1860; ANMT, CUCMS, 1995 060 1323, n.d., Excerpts of the Reports of the Director General.

56. Nubarian, *Mémoires de Nubar Pacha*, 227; TNA, FO 423-1, Constantinople, 27 June 1863, Sir H. Bulwer, to Earl Russell, 210.

57. "On 21 Ramadan 1275 h. corresponding to 25 April 1859," in Sami, *Taqwim al-Nil*, vol. 3, part 1, 326.

58. De Lesseps, *Lettres, journal et documents*, vol. 4, 12. Entry is dated 23 January 1861.

59. ANMT, CUCMS, 1995 060 1323, n.d., Excerpts of the Reports of the Director General. See Montel, *Le chantier du Canal de Suez*, 42.

60. "The Canal across Egypt," *The Times*, 6 June 1861, 10.

61. ANMT, CUCMS, 1995 060 1323, n.d., Excerpts of the Reports of the Director General.

62. Montel, *Le chantier du Canal de Suez*, 42; Bonin, *History of the Suez Canal Company*, 68.

63. ANMT, CUCMS, 1995 060 1323, n.d., Excerpts of the Reports of the Director General; 1995 060 4136, Toussoum, Ismail Hamdy, 12 May 1863, to Sciama, Engineer-in-chief; IPOCAN,

B1956-1961, Alexandria, 10 April 1862, Consul General Schreiner, to Count Rechberg; TNA, FO 423-1, Alexandria, 1 April 1862, Colquhoun, to Lord J. Russell; Nubarian, *Mémoires de Nubar Pacha*, 227.

64. E. Sallior, *La vérité sur l'Isthme de Suez, lettre à messieurs les actionnaires de la société anonyme du percement de l'Isthme de Suez* (Paris: E. Dentu, 1864), 56–57.

65. Nubarian, *Mémoires de Nubar Pacha*, 227. Another source corroborates that there were twenty thousand indigenous workers on average. Leonardo Gallo Da Calatafimi, *L'Egitto antico e moderno* (Catania, Italy: Tip. Di Eugenio Coco, 1891), 170.

66. Mikhail, "Unleashing the Beast," 345; Owen, *The Middle East in the World Economy*, 143. For a more detailed discussion of workers' living conditions and actions on the worksites, see Carminati, *Seeking Bread and Fortune in Port Said*.

67. De Lesseps, *Lettres, journal et documents*, vol. 4, 236, Paris, 23 May 1862, to Layard, under-secretary of the state at the Foreign Office, London.

68. ANMT, CUCMS, 1995 060 1323, n.d., Excerpts of the Reports of the Director General.

69. DWQ, QS, 5009-000208, 6 April 1863, Ali Pacha, to representatives of the sultan in Paris and London (copy of Annex to no. 534-1863 of the Ministry of Commerce from the "Alte Akten des Handelsministeriums Suezkanal 1860–1875").

70. Owen, *The Middle East in the World Economy*, 143.

71. "Hatt-i Sharif of Gulhane," 3 November 1839, in *Manuale di diritto pubblico e privato ottomano*, ed. Domenico Gatteschi, Castelnuovo, and Leoncavallo (Alexandria: Minasi, 1865), 253.

72. Stanford J. Shaw and Ezel Kural Shaw, *History of the Ottoman Empire and Modern Turkey*, vol. 2, *Reform, Revolution, and Republic: The Rise of Modern Turkey, 1808–1975* (Cambridge: Cambridge University Press, 1976), 101, 227.

73. TNA, FO 423-1, London, 10 February 1863, Earl Russell, to Colquhoun; DWQ, QS, 5009-000208, Shawwal 1279 / March–April 1863, Grand Vizier, to Viceroy of Egypt.

74. The fact that all foreign warships were barred from entering the "Constantinople canal, the Dardanelles, and the Black sea inlet" was "an ancient rule" of the Ottoman Empire, sanctioned in the Ottoman-British peace treaty of Kala-I Sultaniye signed on 5 January 1809. Thereby, this principle became part of international law. In the London agreement of 12 July 1840 (aimed to obtain the Egyptian withdrawal from Syria), others besides the British and the Ottomans (Russians, Austrians, Prussians) also accepted that the straits would be closed to warships in war as in peace. See Gatteschi, Castelnuovo, and Leoncavallo, *Manuale di diritto pubblico e privato ottomano*, 114; and Shaw and Shaw, *History of the Ottoman Empire and Modern Turkey*, 13, 57.

75. DWQ, QS, 5009-000208, Shawwal 1279 / March–April 1863, Grand Vizier, to Viceroy of Egypt; QS, 5009-000208, 6 April 1863, 'Ali Pasha, to representatives of the sultan in Paris and London (copy of Annex to no. 534-1863 of the Ministry of Commerce from the "Alte Akten des Handelsministeriums Suezkanal 1860–1875").

76. Percy Fitzgerald, *The Great Canal at Suez, Its Political, Engineering, and Financial History: With an Account of the Struggles of Its Projector, Ferdinand de Lesseps*, vol. 2 (New York: AMS Press, 1978), 2; TNA, FO 423-1, Alexandria, 24 January 1863 (No. 134), Colquhoun, to Earl Russell.

77. Sven Beckert, *Empire of Cotton: A Global History* (New York: Knopf, 2015), 256; Robert L. Tignor, *Egypt: A Short History* (Princeton, NJ: Princeton University Press, 2010), 229; Shaw and Shaw, *History of the Ottoman Empire and Modern Turkey*, 144–45; Roger Owen, *Cotton and the Egyptian Economy, 1820–1914: A Study in Trade and Development*

(Oxford: Clarendon Press, 1969), 89–121. For a different reading of conventional narratives about the long-term continuities of Egypt's cotton economy, see Jakes, *Egypt's Occupation*, 7–8.

78. TNA, FO 423-1, Constantinople, 27 June 1863, Sir H. Bulwer, to Earl Russell; F. Robert Hunter, "Egypt under the Successors of Muhammad Ali," in *The Cambridge History of Egypt*, ed. M. W. Daly, vol. 2, *Modern Egypt from 1517 to the End of the Twentieth Century* (Cambridge: Cambridge University Press, 1998), 193.

79. François-Philippe Voisin, *Le canal de Suez I*, vol. 1 (Paris: Vve C. Dunod, 1902), 208.

80. DWQ, QS, 5009-000207, no place, n.d., no author; Landes, *Bankers and Pashas*, 184.

81. Nubarian, *Mémoires de Nubar Pacha*, 235; Hallberg, *The Suez Canal: Its History and Diplomatic Importance*, 203–7; Voisin, *Le canal de Suez I*, vol. 1, 232. Nubarian argues that the Company, in turn, was supposed to allocate the sum of 4.5 million francs to the Egyptian government for the fellahin's arrears, thus acknowledging that workers had not been regularly paid. However, I could not find other sources corroborating his claim. Nubarian, *Mémoires de Nubar Pacha*, 238, 240.

82. IPOCAN, Bundle 1866–1868, Cairo, 26 January 1866, Consolato d'Italia in Cairo, L. Macciò, to Italian Ministry of Foreign Affairs, Florence; Nubarian, *Mémoires de Nubar Pacha*, 241.

83. DWQ, Watha'iq 'Abdin, 0069-004751, Alexandria, 13 June 1866, Cachet du Ministre Affaires Étrangères, signed by Secretary Gaudard.

84. Nubarian, *Mémoires de Nubar Pacha*, 239.

85. IPOCAN, B1866–1868, Cairo, 26 January 1866, Macciò, Italian Consul, to Italian Ministry of Foreign Affairs.

86. Nubarian, *Mémoires de Nubar Pacha*, 238; Charles-Roux, *L' Isthme et le Canal de Suez*, vol. 1, 487, Fontainebleu, 6 July 1864, "Sentence arbitrale de l'Empereur Napoléon III."

87. Landes, *Bankers and Pashas*, 224. In 1865, Company sources still declared that "the Ouady," a tract of land that was not situated on the isthmus itself but was necessary to the establishment of the sweet-water canal, was "a vast property *belonging to the Company*." Doctor Aubert-Roche, "Rapport," *L'isthme de Suez*, 15–18 July 1865, 215. Emphasis added.

88. ANMT, CUCMS, 1995 060 1323, n.d., Excerpts of the Reports of the Director General. A decree in January 1892 formally suppressed the corvée in the whole country, DWQ, DA'U, 4003-030758, "Decret du 28 Janvier 1892." However, this decree did not actually eliminate labor conscription and the Anglo-Egyptian government's reliance on it. Nathan J. Brown, "Who Abolished Corvée Labour in Egypt and Why?," *Past & Present* 144 (1994): 116–37; Jakes, *Egypt's Occupation*, 51.

89. Nubarian, *Mémoires de Nubar Pacha*, 227, 232; ANMT, CUCMS, 1995 060 4136, Direction générale des travaux, "Évaluation du prejudice qu'éprouverait si le Gouvernement Égyptien cessait d'intervenir dans le recruitement des ouvriers pour la construction du Canal maritime de Suez," n.d.

90. M. A. Lavalley, *Extrait du compte rendu des travaux de la Société des Ingénieurs Civils: séances des 7 et 21 Septembre 1866* (Paris: Imprimerie Bourdier et cie., 1866), 1, 9; Nubarian, *Mémoires de Nubar Pacha*, 239.

91. Caroline Piquet, *Histoire du canal de Suez* (Paris: Perrin, 2009), 54.

92. George Edgar Bonnet, *Ferdinand de Lesseps* (Paris: Plon, 1951), 395.

93. IPOCAN, 1861, Vienna, Ministero Affari Esteri, Canale di Suez 1861–1862, Archivio Politico Alessandria, Fasc. XXXVII/130, Report of Consul General Schreiner to Count Rechberg, Alexandria, 10 April 1862.

94. De Lesseps, *Lettres, journal et documents*, vol. 4, 355–56, Séance extraordinaire du Conseil d'Administration de la Compagnie du Canal Maritime de Suez du 29 Octobre 1863.

95. ANMT, CUCMS, 1995 060 4136, Direction générale des travaux, "Evaluation du prejudice qu'éprouverait . . .," n.d. See Mohamed Sabry, *L'Empire égyptien sous Ismaïl et l'ingérence anglo-française 1863–1879* (Paris: Geuthner, 1933), 283.

96. Bartolotti, "Le Chantier du siècle," 47; Tignor, *Egypt: A Short History*, 229; Modelski, *Port Said Revisited*, 27.

97. Ernest Desplaces, "Chronique de l'Isthme," *L'isthme de Suez*, 1 May 1864, 221.

98. Modelski, *Port Said Revisited*, 28; ANMT, CUCMS, 1995 060 0089, Procès-verbaux des séances, Commission consultative internationale des travaux, Réunion de la commission des 20 et 21 Octobre 1899, 79; Céline Frémaux, "Town Planning, Architecture, and Migrations in Suez Canal Port Cities," in *Port Cities: Dynamic Landscapes and Global Networks*, ed. Carola Hein (New York: Routledge, 2011), 161.

99. Bartolotti, "Le Chantier du siècle," 47; Desplaces, "Chronique de l'Isthme," 221.

100. Ritt, *Histoire de l'isthme de Suez*, 259; TNA, FO 423-1, Alexandria, 26 April 1860, Robert G. Colquhoun, to Lord J. Russell.

101. Frémaux, "Town Planning," 161; Huber, *Channelling Mobilities*, 111.

102. ANMT, CUCMS, 1995 060 0089, Procès-verbaux des séances, Commission consultative internationale des travaux, Réunion de la commission des 29 et 30 October 1900, 84; ANMT, CUCMS, 1995 060 0090, Procès-verbaux des séances, Commission consultative internationale des travaux, Réunion de la commission des 4 et 5 Novembre 1902, 67–68.

103. TNA, FO 423-1, Alexandria, 11 March 1864, Rev. E. J. Davis, Chaplain in Alexandria, to Mr. Layard.

104. Headrick, *The Tools of Empire*, 154; ANMT, CUCMS, 1995 060 0089, Procès-verbaux des séances, Commission consultative internationale des travaux, Réunion de la commission des 29 et 30 October 1900, 84.

105. Montel, *Le chantier du Canal de Suez*, 1999, 287; ANMT, CUCMS, 1995 060 4136, Direction general des travaux, "Évaluation du prejudice qu'éprouverait . . .," n.d.

106. Ritt, *Histoire de l'isthme de Suez*, 288; Mangin, "Percement de l'isthme de Suez," 449.

107. "Conférence de M. Borel," *L'isthme de Suez*, 15–18 February 1867, 63; Gaston Jondet, *Le port de Suez* (Cairo: Institut Français d'Archéologie Orientale, 1919), 88; Najm, *Bur Sa'id*, 58.

108. Joel Beinin and Zachary Lockman, *Workers on the Nile: Nationalism, Communism, Islam, and the Egyptian Working Class, 1882–1954* (Princeton, NJ: Princeton University Press, 1987), 26; Landes, *Bankers and Pashas*, 88.

109. *L'isthme de Suez*, 15–19 July 1867, Aubert-Roche, "Rapport," 227; ibid., 15 November 1868, Correspondent, "La Marche des Travaux dans l'Isthme," 389; ibid., 15–18 February 1867, "Conférence de M. Borel . . .," 63; Ritt, *Histoire de l'isthme de Suez*, 318; *L'isthme de Suez*, 15–18 February 1867, "Conférence de M. Borel . . .," 63; ASDMAE, ARDCE, CC, AV, B18, 1864-1866, Suez, 4 May 1866, the Italian Vice-Consul in Suez to the Consul in Cairo; Robert Franz Foerster, *The Italian Emigration of Our Times* (Cambridge, MA: Harvard University Press, 1919), 212; *L'isthme de Suez*, 15 November 1865, "Conférence de M. Ferdinand de Lesseps à Lyon," 381; ibid., 1 May 1864, Daniel A. Lange, "Chronique de l'Isthme," 222; APF, Fondo S. C., Egitto, Copti, Vol. 21, Gerusalemme S. Salvatore, 15

febbraio 1877, da Fr. Gaudenzio, Custode di Terra Santa a F. Bernardino da Portogruaro Ministro Generale Ordine Frati Minori, Roma, 1197v. For a reference to an unspecified "part" of Germany as a workers' departure point, see Ritt, *Histoire de l'isthme de Suez*, 318. On Spanish workers, see Centre des Archives Diplomatiques de Nantes (CADN), Archives Rapatriés de l'Agence Consulaire de Ismaïlia (ARI), Carton (C) 1, El Ferdane, 14 December 1861, Riche, Sanson, Guiter, Inquiry. CADN, ARI, C26, Lugano per Arazio, Cantone Ticino, Switzerland, 6 February 1866, Francesco Lucchini, to the Police Commissioner in Ismailia.

110. Jondet, *Le port de Suez*, 87.
111. "Société des Ingénieurs Civils, procès-verbaux de la séance du 7 Octobre 1864," *L'isthme de Suez*, 1 November 1864, 444–45; Landes, *Bankers and Pashas*, 180; Halford Lancaster Hoskins, *British Routes to India* (New York: Octagon Books, 1966), 365.
112. Huber, *Channelling Mobilities*, 114.
113. Joseph Conrad, *An Outcast of the Islands* (New York: D. Appleton & Co., 1896), 10; Maya Jasanoff, *The Dawn Watch: Joseph Conrad in a Global World* (London: William Collins, 2018), 95–96.
114. Headrick, *The Tools of Empire*, 154.
115. I am here indebted to Barak, "Three Watersheds in the History of Energy," 444, 451; and Barak, *Powering Empire*, 84.
116. Montel, *Le chantier du Canal de Suez*, 287.
117. Aaron Jakes, "Review Article: A New Materialism? Globalization and Technology in the Age of Empire," *International Journal of Middle East Studies* 47, no. 2 (2015): 378.
118. Dirk Hoerder, *Cultures in Contact: World Migrations in the Second Millennium* (Durham: Duke University Press, 2002), 12.
119. On the implications of Western perceptions of technological superiority, see Adas, *Machines as the Measure of Men*, 339–40.
120. John Donoghue and Evelyn P. Jennings, *Building the Atlantic Empires: Unfree Labor and Imperial States in the Political Economy of Capitalism, ca. 1500–1914* (Leiden: Brill, 2016), 2, 7; Sidney Chalhoub, "The Politics of Ambiguity: Conditional Manumission, Labor Contracts, and Slave Emancipation in Brazil (1850s–1888)," *International Review of Social History* 60, no. 2 (2015): 161–65; Marcel van der Linden, "The Promise and Challenges of Global Labor History," *International Labor and Working-Class History* 82 (2012): 64; Robert J. Steinfeld, *Coercion, Contract, and Free Labor in the Nineteenth Century* (Cambridge: Cambridge University Press, 2001); Tom Brass and Marcel van der Linden, eds., *Free and Unfree Labour: The Debate Continues* (Bern: Peter Lang, 1997).

BIBLIOGRAPHY

Adas, Michael. *Machines as the Measure of Men: Science, Technology, and Ideologies of Western Dominance*. Ithaca, NY: Cornell University Press, 1989.

Barak, On. *Powering Empire: How Coal Made the Middle East and Sparked Global Carbonization*. Oakland: University of California Press, 2020.

Beinin, Joel, and Zachary Lockman. *Workers on the Nile: Nationalism, Communism, Islam, and the Egyptian Working Class, 1882–1954*. Princeton, NJ: Princeton University Press, 1987.

Bilici, Faruk. *Le canal de Suez et l'Empire ottoman*. Paris: CNRS Editions, 2019.

Carminati, Lucia. "Port Said and Ismailia as Desert Marvels: Delusion and Frustration on the Isthmus of Suez, 1859–1869." *Journal of Urban History* 46, no. 3 (2019): 622–47.

Carminati, Lucia. "Suez: A Hollow Canal in Need of Peopling. Currents and Stoppages in the Historiography, 1859–1956." *History Compass* 19, no. 5 (2021): 1–14.

Curli, Barbara. "Dames Employées at the Suez Canal Company: The 'Egyptianization' of Female Office Workers, 1941–56." *International Journal of Middle East Studies* 46, no. 3 (2014): 553–76.

Farnie, D. A. *East and West of Suez: The Suez Canal in History, 1854–1956*. Oxford: Clarendon Press, 1969.

Frémaux, Céline. "Town Planning, Architecture, and Migrations in Suez Canal Port Cities." In *Port Cities: Dynamic Landscapes and Global Networks*, edited by Carola Hein, 156–73. New York: Routledge, 2011.

Gamal-Eldin, Mohamed. "Cesspools, Mosquitoes and Fever: An Environmental History of Malaria Prevention in Ismailia and Port Said, 1869–1910." In *Seeds of Power: Explorations in Ottoman Environmental History*, edited by Onur İnal and Yavuz Köse, 184–207. Winwick, Cambridgeshire: White Horse Press, 2019.

Headrick, Daniel R. *The Tools of Empire: Technology and European Imperialism in the Nineteenth Century*. New York: Oxford University Press, 1981.

Huber, Valeska. *Channelling Mobilities. Migration and Globalisation in the Suez Canal Region and Beyond, 1869–1914*. Cambridge: Cambridge University Press, 2013.

Landes, David S. *Bankers and Pashas: International Finance and Economic Imperialism in Egypt*. London: Heinemann, 1958.

Mikhail, Alan. *Nature and Empire in Ottoman Egypt: An Environmental History*. Cambridge: Cambridge University Press, 2011.

Mitchell, Timothy. *Colonising Egypt*. Berkeley: University of California Press, 1988.

Montel, Nathalie. *Le chantier du Canal de Suez: 1859–1869: Une histoire des pratiques techniques*. Paris: Presses de l'École nationale des ponts et chaussées, 1999.

Mubarak, 'Ali. *Al-Khitat al-Tawfiqiyya al-Jadida li-Misr al-Qahira wa-Muduniha wa-Biladiha al-Qadima wa-l-Shahira*. Vol. 10. Cairo: al-Matba'a al-Kubra al-Amiriyya, 1887.

Piaton, Claudine. *L'Isthme et l'Égypte au temps de la compagnie universelle du canal maritime de Suez (1858–1956)*. Paris: IFAO du Caire, 2016.

Piquet, Caroline. *Le Canal de Suez, une voie maritime pour l'Égypte et le monde*. Paris: Erick Bonnier Editions, 2018.

Shinnawi, 'Abd al-'Aziz Muhammad. *Al-Sukhrah fi Hafr Qanat al-Suways*. Alexandria: Munsha'at al-Ma'rifa al-Haditha, 1958.

CHAPTER 8

RETHINKING THE GREEKS OF EGYPT

Individuals and Community

ANTHONY GORMAN

THE Greeks stand out as one of Egypt's most significant resident ethnic communities in the modern period. Along with others, such as the Armenians, Syrians, Maltese, and Italians, they emerged as a distinctive feature of multicultural Egyptian society and a common element across much of the Eastern Mediterranean in the nineteenth and twentieth centuries. The nature of this Greek presence continues to attract the attention of scholars, even if for different reasons. For some, the Greeks of Egypt are perceived as emblematic of a cosmopolitan milieu or an expression of a superior level of Hellenic culture. For others, they were beneficiaries, if not accomplices, of the colonial order founded with the British occupation of 1882. Larger and more diverse than the other ethnic communities, the Greeks of Egypt nevertheless have ultimately been regarded as a unity, whether a colony, a community, or another type of collective. However, the complex character of the Egyptian Greek population suggests that rather than seeking to reduce it to a single discrete community, an analysis of individual profiles might offer an alternative, complementary and more organic perspective. This suggestion is borne out by case studies of three Egyptian Greeks—Apostolos Skouphopoulos, medical doctor, labor leader, and littérateur in Port Said; Giorgis Dimou, artist, writer, and political activist in Cairo; and Semele Tsotsou, feminist and founding director of a school for the deaf in Alexandria—each of which illustrates an interactive engagement across Egyptian society well beyond the confines of the Greek community.[1]

HISTORICAL BACKGROUND

The modern presence of Greeks in Egypt was principally the result of the open migration policy operated during the nineteenth century by Muhammad 'Ali and his successors that encouraged those looking for economic opportunity or political haven to settle in the country. From a few thousand at the beginning of the nineteenth century, numbers grew steadily into the twentieth century, officially peaking near the end of the 1920s, when just over ninety thousand ethnic Greeks were recorded as living in Egypt.[2] By this time, they had assumed a prominent role in many aspects of Egyptian life in a way that exemplified the pluralist character of Egyptian society as well as the political, economic, and social transformation that it was undergoing.

Most Egyptian Greeks lived in urban areas, notably in Alexandria and Cairo as well as on the Suez Canal, but significant numbers populated Delta cities, such as Mansoura and Kafr al-Zayat, and smaller towns in Upper Egypt. In many of these places, Greeks established an institutional communal body, the *Kinotita* (community, plural *Kinotites*), generally financed and managed by its wealthier members, to serve as a center of community life, often supporting a school, church, and various social organizations. The first *Kinotita*, founded in Alexandria in 1843, would be followed by many others scattered throughout the country.[3] In addition to this institutionalized presence, a great profusion of associational life, which included charitable and occupational bodies, cultural clubs, literary salons, and local brotherhoods, flourished, particularly in the cities. A prolific Greek-language press and publishing sector further testified to the breadth and depth of Egyptian Greek life in different political, social, cultural, and economic fields of activity.

The Literature

Academic literature has characterized this Egyptian Greek presence in several ways.[4] Historians of Egypt have most often cast the Greeks as a conspicuous example of the resident foreign minorities, including the Italians, Maltese, and Armenians, whose presence and prosperity was generally located and explained within a colonial framework, especially after the British occupation of 1882. Different aspects of this characterization have been stressed. Some works have emphasized the critical importance of foreign nationality and, thus, entitlement to the legal and economic privileges of the Capitulations that exempted foreign nationals from local criminal law and customs duties.[5] In this context, the Treaty of Montreux in 1937, which abolished these rights and set in train the dissolution of the Mixed Courts, a judicial body set up in 1875 to deal with cases involving Egyptian and foreign nationals, is seen as a key turning point for the future of local foreigners. Other analyses have given greater weight to the Egyptian Greeks' economic role in forming an important part of a comprador bourgeoisie or a middleman minority that was part of expanding international capitalism and imperial economic interests.[6] Here, Greek fortunes are often measured according to the relationship between the institutional Greek community and colonial authority, sometimes spoken of in terms of political loyalties toward British interests or those of the Greek state (as opposed to the Egyptian state) or of their connections with larger imperial networks.

Scholarship specifically dedicated to the Greeks of Egypt offers a more detailed and complex picture that varies greatly in quality, from modest studies of particular institutions, local communities, and individuals (most often community benefactors or captains of the cotton industry) to grander surveys of personalities and associations.[7] Usually the work of Greek authors, these accounts have the advantage of drawing on Greek-language sources such as the local press, personal memoirs, and literary works and so provide important insights into Egyptian Greek life of which national histories of Egypt remain largely unaware. On the other hand, they are often characterized by a certain insular quality—Arabic-language sources are almost never used—being more concerned with the dynamics of local Egyptian Greek communities or of the Greek community in Egypt writ large, or with the celebrated achievements of the Greek presence in Egypt as an iconic outpost of Hellenism—almost inevitably so in the case of Alexandria, often with close reference to comparative developments in metropolitan Greek culture and politics.

The two-volume work of Athanasios Politis, an authoritative historical and contemporary account of the Greek community of Egypt published both in Greek and in French translation during the interwar period, is an early example of this approach.[8] A Greek diplomat based in Egypt, Politis focused his second volume on the Greek contribution to various sectors of the Egyptian economy, such as agriculture, commerce, financial services, and industry, with the Greek cast as a "pioneer of civilisation." A later work by Manolis Yalourakis, written when the Greek community of Egypt was in steep decline, adopts a similar if more subdued approach that presents a survey of the organizations and achievements of the Egyptian Greek community, again across a wide range of fields of activity.[9]

More recent work represents an important, if qualified, advance on this strong Hellenocentric focus. Pandelis Glavanis explored divisions within the Egyptian Greek elite class and its relationship with British and Egyptian authorities.[10] Alexander Kitroeff sought to locate the Greeks as a minority community within an Egyptian context by highlighting their ethnic character and class dynamics.[11] However, the period chosen, namely the years between the 1919 Revolution and the Treaty of Montreux in 1937, is determined specifically by the colonial backdrop, and the title of the work makes clear that the narrative depicts Greeks more *in* Egypt than *of* Egypt.[12] A more recent study by Kitroeff has taken on a broader chronological framework that suggests a more integrated perspective. However, some of the standard themes of the community leadership of the Greek plutocracy, the idiom of the Greek contribution to the Egyptian state, and the central importance of community identity remain conspicuous.[13]

Some scholars have taken on a more specific focus, particularly education and intellectual life, providing nuanced analyses and representing significant contributions to the literature.[14] Other works are less concerned with the historical presence of the Greeks of Egypt and more focused on the circumstances and manner of their departure, an influential theme in personal and community publications as well as the academic literature.[15] The study by Angelos Dalachanis offers a definitive examination of the circumstances of the "exodus" in the decades after World War II.[16] Floresca Karanasou places the Greeks of Egypt within a diasporic framework and is less concerned with the Egyptian context and more with national delineation.[17] Ultimately, while these studies draw on important Greek-language sources, including substantial archival materials, their focus is determined by a concern with the actions of the institutional Greek community and the policies of the Greek state, with comparatively little attention given to the Egyptian context.[18]

CRITIQUING THE COLLECTIVE, INSERTING THE INDIVIDUAL

Despite the critical insights these works have offered into the complex circumstances of Egyptian Greek life, each is largely governed by a collective conception of this particular Greek presence. For some, it is conceived as a colony serving, in some sense, as an extension of Greek culture or even the Greek state; for others, it is a distinct national minority protected by British imperium. In more specific terms, it is embodied in the formal institution of the *Kinotita* or of a social collective dominated by the ethos and power of the wealthy community leadership of a discrete, rather insulated, society.

However, such perspectives are based on assumptions that seek to create a center of gravity and a collective identity that arguably overdetermine the group's unity and shared character. The single term *Greek* is asked to shoulder a heavy burden of meaning that includes ethnic, religious, and language uniformity, usually invoked to support a national, even geographic, affiliation. This approach can create certain distortions and elisions. Egyptian Greeks migrated to Egypt from many parts of the Ottoman Empire and Mediterranean littoral and only after 1830 from a small, if expanding, Greek state. In time, many would be born in Egypt itself. For various reasons, by the beginning of the twentieth century, Egyptian Greeks held a range of nationalities—chiefly Greek, but also Egyptian, Ottoman/Turkish, Italian, and British—that not only expressed this diversity of backgrounds but implied with them different prospects and possible trajectories.[19] In terms of religious affiliation, most ethnic Greeks were Orthodox, but there were also significant Catholic and Jewish communities; Greek language might be taken as near universal, but not all Greeks were formally educated in the Greek community school system in Egypt, and multilingualism was relatively common.[20] Further, the emphasis on a national or ethnic community overlooks, or at best underplays, some of the internal political, social, economic, and even personal differences among Egyptian Greeks.[21] The political instability of the Greek state itself throughout the interwar period, followed by the German and then British occupations, and by a civil war afterward, seriously challenged a clear sense of national identity. Finally, a community approach runs the risk of not fully recognizing the widespread, if perhaps unsystematic and asymmetrical, pattern of Greek engagement with the broader Egyptian society, particularly its Arabophone majority and other minority communities. Ultimately, in seeking to distill a collective sense, this national framework threatens to overlook the complex interrelations within a multiethnic and multilingual society and the pattern of heterogeneous relations between individuals.

The Egyptian Greek presence was marked by great social and economic diversity. While often celebrated in the literature by reference to its successful cotton merchant and banking families, it ranged widely from cigarette rollers to wealthy merchants, from local grocers (epitomized in the familiar figure of the *baqqal rumi*) to industrialists, from police officers to drug traffickers, from intellectual and artistic circles to the professional classes of doctors, lawyers, pharmacists, and teachers, from both the public and the private sector.[22] Partly explained by the breadth of opportunity available in Egypt during this period, this heterogeneity was also a function of the diversity of origins, qualifications, and experience that characterized the Egyptian Greek population. Their familiarity with the conditions and complexities of late Ottoman and Mediterranean society facilitated their adaptation to the Egyptian environment well beyond simply taking any advantages that British colonial rule may have offered.

This chapter offers the case studies of three individuals who were neither part of the celebrated commercial Egyptian Greek elite nor drawn from the majority working class, but whose life trajectories nevertheless capture important elements of the diversity and complexity of the Egyptian Greek experience. Two of them migrated to Egypt from different parts of the Ottoman Empire as young adults at the end of the nineteenth century, while the third was born in Egypt. They lived in three different cities—Port Said, Cairo, and Alexandria—were multilingual, and were active in a range of contrasting and common fields—medicine, labor, art, political activism, and education—that connected them with and beyond the titular Greek community through personal contacts and professional networks. Their individual courses illustrate the interconnected and entangled quality of Greek life across the wider Egyptian society. As such, the pointillist approach adopted here seeks to distance itself from an emphasis on collective identity and instead explores the differentiated picture of Egyptian Greek life and its range of political, economic, cultural, and social roles and interactions across different levels of engagement within Egyptian society. Each case study draws on a diversity of sources in Arabic, Greek, and other languages, particularly from Egyptian Greek publications, and local and international archival materials, to present a complex and multilayered study of these individual lives.

APOSTOLOS SKOUPHOPOULOS: DOCTOR, COUNCILOR, UNION LEADER, AND MAN OF LETTERS

Apostolos Skouphopoulos (Απόστολος Σκουφόπουλος) is best known to historians of Egypt as a radical labor leader on the Suez Canal immediately after World War I.[23] While this was undoubtedly an important aspect of his public life, Skouphopoulos's professional career and private interests engaged with a much wider range of political, social, and cultural activities. Born in 1882 in Kasaba (now Turgutlu), some 50 kilometers west of Smyrna (Izmir), Skouphopoulos was educated in Smyrna, first at the Greek Evangelical School and then at the missionary American College, before migrating to Egypt as a young man for reasons unknown.[24] By 1902, he was living in Port Said, at that time a city of roughly fifty thousand people, about 70% of whom were Egyptian, almost 10% Greek, and the remainder made up of other, mainly European nationals. Skouphopoulos would remain in the city for the rest of his life, dedicating himself to community affairs, matters of local government, the labor movement, and a range of cultural activities.

Skouphopoulos first appeared in the local record in December 1902 as the author of an article on the Chinese economy published in *Emporikos Minitor*, an Alexandrian commercial journal.[25] In May 1903, he launched his own newspaper, *I Foni tou Laou* (The Voice of the People), a biweekly that focused on international affairs but folded after only about six issues.[26] Already showing himself to be a man of considerable drive, Skouphopoulos then turned to the study of medicine at the American University of Beirut (then the Syrian Protestant College), where he graduated in 1907. He would later specialize in gynecology in Vienna, Berlin, and Paris.[27]

The decision to pursue medicine was not unusual for someone of his intellectual gifts. Greek names were conspicuous among the ranks of the medical profession in Egypt: Greeks accounted for about 13% of all doctors in the country in the late 1920s, while representing less than 1% of the general population.[28] Most (just over 80%) studied in Athens, presumably for linguistic reasons, while others, like Skouphopoulos, attended an Ottoman medical school in Istanbul or Beirut, or studied in Europe (chiefly France). The majority worked in the cities, but Greek doctors were also found in smaller population centers in the Delta and Upper Egypt, sometimes as the area's only registered doctor. In Port Said, they were particularly prominent, representing almost a third of all doctors, a greater proportion even than in Alexandria.[29] A doctor's duties fostered individual relationships with patients and colleagues, especially for those who worked in community hospitals, where they could develop a broad range of social contacts.[30] Doctors also enjoyed certain social status and visibility that facilitated other professional and associated engagements. As educated men (overwhelmingly), they were well represented in scientific and cultural organizations and in public bodies, and often were known for pursuing their own intellectual interests.[31]

Little specific detail is known of Skouphopoulos's own medical practice. Early in his career, in 1913, he played an important role as one of several doctors involved in establishing Sotera, a private hospital affiliated with the local Greek community. He lived and maintained his own office for much of his life at 5 al-Tijara Street (rue du Commerce, later renamed Prince Faruq Street) in the European quarter of Port Said. In addition, for a time, he operated a clinic in the Arab quarter of the city, near the red-light area, which may have informed his later view on brothels and offered opportunities for him to practice his specialisation in gynecology, but this suggestion must remain speculative.[32] For a brief period in the 1930s, he is listed as the owner of the Couppas Pharmacy in Constanineh Street, which suggests a change in his practice.[33]

While his status as a doctor served as a constant in his professional life, the record shows that Skouphopoulos devoted as much energy to community affairs, public administration, and the consideration of various sociological, ethical, and literary questions.[34] In the context of the local Greek community, he was associated with innovative and reformist initiatives. His co-founding of a local Greek Boy Scout group in 1913 exhibited an early concern with youth activities. He also maintained an enduring commitment to the cause of education. In early 1919, he assisted his wife, Eftychia, and others in establishing a Sunday school for (working) girls, and later proposed a higher School of Practical Studies.[35] In matters of local Greek education, he acknowledged the role of the Ministry of Education in Greece but also drew attention to the importance of local requirements, particularly in the teaching of Arabic and English.[36] His call in 1923 for radical reforms in the management of the Port Said *Kinotita* itself, though unsuccessful, reinforces the impression of his progressive voice within the community (Fig. 8.1).[37]

Skouphopoulos did not restrict himself to Greek community affairs. In 1911, the establishment of a municipality in Port Said opened up an avenue of participation in local politics to those qualified. Like the municipality of Alexandria formed two decades before, this body was a somewhat limited exercise in democratic representation and was granted some powers in the provision of local public services and planning.[38] Based on a narrow property franchise, separate elections were held every two years for half of the municipal committee of ten councilors, divided equally between European and Egyptian candidates, to serve four-year terms. Skouphopoulos sat as a member of the first municipal council when he served out the term of an elected Greek member who had stepped down. In the 1921 election, he stood successfully in his own name for a full term. An appreciation of his full record on the council awaits further study, but his appointment as the stand-in president of a large committee dedicated to urban renewal in 1926 suggests that he had established himself as an influential player in the city's affairs.[39] He was elected again as a councilor in the 1930s and continued to serve into the next decade.[40]

Skouphopoulos's political activism was also conducted on a broader canvas. In the schismatic national politics of Greece during World War I, he supported the pro–Entente Venizelist camp and used his oratorical skills to support its cause during the visit of the Greek leader to Port Said in the spring of 1915.[41] It was very likely at this time that Skouphopoulos served as secretary of the Return of the Irredentists (Epistrophi ton Alytroton), an organization presumably supportive of the Great Idea, the policy cherished by Venizelos and others to unite Greeks on both sides of the Aegean within one state.[42] Skouphopoulos's reaction to the Asia Minor campaign, which ended in the rout of the Greek Army by Turkish nationalist forces and the fall of Smyrna in 1922, along with the collapse of Greece's territorial ambitions, is unknown, but already before the end of World War I, his politics were taking a more radical turn. In 1917, he appeared on a list of "undesirable Greeks" recommended for deportation from Egypt by the British authorities because of his political activities.[43] The order was not implemented, but neither did Skouphopoulos temper his behavior. Indeed, from this period onward, he embraced explicitly internationalist pro-labor politics.

FIG. 8.1 Dr Apostolos Skouphopoulos, Port Said, president of the International Workers' Union of the Canal and author of scientific, sociological, and philosophical works. Taken from *Panorama* January–February 1929, with thanks to ELIA.

Skouphopoulos had shown an early interest in workers' organizations in an article on strikes in Europe that he had contributed to *Emporikos Minitor* in 1903.[44] His subsequent record of labor involvement was no doubt informed by his knowledge of international developments as well as his experience of local workers' conditions. In August 1919, Skouphopoulos was elected president of the International Workers' Union of the Isthmus of Suez (IWUIS), a body whose formation was part of a broad surge in syndicalist activity in Egypt immediately following World War I. His appointment suggests that he possessed recognized credentials for the task. A further appointment as president of the International Association of Shop Assistants in 1921 reinforces this impression. In fact, the practice of Greek doctors serving as union representatives, no doubt assisted by the prominence of Greek workers in the labor force, had been already well established at the beginning of the century when organized labor first emerged as an industrial force in Egypt.[45]

Skouphopoulos's place at the head of the IWUIS came at a critical time, when postwar expectations surrounding Egyptian national independence coincided with the rise of communism as an international force. As the operational home of the Suez Canal Company (SCC), Port Said was an obvious location for the development of a strong labor movement. The Phoenix, an earlier union composed solely of Greek workers, had achieved some success during the war. However, the formation of the IWUIS in 1919 with a membership of some four thousand foreign and Egyptian workers, made up of not only SCC workers but also other employees on the canal, signified a more significant industrial power, not just locally but on the Egyptian national scene as well. It was a clear recognition of the standing of the IWUIS that when Joseph Rosenthal (1872–c. 1966), a longtime anarchist and labor organizer, called for a meeting in Alexandria in late February 1921 to establish the Confédération Générale du Travail, a broad coalition of labor forces, Skouphopoulos chaired the occasion.[46] At the following May Day celebrations held in the city at Jardin Rosette, Rosenthal stressed this link by reading out a telegram sent by Skouphopoulos as IWUIS president: "To the sound of the worker's song and amid fine enthusiasm, the proletariat of the Suez Canal salute their Alexandria comrades of the General Federation of Labour. Long live May Day and the workers of every country."[47] The radical instincts expressed here point to Skouphopoulos's involvement in socialist circles during a period that saw the establishment of the Egyptian Socialist Party in 1921 and the Egyptian Communist Party the following year.[48] However, he does not appear to have suffered personally during the subsequent government crackdown against communists in 1924, possibly because his public standing and physical distance from metropolitan Cairo offered him some protection.

Skouphopoulos continued as IWUIS president until 1926, when he was unseated by supposedly more radical union members and replaced by a Greek lawyer, Christy Modinos, the son of Polis Modinos, himself a Greek doctor and former union leader. If accurately characterized, this change of leadership suggests some disagreement over goals and strategies within the union. However, by 1931, Skouphopoulos was back as president, leading negotiations between the SCC and *tacherons* (temporary workers) regarding working conditions. The presence of many Egyptians in this latter group gave the matter heightened importance in Egyptian national politics, and Skouphopoulos liaised with the Cairo-based Wafdist labor lawyer, Husni al-Shintinawi, during the discussions.[49] Skouphopoulos continued as union president until at least the end of the tumultuous 1930s, writing at one point to Prime Minister Mustafa al-Nahhas to express his disappointment in the meager government support offered to workers.[50]

Further to these activities, Skouphopoulos was a leading figure in Port Said's cultural circles, a founding member of the Endefkterion, a Greek cultural club, and the president of the Art Lovers Company. As a considerable man of letters, he also took up the role of literary critic and social and cultural commentator. A gifted linguist fluent in Greek, German, English, French, and Italian (and very likely functional in spoken

Arabic), he published a collection of essays in 1924 that demonstrated a deep concern with ethical and sociological questions.[51] More often, he preferred to contribute articles to the Egyptian Greek-language press that frequently appeared throughout the 1920s and 1930s.[52] In 1931, his presence among a number of other Egyptian Greek intellectuals to support the launch of *Panegyptia*, a Greek-language review edited by Stephanos Pargas and published in Alexandria, placed him in unmistakeably liberal circles. His contributions over subsequent years spoke to his varied interests: Port Said community affairs, the work of Goethe, labor matters, and other topical issues. In response to a question about the abolition of brothels in Egypt in 1932, a topic then under considerable public discussion, Skouphopoulos was particularly disparaging of the part played by "professional moralists" and "hedonists" in the debate and deeply critical of brothels as places that deprived prostitutes of their personal and social freedom and failed to secure their legal, ethical, and physical rights, or those of any illegitimate children.[53]

Skouphopoulos's interest in literature largely focused on Western writers, particularly German and Greek, such as Heine and Goethe, and Palamas and Kavafy, respectively. He authored a play in Italian, wrote poetry, and lectured on issues of philosophy and literature. However, he appears to have also maintained connections with the Egyptian literary establishment, as evidenced during a visit of the Indian Nobel Prize winner Rabindranath Tagore to Egypt. Tagore had stopped in the country for a few days on his way home to India after a European tour at the end of 1926.[54] First feted in Alexandria, then in Cairo, by many Egyptian politicians and literary figures, among them Sa'd Zaghlul, Ahmad Lutfi al-Sayyid, and 'Abbas Mahmud al-'Aqqad, he spent his last day in Port Said in the company of the Egyptian modernist poet Ahmad Abu Shadi and Skouphopoulos. In a conversation later recorded by Abu Shadi, Skouphopoulos debated the concept of world literature with Tagore. A formal group photograph of Tagore, Abu Shadi, and Skouphopoulos, nattily dressed in suit and bow tie, marked the occasion. While the exact circumstances of this meeting are unclear, Skouphopoulos's presence suggests both a close acquaintance with Abu Shadi and a familiarity within Egyptian literary circles.[55]

Skouphopoulos maintained his various commitments to his medical practice, the presidency of the union, and local government affairs, as well as his intellectual pursuits throughout the 1930s. A resident of Port Said, where he lived for more than forty years, he was able to apply his talents in a city that offered particular opportunities. His son Emilios, registered as a trainee lawyer before the Mixed Courts in 1934, continued the family tradition by pursuing a career that, like medicine, facilitated contacts across and beyond community boundaries. Apostolos Skouphopoulos died in 1944 or 1945,[56] leaving behind a considerable and varied record of public and personal achievement that exemplified the multidimensional character of Egyptian Greek life. Born in Asia Minor and the product of Greek Orthodox and American missionary education systems, his life in Egypt exhibited a course that extended well beyond a Greek milieu to engage with different aspects of a pluralist Egyptian society.

GIORGIS DIMOU: ART AND POLITICS

An artist, author, and activist, Giorgis Dimou (Γιώργης Δήμου) illustrates the case of an Egyptian Greek leftist immersed in Egyptian, Greek, and international political struggles during the interwar period. The son of a stonemason of Thracian origin, Dimou was born in Cairo in 1911 and grew up in the popular quarter of 'Abdin. The experience brought him into direct contact with the ethnic diversity of the neighborhood, where, among other things, he acquired a knowledge of spoken Arabic. It also radicalized his social and political conscience and imbued him with a lasting sympathy for the plight of workers.[57] Dimou himself attended the Greek-language Ambeteios School, which was founded in 1854 following an endowment from the Syrian Abet Brothers and directed by the Monastery of St. Katerina (and not by the *Kinotita*). Located in Bulaq Street (renamed 26 July), the school catered predominantly to Greek boys at the primary and high school levels, but it also included an Egyptian and a commercial section (the latter which Dimou attended).[58] One of his classmates was poet and novelist of the left Yiannis Hatziandreas (Stratis Tsirkas), with whom he would enjoy a lifetime friendship.[59]

After his graduation from school in 1928, Dimou forsook his commercial training and began developing his artistic talents. He first exhibited his work at the International Exhibition in Cairo in the same year. Around this time, he came under the personal influence of Nikos Nikolaidis (1884–1956), a progressive Cypriot author, poet, and member of the first generation of Egyptian Greek painters, who then lived in Cairo.[60] Associated with the naturalist school, Nikolaidis's work appeared regularly in the pages of *Panorama*, where he established a reputation for Egyptian landscapes.[61] His impact on Dimou had less to do with matters of art and more to do with his introduction of the younger man to local Greek leftist circles, which included Sakellaris Yannakakis, an iconic figure of the Egyptian Communist Party from the early 1920s.

In 1929, Dimou accepted a scholarship at the School of Fine Arts (Scholi Kalon Technon) in Athens, where he was taught by the noted engraver Yiannis Kefallinos.[62] From then until his graduation in 1934, he would spend the academic year in Greece and the summer in Egypt, while producing regular creations for publication in both Egyptian and Greek periodicals. An early example appeared on the cover of the French-language *La Semaine Égyptienne* in 1930, and thereafter his work was published regularly in the review.[63] Among other original artwork, Dimou produced a series of prints for a volume of poetry by Gaston Zananiri in 1932, the memorable felucca on the cover of Stratis Tsirkas's first book of poetry, *Fellahi* (Fellahin), and a portrait of the author Eleni Voiskou for her collection of short stories.[64]

Described by Yalourakis as a painter "of the masses" (*ton mazon*), Dimou himself did not feel a close connection with other painters in Egypt, although he recognized the political character of the work of Menis Angelopoulos.[65] His earliest work was modernist in form, but as his politics became more clearly defined, he was drawn to socialist realism, depicting the life and conditions of male and female workers in both Egyptian and Greek contexts. After his return to Egypt in 1934, he produced several memorable woodcuts, including studies of Egyptian workers unloading timber on the Nile, date palm plantations, an Arab youth, and a group of Arab women. Probably his most remarkable piece was a woodcut of a nationalist demonstration of Egyptian students that so effectively captured the contemporary political atmosphere that it would later be used on the cover of the progressive Cairene review *al-Fajr al-Jadid* (The New Dawn) (Fig. 8.2).[66]

Dimou's political activism was not confined to his art. With the threat of Italian aggression in Ethiopia (Abyssinia) in 1935, he committed himself to the cause of peace and joined the Ligue Pacifiste (Ansar al-Salam). First launched in April 1935, the Ligue, both in Alexandria and Cairo, attracted a largely international membership consisting of progressive Greeks, other Europeans, and Jewish Egyptians.[67] The organization later became affiliated with the international Rassemblement Universel pour la Paix, based in Brussels, and worked with a broad coalition of local organizations that included the Egyptian section of the Women's International League of Peace and Freedom.[68] It supported a greater role for the League of Nations in securing world peace, particularly

FIG. 8.2 Giorgis Dimou, *Student Demonstration*, 1936, illustrating the popular political struggle in Egypt in the mid-1930s. Reproduced with kind permission of Stella and Alexis Dimou.

an end to Italian aggression in Africa and the civil war in Spain, but also called for Egyptian national independence.

In early 1937, Dimou authored numerous articles in *Panegyptia* that upheld the values of the peace movement, particularly in relation to the struggle in Republican Spain. However, his last piece explicitly called on public support for Egyptian demands for independence: "To us, then, the Greeks that drink the water of the Nile, falls a heavy burden. We need to understand that we have patriotic obligations to the country where we were born and where we grew up and live, to the country that hosts and nourishes us [that] we call our second homeland."[69]

Dimou's art manifested a similar pro-peace commitment. In *Politismos*, the monthly bulletin of the Pacifist Unions of Egypt, his woodcut titled *Libation to Death* depicted the close relationship between militarism, capitalism, and the march to war (Fig. 8.3).[70] Political and other reasons took Dimou back to Greece, which since 1936 had been under the Metaxas dictatorship. In 1938, he married Maria (Mario) Koukoudami of Alexandria in Athens; both were arrested and imprisoned soon after by the Greek authorities but were released following intervention by Nikolaidis and allowed to leave for Egypt.[71] However, by the end of the decade, with the cause of peace lost, Dimou,

FIG. 8.3 Giorgis Dimou, *Spondi sto Thanato* (Libation to Death), an antiwar woodcut that linked militarism and capitalism. Taken from *Politismos* September–October 1937, with thanks to ELIA and reproduced with kind permission of Stella and Alexis Dimou.

like other Egyptian Greek communists, departed for Greece, where he remained until the end of the war, staying for a time with the partisans of the communist-led National People's Liberation Army (ELAS) insurgency in the mountains.

After the war, Dimou returned to Egypt, where he reconnected with his leftist network. At the Greek Club of Amateurs (Ellinikos Sillogos Erasitechnon) in Cairo, a revived cultural youth center that embodied the progressive dynamism of the time, he volunteered his services to teach painting to students.[72] Dimou continued to design covers, notably for Orizontes, a progressive publisher in Alexandria, and produce work for the leftist review *Ellin*, but in his painting he departed from the social realist style of the prewar period and turned to bright watercolors. In 1948, he produced a series of lively everyday Egyptian scenes set in the popular quarters of Cairo, at the local water fountain, in the café, and in the market (Fig. 8.4).

Deciding to rejoin the political struggle in Greece, Dimou finally left Egypt in 1948, traveling with other comrades through Italy and Yugoslavia to the communist-held area in northern Greece. With the communist defeat in the Greek Civil War the following year, he moved to Romania with his wife and lived for many years in political exile while he documented the life of Greek refugees and Romanian workers.[73] Dimou relocated to Greece with his family in 1965 and remained there until his death in 2004. At a political level, his life exemplifies some of the dilemmas of the interwar Egyptian Greek left that was caught between the anti-colonial and class struggle in Egypt and

FIG. 8.4 Watercolour, 1948, one of a series of popular scenes Giorgis Dimou produced following his return to Egypt after the war. Reproduced with kind permission of Stella and Alexis Dimou.

the civil war in Greece.[74] Yet, while he would spend the second half of his life outside Egypt, an exhibition held in Athens in 2005–06 dedicated to his life's work showed that his time in Egypt had constituted a very significant period for both his political formation and his artistic creativity.[75]

SEMELE TSOTSOU (D. 1958): HEARING THROUGH THE EYES

The life of Semele Tsotsou (Σεμέλη Τσώτσου) offers yet another Egyptian Greek trajectory, less conventionally political than those of Skouphopoulos and Dimou, but one firmly associated with the emergence of the women's movement and the progressive cause of special education. Born in the European Ottoman city of Kırklareli (Greek name: Saranta Ekklisies) in Eastern Thrace in 1879/1885, Tsotsou migrated to Egypt as a young woman in 1895 and settled in Alexandria.[76] Little is known of her family circumstances or education. Her brother was Radamanthos G. Radopoulos, the historian and longtime general secretary of the Alexandrian *Kinotita*, which suggests her maiden name was Radopoulou and the surname Tsotsou was acquired through marriage. She made her first appearance in the public record in 1912 when she was active in local Greek community affairs in fundraising for a mobile hospital sent to Thessaloniki to treat wounded Greek soldiers during the Balkan Wars (1912–13).

Immediately after World War I, Egyptian Greek women shared the general enthusiasm for new organization and purpose evident throughout the country. In Alexandria, Manna, the Union of Greek Women (Enosis Ellinidon), was formed at the end of 1918 to address various concerns of women in the community. Tsotsou would play a central role in the organization, serving as its general secretary for the first seven years. The following year, she became president of the Night School for Women established by Manna to teach Greek women vocational skills such as foreign languages, stenography, and typing.[77] Consistent with its mission to support women in gaining employment, Manna also operated a nursery where working women could leave their preschool children during the day for a small fee. It was as a result of an encounter with a deaf child at the nursery that Tsotsou would change the focus of her life's work and commit herself to the cause of deaf education.

The history of deaf education in Egypt awaits a detailed study.[78] There is evidence that institutions dedicated to the deaf operated late in the nineteenth century.[79] A significant step occurred around 1906 when ʿAbd Allah Idilbi established a school for the deaf in Cairo, supported by the English Church Missionary Society, which operated for about two years.[80] However, when Tsotsou established the Elpis (Greek for "hope") School for the deaf in the Alexandrian suburb of Sporting in 1934, it seems to have been the first such institution in the city and the only one operating in Egypt at the time.

Tsotsou had prepared for the opening of the school by withdrawing from community activities in 1932 and applying herself to the study of speech therapy. She spent time in Europe, chiefly Austria and probably Paris, where she began studying methods for teaching deaf children. Once the school opened, she continued to be active in expanding and maintaining these professional contacts, attending conferences, for example, in Prague in 1936, and making a trip in 1939 to New York and Washington, which had to be cut short due to the outbreak of World War II.[81]

After a slow start, the Elpis School developed into a significant success over the next decade and more. From the beginning, the school was explicitly open to children of either sex and any nationality or religion. An early press report indicates the presence of Greek, Armenian, and Italian girls and one Egyptian Muslim boy.[82] In time, Elpis would attract pupils from around the Mediterranean and accommodate boarders. By the early 1940s, numbers had grown to thirty students across different levels of instruction. Pupils could be taught in three languages, French, Greek, and Arabic, with all students generally required to do French and another language.[83] After visiting the school in 1934, Ahmad al-Sidudi, the Egyptian editor of the bilingual *Egiptiotis-Ellin-al-Yunani al-Mutamassir*, wrote his impressions of the class: "We visited the school. We waited there [expecting] to see a number of deaf [children] busy drawing certain characters or amusing themselves examining different pictures. Did this happen? Were our expectations realized? No, not at all! What we saw is amazing! We saw deaf [children] reading, writing, conversing, differentiating things, understanding the one speaking to them and answering appropriately, without the least difficulty!"[84]

Initially trained by speech therapist Emil Fröschels in Vienna, Tsotsou would advance her understanding of deaf education by studying the methods of Gérard de Parrel (1883–1956), a leading otologist and physician in Paris, affiliated with the Institut National des Sourds-Muets (Paris Deaf Institute). A proponent of the oralist approach, which had originated in Germany and was dominant in Europe at this time, De Parrel stressed the importance of mimicking the breathing pattern and mouth movement of speech as well as lip-reading as the key to deaf communication and education.[85] Tsotsou would term this method "Hearing with the Eyes." Al-Sidudi further described the scene:

> The method which the Madame Director of the school follows in teaching these deaf [children] is simple but has a great impact. There are pictures and drawings and some children's games and mirrors for the student to see their face when they speak or when the director of the school addresses them. There are things to strengthen the larynx and the lungs, and others to revive the sense of hearing in the student. In short, the methods used for the teaching of the deaf are scientific, simple and at the same time effective, something it is only possible to understand when you witness it.[86]

Tsotsou's methods relied principally on European ideas of deaf pedagogy, but she became aware of the need to develop techniques specifically for the Egyptian situation that she would later liken to the Belgian method of Alexandre Herlin.[87] She was also determined to disseminate her ideas more widely.[88] In 1934, she had published an alpha-betic reader for Greek children, probably the first of its kind in Greek. This was only the first of several works. Two years later, a description of her teaching methods appeared, this time in French.[89] Over time, Tsotsou wrote several books in Greek and French which earned her a reputation as an authority on the education of the deaf. During the war, and in a clear response to its impact, she turned her attention to deafness among adults, publishing a book on lip-reading for those whose hearing had been damaged by war service or illness.[90] More publications would follow.[91]

Tsotsou's school would even be referenced in literature. In his semi-autobiographical work *Out of Egypt*, André Aciman provides a memorable, if at times wry, account of "Madame Tsotsou" and the ethos of the Elpis School that seems broadly consistent with other sources.[92] The narrator, whose mother was deaf and had been educated for some time at the school, apparently as a boarder, remarks, "Under Madame Tsotsou's vigilant egalitarianism, no one was permitted to distinguish between rich and poor, Greek and Arab." If this ethos challenged some contemporary social attitudes, her oralist approach to deaf learning that sought to assimilate the deaf into mainstream hearing society and dismiss the use of sign language showed a more conventional spirit. "Madame Tsotsou defined a successful graduate as one who befriended the hearing over the deaf, who felt less deaf than she truly was, and who experienced an instinctive revulsion toward those who knew no better than to speak with their hands, not their mouths."[93]

During the early years of its operation, the financial basis of the school was somewhat precarious. Initially, Tsotsou funded its operation from her own means with assistance from a committee of Greek women, but additional backing was soon required. Before World War I, her activities had demonstrated her talents as an effective fundraiser, and she came to employ these same skills in attracting support from other sources, such as the Rotary Club, wealthy notables of the city, and the Greek Patriarchate.[94] Tsotsou also sought assistance from the Egyptian Feminist Union (EFU), drawing on personal connections she may have developed in earlier years. In early 1938, the EFU president and founding spirit, Huda Shaʿrawi, visited the school, expressing her enthusiasm for its work and promising to lobby the Egyptian government in its cause.[95] In an article in the EFU's Arabic-language journal, *al-Misriyya* (The Egyptian Woman), Shaʿrawi wrote encouragingly of the work done at Elpis in addressing the great problem that Egypt had with the education of the deaf, a group she estimated at numbering about fifty thousand people. More than simply calling for the financial support of Elpis, she called on the Egyptian government to establish a national network of schools for the deaf employing the methods developed by Tsotsou. Anticipating the objection that the lack of qualified male and female teachers in Egypt might be an obstacle to implementing such an idea, Shaʿrawi proposed that people be trained in Tsotsou's ped-agogical methods at the school itself.[96]

It is not known if there was a specific response to Shaʿrawi's proposal, but by the mid-1940s Tsotsou's methods had been officially recognized and the Elpis School had assumed semi-state status. Tsotsou herself was appointed as inspector of a new state school for the deaf in Cairo and became the director of a teacher training course for deaf children. Her book on the demutization method now appeared in an Arabic edition.[97] By 1947, Elpis was employing five teachers (three Egyptians and two Greeks), and fifteen Egyptians had already graduated from Tsotsou's training course. In the following year, five schools for the deaf were reported in operation in Egypt.[98] In time, a government network of deaf schools expanded across the country.[99] By the time of her death in December 1958, Semele Tsotsou had established herself as a recognized authority in Egypt and an international figure in the field of deaf education, earning her the sobriquet of Friend of the Deaf-Mute (Φίλη των κωφαλάλων, or Filis ton Kofalalon). Other deaf schools were established elsewhere in Egypt, in Mansoura, Aswan, Minya, Suhag, and 'Abbasiyya, as well as in the Arab world, in the West Bank (Qalqiliyya and Hebron), Jordan, and Sharjah.[100] It seems an appropriate tribute to Tsotsou's work that they all adopted the name al-Amal, Arabic for Elpis (hope).

CONCLUSION

Studies of the Egyptian Greeks have routinely stressed the community aspect and national identity of their presence, or as often in Egyptian histories, their minority character aligned in interest, if not in sentiment, with European colonialism in its contest with the Egyptian national movement. An analysis of the lives of three Egyptian Greeks reveals the much greater complexity of this presence by adopting a different vector of enquiry, namely of individual trajectories marked by their own specificities, interconnections, and dynamics.

As a doctor in Port Said, Apostolos Skouphopoulos enjoyed a wide range of contacts with patients and colleagues within but also beyond the local Greek community; as a member of the municipal council, he engaged with the issues of local government and the concerns of constituents; as a labor leader, he represented Greek, Egyptian, and other workers, meeting with union representatives, lawyers, and Suez Canal Company officials and negotiating work agreements; and as a man of letters, he connected with fellow literati and the readers of his writings. Born and educated in Cairo, Giorgis Dimou drew on his direct experience of Cairene life to forge a career as an artist whose work drew inspiration from the plight of the working poor and expressed itself in both urban and rural Egyptian themes. As a political activist during the 1930s, he participated in internationalist peace campaigns in Egypt and wrote supportively of Egyptian independence. With the outbreak of World War II, he was drawn into the Greek national struggle against fascism, a commitment that continued into the postwar years. A girl when she first arrived in Egypt from Ottoman Europe, Semele Tsotsou moved from her initial involvement in Greek women's organizations of Alexandria to take up a calling as an educator of deaf children that greatly expanded her horizons and influence. In doing so, she established herself as a noted practitioner in special needs education, the mentor of an expanding Egyptian state network, and an authority in the international field of pedagogy of the deaf.

Analyzing these three individual trajectories reveals a different dimension of the Egyptian Greek presence. Moving beyond the framework of community and national minority discourse, which has dominated the understanding of ethnic minorities of Egypt, it highlights connections mediated not simply by communal or ethnic identity but by a more complex interplay of professional, personal, and political relationships played out locally, nationally, and internationally. In other words, it highlights a more interconnected, interactive, and interpersonal world. Such an approach might also usefully be applied to the cases of other communities in Egypt that were characterized by a comparable diversity and dynamism in their professional, public, and even private lives. Rather than being seen as insulated, privileged peoples or reduced to collective beneficiaries of a colonial order, these groups were constitutive elements of a vibrant multicultural Egyptian society in a late Ottoman and early post-Ottoman age.

NOTES

1. The term *Egyptian Greek* will be used throughout and preferred to the archaic *Ægyptiote Greeks*, as an equivalent to the local and contemporary Greek usage of *Egyptiotes Ellines*. I would like to thank the editors and Katerina Trimi-Kyrou for their comments on an earlier draft and Mathilde Pyrli of ELIA-MIET (Hellenic Literary and Historical Archive) for her assistance in collecting materials.

2. *Population Census of Egypt, 1927* (Cairo: Government Press, 1931).

3. Alexander Kitroeff lists more than thirty separate *Kinotites* established in Egypt. Alexander Kitroeff, *The Greeks in Egypt, 1919-1937: Ethnicity and Class* (London: Ithaca, 1989), 189.

4. For earlier thoughts on this historiographical issue, see Anthony Gorman, *Historians, State and Politics in Twentieth Century Egypt: Contesting the Nation* (London: Routledge Curzon, 2003), 174-95.

5. See, e.g., Arthur Goldschmidt Jr., *Modern Egypt: The Formation of a Nation-State* (Boulder, CO: Westview, 1988), 27, 67.

6. See, e.g., Marius Deeb, "The Socioeconomic Role of the Local Foreign Minorities in Modern Egypt, 1805-1961," *International Journal of Middle East Studies* 9, no. 1 (1978): 11-22; Robert L. Tignor, "The Economic Activities of Foreigners in Egypt, 1920-1950: From Millet to Haute Bourgeoisie," *Comparative Studies in Society and History* 22, no. 3 (1980): 416-49; and Nabil 'Abd al-Hamid Sayyid Ahmad, *al-Nashat al-Iqtisadi li-l-Ajanib wa-Atharuhu fi al-Mujtama' al-Misri min 1922 ila 1952* (Cairo: al-Hay'a al-Misriyya al-'Amma li-l-Kitab, 1982).

7. See, e.g., Tasos P. Palaiologos, *O Egiptiotis Ellinismos, Istoria and Drasis (753 P.Kh.-1953)* [Egyptian Hellenism, History and Activity], vol. 1 (Alexandria: Adelphon Velentza, 1953); and I. M. Chatzifotis, *Alexandreia, Oi Dio Eones tou Neoterou Ellinismou 190s-200s eon* [Alexandria, Two Centuries of Modern Hellenism 19th-20th centuries] (Athens: Ellinika Grammata, 1999).

8. Athanasios G. Politis, *O Ellinismos ke I Neotera Egiptos* (Alexandria: Grammata, 1927, 1930); Politis, *L'Hellénisme et L'Égypte moderne*, 2 vols. (Paris: Félix Alcan, 1929-30). See also Gorman, *Historians, State and Politics*, 189.

9. Manolis Yalourakis, *I Egiptos ton Ellinon* [Egypt of the Greeks] (Athens: Mitropolis, 1967).

10. Pandelis Michalis Glavanis, "Aspects of the Economic and Social History of the Greek Community in Alexandria during the Nineteenth Century" (PhD diss., University of Hull, 1989), which drew on the work of Stratis Tsirkas, *O Kavafis ke i epochi tou* (Athens: Kedros, 1958).

11. *The Greeks in Egypt, 1919–1937,* iv.

12. My phrasing recalls the comment by P. J Vatikiotis, himself a Greek born in Palestine but with Egyptian family connections, about radical Egyptian Greek activists during World War II that they "were resident in Egypt, but they were not of Egypt." See P. J. Vatikiotis, "The New Western Historiography of Modern Egypt: Review Article," *Middle Eastern Studies* 27, no. 2 (1991): 324. Vatikiotis held a similar though more generalized view of an insulated community in his "Greek Communities in Arab Lands," *Greek Gazette* 15 (1981): 1, 4–7.

13. Alexander Kitroeff, *The Greeks and the Making of Modern Egypt* (Cairo: American University in Cairo Press, 2019), 18–19. The prominent place given to the genealogical tree of the Choremi-Benaki family, the plutocratic class par excellence, reinforces this view.

14. See, e.g., Manolis Maragoulis, *"Keros na synchronisthomen," I Egiptos ke I egiptiotiki dianoisi (1919–1939)* (Athens: Panepistimiakes Ekdoseis Kiprou, Gutenberg, 2011).

15. See, e.g., Dan Georgaka, Alexander Kitroeff, and Matoula Tomara-Sideris, eds., special issue, *Journal of the Hellenic Diaspora* 35, no. 2 (2009).

16. Angelos Dalachanis, *The Greek Exodus from Egypt: Diaspora Politics and Emigration, 1937–1962* (New York: Berghahn, 2017). A Greek version was also published.

17. Floresca Karanasou, "The Greeks in Egypt: From Mohammed Ali to Nasser, 1805–1961," in *The Greek Diaspora in the Twentieth Century,* ed. Richard Clogg (London: Palgrave Macmillan, 1999), 24–57.

18. One important exception is the study of Sayyid 'Ashmawi, *al-Yunaniyyun fi Misr 1805–1956* (Cairo: Ein, 1997), which uses a good range of Arabic language material, notably poetry and other literature.

19. The 1917 census lists 68.3% of all ethnic Greeks as holding Greek nationality, followed by Egyptian (21.32%), Ottoman (5.51%), British (2.93%), and Italian (1.97%) nationals. By the time of the 1937 census, Greek nationals had increased to 75.8% of the total, with Egyptians at 16.9%. *The Census of Egypt Taken in 1917* (Cairo: Government Press, 1920), Table VII.

20. Roughly two-thirds of Egyptian Greek children attended Greek schools in Egypt.

21. Apostolos Skouphopoulos would refer to this lack of solidarity in the context of Port Said, "E Aposeis tou Dros k. Skouphopoulou dia ta parikiaka en Port-Said," *Panegyptia,* 28 January 1933, 6.

22. Giorgis Athanasiadis, in the 1940s, described the Greek community as being made up of 5% upper bourgeoisie, 35% petit bourgeoisie, and 60% working poor, in Efthymios Souloyiannis, *I Thesi ton Ellinon stin Egipto* (Athens: Dimos Athinaion, 1999), 58.

23. Joel Beinin and Zachary Lockman, *Workers on the Nile: Nationalism, Communism, Islam, and the Egyptian Working Class, 1882–1954* (Cairo: American University in Cairo Press, 1998), 109, were the first to bring attention to this role in English-language scholarship.

24. 'Apostolos V. Skouphopoulos,' Biographical note, Panos Xenos Archive, ELIA.

25. Apostolos Skouphopoulos, "To Emporion en Siniki," *Emporikos Minitor* 1, 14 December 1902, 23–24.

26. Its masthead adapted a quote from *Oedipus Rex* (l. 314–15): "To help man by whichever way you can is the best of labors."

27. Skouphopoulos, Biographical note.

28. Calculation and following discussion based on Ministère de l'Intérieur–Administration de l'Hygiène Publique, *Listes officielles des médecins, vétérinaires, dentistes, pharmaciens, aides-pharmaciens et sages-femmes, en Égypte au 31 Dec 1925* (Cairo: Imprimerie Nationale, 1928). Souloyiannis states that for an earlier period (1879–1908), the percentage of Greek doctors was even higher (22.5), Souloyiannis, *I Thesi ton Ellinon stin Egipto*, 59. For a survey of the role played by Greek doctors in Egypt characteristically emphasizing their scientific achievements and professional services to the country, see Yalourakis, *I Egiptos ton Ellinon*, 419–25.

29. Ministère de l'Intérieur–Administration de l'Hygiène Publique, *Listes officielles des médecins, vétérinaires, dentistes, pharmaciens, aides-pharmaciens et sages-femmes, en Égypte au 31 Dec 1925*.

30. See, e.g., the case of Dr. Spiridon Tombler of the Greek Hospital in Cairo, whose funeral cortege was followed by many Egyptians. Giorgis Athanasiadis, *I Proti Praxi tis ellinikis tragodias (Mesi Anatoli 1940–1944)* (Athens: Sinchroni Epochi, 1994), 26–27.

31. Note, e.g., the case of Dr. Nikolaos Mavris, a doctor in al-Zaqaziq, who became an authority on popular Egyptian songs. See Anthony Gorman, "Cultural Communicators: The Greek Arabists of Interwar Egypt," in *Cultural Entanglement in the Pre-Independence Arab World*, ed. Anthony Gorman and Sarah Irving (London: I. B. Tauris, 2021), 204.

32. Themis Matsakis, Autobiography ms, 59. Panos Xenos Archive, ELIA.

33. *The Egyptian Directory 1934* (Cairo: Max Fischer, 1934).

34. This impression is somewhat supported by the fact that Skouphopoulos is not discussed by Yalourakis in his section on the medical achievements of Greek doctors (although he is mentioned elsewhere).

35. Dimitrios K. Chaldoupis, *Anamniseis ke Chronika Port-Said* (Alexandria: N. Mitsanis, 1939), 173, 187.

36. "E Aposeis tou Dros k. Skouphopoulou," *Panegyptia*, 28 January 1933, 6.

37. Chaldoupis, *Anamniseis ke Chronika Port-Said*, 187.

38. Gabriel Baer, "The Beginnings of Municipal Government in Egypt," *Middle Eastern Studies* 4, no. 2 (1968): 118–40; Ioan. I. Soultanakis, *To Lefkoma ton Paristhmion Poleon Port Said, Ismailias kai Souez* (Leipzig: n.p., 1922), 116.

39. Chaldoupis, *Anamniseis ke Chronika Port-Said*, 140, 183, 203. Skouphopoulos was also a member of the committee that discussed the establishment of Port Fu'ad, Diya' al-Din Hassan al-Qadi, *Mawsu'at Tarikh Bur Sa'id*, vol. 1 (Cairo: al-Hay'a al-Misriyya al-'Amma li-l-Kitab, 2015), 170–71.

40. E. J. Blattner, *Le Mondain Égyptien* (Cairo: F. E Noury 1939 and 1943), s.v. "Skouphopoulos."

41. Chaldoupis, *Anamniseis ke Chronika Port-Said*, 157. Venizelos had resigned as Greek prime minister in March 1915 and was conducting a campaign in the lead-up to elections in June. It is unlikely that Greek nationals in Egypt could vote unless they were in Greece at the time of the poll.

42. Soultanakis, *To Lefkoma ton Paristhmion*, 230.

43. The National Archives, London, Kew (TNA), Foreign Office (FO) 286/658, Undesirable Greeks in Egypt, 21 October 1917.

44. "E Apergie, scheseis kephaliou kai ergasias," *Emporikos Minitor* 16, 29 October 1903, 154–56.

45. See *al-Ahram*, 28 December 1901, which lists a number of union presidents, among them Dr. Zorbanos (shoemakers), Dr. Kyriazi (cigarette rollers), and Dr. Pistis (tailors).

46. Benin and Lockman, *Workers on the Nile*, 139.

47. TNA, FO 371/6297, Defence Security Intelligence Report [Green paper], 12 May 1921.

48. Caroline Piquet, *La Compagnie du canal de Suez* (Paris: PUPS, 2008), 331, notes that Skouphopoulos (incorrectly identified as a lawyer) participated in Group d'Études Sociales, a socialist discussion group, in Cairo in 1921.

49. Marius Deeb, "Labour and Politics in Egypt, 1919–1939," *International Journal of Middle East Studies* 10, no. 2 (1979): 193.

50. Piquet, *La Compagnie*, 343–44 (letter written in February 1937).

51. *Palies kai kainourgies Idees* (Alexandria: Grammata, 1924). Skouphopoulos's familiarity with Arabic seems a reasonable inference from the autobiography of his close friend, Themis Matsakis (Panos Xenos archive, ELIA).

52. Skouphopoulos is also reported to have published articles in English, French, and US American periodicals. Skouphopoulos, Biographical note.

53. "Peri ton oikon anochis," *Panegyptia*, 12 November 1932, 5.

54. Md. Badiur Rahman, "Egypt," in *Rabindranath Tagore, One Hundred Years of Global Reception*, ed. Martin Kämpchen and Imre Bangha (New Delhi: Orient BlackSwan, 2014), 145–47.

55. For Abu Shadi's account and photograph, see Ahmad Zaki Abu Shadi, *Masrah al-Adab* (Cairo: n.p., n.d.), 4–14; Shaden M. Tageldin, "Abū Shādī, Tagore, and the Problem of World Literature at the Hinge of Afroeurasia," *Journal of World Literature* 4, no. 3 (2019): 350–73.

56. Sources differ on his year of death but not the month (November).

57. For Dimou's childhood, see Giorgis Dimou, "Ta Paidika Ekeina Chronia," *Charaktika/ Schedia, Keimena/Epistoles* (Athens: Morphotiko Idrima Ethnikis Trapezis, 2004), 79–111.

58. Souloyiannis, *I Thesi ton Ellinon stin Egipto*, 87.

59. Tsirkas's most famous work, the trilogy *Drifting Cities* (*Akivernites Politeies*), was published in the early 1960s.

60. Egyptian Greek artists have received little attention in the literature on modern Egyptian art. For a survey of Egyptian Greek painters, see Yalourakis, *I Egiptos ton Ellinon*, 533–53.

61. For some examples of Nikolaidis's work, see "Kallitechnia," *Panorama* (Cairo-Alexandria), June 1931, 25.

62. Born in Alexandria in 1894, Kefallinos had taken a position at the School of Fine Arts in Athens in 1930 and worked there until his death in 1957. For the following biographical details on Dimou, see Anna Matthaiou and Popi Polemi, "O zografos-charaktis Giorgis Dimou," *ArcheioTaxio* 4 (2002): 61–63.

63. See, e.g., "Ils briseront les chaines," used to illustrate an article by Georges Henein, "Pour l'indépendance du monde," *Le Semaine égyptienne*, 25 March 1942, 60. Dimou himself was not associated with the surrealist movement.

64. Gaston Zananiri, *Rythmes dispersés* (Cairo: Le Semaine égyptienne, 1932); Stratis Tsirkas, *Fellahoi* (Alexandria: n.p., 1937); Lena Voiskou, *Alaska* (Cairo: Photos, 1938). The latter two covers are reproduced in Dimou, *Charaktika/Schedia, Keimena/Epistoles*, 33, 64.

65. Dimou, interview with the author, 8 April 1994, Athens. Menis Angelopoulos (1900–1990) lived and worked in Alexandria for many years and was notable for depicting different aspects of Egyptian life. He was a member of L'Atelier, an art society set up in Alexandria in 1935 that included Greek painter Thalia Flora-Karavia as well as Egyptians Mahmud Sa'id, Muhammad Naji, and others. See *Panegyptia*, 16 February 1935. For Yalourakis on Dimou, see *I Egiptos ton Ellinon*, 552.

66. *Al-Fajr al-Jadid* 1, no. 13 (1945): 1. The periodical was associated with a communist group in Cairo later known as the Workers' Vanguard (Tali'at al-'Ummal). The correct title of the woodcut itself is unclear. *Al-Fajr al-Jadid* captioned it "The National Revolution" and so associated it with the events of 1919. Elsewhere, in Dimou, *Charaktika/Schedia, Keimena/ Epistoles*, 60, it was titled "13 November 1935," a notable day of Egyptian protest against the British occupation following a speech by Mustafa al-Nahhas. Asked what the work depicted, Dimou himself said that this was a scene he saw many times in the streets in the mid-1930s. Interview with the author, 8 April 1994, Athens.

67. Tareq Y. Ismael and Rifa'at El-Sa'id, *The Communist Movement in Egypt, 1920–1988* (Syracuse, NY: Syracuse University Press, 1990), 33.

68. For some activities of the WILPF, see Margot Badran, *Feminists, Islam, and Nation: Gender and the Making of Modern Egypt* (Cairo: American University in Cairo Press, 1996), 226.

69. "Prepi na proaspisome tin Egiptiaki Eleftheria!," *Panegyptia*, 24 July 1937, 6–7.

70. "Spondi sto Thanato," *Politismos* 12–13 (1937): 29.

71. Matthaiou and Polemi, "O zografos-charaktis," 63. After the war, Koukoudami would work as a journalist for *Rizospastis*, the official organ of the Communist Party of Greece.

72. Interview of author with Miltos Kritikos (an active member in Egyptian Greek progressive circles), 16 April 1999, Athens. On the Greek Club of Amateurs, see Anthony Gorman, "Egypt's Forgotten Communists: The Postwar Greek Left," *Journal of Modern Greek Studies* 20, no. 1 (2002): 4.

73. As a result of their association with Kostas Karagiorgis, Dimou and his wife would also suffer adversely following his fall in the Greek Communist Party in the 1950s. Matthaiou and Popi, "O zografos-charaktis," 63.

74. For a more detailed study of the Egyptian Greek left of this period, see Gorman, "Egypt's Forgotten Communists."

75. Exhibition Programme, *Giorgis Dimou, Charaktika ke Schedia* [Engravings and Drawings] (Cultural Foundation of the National Bank [MIET]), 19 October 2005–6 January 2006.

76. For the following, see Despinas Sevastopoulou, *I Alexandreia pou fevgei . . .* (Alexandria: Le Progrès, 1953), 315–16, who gives 1879 as her birthdate, while Yalourakis says 1885, *I Egiptos ton Ellinon*, 470.

77. Souloyannis, *I Thesi ton Ellinon stin Egipto*, 85.

78. For a basic discussion, see Lesley Lababidi in collaboration with Nadia El-Arabi, *Silent No More: Special Needs People in Egypt* (Cairo: American University in Cairo Press, 2002).

79. Volta Bureau, *International Reports of Schools of the Deaf Made to the Volta Bureau, December 1895* (Washington: Gibson Bros, 1896), 6–7; Emad Gaan, *Inclusive Education in the Middle East* (New York: Routledge, 2011), 4–5.

80. E. A. F., "School Items," *American Annals of the Deaf* 53, no. 5 (1908): 499; H. Dominic W. Stiles, "Abdulla Iddleby/Ydlibi and the Cairo Deaf School," Institute & Action on Hearing Loss Libraries, accessed 28 March 2020, https://blogs.ucl.ac.uk/library-rnid/2015/07/10/abdulla-iddlebyydilbi-and-the-cairo-deaf-school/.

81. "A School for the Deaf in Egypt," *Volta Review* 43, no. 2 (1941): 98.

82. Ahmad al-Sidudi, "Madrasa al-Sam'/'I Scholi kophalalon tis Kas Semelis Tsotsou,'" *Egiptiotis Ellin* (December 1934) [Arabic original and Greek translation], 1, 4.

83. "A School for the Deaf," 98. Tsotsou was unable to speak English but reportedly knew six languages, likely Greek, French, Turkish, German, Arabic, and possibly Bulgarian or Italian.

84. Al-Sidudi, "Madrasa al-Sam'."

85. Oralism, which stressed the mimicking of speech, as opposed to manualism, which advocated the use of sign language, had been dominant in Europe since the International Congress of the Deaf in Milan in 1880. See British Sign Language Broadcasting Trust, *History of Deaf Education, Part 2*, accessed 14 April 2020, https://www.bslzone.co.uk/watch/history-deaf-education-2/.

86. Al-Sidudi, "Madrasa al-Sam."

87. "A School for the Deaf," 98.

88. *To "Proton" ke to "Pachi" Alphavitikon Anagnosmatarion dia ta Adikimena Ellinopoula* (Alexandria: Patriarchikon Tipografeion, 1934).

89. Semely Th. Tsotsou, *Pour les sourds-muets. Méthode de démutisation* (Alexandria: Lithographie d'Ancre, 1936).

90. *Méthode Pratique de Lecture Labiale. Pour les Victimes de l'Artillerie de la Guerre et pour ceux qui entendent mal* (Alexandria: n.p., 1943). It is not known to what extent she may have practiced these methods.

91. *I Chileoanagnosis i i akoi dia ton ophthalmon, Praktiki methodos dia kophous* (Alexandria: Emporiou, 1944); *Yia to kophalalo pedi (Methodos xemougomatos)* (Alexandria: Emporiou, 1951); *Therapia tis vradiglossias* (Alexandria: Emporiou, 1956).

92. *Out of Egypt* is a semi-autobiographical account of life in Egypt in the 1940s and 1950s, André Aciman, *Out of Egypt* (London: Harvill Press, 1994).

93. In a more critical vein, Aciman describes Tsotsou as "an obdurate middle-class idealist," Aciman, *Out of Egypt*, 89.

94. "Rotary around the World," *The Rotarian* (1938): 51.

95. KNK, "I Elpis," *Panaigyptia*, 22 January 1938, 10.

96. "Dar al-Amal," *al-Misriyya*, republished in *Egiptiotis Ellin–al-Yunani al-Mutamassir*, 31 January 1938, along with a Greek translation "ο Οίκος της Ελπίδος." [transliteration: o Oikos tis Elpidis].

97. "The Deaf in Egypt," *Volta Review* 49, no. 1 (1947): 35.

98. Higgins lists the following: Institute for the Deaf, Matariyya, Cairo; Institute for the Deaf, Rasafa St., Muharram Bey, Alexandria; a second School of the Deaf in Cairo; School for the Deaf, Helwan; and Elpis. Francis C. Higgins, "Schools for the Deaf in the World," *American Annals of the Deaf* 93, no. 1 (1948): 55. Lababidi provides different places and dates: al-Amal, Hilwan est. 1936, al-Kablat (possibly Matariyya), est. 1957. Lababidi, *Silent No More*, 38–43.

99. Yalourakis, *I Egiptos ton Ellinon*, 470.

100. An online search on "madrasa al-amal li-l-sam," accessed 15 March 2020.

BIBLIOGRAPHY

Abdulhaq, Najat. *Jewish and Greek Communities in Egypt: Entrepreneurship and Business before Nasser*. London: I. B. Tauris, 2016.

'Ashmawi, Sayyid. *Al-Yunaniyyun fi Misr 1805–1956*. Cairo: Ein, 1997.

Dalachanis, Angelos. *The Greek Exodus from Egypt: Diaspora Politics and Emigration, 1937–1962*. New York: Berghahn, 2017.

Deeb, Marius. "The Socioeconomic Role of the Local Foreign Minorities in Modern Egypt, 1805–1961." *International Journal of Middle East Studies* 9, no. 1 (1978): 11–22.

Georgaka, Dan, Alexander Kitroeff, and Matoula Tomara-Sideris, eds. Special issue, *Journal of the Hellenic Diaspora* 35, no. 2 (2009).

Gorman, Anthony P. "Cultural Communicators: The Greek Arabists of Interwar Egypt." In *Cultural Entanglement in the Pre-Independence Arab World*, edited by Anthony Gorman and Sarah Irving, 195–216. London: I. B. Tauris, 2021.

Gorman, Anthony P. "Egypt's Forgotten Communists: The Postwar Greek Left." *Journal of Modern Greek Studies* 20, no. 1 (2002): 1–27.

Issawi, Charles Philip. "The Greeks in the Middle East." In *Cross-Cultural Encounters and Conflicts*, 101–18. New York: Oxford University Press, 1998.

Karanasou, Floresca. "The Greeks in Egypt: From Mohammed Ali to Nasser, 1805–1961." In *The Greek Diaspora in the Twentieth Century*, edited by Richard Clogg, 24–57. London: Palgrave Macmillan, 1999.

Kitroeff, Alexander. *The Greeks and the Making of Modern Egypt*. Cairo: American University in Cairo Press, 2019.

Kitroeff, Alexander. *The Greeks in Egypt, 1919–1937: Ethnicity and Class*. London: Ithaca, 1989.

Politis, Athanase G. *L'Hellénisme et L'Égypte moderne*. 2 vols. Paris: Félix Alcan, 1929–30.

Tignor, Robert L. "The Economic Activities of Foreigners in Egypt, 1920–1950: From Millet to Haute Bourgeoisie." *Comparative Studies in Society and History* 22, no. 3 (1980): 416–49.

Yalourakis, Manolis. *I Egiptos ton Ellinon*. Athens: Mitropolis, 1967.

CHAPTER 9

GENDERING THE HISTORY OF THE LABOR MOVEMENT

HANAN HAMMAD

In July 1948, woman labor activist Zaynab al-ʿAskari wrote in the leftist periodical *Kifah al-Umma* (Nation's Struggle), "Finally for the first time in our history we witness in-dependent women's movements championing working women's struggles."[1] Al-ʿAskari pointed at the protests of women workers and the wives, sisters, and mothers of the male workers who were detained once war broke out in Palestine in the summer of 1948. Protesting women demanded the release of their men, visitations to the detainees, and financial support for their families until release. Bourgeois feminist organiza-tions, lacking affinity with the working class, did not effectively respond to the women laborers' call for support. The press, under martial censorship, could not report this pro-test or any labor activism.

Nevertheless, working women confirmed the leadership of their movement, as male activists and leaders of many trade unions welcomed representatives of the protesting women and publicly supported their demands. Detained workers themselves followed women's leadership and went on a hunger strike to pressure authorities to accept their demands. The women's labor movement successfully pressured the government to provide each detained worker's family with five Egyptian pounds to help cover living expenses while their breadwinners were behind bars without trial. Al-ʿAskari represented a clear gendered-classed discourse that spoke for experiences, conscious-ness, and views drastically different from the upper- and middle-class women in the feminist movement and the male-dominated labor movement of the interwar period. She wove nationalist, feminist, and working-class views together into one agenda that highlighted women in workers' families as leaders on the frontline of the labor movements.

The visibility of women's leadership and participation in the wave of labor protests that swept across Egypt before the January 2011 revolution has captured scholars' at-tention and propelled them to research gender in the labor movements of twenty-first-century Egypt. This recent scholarship rightly argued that gender relations inside and outside the workplace shaped the dynamics of workers' collective action, mobilization, and protests.[2] Despite the contribution of this scholarship, it mistakenly assumed that women's labor activism is a new phenomenon that emerged out of structural changes in the economy that increased the number of women workers while their working and living conditions deteriorated.[3] Scholars of the history of the Egyptian working class have overlooked women workers' leadership and active contributions to Egypt's vibrant labor movements predating the recent struggles against Mubarak's regime in the 2000s. In his pioneering work on the history of the labor movement in Egypt, historian Raouf Abbas reported that he had no information on any women's labor activism in Egypt. He wrote, "I did not hear of any existence of a labor union of women workers even during peak activism. Programs of [male] labor unions that appeared during the interwar period did not care to organize women workers, probably due to the limited number of women working in the industry. Women worked only in cotton ginning and textile factories where they performed secondary tasks. Thus, they [women] were not substantially present to attract labor organizers to form women-only trade unions. At the same time, social traditions prevented women from participating with men workers in the same unions."[4]

This quotation from Abbas reflects two recurring challenges in writing labor and women's histories: the lack of sources documenting working-class activism and gender biases in interpreting available sources. Both challenges have fortified the false assumptions that only men participated in Egyptian labor activism and that the women's movement ignored working-class struggles. Until recently, the history of labor, the history of women, and the emerging history of capitalism have been separate terrains of inquiry. Social and labor history that flourished in the 1970s and 1980s focused on political and economic structures but paid scant attention to female laborers and was eclipsed by cultural history in the 1990s.

Labor historians have argued that the industrial working class in Egypt emerged through Egypt's integration into the global capitalist system, allowing an influx of investments in industrial and transport enterprises, followed by workers engaging in collective actions. They have focused on organized factory workers, labor politics, partisan ideologies, and the institutional history of the Egyptian working class. Meanwhile, they gave little attention to workers' social life outside the workplace and trade unions.[5] Historians have also demonstrated that policies and attitudes toward Egyptian workers in the first half of the twentieth century often configured these workers as classed individuals, leaving the question of gender consciousness and women's labor activism out. Women's history benefited from the cultural history that underlines the politics of identity and representation. Historians of gender in twentieth-century Egypt have tended to focus on the activism of upper- and middle-class women and the legal and institutional structures that contributed to changes or stagnation of gender regimes.[6] This vibrant intellectual history has limited its scope and sources, undermining how class, as a socioeconomic category, operated in socioeconomic and cultural structures, thus paying little attention to female industrial workers who carved out their spaces in masculine mechanized factories. Emerging histories of capitalism that draw on the analytical tools of cultural studies to research socioeconomic histories can potentially reconcile social and cultural histories. However, although histories of gender and women must be an integral part of the history of capitalist society, these new histories of capitalism rarely address sex and gender.[7]

Gendering the history of the Egyptian labor movement involves, in part, tracing the origin and development of women's labor activism in the interwar period and experiences of proletarianization, or dependency on the sale of labor power for survival. It also means counting the emotional, social, economic, and political labors shouldered by women to sustain the labor movement and male activists. By widening the scope of analysis beyond factory struggles, industrial working-class women and labor activism can be reconceptualized. For instance, women in workers' families creatively employed gendered traditions to win public awareness and sympathy for their causes. Their practices illuminate working-class women's immense contributions to labor history and how their gendered practices enhanced their activism rather than presenting barriers to it. Underlining how gender shaped working-class activism shows that gender is fundamentally crucial to shaping working-class history and culture, just as class is important to understanding the histories of women.[8]

THE CHALLENGE OF SOURCES

Scholars of Egyptian labor history have struggled with persistent lack of access to primary documents produced by labor activists. During its endless campaigns against labor and leftist movements, the Egyptian state police confiscated activists' papers, books, and artifacts without either returning them or depositing them in publicly accessible inventories. Despite repeated promises to share confiscated archives of the Egyptian left with the public, police departments, in constant battle with labor activism and communist movements throughout the twentieth century, have rejected all researchers' attempts to access these materials.[9] Meanwhile, activists who managed to save some sources tirelessly hid them out of fear of police raids and confiscations. As a result, some activists respond with suspicion when scholars ask to access and draw on those materials.

Despite the state's hostility toward labor activism, President Husni Mubarak's regime (r. 1981–2011), with its democratic façade, allowed veteran labor and communist activists to have the accounts of their experiences in labor and nationalist movements published. Countering the dominance of the Islamist movement over oppositional politics, independent and leftist research centers mushroomed in parallel with the expansion of civil society from the early 1990s and invested in recovering the history of the Egyptian left. Leaders of labor movements from different generations finally had a chance to have their accounts published, relying on memories or extractions from the few primary sources that survived police raids and confiscation campaigns. Factionalism among Egyptian leftists also posed barriers to making these fractured personal archives available to all scholars. Each faction granted access to its archives in personal depositories only to scholars deemed trustworthy or willing to accept the faction's views uncritically. While this factionalism still colors the published testimonies and volumes of documents, the fractured archives provide a wealth of sources that could energize agendas for researching labor history. Programs and pamphlets of clandestine groups and historical voices that had been silenced in personal hoards or police headquarters since the interwar period were published and became available to scholars for the first time.

The sources to reconstruct women's history in the Egyptian labor movement, and thereby reconceptualize proletarian women and labor activism, include the collection of documents the communist writer and activist Abu Sayf Yusuf published in a volume on the history of the leftist organization Tali'at al-'Ummal (Workers' Vanguard) between 1941 and 1957, the collection of documents and testimonies included in several volumes compiled by the Committee of Documenting the History of the Egyptian Communist Movement until 1965, and the documents and historical writings about textile workers by labor activist Taha Sa'd 'Uthman. Notwithstanding how memories and personal, partisan, and ideological biases could have shaped and colored the activists' accounts of their experiences narrated in these sources, these accounts are valuable considering the scarce archival sources that are accessible. The challenge scholars face when subjecting them to gender analysis is that they contain only limited or silenced voices of women labor activists. Male comrades still dominate the crafting of the canonical narrative of the Egyptian labor movement and working-class struggles. Male professional scholars who edited those volumes expressed, with a few exceptions, no interest in unearthing women's experiences. Nonetheless, reading these accounts against the grain can open doors to excavate the experiences of women activists in the labor movement and among the industrial working class.

Women joined the industrial labor force in large numbers from the advent of industrialization and the emergence of mechanized factories in the second half of the nineteenth century. Women's work intensified with the integration of Egypt into the global economy at the close of the nineteenth century. A work incident on 8 October 1864 revealed that the entire labor force of one floor in a factory was female. On that day, a girl worker lost her life as her body was crushed by a machine in an Alexandrian cotton press factory while working after dark.[10] Women laborers were concentrated in two major industries at the time—cotton ginning and tobacco factories—and many women worked in agriculture, including seasonal mobile work (*tarahil*). The spread of local industry during and following World War I increased the number of industrial workers. With the establishment of Bank Misr in 1921 to lead the industrialization drive along with the Egyptian Industrial Federation, thousands of urban and rural poor women workers became visible in different industries throughout the country.

Contradictory and unreliable information about women's participation in industrial work is an obstacle to writing women into labor history. For example, the first census to count Egyptian industrial workers in 1907 reported only fifteen women workers in the tobacco industry. Yet other sources suggest that twenty women worked in one of the thirty-seven cigarette factories at that time.[11] Lack of accuracy continued in the following censuses. The 1947 census documented 1,379 female industrial workers in al-Mahalla al-Kubra, even though 2,000 women worked at the Misr Spinning and Weaving Company (MSWC) alone. Women dominated the labor force at MSWC's gauze factory from its inauguration in 1930. Thousands of women and girls in al-Mahalla al-Kubra worked in small mechanical and handloom weaving factories for wages or as unpaid household labor.

State statistics reflected inefficiency and biases that undercounted working women. Authorities' ambivalence toward women working for wages and the uncertainty about how to categorize new urban social groups contributed to undercounting female industrial workers in the early and mid-twentieth century.[12] For instance, in his survey on the living conditions of factory workers outside Cairo, Saʻd Habib, a male inspector in the Labor Department in the mid-twentieth century, devoted a chapter that was purportedly on women workers but in reality was a diatribe against them. Habib denied women's right to work or any other women's right and dismissed women's demand for equal pay because "women are physically, intellectually, and mentally inferior to men."[13] Habib did not recognize that women constituted a substantial part of the industrial labor force that his survey professed to cover. Nevertheless, he called for making work available for poor women because "it is better for a woman to work than to fall, better to toil away to earn the substance of living than to sell her honor for a living."[14]

State bureaucrats were not the only source of ambivalence about women's work. Women themselves, intentionally or not, hid their factory work, being unaware of its value or avoiding social stigma. Some women quit working once they got married and even hid their history of factory work to avoid such stigma. Factory owners also tended to hide workers from state officials to avoid legal obligations. Employers enforced long work hours and night shifts and hired child laborers younger than the minimum age. The invisibility of women workers in state records and social consciousness constitutes part of the experience of industrial women workers in Egypt, which highlights the importance of gendering the labor movement and writing female workers into women and labor histories.

WOMEN'S LABOR AND LAW

The legal apparatus was faster than censuses and male activists to acknowledge women's participation in industrial labor. The visibility of women and girls in hazardous industrial workplaces drew public attention as early as the 1860s. Following the incident mentioned above of a girl being crushed in a cotton pressing factory in 1864, the courts instructed the government to disallow women's work after dark.[15] The 1904 labor law was the earliest act to protect women and children in hazardous workplaces. Five years later, in 1909, Law No. 14 explicitly limited work hours for women and children in burgeoning cotton ginning factories.

After the 1919 revolution, the short-lived Wafd government, led by nationalist leader Sa'd Zaghlul, formed the Nile Valley Workers' Union Federation in 1924. The general secretary of the Central Committee of the Wafd Party, 'Abd al-Rahman Fahmi Bey, led the federation.[16] The upper-class bey sought to empower himself among elite politicians by leading the labor trade unions. The Wafd Party's goal was to assert its popularity among workers and contain communist activism, particularly after the first Egyptian Communist Party formed the first labor union in 1921 in Cairo and then moved its base of operations to Alexandria.[17] Although the Wafdist union was ineffective in organizing workers—its main aim was to bring workers under the control of the Wafd government—it recognized women's participation in the industrial workforce. In its newspaper *Ithad al-'Ummal* (Workers' Union Federation), it dedicated a section to women workers. The federation and its mouthpiece encouraged female workers to organize themselves into a women's labor union. However, the Wafd federation and its dependent unions never sought to act on this call; no union member of the federation included a female leader or women members.

From its inception in the 1920s, the Egyptian Feminist Union (EFU) was the dominant organization to recognize women's rights, but it stayed away from working-class women's aspirations.[18] Despite the barriers, women-only organizations emerged, as did political party programs focused on women workers. Among political parties and feminist organizations of the period, al-Hizb al-Watani al-Nisa'i (the National Feminist Party [NFP]), founded by Fatima Ni'mat Rashid in 1942, championed women workers' rights. A veteran feminist and former activist in the EFU who wrote for its outlet, *l'Egyptienne*, and edited its Arabic journal, *al-Misriyya*, Rashid was one of the leftists and radical feminists. She founded the NFP as the first party devoted to women's political rights.[19] The party had a predominantly middle-class membership, including lawyers, teachers, journalists, and writers. According to one historical account, it did not enjoy a broad appeal despite its broadening feminist base.[20] Rashid also established close ties with Marxists, and her party maintained close contacts with communist activists during the 1940s, including writers Ahmad Rushdi Salih and Abu Sayf Yusuf and labor lawyer Yusuf Darwish. Thus, when those three activists established their communist labor organization Tali'at al-'Ummal (Workers' Vanguard) in 1946, the organization interacted with Rashid and the NFP.[21] The NFP maintained connections with workers' and peasants' parties, adopted a platform for economic and social reforms, fought illiteracy, and called for hygienic living standards among working-class women of Greater Cairo. It called for equal labor rights for men and women workers, including equal wages and women's rights to form and join labor unions.[22]

The NFP recognized and attempted to benefit from already vibrant activism among female workers in the interwar period. Women workers launched their movement, demanding a nine-hour workday as early as 1927.[23] Although many details about this movement, which lasted more than two years, are still lacking, it effectively pushed for improved work conditions and reduced work hours for women and children. The demand occupied the top priority of the committee that the government formed in 1929 to investigate labor issues in Egypt. 'Abd al-Rahman Rida Pasha chaired the committee, which suggested a legal ban on employing women and minors in hazardous health work on night shifts. The committee's report recognized working women's rights in a three-week maternal holiday with half pay and two ninety-minute breaks every workday to nurse their babies. Those rights became law in 1933 after Harold Butler, deputy director of the International Labor Office, visited Egypt on the invitation of the government to advise on the situation of Egyptian workers. Butler reported that most women working in ginning factories were fifteen- to nineteen-year-old girls, and child labor laws should cover them.[24]

Law No. 48 and Law No. 80 in 1933 were the first comprehensive labor laws regulating women's and children's work in industry and trade. Subsequently, Law No. 147 in 1935 regulated work hours in retail stores and health services. Though it granted women and children a weekend and annual holiday, employers did not follow its regulations, and only a few big establishments in Cairo and Alexandria granted workers weekend breaks.[25] A lack of government inspections or supervision, particularly outside the two big cities, allowed employers to violate laws, making women and children work longer than the maximum work hours and at night, with no weekly holiday. Employers ignored health conditions in workplaces and hired children younger than the legal age without medical examination proving their physical ability to work.[26]

WOMEN IN LABOR

The rising number of women working in industry enhanced the social acceptance of women and even their own preference to work in factories rather than domestic service. The militant labor movements of the late 1930s and the 1940s witnessed intensive participation among women and forced the government to recognize labor unions. Female workers participated in and supported labor platforms that included the rights and demands of women workers in addition to the demands shared with male workers.[27] Thus, women became more visible in strikes along with their male colleagues.

Foreign owners of some factories in Shubra al-Khayma, in northern Cairo, had to leave Egypt to join the army of their country of origin during World War II. They laid off their Egyptian workers in large numbers, leaving the workers to face unemployment and skyrocketing living costs. Workers gathered in the Textile Labor Union on 14 September 1939 and launched a sit-in strike to protest. Female workers participated in the protest, and male and female workers from different parts of the country expressed their solidarity with the workers by sending supporting messages to the press.[28]

In 1942, male and female workers in the Egyptian Jute Company, a wool textile factory in the Musturud area of southern Cairo, went on a desegregated strike, undermining conservative social traditions. After limiting women's work to preparation sections, the factory owners started employing women to operate looms and paid them half the wages of men. This step triggered men workers' greatest fears. Men always worried that factories would replace them with women for lower wages. This concern was not unrealistic, as the average daily wage for women in 1938 was 4.3 piasters, less than half that of men (8.8 piasters), which itself did not cover the cost of living.[29] The factory's labor union thoughtfully avoided tension with women weavers by demanding equal pay for all. Male and female workers worked together in solidarity. They participated in the strike for equal pay for male and female workers, assigning the operation of looms to men only and assigning women workers to less-tiring tasks.[30] Attempting to contain the strike, the government sent a committee to mediate between the workers and the factory owners. Female and male workers negotiated with the mediators, known as the al-Tawfiq Committee, which accepted all workers' demands except equal pay, intending to stir division among workers.[31]

Women workers decided to extend the strike despite police violence. They eventually ended their strike fifteen days later, and men continued the strike for another ten days. Management at the factory rescheduled women's hours differently from men's hours to abort any future cooperation and solidarity between male and female workers. It deployed police power to force women to sign pledges not to participate in future strikes. Eventually, the company moved sections that relied on women's work to a different area and hired new women workers. The separation of male and female workers weakened the collective negotiation power of all workers. In 1947, new female workers saw a reduction of their annual holiday from ten to seven days.[32]

With increased women's participation in expanding industries in the early 1930s, women workers developed organic leadership. Women's activism to form and empower labor unions varied from one industrial site to another, and there are contradicting accounts about women's participation in unions. According to one account, the Union of Mechanical Textile Workers in Greater Cairo did not have any female membership from its establishment until it was disbanded in April 1945.[33] During the same period, women and men in several small textile factories in Alexandria, including all-women workers of the flannel underwear factory, formed one union named the Trade Union of Mechanical Textile Workers. Women members participated in the election to choose its board and leadership.[34] Meanwhile, the account of woman worker activist Zaynab al-'Askari confirms that women workers in the Shubra al-Khayma area were eager to join labor unions in 1944, and they worked hard to convince the all-male members of the union boards to accept women's membership. By 1945, women had succeeded in this effort and were able to join the trade unions. Al-'Askari launched her labor activism when she worked in textile factories in Shubra al-Khayma in the late 1930s. In vibrant labor activism that reflected increasing class and gender consciousness, all of the textile workers, and particularly women, affirmed her leadership. In 1945–46, she led labor strikes and demonstrations in Shubra al-Khayma, which forced factory owners to discuss workers' demands with elected factory committees. Workers elected al-'Askari to represent them for the Polytex Textile Factory, and she succeeded in attaining some of the workers' demands.[35] According to one account, she was the first woman to lead women workers in labor protests alongside male workers. Her primary influence was to mobilize women workers and convince them to participate in labor strikes and demonstrations that demanded workers' rights and the release of detained labor activists. She met activist

Mahmud al-'Askari in a communist circle in Shubra al-Khayma, and they got married in 1946 and had three children together.

Female workers in the Misr Silk Textile Company in Damietta, along the Mediterranean coast in northern Egypt, encouraged their eighty-six colleagues to join the labor unions.[36] The company's labor union invited al-'Askari to meet their women workers to exchange experiences and thoughts on continuing their struggles along with their male counterparts for a wage increase. Six of the women workers in Damietta continued their communication with women activists in Shubra al-Khayma, al-'Askari in particular. Echoed in al-Mahalla al-Kubra, women workers of the MSWC also joined the labor union of the company workers, though there is no evidence that they participated actively. However, the council of that labor union did not have a record of standing with or advocating for workers' interests and became widely known for its dependency on the company's administrators, from whom it received instructions. In al-Mahalla, women workers of MSWC received a financial gift from the trade union upon getting married and leaving work. The money was partial compensation for the membership fees they paid during their years of work.[37]

WOMEN-ONLY WORKERS' ASSOCIATION

The first labor union for women workers, Rabitat 'Amilat al-Qutr al-Misri (The Association of Egypt's Women Workers [AEWW]), emerged in 1946 under the leadership of textile worker Hikmat al-Ghazali. The association, which made its headquarters in downtown Cairo, was close to militant leftists.[38] Al-Ghazali started as a textile worker in Shubra al-Khayma in the early 1940s, earned a degree in social work, and married a communist lawyer. The association circulated leaflets and pamphlets urging male and female laborers to work together. Its public agenda had two overlapping classed and gendered goals. The first goal was to unify workers in powerful labor unions to improve the living and working conditions of the entire working class. The second goal was to empower women workers to earn equal pay for the same work and equal rights to unemployment insurance, medical healthcare, a pension, and affordable services such as daycare, kitchens, and laundromats. The organization attracted women workers who felt comfortable participating in labor activism in a homosocial milieu that conformed with the traditional social expectations of women-only gatherings. Combining social respectability and keenness for participation, women workers maintained traditional modesty and attended meetings dressed in *milayya laff*—black overwrap sheets that working-class urban women put on over their clothes, neither completely closed nor blatantly open—signifying modesty and authenticity among popular-class women.[39] Due to the link between the association and militant labor and leftist activists, Prime Minister Isma'il Sidqi disbanded it during his campaign against communism in July 1946. The regime accused the association of being a cover for illicit communist activism.[40]

Despite its short life, the AEWW promoted the Congress of the Egyptian Workers' Union, which functioned as a union federation and mobilized workers behind it.[41] The association played a crucial role in organizing women workers and unifying the labor movement at a critical moment. In his account of the attempt to establish a unified federation for labor unions in the 1940s, Taha Sa'd 'Uthman highlighted the role of the association's leader, Hikmat al-Ghazali, in unifying workers across divided factions. At the World Union Conference in Paris in 1946, competing and divided Egyptian delegates claimed to represent Egyptian workers. Upon their return, a group called for a meeting to discuss the preparation for May Day and announce the Congress of the Egyptian Workers' Unions. The factionalism that appeared among Egyptian delegates in Paris spilled over, and some of them boycotted the meeting without previous notice. Simultaneously, many representatives of the provincial labor unions came to Cairo eager to participate. Al-Ghazali courageously attended, although the event became dangerous as police surrounded the initial location, and organizers succeeded in holding the meeting elsewhere. Maneuvering within Law No. 85 of 1942, which banned forming a unifying federation of labor unions, activists deliberately avoided the word *federation*. They named their unifying organization the Congress of the Egyptian Workers' Unions.

'Uthman applauded al-Ghazali for attending the meeting, at which she gave 'Uthman all documents, minutes, and membership fees that the committee received, while some male activists boycotted and tried to keep those records away from the newly born federation. Representing the women workers' association, al-Ghazali delivered a speech fueling the call for unity among all men and women workers and for unionization of women so that women could achieve "equality with men in payment and vote . . . the association strives to rid women from exploitation by men and employers."[42] The association actively participated in the vibrant and militant labor movement, calling for the release of arrested labor activists, the limitation of work hours to forty hours per week for full pay, and the recognition of May Day as a paid holiday for all workers. It encouraged women workers to get involved in labor elections and form factory committees and "male and female workers [to] stay united."[43]

The AEWW also contributed to the establishment of Jam'iyyat Rabbat al-Buyut (Housewives' Association), a group of neighborhood-based associations aimed at pressuring the government to control prices and provide sufficient quantities of basic living supplies at moderate prices for working-class families.[44] The association also participated in the nationalist movement and joined the Committee of Students and Workers, which played a significant part in organizing the popular demonstrations and protests against the British occupation in the 1940s. Al-Ghazali and many association members, including many leftist women, demonstrated against Prime Minister Mahmud Fahmi al-Nuqrashi in downtown Cairo upon his failure to address the nationalist question at the United Nations in September 1947. Participants in the demonstration waved signs that read "Free Palestine, Viva Nile Unity, Down with Colonialism, Women Are Half of Society, Viva Men's and Women's struggle, Colonialism is the People's Enemy."[45]

Hikmat al-Ghazali's activism challenged patriarchal anxiety among her male colleagues and comrades. While communist factions attempted to undermine one another, splitting labor activists and undermining collegial coordination and support, some launched gossip campaigns against al-Ghazali. Some activists of the Workers' Vanguard organization accused al-Ghazali of employing "dishonorable" methods, a campaign that Taha Sa'd 'Uthman, an activist of the group, strongly refuted in 1998, fifty years after the events.[46]

LABOR OF LOVE AND ACTIVE SUSTAINABILITY

Labor historians and activists considered social traditions barriers to women's participation in labor struggles.[47] They narrowed their understanding of activism to attending organizational meetings, usually in male-only spaces such as coffee shops and *buza* taverns, running for union board elections, and leading strikes and protests. This narrow vision ignores how women used the same gender-based traditions to play crucial roles in facilitating activism and supporting male workers' protests. We need to reconceptualize labor activism to appreciate women's hard labor in sustaining workers' movements through shouldering and providing social, economic, emotional, and political support that sustained male and female activists. Women's labor was largely invisible, and there was no way to measure and count it even when noticed.

Female workers and women in the households of industrial workers were often critical factors in continuing labor activism even when women workers were not visible at organizational meetings or strikes. In the MSWC in al-Mahalla al-Kubra, the largest textile compound in the country, female laborers supported their colleagues in weaving factories and maintenance workshops when they launched a two-week strike for an eight-hour workday in 1938. Women workers shared their savings with striking male coworkers so that the latter could support their families while unpaid.[48] Women were better positioned than male colleagues to provide financial support to striking workers. Although male and female workers were both in poverty and women were paid even less, social traditions allowed, even encouraged, working women to save part of their wages. Those meager savings helped the woman's family to buy clothing and household items upon her marriage. Thus, women workers in the MSWC had a little savings to support their striking colleagues.[49] This form of invisible solidarity was crucial in supporting striking workers and galvanizing female workers' awareness of being part of the labor community and movement with common interests.

Upon the declaration of the establishment of the State of Israel on 15 May 1948, Egypt imposed an emergency law and arrested many leftist and labor activists. Wives and mothers of the detainees, mostly textile workers in Greater Cairo, formed an organization named Jam'iyyat Usar al-Mu'taqalin al-Shuyu'iyyin (Association of the Families of the Communist Detainees). Hikmat al-Ghazali, whose husband was among the communist detainees, was active in the association, demonstrated in Cairo's streets, wrote to the press, and delivered petitions to the government asking it to release their men and raise public awareness about their living conditions. Women protested in challenging conditions as emergency laws posed restrictions on the press and civil society. Women labor activists acted with no support from formal organizations, as authorities prevented the progressive Women's National Party from assembling.[50] The wives visited Egypt's Society for Protecting Women and Children, asking its support in releasing the men so wives would not fall into moral corruption. Representatives of the organization received them but could not act on their behalf.[51] Only the leftist periodical *Kifah al-Umma* (Nation's Struggle) published messages of protest from wives to the government.[52]

Women provided supply lines to incarcerated men and revealed abuses they faced in the Haykisteb Detention Center on the outskirts of Cairo. To intimidate the women, officers verbally abused them, forcing them to descend from the visitation car and leaving them in the middle of the desert road without transportation after visiting their men. Emboldened women shamed the abusing officers and asked the general martial ruler to investigate the incident and the deteriorating health conditions of the detainees.[53] Women's activism pressured the government to allow detainees to use pens, scrap papers, and newspapers. It allowed them to keep money, dress in plain clothing, and move freely inside the detention yards and improved the quality of their food.[54]

To raise public awareness about the detainees and maneuver around the press censorship and the emergency law restrictions against public protests, women drew on the gendered social traditions of funerals. Many women moved through public streets dressed in black, weeping and wailing as if they were in a funeral procession. Whenever passersby asked them who died, they talked about the political prisoners and the vulnerability to infectious diseases in prison. Several infectious diseases, particularly relapsing fever, were rampant in Egypt's densely populated and unhygienic urban areas.[55]

Political prisoners lingered in detention until 1950, when the coalition government released some of them. Upon the formation by the Wafd of a new government, news reached families that the Ministry of Interior Affairs intended to keep several detainees and transfer them to the detention center in the far oasis (al-Wahat prison). Women organized a large protest demonstration in downtown Cairo and had a sit-in protest outside the residency of Prime Minister Mustafa al-Nahhas until he came out and promised to release all political prisoners the following day, which he did.[56]

'Aysha Ahmad al-Wakil employed gendered traditions to support a labor movement when her son, Ahmad Salim Salim, participated in the massive strike of textile workers in Cairo and Shubra al-Khayma in 1946. She wanted to help workers stop newly recruited replacement workers from reaching factories and breaking the strike. Worker activists in the Representative Committee of Textile Workers in Cairo and Its Suburbs planned to hit buses bringing replacement workers with bottles full of sand. 'Aysha hosted striking workers and hid them in the backyard of her single-room home so that the police could not arrest them while they filled bottles with sand. 'Aysha utilized her creativity to ensure that workers and their tools were safe. She borrowed *milayya laff* from many of her neighbors so male workers could disguise themselves as women. The plan succeeded. Workers managed to escape police surveillance and, accompanied by 'Aysha, arrived at their destinations safely with sand bottles.[57]

Over the years, 'Aysha frequently hosted workers eluding police arrest and claimed them as her own children for protection. She hid their clandestine publications and burned them at the right time lest police confiscate the material and use them as evidence for outlawed labor and communist activities. She became active in Jam'iyyat Rabbat al-Buyut, which collected signatures from the public and mobilized demonstrations to protest the cost of living, particularly the prices of foodstuff. One of its demonstrations culminated in delivering to parliament a petition for members to reject the government's decision to raise prices. In 1951, 'Aysha participated in a delegate meeting with the minister of supplies to protest an increase in bread prices from five to eight *millims*.

Women workers provided crucial logistical support to male participants in sit-in strikes. While male workers had sit-ins inside factories, women workers demonstrated outside to attract public attention, visited press offices to publicize strikes, submitted workers' demands to government departments, and collected food from families to deliver to striking workers inside factories.[58] Many of those actions were courageous, as police forces usually put factories under siege to cut supplies and pressure workers to end strikes. Women also took advantage of the social traditions that compromised the police's willingness to overtly attack women in public. It was also upon the mothers, wives, sisters, and daughters of striking workers to pool sources and prepare meals and provisions to keep striking workers alive and well inside factories.

In some cases, married worker couples championed labor activism together, or wives picked up the baton after husbands were detained. The information available about a few couples provides good examples of gendered labor activism and the crucial role women had in the movement even when their struggles were invisible behind the scenes and when men's struggles only took the fore. The new owner of the Nuzhah Textile Company in Alexandria fired Muhammad Fahmi al-Mahdi, the president of the workers' union. Al-Mahdi and his wife, who worked in the same factory, went on a hunger strike. Police failed to manipulate the wife by promising to hire her husband in a more lucrative job in the transportation sector if they both ended the strike. The wife informed her colleagues of the corrupt offer, which energized workers' solidarity and encouraged some to join the hunger strike and sit-in protest. Eventually, the government mediated an agreement between workers and the owner to reinstate all workers and give them half pay for the strike days.

While her husband, Mahmud al-'Askari, was in detention in the late 1940s, Zaynab al-'Askari's manager in the wool textile factory where she worked and the head of the Labor Department there attempted to manipulate and intimidate her into divorcing her husband. She was steadfast against all promises to grant her promotions and significant raises. The manager demoted and transferred her to a factory branch far from home in retaliation for her rejection.[59] As Taha Sa'd 'Uthman summarizes it, "Women workers who shouldered labor activism faced huge pressure and attacks and were fought in their livelihoods."[60]

In the early 1940s, textile factories were a hotbed of labor protests to form workers' unions. Police frequently arrested protesting workers and threatened to arrest women in the families of those who escaped before police raids. Detaining or threatening to detain women in police stations by itself fueled workers' protests. Meanwhile, women had to handle the situation spontaneously during the absence of their male relatives and sometimes without previous experience. Two months after her move from her village to Shubra al-Khayma to live with her husband, Taha Sa'd 'Uthman's wife faced police forces storming her home. Realizing that her husband was not at home, police left before returning to threaten to arrest her unless she informed them of her husband's whereabouts. The young rural wife had barricaded the door with all available furniture so the policemen could not enter the house to arrest her. Finally, her husband arrived and surrendered himself to the police. 'Uthman was one of the leaders of the ongoing labor strike in textile factories in Shubra al-Khayma in September 1939.[61] Police threatened to attack the sister and mother of one worker, 'Abd al-Mun'im Ibrahim, secretary of the union of the Egyptian National Textile Company in Alexandria, in the summer of 1946.[62]

Women had to shoulder manifold burdens when their husbands were fired or imprisoned due to labor and political activism. Some women spontaneously participated in this activism, and their experiences of proletarianization are important but invisible. Women provided food, cash, cigarettes, and other basics to male relatives whose activism resulted in detentions and imprisonment. More than material support, women provided emotional support that gave imprisoned male labor activists the certainty and peace of mind they needed at their lowest moment. An illustrative example is Zaynab Ibrahim 'Ali Gharraba, who had married industrial worker Fikri al-Khuli when he worked in the al-Mahalla textile factory in the mid-1930s. Al-Khuli had to leave al-Mahalla for Shubra al-Khayma after facing prosecution due to his unionist activism in the early 1940s. He lived an epic journey of labor activism, detention, escape, and reimprisonment from 1948 through the 1960s. Upon his detention for the first time in Shubra al-Khayma in 1948, his wife joined both the job market to feed their children and the movement to support detained workers, including her husband. Gharraba joined wives and mothers of workers in their protests outside the Ministry of Interior Affairs, courthouses, and detention centers. This protest by women forced the government to grant them financial support because the police detained their husbands and sons, depriving families of their primary livelihood.

Under President Gamal Abdel Nasser (r. 1954–70), al-Khuli was arrested and later escaped from the detention center in Rud al-Faraj in Cairo. Police arrested his wife, Zaynab Gharraba, and detained her to force her husband to surrender himself. Upon her release, she activated the protest movements of detained workers' mothers and wives. Gharraba and other activists, including Zaynab al-'Askari, formed a women's committee to support detained workers and their families. Women exchanged experiences and advice on facing police raids and coping with the uncertainty of having their men behind bars. They cooperated and developed individual tactics and collective movements to defend themselves and their male relatives. The group raised funds through donations and selling foodstuff and used the revenues to support families. The group frequently protested and communicated messages from detained workers to their families.[63] The movement succeeded in pressuring police to release at least two workers. When she learned, in the early 1960s, that authorities released political prisoners if they agreed to denounce their political ideologies publicly and promised never to resume their activism, Zaynab Gharraba visited her husband in prison to encourage him not to accept such an offer. Gharraba's emotional support and encouragement for her husband were crucial to keeping his morale up during the long years in prison. While al-Khuli lingered in Nasser's prisons, Gharraba managed to support all their children in pursuing a college education, except her eldest daughter, who worked in the factory.[64]

Conclusion

Women have participated in and contributed to labor movements in Egypt since the rise of modern industry following World War I, whether as factory workers or members of worker families. Their activism combined and reflected their gendered and classed positionalities. These women's communal and social consciousness were anchored in their dependence on the sale of labor power for survival (i.e., they experienced proletarianization).[65] Their multifaceted proletarian experiences as women, workers, and members of working-class families and communities informed their activism. They maneuvered within the social patriarchy that limited their access to male-dominated spaces by expanding their agency in manipulating the same gender regime to actively defend their labor rights and protect their male coworkers, husbands, brothers, and sons. They stood up to the police force, and when political repression forced their male relatives behind bars, they pooled their resources and shared knowledge to launch collective action. When women had to stay home, they prepared meals for protesting or imprisoned men and cared for their children—practices that should be understood as activism rather than mere domestic chores.[66] Their labor and support offered their families and imprisoned men provisions and love. We should acknowledge the mental and emotional toll that those women paid and avoid the pitfall of romanticizing their resilience and resistance. Studying labor history through a gender lens and centralizing women's experiences in researching labor movements enrich our understanding of the proletarianization of Egypt's populations.

Acknowledgment

I dedicate this chapter to Professor Joel Beinin and the memory of the late Professor Raouf Abbas, two great labor historians, teachers, and mentors.

NOTES

1. Zaynab al-'Askari, "al-Haraka al-Nisa'iyya fi al-Hala al-Hadira," *Kifah al-Umma*, 15 July 1948, 4.
2. Marie Duboc, "Where Are the Men? Here Are the Men and the Women! Surveillance, Gender, and Strikes in Egyptian Textile Factories," *Journal of Middle East Women's Studies* 9, no. 3 (2013): 28–53.
3. Joel Beinin, "Egyptian Workers and January 25th: A Social Movement in Historical Context," *Social Research* 79, no. 2 (2012): 323–48.
4. Raouf Abbas, *al-Haraka al-'Ummaliyya fi Misr: 1899–1952* (Cairo: Dar al-Kitab al-'Arabi li-l-Tiba'a wa-l-Nashr, 1968), 128.
5. Ibid., Abbas, *al-Haraka al-'Ummaliyya al-Misriyya fi Daw' al-Watha'iq al-Baritaniyya, 1924–1937* (Cairo: 'Alam al-Kutub, 1975); Ellis Goldberg, *Tinker, Tailor, and Textile Worker: Class and Politics in Egypt, 1930–1952* (Berkeley: University of California Press, 1986); Joel Beinin and Zachary Lockman, *Workers on the Nile: Nationalism, Communism, Islam, and the Egyptian Working Class, 1882–1954* (Princeton: Princeton University Press, 1989); Joel Beinin, *Workers and Peasants in the Modern Middle East* (New York: Cambridge University Press, 2000); Joel Beinin, "Egyptian Textile Workers: From Craft Artisans Facing European Competition to Proletarians Contending with the State," in *Covering the World: A Global History of Textile Workers, 1650–2000*, ed. Lex Heerma van Voss et al. (Burlington: Ashgate Press, 2009).
6. See, e.g., Margot Badran, *Feminists, Islam, and Nation: Gender and the Making of Modern Egypt* (Princeton: Princeton University Press, 1995); Selma Botman, *Engendering Citizenship in Egypt* (New York: Columbia University Press, 1999); and Beth Baron, *Egypt as a Woman: Nationalism, Gender, and Politics* (Berkeley: University of California Press, 2005).
7. Omar Youssef Cheta, "The Economy by Other Means: The Historiography of Capitalism in the Modern Middle East," *History Compass* 16, no. 4, April 2018, https://doi.org/10.1111/hic3.12444.
8. Alice Kessler-Harris, *Gendering Labor History* (Urbana: University of Illinois Press, 2007).
9. Nawal 'Abd al-'Aziz Radi, *Adwa' Jadida 'ala al-Haraka al-'Ummaliyya* (Cairo: Dar al-Nahda al-'Arabiyya, 1977).
10. Liat Kozma, "Girls, Labor, and Sex in Precolonial Egypt, 1850–1882," in *Girlhood: Global History*, ed. Colleen A. Vasconcellos and Jennifer Helgren (New Brunswick, NJ: Rutgers University Press, 2010), 344–62.
11. Beinin, *Workers and Peasants*, 68.
12. Ibid., 68–69.
13. Sa'd 'Abd al-Salam Habib, *Mashakil al-'Amal wa-l-'Ummal* (Cairo: Maktabat al-Nahda al-Misriyya, 1951), 88.
14. Ibid., 94.
15. Kozma, "Girls, Labor, and Sex in Precolonial Egypt," 344–62.
16. For more on the federation, see Amin 'Izz al-Din, *Tarikh al-Tabaqa al-'Amila al-Misriyya mundhu Nasha'tihha hatta Sanat 1970* (Cairo: Dar al-Ghad al-'Arabi, 1987), 346–60.
17. 'Abd al-Salam 'Abd al-Halim 'Amir, *Thawrat Yulyu wa-l-Tabaqa al-'Amila* (Cairo: al-Hay'a al-Misriyya al-'Amma li-l-Kitab, 1987), 35.
18. Anthony Gorman, *Historians, State and Politics in Twentieth Century Egypt: Contesting the Nation* (London: Taylor & Francis, 2012), 139.

19. For more on the early years of Rashid's activism, see Isma'il Ibrahim, *Sahafiyyat Tha'irat* (Cairo: al-Dar al-Misriyya al-Lubnaniyya, 1997), 77–83.

20. Margot Badran, *Feminism in Islam: Secular and Religious Convergences* (London: One World Publications, 2013).

21. Abu Sayf Yusuf, *Watha'iq wa-Mawaqif min Tarikh al-Yasar al-Misri, 1941–1957: Madda li-Tarikh Munazamat Tali'at al-'Ummal* (Cairo: Sharikat al-Amal li-l-Tiba'a wa-l-Nashr, 2000), 867.

22. Dar al-Mar'a al-'Arabiyya, *al-Mar'a al-'Arabiyya fi Muwajahat al-'Asr: Buhuth wa-Niqashat al-Nadawat al-Fikriyya Allati Nazamatha Nur* (Cairo: Dar al-Mar'a al-'Arabiyya li-l-Nashr, 1996), 112.

23. Yusuf Idris, *Shahid 'Asruh* (London: Hindawi Foundation CIC, 2018), 151–54.

24. Harold Butler, *Report on Labour Conditions in Egypt with Suggestions for Future Social Legislation* (Cairo: Government Press, 1932), 12.

25. Habib, *Mashakil al-'Amal wa-l-'Ummal*, 81–82.

26. Ibid., 87.

27. Taha Sa'd 'Uthman, *Min Tarikh 'Ummal Misr: Mudhakkirat wa-Watha'iq* (Cairo: Maktabat Madbuli, 1983), 205.

28. Ibid., 28–30. See also *al-Ahram*, 17 September 1939; and *al-Misri*, 16 and 17 September 1939.

29. Charles Issawi, *Egypt at Mid-Century: An Economic Survey* (Oxford: Oxford University Press, 1954), 171; Abbas, *al-Haraka al-'Ummaliyya fi Misr*, 187.

30. 'Uthman, *Min Tarikh 'Ummal Misr*, 205.

31. "Harakat 'Amilat Masna' min Masani' Shubra al-Khayma," *Kifah al-Sha'b* 10, 4 October 1947, 5–8.

32. "Harakat 'Amilat Masna' min Masani' Shubra al-Khayma," *Kifah al-Sha'b* 20, 28 December 1947, 3–5.

33. 'Uthman, *Min Tarikh 'Ummal Misr*, 205.

34. Ibid., 201.

35. Yusuf, *Watha'iq wa-Mawaqif*, 869–70.

36. "Akhbar Niqabiyya: al-'Amilat fi Dumyat," *Kifah al-Sha'ab* 13, 14 October 1947, 5–8.

37. Hanan Hammad, *Industrial Sexuality: Gender, Urbanization, and Social Transformation in Egypt* (Austin: University of Texas Press, 2016), 92.

38. 'Uthman, *Min Tarikh 'Ummal Misr*, 206–7.

39. Taha Sa'd 'Uthman, "Min Tarikh al-Haraka al-Nisa'iyya: al-'Amilat fi Sina'at al-Nasij," *al-Mar'a al-Jadida* 4, February 1990, 16.

40. Ramsis Labib, ed., *Misriyyat fi al-Sujun wa-l-Mu'taqalat: al-Mar'a al-Misriyya wa-l-Yasar* (Cairo: Markaz al-Buhuth al-'Arabiyya wa-l-Ifriqiyya, 2007), 114.

41. Joel Beinin and Zachary Lockman, *Workers on the Nile*, 2nd ed. (Cairo: American University in Cairo Press, 1998), 345.

42. *Al-Mu'tamar: Nashra ghayr Dawriyya* 6, 18 May 1946, in *al-Haraka al-'Ummaliyya fi Misr*, 142–43.

43. Nida' min Rabbitat 'Amilat al-Qutr al-Misri, unpublished leaflet.

44. Labib, *Misriyyat fi al-Sujun wa-l-Mu'taqalat*, 114.

45. "Fatat Tahtif 'ala Sahwat Hisn," *al-Ithnayn*, 29 September 1947; Taha Sa'd 'Uthman in Labib, *Misriyyat fi al-Sujun wa-l-Mu'taqalat*, 114. See also Sa'id Khayyal, ed., *Mudhakkirat Inji Aflatun* (Cairo: Dar Su'ad al-Subah, 1993), 84–85.

46. 'Assim al-Dusuki, ed., *Shahadat wa-Ru'a VII* (Cairo: Markaz al-Buhuth al-'Arabiyya wa-l-Ifriqiyya, 2006), 37. See also Taha Sa'd 'Uthman, *Niqabiyyun wa-Ishtrakiyyun Yatakallamun:*

Shahadat Waqiʻiyya (Cairo: Markaz Dirasat al-Tanmiyya al-Siyasiyya wa-l-Dawliyya, 1997); and Taha Saʻad ʻUthman, "Mudhakkarat wa-Wathaʼiq fi Tarikh al-Tabaqa al-ʻAmila," *al-Katib* 136 (July 1972): 158–59.

47. For the discussion among activists over the issue, see Yusuf, *Wathaʼiq wa-Mawaqif*, 868–69.
48. Fikri al-Khuli, *al-Rihla* (Cairo: Dar al-Ghad, 1987), 173–76.
49. Ibid., vol. 3 (Cairo: Dar al-Ghad, 1991), 173–76.
50. Yusuf, *Wathaʼiq wa-Mawaqif*, 873.
51. "Akhbar La Tunshar fi Zil al-Ahkam al-ʻUrfiyya," *Kifah al-Umma*, 14 June 1948, 4.
52. "Akhbar La Tunshar fi Zil al-Ahkam al-ʻUrfiyya," *Kifah al-Umma*, 15 September 1948, 4.
53. "Al Haraka al-Nisaʼiyya fi Nisf ʻAmm," *Kifah al-Umma*, 14 June 1948, 4.
54. "Akhbar La Tunshar fi Zil al-Ahkam al-ʻUrfiyya," *Kifah al-Umma*, 15 September 1948. See also Taha Saʻd ʻUthman, "Jamʻiyyat Usar al-Muʻtaqalin," in *Misriyyat fi al-Sujun wa-l-Muʻtaqalat*, 115–17.
55. Yusuf, *Wathaʼiq wa-Mawaqif*, 871. The incident could have inspired filmmaker Salah Abu Sayf in *La Waqt li-l-Hub* (*No Time for Love*, 1963).
56. ʻUthman, "Jamʻiyyat Usar al-Muʻtaqalin," 115–17.
57. Taha Saʻd ʻUthman, "Umm Ahmad Salim Salim," in *Misriyyat fi al-Sujun wa-l-Muʻtaqalat*, 72–76.
58. Labib, *Misriyyat fi al-Sujun wa-l-Muʻtaqalat*, 112–13.
59. ʻUthman, *Min Tarikh ʻUmmal Misr*, 208.
60. Ibid.
61. Ibid., 28–31.
62. Ibid., 200.
63. Zinat al-ʻAskari, "Zaynab al-ʻAskari: ʻAmila Munadila Misriyya," in *Misriyyat fi al-Sujun wa-l-Muʻtaqalat*, 101–3.
64. Mahmud Midhat, "Zaynab Ibrahim ʻAli Gharraba: Umm Faruk," in *Misriyyat fi al-Sujun wa-l-Muʻtaqalat*, 95–100.
65. Charles Tilly, "Did the Cake of Custom Break?," in *Consciousness and Class Experience in Nineteenth-Century Europe*, ed. John M. Merriman (New York: Holmes & Meier, 1979), 29.
66. Jessica Winegar, "The Privilege of Revolution: Gender, Class, Space, and Affect in Egypt," *American Ethnologist* 39, no. 1 (2012): 67–70; Nadine Naber, "The Radical Potential of Mothering during the Egyptian Revolution," *Feminist Studies* 47, no. 1 (2021): 62–93.

Bibliography

Abbas, Raouf. *Al-Haraka al-ʻUmmaliyya fi Misr: 1899–1952*. Cairo: Dar al-Kitab al-ʻArabi li-l-Tibaʻa wa-l-Nashr, 1968.

ʻAmir, ʻAbd al-Salam ʻAbd al-Halim. *Thawrat Yulyu wa-l-Tabaqa al-ʻAmila*. Cairo: al-Hayʼa al-Misriyya al-ʻAmma li-l-Kitab, 1987.

Badran, Margot. *Feminists, Islam, and Nation: Gender and the Making of Modern Egypt*. Princeton: Princeton University Press, 1995.

Baron, Beth. *Egypt as a Woman: Nationalism, Gender, and Politics*. Berkeley: University of California Press, 2005.

Beinin, Joel. "Egyptian Workers and January 25th: A Social Movement in Historical Context." *Social Research* 79, no. 2 (2012): 323–48.

Beinin, Joel. *Workers and Peasants in the Modern Middle East*. New York: Cambridge University Press, 2000.

Beinin, Joel, and Zachary Lockman. *Workers on the Nile: Nationalism, Communism, Islam, and the Egyptian Working Class, 1882–1954*. Princeton: Princeton University Press, 1989.

Botman, Selma. *Engendering Citizenship in Egypt*. New York: Columbia University Press, 1999.

Cheta, Omar Youssef. "The Economy by Other Means: The Historiography of Capitalism in the Modern Middle East," *History Compass* 16, no. 4 (April 2018): e12444. https://doi.org/10.1111/hic3.12444.

Duboc, Marie. "Where Are the Men? Here Are the Men and the Women! Surveillance, Gender, and Strikes in Egyptian Textile Factories." *Journal of Middle East Women's Studies* 9, no. 3 (2013): 28–53.

Al-Dusuki, 'Assim. *Shahadat wa-Ru'a VII*. Cairo: Markaz al-Buhuth al-'Arabiyya wa-l-Ifriqiyya, 2006.

Goldberg, Ellis. *Tinker, Tailor, and Textile Worker: Class and Politics in Egypt, 1930–1952*. Berkeley: University of California Press, 1986.

Hammad, Hanan. *Industrial Sexuality: Gender, Urbanization, and Social Transformation in Egypt*. Austin: University of Texas Press, 2016.

Issawi, Charles. *Egypt at Mid-Century: An Economic Survey*. Oxford: Oxford University Press, 1954.

Kozma, Liat. "Girls, Labor, and Sex in Precolonial Egypt, 1850–1882," in *Girlhood: Global History*, edited by Colleen A. Vasconcellos and Jennifer Helgren, 344–62. New Brunswick, NJ: Rutgers University Press, 2010.

Labib, Ramsis. *Misriyyat fi al-Sujun wa-l-Mu'taqalat: al-Mar'a al-Misriyya wa-l-Yasar*. Cairo: Markaz al-Buhuth al-'Arabiyya wa-l-Ifriqiyya, 2007.

Naber, Nadine. "The Radical Potential of Mothering during the Egyptian Revolution." *Feminist Studies* 47, no. 1 (2021): 62–93.

Tilly, Charles. "Did the Cake of Custom Break?," in *Consciousness and Class Experience in Nineteenth-Century Europe*, edited by John M. Merriman, 17–41. New York: Holmes & Meier, 1979.

'Uthman, Taha Sa'd. *Min Tarikh 'Ummal Misr: Mudhakkirat wa-Watha'iq*. Cairo: Maktabat Madbuli, 1983.

Winegar, Jessica. "The Privilege of Revolution: Gender, Class, Space, and Affect in Egypt." *American Ethnologist* 39, no. 1 (2012): 67–70.

Yusuf, Abu Sayf. *Watha'iq wa-Mawaqif min Tarikh al-Yasar al-Misri, 1941–1957: Madda li-Tarikh Munazamat Tali'at al-'Ummal*. Cairo: Sharikat al-Amal li-l-Tiba'a wa-l-Nashr, 2000.

CHAPTER 10

DAMS, DITCHES, AND DRAINS

Managing Egypt's Modern Hydroscape

NANCY Y. REYNOLDS

IN mid-October 1969, the Egyptian daily newspaper *al-Ahram* reported that a child had fallen into a sewer drain.[1] According to the article, the five-year-old boy, Khalid, was walking home with his father, a merchant named Sha'ban 'Atiyya Darwish, on the evening of 11 October along Qubba Palace Street in the Zaytun neighborhood of Cairo, when his foot slid into the open drain and he tumbled in. After rescue officials searched drains and pipes frantically for three hours, the boy's body surfaced ten kilometers away at the Amiriyya station. The tragedy of Khalid's body's circulation in the hydraulic system made visible the complex hidden topography of water control, a regime that was changing in the 1960s.

The porosity of dense urban infrastructure had long been a hazard in Cairo; cesspools, an earlier form of sewage management, were often poorly marked in city streets during the nineteenth century—at times people slipped into them and were gravely injured.[2] Unlike the freestanding units of waste collection represented by cesspools, or even urban canals that often carried both waste and drinking water to and from urban dwellings in the nineteenth century, the city's sewers in the 1960s were part of a vast and highly connected system of below-ground pipes, street drains, and newly renovated treatment centers, whose operations were largely coordinated by state officials. Egyptians were increasingly aware that their water needs were serviced as part of a larger and newly configured national system. The country had celebrated the completion of the first stage of construction on a massive hydroelectric dam in the south in May 1964—a project that involved the closure and diversion of the nation's primary water source, the Nile, into a newly dug channel. The closing of the river allowed state officials to impound water from a record-high Nile annual flood that summer, which, with the dam's increasing pressure on the water table, caused massive flooding in Cairo early in the fall of 1964 and again in the spring of 1965. The drains of Cairo—and the substation where Khalid's body surfaced—had been under constant repair over the past four years as a result, as farmers struggled with waterlogged and salty fields. The local points at which the interconnected hydraulic system erupted to the surface, such as drains in city streets or ditches in rural fields, thus presented points of interaction between the system and many residents, for whom the long stretches of closed water circulation were otherwise invisible.[3]

Although on opposite ends of the water system, dams and drains were integrally connected as forces and even as sites of agency in Egypt's modern hydraulic regime— or the integration of most of the country into a single "hydroscape," a term coined by water politics scholars to refer to the hybrid spaces created through the technology and technological expertise of large-scale projects to manage rivers.[4] How human bodies participate in infrastructure, both formally and informally—as experts, labor, obstacles, and casualties—is crucial to understanding the hydroscape and the nature of power in modern societies. The findings of a series of new studies of Egypt's water history, as well as research through archives, the press, and engineering reports, enable a critical biography of the hydroscape in modern Egypt. Such a biography tracks an arc of change that follows the interplay between local points of opening and control versus the functioning of the larger system: early modern local management within the broader Ottoman system gradually gave way to more centralized control, or at least aspirations of control, by Egyptian and British state officials and experts as they constructed ever-larger water management projects on the Nile in the first half of the twentieth century. Through its partial failure, this new technology ultimately returned some measure of control to local water users by the early twenty-first century.

The 1960s was a crucial turning point in this larger story, as that decade witnessed the remaking of earlier and aging colonial hydrological infrastructure in the capital city (the decrepit sewer system of Greater Cairo originally installed by the British between 1907 and 1915), in the south of the river valley (the new Aswan High Dam that replaced the British-constructed low dam built in 1898–1902), and in the agricultural areas across the country (the canal and drainage systems that linked the river to the fields).[5] These 1960s projects were attempts to accommodate the realities of the postcolonial period— its rapid population growth and the push to transform Egypt from a monocultural agricultural economy into an industrial one—and reoriented work on the river system from removing silt to managing scour. The stories of these different water systems are usually told separately. The water, however, flows in the hydroscape as a single system, and although the relationship of the system to local points varies, each reflects the evolving struggle between experts and users.

THE WATER OF EGYPT: THE NATURE OF EGYPT'S HYDROSCAPE

Except for a small amount of rainfall along the northern coast and groundwater aquifers supplying oases in the Western Desert, Egypt depends wholly on the water of a single long river to irrigate its agricultural fields and to provision its villages, towns, and cities. Roughly 96% of water used in Egypt comes from this river, the Nile. Most of Egypt's water is used for agriculture—somewhere between 85 and 90% of the water taken from the Nile in the country. In the year 2000, the industrial sector used another 6% of the water, and municipalities consumed 8% (for personal drinking, household use, etc.).[6] The Nile has historically brought more than just water into Egypt. From the volcanic rocks upstream in Ethiopia, the rains washed rich suspended particulate matter (a mixture of silt, sand, and clay) that has slowly built up the Nile floodplain and the Egyptian Delta.[7] The unpredictability of the river's annual flow is compounded by the variable volume of the river over the "water year" (which runs from July to July on the Nile due to the timing of the flood): over 80% of the water discharged by the river comes during the annual flood, which reaches Egypt between August and October; only 20% of the river's total discharge occurs in the other nine months of the year.[8] The annual flood flushed out toxins and residues from fields and towns and brought new supplies of water into local canals.

While the ecological fact of the need for Nile water and silt has remained constant over millennia, the mechanisms of river control, and its broader context, have altered significantly. As John Waterbury put it in the 1970s, "For 7,000 years, or perhaps longer, the inhabitants of the Nile Valley have been mastering their river in order to master their land. But each technological advance has eventually entailed ecological setbacks."[9] The Middle East has long been linked to theories, such as Karl August Wittfogel's "Oriental despotism," that attribute the rise of powerful, centralized, and bureaucratic states to river control and irrigation works. Tracking the relationships of state to river and of water to power remains a robust mode of inquiry in water politics and environmental history scholarship and continues to inform strands of Middle Eastern history.[10] Whereas scholars once assessed water management through a cause-and-effect model tabulated on a balance sheet, more recent explanations focus on the co-constitution of human and natural change in the Nile Valley as well as the centrality of water management as a force shaping the broader political, socioeconomic, and cultural history of Egypt.[11]

Few scholars have analyzed Egypt's hydroscape as a unit, although many have written biographical studies of the Nile itself or linked Egypt's identity unequivocally with the river. If Herodotus's claim that "Egypt is the gift of the Nile" is the most famous, the colonial epics and more recent Egyptian studies on the relationship of the Nile to Egypt's "national character" are just as influential.[12] Jessica Barnes has noted that these various iterations of hydropolitical analysis, with their focus on governmental expertise, generally neglect the nature of water itself.[13] To track the oscillation in hydroscape governance between centralized and more diffuse user control requires conceptualizing a unit of water landscape that incorporates water as it cycles in the river; in the fields; under the ground; in the sewers, pipes, and drains of urban areas; and even in the bodies of humans, animals, and plants. To do so is not to argue for a totalizing force that overdetermines Egyptian politics and history but rather to follow the water to chart the intersections of fields of power and their change over time.

From ancient times until the nineteenth century, irrigation technology was primarily directed to managing the highest levels of the flooding river: building levees, managing flood basins, dredging natural river channels, and erecting small earthen dams and short canals to retain and direct existing flows of water.[14] These hydraulic works required significant labor and regional coordination, although much of the work of daily water control was performed by individuals or small groups working in specific fields. As Alan Mikhail has demonstrated, the Ottoman imperial state relied heavily on the local knowledge of canal users to determine the engineering works needed to maintain the system. As such, the irrigation network was a site through which, paradoxically, "Egyptian peasants . . . controlled Ottoman bureaucrats—not the other way around—in the determination and execution of repairs to irrigation works in the countryside."[15] The importance of peasant knowledge of local conditions—"a coordinated localism" managed by the imperial center—left a broad scope for agency in the hands of local users of irrigation works, in contrast to the despotic and top-down model of water governance projected by both the Oriental despotism of Wittfogel or the decline narratives of Ottoman history.[16]

Various local and international economic, political, social, and ecological factors radically transformed this regime of fluvial management in the early nineteenth century. The reconstruction of the Mahmudiyya Canal, which carried river water to Alexandria, was a massive state-directed effort completed in 1819–20 at the cost of the lives of one-third of the 300,000 peasants forced to build it.[17] The new local ruler, Mehmet Ali, and his successors continued to develop new hydraulic public works projects and an ever-growing bureaucracy and professionalized engineering corps to support the expansion of summer commercial crops, such as cotton and rice, which require water at times when the flood cycle is low; in other words, they began to manage the river at its lowest levels. Between 1798 and 1833, the land available for summer cropping more than doubled, from 250,000 feddans to 600,000 feddans, supported by 240 miles of deep irrigation canals that the state excavated and had to annually maintain, using compelled peasant labor.[18]

Funneling water from the river into this new canal system remained a challenge, since the valley's slope was so gradual and the water level so low. Throughout the nineteenth century, Egyptian and later British engineers oversaw Egyptian labor to construct new barrages and dig sediment from canals as irrigation on the cycle of the annual river flood (known as "basin irrigation") gave way to year-round or "perennial" irrigation to accommodate the growth of export-oriented agriculture and expand the amount of cultivation to meet the country's growing and urbanizing population.[19] Beginning in the Delta, the conversion to perennial irrigation slowly expanded to Middle and Upper Egypt by the twentieth century, reaching four-fifths of the country by the early 1950s.[20] Perennial irrigation intensified peasant labor and radically altered the ecology of the fields and the river itself: the annual flooding had allowed for washing and aeration of the soil that prevented salt deposits and for natural drainage that kept the water table low, both of which also mitigated against the growth of waterborne parasites, such as those that cause schistosomiasis and hookworm, and the growth of plants that harbored malaria-bearing mosquitoes and cotton bollworm. This switch in irrigation took a heavy toll on the farmers' bodies, creating, as Jennifer Derr describes it, new "ecologies of pain."[21]

An Early Twentieth-Century Colonial Hydroscape

New agricultural practices increasingly bifurcated management of the rural hydroscape between local users and government officials in the closing decades of the nineteenth century. The branches of government involved in water management grew, and several expanded their purview to other domains.[22] Centralized control of the water commons was not enacted through pricing but through more complex distribution forces. Farmers incurred no charge to use irrigation water, as its cost was covered by the land tax levied on all cultivated land, but its distribution was tightly controlled from its source at the regional level to local canals.[23] The large-scale hydraulic works constructed at the turn of the century, most notably the British dam at Aswan, relocated much of the decision-making about water distribution from farmers into the hands of state employees. While the nationalist movement challenged this consolidation as part of its broader call for political sovereignty, the hydroscape continued to develop as an increasingly complex built space that concentrated control of land, wealth, and local political power.

The distribution of authority in turn-of-the-century irrigation roughly corresponded to the different levels of the canals. As water traveled from the river's main channel into smaller canals, it moved from more centralized control to the domain of local users in four levels of waterways. Government officials, agricultural inspectors, and irrigation engineers, all organized through the Irrigation Department of the Ministry of Public Works (headquartered in Cairo), managed the first three: the main channel or branches of the river, the primary canals, and the secondary (branch or distributary) canals. The frontier of control was the local or tertiary canal, known as the *misqa*.[24] Once the water reached the *misqa*, village officials and local cultivators negotiated the rotation of its movement into individual fields; each *misqa* canal might irrigate 25–30 feddans worth of fields directly through temporary field ditches or furrows.[25] Social power and complex negotiations among local users determined the order to cut and re-block canal banks, operate and direct animal- or human-powered water wheels or other lifting devices, or connect to and operate steam, diesel, or electrical and mechanical pumps.[26] The order of waterings affected both the volume of water available and its quality—as the water moved from the field back to the canal and onto a new field, it became increasingly saline and less nourishing to crops.

Water-lifting technologies to irrigate fields during the low Nile season or those above the reach of canals both changed and expanded in the modern period, transforming patterns of landowning and agricultural work. Employing human and animal labor, these devices enlarged the role of local end-users in irrigation, perhaps offering more agency but, more importantly, intensifying the labor directed to cropping. Historically, farmers lifted water either through pots, buckets, or scoops attached to long poles (the *shaduf*) or fitted into a water wheel (the *saqiyya, tambusha,* or *tabut*), or pumped the water through manual crank pumps, such as the Archimedean screw (the *tanbur*), or automatic pumps powered by steam, diesel, or electric motors.[27] Although water wheels historically had been turned by animal power (mostly oxen, cows, buffalos, and, occasionally, camels), human labor could also be employed when disease and state levies decimated rural stocks of domesticated agricultural animals.[28] Over time, human labor would be replaced by machine labor. By the late nineteenth century, large landowners began to expand away from the older devices lifting water into furrows to the use of motorized pumps feeding pipes under their fields. The environmental forces that shifted labor from animal to human to mechanized lifting power combined with what Ghislaine Alleaume has called the "geometric rationalization of space," produced by developing the new infrastructural grid of irrigation works, to dispossess smallholders. "Large estates were thus the best instruments and the first beneficiaries of the hydro-agricultural revolution in the nineteenth century."[29] The consolidation of large estates through mechanical pumping would transform Egyptian social and political power through at least the mid-twentieth century, if not until today.[30]

The regional developments in irrigation infrastructure became coordinated into a single hydraulic regime with the building of dams at Aswan to store Nile water for summer cropping. British engineers designed the first, or low, Aswan dam, known as Khazan Aswan, which was built in 1898–1902 with mostly Egyptian labor (roughly ten thousand Egyptians from all over the country), alongside Greek workers and Italian stonemasons, supervised by British engineers. The enormous masonry dam was fitted with 180 sluices that allowed most of the river's floodwater, with its heavy load of silt, to pass downstream; closure of the sluice gates then retained the tail of the flood in the reservoir so that it could be distributed in the spring and summer, when the river level was low. In the first few years, additional engineering projects along the river were required to correct the deep scouring of the fast-moving water released through the dam, and the dam itself had to be widened and supported to prevent its collapse.[31] To meet the growing demand for summer irrigation water, the crest of the dam was raised twice (in 1912 and 1933) in major and complex engineering projects to enlarge its reservoir's capacity, ultimately to 5.7 billion cubic meters, and to build large barrage works downstream to manage the new regime of water discharge (its timing, volume, and velocity) and trap floodwater for regional use in summer cropping: at Asyut (1902), Zifta (1903), Isna (1909), Naj' Hammadi (1930), and Idfina (1951).[32]

Each stage of dam building displaced people living upstream, as the reservoirs flooded the river valley in the area known historically as Nubia. Although somewhat ethnically and linguistically diverse, Nubians had a political, ethnic, and historical identity distinct from both Egyptians and Sudanese. By the 1970s, more than 150,000 Nubians in Egypt and Sudan would be forcibly displaced by the dams to interior land reclamation projects, mostly at Kum Umbu in Egypt and Khashm al-Qirba in Sudan.[33]

Derr has argued that the building of Khazan Aswan marked the ascendency of British colonial irrigation expertise in Egypt by making "permanent the vision of the perennial Nile that was the fantasy of British colonial officials in the late nineteenth century," resolutely linking British colonial officials with colonial capitalists, and marking a transition of sovereignty over the Egyptian hydroscape.[34]

Within a decade, however, nationalist demands for independence would also come to center on Egyptian sovereignty of the Nile's waters, mostly focused on the issue of British-Egyptian control of Sudan and British plans to develop new dams and irrigation works on the river's upstream sources, mainly to store water in less arid environments and to expand the cotton-growing regions of Sudan rather than continue to raise the Aswan dam solely to store additional water.[35] This basin-wide over-year storage program became known after 1920 as the Century Storage Scheme.[36]

Egyptian engineers portrayed this conflict as a contest of national sovereignty, one in which they felt they could directly intervene as individual agents.[37] In 1928, amid this controversy, an Egyptian engineer, Ibrahim Zaki, sent to the local press a pamphlet criticizing upstream British irrigation works, including the Jabal Awliya' project; he titled the forty-eight-page work "Egypt's Enslavement [isti'bad misr] by English Irrigation Projects."[38] Compiling a detailed collection of official statements and publications by British and Egyptian irrigation authorities, Zaki argued that "the result of British irrigation projects in the near future is Egypt's perpetual dispossession [hirman] of the waters and silt of the Blue Nile and the allocation of that to Sudan" for land reclamation.[39] The dams that the British proposed to construct in Sudan, he claimed, would "rule over the waters of Egypt."[40] Ultimately, a water agreement would be signed in 1929 that would guarantee Egypt water to irrigate all its lands under perennial irrigation (totaling some five million acres at that time) and state that Egypt's water needs would take priority over Sudan's and any other upstream river control projects.[41] The low dam's second heightening, completed in 1933, would be led by an Egyptian industrialist, Ahmad 'Abbud.[42]

Downstream on the Damietta or eastern branch of the Nile in the Delta where Mit Ghamr lies across the river from the town of Zifta, overlapping transformations of irrigation infrastructure revealed the extent to which the river had become almost fully engineered by the state by the early twentieth century. The different types of barrages constructed at this small bend in the river reflected not only the topography of the river's course but also the economic importance and agricultural density of the region, which had long been settled.[43] Mit Ghamr was an old town with a history of robust trade in cotton and cottonseed and the manufacture of a variety of fabrics.[44] Zifta was also a large regional center for villages on the river's west bank, and it housed an important Coptic church, an international community of traders, and a thriving cotton industry. It supported in the 1880s, according to 'Ali Mubarak, a large agricultural district famous for the variety of crops it produced, including cotton, wheat, barley, maize, fenugreek, lupines, and vegetables on over 3,236 feddans irrigated by water from the Nile and its canals, plus two sweet water springs; eleven waterwheels moved the water from canal to field. It was also the location of a road bridge over the river that served an array of local villages.[45] One of the early canals was a summer, or *sayfi*, canal called Buhiya Canal, which originated in this region and cut northeast through the eastern Delta, toward Mansoura.[46] In 1885 the state built a temporary stone barrage at Mit Ghamr that funneled "the whole supply of the [Damietta] branch . . . down the canals between 1885 and 1889"; practically no water flowed over the barrage during the summer until the small stone crest at its top was removed to allow the annual flood to pass over it.[47] By contrast, the Zifta Barrage was a permanent elevation barrage built later, in 1903, as part of the downstream works to support the new regime of river regulation made possible by Khazan Aswan.[48]

By 1913, Zifta and Mit Ghamr lay at the crossroads of a series of major canals in the Delta. The Rayyah al-Tawfiqi (one of the three main arterial feeder canals from the Delta Barrages), built in the 1850s and reconstructed in 1887–89 to connect "all the northern canals of the Eastern Delta with the canal system taking off from above the Delta Barrages,"[49] passed through Banha and onto Mit Ghamr, where the Mansuriyya Canal carried the water farther north. Across the river, the Sahil Canal ended at Zifta, and just below the town, the Bahr al-'Abbasi headed northwest toward al-Mahalla al-Kubra. Not far to the west passed the Manufiyya feeder canal. The barrage below Zifta and Mit Ghamr raised the head of the river's branch to fill both the Bahr al-'Abbasi and the Buhiya canals.[50] Landowners constructed large cotton-growing estates, or *'izbas*, in areas serviced by these new summer canals. Moving from his family's estate at Kafr Tanbul, Mustafa Fuuda established his own estate nearby at Balamun in 1927; by 1929, 60% of the villages in the Nile Delta were organized as *'izbas*.[51] As one Egyptian geographer put it in 1961, "The opening decades of the century may well be designated the 'era of dams and barrages."[52] These new river works fundamentally altered, even inverted, the Nile's regime so that its "seasons of flood and cultivation are diametrically opposed."[53]

THE "CAPTIVE NILE" OF THE 1960S

From 1904 until 1956, the Nile was administered as a single planning unit—as a basin, a construct made possible by the scope of British imperial control of the major territories in the watershed (for the While Nile). This British "water imperialism," Terje Tvedt has noted, allowed "political leaders . . . to regard this widely varying resource as one hydrological and political unit, with far-reaching consequences for the peoples who for generations had been living along the banks of the river as if the river and its tributaries were local water courses."[54] The building of the Aswan High Dam (al-Sadd al-'Ali) at midcentury, however, altered the relationship of Egypt to the Nile Basin politically and materially.

The High Dam allowed the state to remake the Nile into a national river by creating a new river "source" (its reservoir, Lake Nasir) largely within the bounds of the nation and generating a fixed "artificial flood" each year.[55] In other words, the High Dam, in the

1950s and 1960s, turned the water system of Egypt into a national hydroscape through two radical changes to the administration of the Nile. First, nationalist agitation finally succeeded in fully eliminating the British colonial presence in Egypt, in large part through the nationalization of Egyptian waterways—both the Nile, via the building of the High Dam to conserve over-year storage within Egypt's national boundaries, and the Suez Canal, nationalized in 1956 to provide local funding for the High Dam project and establish the local and international political authority of the country's anticolonial revolution and its leader, Gamal Abdel Nasser. Second, the High Dam's capture of the full discharge of the annual flood changed the entire downstream hydrological regime: it flattened out the water flow's seasonal variation and altered its content. Irrigation officials no longer struggled with dredging silt from the canals but now had to contend with the clear-flowing water (its speed, lack of sediment, and waterlogging).

The new hydrological regime's effect on drains in fields and cities was profound. Cairo's old colonial-era sewer system largely collapsed in the 1960s, requiring massive restructuring and rebuilding, and drainage facilities became the primary target of national and international water experts attempting to rescue Egyptian fields from waterlogging and salinization. While the High Dam seemed to offer the Egyptian state full centralized control of the release and flow of Egypt's water, these secondary effects on the hydroscape slowly returned some control to local users in Egypt's fields and cities.

The High Dam functioned as an important technology and symbol of Egypt's postcolonial transition. Signaling the nation's independent sovereignty, the dam provided the new regime with a dramatic opportunity to assert postcolonial independence and position itself within an emerging system of Cold War "development."[56] Exponential population growth also drove international donor experts and Egyptian officials to build the dam: feeding a growing population within the limits of the Nile Valley demanded both expansion of arable land and further intensification of existing cultivated land by increased irrigation. By the 1950s, Egypt's population had doubled from about 10 million since Khazan Aswan opened and was projected at that time to grow at 2.5 to 3% annually; by 1960, it reached 26 million and was expected at that time to reach about 70 million in 1993.[57] Egypt's cities especially grew enormously larger and denser in the 1950s and 1960s, aided by rapid migration from the overburdened agrarian zones as well as sanitation and medical reforms that lengthened urban residents' life expectancy, especially in Cairo.

Increasing agricultural resources to support the growing population dovetailed with the perceived need to fully regulate the discharge of the river by "mastering" the annual flood: gaining control of all the river's discharge (water and silt) as well as regularizing its release across the seasons and from year to year. Even with the expanded irrigation grid, by midcentury, almost 40% of the river water flowed into the Mediterranean Sea during the yearly flood season.[58] Irrigation officials condemned this discharge into the sea "as waste" of a needed resource.[59] Just as important was standardizing the irregular volume of the annual flood. Although the average measured annual discharge of the Nile in the century between 1878 and 1977 was 84 billion cubic meters, the flow had ranged in that period between nearly double that volume (155 billion cubic meters in 1878–79) and half of it (42 billion cubic meters in 1913–14).[60] The shift from seasonal to over-year storage made possible by the High Dam would finally manage this unpredictability in volume and permit greater water distribution for summer cropping. Equally significant was the elimination of silting to block water flow in downstream canals. As one foreign policy expert put it in the years after the High Dam opened, a new "captive Nile" had emerged.[61]

The High Dam was built four miles upstream of Khazan Aswan at the first cataract on the Nile. An enormous rock-fill dam, it is often described as an engineering feat, either by reference to its metrics (111 meters high; a kilometer broad at the base; 3.8 kilometers long at the top; requiring 42.7 million cubic meters of construction materials; creating one of the largest reservoirs in the world) or to its monumentality, and likened to other natural and human-created "wonders."[62] Writing in the late 1970s, Richard Benedick presented the dam using both strategies: "By any standards, the Aswan High Dam is one of the engineering wonders of the world; there is no comparable structure in terms of impact on the life of an entire country. One of the world's largest man-made constructions, it is a veritable artificial mountain of rock and sand; here, at the first cataract of the Nile and the traditional southern outpost of the pharaohs before the sands of Nubia, modern Egypt erected a gargantuan quasi-pyramidal structure 17 times larger in volume that the Great Pyramid of Giza."[63] On the dam's east side, the hydroelectric powerhouse sits across the diversion channel. The turbines were installed between 1968 and 1970, and the powerhouse reached total power production in the middle 1980s. In 1974, before the country had developed other significant sources of power, the dam supplied 53% of Egypt's total electric power use; much of that power went to service a new fertilizer plant, in part to replace the nutrients lost to Egypt's soils due to the dam and the overall irrigation regime, in addition to servicing chemical plants at Aswan and providing electricity downstream in Cairo, Alexandria, and Port Said, along with some villages.[64]

Historians have argued that the political "battle of the high dam" to secure funding and establish a new water rights convention was "harsher" than the battle against nature in the technical struggle to build the dam.[65] Nevertheless, the actual construction project, first managed by Soviet hydraulic expertise and later largely transitioned to Egyptian engineering firms, including 'Uthman Ahmad 'Uthman's Arab Contractors, was massive and stretched over the 1960s.[66] At the height of construction in 1962–63, more than thirty thousand workers labored under harsh and often dangerous conditions at the site.[67] The dam's construction entirely remade the region of Aswan as a whole, including the forced relocation of residents and the more-publicized rescue of ancient monuments behind the dam in historic Nubia.

Full regulation of the streamflow and end of the annual flood fundamentally altered the hydroscape and its management.[68] In material terms, the dam's retention of the river's silt radically reordered the kinds of labor and maintenance required by the irrigation network. After two centuries or more of forcing Egyptian laborers to dredge canals of built-up sediment, the water downstream of Aswan flowed nearly clear, not silting up the irrigation grid but rather cutting into its banks with its newfound velocity.[69] New elements of the hydraulic infrastructure were constructed, and older barrages were shored up. The state built a new feeder canal, the Nubariyya, in the western side of the Delta and established new pumping works northwest of Cairo in Tahrir Province, both with the goal of converting desert to agricultural land, although, ultimately, these projects were not fully successful because the quality of the soils and the topography caused waterlogging or prevented successful cultivation.[70] The temporality of canal labor also changed: canals were closed for only one week rather than three each year for cleaning and rehabilitation, which led to increased waterlogging of fields. Also, the diminished turbidity and different quality of the water (higher levels of dissolved solids and phytoplankton) coming down the river led to the growth of aquatic vegetation (including water hyacinths) that needed clearing rather than silt.[71]

The state expected that the High Dam would expand the agricultural area of Egypt by reclaiming 1.3 million feddans and allow for the conversion of 700,000 feddans from basin to perennial irrigation, thereby increasing the productivity of these lands. Specifically, it aimed to expand the area under cultivation for rice—a water-intensive crop that can be used in land reclamation—as well as to improve conditions for navigating the Nile year-round.[72] The new hydraulic regime led to a return to state control over the crop mix in the 1950s and 1960s, which was enforced through the "nationwide cooperative system established in 1963."[73] Agricultural expansion, ultimately, was much less than predicted: in fact, the amount of cultivated land declined between 1960 and 1975 from more than 6 million to 5.9 million feddans, due to the expansion of building in Cairo and the Delta; the conversion of about 120 square kilometers annually of agricultural land to soil harvested for brickmaking once annual silt deposits disappeared; and the high salinity of some agricultural land, which compromised its fertility. Some of this land loss was offset by the intensification of land cultivation; croppings, for example, expanded from 9.3 million feddans in 1952 to 11.2 million feddans in 1982.[74] The technical feat of channeling and controlling the water's entire flow also necessitated new international agreements to determine the exact amount of the Nile's water that Egypt could claim. The British Empire's control over both Egypt and Sudan in the early twentieth century had facilitated this division; the first postcolonial agreement was signed by Nasser in Cairo on 8 November 1959. The Agreement for the Full Utilization of the Nile Waters between Egypt and Sudan gave Egypt a fixed annual share of Nile water—55.5 billion cubic meters (bcm).[75]

DRAINING EGYPT'S WATERLOGGED FIELDS AND CITIES

The expansion of perennial irrigation's highly engineered and increasingly centralized hydraulic network led in turn to the growth of an equally complex and extensive network of artificial drainage to serve Egypt's fields and maintain their fertility by removing water pooled at the surface and lodged near plant roots.[76] According to Gamal Hamdan in 1961, "Until World War I, drainage was a very secondary question, but has since leapt into the forefront. Everywhere, the fellah now asks for a drain."[77] Field drainage was modified in two primary ways in the twentieth century: expanded spatially to maintain soil quality and pushed underground to free up more surface land for cultivation. Field drainage infrastructure soon became nearly as extensive as the system that brought fresh water to the fields, especially once flushing by the annual flood stopped in the 1960s.[78] Moreover, the gradual slope of the Delta toward the north and the fact that much of the land near the coast was below sea level required the establishment of electric pumping stations to push drainage water into the sea, since gravity alone could not discharge it.

Early field ditch drains reduced the amount of land that could be farmed, thus directly undermining the irrigation system's very goal of agricultural expansion. By the 1960s, this loss of valuable land had become acute, even reaching one-tenth of each field.[79] Pipe drains, which lay underground in the fields in soil-covered trenches, were increasingly installed in the second half of the twentieth century to prevent land and water waste.[80] Subsurface drainage through pipes, then, reversed land loss and worked more effectively, as it did not need to be cleared of weeds and other materials that could hamper water flow in open ditches. It was, however, expensive and required more specialized technologies for installation and maintenance.[81] There were also other limits to drains. Within individual fields, drains created an uneven cultivation geography, since drainage efficiency diminished across individual fields: while cotton could be grown on either side of a drain, field edges could support only reclamation crops, such as rice.[82] By 1971, the drainage network was substantial throughout the country.[83] By the 2010s, about 60% of Egypt's agricultural land was served by subsurface drainage and 40% by surface drains.[84]

Drainage technology came increasingly under state control after the late nineteenth century to compel implementation by smaller landholders, who were less willing to convert usable land to drainage.[85] Over time, however, drainage networks became less centralized, marking a sharp shift away from the river control and irrigation networks, which remained concentrated under state authority. The power of a large dam, Barnes argues, "stems from the concentration in space of the technologies for managing the flow of water through the country. . . . In contrast, while the subsurface drainage program has made Egypt's subterranean flow controllable, it is a diffuse network of control. There are nodal points—the manholes for inspection, the joints between different pipes—but there is no one site where this flow can be turned on and off."[86] Despite the increasing diffusion of control, drainage brought a new generation of international water experts into Egypt's hydroscape. In 1971, just as the High Dam was officially completed, the World Bank began a series of US-funded subsurface drainage projects to reclaim Delta farmland, a program that eventually grew to include other partners (such as the Netherlands and European and African funders) and has continued into the 2000s and expanded out of the Delta to become national in scope.[87] Thus, the new national hydroscape, brought into being by the High Dam, ultimately invited a new form of neoliberal international water expertise to "fix" its ecological consequences.

The river control and irrigation networks that compromised drainage in Egypt's fields also affected the circulation of water in Egypt's cities. When Khalid fell into Cairo's sewer in 1969, the city's drains were undergoing repair as part of an ongoing process to manage the system after the construction of the Aswan High Dam. Cairo's drains were part of a combined system that carried both runoff water and sewage out of the city and ran separately from a parallel grid to supply fresh water from the river and, to a lesser extent, from deep-welled aquifers, for drinking, cleaning, or industrial uses by urban residents.[88] The upstream dams, the cessation of the annual flood, and the lack of field drainage increasingly put pressure on the country's water table. Its unmanageable rise, along with other factors, caused segments of the urban water system of Cairo, originally installed by the British between 1907 and 1915, to collapse by 1965. The failure of the sewer systems is often recounted as a coda to histories of Cairo to preview the wider breakdown of the city's infrastructure due to population expansion and massive in-migration from the countryside, as well as the limits of socialist planning under Nasser and the corruption that followed in Anwar al-Sadat's and Husni Mubarak's eras. This narrative is almost always part of a story of disease and public health.[89] However, river control and urban water projects were interlinked in important ways in the 1960s, including their colonial legacies.

The British sewer project and the properties of the urban hydroscape that came into the state's view during its design and construction were largely prompted by colonial anxieties about the health of locally resident foreigners and concerns over the repeated disease epidemics of the late nineteenth century. As Shehab Ismail documents convincingly, the cholera epidemics between 1883 and 1902 led to increasing scrutiny of the nature of Cairo's subsoil, the routes of human waste disposal and potable water provision within it, and the relationship of those routes to the Nile itself. Proposals for new sanitary infrastructures, both sewage systems and sources for drinking water, entailed a series of intertwined decisions about the relationship of the two water systems through underground drainage into the river. Both water provisioning and sewage removal deepened "a bifurcated urban landscape" in the city, which was marked by colonial assumptions about consumption according to class and culture.[90] As Ismail notes, the decisions and designs in constructing the new colonial sewers were political acts intended to "civilize" Egyptians. According to liberal European engineers, "sanitary uplift" would be created by the expansion of domestic privacy in plumbing and the decline of more collective hygiene.[91] Limited to certain sectors of the city and its capacity overdetermined by racialized assumptions about consumption and cleanliness, the new colonial system was insufficient from the outset, even as it remade portions of the cityscape.

The city flooded twice in the "water year" of 1964–65. While urban flooding was not unknown in Cairo—a particularly wide-scale collapse of the sewers had occurred in 1934[92]—this year, 1964–65, was unusual for several reasons: urban flooding occurred both during high and low points of the river, while the nation celebrated its technical mastery of its hydrological regime with the completion of the first stage of High Dam construction. A long-term increase of the groundwater table was largely to blame. According to Egyptian geologists in the late 1970s and 1980s, Egypt's water table rose between 1930 and 1980 from a depth of fourteen meters from the surface to less than five meters from the surface. By 1980, the water table in Cairo, for instance, was less than two meters below the surface.[93]

The first flooding of the streets of Cairo in the water year occurred in September 1964. Just months after the diversion of the Nile River into the channels for High Dam construction, the river produced its largest flood of the century, and by the end of September, the Nile ran two meters higher than the city.[94] In April 1965, many of the same streets were again inundated with sewage as the city flooded a second time, mostly due to a collapse of the drainage system. The old pipes and pumping stations in many districts of the city could not keep pace with the surging sludge that urban expansion and population growth produced. The flooding hit several of Cairo's low-lying neighborhoods the hardest. The 1964–65 urban floods and overflows prompted the emergency formation of the Permanent Cairo and Giza Drainage Committee to oversee the "hundred-day drainage projects" to repair the city's sewerage grid in the spring of 1965.[95] The committee was chaired by the state's minister of electric power, 'Izzat Salama, who represented perhaps the highest level of state infrastructure, the High Dam. Completing major projects nearly a month ahead of schedule, in July the committee oversaw the inauguration of new drainage projects in Giza and in the "northern districts" of Cairo, as well as pipeline repairs on major streets. Salama and his engineers declared their total control of the urban waterscape in 1965, although drainage problems continued well into the 1980s and even plague the city to this day.[96]

THE FUTURE OF HYDRO-IRREGULARITY

Widely fluctuating Nile flood levels in the 1970s and early 1980s convinced many Egyptians that eliminating the annual flood by impounding the river's waters in the reservoir had "saved the country." In the early 1980s, a series of low Niles brought widespread drought to much of eastern Africa. Many Egyptians believed that the High Dam prevented drought in Egypt since the dam's reservoir had filled earlier than expected due to record-high floods in 1964 and 1975.[97] The reservoir replenished thanks to more regular rains in the 1990s, although, by the 2000s, the problem had become one of excess water in years of strong flooding. State officials, worried about raising farmers' expectations of more water, for instance, or about damage to the infrastructure below the dam, have in recent years diverted excess river water to the desert to evaporate rather than send it downstream.[98] Regardless of stored capacity, the state releases the same amount of water each year. Control of the Nile's waters has re-emerged as an area of international conflict and struggle. The Grand Ethiopian Renaissance Dam (GERD) has been under construction in the headwaters of the Blue

Nile (responsible for the bulk of the water of the Nile in Egypt) in the highlands of northern Ethiopia since 2011, although its impact on the Egyptian hydroscape remains unclear.[99] As such, Egypt faces problems of both water scarcity and water abundance in the twenty-first century.[100]

Widening the view of Egypt's hydraulic regime, therefore, brings together water narratives that are usually recounted and even experienced separately. Since the early modern or Ottoman period, control of Egypt's irrigation regime had been shifting from forms of local control and expertise to more centralized state coordination of the system as the fluvial environment was increasingly engineered into a new hydraulic regime, one governed by new seasonal cycles and water tempos as much as a new and expanded logic of control. However, the failures of the large dams in the country's south, such as waterlogging, scouring of the riverbed, and lower yields due to salinity and nutrient loss in fields, paradoxically shifted water system control back to the end-users over the following half century. The ongoing struggle becomes visible by tracking the transformation and management of Egypt's hydroscape along narrative registers of both the local surface encounters and the broad infrastructural system that emerged in direct conflict in the 1960s. The "captive Nile" and its new artificial flood also fundamentally reordered the work of irrigation from clearing silt to managing swift water that scoured banks and barrages and refused to drain from fields.

Increased centralized control by the state unified the country into a national hydroscape and led to global changes in water politics. The new centralized regime of water management that emerged between 1898 and 1971 "represented [one] of the most powerful transformations of the twentieth century," according to Timothy Mitchell. "The building of the original barrage at Aswan in 1898–1902 helped inaugurate around the world an era of engineering on a new scale. Schemes to block the flow of large rivers were to become the century's largest construction projects. Dams were unique in the scope and manner in which they altered the distribution of resources across space and time, among entire communities and ecosystems. . . . For many postcolonial governments, this ability to rearrange the natural and social environment became a means to demonstrate the strength of the modern state as a techno-economic power."[101] As each new technological stage of fluvial management invited more and different forms of intervention, a paradoxical alignment of a strong state and diffuse control brought new actors into water control. It is this engineered and hybrid quality that most firmly marks the hydroscape in modern Egypt. The awkward and contradictory locations for human agency in this system come in and out of view at crucial junctures but, nevertheless, remain deeply connected as forms of power.

Acknowledgment

The author thanks Beth Baron and Jeffrey Culang for excellent editorial guidance and the ACLS, the Mellon Foundation, and Washington University in St. Louis for research support.

Notes

1. "Tifl Yasqut fi Balu'a; al-Miyah Tajrufuhu 10 Kilumitrat," *al-Ahram*, 12 October 1969, 9.

2. Khaled Fahmy, "An Olfactory Tale of Two Cities: Cairo in the Nineteenth Century," in *Historians in Cairo: Essays in Honor of George Scanlon*, ed. Jill Edwards (Cairo: American University in Cairo Press, 2002), 175, 185 note 55.

3. Brian Larkin, "The Politics and Poetics of Infrastructure," *Annual Review of Anthropology* 42 (2013): 327–43.

4. Ravi Baghel, *River Control in India: Spatial, Governmental and Subjective Dimensions* (New York: Springer 2014), 17. Marcus Nüsser delineates a genealogy for the term *technological hydroscapes* in *Large Dams in Asia: Contested Environments between Technological Hydroscapes and Social Resistance* (New York: Springer, 2014), 6. See also Erik Swyngedouw, *Liquid Power: Contested Hydro-Modernities in Twentieth-Century Spain* (Cambridge, MA: MIT Press, 2015).

5. On the 1960s as the global highpoint of dam building, see J. R. McNeill, *Something New under the Sun: An Environmental History of the Twentieth-Century World* (New York: W. W. Norton and Co., 2000), 159.

6. Hosam E. Rabie Elemam, "Egypt and Collective Action Mechanisms in the Nile Basin," in *River Nile in Post-Colonial Age: Conflict and Cooperation among the Nile Basin Countries*, ed. Terje Tvedt (New York: I. B. Tauris, 2010), 219; Jessica Barnes, *Cultivating the Nile: The Everyday Politics of Water in Egypt* (Durham, NC: Duke University Press, 2014), 1, 5; *Food and Agriculture Organization of the United Nations*, AQUASTAT country report for Egypt, 2016, accessed 15 July 2019, http://www.fao.org/nr/water/aquastat/countries_regions/EGY/print1.stm.

7. John Waterbury, *Hydropolitics of the Nile Valley* (Syracuse, NY: Syracuse University Press, 1979), 24; Gamal Hamdan, "Evolution of Irrigation Agriculture in Egypt," in *A History of Land Use in Arid Regions*, ed. Laurence Dudley Stamp (Paris: UNESCO, 1961), 136; John Cooper, *The Medieval Nile* (Cairo: American University in Cairo Press, 2014), 1.

8. Waterbury, *Hydropolitics*, 22–23.

9. Ibid., 12.

10. For a discussion of these trends, see Alan Mikhail, *Nature and Empire in Ottoman Egypt* (Cambridge: Cambridge University Press, 2011), 16–17, 31–34; and Jennifer L. Derr, *The Lived Nile: Environment, Disease, and Material Colonial Economy in Egypt* (Stanford: Stanford University Press, 2019), 68–69.

11. Alan Mikhail, *Under Osman's Tree: The Ottoman Empire, Egypt, and Environmental History* (Chicago: University of Chicago Press, 2017), 19; Timothy Mitchell, "Can the Mosquito Speak?" in *Rule of Experts: Egypt, Techno-Politics, Modernity* (Berkeley: University of California Press, 2002).

12. River epics range from Emil Ludwig's *The Nile: The Life-Story of a River*, originally published in Dutch in 1935 and then English translation in 1937 (Crows Nest, Australia: Allen & Unwin), to works such as Robert Twigger, *Red Nile: A Biography of the World's Greatest River* (New York: St. Martin's Press, 2013) or Egyptian geologist Rushdi Sa'id's *Nahr al-Nil*, 2nd ed. (Dar al-Hilal; Oxford: Pergamon Press, 2001). On the Nile and Egypt's character, see Amin Sami's multivolume *Taqwim al-Nil*, published in Cairo between 1916 and 1936, and Gamal Hamdan's four-volume *Shakhsiyyat Misr: Dirasa fi 'Abqariyyat al-Makan*, published in Cairo in the 1980s.

13. Barnes, *Cultivating the Nile*, 26. See also Ben Orlove and Steven C. Caton, "Water Sustainability: Anthropological Approaches and Prospects," *Annual Review of Anthropology* 39 (2010): 404.

14. Karl C. Butzer, *Early Hydraulic Civilization in Egypt: A Study in Cultural Ecology* (Chicago: University of Chicago Press, 1976), 47.

15. Mikhail, *Nature and Empire in Ottoman Egypt*, 62.

16. Ibid., 33; Mikhail, *Under Osman's Tree.*

17. Mikhail, *Nature and Empire*, 242–90; Cooper, *Medieval Nile*, 48–74.

18. Derr, *The Lived Nile*, 17.

19. H. E. Hurst, *The Nile* (London: Constable, 1952), especially chapter 3; Nicholas S. Hopkins, "Irrigation in Contemporary Egypt," in *Agriculture in Egypt: From Pharaonic to Modern Times*, ed. Alan K. Bowman and Eugene Rogan (Oxford: Oxford University Press, 1999), 367–85. This notion of the "perennial Nile" is the premise of Derr, *The Lived Nile.*

20. Hurst, *The Nile*, 46.

21. Derr, *The Lived Nile*, 6.

22. For the various ministries involved in Egypt's water management, see Barnes, *Cultivating the Nile*, 17.

23. Hurst, *The Nile*, 65; Yusuf A. Shibl, *The Aswan High Dam* (Beirut: Arab Institute for Research and Publishing, 1971), 43.

24. Hurst, *The Nile*, 65.

25. Ibid.

26. Nicholas S. Hopkins, *Agrarian Transformation in Egypt* (Boulder, CO: Westview Press, 1987), especially chapter 7; Barnes, *Cultivating the Nile*; Hurst, *The Nile*, 42–45; Derr, *The Lived Nile*, 101–3.

27. Hurst, *The Nile*, 42–45; Derr, *The Lived Nile*, 101–03; Ahmad al-Hitta, *Tarikh al-Zira'a al-Misriyya fi 'Ahd Muhammad 'Ali al-Kabir* (Cairo: Dar al-Ma'arif, 1950), 14.

28. Alan Mikhail, *The Animal in Ottoman Egypt* (Oxford: Oxford University Press, 2014), 39.

29. Ghislaine Alleaume, "An Industrial Revolution in Agriculture? Some Observations on the Evolution of Rural Egypt in the Nineteenth Century," in *Agriculture in Egypt: From Pharaonic to Modern Times*, ed. Alan K. Bowman and Eugene Rogan (Oxford: Oxford University Press, 1999), 338.

30. Samera Esmeir, *Juridical Humanity: A Colonial History* (Stanford: Stanford University Press, 2012); Derr, *The Lived Nile.*

31. On the building of the low dam, see Derr, *The Lived Nile*, chapter 2; and Waterbury, *Hydropolitics*, 33.

32. Waterbury, *Hydropolitics*, 3.

33. Hussein M. Fahim, *Egyptian Nubians* (Salt Lake City: University of Utah Press, 1983).

34. Derr, *The Lived Nile*, 72–73.

35. Ibid., 61–64.

36. Waterbury, *Hydropolitics*, 64.

37. On the general political and nationalist furor of the 1920s around the Jabal Awliya' dam on the White Nile, see Robert L. Tignor, "Nationalism, Economic Planning, and Development Projects in Interwar Egypt," *The International Journal of African Historical Studies* 10, no. 2 (1977): 185–208.

38. The full title of the pamphlet was *Isti'bad Misr bi-Mashru'at al-Rayy al-Injliziyya. Isti'bad* may also be translated as "subjugation," although the British Interior Ministry officials in Cairo chose to translate it as "Enslaving Egypt by British Irrigation Projects" when they forwarded a copy of the Arabic pamphlet to the British Embassy in Cairo in November 1928. The British prided themselves on abolishing slavery in Egypt as part of their civilizing colonial mission, as well as abolishing forced (corvée) labor. On Egypt's relationship to

Sudan, especially under British occupation, see Eve Troutt Powell, *A Different Shade of Colonialism* (Berkeley: University of California Press, 2003). The pamphlet is enclosed in The British National Archives, London, Kew (TNA), Foreign Office (FO) 141/577/ C376586, Cairo, 8 November 1928, Keown-Boyd to Smart/High Commissioner.

39. Zaki, "Ist'bad Misr," 16.

40. Ibid., 23.

41. Derr, *The Lived Nile*, 64.

42. Robert Vitalis, *When Capitalists Collide: Business Conflict and the End of Empire in Egypt* (Berkeley: University of California Press, 1995).

43. These towns appear across the river branch (then the Tinnis branch) on al-Idrisi's map of the Delta in 1154. See Cooper, *Medieval Nile*, figure A1.7.

44. 'Ali Mubarak, *al-Khitat al-Tawfiqiyya al-Jadida li-Misr al-Qahira wa-Muduniha wa-Biladiha al-Qadima wa-l-Shahira*, vol. 16 (Bulaq: al-Matba'a al-Kubra al-Amiriyya, 1886), 79–80. The town at that time was named Minya al-Ghamr; on the name change, see Muhammad Ramzi, *al-Qamus al-Jughrafi li-l-Bilad al-Misriyya min 'Ahd Qudama' al-Misriyyin ila Sanat 1945*, part 2 (Cairo: al-Hay'a al-Misriyya al-'Amma li-l-Kitab, 1994), 263.

45. Mubarak, *al-Khitat*, vol. 11, 95.

46. Rivlin, *Agricultural Policy*, 232.

47. Willcocks and Craig, *Egyptian Irrigation*, vol. 2, 631–32.

48. Shibl, *Aswan High Dam*, 39. The Zifta Barrage is illustrated in Willcocks and Craig, *Egyptian Irrigation*, vol. 2, facing 664 in plate 164.

49. Willcocks and Craig, *Egyptian Irrigation*, vol. 2, 572.

50. Ibid., vol. 1, plate 31 (Map of Lower Egypt and the Fayum).

51. Mona Abaza, *The Cotton Plantation Remembered: An Egyptian Family Story* (Cairo: American University in Cairo Press, 2013), 82.

52. Hamdan, "Evolution of Irrigation Agriculture," 127.

53. Ibid.

54. Tvedt, *The River Nile in the Post-Colonial Age*, 3.

55. United Arab Republic, Maslahat al-Ist'lamat, *The High Dam: Bulwark of Our Future* (Cairo: Ministry of Information, 1963), 6.

56. Ahmad Shokr, "Hydropolitics, Economy, and the Aswan High Dam in Mid-Century Egypt," *Arab Studies Journal* 17, no. 1 (2009): 9–31.

57. Gilbert F. White, "The Environmental Effects of the High Dam at Aswan," *Science* 30, no. 7 (1988): 6.

58. Richard Elliot Benedick, "The High Dam and the Transformation of the Nile," *Middle East Journal* 33, no. 2 (1979): 122; Hamdan, "Evolution of Irrigation Agriculture," 140.

59. See, e.g., Hamdan, "Evolution of Irrigation Agriculture," 125, 140; and UAR, Maslahat al-Ist'lamat, *The High Dam*, 6–8.

60. John Waterbury, *The Nile Stops at Aswan*, part 1 (Hanover, NH: American Universities Field Staff, 1977), 10.

61. Benedick, "The High Dam," 127.

62. See Waterbury, *Hydropolitics*, Table 8: "The High Dam in Figures," 111.

63. Benedick, "High Dam," 123; Waterbury, *Hydropolitics*, 111.

64. White, "Environmental Effects," 11.

65. Tahir Abu Fasha, *Qissat al-Sadd al-'Ali*, 2nd ed. (1960; reprint, Cairo: General Authority for Cultural Palaces, 2010), 61.

66. Elizabeth Bishop, "Talking Shop: Egyptian Engineers and Soviet Specialists at the Aswan High Dam" (PhD diss., University of Chicago, 1997).

67. Alia Mossallam, "We Are the Ones Who Made This Dam 'High'! A Builders' History of the Aswan High Dam," *Water History* 6, no. 4 (2014): 297–314.

68. Abdelazim Negm, Mohamed Elsahabi, and Mohamed Salman Tayie, "An Overview of Aswan High Dam and Grand Ethiopian Renaissance Dam," in *Grand Ethiopian Renaissance Dam Versus Aswan High Dam: A View from Egypt*, ed. Abdelazim M. Negm and Sommer Abdel-Fattah (Cham, Switzerland: Springer Nature, 2019), 7.

69. S. Shalash, "The Effect of the High Aswan Dam on the Hydrological Regime of the River Nile," *IAHS-AISH Publication* 130 (1980): 244.

70. White, "Environmental Effects," 34.

71. Ibid., 11, 35–36.

72. United Arab Republic, Ministry of National Guidance, *The Yearbook 1966* (Cairo: Information Administration, 1966), 97–98.

73. Roger Owen, "A Long Look at Nearly Two Centuries of Long Staple Cotton," in *Agriculture in Egypt*, 356–57.

74. White, "Environmental Effects," 11, 34. The figures for "cropped land" are obtained by "counting land cultivated in each crop season separately," 34.

75. Elemam, "Egypt and Collective Action," 219; Waterbury, *Hydropolitics*, 72–73; Tvedt, *The River Nile*, 7.

76. Barnes, *Cultivating the Nile*, 141.

77. Hamdan, "Evolution of Irrigation Agriculture," 129.

78. Hurst, *The Nile*, 63–64; Hamdan, "Evolution of Irrigation Agriculture," 129.

79. Hamdan, "Evolution of Irrigation Agriculture," 129.

80. Hurst, *The Nile*, 64.

81. Barnes, *Cultivating the Nile*, 147–50.

82. Hamdan, "Evolution of Irrigation Agriculture," 133.

83. Shibl, *Aswan High Dam*, 39–40.

84. Barnes, *Cultivating the Nile*, 143.

85. Ibid., 147.

86. Ibid., 158.

87. Ibid., 149.

88. André Raymond, *Cairo*, trans. Willard Wood (Cambridge, MA: Harvard University Press, 2000), 358.

89. Janet Abu-Lughod, *Cairo: 1001 Years of the City Victorious* (Princeton, NJ: Princeton University Press, 1971); Raymond, *Cairo*; Shehab Ismail, "Engineering Metropolis: Contagion, Capital, and the Making of British Colonial Cairo, 1882–1922" (PhD diss., Columbia University, 2017).

90. Ismail, "Engineering Metropolis," 155. See also Shehab Ismail, "Epicures and Experts: The Drinking Water Controversy in British Colonial Cairo," *Arab Studies Journal* 26, no. 2 (2018): 8–42; and Ismail, "Engineering Heterotopia," *International Journal of Middle East Studies* 47 (2015): 566–69.

91. Ismail, "Engineering Metropolis," 274.

92. "Cairo's Drainage System Breaks Down; Serious Privations Menace Flooded City," *The New York Times*, 17 September 1934, 11.

93. "Egypt's Cultural Heritage Is at Risk," *New Scientist* 87, 10 July 1980, 98; Thomas Naff papers, The Middle East Water Collection, Oregon State University Libraries, accessed

through Oregon Digital, 7 September 2020, https://oregondigital.org/downloads/oregon digital:df70pn89t.

94. See *al-Ahram*, 24 September 1964, 3.

95. On the constitution of the committee and discussion in the People's Assembly, see "Miyah al-Tafh Satakhtafi fi al-Qahira wa-l-Giza," *al-Ahram*, 29 April 1965, 6.

96. "Aly Sabry Opens 'One-Hundred-Day' Drainage Projects," *Egyptian Gazette*, 21 July 1965, 2; Raymond, *Cairo*, 358–59; Christophe Boltanski, "Rehabilitation des égouts du Caire," *Observatoire Urbain du Caire Contemporain, CEDEJ: Lettre d'information* 14 (1988): 8–9.

97. "Drought Averted Thanks to H. Dam," *Egyptian Gazette*, 23 July 1985, in clippings file, Thomas Naff papers, The Middle East Water Collection, Oregon State University Libraries, Oregon Digital, accessed 7 September 2020, https://oregondigital.org/downlo ads/f0df70q408p?file=thumbnail. On the earlier than expected filling of the reservoir, see also White, "Environmental Effects," 7–8.

98. Barnes, *Cultivating the Nile*, chapter 2.

99. On the GERD struggle, see Negm and Abdel-Fattah, eds., *Grand Ethiopian Renaissance Dam Versus Aswan High Dam*; and Muhammad Saliman Tayiʻ, *Misr wa-ʻAzmat Miyah al-Nil* (Cairo: Dar al-Shuruq, 2012).

100. Barnes, *Cultivating the Nile*, 138–39.

101. Mitchell, "Can the Mosquito Speak?," 21.

BIBLIOGRAPHY

Abu-Lughod, Janet L. *Cairo: 1001 Years of the City Victorious*. Princeton, NJ: Princeton University Press, 1971.

Baghel, Ravi. *River Control in India*. New York: Springer, 2014.

Barnes, Jessica. *Cultivating the Nile: The Everyday Politics of Water in Egypt*. Durham, NC: Duke University Press, 2014.

Bowman, Alan K., and Eugene Rogan, eds. *Agriculture in Egypt*. Oxford: Oxford University Press for the British Academy, 1999.

Butzer, Karl W. *Early Hydraulic Civilization in Egypt: A Study in Cultural Ecology*. Chicago: University of Chicago Press, 1976.

Cooper, John P. *The Medieval Nile: Route, Navigation, and Landscape in Islamic Egypt*. Cairo: American University in Cairo Press, 2014.

Derr, Jennifer L. *The Lived Nile: Environment, Disease, and Material Colonial Economy in Egypt*. Stanford, CA: Stanford University Press, 2019.

Fahim, Hussein M. *Egyptian Nubians*. Salt Lake City: University of Utah Press, 1983.

Hopkins, Nicholas S. *Agrarian Transformation in Egypt*. Boulder, CO: Westview Press, 1987.

Huber, Valeska. *Channelling Mobilities: Migration and Globalisation in the Suez Canal Region and Beyond, 1869–1914*. Cambridge: Cambridge University Press, 2013.

Little, Tom. *High Dam at Aswan: The Subjugation of the Nile*. New York: John Day, 1965.

Mikhail, Alan. *Nature and Empire in Ottoman Egypt: An Environmental History*. Cambridge: Cambridge University Press, 2011.

Mitchell, Timothy. *Rule of Experts: Egypt, Techno-Politics, Modernity*. Berkeley: University of California Press, 2002.

Mossallam, Alia. "We Are the Ones Who Made This Dam 'High'! A Builders' History of the Aswan High Dam." *Water History* 6, no. 4 (2014): 297–314.

Negm, Abdelazim, and Sommer Abdel-Fattah, eds. *Grand Ethiopian Renaissance Dam versus Aswan High Dam: A View from Egypt*. Cham, Switzerland: Springer Nature, 2019.

Shokr, Ahmad. "Hydropolitics, Economy, and the Aswan High Dam in Mid-Century Egypt." *Arab Studies Journal* 17, no. 1 (2009): 9–31.

Tvedt, Terje. *The River Nile in the Age of the British: Political Ecology and the Quest for Economic Power*. New York: I. B. Tauris, 2004.

Tvedt, Terje, ed. *The River Nile in the Post-Colonial Age: Conflict and Cooperation among the Nile Basin Countries*. New York: I. B. Tauris, 2010.

Waterbury, John. *Hydropolitics of the Nile Valley*. Syracuse, NY: Syracuse University Press, 1979.

White, Richard. *The Organic Machine: The Remaking of the Columbia River*. New York: Hill and Wang, 1995.

PART III

LAW AND SOCIETY

CHAPTER 11

HOSTAGES OF CREDIT

The Imprisonment of Debtors in the Khedival Period

OMAR CHETA

In nineteenth-century legal parlance, an imprisoned debtor could be referred to as a "hostage" (*rahina*) of his creditor.[1] It was the government, however, that incarcerated debtors. In other words, debtors' prisons embodied state power in the service of private capital. The history of the modern state is commonly documented through the prism of its intrusion into the lives of individuals. Michel Foucault has theorized the defining features of this process in relation to modern institutions such as the school, the hospital, and, most notably, the prison.[2] Scholars of the colonized world elaborated on, revised, and often transcended these Foucauldian points of departure. State-building in nineteenth-century Egypt, in particular, has become a solid foundation for historical knowledge production about the modern state and its power, not least because of the massive archive it has generated. Studies of modern institutions (e.g., the army and the factory) and fields of knowledge (e.g., anthropology, law, and medicine) that pay particular attention to practices of state power and the incredible social costs they generated have profoundly deepened our understanding of the history of Egypt and its surroundings.[3] In the same vein, Rudolph Peters has written extensively on the history of the prison—that quintessentially modern and persistently contemporary institution.[4] Curiously, however, the imprisonment of debtors, a practice at the intersection of state power and commercial capitalism, both hallmarks of nineteenth-century Egyptian history, has remained virtually unstudied.

In a rough sense, the historical trajectory of precolonial nineteenth-century Egypt can be described as a movement from aggressive modern state-building with an agricultural monopoly at its core under Mehmed ʿAli (r. 1805–48) to a more measured elaboration of that state structure in the context of commercial capitalism under his successors, the khedives.[5] Centralized state prisons have an uncontested place within this historical narrative. Modern states invariably rely on incarceration not only as a main form of punishment for those transgressing the law but also to solidify their grip over suspects while investigations and trials follow their course. Egypt and the late Ottoman Empire were no exception to this general rule.[6] However, this neat justification for the ubiquity of prisons requires refinement once we consider one category of prisoners: debtors. Merchants, in particular, were permanently embedded within circuits of credit. They borrowed money to circulate goods across time and space, and, if successful, generated profits that they used to simultaneously pay these debts and re-enter the business cycle with newly acquired debts. Whenever that process failed, which was a frequent occurrence, debtors and creditors renegotiated original plans, revised payment timetables, or even took their losses and drew new schemes. Imprisonment was a dangerous escalation. It likely marked the end of amicable business relations between creditor and debtor and signaled to the larger merchant community that both were risky potential business partners—the creditor for not recognizing the cyclical character of credit-fueled business, and the debtor for failing to fulfill his or her promise.

Although it may seem antithetical to the logic of commerce, debtor imprisonment was prevalent even within the centers of capitalism. At the heart of the scholarly exploration of this practice around the world is a fascination with the particular historical moment in which bankruptcy ceased to be seen legally and socially as a moral failure and instead became considered an economic failure. The moment of this reconceptualization is arguably the moment in which the function of imprisoning debtors would either end or undergo a radical redefinition. In North America, the first indications of widespread opposition to the idea of debt as a moral failing only appeared in the second half of the eighteenth century. Bruce Mann argues that even though diminished, "the redefinition of insolvency from sin to risk, from moral failure to economic failure" is still incomplete.[7] Nineteenth-century London was the site of notorious debtors' prisons, some with medieval roots, such as the privately owned and operated Marshalsea, which housed some of the poorest debtors of the capital city of the British Empire and modern industry.[8] In France, for several decades after the French Revolution, insolvent debtors continued to be stigmatized. There, imprisonment for private debts in state-controlled prisons was legal until 1867. By then, not only did legal and social views shift toward a depersonalized view of credit as "an economic necessity and a human right," but also, as Erika Vause has shown, "mechanisms and institutions for handling the risks of debt" became more sophisticated.[9]

The utility of these comparative references to Egypt derives from the country's place within the modern world economy, primarily as an exporter of cotton to British industrial sites,[10] and from the fact that the khedival and Ottoman law regimes were based directly on French models.[11] Yet a sound explanation of debtor imprisonment should also take into account the long history of shari'a-informed and Ottoman practices governing bankruptcies and enforcing debt collection. For example, studies from across the early modern Ottoman Empire emphasize the marginality of moral understandings of credit relations, including interest-bearing loans, in shari'a court practices.[12] As Munther al-Sabbagh has aptly explained in relation to sixteenth-century Palestine and Syria, "the courts were interested in maintaining overall order of the market and rather disinterested in regulating market morality."[13] Additionally, the prominence of extraterritorial privileges in the context of European imperialism accentuated the practical difficulties of resolving disputes over debts between Ottoman subjects on the one hand and European subjects and protégés on the other.[14]

A range of sources—archival, legal, and narrative—enable us to reconstruct the logic and practice of imprisoning debtors in khedival Cairo. Such an effort builds on Rudolph Peters's groundbreaking studies of nineteenth-century Egyptian prisons, which form a small part of his larger agenda of excavating the origins of Egyptian criminal law.[15] By carefully and systematically combining examples from nineteenth-century court documents and fatwas with mainly brief and incidental references in contemporaneous European travelers' accounts and modern scholarship, three fundamental questions about the history of debtors' prisons can be addressed: Why were debtors imprisoned? Under what conditions? How did they regain their freedom? On the question of debtor imprisonment, the khedival legal system resembled pre-nineteenth-century shari'a practices in significant ways. The khedival state encompassed a sophisticated bureau-cratic apparatus, a new capacity for legal enforcement, and a law regime that separated commercial matters from the civil legal sphere. As a result, mechanisms of debt collection, including imprisonment, for those who borrowed money to invest it or alleviate hardship would follow different paths. However, the particular history of imprisonment in shari'a practice, the function of imprisonment under nineteenth-century commer-cial law, the khedival state's commitment to standardize Hanafi law, and the continued relevance of Islamic legal opinions in civil affairs led to a convergence of the logics and practices of imprisoning commercial and civil debtors. The close study of this one practice—the imprisonment of debtors—sheds light on what such grand labels as legal reform and secularization meant on a social level. It is worth noting that the debtors at the center of this study were all Ottoman subjects who were either sued by their compatriots or by Europeans and their protégés.[16]

ENTERING DEBTORS' PRISON

To begin with, we must distinguish between debtors' prison as a site of incarceration that was exclusive to debtors and the practice of detaining debtors in prisons alongside convicts and pretrial detainees who were accused of any legal offense. There is evidence that some insolvent debtors were indeed locked up in exclusive spaces, but this specific treatment was neither a consistent nor a universal practice. In any case, debtors who ex-perienced this fate were held in government prisons.[17] Despite their official character, these incarceration sites were scattered, uneven, and decentralized. Many were not orig-inally built to be prisons but were rather repurposed to serve a sometimes short-term function. This apparent disorder led Peters to note the incongruence between the cen-trality of the prison to the penal system and the absence of a clear justification for its role within the bureaucratic culture. Similarly, he speculated that prisoners must have suffered little by way of social stigma because of the seeming randomness of the prac-tice of incarceration, especially when applied by an oppressive government. During the second half of the nineteenth century, the purpose and condition of imprisonment shifted in ways that reflected political reconfiguration, medical discoveries, and legal reforms. By the late 1850s, it was becoming a more common practice for members of the poorer classes and enslaved individuals to sue members of the ruling elite, and in 1861 imprisonment formally replaced flogging as a means of legal punishment.[18] Life conditions within the prisons also generally improved. Prison administration was consolidated, and public health became a major factor in how the prisons were run. Archival records reveal details about the multiple locations of prisons within cities, their internal organization, and their regulation of visitations and provisions. Yet debtors appear only incidentally within these records.

European travelers to Egypt during the nineteenth century were ignorant of the complexity of the ongoing reconfiguration of state institutions. The accounts they left behind often paid attention to the place of law in society as they observed or heard about it. Still, these accounts, if read critically, are revealing. Edward William Lane, a notable orientalist who spent several years in Egypt during the 1820s and 1830s, wrote about the imprisonment of criminals and of debtors in distinct ways. Regarding the former, he mentioned "numerous guard-houses" in Cairo, where "persons accused of thefts, assaults, &c." were confined until they were subjected to interrogation and, potentially, conviction. Punishment, however, was a different matter. "It usually consist[ed] in [the convicts] being compelled to labour," conscripted into the army, or, in the case of crimes committed against the governor, killed.[19] In contrast to these actual observations, Lane's comment on the imprisonment of debtors recounted the Islamic learned opinion, "The debtor is imprisoned for non-payment of his debt; but if he establish [*sic*] his insolvency, he is liberated."[20] The French abolitionist Victor Schoelcher, who visited Egypt in the mid-1840s, noted the radically uneven treatment of prisoners, with the rich having their own "furnished rooms and even servants or slaves," while the poor were "detained in a dark ward" during the day and "chained" during the night.[21] Lady Duff-Gordon, the translator of several books from German and author of the popular *Letters from Egypt* who spent the 1860s in Upper Egypt, mentions imprisonment in several of her letters, mainly to highlight the arbitrariness of Egypt's legal system. Writing from Luxor in 1864, she commented that "if the prisoner can bribe high, he is apt to get off."[22] A few years later, on the occasion of the release of a man after he spent three years in a Cairo prison, she remarked that "so many honest men go to prison that it is no presumption at all against a man."[23] Interestingly, she recorded that a group of women whose husbands were imprisoned for not paying taxes were supplying them with "their dinner *à tour de rôle*."[24] The core of these observations is generally consistent with the archival discoveries: imprisonment was becoming more widespread from the mid-nineteenth century, but the experience of it was not uniform, prisoners were not completely cut off from their relations while confined, and popular attitudes toward imprisonment may have been nonjudgmental.

To capture a glimpse of imprisoned debtors among a general and diverse population of prisoners, and to understand why and how they ended up in prison in the first place, we need to turn to other historical sources. The nineteenth century was a period of legal transformation. It witnessed a reduction of the jurisdictional domain of shari'a courts and the adoption of new French-inspired Ottoman and khedival laws. Beneath this veneer of secularization, the khedival state expanded its appointment of Muslim jurists (Hanafi muftis to be exact) "to the various levels of the judiciary and the administration"[25] and in deploying the shari'a-sanctioned concept of *siyasa*, which allows the ruler to supplement Islamic jurisprudence "with extra measures intended to . . . uphold the interests of the state."[26] This dynamic manifests itself in the realm of debt collection and bankruptcies in counterintuitive ways. By the mid-nineteenth century, shari'a courts—historically indispensable sites for registering contracts and adjudicating related disputes—were no longer authorized to hear commercial cases, including those revolving around debt collection. Instead, these cases were heard by state-organized merchant courts according to the Ottoman Code of Commerce and with no explicit reference to shari'a. This jurisdictional shift, as I will explain shortly, brought about new procedures for imprisoning debtors and liquidating assets. Yet, significantly, it did not result in a radical shift in the legal logic of dealing with insolvent debtors, which focused on enforcing debt collection rather than punishing the presumed immorality of the debtor. Furthermore, the office of the Grand Mufti, a Hanafi jurist, continued to explain the legal conditions for imprisoning delinquent debtors in his answers to inquiries about the shari'a-sanctioned mechanisms of debt collection from individuals and state agencies.

As such, while the khedival state decisively removed commercial litigation from the jurisdiction of shari'a courts and transferred it to specialized merchant courts in the mid-1840s, it preserved, at least in form, the longstanding shari'a-sanctioned practice of imprisoning delinquent debtors. Historically, in fact, the Islamic legal tradition has reserved imprisonment primarily for debtors rather than other offenders. In practice, judges, with the support of jurists, imprisoned delinquent debtors in order to pressure them to pay what they owed and released them when they became convinced of their insolvency. Historically, debtors' prisons existed, they were under the control of shari'a court judges, men and women debtors were confined to separate spaces, and debtors were allowed to receive guests while in prison. Depending on the legal school being followed, the state (through the court) or the creditor was responsible for financially maintaining the imprisoned debtor. This variation notwithstanding, and although it was not a final punishment but rather a strategy to force payment, imprisonment was meant to constitute "harsh treatment."[27] Five centuries before these khedival policies, the Mamluk state made the imprisonment of debtors the prerogative of state-organized (*siyasa*) courts rather than the usual shari'a courts, thus opening the door for the use of torture to extract money, which was not allowed by the main schools of law.[28] Later, under the Ottomans, the practice of imprisoning debtors continued under a slightly different arrangement. In the seventeenth century, debtors were imprisoned when their creditors proved their financial delinquency in the shari'a court. An employee of the court then carried out the decision of imprisonment not in a space under the control of the judge but rather in "a jail operated by one of the military regiments."[29] By the nineteenth century, the practice of imprisoning debtors had had a long and uninterrupted genealogy within Islamic legal theory and practice.

Despite heated debates over its exact scope and influence in khedival Egypt, shari'a continued to play an important role within the legal landscape. From the state's point of view, litigation over commercial debts was only to take place within the merchant courts. Yet debt was not necessarily a commercial matter, and disputes over debt were not always resolved through lawsuits. Therefore, it is not surprising that nineteenth-century fatwa collections would continue to address questions related to debtor imprisonment. Of those, the legal opinions of Muhammad al-'Abbasi al-Mahdi deserve particular attention. A Hanafi jurist, al-Mahdi served as Egypt's Grand Mufti for the better part of five decades between 1848 and his death in 1897. As a senior and remarkably enduring government official, he was responsible for ensuring the conformity of government policy with shari'a, specifically Hanafi doctrine. Simultaneously, he answered questions from the public about Islam and practically any aspect of social life. Unsurprisingly, then, al-Mahdi addressed debtors and prisons. The image that emerges from reading his opinions on the subject could be summarized as follows: It was within the rights of a creditor to imprison his or her debtor if that debtor failed to pay back a debt. The creditor had to convince the judge of the validity of the case, and it was the judge who imprisoned the debtor on behalf of the creditor. The purpose of the imprisonment was to force payment of the debt. The creditor could instruct the judge to release the prisoner at any time. If the imprisonment proved futile because the debtor was revealed to be genuinely unable to pay his or her debt, the judge was entitled to unilaterally release the prisoner (*li-l-qadi qubul al-bayyina . . . wa-itlaquh*). This procedure applied regardless of the nature of the debt—that is, whether or not it was commercial.[30] Al-Mahdi's opinions are significant because they show the continuity of the shari'a-sanctioned position on the matter, whether with noncommercial debts that were being investigated by the shari'a courts or general debts that were being settled outside of state institutions among individuals who opted to follow the sound shari'a opinion.

We can conclude with confidence, then, that noncommercial debtors—for example, those who borrowed money based on need or to acquire a service or commodity—found themselves, on occasion, threatened by their creditors, who had acquired fatwas indicating the appropriateness of imprisonment, or were indeed imprisoned temporarily under the orders of shari'a court judges. In the realm of commerce, merchant court and consular archives contain evidence of an established procedure that led to the imprisonment, and eventual release, of insolvent merchants who were suspected of delinquency. Internal khedival state correspondence further confirms that this procedure was carried out. The existence of this little-known process sheds light on the legislative foundations of the khedival judicial system. While shari'a continued to be invoked in relation to what in modern legal terminology is called a noncommercial debt—referred to in archival documents as "civil debt" (*dayn madani*)—French and Ottoman legal codes were cited to justify the imprisonment of merchants. For example, in February 1868, after three months of trying unsuccessfully to collect his debts, a Cairo-based merchant, Nicola Grima, issued an ultimatum to his debtor, Hasan Pasha Yakan Sirri, which was consistent with "French law" (*tibqan li-l-qanun al-faransawi*), that if he did not receive the amount he had lent as well as the accrued interest "within twenty-four hours," he would deploy all available "legal means against [Hasan's] assets *or his person*."[31] This was not an empty threat but part of a recognized strategy. Since the defendant was an Ottoman subject, he could only be sued before a state-organized court. Nicola had already sought the support of the British consul, who helped him bring a lawsuit against Hasan before the merchant court, where imprisonment was a potential outcome.[32] When he issued his ultimatum, the court had already ruled in his favor and notified Hasan of his responsibility to pay back the debt. Armed with the merchant court decision, Nicola was now preparing to approach the police department to put it into action.

The direct reference to "French law" was not out of place in merchant court proceedings. The 1857 statute of the court had specified a clear ranking of the laws to be applied. The merchants presiding over the court were to rule first according to the established norms of commerce that they knew and practiced by virtue of their vocation. Next, they should follow the clauses of the 1850 Ottoman Code of Commerce and the khedival state-issued statute of the merchant court. If these sources were insufficient to help them reach a decision, they were expected to "follow the relevant articles of the French Law."[33] In that sense, Nicola's reference to French law was neither uncommon nor invalid but probably uncalled for. Typically, the merchant court did not have to look beyond Ottoman law, itself based on French law, to resolve such cases. In cases of bankruptcy, the court ordered the imprisonment of the debtor as part of the broader resolution of the case. The following excerpt from a different but near-contemporaneous merchant court entry reflects, in compressed and formulaic language, the standard course of action that members of the court followed in such cases:

> The case of the debts due to named individuals from Khawaja Jurji Na'um the grocer . . . which has been referred to the court by the Cairo police department . . . 23 [Ramada]N [12]88, number 23
>
> The documents of the case have been consulted[34]
>
> Article [147], article [150], and article [170] of the [Ottoman] Code of Commerce have been consulted[35]
>
> It has been decided by the unanimous opinion of the members of the court to declare Khawaja Na'um bankrupt and to imprison him . . . to appoint one of us, Khawaja Jabru, as a bankruptcy trustee and [one of the creditors] Khawaja Dimitri Kasartridi the Greek as a temporary representative for the creditors [and granting him] fifteen days to gather the creditors.[36]

If the court's decision was carried out without hindrance, the next steps would be for the creditors to agree within the following two weeks on one or more of a set of actions: liquidating the commercial assets of Jurji to pay themselves; temporarily sequestrating the assets; agreeing to reschedule the debt, usually after forfeiting part of the amount they were entitled to; or accepting the involvement of a guarantor who would vow to use his or her own money or relationship with Jurji to ensure payment at a specified later date. Numerous creditors continually sought the help of the merchant courts to collect their debts. Whenever there was sufficient reason for a declaration of bankruptcy (*i'lan taflisa*), imprisonment was part of the resolution.

The imprisonment of commercial debtors, then, was a consequence of their official designation by the merchant court as bankrupt (*muflis*). Similar to the shari'a logic, imprisonment followed from recognizing that the debtors may have the ability to pay back their debts but are choosing not to do so. For example, they may own assets or be successfully engaged in another business that could be redirected to pay their debts. As one creditor specified in a petition, his debtor should be imprisoned "if necessary."[37] Similarly, a silk merchant argued during a court session that his debtors should be "constrained through imprisonment and other means, and should not leave until they pay the amount [of the debt] (*al-tadyiq 'alayhim bi-l-sijn wa-ghayrihi wa-la yabrahu ma lam yadfa'u*)."[38] The conditions of these temporary imprisonments changed, however, if the debtors in question were suspected of criminal intentions or acts related to their bankruptcy. Anton Nicolopulo, for instance, was suspicious of his business partner, Hasan Khabir Muhammad 'Uraybi. They used to conclude their deals in Cairo, where Anton would pay in advance for commodities that Hasan would later ship from his base in Aswan, more than five hundred miles away. But Hasan used to disappear for unspecified periods of time and sometimes sent the promised goods using a different name. When these unusual dealings resulted in growing unpaid debt, Anton was keen on imprisoning Hasan, not because he could prove his delinquency but "to ensure the promptness [of the resolution] in light of the debtor's untrustworthiness (*'adam istiqamat al-madyun*)."[39] Put differently, Hasan was to be detained because of the flight risk. Other debtors were subjected to different conditions of imprisonment because they were charged with fraud (*ihtiyal*) or betrayal (*khiyana*).

In Debtors' Prison

Reconstructing the experience of debtors during imprisonment is difficult because it relies on reconciling two empirical findings. On the one hand, debtors were imprisoned as a matter of routine and on a large scale, a fact that can be gleaned from an 1869 state decree that stipulated stricter conditions for imprisoning debtors in an attempt to remedy their "frivolous arrest."[40] On the other hand, there was no centralized prison authority, at least until 1865, and even then only a limited one existed. Collated anecdotal evidence offers some glimpses of the situation on the ground. Cairo probably had one standalone prison that only housed debtors. Some shari'a courts also had debtors' prisons under their control.[41] Yet in Cairo, as in other urban centers, debtors were incarcerated in other general prisons as well, even if they were sometimes held in separate wards. Government orders from the first half of the nineteenth century show that they were sometimes incarcerated in the prison of the Alexandria Arsenal.[42] Court proceedings include references to debtors being held within the merchant court (*sijn al-majlis*),[43] in the prison of the Cairo police department (*sijn al-dhabtiyya*),[44] and in prisons attached to different governorates (*sijn al-muhafaza* or *sijn al-diwan*).[45] Information on the imprisonment of women debtors is scant. It was likely that women who incurred debts through fraudulent means were imprisoned alongside women criminal convicts in the *iplikhane*, the textile workshop in Bulaq that served as a women's prison.[46] European debtors, whether subjects or protégés, were likely held in their respective consulates.[47]

These archival fragments provide essential context for critically reading A. A. Paton's rare description of his visit to a debtors' prison in Cairo. Paton arrived in the city in 1839 as a private secretary to the British consul-general and spent the next seven years in the region as a diplomat, an orientalist, and a writer, "having received most liberal encouragement to travel in Egypt, Syria, and other parts of the Ottoman Empire, for *The Times*."[48] Like other orientalists, he downplayed the possibility that his effort to pass as a local would be detected by his local interlocutors. That said, the skeleton of his account confirms and offers social depth to archivally based knowledge.[49] Paton recounts that the debtors' prison he visited was located next to a shari'a court. Petitioners holding stacks of sealed documents stood outside. Paton's attempt to enter the premises prompted the guard to question "which of the prisoners we wanted?" While he claims to have entered the building after bribing the guard, the whole episode suggests that meeting with prisoners in person to negotiate a settlement, for example, was common practice.[50] Inside the premises, the guard led him "into a dark passage," after which he entered through the "door with a large wooden bolt" to find himself "among the prisoners." The cell from the inside was "about twenty feet high, the light being admitted by two barred unglazed windows, close to the roof. The walls were perfectly bare, and in the upper corner of the room a spider's web of thick texture fluttered in the slight breeze which ventilated the apartment. On the floor were the mats, carpets, and cushions of the prisoners."[51] Once inside, he heard from a few debtors about living off charity and worrying about their children outside. Yet he also noticed that the prisoners, all men, were of different social status: "a Bedouin," "a miller," "a very young man," "a well-dressed townsman" who suspected that Paton was an agent of Mehmed 'Ali, "a man with weak eyes, a grey beard, and green turban," and "a soldier of fortune." Paton "ordered a pilaff [*sic.*] for the poorer prisoners, and coffee to be served all round." He may have been charitable or was trying to earn their trust. Either way, he understood correctly that eventually they would all be "liberated."[52]

Prolonged pretrial and presentencing detention had been an ongoing problem in Egypt since at least the mid-1830s. In 1849, a few years after Paton visited the debtors' prison, the government tried to fight this phenomenon, partly because the detainees, who were "the providers for their families . . . lead their dependents to fall into destitution and misery."[53] Aware of the persistence of the problem, Sa'id Pasha (r. 1854–63) instructed the Cairo Governorate in 1856 to ensure the speediness of court trials. He looked beyond the concern with material conditions, stressing that he wanted to pacify the prisoners.

Commercial debtors, in particular, would have been affected by this government interest. They could be detained before the merchant court decided on their bankruptcy, for example, because their mobility deemed them a flight risk. Even after the court decided to declare their bankruptcy, their imprisonment was temporary by definition because it would end with them paying off their outstanding debts either voluntarily or through the liquidation of their assets. Saʿid Pasha instructed that pretrial detainees and debtors should be treated more leniently compared to criminal convicts. He reminded his officials to "consider the statuses of people (*darajat ahwal al-nas*) in prison so that they are not all humiliated equally. There must be a distinction between them. . . . Murderers, highway robbers and their likes . . . should be placed in the worst part of the prison. They are to be subjected to partial and total confinement. Those who are in prison while their case is pending, or for a debt and are awaiting a guarantor, should not be imprisoned with [the convicted criminals]."[54] The governor also urged prison officials to explain to the prisoners why they were being held in the hope that being informed would make them less likely to burden the judicial system with complaints and contestations.[55]

For imprisoned debtors, such explanations, if given, probably meant very little. Unlike other prisoners, who were confined as a form of punishment, debtors lost their freedom as part of a larger procedure that led to their financial impoverishment. If the debtor had dependents, they would be deprived of essential income while their provider was incarcerated. The limited duration that debtors spent in prison corresponded with the time that creditors had to liquidate some or all of their commercial assets. In the case of commercial debtors, the merchant court appointed a bankruptcy trustee to ensure the proper handling of this procedure. Typically, the liquidation of a debtor's assets was conducted through auction to ensure the highest possible price was collected.[56] However, these built-in guarantees and the explanations that prison officials were supposed to provide were not always sufficient to protect imprisoned debtors from exploitation. The predicaments that ensued were also not easily resolved by government officials.

Early in al-Mahdi's tenure as Grand Mufti, Majlis al-Haqqaniyya sought his opinion on a debt-related question. A man had been imprisoned for defaulting on his debt, and while he was confined, as per standard procedure, his creditors sold his "slaves, cattle, and other [possessions]" on the market to pay themselves. However, as the imprisoned debtor later proved, the sales were unlawful because his possessions were sold for subpar prices (*bayʿaha bi-l-bakhs*). Considering this discovery, the court issued a new decision obligating the buyers of the debtor's possessions to either return them or pay additional amounts to make up for the price difference. The buyers, expectedly, refused to comply, citing various practical problems. For example, enough time had passed for the young cattle to have matured and for the mature ones to have fallen sick or died. They implied that the court's new decision amounted to a punishment of legal market exchanges, which they had engaged in with the court's approval in the first place. In his fatwa, al-Mahdi reaffirmed the court's second decision, effectively handing off the problem to the bureaucrats.[57]

Similar problems occurred in the merchant courts, albeit in a slightly different fashion. When Hasan al-Shirbini was imprisoned on suspicion of acquiring a debt through fraudulent means, his creditors acted quickly and aggressively to liquidate his assets during his confinement. Upon his release, Hasan managed to partially reverse these actions against him, but, unlike in al-Mahdi's fatwa, the dispute revolved around Hasan's right not only to reclaim the assets he lost unjustly but also to claim additional amounts in damages. The dispute also concerned the responsibility of the creditors' representative in managing the auction that led to Hasan's dispossession.[58]

Estimating a fair price or the correct value of damages was not impossible. More difficult to determine were the opportunities that imprisoned merchants missed or the ongoing business deals that were interrupted and, inevitably, resulted in more debts. Muhammad Effendi Abu Dihya al-Wastani, a cotton merchant, was imprisoned in Zaqaziq in November 1865. Meanwhile, ignorant of this development, a business agent arrived in town from Cairo. He had a simple task to accomplish: deliver to Muhammad the bags (*al-akyas al-fawarigh*) that he was to fill with 150 kantars of cotton and send to Sa'd Levi Menasce, an advance buyer in Cairo.[59] Muhammad's imprisonment, in relation to another dispute, led potentially to financial losses incurred by the creditor-buyer, Sa'd, who must have been embedded within other networks of credit while leading the debtor-seller Muhammad to drown further in debt because he had now failed to fulfill his promise to another creditor. Even one single day could make a difference in such debt-related disputes, as can be seen in another case. For two years, 'Ali Hasan Salam had been unsuccessfully trying to reclaim a certain debt from Sulayman Effendi al-'Isawi. By February 1874, the creditor, 'Ali, found himself in prison for defaulting on a payment to another merchant, named Muhammad Ja'far. Remarkably, the next morning, Sulayman, who had been evasive for two years, showed up in the merchant court and deposited one-third of the amount that he owed to his now-imprisoned creditor, Ali, potentially allowing him to pay back at least a portion of the debt that had led to his incarceration. After his release from debtors' prison, 'Ali sued Sulayman again and managed to receive a favorable court ruling from the merchant court that would have helped him reclaim the remaining two-thirds of the debt from Sulayman.[60]

EXITING DEBTORS' PRISON

Every instance of debtor imprisonment was meant to pave the way for a financial resolution, which aimed to recompense the creditor within a short amount of time. Regardless of whether that goal was achieved, debtors were eventually released from prison. While debtors probably did not worry about perishing in prison, they did worry about their dependent families, the fate of their assets that were now in the hands of creditors, and their financial prospects after regaining their freedom. Moreover, the exact duration of their imprisonment and the terms of their eventual release remained unknown until leaving prison was imminent. Debtors could be released for paying back their debts partially or wholly. They could also be set free if a trustworthy guarantor committed to supporting them. In some cases, indebted merchants were allowed to leave prison temporarily in order to raise money, with the hope that they would be able to pay back their

debts. Some, unsurprisingly, tried to escape. Others, having failed to pay their debts because they genuinely could not afford to, were freed because both their creditors and the
legal system concluded that a longer imprisonment served no purpose.

For merchants, in particular, each of these outcomes influenced how they could reengage in the commercial economy after a period of incarceration. The most straightforward scenario—discussed in the previous section—placed the debtors in prison while
the creditors liquidated their assets. Once the creditors paid themselves, the debtors
were set free, with diminished capital and a tarnished reputation. Their ability to reengage in commercial ventures now depended on their success in accumulating capital,
probably through entering into business partnerships or getting themselves indebted
anew. It would be reasonable to speculate that they entered into these arrangements
from a position of relative weakness and, thus, on unfavorable terms. In the case of
failure, this scenario of brief imprisonment and the liquidation of assets may have been a
path toward exiting the commercial economy altogether.

A more appealing option for an imprisoned debtor was probably to secure *daman
al-hudur*, or "the guarantee of attendance." This standard term in merchant court terminology referred to the scenario whereby a guarantor, typically a merchant in good
standing, pledged that the indebted merchant, once released from prison, would return
to it or the court if summoned. The point of this temporary release was to allow the indebted merchant to find money to pay his or her creditors. If, in freedom, they evaded
this commitment or disposed of any of their frozen assets, the "guarantor of attendance"
became financially liable.[61] The path to immediate but temporary freedom was not only
a matter of merchant court practice but was also consistent with both state policy and
shari'a.

In 1856, Egypt's governor Sa'id Pasha instructed the governor of Cairo to "never imprison anyone unnecessarily (*la yahsul sijn ahadan mutlaqan bi-ghayri mujib*). For he
who could be released through . . . a guarantor . . . accept the guarantee and do not imprison [him] . . . so that no one would be adversely affected by being delayed, having to
present a complaint, or [doing] something similar"—actions that were to be anticipated
by "any perceptive and enlightened person."[62] The official recognition of imprisonment
as a counterproductive punitive measure found its counterpart in the shari'a concept of
kafala, a term used interchangeably with *daman*.[63] Al-Mahdi's answers to questions on
contract enforcement and debtor imprisonment provide further evidence of the prevalence of this form of guarantee in practice.[64]

Typically, an imprisoned debtor petitioned the government agency that imprisoned
him or her to be released, citing either an inability to raise money while being confined
or an unreasonably long duration of imprisonment. A particularly effective strategy
was for the imprisoned debtors to request a daily allowance from their creditors to
support themselves in prison and alleviate the suffering of their families who had lost
all financial support. Merchant courts, in particular, seem to have been responsive to
this argument and would communicate to the creditors that if they did not provide for
imprisoned debtors, the court would release them.[65] In response, the imprisoning department, sometimes without recognizing the content of the petition, would order the

release of the debtor, which was conditional upon securing "the guarantee of attendance," setting a date by which the debtor was to return to the court or police station to
pay what was owed and, significantly, justifying why temporary release was on the table
in the first place.[66]

In February 1862, for example, the merchant court of Cairo met to discuss the fate of
twelve imprisoned debtors who had petitioned to be released.[67] In its decision, the court
acknowledged that it had not been convening regularly, which may have resulted in unnecessarily long imprisonments for some debtors, the longest being seven months. It
then ordered the release of most of them if they could provide "the guarantee of attendance." Two prisoners were excepted: Rizq 'Iwaz, whose release was conditional upon the
approval of the trustee of his bankruptcy because he was suspected of fraud, and Sarkis
Sikizan, who used his position as an agent for the estate (daira) of Mustafa Pasha to acquire goods from several wholesale merchants for his own private venture. In June of
the same year, the court reconvened to discuss more petitions, this time in the context
of the approaching "'Id Allah al-Akbar," which would occur three days later. It would be
appropriate, the court stated, to release the imprisoned debtors who could present the
appropriate guarantees for ten days. Some of those who benefited from the occasion had
been released temporarily earlier in February and probably were back in prison having
failed to pay off all of their debts.[68] One of the few who would not be released was the
same Rizq 'Iwaz, whose reprieve was conditional, as it had been the first time, upon the
decision of his creditors. Evidently, the only exceptions to the logic of temporary imprisonment so integral to debtor prisons were those who engaged in criminal activity—
what we would call today "white-collar crimes."

So far, these cases show creditors using the government infrastructure to extract private capital from debtors. This process was modified by either the law—for example,
shari'a or commercial law—or the initiative of the debtors who won attention for their
own plight and provided guarantees. In a telling case from 1854, the creditors of Hasan
al-Saqqa petitioned the police department to release him from prison (initially sijn al-
diwan and later sijn majlis al-tujjar) for twenty days. Hasan's case was complicated. He
was indebted to at least seven different people simultaneously and may have tried to play
them against each other. He explained to one group that he could not pay them back because other creditors had raided his place in Tanta and taken valuable goods, through a
combination of "treachery and coercion." The matter was then investigated, initially by
guild leaders and later by the merchant court, but it remained unresolved because some,
but not all, of the creditors convinced the investigators through textual evidence and
witness testimonies that they had acquired the "stolen" goods amicably. This uncertainty
led to the imprisonment of Hasan until the debts were paid because he had a history of
insolvencies and, regardless of the exact details, had "unjustly wasted the money (al-mal
thahaba bidun wajh haqq)." In other words, he was imprisoned because of his private
dispute with his creditors and not because of fraud, a crime that the state would have
punished through imprisonment. At that point, while Hasan al-Saqqa was still in prison
at the behest of the creditors, one Ibrahim Effendi 'Abd al-'Al, who owned the largest
portion of the debt, learned of the passing of Hasan's wife and saw an opportunity. He

argued for Hasan's temporary release from prison and offered "the guarantee of attendance" to allow the debtor to collect his wife's inheritance. Ibrahim then claimed half of the inheritance, although it is unclear whether he did so to his own benefit exclusively or that of other creditors as well. Either way, his next move was to spearhead the reorganization of the debt with the other creditors, who agreed to forgive one-third of the total debt and hold off the collection of the remaining amount for six months, after which they would collect it in installments over one year.[69]

Temporary and restricted release from debtor prison was, in official practice and policy, and in Islamic legal thought, meant to facilitate the reintegration of insolvent debtors into the commercial economy by implicating other merchants, who were doing better and likely enjoyed superior reputations, as guarantors. However, because the commercial economy was founded on the ubiquity of overlapping debt relations, which were overwhelmingly private legal matters between merchants and businesses, the decision to temporarily imprison or release a debtor affected not only insolvent merchants but also their creditors. As seen in the case of Hasan, it was not uncommon for a merchant to be indebted to multiple groups of creditors simultaneously. If one group, motivated by its need to reclaim part of an outstanding debt in the short term, moved to imprison a debtor to force him or her to pay, that decision could clash with the interests of another group that preferred waiting because it was more confident that payments were on the way.

For instance, 'Abd al-Ghani al-Jazzar was indebted simultaneously to Ahmad Dawud al-Hajjar and the estate of the recently deceased Anton Manolli. Because Ahmad moved first, he managed to put 'Abd al-Ghani in the prison of the Cairo merchant court until his debt was paid back. Accordingly, the imprisoned debtor reached out to a business partner who, he claimed, would pay the required amount. Meanwhile, knowingly or not, Ahmad got in the way of Manolli's heirs, who were now instructed by the merchant court to wait until the ongoing episode of imprisonment and repayment was concluded before making a move to reclaim their debt.[70] This dynamic was even more complicated when the creditors lived in different provinces, as was the case with Hanna 'Awda. In the spring of 1866, Hanna failed to pay a debt he owed to a certain Khawaja Yusuf and only avoided prison due to the intervention of his guarantor, al-Mu'allim Sam'an Jirjis Dahbura, who pledged in writing that Hanna would return to the Cairo police department with the owed amount of money within sixty-one days. Soon after this two-month release from prison was arranged, the British consulate in Jerusalem wrote to the Cairo police department requesting that it transfer Hanna to its counterpart in the administratively independent sanjak, with the goal of obliging him to pay an outstanding debt he owed to Giacomo Banajotti, a British protégé and employee at the same consulate.[71] The police department replied that "appropriate measures will be taken (*tajri al-usul majraha*)" only after the original debt was settled at the end of the two-month period.[72]

These two examples show a particular method of diffusing the potential conflict between different groups of creditors over the fate of a debtor: a state apparatus that uses its power to imprison individuals not only to ensure restitution but also to set an order of priorities for this restitution. A particularly illuminating case that sheds light on the limitations of this mechanism and potentially hints at the relevance of gender in court decisions of imprisonment can be gleaned from a fatwa that al-Mahdi issued in 1858.[73] The question that the Grand Mufti received described a woman who, having failed to pay back a debt on time, rescheduled it with the support of a guarantor who accepted liability for the debt if she failed to abide by the rescheduled installments. With the new terms in effect, the woman stopped paying, and when the creditors approached her guarantor, he too did not pay. The creditors, therefore, sued the guarantor before a shari'a judge, who ruled to imprison the guarantor to pressure him to pay. But the imprisonment yielded no results, and the guarantor continued to insist that he genuinely did not have the money or even the assets that could be liquidated to raise the needed amount. The specific question that al-Mahdi had to answer was that if the judge concluded that the imprisoned guarantor was indeed financially incapable of repaying the debt, should the creditors drop their claim, and, by extension, should the judge release the guarantor from prison? Al-Mahdi answered, "Yes. If his hardship (i'sar) was proven in a shari'a-sanctioned way, [the creditors will] await his ease (yasar). He is not to be asked [for the outstanding debt] as long as this is the case. The most that could be done (ghayat al-'amr) is for the creditor to keep him under pursuit (yulazimahu) . . . after the judge releases him from prison. . . . [There is] no difference in treatment between debtor and guarantor of debt."[74] The final sentence is particularly interesting because it highlights the equal liability of debtor and guarantor regardless of their gender difference. Yet the actual situation described in the question shows that the creditors' attention had shifted completely from the original debtor, a woman, to the guarantor, a man. One can only speculate whether this shift reflected the higher financial worth of this particular guarantor or the expectation that keeping this man "under pursuit" would be more practical, for example, because he would be more easily traceable in the social sphere than the woman debtor.

The fatwa further confirms that, similar to the state-enacted laws governing the merchant courts, debtor imprisonment was not an end in itself but a means of extracting money. Al-Mahdi offered versions of this fatwa consistently to questioners who raised the issue of the inability of imprisoned debtors to pay or support themselves and their dependents due to genuine financial hardship. This is not to say, however, that imprisonment served no purpose. As he explained on more than one occasion, imprisonment preceded the proof of hardship—if a debtor failed to pay a debt, the creditor had a right to imprison him or her, but if, while in prison, the judge became convinced "in a shari'a-sanctioned way (bi-l-wajh al-shar'i)," such as through the testimony of witnesses, that the debtor was indeed unable to pay, he (i.e., the judge) would unilaterally let the debtor go.[75]

Conclusion

Merchant court records, fatwas, bureaucratic and consular communication, and travelers' accounts offer a reasonably coherent picture of the logic behind and the practice of debtor imprisonment in mid-nineteenth-century Cairo. Individuals unable to meet their private financial obligations could end up in prison for weeks or months. Enduring shari'a-mandated (especially Hanafi) practices included imprisoning recalcitrant debtors on behalf of creditors as a way of pressuring them to scrape together enough funds to pay back their debts. Those prisoners were released after the debt was paid, a guarantor agreed to back the debtor, or the judge became convinced that the prisoner was indeed insolvent. State-organized merchant courts adopted the same logic in relation to commercial (not civil) debts but attributed it to Ottoman, and by extension French, commercial law. They imprisoned insolvent debtors as part of a creditor-led but state-supervised resolution that centered on liquidating the prisoners' market-related assets.

In practice, imprisoned debtors seemed to have a clear path to freedom as long as they had not committed fraud. It usually started with the debtors complaining that they were unable to support themselves or their dependents while incarcerated and, more effectively, relied on securing a "guarantee of attendance," or a viable pledge that they would return to court or prison if summoned. What they lost during their sometimes short period of incarceration was not always redeemable, however. Assets that creditors misidentified as business-related and sold may have been personal—for example, a storehouse may have been a residence. Similarly, while held away from the marketplace, merchants often defaulted on debts to other creditors and, in the process, lost business deals and, likely, a part of their reputation. Their families' suffering cannot be gleaned from the archival evidence but must have been a factor as well.

Debtor imprisonment in khedival Cairo was not open-ended. It may have lasted for as long as seven or nine months in the case of some insolvent merchants, but these extended periods seem to have been uncommon and themselves grounds for releasing the debtor. Nor was imprisonment primarily a form of punishment. True, it temporarily separated the person from their family and social network, prevented them from work, and left them in doubt about the material and reputational damage they would suffer once they left prison. But from a legal standpoint, this suffering was incidental to the desired outcome, which was repayment of the outstanding debt. Although imprisonment was authorized and managed by state agencies such as the merchant court and the police department, it only occurred at the request of the creditors, who were also expected to financially maintain their debtors while in state prison. During the period of incarceration, creditors could liquidate the debtors' assets to recoup their money. Debtors could avoid or shorten this period if they were well connected and could get a guarantor to vouch for them. Khedival and Ottoman laws were consistent with the historical shari'a position that limited the resolution to the expropriation of property and not of labor as a consequence of bankruptcy. So, while debtors were often incarcerated in sites where labor was required, such as the Alexandria Arsenal for men, and potentially the *iplikhane* for women, there is no evidence in the archival record that they were expected to work. At least formally, temporary imprisonment by the state was not an intermediary stage that led to death, enslavement, or long-term bondage.

Overall, the khedival state in Egypt, like the Ottoman imperial center in the nineteenth century, was becoming more reliant on imprisonment as an instrument of government rule. The growing scale and effect of incarceration and the novelty of modern prisons have understandably attracted the attention of historians. Less consideration has been given to a particular subcategory of prisoners—debtors—who were scattered among multiple places of detention and for whom the function of imprisonment was only to facilitate a financial resolution. While most inmates were experiencing a novel historical phenomenon—that of being in a modern prison—imprisoned debtors personified a historical continuity. Those imprisoned because of a civil debt continued to be subjected to shari'a, which historically deployed imprisonment as a means of pressuring delinquent debtors. Others who defaulted on commercial debts and who, according to the khedival legal regime, were no longer under the jurisdiction of shari'a were subject to the particular mechanisms of Ottoman and French law, for example, with regards to the procedure of liquidating assets. However, the experiences of both civil and commercial debtors were generally similar, pointing to a convergence between shari'a and khedival (and Ottoman) logics when it came to debtors' prisons.

Notes

1. See, e.g., the references to Husayn Shayba and his son and, in a separate case, to Salih Agha al-Siyaji in Dar al-Watha'iq al-Qawmiyya (DWQ), 3036-000409, *Qayd al-Qararat al-Intiha'iyya*, 6 Sha'ban 1278 / 25 February 1862. While the term is not used consistently in legal documents, it constitutes an apt description of the relationship between creditor and debtor, as will be detailed in this chapter.

2. See Diana Taylor, *Michel Foucault: Key Concepts* (New York: Routledge, 2014); and especially Michel Foucault, *Discipline and Punish: The Birth of the Prison* (New York: Vintage, 1995).

3. On the army and the factory, see, e.g., Khaled Fahmy, *All the Pasha's Men: Mehmed Ali, His Army and the Making of Modern Egypt* (Cairo: American University in Cairo Press, 2002); and Hanan Hammad, *Industrial Sexuality: Gender, Urbanization, and Social Transformation in Egypt* (Austin: University of Texas Press, 2016). Hammad deals with the interwar period, but her work is exemplary for its exploration of the intersection between modern state policing practices that have their roots in the nineteenth century and private industrial interests. On fields of knowledge, see, e.g., Omnia El Shakry, *The Great Social Laboratory: Subjects of Knowledge in Colonial and Postcolonial Egypt* (Stanford, CA: Stanford University Press, 2007); and Khaled Fahmy, *In Quest of Justice: Islamic Law and Forensic Medicine in Modern Egypt* (Oakland, CA: University of California Press, 2018).

4. Rudolph Peters, "Egypt and the Age of the Triumphant Prison: Judicial Punishment in Nineteenth-Century Egypt," *Annales Islamologiques* 36 (2002): 253–85; Rudolph Peters, "Prisons and Marginalisation in Nineteenth-Century Egypt," in *Outside In: On the Margins of the Modern Middle East*, ed. Eugene Rogan (London: I. B. Tauris, 2002), 31–52; Rudolph Peters, "Controlled Suffering: Mortality and Living Conditions in 19th-Century Egyptian Prisons," *International Journal of Middle East Studies* 36, no. 3 (2004): 387–407.

5. Ehud R. Toledano, *State and Society in Mid-Nineteenth-Century Egypt* (New York: Cambridge University Press, 1990). Historians cite multiple dates to mark the end of the khedival period: 1879 when Khedive Isma'il was deposed, 1882 when the British Empire occupied Egypt militarily, and 1914 when the same empire declared Egypt a British protectorate. The archival research for this chapter spans the period before 1882.

6. For studies focusing on the Ottoman imperial center, see Kent Schull, *Prisons in the Late Ottoman Empire: Microcosms of Modernity* (Edinburgh: Edinburgh University Press, 2014); and Ufuk Adak, "Central Prisons (*Hapishane-i Umumi*) in Istanbul and Izmir in the Late Ottoman Empire: In-Between Ideal and Reality," *Journal of the Ottoman and Turkish Studies Association* 4, no. 1 (2017): 73–94.

7. Bruce Mann, *Republic of Debtors: Bankruptcy in the Age of American Independence* (Cambridge, MA: Harvard University Press, 2002), 5.

8. Jerry White, *Mansions of Misery: A Biography of the Marshalsea Debtors' Prison* (London: Vintage, 2016).

9. Erika Vause, *In the Red and in the Black: Debt, Dishonor, and the Law in France between the Revolutions* (Charlottesville: University of Virginia Press, 2018), 248.

10. E. R. J. Owen, *Cotton and the Egyptian Economy, 1820–1914: A Study in Trade and Development* (Oxford: Clarendon Press, 1969).

11. On nineteenth-century legal reforms in the Ottoman center, see Avi Rubin, "Legal Borrowing and Its Impact on Ottoman Legal Culture in the Late Nineteenth Century," *Continuity and Change* 22, no. 2 (2007): 279–303; and Rubin, "Ottoman Judicial Change in the Age of Modernity: A Reappraisal," *History Compass* 7, no. 1 (2009): 119–40.

12. See, e.g., Ronald C. Jennings, "Loans and Credit in Early 17th Century Ottoman Judicial Records: The Sharia Court of Anatolian Kayseri," *Journal of the Economic and Social History of the Orient* 16, no. 2–3 (1973): 168–216; and Munther H. Alsabbagh, "Before Banks: Credit, Society, and Law in Sixteenth-Century Palestine and Syria" (PhD Diss., University of California Santa Barbara, 2018), accessed 3 June 2021, https://escholarship.org/uc/item/3qw371fm.

13. Alsabbagh, "Before Banks," 161. The author further shows that usury was also demoted in contemporaneous polemical works on vice. Ibid., 111.

14. For a recent discussion of disputes involving European creditors in the Ottoman Empire, see Michael Talbot, *British Ottoman Relations, 1661–1807: Commerce and Diplomatic Practice in Eighteenth Century Istanbul* (Woodbridge, UK: Boydell Press, 2017), 173–210.

15. For a general appraisal of Rudolph Peters's scholarly oeuvre, see Khaled Fahmy, "Rudolph Peters and the History of Modern Egyptian Law," in *Legal Documents as Sources for the History of Muslim Societies: Studies in Honour of Rudolph Peters*, ed. Maaike van Berkel et al. (Leiden: Brill, 2017), 12–35.

16. It is also important to note that nationality did not necessarily imply religious difference. An Ottoman may be a non-Muslim, and a European subject or protégé may be a Muslim, as with South Asian merchants conducting business in Egypt.

17. The terms referring to both the act and place of incarceration most commonly found in the archival documents are *habs* and *sijn*. Because they are used interchangeably during this period, I have opted to translate them both as *prison* whenever they referred to the place of incarceration. For simplicity, I have chosen to avoid near-synonyms such as *jail* or *gaol*.

18. See Fahmy, *In Quest of Justice*, 226–70, esp. 226–33, which includes an account of the successful legal pursuit of 'Umar Bey Wasfi by a group of enslaved individuals that led

to his banishment from Egypt on the charge of murdering two of their peers; Ehud R. Toledano, "Shemsigul: A Circassian Slave in Mid-Nineteenth-Century Cairo," in *Struggle and Survival in the Modern Middle East*, ed. Edmund Burke III and David N. Yaghoubian (Berkeley: University of California Press, 2006).

19. Edward William Lane, *An Account of the Manners and Customs of the Modern Egyptians: The Definitive 1860 Edition* (Cairo: American University in Cairo Press, 2003), 111.

20. Ibid., 104.

21. Quoted in Rudolph Peters, "Controlled Suffering," 394. Peters speculates that the better treatment may have been reserved for debtors.

22. Lady Duff Gordon, *Letters from Egypt* (New York: McClure Phillips & Co., 1902), 154.

23. Ibid., 257.

24. Ibid., 342.

25. Rudolph Peters, "Muhammad al-ʿAbbasi al-Mahdi (d. 1897), Grand Mufti of Egypt, and his al-Fatawa al-Mahdiyya," *Islamic Law and Society* 1, no. 1 (1994): 74.

26. Fahmy, *In Quest of Justice*, 27.

27. Irene Schneider, "Imprisonment in Pre-Classical and Classical Islamic Law," *Islamic Law and Society* 2, no. 2 (1995): 157–73.

28. Yossef Rapoport, "Royal Justice and Religious Law: Siyasah and Shariʿah under the Mamluks," *Mamluk Studies Review* 16 (2012): 100–102.

29. James E. Baldwin, *Islamic Law and Empire in Ottoman Cairo* (Edinburgh: Edinburgh University Press, 2017), 70–72.

30. Muhammad al-ʿAbbasi al-Mahdi, *al-Fatawa al-Mahdiyya fi al-Waqaʾiʿ al-Misriyya*, vol. 3 (Cairo: al-Matbaʿa al-Azhariyya al-Misriyya, 1883–85). See especially 231–40.

31. The National Archives, London, Kew (TNA), Foreign Office (FO) 841/29, File 24, Grima, N (British) vs. Sary, Hassan Pasha Yeghen (Ottoman), 1868. Emphasis added. The document cited here was sent by Nicola to the merchant court of Cairo, and a copy of it was preserved in the consulate since the latter served as an intermediary between the British plaintiff and the state-organized court. This context applies to later references to British consular archives in this chapter.

32. TNA, FO 841/28, File 146, Grima, N (British) vs. Sary, H. Pasha Yakan (Ottoman), 1867.

33. "Laʾihat al-Arbaʿin Band," published in Ahmad Fathi Zaghlul, *al-Muhamah* (Cairo: Matbaʿat al-Maʿarif, 1900), appendix, 45–52.

34. These typically included contracts (Arabic: *kuntratat*, singular: *kuntratu*; Italian: *contratto*) and/or promissory notes (Arabic: *kambiyalat*, singular: *kambiyala*; Italian: *cambiale*).

35. In this particular entry, the exact articles were left blank, but I was able to fill them in based on similar case summaries and by consulting the Ottoman code of commerce. The three articles in question were consistently referred to in cases of bankruptcy. It is unclear to me why they were sometimes left unwritten: "article [blank], article [blank] and article [blank]."

36. DWQ, 3036-000503, *Daftar Qayd Madhbatat al-Ahkam al-Sadira min Majlis Tujjur Misriyya*, 15 Shawwal 1288 / 28 December 1871.

37. TNA, FO 841/27, File 93, Coen G. (British) vs. Kader M. A. (Ottoman), 1867.

38. DWQ, 3036-000206, *Daftar Qayd al-Khulasat al-Intihaʾiyya bi-Majlis Tujjur Misriyya*, 1 Shaʿban 1290 / 24 September 1873.

39. TNA, FO 841/35, File 14, Nicolopulo, A & Others (British) vs. Oreb, Hassan Heber Moh. (Ottoman), 1871.

40. Rudolph Peters, "Egypt and the Age of the Triumphant Prison," 264.

41. Peters, "Controlled Suffering," 390–91.

42. Peters, "Egypt and the Age of the Triumphant Prison," 264, 273; Peters, "Prisons and Marginalisation," 31–52.

43. For one example, see DWQ, 3036-000503, 5 Jumada I 1289 / 11 July 1872.

44. For one example, see, DWQ, 3036-000419, *Qayd al-Qararat al-Intiha'iyya*, 29 Dhu al-Qa'da / 27 December 1875.

45. See, e.g., DWQ 3036-000420, *Daftar Qayd al-Qararat al-Ibtida'iyya bi-Majlis Tujjar Misriyya*, 21 Jumada I 1279 / 13 November 1862; and DWQ 3036-000125, *Khulasat wa-Qararat wa-Ifadat*, 17 Muharram 1272 / 29 September 1855.

46. DWQ, 0019-000628, [No Title], Correspondence from Majlis al-Khususi to Nazir al-Dakhiliyya, 1290/1873–74].

47. For examples of consular-operated prisons at the turn of the twentieth century, see Elizabeth H. Shlala, *The Late Ottoman Empire and Egypt: Hybridity, Law and Gender* (New York: Routledge, 2018).

48. A. A. Paton, *History of the Egyptian Revolution, From the Period of the Mamelukes to the Death of Mohammed Ali*, vol. 1 (London: Trubner & Co., 1870), v–viii.

49. Ibid., vol. 2, 264–66.

50. Incidental references to such visitations include a case of theft, the target of which was a woman in the vicinity of a Cairo prison, who was on her way to deliver money to two imprisoned relations. Fahmy, *In Quest of Justice*, n. 89, 339.

51. Paton, *History of the Egyptian Revolution*, vol. 2, 264–65.

52. Ibid., 265–66.

53. Quoted in Fahmy, *In Quest of Justice*, 248.

54. DWQ, 3036-000407, *Qayd al- Lawa'ih wa-l-Awamir al-Mustadima*, 3 Safar 1273 / 3 October 1856.

55. Ibid., for additional references to the same point, see Peters, "Egypt and the Age of the Triumphant Prison," 273.

56. For representative examples, see DWQ, 3036-000503, 19 Dhu al-Qa'da 1288 / 30 January 1872; 21 Rabi' II 1289 / 28 June 1872; 5 Jumada I 1289 / 11 July 1872; and 18 Jumada II 1289 / 23 August 1872.

57. Al-Mahdi, *al-Fatawa al-Mahdiyya*, vol. 5, 72, 11 Jumada II 1265 / 4 May 1849.

58. DWQ, 3036-000206, 3 Rabi' II 1291/19 May 1874 and 20 Ragab 1291 / 1 September 1874.

59. TNA, FO 841/22, File 89, Menasce, S. L. (British) vs. El Wastani, M. Eff. Abudehie (Ottoman), 1865.

60. DWQ, 3036-000419, 29 Dhu al-Qa'da 1292 / 27 December 1875.

61. Also written as *damanat al-hudur*. For a representative example, in which the concept is explained as part of court proceedings, see DWQ, 3036-000409, 6 Sha'ban 1278 / 25 February 1862.

62. DWQ, 3036-000407, 3 Safar 1273 / 3 October 1856. The concept of *daman al-hudur* is to be contrasted with *daman gharim*, which entails direct financial liability by the guarantor if the original debtor failed to meet his or her obligation.

63. Note that *daman al-hudur* was a general term used in cases of incarceration and not limited to imprisoned debtors. For a concise explanation of "Guaranty, Suretyship (*kafala*)" in Islamic law, see Wael B. Hallaq, *Shari'a: Theory, Practice, Transformations* (New York: Cambridge University Press, 2009), 258–61.

64. For multiple examples, see al-Mahdi, *al-Fatawa al-Mahdiyya*, vol. 3, 198–220.

65. For multiple examples, see DWQ, 3036-000503, 18 Rajab 1288 / 3 October 1871; 9 Sha'ban 1288 / 24 October 1871; 21 Shawwal 1288 / 3 January 1872; 19 Dhu al-Qa'da 1288 / 30 January 1872; 19 Dhu al-Hijja 1288 / 29 February 1872; and 2 Jumada II 1289 / 7 August 1872.

66. Note that the state occasionally granted general amnesties as a way of dealing with overcrowded prisons. Peters, "Egypt and the Age of the Triumphant Prison."

67. DWQ, 3036-000409, 6 Sha'ban 1278 / 25 February 1862.

68. DWQ, 3036-000409, 7 Dhu al-Hijja 1278 / 4 June 1862.

69. DWQ, 3036-000125, 17 Muharram 1272 / 10 October 1854.

70. DWQ, 3036-000001, *Sadir*, 1270–71/1853–55.

71. On the administrative status of Jerusalem in the late Ottoman Empire, see Butrus Abu-Manneh, "The Rise of the Sanjak of Jerusalem in the Late Nineteenth Century," in *The Israel/Palestine Question: A Reader*, ed. Ilan Pappé (New York: Routledge, 2007), 40–50.

72. TNA, FO 841/23, File 34, Banajotti, Giacomo (British) vs. Ode, Hanna & Others (Ottoman), 1866.

73. Al-Mahdi, *al-Fatawa al-Mahdiyya*, vol. 3, 198–220, 2 Dhu al-Hijja 1274 / 14 July 1858.

74. For an exploration of the concept, see Farhat Ziadeh, "Mulazama or Harassment of Recalcitrant Debtors in Islamic Law," *Islamic Law and Society* 7, no. 3 (2000): 289–99.

75. For multiple examples spanning December 1849–July 1855, see al-Mahdi, *al-Fatawa al-Mahdiyya*, vol. 3, 231–40.

BIBLIOGRAPHY

Ayoub, Samy A. *Law, Empire, and the Sultan: Ottoman Imperial Authority and Late Hanafi Jurisprudence*. New York: Oxford University Press, 2019.

Bishara, Fahad Ahmad. *A Sea of Debt: Law and Economic Life in the Western Indian Ocean, 1780–1950*. New York: Cambridge University Press, 2017.

Cannon, Byron. *Politics of Law and the Courts in Nineteenth-Century Egypt*. Salt Lake City: University of Utah Press, 1988.

Chalcraft, John T. *The Striking Cabbies of Cairo and Other Stories: Crafts and Guilds in Egypt, 1863–1914*. Albany: State University of New York Press, 2005.

Fahmy, Khaled. *In Quest of Justice: Islamic Law and Forensic Medicine in Modern Egypt*. Oakland: University of California Press, 2018.

Hunter, F. Robert. *Egypt under the Khedives, 1805–1879: From Household Government to Modern Bureaucracy*. Cairo: University of Pittsburgh Press, 1984.

Peters, Rudolph. *Shari'a, Justice and Legal Order: Egyptian and Islamic Law: Selected Essays*. Leiden: Brill, 2020.

Rubin, Avi. *Ottoman Nizamiye Courts: Law and Modernity*. New York: Palgrave Macmillan, 2011.

Schull, Kent F. *Prisons in the Late Ottoman Empire: Microcosms of Modernity*. Edinburgh: Edinburgh University Press, 2014.

Shlala, Elizabeth H. *The Late Ottoman Empire and Egypt: Hybridity, Law and Gender*. New York: Routledge, 2018.

Toledano, Ehud R. *State and Society in Mid-Nineteenth-Century Egypt*. Cambridge: Cambridge University Press, 1990.

Vause, Erika. *In the Red and in the Black: Debt, Dishonor and the Law in France between Revolutions*. Charlottesville: University of Virginia Press, 2018.

CHAPTER 12

....

AN ERASED EXPERIMENT

Penal Legislation between 1823 and 1883

....

EMAD AHMAD HELAL

EGYPT experienced remarkable penal legislation from the early 1820s to the early 1880s. Studies dealing with this experience have overlooked the precursors or preludes of the great penal laws of Muḥammad ʿAlī, however, such that it came to be seen as unrelated to what preceded it. These studies have also situated these legislations in the wrong context, for they dealt with them as a mere attempt to get rid of Sharīʿa and transition to modern European law. During its legislative experience, however, Egypt was not affected by Europe or the Ottoman Empire, but rather by its local environment, economic conditions, social norms, and political situation. The process of developing penal legislation in Khedival Egypt went through five successive and overlapping stages, each differing in its form and promulgator.

When the Egyptian penal legislation reached its most appropriate and closest point to the nature of the Egyptian society, Egypt fell under British occupation. The British reformulated the Egyptian judicial system. In 1883, they replaced the previous legislative experience with a penal law unrelated to Egyptian society that was a literal translation of the French penal law issued in 1810. Consequently, the British sent Egypt back to ground zero, and Egyptian legislators needed another experiment, which took half a century of developing and amending, in order to reach a suitable formula for Egyptian society.

In the records of the trial of Sulaymān al-Ḥalaby, who had been accused of assassinating the leader of the French campaign to Egypt, General Kléber, the French claimed that the judicial system in Ottoman Egypt was in utter chaos, that it was the habit of the country to threaten accused people and subject them to torture, and that the punishments were savage and included cutting people in half, skinning them alive, and impaling them. They used this rationale to justify savage punishments for al-Ḥalaby.[1] Based on a review of thousands of records of the Islamic courts (maḥākim, singular maḥkama), which were the only judicial body in Ottoman Egypt, it is possible to state confidently that no judge of maḥākim (qāḍī, plural quḍāt) ever used such barbaric means in investigations or punishment and that the first and only judge in the history of Egypt to sit on the bench wearing the judge's robe, order the torture of the accused, and rule him to be impaled was the French general René in the trial of al-Ḥalaby.[2]

In the turmoil and political unrest that occurred occasionally between Egyptians and the French occupation forces, or between Muḥammad ʿAlī Pasha and the Mamluks, as a result of the conflict between pashas and military regiments or Mamluk households, many murders and brutal reprisals occurred outside the law. *Maḥākim* could not punish the perpetrators, but it would be a fallacy to say that these were the rulings of *quḍāt*. Apart from that, the judicial and legal system was the most stable system in Egypt during the Ottoman period and the first three decades of Muḥammad ʿAlī's era. *Maḥākim* were competent to hear all kinds of criminal cases, and *quḍāt* had the power to issue death sentences (*qiṣāṣ*), blood money (*diyya*), and other Islamic punishments (*ḥudūd*, singular *ḥadd*) like cutting off the thief's hand and whipping the wine drinker. *Qiṣāṣ* was carried out by cutting off the head with a sword with one blow, without torture or mutilating the body, according to the rules of the Hanafi school of thought.[3]

Over the past century, many studies have been published about the history of legislation in the era of Muḥammad ʿAlī and penal legislation in particular. These studies uncovered many unknowns and filled in many gaps.[4] The beginnings of penal legislation in the era of Muḥammad ʿAlī remain a mystery, however. For many decades, the prevailing argument was that Muḥammad ʿAlī ruled Egypt for a quarter of a century without any law or system that dealt with criminal cases and that he and his administration judged criminal cases without any reference to law or Sharīʿa. Central to this argument was that in January 1830 the Peasant Cultivation Regulation (Lāʾiḥat Ziraʿat al-Fallāḥ [LZF]) appeared suddenly as the first penal law to address crimes in the rural sector.[5] Then, after eight years, Muḥammad ʿAlī issued another regulation, the Law of Civil Administration (al-Siyāsit-Nāmah al-Mulkiyya [S-NM]), to address crimes in the urban sector.[6] Finally, in 1845, Muḥammad ʿAlī issued the first comprehensive penal code, the Selections Law (Qānūn al-Muntakhabāt [QM]), followed by two main comprehensive codes: the ʿAbbās Code in 1849 and the Sultanic Law (Qānūn-Nāmah al-Sultānī) in 1852, which continued to be applied until the British occupation.[7]

However, this long-held argument, which offered an incomplete understanding of the development of penal legislation in Khedival Egypt before the British occupation, has been undermined more recently. Relying on the documents of judicial institutions from that period, a newer literature analyzed the political and social contexts of many unknown laws. The first of these studies, by Rudolph Peters, revealed a criminal law issued on 20 September 1829, four months before LZF.[8] Peters did not discuss the preconditions of its promulgation or whether there were any other preceding laws. Rather, he made a similar mistake as the scholars who considered the LZF the first criminal law of Muḥammad ʿAlī. This law comes in the third stage of the development of penal legislation during the era of Muḥammad ʿAlī.

When Muḥammad ʿAlī Pasha took power in Egypt in 1805, *maḥākim* were the only judicial institution in Egypt. There was no written penal code, and Sharīʿa in the jurisprudence text (*fiqh*) books was their only reference. *Maḥākim* continued to operate unaffected by politics between 1801 and 1829. *Maḥākim* records indicate that *quḍāt* took up various criminal cases and judged according to Sharī'a. These cases included murder,[9] beating leading to wounds[10] or miscarriage,[11] rape,[12] and theft of animals or crops. When the *qāḍī* judged a case by *ḥadd*, the governor had to apply it.[13]

THE NEED FOR A POSITIVE LAW

During the first years of his rule, and in parallel with *maḥākim*, Muḥammad 'Alī gradually began to give his administrators a judicial role under the term *ta'zīr* (plural *ta'āzīr*). In Sharī'a, *ta'zīr* is the authority to set a discretionary punishment for all crimes that Sharī'a prohibits but for which it does not provide an explicit punishment, like bribery, embezzlement, fraud in buying and selling, and perjury. Sharī'a gave the right of *ta'zīr* to both the *qāḍī* (*ḥākim al-shar'*, plural *ḥukkām al-shar'*) and the governor (*ḥākim al-siyāsa*, plural *ḥukkām al-siyāsa*).[14] In a period of chaos and insecurity, Muḥammad 'Alī did not need a penal code because he himself would not respect it. However, as he shored up his rule in the 1820s, Muḥammad 'Alī realized that *maḥākim*, through its traditional mechanisms, would not be able to help him build the modern and central state that he sought to create. The *maḥākim* would not help him to control people's bodies, wealth, and lands—control that he sought to achieve by forcing them to grow the crops he wanted, pay the taxes and fines he imposed, perform the forced labor he assigned, and serve in the army he would later establish. If someone refused to do any of these duties, the *qāḍī* would not consider it a crime.

Therefore, Muḥammad 'Alī began stripping *maḥākim* of their right of *ta'zīr* and adding it gradually to *ḥukkām al-siyāsa*. Thus, the role of *ḥukkām al-shar'* in the criminal field was limited to cases involving disputes between people, the punishment for which was always *qiṣāṣ* or *diyya* (such as murder, breaking a tooth, poking an eye, stumping a nose, or breaking a hand or finger), and *ḥudūd* cases (such as theft, adultery, or drinking alcohol). *Ḥukkām al-siyāsa* monopolized the right to hear all disputes between people and the government (such as administrative corruption, tax evasion, draft evasion, and public works). However, *ḥukkām al-siyāsa* had no experience in the traditions of the Sharī'a judiciary or knowledge of the criteria for applying *ta'zīr* sentences.[15] As a result, some of them imposed exaggerated penalties that were incommensurate with the scale of the crime committed, while others gave negligent punishments, making them non-deterrent. This necessitated determining a punishment for each offense and obliging *ḥukkām al-siyāsa* to enforce it. Accordingly, the need to legislate specific penalties for such crimes and infractions arose.

The pasha and his men made great legislative efforts to address these crimes and infractions by instituting many acts, laws, regulations, and codes. Muḥammad 'Alī entrusted *ḥukkām al-siyāsa* to new civilian courts, which would apply it individually at first and then collectively. However, he did not dare call the civilian court *maḥkama* lest he be accused of transgressing Sharī'a, so he simply called it an association (*jam'iyya*) or council (*majlis*). The legislation comprised positive laws under the guise of Sharī'a,[16] within the framework of *taʿzīr*, and under the title of "Siyāsit-Nāmah" (S-N), whose literal translation is "the book of *siyāsa*." The word *siyāsa* is a distortion of the word *yasa*, which is the law that Genghis Khan laid down for the Mongols. *Yasa* was the first positive law to be applied in the lands of Islām. It was widely applied in the Mamluk era alongside the Sharīʿa.[17] The process of developing penal legislation in Khedival Egypt went through five stages, which I will explain in the following sections.

Muḥammad ʿAlī's Penal Acts

Muḥammad ʿAlī issued thousands of decrees, most of which were directives and assignments for the administration. Some took the form of adjudications that imposed a specific punishment on a specific person.[18] A few took the form of a "penal law" but contained one article to be applied to everyone who committed the crime in question. I call it in Arabic *amr-qānūn* (law-decree), but in my view, the English term *act* combines the two meanings of law and decree. Issued in the 1820s, these acts form the first stage of Egyptian penal legislation and were always overreactive, harsh, and exaggerated.

In the beginning, the acts did not stipulate explicit penalties but were merely threats. For example, in October 1816, the pasha obliged peasants to sell their crops exclusively to him at his price. He also ordered administrators not to accept gifts or take anything from peasants without paying him, as was their habit. Because he did not want anyone but himself to benefit from plundering peasants, the order stipulated that "whoever does that from the peasants or the men of administration would suffer more harm even if he is a nobleman."[19] When an Ottoman firman arrived in Egypt during Ramadan of 1235 / June 1820, in which the sultan determined the value of the currency in circulation in Egypt, Muḥammad ʿAlī stated that anyone who exceeded that value would face severe punishment, but he did not specify the nature, size, or extent of that punishment.[20]

Finally, on 4 November 1823, Muḥammad ʿAlī issued an act (*amr-qānūn*) to his deputy (*katkhuda*) in which he specified exile as a penalty for money changers who exchanged currency with more value.[21] This was the first penal act in the Muḥammad ʿAlī era to specify a clear penalty for a crime. The second one came two years later, on 23 January 1826. The pasha wrote to all administrators in the countryside, informing them that he was dividing Egypt into governorates (*mudīriyyāt*, singular *mudīriyya*), sections (*aqsām*, singular *qism*), and villages to facilitate construction and cultivation. He also informed them of his decision to visit all regions of the country and stated that if he found negligence from a governor (*mudīr*), a section's head (*naẓir qism*), or a village's shaykh, he would gather them in the field where that delay or negligence manifested and order that a pit be dug to bury them alive on top of the testimonies.[22] Although this act was never enforced, it could be counted among the acts that set a specific penalty for a specific offense. The third act came on 6 October 1827. It was stranger than the previous one. It did not specify a penalty but rather a reward for whoever provided information about unregistered lands cultivated by a village's shaykh or peasant without paying taxes.[23]

At this rate, it would have taken the pasha several centuries to treat all crimes and infractions. However, the year 1244/1828–29 witnessed a leap in legislation, and the rate of penal acts issued accelerated. On 17 August 1828, the pasha issued an act intended to stop Bedouin raids on villages. He ordered the punishment of Bedouins whose live-stock destroyed peasants' crops by having them pay five times the price of the destroyed crops,[24] which was not based on Sharī'a, in which the fine is only the price of the perished crops. Because agricultural land taxes were the main resource for the treasury, Muḥammad 'Alī was keen to cultivate every acre of Egypt's irrigable land. Moreover, on 17 August 1828, he issued an act stipulating that when there is uncultivated land in a vil-lage, the village shaykh, as well as the *nāẓir al-qism*, should be punished by paying the assessed tax on that land,[25] which was not a crime according to Sharī'a.

Furthermore, peasants fleeing from their villages constituted one of the most impor-tant problems for which penal acts were issued. On 19 February 1829, the pasha issued an act to punish a shaykh, who had hidden a fleeing peasant from another village and had not reported him, with one hundred lashes and a fine of one hundred piasters to be paid to the spy (*baṣṣāṣ*) who reported the fugitive.[26] On 12 April 1829, he issued an act ordering a beating of five hundred whips for anyone who dared to slaughter animals outside the slaughterhouse and did not pay taxes on them. He likewise punished the butcher who did it and the shaykh of the neighborhood in which the crime happened, sending them to jail for life in Alexandria's *līmān*.[27] This punishment was significantly greater than the crime but was insufficient in the pasha's eyes.

Hukkām al-siyāsa had no judiciary experience or knowledge of the criteria for applying *ta'zīr* sentences. It is therefore comical that when the *nāẓir qism* of al-Shabbāsāt caught the shaykh of Kafr Majar hiding two peasants who had fled from another vil-lage, he was bewildered: if the punishment was applicable to the crime of hiding a single peasant, should it be doubled when two peasants were hidden, or was it applied as is, no matter how many peasants the shaykh hid? The *nāẓir* had to inquire with the pasha about this issue. The pasha's response was even more comical, as he issued an order to the *nāẓir* on 16 August 1829 to beat the shaykh with two hundred lashes and fine him only one hundred piasters, while taking another hundred piasters from the department's treasury and giving it all to the *baṣṣāṣ*.[28]

On another occasion, the *nāẓir qism* of Tanta told the pasha that he had found two peasants in Bedouin clothes residing with one of the tribal shaykhs. Muḥammad 'Alī believed that the previous orders of the village shaykhs might not be an effective de-terrent against the Bedouins. On 24 July 1829, he issued another legislative decree to all the provincial governors, instructing them to arrest any Bedouin who had con-cealed a peasant fleeing his village, as well as the shaykh of his tribe, and send them to Alexandria's *līmān* for life, and to send the peasant back to his village.[29]

While Muḥammad 'Alī was issuing legislative acts at an accelerated rate, *hukkām al-siyāsa* in the provinces were giving their opinions on crimes for which no punitive acts were issued. The result was disastrous. For example, the *nāẓir qism* of Mīt Ghamr, who was a relative of the pasha, had a man beaten with more than eighteen hundred lashes for forging a receipt. The man died as a result. On 13 August 1829, Muḥammad ʿAlī reprimanded the *nāzir* for his action, informing him that when such crimes occurred, he should present them to him for a verdict.[30]

This means that the pasha obliged *ḥukkām al-siyāsa* not to set their own penalties but to abide by the texts of his previously issued penal decrees. The accelerated rate at which legislative decrees were issued was not sufficient, so Muḥammad ʿAlī had to search for alternatives. First, he allowed his senior personnel to lay down laws, and later he established legislative councils for this purpose. Simultaneously, he continued to issue legislative decrees in cases about which he was extremely angered, and he would issue severe punishments disproportionate to the crime. For example, when he learned that some young men were trying to avoid military service recruitment by putting rat poison in their eyes, making themselves blind, he issued a penal act on 11 February 1830 forbidding perfumers from selling rat poison and punishing those who sold it or used it in their eyes with life imprisonment.[31] When he learned that people were still slaughtering animals outside the slaughterhouse, he issued another act on 15 April 1830 that established execution as a punishment for this practice.[32] And when reports were brought to him about the spread of theft in the Egyptian countryside, with thieves daring to break into al-Maḥalla al-Kubra's police station and steal the treasury, the pasha became furious and issued a legislative act on 23 April 1832 ordering the crucifixion of every thief who stole, after the first occurrence.[33] Although these exaggerated overreactions did not achieve the desired justice, they shed light on an important aspect of the legislative authority in Muḥammad ʿAlī's era.

Individuals' Regulations

The pasha allowed *ḥukkām al-siyāsa* to propose administrative and organizational regulations. If he was convinced of a regulation's value, he would promulgate it by decree as a regulation in effect. Hence, the second stage of the Egyptian penal legislation took the form of administrative and organizational regulations drawn up by senior personnel to define the tasks of associations and employees, price goods and products, and chart the manner of work in the various departments and regions. Its relationship to the development of penal law is limited to the punitive articles it includes for those who did not follow those tasks, prices, or methods. I call them individuals' regulations (Lawāʾiḥ al-Afrād) because they were drawn up by specific individuals and carried their names.

Most of these regulations are unknown because they were soon obsolete due to the issuance of new regulations in the subsequent legislative stage. However, some of them continued in effect, and their full texts or summaries have reached us. The best example of this is the individuals' regulations adopted by the LZF. A careful reading of the LZF indicates that it consists of several partial individuals' regulations.

The first Egyptian legislator was Major General Maḥmūd Bey ʿIzzat, the minister of war (nāẓir al-jihādiyya),[34] who put in place several important regulations. First, he organized the state (wilayat) of Qaliyyūbiyya, the name of which he changed to Commandarity (maʾmūriyyat) of Qaliyyūbiyya, governed by a commander (maʾmūr, plural maʾmūrīn). Then he divided it into aqsām, each governed by a nāẓir (plural nuẓẓār), and divided each qism into akhṭāṭ (singular khaṭṭ, large village), administered by a ruler of khaṭṭ, similar to the shaykh of shaykhs (later the mayor) and assisted by a deputy (qaʾim maqām). Finally, he wrote a detailed regulation concerning the new ad-ministrative division, specifying the tasks entrusted to each peasant, shaykh, nāẓir, and maʾmūr. The pasha approved it, and it has remained the basis for the administrative or-ganization of Egypt. This regulation also became the basis on which the LZF determined the tasks of administrators in the countryside. LZF recognized him as Maḥmūd Bey, "the nāẓir of jihād abād and the organizer of al-Qaliyyūbiyya."[35]

Afterward, Maḥmūd Bey proposed a new administrative system for the villages of Egypt and applied it to the village of Kalabshū, now Rawda in Gharbiyya Governorate. He divided the village's land into twenty-four parts, carats, and then distributed the peasants of the village evenly among those carats, which were in turn distributed among the village shaykhs. He formulated this process in a regulation known as Maḥmūd Bey's Regulation to Amend Kalabshū, in which he specified the tasks of each shaykh and the penalties imposed on them if they fell short or did not fulfill them. For example, the reg-ulation stipulated that "If there is negligence by one of the shaykhs, he is reprimanded in front of his peers, and if the infraction is repeated, he is delivered one hundred lashes." He submitted the reorganization to the pasha, who approved it as a general regula-tion to be applied in all the villages of Egypt under the title of Lāʾiḥat Taʿdīl al-Nawāḥī wa-Taqsīmiha bi-Istiḥqāq al-Qirāt Faddān (Regulation to Amend the Villages and Dividing It into Carats by Its Merit per Acres), which later became an essential chapter in the LZF.[36]

Finally, Maḥmūd Bey reached the stage where he had the experience that qualified him to draft a complete penal code. This code cataloged the crimes and infractions that might be committed by peasants, carat shaykhs, and senior village shaykhs, as well as the penalties that ḥukkām al-siyāsa should impose on them. This important penal code begins by clarifying the name of its author and the reason for establishing these penalties: "It is heard that criminals whom ḥukkām need to discipline are being beaten more than the average, causing harm to them. To prevent this treachery, it was required to set limits for penalties for all crimes. Moreover, maʾmūrīn, nuẓẓār aqsām, and ḥukkām akhṭāṭ should be warned not to punish any criminal more than what is specified. If any of them beats a criminal more than his limits, he should be punished by the same punishment."[37]

Subsequently, Maḥmūd Bey began listing the crimes and infractions and the penalties specified for each. The purpose of this code was to legalize taʿzīr and determine their value so that there was no difference in penalties between different regions. This part clearly affirmed that the jurisdiction of the qāḍī would remain the same in cases of qiṣāṣ and *ḥudūd.* It stipulated that cases of premeditated and accidental murder, wounds, indecent assault, rape, abortion, and other infractions that have a specific penalty in Sharī'a would be referred to the *qāḍī* and that the *ḥakim al-siyāsa* would have to implement whatever the *qāḍī* ruled. It included about sixty unnumbered articles dealing with two types of crimes. The first type concerned crimes related to the rights of farmers: moving borders, crop burning, breaking waterwheels, stealing fruits, grain, chickens, and sheep, and using the farmer's livestock without consent. The second type concerned crimes related to the government's rights regarding peasants. It set penalties for those who refrained from paying taxes, protected fleeing peasants and thieves, and lied or provided incorrect information to the rulers, as well as for the shaykhs who neglected to do their job or plundered from peasants. This penal code literally constituted the punitive part of LZF.[38]

Another great Egyptian legislator, 'Uthmān Bey Nūr al-Dīn, suggested to the pasha that he establish a school for the war staff. The pasha established it in 1825 in a place close to al-Khānka, known as Jihād Abād, and appointed 'Uthmān Bey the head of the school,[39] with the title Chief of the Men of Jihad Abād (*kabīr rijāl jihād abād*).[40] Soon his position evolved to become Head of the Men of the Army (*ra'īs rijāl al-jihādiyya*). Later, in 1831, he became the Commander-in-Chief of the Egyptian fleet.[41] 'Uthmān Bey proposed a regulation that defined the functions of senior administrators, *ma'mūrīn* and *nuẓẓār*, and the penalties to be imposed on them in case they neglected those tasks assigned to them. This regulation was accepted and later became a major chapter in the LZF under the title "*Ma'mūrīn's* Tasks, Extracted from the Regulation of 'Uthmān Bey, *Kabīr Rijāl Jihād Abād*."[42] In fact, Amīn Sāmī mentioned two regulations that the pasha approved on 21 April 1828, one entitled Regulation of Tasks and *Ḥudūd* of *Ma'mūrīn* in Lower and Upper Egypt's *Ma'mūriyyāt* and the other entitled Regulation of Tasks and *Ḥudūd* of *Nuẓẓār* in Lower and Upper Egypt's *Aqsām*.[43]

In addition, 'Uthmān Bey assumed the task of arranging the financial management of the Zifta *qism*. Thus, he prepared a regulation that included lists showing the census of the people of the *qism*, the enumeration of their livestock, their palm trees, and their lands, and the total taxes imposed on them. Muḥammad 'Alī admired this regulation and ordered that it be circulated within all the *aqsām* of Egypt.[44] This was the beginning of a general census of population, livestock, and palm trees.

The LZF indicates that there are many other individuals' regulations. For example, an essential chapter in the LZF, "Peasant's Agricultural Operations in Upper Egypt," was entirely based on the Senior Shaykhs of Upper Egypt's Regulation, which was set by seven shaykhs whose names are mentioned in it.[45] The LZF also referred to other unnamed regulations when it described the method of henna cultivation based on Maḥmūd Bey's Regulation and mentioned that the method of henna cultivation was not found in any other regulation.[46]

In addition, many other individuals' regulations were not related to rural matters and, as such, were not included in the LZF. For example, the regulation of Mustafa Bey, the governor of Cairo, was issued on 19 January 1830 to determine food prices and penalties for sellers who did not adhere to the price. This regulation put an end to the absolute discretionary power of *al-muḥtasib*, to whose punishments—which ranged from cutting off ears or noses to flogging—al-Jabartī often referred.[47]

The number of individuals' regulations paved the way for the emergence of the third stage of punitive legislation. As a result, the individuals' regulations decreased but did not entirely disappear, with some continuing to appear occasionally.[48]

PARTIAL LEGISLATIONS OF MAJLIS AL-MASHŪRA

The third stage of penal legislation started a few days after Muḥammad ʿAlī established the Advisory Council (Majlis al-Mashūra [MM]), also known as al-Majlis al-ʿUmūmī, al-Majlis al-ʿĀlī, or Majlis al-Mulkiyya, with legislative authority on 2 September 1829, to indicate the shift from individuals' legislation to institutional legislation. This stage is represented in punitive laws to treat crimes and infractions in a specific sector of the society, or in a group of previous individuals' regulations compiled and reformulated by MM.

The first law of this type was issued ten days after MM was established to deal with the rural sector and stop peasants from fleeing villages to escape paying taxes or contributing labor to public works. Therefore, MM introduced the idea of a financial mortgage taken from peasants and not returned until they have paid what they owe. However, sometimes the peasant escaped and the mortgage was not enough to cover what he owed. As a result, MM devised the principle of "Family Solidarity in Punishment," according to which the son paid the debts owed by his fugitive father, and if he was unable to do so, the brother or any of his relatives was responsible.[49]

On the same day, MM issued another one-article penal law dealing with corruption in the administrative sector. The law forbade administrators from exploiting peasants for their own work without pay. It stipulated that the perpetrator should be punished by having to pay double the peasant's wages and deliver the payment to the peasant.[50] This law was an introduction to the third law of MM.

The Collection of Criminal Matters' Register (CCMR), which I discovered, edited, and published,[51] records three laws titled S-N. The oldest was issued on 20 September 1829, so I named it "the first S-N." Rudolph Peters considered it "Meḥmed Alī's First Criminal Legislation," but it is the third law in the third stage. The first S-N was issued to fight corruption in the administrative sector in particular and in the urban sector in general. Its goals were, first, to prevent employees from exploiting people and plundering their money, and second, and more importantly, to prevent them from plundering the government's funds. The importance of the second goal is clear from the degree of the punishment. A *maʾmūr* who plundered a peasant's money would be imprisoned for six months, but if he plundered the government's money, he would be imprisoned for a year.

Peters reproduced the first S-N in twenty-two articles, including twelve articles that were issued later upon different occasions, while the original law, in all sources, did not exceed ten unnumbered articles. These articles dealt with the crimes of theft and embezzlement that the *ma'mūrīn*, *nuẓẓār*, shaykhs, and Coptic cashiers might have committed. It criminalized the plundering of people's money, currency fraud, and road blockages, and punished the murderer, whose accusation is not proven by the *qāḍī* according to Sharī'a's requirements, with life imprisonment in Alexandria's *līmān*. The most important thing to note in the first S-N is that it established the bases of discrimination between criminals in terms of their status and religion. For the same crime, notables had different punishments from commoners, Turks from Egyptians, and Muslims from Copts.[52]

The first test of the first S-N took place less than two weeks after its issuance when the *ma'mūr* of al-Gharbiyya reported to Muḥammad 'Alī Pasha that several people had died when inflicted with the punishment of severe beating. Muḥammad 'Alī hurriedly wrote to him on 16 October 1829 to reprimand him and concluded his letter by stating, "If I discovered that you have beaten someone in excess of what is prescribed by law and he dies, know that I will take revenge on you."[53] This suggests that Muḥammad 'Alī was keen that officials and administrators follow the text of the new law and not override the penalties stipulated therein. It also indicates that Egypt moved from the stage of discretionary *ta'zīr* to the codified *ta'zīr*, and the LZF confirmed this in the introduction of its punitive part.[54]

The fourth law of MM was issued four months after the first S-N to deal with the problems of the rural sector and compile the disparate regulations of individuals that had been issued in this regard.[55] All historians except Peters considered the LZF Muḥammad 'Alī's first penal legislation. As written on its cover, it was printed at the end of Rajab 1245 / 25 January 1830, with the title Peasant Cultivation Regulation and Management of *Siyāsa*'s Adjudications with the Purpose of Success, and it consisted of two parts. The first part was the sixty-page constitution, which set the framework for action in the rural sector and was mainly based on the individuals' regulations previously issued in this regard, as mentioned before. The second part was the punitive part, which included all the penalties imposed on peasants and administrators if they did not perform the tasks assigned to them in the first part. It was literally the regulation of Maḥmūd Bey. The LZF clearly confirms that all cases of *qiṣāṣ*, *diyyat*, and *ḥudūd* must be referred to the *qāḍī*.[56] Gabriel Baer thought that the punitive part of the LZF was reprinted and published in Sha'ban 1245 under the title Qānūn al-Filāḥa, but in fact there is no law called Qānūn al-Filāḥa; it is just an abbreviated name of the LZF given by the collectors of QM, who stated that it was published in Sha'ban, and this is logical because it was printed on the last day of the previous month. Baer compared the LZF with Qānūn al-Filāḥa, but he was actually comparing Mahmūd Bey's Penal Regulation and the first fifty-five articles of the QM.

The first S-N failed to achieve its goals, and it required many amendments and additions. The first amendment was the fifth law of MM. It was a one-article law issued on 14 February 1830 as an appendix to the first S-N. It was nothing more than a clarification or completion of the third article that stipulated that anyone who embezzled a thousand piasters or more would be imprisoned for one year. It did not, however, specify a penalty for those whose embezzlement was less than a thousand piasters. This is what that appendix explained in detail.[57]

The sixth law, the Roma Law (Qānūn al-Nawar), dealt with the crimes of a different sector of society. The date of its issuance is unknown, but it was probably issued on 14 February 1830 or shortly thereafter, according to its order in the register. Peters considered it part of the first S-N, but it is neither a part nor an appendix of the first S-N or the LZF. It is an independent law that determined the penalties that should be imposed on the Roma, escaped slaves, Moroccans who were practicing astrology and magic, and peasants who were begging.[58] This law punished groups, not individuals, for the crime of theft associated with vagrancy. It inflicted a punishment on them, whether the accusation was proven against all of them, some of them, or none of them.

Until 1834, prostitution was not a crime or even an infraction under the government of Muḥammad ʿAlī. On the contrary, it was a source of income for the state through taxes imposed on prostitutes. However, on 28 May 1834, MM promulgated its seventh law to prohibit prostitution. The law stipulated a punishment of fifty lashes for any prostitute caught practicing adultery, three hundred lashes for any man who caught with her, and another three hundred lashes for the neighborhood shaykh who was neglected to prevent prostitution.[59] This law also represents an important milestone in the history of Egyptian criminal legislation. For the first time, we find a law that deals with ethical issues not directly related to the interests of Muḥammad ʿAlī's government and thus deprives the state of a financial resource.

Unlike the LZF in the rural sector, the first S-N and its appendix failed to solve the problems and infractions of the urban and administrative sectors. Therefore, MM decided to replace it with a more comprehensive law. On 10 February 1835, Muḥammad ʿAlī Pasha approved the new law in a decree that was printed in Dhu al-Qiʿdah 1250 / March 1835. This law is unknown to historians. The only source that recorded it was the CCMR, which referred to it as one of the series of S-N laws.[60] The decree defined it as the "Civil Administration Law" (Qānūn al-Mulkiyya),[61] but I prefer to call it the second siyāsit-nāmah in order to distinguish it from the first S-N of 1829 and the third one (S-NM) of 1837. It consisted of twenty-two articles on multiple aspects of crimes committed in the urban and administrative sectors. Some of them are mentioned in the first S-N, such as embezzlement, bribery, and falsification of records and receipts, while others are not mentioned, such as laziness of employees, damaging the government's equipment, and slandering.

The second S-N confirmed what was stated in the first S-N regarding distinctions between criminals in terms of their status and religion. It added a new social dimension by distinguishing between ordinary people and nobles and by creating special courts for the latter. Nevertheless, it became the basis on which the third S-N was built since all of its articles were fully contained in the third S-N after modifications in wording.[62]

The LZF was the constitution of action and the penal law of the rural sector, while the first and second S-Ns failed to play the same rule in the urban sector. Accordingly, an urgent need emerged to reorganize the central administration and governmental bodies and set appropriate penalties for infractions committed in the urban sector, following the same pattern of the LZF. MM issued a third S-N in Rabī' al-Awwal 1253 / June 1837 titled S-N of Civil Administration (S-N al-Mulkiyya). Historians considered it the first constitution of the Egyptian government, and it consisted of three chapters. The first chapter, titled "Basic Arrangements," consists of nine articles regulating the management of the various *divans* and bodies. The second chapter, titled "The Process," consists of thirty-one articles specifying the tasks entrusted to the heads of the *divans* and employees. The third chapter, titled "*Siyāsit-Nāmah*," is the punitive one. It consists of an introduction and twenty-one articles that deal with the same topics mentioned in the second S-N. The S-NM equalized the punishment among criminals regardless of their social origins, but it intensified the punishment for all.[63]

Administrators were responsible for weekly, monthly, and annual submission of reports to the office of the pasha. As various directorates were overdue in submitting periodic reports, Muḥammad 'Alī ordered the Revenue Bureau (Diwān al-Irādāt) to set a regulation to punish those who were late in submitting reports. The regulation was issued on 18 August 1839 but was not distinctive, so I call it the First Engagements' Regulation, as there are subsequent legislations that dealt with the same topic bearing the name Engagements' Regulation. The First Engagements' Regulation affirmed that it is the responsibility of the chief clerk of the directorate (*bashkatib*) in cases of delay in submitting reports and fixed a penalty of fifteen days of imprisonment for the first offense. However, if the infraction was repeated, the punishment would be doubled.[64]

PARTIAL LEGISLATIONS OF AL-ḤAQQĀNIYYA ASSOCIATION

Egyptian criminal legislation took a big leap forward when Muḥammad 'Alī established the first modern judicial institution in Egypt, the Fairness Association (Jam'iyyat al-Ḥaqqāniyya), on 14 February 1842, to serve as a supreme court in addition to assuming legislative authority.[65] We can count seventeen regulations and partial criminal laws that al-Ḥaqqāniyya issued in two and a half years before it came to the fifth stage. The issuance of this multitude of laws after the collapse of Muḥammad 'Alī's empire in 1840 makes us wonder whether the state of Muḥammad 'Alī really ended or whether Muḥammad 'Alī's projects transformed from an imperial type to a local one in Egypt. Actually, it was a stage of transformation in which Muḥammad 'Alī began to focus his reform efforts on Egypt as it became exclusive to him and his family. While he neglected projects of an imperial nature, such as military conscription, expanded education, and mass manufacturing, he undertook major projects of a local nature in many fields that he had not been interested in before, such as population census, summer irrigation, land ownership, and legislation in sectors that were not a priority in previous stages.

Muḥammad ʿAlī expanded the cultivation of summer crops, which depended on the Nile waters that came from tropical sources in the off-season of the flood. When the flood season began, the summer crops would be mature and close to harvest. In order to prevent them from being damaged by the floodwater, they were surrounded by high embankments, and they needed constant guarding throughout the four months of the flood. Hence, embankments were one of the areas that al-Ḥaqqāniyya dealt with by issuing two laws regarding them. The first was the Embankments Regulation (Lāʾiḥat al-Jisūr), issued in August 1842 to specify the responsibilities of peasants and shaykhs toward the maintenance, restoration, and guarding of embankments. It also included five punitive articles detailing the penalties to be imposed on the peasants and shaykhs in case they breached its rules. The text of this regulation does not seem to be available, but I found the five punitive articles that were elected within QM (articles 76–80).[66] The second regulation was the Embankments Operations Law (Qānūn ʿAmaliyyāt al-Jisūr), issued in January 1843 to specify the tasks of irrigation engineers. It included eleven punitive articles detailing the penalties to be imposed on the engineers in case of infraction (QM 87–97).[67]

Although many administrative matters were regulated in previous laws, neglect and delay in completing work after the specified dates was a dominant feature of the administrative apparatus under Muḥammad ʿAlī. Therefore, al-Ḥaqqāniyya issued a series of eight laws and regulations to punish those who neglected or delayed work. The first was issued in November 1842 as an appendix of an unknown law to punish negligent or sluggish employees. It is not clear which original law the appendix was attached to, but it was likely an administrative regulation issued on 30 August 1841 to organize work in the various *divans*. The appendix was the punitive part of it, which contained six articles that were selected in QM (articles 81–86).[68] The second law was the Second Engagements' Regulation, which was issued in January 1843 to punish employees who were late in completing the tasks assigned to them within the specified dates. It distinguished between junior and senior employees, making the punishment of juniors corporal, with one stick for each day of delay, while making the punishment of seniors financial (QM, article 110).[69] The third was the Third Engagements' Regulation, which was issued in February 1843 to emphasize the punishments in the second one, and, as such, al-Ḥaqqāniyya selected noting from it in QM.[70] The fourth was the Delay Law, which was issued in October 1843 to punish administrators who delayed in finishing works (QM 116).[71] The fifth was the Delay Law for military personnel, which was also issued in October (QM 111).[72]

Furthermore, al-Ḥaqqāniyya issued the Regulation of the Auxiliary *Shūra Divan*'s Jobs in April 1843.[73] It contained eighteen articles to organize the management process in the *divan* and the penalties for the violating officials. In April 1844, al-Ḥaqqāniyya selected the punitive articles from this regulation and printed them in a separate law, titled *Siyāsa* of the Regulation (Siyāsat al-Lāʾiḥa), which was later selected in QM (articles 98–106).[74] The *Siyāsa* of the Regulation represents an important turning point in the history of criminal legislation in Egypt, as al-Ḥaqqāniyya no longer issued mixed regulations that contained administrative and punitive articles, but rather separate pure punitive laws.

In the administrative sector, al-Ḥaqqāniyya dealt with the issue of employees being dismissed from their jobs and issued two laws on this concern. The first was issued in May 1843, stipulating that if they were reinstated at a later time, they were not entitled to get a salary for the term of dismissal and that the manager who assisted them in that matter would be punished (QM 107).[75] The second law was issued on 5 October 1844 to deal with employees who were sentenced to imprisonment or expulsion from their job. It stipulated the confiscation of their remaining salaries and benefits (QM 195).[76]

Al-Ḥaqqāniyya gave special attention to the management of agricultural holdings after Muḥammad ʿAlī reformulated the agricultural ownership system and created new types of agricultural holdings. It issued two laws in this regard: the first was Qānūn al-Jafālik, on March 1843, to organize the process of managing al-Jafālik (the royal family members' domains) and specify the penalties that would fall on those who breached the law.[77] The second was the Delay Law for *Nuẓẓār* of the Noblemen's Covenant Farms (*nuẓẓār al-ʿuhad*), which was issued in January 1844 (QM 117).[78]

Because of the pasha's desire to organize the process of presenting reports to him, al-Ḥaqqāniyya issued two laws in this regard. The first was the Law of Presenting to the Supreme Doorsteps (Qānūn al-ʿArḍ ʿala al-Aʿtāb al-Saniyya), which was issued in June 1843 (QM 108–09).[79] The second was the Law of Prying, issued in April 1844 to punish employees who presented matters not related to their job (QM 120).[80]

Finally, al-Ḥaqqāniyya issued three different laws of a local nature. The first was Qānūn-Nāmah-Siyāsa, which was issued in October 1843 to deal with offenses committed by those who collected taxes and royalties from craftsmen (*al-multazimīn*). Later, al-Ḥaqqāniyya selected all its articles in QM (articles 112–15).[81] The second was the Fleeing Law, issued in January 1844 to punish fleeing farmers (QM 118).[82] The third was the Currencies Law (Qānūn al-Maskukāt), which was issued in March 1844 to abolish the arbitrary penalty imposed by the Decree-Law, issued in May 1830 to execute those who abuse the French Riyal in excess of its value. The new punishment was a fine of five times the profit made by the seller, increased to ten in case of return (QM 119).[83]

In an exceptional case, the *divan* of finance entered the field of punitive legislation, placing three significant laws that were later selected by al-Ḥaqqāniyya within the QM. The first was issued on 25 June 1844 regarding thefts that occurred in villages. It stipulated that if a theft crime occurred and the village shaykh did not arrest the thief, he must pay the value of the stolen items. The *divan* of finance had devised a new punishment for the thieves: to exile them to Fazughli on the Sudanese-Ethiopian border for two to five years. If the thief had a history of theft and took the crime of blocking roads as his trade, he would be sent to Fazughli for the duration of his life (QM 121).[84]

The second law was issued on 13 October 1844 to generalize the punishment concerning exile to Fazughli. The law stipulated that an employee who stole government money and was sentenced to prison in Alexandria's *līmān* for a certain period according to laws must serve that period in Fazughli instead of the *līmān*. It also stipulated that the thief who had taken looting, raiding, and blocking roads as a trade should not be executed, but rather sent to Fazughli to work in the mountains for the duration of his life. It thus rescinded Muḥammad 'Alī's penal act (*amr-qānūn*), issued on 23 April 1832, which stipulated the execution of thieves who returned to thievery after the first occurrence (QM 196–97).[85]

The third law, titled the *Līmān* Law, determined how to manage and guard the Alexandria arsenal and specified the type of criminals to be sent to Fazughli, most of whom were sentenced to life imprisonment, while most of those to be sent to the arsenal were sentenced to prison for a more limited period. This law was not dated, and it was clearly issued days before the promulgation of QM, but it was not published. When the QM was issued, the law was included in it and published as part of it (articles 198–302).[86]

Comprehensive Laws

The legislative environment reached the point of saturation; al-Ḥaqqāniyya could no longer handle partial legislation scattered among different laws and regulations. As a result, al-Ḥaqqāniyya began to move toward the idea of developing a comprehensive penal code covering all crimes in all sectors. The first attempt was the Ninth of Sha'bān 1260 Law, issued on 9 Sha'bān 1260 / 24 August 1844. It was an unconventional law since it was, on the one hand, a comprehensive penal code that dealt with various crimes in multiple sectors and, on the other hand, the first criminal procedure code in Egypt. It regulated the process of implementing penalties and defined the procedures to be followed during implementation. The original text does not seem to be available, but I found a selected edition in QM. It consists of seventy-three articles in QM (articles 122–94)[87] without any deletion, addition, or amendment. Its articles were arranged thematically and could be easily divided into two parts.

The first part consisted of fifteen articles concerned with setting some legal principles related to the methods of implementing penalties and the rights of criminals, as it treated the criminal as a human being and preserved rights for him or her that were not respected by previous laws. This law also respected the criminal's religion and personal circumstances, forbidding execution on religious holidays and necessitating the postponement of the death penalty for a pregnant woman until after she gave birth. Though the Sharī'a stipulates these principles, this was the first time that they were stipulated by Egyptian positive law. The second part consisted of fifty-eight articles and dealt with some crimes that previous laws had dealt with as well as new crimes that no previous law had addressed. Most importantly, this law established Sharī'a penalties such as *qiṣāṣ* and *diyya*.

Although I classify it as a comprehensive law, it neglected some crimes, such as administrative corruption, embezzlement, and bribery, with which previous partial laws dealt. Undoubtedly, the Ninth of Sha'bān 1260 Law was an important qualitative leap in the history of Egyptian criminal legislation, as it opened the door wide to the development of a more comprehensive penal code.

When we reach the end of 1260/1844, we find a large array of partial laws and regulations. Each dealt with one or several crimes in one or several sectors, sometimes in a repetitive or contradictory fashion, but they were all scattered in registers, printed brochures, or single papers. Al-Ḥaqqāniyya realized an urgent need to select and compile these laws into one single and comprehensive law. Accordingly, the second comprehensive law appeared. The Selections Law (QM) was issued on the first of al-Muḥarram 1261 / 10 January 1845. Although it was a comprehensive penal code containing 203 articles,[88] it did not completely eliminate the spirit and method of the old legislation. In fact, it was a selection of old regulations that were completely or partially replicated. Its articles were arranged chronologically, rather objectively. The first fifty-five articles were selected from the LZF, followed by twenty articles from the third S-N, with some modifications in language and punishment. Al-Ḥaqqāniyya selected the penal articles from its administrative regulations before adding the full text of all of its penal laws (which I mentioned in the fourth stage) without any modification, including the Ninth of Sha'bān 1260 Law.

Baer mentioned that at the end of 1259 (or beginning of 1844), Muḥammad 'Alī issued a law called the General Law (Qānūn 'Āmm), which was a summary of his penal laws. However, this law was not published until Rajab 1265 / May 1849, which is half a year after 'Abbās Pasha assumed power. Therefore, this law was known among the Europeans as Abbās's Law. Baer did not find the Arabic text of this law but indicated that it was divided into six chapters comprising eighty-eight articles.[89] Amīn Sāmī also stated that this comprehensive law was issued at the end of 1259, but he asserted that it was divided into ten chapters comprising ninety articles. He also confirmed that the law was not published until Rajab 1265 but that it was in force since its issuance.[90]

These assertions should be problematized, for it is illogical and unjustified for al-Ḥaqqāniyya to issue three comprehensive penal codes that deal with the same subjects and the same penalties within one year: this Common Law, the Ninth of Sha'bān 1260 Law, and the QM. Al-Ḥaqqāniyya did not select any article from this Common Law in the QM. However, it selected all the articles of the Ninth of Sha'bān Law in the QM, which means that this law did not exist, nor was it in force since its promulgation, as Sāmy mentioned. Confirming this point, there was no trace of this law in the records of al-Ḥaqqāniyya, which was carrying out the task of legislation in the year 1259.

When this law was issued in Rajab 1265, the al-Daqahliyya director wrote to the Council of Judgments (Majlis al-Aḥkām [MA]) requesting copies of it to be applied in his directorate. The council replied that the schools' *divan* would send it to him and indicated in that correspondence that this law had been "regulated by the Private Council (al-Majlis al-Khusūsy) before His Excellency (Afandina), the Guardian of Blessings."[91] However, the Private Council was founded in al-Muḥarram 1263 / January 1847, not 1259. After a careful search in the records of MA, which 'Abbas Pasha founded in Rabī' al-Ākhar 1265 to replace al-Ḥaqqāniyya in its judicial rule, I found that the records of 1265–66 mention this law clearly, calling it the New Law or the New *Ḥudūd* Law.[92] I have successfully compiled the full Arabic text of this law from CCMR, which referred to it as the Law of Rajab 1265.

I noted through its text that this law includes ninety numbered articles, not eighty-eight as Baer mentioned. In Article No. 23, the following appears: "If someone attended MA and complained of the injustice . . ."[93] Once again, MA did not exist in 1259. On the other hand, it is noteworthy that on its issuance this law superseded all the criminal laws issued before it, including the QM. Therefore, MA sent the cases brought before it and judged following QM back to the regions, asking them to reconsider the New Ḥudūd Law.[94] This means that the New Ḥudūd Law was not in force before Rajab 1265 as Sāmy stated.

Although Tanẓīmāt in the Ottoman Empire began in the era of Muḥammad ʿAlī, it was only applied in Egypt during the reign of Saʿīd. The first Ottoman Penal Code, which Muḥammad ʿAlī ignored, was issued on 3 May 1840, and the second law, which ʿAbbās ignored, was issued on 17 February 1851. ʿAbbās argued that Egyptian law was better than the Ottoman law. This caused a crisis in relations between Egypt and the Ottoman Empire, resulting, after long negotiations, in a special amended version of the Ottoman Penal Code per the conditions of Egypt, which was printed in early Rabīʿ al-Ākhar 1271 / late December 1854. This law seemed to have multiple names. Baer points out that this law was known among the Europeans as Saʿīd's Law,[95] but the formal title of the printed version is Qānūn-Nāmah al-Sultānī.[96] However, its name in the CCMR is al-Qānūn al-Hamayūny, and in the other records of MA it is referred to as Qānūn al-Tanẓīmāt, and sometimes as simply the Law.[97]

This law consists of eighty-four articles distributed among five chapters and divided thematically. Thus, in terms of form, this law was superior to the QM and the Law of Rajab 1265 (ʿAbbās's Law) in terms of comprehensiveness, nonrepetition, noncontradiction, and objective tabulation. But in terms of content, it was less mature than the QM and ʿAbbās's Law, as we find it differentiating between people's punishments according to their grades and ranks. For example, the second article of the second chapter clearly distinguishes between penalties for notables and those for ordinary people. This law is also distinctive among all previous Egyptian laws in that it established the Ḥadd of Sharīʿa for drinking alcohol.[98]

Qānūn-Nāmah al-Sultānī continued in force until the British occupation in September 1882, with some partial modifications from time to time.[99] In 1876, the Mixed Penal Code was issued to be applied in the "Mixed Courts," which specialized in handling cases related to foreigners. It ignored this long history of Egyptian legislative experience and copied the French Penal Code issued in 1810. In October 1882, under British and European pressure, the Egyptian government formed a committee that designed the new judicial system, in which they dared to rename the new majālis as maḥākim, the term that was exclusively reserved for Sharīʿa courts. On 13 November 1883, the National Penal Code, a modified version of the Mixed Penal Code, was issued. The authors of that law ignored half a century of Egyptian legislative history—which was based on trial and error, by issuing laws, regulations, leaflets, amendments, and appendices—during which Egyptian legislators, individuals, and councils could reach a legal formula appropriate to Egypt's circumstances. Thus, Egypt returned to ground zero to begin a new phase of amendments and additions to fill the gaps and defects that appeared after the application of the National Penal Code.[100]

Conclusion

Through this study, we find that Muḥammad ʿAlī assumed the role of a legislator in the first stage by issuing decrees with a legislative character. Then he allowed his senior personnel to set regulations and laws, and later he established legislative councils to carry out this sensitive task. The legislative councils moved Egypt from overreactive and partial legislation to comprehensive, collective, and rational legislation.

The criminal laws of Muḥammad ʿAlī and his successors were neither transmitted from Europe nor influenced by it. Rather, these laws were local in character, language, and style, fulfilling needs revealed by actual practice. This legislation was not aimed at diminishing the authority of *maḥakim* to hear criminal cases or replacing Sharīʿa with secular law. Rather, it came as a part of Sharīʿa and within its framework to determine the types of cases that were referred to Sharīʿa and those that came under the jurisdiction of *ḥukkām al-siyāsa* under the term of *taʿāzīr*. In addition, it did not leave the discretionary punishment open to the *ḥukkām al-siyāsa* but rather specified for each crime the appropriate type of discretionary punishment and obligated the administration to carry it out. There is no doubt that this philosophy remained in effect even after the establishment of civil courts. As stated in Article 1 of the Penal Code issued in 1883, "Accordingly, in this law, the degrees of punishment (*taʿāzīr*) that the governors (*awliyāʾ al-amr*) have the legal authority to determine, and this is without prejudice in any case to the rights established for each person under the noble Sharīʿa."[101] But it was not a determination; rather, it was copied from the French Penal Code, and thus it needed to be redetermined, reconsidered, and amended.

Notes

1. *Mujammaʿ al-Taḥrīrāt al-Mutaʿlliqa ila mā Jara bi-Iʿdām wa-Muḥākamat Sulaymān al-Ḥalaby Qātil Sāry ʿAskar al-ʿĀmm Kléber* (Cairo: Maṭbaʿat al-Jumhūr al-Faransāwy, 1800).
2. For more details, see Emad Ahmad Helal, "al-Qaḍāʾ al-Jināʾī al-Miṣrī fī al-ʿAṣr al-ʿUthmānī," *Banha University Magazine* 42, October 2015, 959–1022.
3. Ibid.
4. Aḥmad Fatḥy Zaghlūl, *al-Muḥāmāh* (Cairo: Maṭbaʿat al-Maʿārif, 1900); ʿAzīz Khanky, *al-Tashrīʿ wa-l-Qaḍāʾ qabla Inshāʾ al-Maḥākim al-Ahliyya* (Cairo: al-Maṭbaʿa al-ʿAṣriyya, 1940); Shafīq Shiḥāta, *Tārīkh Ḥarakat al-Tajdīd fī al-Nuẓum al-Qānūniyya fī Miṣr Munẓu ʿAṣr Muḥammad ʿAlī* (Cairo: Dār Iḥyāʾ al-Kutub al-ʿArabiyya, 1961); Gabriel Baer, "Tanzimat in Egypt, The Penal Code," *Bulletin of the School of Oriental and African Studies* 26, no. 1 (1963): 29–49; Latīfa Muḥammad Sālim, *al-Niẓām al-Qaḍāʾī al-Miṣrī al-Hadīth, 1875–1914*, vol. I (Cairo: Markaz al-Dirāsāt al-Siyāsiyya wa-l-Istrātijiyya bi al-Ahrām, 1984).

5. Baer, "Tanzimat in Egypt," 29; Zaghlūl, *al-Muḥmāh*, 203; Helen Anne B. Rivlin, *The Agricultural Policy of Muḥammad 'Alī in Egypt* (Cambridge, MA: Harvard University Press, 1961), 89–101.

6. Zayn al-'Ābdīn Shams al-Dīn Najm, *al-Siyāsit-Nāmah* (Cairo: Dār al-Kitāb al-Jāmi'ī, 1996); Baer, "Tanzimat in Egypt," 30.

7. Baer, "Tanzimat in Egypt," 30–31, 41–42; Zaghlūl, *al-Muḥmāh*, 159; Khanky, *al-Tashrī' wa-l-Qaḍā'*, 2, 11; Shiḥāta, *Tārīkh Ḥarakat al-Tajdīd*, 105; Sālim, *al-Niẓām al-Qaḍā'ī*, 16.

8. Rudolph Peters, "For His Correction and as a Deterrent Example for Others, Mehmet 'Alī's First Criminal Legislation (1829–1830)," *Islamic Law and Society* 6, no. 2 (1999): 164–92.

9. Dār al-Wathā'iq al-Qawmiyya (DWQ), Maḥkamat al-Bāb al-'Alī (MBA), register 325, pp. 107–08, document 206, year 1218/1803; and p. 232, doc. 473, 1217/1802. DWQ, Maḥkamat al-Diwān al-'Alī, register 4, p. 5, doc. 25, 1228/1813, with the sentence of *diyya*; and p. 18, doc. 149, 1228/1813, with the death sentence (*qiṣāṣ*).

10. DWQ, MBA, register 346, p. 19, doc. 42, 1227/1812; DWQ, Maḥkamat Damanhour, register 12, p. 55, doc. 79, 1222/1807.

11. DWQ, MBA, register 327, p. 224, doc. 559, 1218/1803.

12. DWQ, MBA, register 335, p. 90, doc. 208, 1218/1804.

13. DWQ, MBA, register 335, p. 26, doc. 59, about stealing a donkey, and in the same register, p. 72, doc. 161, about stealing a camel, year 1219/1804; 'Abd al-Raḥmān al-Jabartī, *'Ajā'ib al-Āthār fī al-Tarājim wa-l-Akhbār*, vol. IV, ed. 'Abd al-Raḥīm 'Abd al-Raḥmān (Cairo: Dār al-Kutub al-Miṣriyya, 1998), 231.

14. Muḥammad Abu Zahra, *al-Jarima wa-l-'Uqūba fī al-Fiqh al-Islāmī*, "al-'Uqūba" (Cairo: Dār al-Fikr al-'Arabī, 2006), 79–81.

15. For more details on Ta'zīr, see Abu Zahra, *al-Jarima wa-l-'Uqūba*, 81–82.

16. By positive law I mean a statute that has been laid down by a legislature, court, or other human institution and can take whatever form the authors want. It was similar to secular law, but I cannot call it secular because it derived its legitimacy from Sharī'a.

17. Aḥmad Ibn 'Alī al-Maqrīzī, *al-Mawā'iẓ wa-l-I'tibār bi-Dhikr al-Khutat wa-l-Āthār*, vol. II (Cairo: al-Maṭb'a al-Amiriya, 1270/1853), 219–20.

18. *Al-Awāmir wa-l-Mukātabāt al-Ṣādirah min 'Azīz Miṣr Muḥammad 'Alī*, vol. I, ed. a group of researchers under the supervision of Raouf Abbas (Cairo: Egyptian National Library and Archives, 2005), 61.

19. Amīn Sāmy, *Taqwīm al-Nīl*, part II (Cairo: Dār al-Kutub al-Miṣriyya, 1928), 256.

20. Ibid., 283.

21. Ibid., 310.

22. Ibid., 320.

23. Ibid., 330.

24. *Al-Awāmir wa-l-Mukātabāt*, 227.

25. Ibid., 228.

26. Emad Ahmad Helal, "Irhāṣāt lā'iḥat zira'at al-Fallāḥ, al-Tashrī' al-Jinā'y fi Miṣr, 1805–1830," *al-Ruznāmah* IV (2006): 249–303.

27. Ibid., 257.

28. *Al-Awāmir wa-l-Mukātabāt*, 274.

29. Wizārat al-Thaqāfa wa-l-Irshād al-Qawmī, *Diwān al-Ma'iyya al-Saniyya, al-Sijill al-Awwal min 6 Muḥarram 1245 ila 8 Rajab 1246* (Cairo: Maṭbū'āt Dār al-Wathā'iq al-Qawmiyya, 1960), 14–15.

30. *Al-Awāmir wa-l-Mukātabāt*, 271.

31. Sāmy, *Taqwīm al-Nīl*, 362.

32. *Al-Awāmir wa-l-Mukātabāt*, 292.

33. Emad Ahmad Helal, *Wathā'iq al-Tashrī' al-Jinā'ī al-Miṣrī, Sijill Majmū' Umūr Jinā'iyya*, Silsilat Dirāsāt Wathā'iqiyya, vol. 3 (Cairo: Dar al-Wathā'iq al-Qawmiyya, 2011), 195–96.

34. For more details about him, see al-Jabartī, *'Ajā'ib al-Āthār*, 319, 321, 323, 332, 336, 349, 417; and Sāmy, *Taqwīm al-Nīl*, 404–6.

35. *Lā'iḥat Zīrā'at al-Fallāḥ wa-Tadbīr Aḥkām al-Siyāsa bi-Qaṣd al-Najāḥ*, LZF (Būlāq: Maṭba'at Ṣāhib al-Sa'āda, end of Rajab 1245 / January 1830), 18.

36. Ibid., 34–41.

37. Ibid.

38. Ibid., 61–76.

39. 'Abd al-Rḥamān al-Rāfi'ī, *'Aṣr Muḥammad 'Alī*, 4th ed. (Cairo: Dar al-Ma'ārif, 1982), 386–88.

40. This was his title in LZF, 58.

41. *Al-Awāmir wa-l-Mukātabāt*, 341; Sāmy, *Taqwīm al-Nīl*, 375.

42. LZF, 58–60.

43. Sāmy, *Taqwīm al-Nīl*, 335.

44. *Al-Awāmir wa-l-Mukātabāt*, 253.

45. LZF, 20.

46. Ibid., 18.

47. Sāmy, *Taqwīm al-Nīl*, 360; al-Jabartī, *'Ajā'ib al-Āthār*, 419.

48. See, e.g., Bedouin Shaykhs' Law on Ṣafar 23, 1249, in al-Jabartī, *'Ajā'ib al-Āthār*, 413; and 'Abd al-Raḥman Bey's Regulation on Rabī' al-Awwal 7, 1253 / June 12, 1837, in Helal, *Wathā'iq al-Tashrī'*, 221–22, 462–63.

49. Sāmy, *Taqwīm al-Nīl*, 353.

50. Helal, *Wathā'iq al-Tashrī'*, 249.

51. Ibid.

52. DWQ, Diwān al-Khidīwī, Sijill Qayd al-Khulāṣāt Turkī, no. 12, archival code 0004-000751, 1–2, and no. 23, code 0004-000762, 12–14; Sāmy, *Taqwīm al-Nīl*, 354; Zaghlūl, *al-Muḥmāh*, 163–64; Peters, "For His Correction," 164–92.

53. *Al-Awāmir wa-l-Mukātabāt*, 276; Sāmy, *Taqwīm al-Nīl*, 356.

54. LZF, 61.

55. Sāmy, *Taqwīm al-Nīl*, 362.

56. LZF, 63, 65, 68, 70.

57. Helal, *Wathā'iq al-Tashrī'*, 295.

58. DWQ, Diwān al-Khidīwī, Sijill Qayd al-Khulāṣāt Turkī, no. 23, code 0004-000762, 15–17.

59. Emad Ahmad Helal, *al-Baghāyya fī Miṣr: Dirāsa Tārīkhiyya Ijtimā'iyya, 1834–1949* (Cairo: al-'Arabī for Publishing, 2001), 157.

60. Helal, *Wathā'iq al-Tashrī'*, 107–8.

61. Sāmy, *Taqwīm al-Nīl*, 431.

62. Emad Ahmad Helal, "al-Siyāsat-Nāmah al-Thāniyya, Ṣafḥa Majhūla min Tārīkh al-Tashrī' al-Jinā'ī fī 'Aṣr Muḥammad 'Alī, " *al-Ruznāmah* VIII (2010): 249–303.

63. Ibid., 59–70; Zaghlūl, *al-Muḥmāh*, 4–26 Mulḥaqāt.

64. *Al-Awāmir wa-l-Mukātabāt*, 347–49.

65. Sālim, *al-Niẓām al-Qaḍā'ī*, 16.

66. Filīb Jallād, *Qāmūs al-Idāra wa-l-Qaḍā'*, vol. III (Alexandria: Maṭba'at Yanny Lāghudāks, 1895), 359–60; Zaghlūl, *al-Muhmāh*, 116–17 Mulḥaqāt.

67. Jallād, *Qāmūs al-Idāra*, 361–63; Zaghlūl, *al-Muhmāh*, 119–24 Mulḥaqāt.

68. Jallād, *Qāmūs al-Idāra*, 360–61; Zaghlūl, *al-Muhmāh*, 117–19 Mulḥaqāt.

69. Jallād, *Qāmūs al-Idāra*, 365; Zaghlūl, *al-Muhmāh*, 129 Mulḥaqāt.

70. Helal, *Wathā'iq al-Tashrī'*, 367.

71. Jallād, *Qāmūs al-Idāra*, 367; Zaghlūl, *al-Muhmāh*, 132 Mulḥaqāt.

72. Jallād, *Qāmūs al-Idāra*, 367; Zaghlūl, *al-Muhmāh*, 129–30 Mulḥaqāt.

73. *Lā'iḥat Waẓā'if Diwān Shūra al-Mu'āwana* (Cairo: Maṭba'at Būlāq al-Amīriyya, 1259/1843).

74. Jallād, *Qāmūs al-Idāra*, 363–64; Zaghlūl, *al-Muhmāh*, 124–27 Mulḥaqāt; Shiḥāta, *Tārīkh Ḥarakat al-Tajdīd*, 106.

75. Jallād, *Qāmūs al-Idāra*, 364–65; Zaghlūl, *al-Muhmāh*, 127 Mulḥaqāt.

76. Jallād, *Qāmūs al-Idāra*, 375; Zaghlūl, *al-Muhmāh*, 150 Mulḥaqāt.

77. *Qānūn al-Jafālik* (Cairo: Maṭba'at Būlāq al-Amīriyya, 1259/1843); Baer, "Tanzimat in Egypt," 26.

78. Jallād, *Qāmūs al-Idāra*, 367; Zaghlūl, *al-Muhmāh*, 133 Mulḥaqāt.

79. Jallād, *Qāmūs al-Idāra*, 365; Zaghlūl, *al-Muhmāh*, 127–28 Mulḥaqāt.

80. Jallād, *Qāmūs al-Idāra*, 368–69; Zaghlūl, *al-Muhmāh*, 135 Mulḥaqāt.

81. Jallād, *Qāmūs al-Idāra*, 366; Zaghlūl, *al-Muhmāh*, 130–31 Mulḥaqāt.

82. Jallād, *Qāmūs al-Idāra*, 367–68; Zaghlūl, *al-Muhmāh*, 133–34 Mulḥaqāt.

83. Jallād, *Qāmūs al-Idāra*, 368; Zaghlūl, *al-Muhmāh*, 134–35 Mulḥaqāt.

84. Jallād, *Qāmūs al-Idāra*, 369; Zaghlūl, *al-Muhmāh*, 163–37 Mulḥaqāt.

85. Jallād, *Qāmūs al-Idāra*, 375–76; Zaghlūl, *al-Muhmāh*, 150–51 Mulḥaqāt.

86. Jallād, *Qāmūs al-Idāra*, 375–76; Zaghlūl, *al-Muhmāh*, 150–51 Mulḥaqāt.

87. Jallād, *Qāmūs al-Idāra*, 376–78; Zaghlūl, *al-Muhmāh*, 152–55 Mulḥaqāt.

88. See its full text in: Jallād, 359–78; Zaghlūl, *al-Muhmāh*, 100–55 Mulḥaqāt.

89. Baer, "Tanzimat in Egypt," 32.

90. Sāmy, *Taqwīm al-Nīl*, part III, vol. I (Cairo: Dār al-Kutub al-Miṣriyya, 1355/1936), 22.

91. DWQ, MBA, register no. Sīn7/1/1, archival code 0020-000751, p. 69, doc. 86, in Sha'bān 14, 1265 / July 5, 1849.

92. Ibid., p. 156, docs. 63, 64, in Sha'bān 13–14, 1265 / July 4–5, 1849.

93. Helal, *Wathā'iq al-Tashrī'*, 384.

94. DWQ, MBA, archival code 0020-000001, p. 83, doc. 47, p. 104, doc. 3. 1265.

95. Baer, "Tanzimat in Egypt," 38.

96. *Qānūn-Nāmah al-Sultānī* (Cairo: Maṭba'at Būlāq al-Amīriyya, fī Awā'il Rabī' al-Ākhar, 1271 / late December 1854).

97. DWQ, MBA, register no. sīn7/29/4, p. 2, doc. 317, p. 6, doc. 331, 1271/1855.

98. *Qānūn-Nāmah al-Sultānī*; Baer, "Tanzimat in Egypt," 38–44.

99. Helal, *Wathā'iq al-Tashrī'*, 67–68.

100. Shiḥāta, *Tārīkh Ḥarakat al-Tajdīd*, 63; Sālim, *al-Niẓām al-Qaḍā'ī*, 24.

101. *Qānūn al-'Uqūbāt al-Ṣadir 'Alayhi al-Amr al-'Āly al-Mu'arrakh 13 Muḥarram 1301 (13 November 1883) wa-Ta'dīlātuh* (Cairo: Maṭba'at Būlāq al-Amīriyya, 1896).

BIBLIOGRAPHY

Amos, Maurice S. "Legal Administration in Egypt." *Journal of Comparative Legislation and International Law* 12, no. 4 (1930): 168–87.

Baer, Gabriel. "Tanzimat in Egypt, the Penal Code." *Bulletin of the School of Oriental and African Studies* 26, no. 1 (1963): 29–49.

Baer, Gabriel. "The Transition from Traditional to Western Criminal Law in Turkey and Egypt." *Studia Islamica* 45 (1977): 139–58.

Brown, Nathan J. *The Rule of Law in the Arab World: Courts in Egypt and the Gulf.* Cambridge: Cambridge University Press, 1997.

Cannon, Byron. *Politics of Law and the Courts in Nineteenth Century Egypt.* Salt Lake City: University of Utah Press, 1988.

Fahmy, Khaled. "The Anatomy of Justice: Forensic Medicine and Criminal Law in Nineteenth Century Egypt." *Islamic Law and Society* 6 (1999): 224–71.

Fahmy, Khaled. "Justice, Law and Pain in Khedival Egypt." In *Standing Trial: Law and the Person in the Modern Middle East*, edited by Baudouin Dupret, 85–116. London: I. B. Tauris, 2004.

Helal, Emad Ahmad. *al-Fallāh wa-l-Sulta wa-l-Qānūn.* Cairo: Dār al-Kutub wa-l-Wathāʾiq al-Qawmiyya, 2007.

Helal, Emad Ahmad. *Wathāʾiq al-Tashrīʿ al-Jināʾī al-Miṣrī, Sijill Majmūʿ Umūr Jināʾiyya.* Silsilat Dirāsāt Wathāʾiqiyya, vol. 3. Cairo: Dār al-Wathāʾiq al Qawmiyya, 2011.

Hill, Enid. "Courts and the Administration of Justice in the Modern Era." In *The State and Its Servants: Administration in Egypt from Ottoman Times to the Present*, edited by Nelly Hanna, 98–116. Cairo: American University in Cairo Press, 1995.

Kramers, J. H. "Droit islamique et droit de l'islam." *Archives de l'Histoire du Droit Oriental* I (1937): 401–14.

El-Nahal, Galal H. *The Judicial Administration of Ottoman Egypt in the Seventeenth Century.* Minneapolis: Bibliotheca Islamica, 1979.

Peters, Rudolph. *Crime and Punishment in Islamic Law: Theory and Practice from the Sixteenth to the Twenty-First Century.* Cambridge: Cambridge University Press, 2005.

Peters, Rudolph. *Shariʿa Justice and Legal Order, Egyptian and Islamic Law: Selected Essays.* Leiden: Brill, 2020.

Sālim, Latīfa Muḥammad. *Al-Niẓām al-Qaḍāʾī al-Miṣrī al-Hadīth, 1875–1914*, vol. I. Cairo: Markaz al-Dirāsāt al-Siyāsiyya wa-l-Istrātijiyya bi al-Ahrām, 1984.

Shihāta, Shafīq. *Tārīkh Ḥarakat al-Tajdīd fī al-Nuẓum al-Qānūniyya fī Miṣr Munẓu ʿAṣr Muḥammad ʿAlī.* Cairo: Dār Iḥyāʾ al-Kutub al-ʿArabiyya, 1961.

Toledano, Ehud R. "Law, Practice, and Social Reality: A Theft Case in Cairo, 1854." In *Studies in Islamic Society: Contributions in Memory of Gabriel Baer*, edited by G. R. Warburg and G. Gilbar, 153–74. Haifa, Israel: Haifa University Press, 1984.

Zaghlūl, Aḥmad Fatḥy. *al-Muḥmāh.* Cairo: Maṭbaʿat al-Maʿārif, 1900.

....

CHAPTER 13

MARRIAGE AND FAMILY BETWEEN THE MID-NINETEENTH AND EARLY TWENTY-FIRST CENTURIES

....

KENNETH M. CUNO

DURING the late nineteenth and early twentieth centuries, the ideal of the modern conjugal family gained currency in Egypt. Initially promoted by modernist intellectuals and then taken up in the burgeoning periodical press, this family form consisted of a monogamous couple and their children in an independent household. Since at least the 1940s, it has been signaled by the term *usra*.[1] The conjugal family ideal (if not always the reality) eclipsed the extended patrilineal family and the multifamily or joint household among the upper and middle classes. There was a parallel transformation in marriage practices, such as an upper-class trend toward monogamy, an increase in the age of marriage for both sexes, and, after World War I, a preference for neolocal households among young married couples. The conjugal family ideal gained even more social influence after the war, with the expansion of education, the further development of publishing, and, later, radio, film, and television.

Male 'ulama' and politicians influenced by the Islamic modernist ideas of Muhammad 'Abduh (Grand Mufti 1899–1905) carried out the initial stage of codification of the personal status law governing marriage and divorce in the 1920s. The personal status law is based on religious law, which empowers fathers and husbands over female and minor male relations. Changing it has been difficult because of the sensitivity of issues of family and religion. Political polarization, the anticolonial struggle, revolution, and wars delayed further reform of the personal status law until the last quarter of the twentieth century, when female advocates of women's rights promoted it in the face of stiff resistance from social and religious conservatives. Reformers and conservatives alike appealed to the welfare of the conjugal family within a larger discursive context of "marriage crisis," which is not only about the family. The conjugal family is now regarded as the bedrock of society; hence, the nation's well-being depends upon the stability and soundness of family life. Secularists and Islamists alike raise alarms over the cost of marriage, delays of marriage or nonmarriage, informal and clandestine "religious" (*urfi*) marriages, and divorce that supposedly reflect the corrosive effects of urban life, popular culture, and foreign influence.

THE LATE OTTOMAN PERIOD

Handbooks on marriage and marital relations, composed by 'ulama' for the guidance of judges and husbands, circulated in manuscript form during the Ottoman era, and several were printed in the late nineteenth and early twentieth centuries.[2] In addition to listing the legal essentials of marriage—a bride and groom free to marry, a properly worded contract, qualified guardians, an agreed bridal gift or dower (*mahr* or *sadaq*), and qualified witnesses—this literature also listed the obligations of the spouses toward one another, in what Nadia Sonneveld has called "the maintenance–obedience relationship."[3] Upon payment of a portion of the dower, and provided the bride was physically mature enough for sexual relations, her husband was due her obedience, which included residing with him and not leaving the marital home without his permission, as well as sexual submission. For his part, the husband owed his wife and their children maintenance (*nafaqa*), which included the provision of food, clothing, and appropriate housing.

Some handbooks offered additional guidance on how to achieve good marital relations. They encouraged guardians to allow prenuptial meetings between a prospective bride and groom, with her face and hands uncovered, to enable them to develop some congeniality. A young woman should not be married off to a much older man, in the interest of compatibility.[4] The handbooks left no doubt about the authority of the husband, comparing the wife to a slave or a prisoner, as she was in the custody (*'isma*) of her husband, and emphasized the ability of the husband to enjoy his wife (*milk al-muta'*) and to confine her to the home (*milk al-hubs*). Husbands, however, were encouraged to treat their wives with kindness, not correct them harshly, and so on.[5]

Women or their marriage guardians could mitigate this regime of male authority during prenuptial negotiations by inserting specific stipulations into the marriage contract. The most common stipulations deterred the husband from marrying additional wives or taking slave concubines, either by making divorce conditional on those actions (*ta'liq al-talaq*) or by delegating the prerogative of repudiation to the wife (*tafwid al-talaq*). In the latter case, she was said to have custody of herself (*'ismatuha fi yadiha*). Other common stipulations included the bride's ability to live near her family, to visit outside the home and receive visitors, and to maintain contact with children from a former marriage.[6]

The operation of the Shari'a courts also allowed for flexibility in the application of the norms of marriage and divorce. Hanafi chief judges presided, along with deputy judges representing the other Sunni schools of law, which permitted women and men to venue shop for the most advantageous doctrine.[7] For example, the Hanafi school allowed an adult woman to arrange and contract her own marriage, while the others required this to be done by a marriage guardian (*wali al-nikah*). The Hanbali school permitted stipulations to be written directly into the marriage contract, while the Hanafi and Maliki schools allowed equivalent conditions to be included in separate agreements. Men could divorce their wives at will by repudiation (*talaq*), which entailed payment of the delayed portion of her dower, continued maintenance for a waiting period of three months, during which a pregnancy would become apparent, and child maintenance. *Talaq* pronounced once or twice resulted in a revocable divorce. *Talaq* pronounced three times was final, as was a revocable divorce not rescinded in ninety days. Women had to persuade a judge to divorce them from their husbands for cause. The only cause recognized by the Hanafi school was impotence, which was nearly impossible to prove, but the Maliki and Shafi'i schools allowed women to obtain a divorce for desertion, non-support, or abusive treatment. Maliki judges would also divorce a couple for incompatibility, only after exhausting all possibility of reconciliation. Women had two other options: *mubara'a* and *khul'*. In the former, a woman offered to give up some of her financial compensation to induce her husband to repudiate her; in the latter, she gave up the delayed portion of the dower and/or the temporary maintenance she was due.[8]

In the handbooks and in Muslim jurisprudence, marriage was necessary for procreation and licit sexual activity. This literature privileged the extended patrilineal family over the conjugal family by providing for a regime of separate property in marriage and by favoring male agnates in inheritance. It exempted women from housework and childcare if they were unwilling to perform it;[9] servants and slaves carried out those tasks in the families that could afford them. Polygyny and the ease with which men divorced made marital instability the norm; incomplete data from around the turn of the twentieth century indicate a crude divorce rate of between three and five per thousand population.[10]

RE-IMAGINING THE FAMILY

Modernist intellectuals in Egypt and other Ottoman provinces began to articulate a family ideology in the second half of the nineteenth century. Drawing on post-Enlightenment European social science, and in dialogue with premodern writings, they identified the conjugal family as the basic unit in society, especially as the site where the intellect and character of children—the future of the nation—were formed. Consequently, the modernists advocated monogamy and discouraged divorce, out of a belief that harmony and stability in conjugal family life provided the best environment for childrearing. Moreover, they invested mothers with the vocation of early childhood

care, a task that required the education of women. Rifa'a Rafi' al-Tahtawi, a career government servant, educator, and translator who had studied in France, became an advocate of universal elementary education for girls and boys.[11] The education of girls was
to prepare them for a domestic role, not employment outside the home. In addition,
he wrote, educated women would more easily become companionate wives, ensuring
the harmony and stability of families. 'Ali Mubarak, also an educator who had studied
in France, voiced the same concerns.[12] Later in the century, religious modernists like
Jamal al-Din al-Afghani and his student Muhammad 'Abduh also wrote of women's
education as necessary for them to fulfil their role as housekeepers and mothers.[13] As
mufti, 'Abduh advocated reforms in the family law to strengthen the cohesion of conjugal families, such as discouraging easy divorce by men and restricting polygyny, which
he saw as destructive of family life and a cause of divorce. 'Abduh believed that the misbehavior of men caused many problems in family life, and so he proposed measures to
enable the courts to enforce the payment of maintenance more effectively and to enable
women to obtain a divorce due to nonsupport, desertion, or abusive behavior.[14]

Female intellectuals also emphasized the misbehavior of men. 'A'isha al-Taymur
(1840–1902) asserted that many men were lazy and married for money, shirking their
duty to support their wives. This, she suggested, ought to free a married woman of
the obligation of obedience.[15] The journalist Zaynab Fawwaz wrote in 1905 that men
often deserted their wives and children in favor of a second wife, leaving the former
destitute.[16] Malak Hifni Nasif, a teacher turned essayist under the pen name Bahithat
al-Badiya, complained of dissolute dandies who acquired girlfriends instead of marrying and of the rude behavior of men toward women in public space.[17] These women
agreed with the male modernists' advocacy of women's education and their domestic
ideology, though Fawwaz and Nasif believed that women ought to be able to enter the
professions as well.[18]

The family ideology developed by the women writers and male modernists
anticipated the arguments in *Tahrir al-Mar'a* (The Emancipation of Women, 1899),
by Qasim Amin.[19] Amin restated the importance of the conjugal family for childrearing, the need for family stability and companionate relations, and the importance
of women's education. More controversially, he argued that women need not cover
their hands and faces in public and that they could be in the presence of unrelated
men for a chaste purpose such as education and business and legal affairs.[20] *Tahrir al-
Mar'a* sparked a debate mainly among male intellectuals over the face-veil, critics of
the custom associating it with backwardness while apologists defended it as intrinsic
to Egyptian culture. Women who discussed the issue treated it in less abstract terms.
Nasif opined that women needed to cover in public because men were not yet ready
for them to uncover.[21]

The full development of a family ideology that embraced the conjugal family ideal
and women's domesticity coincided with the era of the British occupation. However,
Egyptian family ideology was a hybrid that also incorporated the maintenance–
obedience relationship. Its construction began well before the occupation. French-
language works were the main vector of European influence.[22] Modernist intellectuals,

women and men, regarded reform of the family as a key to social improvement and national advancement.

CHANGES IN MARRIAGE AND FAMILY FORMATION

Contingent political and social developments favored changes in the family system, especially in the upper and middle classes, and abetted the development of a family ideology. Khedive Isma'il (r. 1863–79) had four contractual wives of slave origin and multiple concubines, but in 1873, he abandoned this Ottoman ruling-class tradition and opted instead for royal endogamy, marrying off Crown Prince Tawfiq and three younger children to members of the extended khedival family. Seven years earlier, the sultan's decree of primogeniture had made Tawfiq the heir apparent, earning him and his father the enmity of the two princes formerly next in line under the old system of succession of the eldest. Isma'il's strategy of royal endogamy aimed to shore up support for the succession of Tawfiq within the extended khedival family. In Ottoman ruling-class culture, a man who married a princess did not take additional wives or concubines. Thus, Khedive Tawfiq (r. 1879–92) became Egypt's first monogamous ruler, and henceforward the khedival family set a public example of monogamy. Europeans praised this change and noted the "irreproachable" domestic lives of later rulers and other monogamous members of the ruling class. Isma'il and Tawfiq allowed them to believe that they had embraced this aspect of Western civilization.[23]

Ruling-class monogamy may have increased in those decades. Just as marriage to a princess entailed monogamy due to her family's status, so did marriage to freeborn daughters of the ruling and upper classes, who, in the late nineteenth century, were educated. Other families insisted on stipulations deterring the husbands of their daughters from marrying additional wives or taking concubines. Concubinage became obsolete after the Anglo-Egyptian convention ended the slave trade, which applied to the traffic in Africans in 1877 and Circassians in 1884. The suppression of the slave trade also meant that middle- and working-class men could no longer purchase a woman for domestic labor and sexual relations in lieu of a contractual wife. The importation of African slaves, most of them women, peaked in the 1860s, and the rate of polygyny (including concubinage) likely did so in that decade as well.[24]

The commonplace assumption that urban upper-class families mainly practiced polygyny is not supported by census data, which show that in the mid-nineteenth century, in the village registers sampled, some 8 to 9% of married men were polygynous, as opposed to fewer than 3% in Cairo. In the villages, polygyny and slave ownership correlated with relatively large landholdings and large multiple-family households, but some working-class men could "afford" plural marriages, evidently because their wives worked, contributing to their own upkeep.[25]

Despite the efforts of Muhammad 'Abduh and the others inspired by him in the early twentieth century, polygyny remains unrestricted in Egypt. However, the writings of the modernists, the example of the khedival family, and the presentation of the conjugal family as a modern ideal in the periodical press turned polygyny into an object of disapproval. The press, which flourished from the last quarter of the nineteenth century, contributed to the formation of a public sphere in which these changing attitudes occurred. The domestic life of Tawfiq's son and successor, Khedive 'Abbas Hilmi II (r. 1892–1914), offers evidence of this change. 'Abbas married a second wife in 1910, but the palace did not reveal his polygyny to protect his public image.[26]

Age at marriage is an important factor in the system of marriage and family formation. The mid-nineteenth-century census registers show that in Cairo, men as well as women married at an earlier age than in the villages sampled. More than half of Cairene women were married before the age of 15, and men before the age of 20. In the villages, both sexes married five or more years later.[27] Early marriage correlated with wealth in urban and rural society; the choice of partner reflected considerations of status and a desire to preserve the family's wealth, especially landed property. The future feminist leader Huda Sha'rawi, who inherited extensive lands from her late father, was married to her much older cousin at the age of thirteen to forestall an offer of marriage from the khedival family.[28] Al-Sha'rawi had to be persuaded to do so for the good of her family, but if the father or grandfather of a minor child (younger than fifteen) was alive, they could betroth him or her legally without need of their consent. The trauma of child marriage experienced by al-Sha'rawi and other upper-class women, along with an international campaign to ban it, led to the enactment of a minimum marriage age in 1923—sixteen for women and eighteen for men.[29] However, a dramatic rise in the age at marriage for both sexes began well before then and was especially marked in urban society. It was not attributable to ideational factors, as it occurred across society, most of which was still illiterate.[30]

The rising age at marriage occurred in tandem with the spread of the conjugal family ideal, and both contributed to the obsolescence of large multiple-family households, which were typical of the urban upper class before World War I. The conjugal family ideal made neolocal marriage desirable and an accoutrement of a modern lifestyle. Patrilocal marriage became less likely in the middle and upper classes as young men delayed marriage to finish their schooling and get started in a career. Delayed marriage among professional men even led to editorial warnings about a "marriage crisis" in the 1920s and 1930s.[31]

The influence on social behavior of the family ideology and its corollaries, the conjugal family ideal and women's domesticity, is an example of what Arland Thornton has called "developmental idealism," the association of a particular family form and culture with "the good life," including wealth and societal advance.[32] However, the contingent political and sociodemographic developments of the late nineteenth century occurred independently of ideational change. In the postwar era, as the educational system and the media expanded, the message of developmental idealism was promoted more widely.

REORGANIZATION OF THE SHARI'A COURTS AND CODIFICATION OF FAMILY LAW

New laws governing the organization and procedures of the Shari'a courts in the nineteenth century produced two significant changes in the application of family law.[33] First, the old system of legal pluralism was abolished by at least the 1840s, and Hanafi jurisprudence was made the sole doctrine upon which cases would be decided. This made the law more uniform, but the exclusive use of Hanafi law disadvantaged married women. They could not petition the court for a divorce even in nonsupport, desertion, or abuse cases. A missing husband was presumed to be alive into his nineties, and so his wife could not remarry. Arrears of unpaid maintenance did not become a debt against the husband unless the rate was set by a judge or in a formal agreement. The second change was the progressive introduction of documentation. Civil registration of marriage and divorce, performed by a registrar (*ma'dhun*), became the norm by the end of the century, and the law of the organization of the Shari'a courts of 1897 instructed the courts not to hear a posthumous claim of marriage or divorce unless it was supported by documentary evidence. Marriages, divorces, and other contracts done the old way in front of notary-witnesses were certified by the courts in documentary form upon the testimony of the witnesses. Although marriages and divorces done out of court were not outlawed, the need for documentation for legal enforcement discouraged informal, extrajudicial arrangements.[34]

In 1875, Muhammad Qadri Pasha published a Hanafi family law reference manual for use in the newly created Mixed Courts.[35] This manual was organized in the manner of the French code, with numbered sections and articles for ease of use. Although it was not enacted as law, Qadri's manual quickly acquired semiofficial status as a "code" of Muslim family law. It was used to teach Muslim family law in the khedival School of Law, along with an explication written by the course instructor. The School of Law taught mainly French law, which was the basis of Mixed Law and the various codes administered in the National Courts organized in 1883. Most of the secular leadership of Egypt in the late nineteenth and early twentieth centuries graduated from the School of Law, where their sole exposure to Muslim family law was in the form of Qadri's manual. Qadri introduced the term personal status (*al-ahwal al-shakhsiyya*, a translation of *statut personnel*) into the Egyptian legal lexicon. The term had only recently begun to be used in colonial Algeria, where a Shari'a-based family law continued to be applied to Muslims within an otherwise French legal system. The Egyptian situation was similar insofar as the issuance of French-inspired law codes reduced the jurisdiction of the Shari'a courts to family and religious law, and the Shari'a courts operated within an overall civil law system.[36]

The idea of codifying Muslim family law arose in the 1890s out of dissatisfaction with the state of application of the uncodified law. Muhammad 'Abduh conducted a study of the Shari'a courts and concluded that the courts needed a more effective system of

ensuring that their decisions were carried out.[37] He identified the irresponsible behavior of men as a prime cause of family problems. They often failed to provide maintenance for their wives and children. If a woman navigated the cumbersome legal system
successfully and won a lawsuit to recover the arrears of maintenance she was due, her
husband could resort to various ruses to avoid payment. Men also married second wives
without the means to support even their first wife. Often, these situations ended in divorce. 'Abduh worried that an unsupported and unsupervised divorcée posed the risk of
immoral behavior.[38] The destitution of women whose husbands had gone missing in the
wars in Crimea, Ethiopia, and Sudan raised the same specter of immorality for another
writer, who noted that the Maliki and Shafi'i schools of jurisprudence allowed a judge to
declare a man deceased if he went missing without a trace for four years but that Hanafi
law offered no such relief to the wives of missing men.[39] In a similar vein, 'Abduh, as
mufti, called for the use of Maliki jurisprudence to enable women in bad marriages—
unsupported, deserted, or abused—to petition a judge for a divorce, something not
permitted in Hanafi law.[40] The memory of the old Ottoman system of legal pluralism
seems to have been behind these proposals.

The codification of Muslim family law began in the next generation. A committee of
senior 'ulama' drafted what became Law No. 25 of 1920 Concerning the Legal Rules of
Maintenance and Some Questions of Personal Status.[41] It mainly addressed the problem
of enforcing maintenance payments and reflected the ideas of 'Abduh by incorporating
Maliki jurisprudence to make unpaid maintenance accrue automatically as a debt
against the husband. The wages and property of the delinquent husband could be
garnished for payment, but if the husband lacked the resources to pay or was absent, the
judge was authorized to divorce the couple. This law also authorized judges to declare a
man gone missing for four years to be deceased, thereby enabling his widow to collect
her share of his estate and remarry.

Law No. 56 of 1923, setting the minimum age of marriage for women and men at sixteen and eighteen, in effect discouraged the forced marriage of minors (less than fifteen
years old). This law, like the law requiring civil registration of marriages and divorces,
did not ban child marriage outright. Rather, it instructed the courts not to hear cases
involving a marriage in which one of the spouses was underage at the time of the contract. Such wording, according to the historical interpretation, sidestepped the question
of human legislators outlawing that which is permitted in divine revelation. Three years
later, the Ministry of Justice ordered the prosecution of persons who gave false testimony regarding the age of marriage.[42]

Law No. 25 of 1929 Concerning Certain Rules of Personal Status addressed some of
the ills identified by 'Abduh in the law of divorce.[43] It rendered null any declaration of
conditional divorce, as well as repudiations pronounced by men accidentally, while
inebriated, or in anger. A triple repudiation declared at one time would now count as a
single, revocable divorce. To be final, a repudiation had to be pronounced three times
with intervals, or as part of a negotiated settlement (*khul'* or *mubara'a*). This law also
expanded women's access to divorce, once again drawing on Maliki jurisprudence to
enable them to petition a judge for a divorce in the case of marital difficulties and

harm suffered in the marriage. The wives of absent and imprisoned men could also request a divorce.

In drafting these laws, legislators adopted the method of selection (*takhayyur*) among the differing legal rules of the four Sunni schools of jurisprudence to achieve the desired result. They stretched this method a bit with the citation of very early jurists to set minimum marriage ages. Yet with these specific exceptions, Hanafi jurisprudence continued to be the basis of Muslim family law. The nineteenth-century laws governing the organization and procedures of the Shariʿa courts specified that in matters not directly addressed by legislation, judges should follow the predominant view in Hanafi jurisprudence. That rule was reiterated in Law No. 78 of 1931 on the organization of the Shariʿa courts, and it has remained a feature of the personal status laws to the present.

The Christian and Jewish Communities

The belief that family law ought to derive from religious law was an artifact of the colonial era, during which the jurisdiction of the Shariʿa was restricted to religious and family law. Colonial administrators, Orientalist scholars, and Muslim religious authorities viewed family law as the "core" or "heart" of the Shariʿa. Colonial officials and, eventually, nationalists believed that the indigenous culture could be safeguarded and the social order maintained by leaving the regulation of the family to local customary and religious law.[44]

The same logic applied to Egypt's Christian and Jewish communities, which had inherited Ottoman-era communal courts that administered their family affairs. Prior to the mid-nineteenth century, during the era of legal pluralism in the Shariʿa courts, Egypt's Christians and Jews resorted to the Shariʿa courts whenever doing so suited their purposes, whether in business or family affairs. Christians of all social strata sometimes registered their marriages as contracts in the Shariʿa courts, declaring their acceptance of the application of Shariʿa to their marriage, and included stipulations like those in Muslim marriage contracts. By doing so, they reserved the option of divorce.[45] After 1856, Christian and Jewish communal courts supposedly had exclusive jurisdiction in personal status cases within their communities when the spouses were of the same denomination. Thus, some Christians and Jews desiring to divorce and remarry availed themselves of the Shariʿa courts by converting to a different denomination within their own faith or to Islam so that Islamic law would apply to their case.

The most vexed issue for Christians was divorce. Coptic law originally permitted divorce only on the ground of adultery, but the medieval Church expanded the causes of divorce to forestall venue shopping and conversion. A code of Coptic law produced in 1896 included multiple grounds for divorce. Nevertheless, in the early twentieth century, Christian men still converted to Islam to be able to divorce their wives by repudiation or to marry a second wife, and some Christians and Jews repudiated their wives in the Shariʿa courts without converting. Law No. 78 of 1931 intended to end this practice by prohibiting the Shariʿa courts from hearing a divorce suit by a non-Muslim against their spouse unless the religious law of both spouses permitted divorce. However, as late as 1952, the Shariʿa court in al-Fayum province allowed a Coptic man to repudiate his wife.[46]

Intramural Coptic politics added to the controversy surrounding the question of divorce. In 1874, a group of prominent lay Copts secured khedival approval for an elected Community Council (al-Majlis al-Milli), which they intended to take the leading role in the supervision of church finances and schools, and personal status matters, thereby reducing the authority of the clergy in nonspiritual affairs. After a brief period of cooperation, there ensued a decades-long struggle between the clergy and lay leadership, the main issues being who spoke for the Coptic community, control of the religious foundations (waqfs), and administration of Coptic personal status law in the communal courts.[47] The lay leadership achieved its greatest influence under the monarchy. They had the most say in the substance of Coptic Orthodox law and in the appointment of judges to the Coptic communal courts. Following earlier precedents, the Supreme Community Council issued a new code of Coptic family law in 1938. In it, the grounds for divorce were adultery; apostasy; the disappearance of a spouse for five years; a prison term of at least seven years; serious illness, mental illness, or impotence; domestic violence; immoral or debauched behavior; mistreatment leading to separation for three years; or a spouse joining a monastic order.[48]

In the Jewish community, the balance of power was even more in favor of the lay leadership over the rabbis. Despite dissatisfaction with communal family law, however, the lay leadership was unable to revise it. Jewish courts in Alexandria and Cairo handled all manner of family law cases, but during the 1930s, the rabbinate court of Alexandria and the Karaite[49] court in Cairo lacked official recognition, and so the Shariʿa courts heard the personal status cases of the Jews of those communities. Owing to these circumstances, and due to the rabbis' relative lack of power, it was not unusual for Jews to have recourse to the Shariʿa courts, out of necessity or in pursuit of more favorable outcomes than were available in the Jewish courts, in such issues as maintenance and child custody. A certain number of Jewish women converted to Islam to escape unsatisfactory marriages.[50]

At the beginning of the twentieth century, fifteen officially recognized religious communities followed nine family laws.[51] These multiple jurisdictions were, on the one hand, a legacy of the Ottoman millet system, which had accorded communal autonomy to the empire's non-Muslim subjects. On the other hand, the persistence of that system, along with the Mixed Courts and numerous consular courts, was also a colonial legacy. Nationalist reformers sought to unify the personal status laws in the 1930s and 1940s, but they failed due to the resistance of Jewish and Christian communal leaders. A step toward unifying the judicial system came pursuant to the Anglo-Egyptian Treaty of 1936, which provided for the phasing out of the extraterritorial legal status of foreign nationals, and with it the Mixed Courts and the consular courts, by 1948. Following the overthrow of the monarchy and the consolidation of Gamal Abdel Nasser's power as president of the new republic (1954–70), Law No. 462 of 1955 on the Abolition of the

Shariʿa and Community Courts completed the unification of the judicial system. As of January 1, 1956, all personal status cases pending before the Shariʿa courts and the various communal courts were transferred to newly created personal status courts within the National Court system. Egyptian courts continue to apply the personal status laws of non-Muslims when the couple are of the same denomination, in cases of marriage and divorce. However, in guardianship, intestate succession, and bequests, Egyptians, regardless of religion, are subject to a uniform law derived from Hanafi jurisprudence.[52]

SOCIAL CHANGE AND PIECEMEAL REFORM

The middle decades of the twentieth century saw no further reforms to the personal status law despite significant urbanization, increased literacy, and the mass movement of women into the waged workforce and professions. Few families were ever able to conform to the ideal maintenance–obedience relationship in which men were supposed to support their family while the wife remained at home. Women in the working class and peasantry had always worked out of necessity. In the second half of the twentieth century, many middle-class women entered the professions, and all had to work to accumulate the funds for marriage, and after marriage to contribute to their household income.

In 1927, a draft revision of the personal status law that would have made polygyny subject to judicial approval, in keeping with ʿAbduh's ideas, was blocked by King Fuʾad (r. 1917–36). In 1945, a similar proposal was also blocked by conservative opposition.[53] Despite widespread social disapproval of polygyny and even criticism by some ʿulamaʾ, political leaders have been unwilling to restrict something expressly permitted in the historical interpretation of the Qurʾan. In 1907, census data indicate that some 6.6% of married Muslim men were polygynous, the proportion declining to less than 2% in 1986, though it may have risen again in the 1990s and 2000s to as much as 3%.[54] However, the census data do not reflect the rate at which men marry second wives because they sometimes do so before divorcing the first wife. In 1979, women acquired the ability to sue for divorce due to their husband's polygyny. The law requires the wife to be informed of a second marriage, but there is no penalty for concealing it. Alaa Al Aswany portrayed this abuse in *The Yacoubian Building* (2002), and other novelists have used polygyny to signal corruption and venality.

The Egyptian Feminist Union (EFU, est. 1923) advocated several reforms in family law, which it argued were compatible with Islam: a minimum marriage age; a longer period of child custody for divorcées; regulation of repudiation; restriction of polygyny; and an end to forced marital cohabitation (known as *bayt al-taʿa* or "house of obedience"). The legislation of the 1920s addressed only the first two concerns. The king's unwillingness to support further reform of the personal status law was consistent with his public stance as a defender of religion and likely also due to the EFU's ties with his nemesis, the Wafd Party. Resistance to reform also came from religious and social conservatives. Muhammad Rashid Rida, Muhammad ʿAbduh's principal collaborator at an earlier time, penned a popular book on women's rights that emphasized male leadership in the family and women's rights and duties within the domestic context. The Muslim Women's Association, founded by Zaynab al-Ghazali in 1936, emphasized female domesticity and insisted on the complementarity of women's and men's roles, a trope that continues to be central in Islamist writings.[55] All sides of the debate appealed to the now hegemonic family ideology, especially the role of women as mothers and homemakers and the importance of the conjugal family to the nation's future.

The revolutionary regime of Gamal Abdel Nasser introduced significant changes to the lives of women. The constitution of 1956 declared women and men to have equal public rights, including the rights to vote, stand for election, and hold public office; and the National Charter of 1962, which articulated the principles of Arab socialism, recognized women as equal to men. The regime encouraged women to pursue secondary and university educations and to enter the workforce and professions. Women were elected to parliament, and Nasser appointed the first female cabinet member. However, the constitution and National Charter also affirmed the family to be the elemental unit of society and committed the state to protecting it, along with motherhood and childhood.[56] Unstated was the perpetuation of inequality in the personal status law, derived from religious law.

As before, reformers approached the personal status law in a piecemeal manner, aiming, among other things, to guarantee a married woman's right to work, to discourage polygyny to reduce the incidence of divorce, and when divorce occurred, to extend the period of a divorcée's maintenance and strengthen her right to child custody and visitation. In the contentious debate over these issues, reformers and conservatives alike appealed to the welfare of the family. An official committee drafted these and other proposals, the only result being an administrative order to cease enforcement of *bayt al-ta'a*, which it described as injurious to the honor of women and a cause of family discord.[57] In Islamic jurisprudence, one of the principal obligations of a married woman is to restrict herself to the marital home, not leaving it without the permission of her husband. It was commonplace for a bride to run off to her family due to a quarrel or mistreatment, and these situations were often resolved through mediation or resulted in bargaining for a divorce. If a "disobedient" wife refused to return, her husband could obtain a judicial order of obedience against her, which exempted him from the obligation of maintenance during her absence. The law of 1897 permitted police enforcement of orders of obedience, a measure supported by Muhammad 'Abduh and others to preserve the integrity of the family. The decision to end enforcement of *bayt al-ta'a* after seventy years reflected the spread of an ideal of family relations based on affection, but it did not otherwise diminish the husband's authority or the principle of wifely obedience.[58]

President Anwar al-Sadat convened another committee to propose changes to the personal status law in the early 1970s, but the reforms stalled in parliament. To break the impasse, al-Sadat issued Law No. 44 of 1979 Modifying Certain Rules of the Personal Status Laws as an emergency decree while parliament was out of session. The most significant reform of the personal status law since the 1920s, it included provisions long advocated by women's rights advocates and liberals.[59] It required a man who pronounced a repudiation to register the divorce within thirty days, and if the wife was absent, the registrar was to inform her of it. This aimed to end the concealment of divorces by men seeking to avoid the payment of temporary maintenance. Now, also, a man who married was required to state his marital status on the marriage certificate. If married, the name of his first wife and her address were recorded. Within twelve months of being informed of her husband's second marriage, the first wife could petition for a divorce on the basis that polygyny caused her harm. This provision intended to curtail clandestine polygyny.

Law No. 44 eliminated the possibility of a return to the enforcement of obedience by making the suspension of maintenance the only consequence possible when a wife refused to live with her husband. It permitted a wife to leave home without the permission of her husband in the circumstances permitted in Shari'a jurisprudence, by custom, out of necessity, or to work, and not to lose maintenance, if that was stipulated in the marriage contract. If she left and refused to return, the law instructed the court to mediate the dispute and to initiate divorce proceedings if the wife so requested.

A wife divorced against her will and without cause was now entitled to compensation (*mut'a*) equivalent to two years' maintenance. A father remained responsible for his children's maintenance until girls were either married or self-supporting and until boys had finished their education or were self-supporting. The right of custody over minor children was granted to the mother, followed by her female relations, ahead of the father and his relations. The mother's right of custody ended when a boy turned ten, and a girl twelve, though a judge could rule it in the children's interest for them to remain in their mother's custody up to the age of fifteen for boys and until marriage for girls.

An especially controversial provision of the law required the father, after a divorce, to provide accommodation for his minor children and their female custodian (usually the mother). In most cases, this meant that they would remain in the family apartment. Men thought that unfair because the tradition was for men to pay for the apartment, including a large initial payment of "key money," while women paid for many of the furnishings. Thus, a divorced man with children would lose control of the apartment, in which he had invested a hefty sum, for the duration of his children's minority.

Critics of Law No. 44 disparaged it as "Jihan's law" because of the involvement of the wife of the president in supporting it,[60] though it contained provisions advocated since the 1960s and even earlier. In 1985, the Supreme Constitutional Court ruled that the promulgation of the law had been unconstitutional: there was no emergency to justify an emergency decree. Shortly afterward, President Husni Mubarak introduced and the parliament passed Law No. 100 of 1985 Amending Several Provisions of the Personal Status Laws, which was nearly identical to the previous law. The two differences were that polygyny was not an automatic cause for divorce, but rather the aggrieved wife had to prove in court that she suffered harm, and the husband was required to provide appropriate housing for his minor children and their female custodian, but it need not be his own apartment.[61]

In 2000, the government revised the printed marriage contract form in use since 1931 to include a blank space for the insertion of stipulations, such as restricting the husband's option of polygyny, guaranteeing the wife's right to work and/or to complete her education, and the like, which had been done routinely in the Ottoman period. The activists promoting this change had lobbied for a checklist of ten stipulations to be included in the form, which would have notified brides of their options, but the blank space was all that could be accomplished in the face of opposition from the religious establishment.[62]

That same year, parliament passed Law No. 1 of 2000 Regulating Litigation Procedures in Personal Status Affairs, known as the "*khul'* law" due to its most controversial provision. Historically, *khul'* involved the husband agreeing to repudiate his wife in exchange for her returning the advance portion of the dower and giving up her right to temporary maintenance. The new law enabled her to obtain a *khul'* unilaterally in court, without her husband's consent and without cause. This offered relief to women seeking to divorce but unable to prove adequate cause to a judge or to convince their husband to repudiate them. Proponents of the reform often cited a figure of 1.5 million women whose divorce suits were stalled in the courts.[63] Another provision in the draft law, omitted in the final version, would have permitted married women to travel without the permission of their husbands. However, in November 2000, the Supreme Constitutional Court invalidated the rule requiring a married woman to obtain the permission of her husband to be issued a passport.[64] Subsequently, the creation of a system of family courts in 2004 intended to provide an accessible, inexpensive, and efficient forum for resolving family disputes, including petitions for *khul'*. In 2005, divorcées gained the right to custody of their children until the age of fifteen,[65] and in 2008, the minimum age of marriage was raised to 18 for women.[66]

Notwithstanding women's participation in the discourse on family and marriage, early twentieth-century reforms to the personal status law were fashioned by male 'ulama' and politicians. In the 1920s, women organized to press for further reform but were resisted by social and religious conservatives backed by the palace. After 1952, the military regimes advanced women's status while curtailing independent women's rights organizations. Since the 1960s, women, often working within state-approved organizations, have had greater success in promoting family law reform. Due to tenacious conservative and religious opposition, they adopted a strategy of piecemeal reform that could be justified as strengthening the family while remaining in conformity with Shari'a. Further changes to the personal status law were in preparation on the eve of the overthrow of Mubarak in 2011. However, some of the proposed changes, like restricting men's right to polygyny and regulating repudiation, were mooted more than a century earlier.[67]

While divorce was always available to Muslim men and became somewhat more accessible to Muslim women after 2000, for Copts, it became more difficult. After 1952, the Church gained exclusive authority to represent the Coptic community in return for its support of the military regime, while the Community Council lost influence and was abolished in 1962.[68] The Church never accepted the 1938 family law, with its multiple causes of divorce, though the law was implemented by the courts. Pope Shenouda III refused to recognize divorces except in the case of adultery or apostasy, which prevented divorced Copts from remarrying within their own denomination. In 2008, the family law itself was amended to restrict the causes of divorce to adultery and apostasy.[69] Coptic men and women converted to another Christian domination or to Islam to be able to divorce and remarry, and the 2008 family law merely encouraged such "religion shopping."[70]

THE FAMILY IN CRISIS?

In the early twenty-first century, marriage continued to be highly valued and nearly universal, but most Egyptians believed their society faced a "marriage crisis" due to multiple causes discussed regularly in opinion columns and depicted in TV serials, films, and social media. A major subject of this discourse since the 1970s has been the high cost of marriage, which requires some couples to delay nuptials and work for years to accumulate the means to set up an independent household. Customarily, the groom pays for the apartment, and the bride provides the furnishings. Additional costs are a gift of jewelry to the bride, the bridal gown, and the public celebration. High youth unemployment and scarce affordable housing are said to contribute to the difficulty of financing a union.[71] However, surveys conducted between 1998 and 2012 show the cost of marriage to have declined significantly since the 1980s,[72] which may be when that impression was formed. Delay of marriage abated in the first decade of the twenty-first century, so couples were engaged for just over a year before marrying.[73]

Before World War I, fathers often negotiated the marriage of their children, and the couple would meet for the first time at their wedding. Nowadays young women and men are involved in selecting their spouse and get to know one another before marriage, though usually the family is still involved in the decision and in settling the financial aspects of the union. Women are expected to become engaged, if not married, in their twenties, and family pressure to do so can lead to a "living room marriage" (*jawwaz al-salon*) in which one is expected to agree to a husband after a few meetings with him. This high-pressure matchmaking was satirized in a popular blog launched in 2006 by Ghada 'Abd al-'Al, who drew from her and her friends' experiences. The blog, *'Ayza Atjawwiz* (I Want to Get Married), became a popular book, and in 2010 it was turned into a serial and aired during Ramadan. At the time, 'Abd al-'Al had remained single past what she called the "expiration date" of 30. Although a growing number of women delay marriage past that age, Egyptian women still marry earlier than women in most Arab countries.[74]

Either to avoid the conventional cost of marriage or to legitimize premarital sexual relations, some youth resort to informal marriages, commonly referred to as "*'urfi*" (customary), "Islamic," or "secret" marriages, which have been a matter of public concern since the 1980s. Because they are clandestine, *'urfi* marriages avoid the involvement of family and civil registration. Supposedly conforming to Islamic norms, such a union permits a couple to engage in licit (in their own eyes) sexual relations, but it puts a woman in a precarious position. The husband may leave her and deny the marriage, refuse the financial compensation a divorce would entail, and deny paternity if she becomes pregnant.[75] In 2005, an *'urfi* marriage between the popular actor Ahmad al-Fishawi and the set and costume designer Hind al-Hinnawi became a cause célèbre when al-Hinnawi brought a paternity suit against al-Fishawi after giving birth to their daughter, Lina. Al-Hinnawi won her case on appeal in 2006, enabling her to divorce al-Fishawi and freeing her to remarry. The decision also ensured that Lina would have a birth certificate with the name of her father. In the face of accusations that she was a gold digger, al-Hinnawi's parents supported her publicly, and her case was taken up by women's and human rights organizations.[76] Since then, a few other middle- and upper-class women have publicized similar paternity suits, though most women lack the resources or social capital to go to court. At the time of al-Hinnawi's case, an estimated fourteen thousand paternity suits were pending, some nine thousand of which were the result of *'urfi* marriages.[77]

Marriage crisis discourse also focuses on divorce, with alarmist headlines such as "A Divorce Occurs in Egypt Every 6 Minutes."[78] Divorces have increased in number along with the married population, but the rate of divorce is relatively low. The frequency of divorce declined dramatically in the second half of the twentieth century, from a relatively high crude rate of more than 4 per 1,000 population to 1.1 per 1,000 in 2000.[79] The family courts seem to have cleared some of the backlogs of women's divorce petitions, accounting for a doubling of the divorce rate to 2.2 per 1,000 in 2015.[80] That year, the crude divorce rate in the United States was nearly twice as high, at 3.6 per 1,000.[81] It is not clear whether the upward trend will continue, but Egyptians still divorce much less often than in the past.

If the data do not justify fears of a marriage crisis, they are nonetheless widespread. Such fears may reflect a perception of Egypt's weakened and more vulnerable position in international politics over the past fifty years and anxiety over changing gender relations in the same period.[82]

NOTES

1. Amira El-Azhary Sonbol, "A History of Marriage Contracts in Egypt," in *The Islamic Marriage Contract: Case Studies in Islamic Family Law*, ed. Asifa Quraishi and Frank E. Vogel (Cambridge, MA: Harvard University Press, 2008), 113, 117 note 3.

2. The handbooks relied upon here are Hasan al-'Idwi al-Hamzawi, *Ahkam 'Uqud al-Nikah*, published at the end of his *Kitab Tabsirat al-Qudat wa-l-Ikhwan fi Wad' al-Yad wa Ma Yashhad lahu min al-Burhan* (Bulaq: al-Matba'a al-Amiriyya, 1859); 'Abd al-Majid 'Ali al-Hanafi b. Shaykh 'Ali Isma'il al-'Idwi, *Matla' al-Badrayn fima Yata'allaq bi-l-Zawjayn* (Cairo: n.p., 1278/1862); Muhammad b. 'Umar al-Nawawi, *Sharh 'Uqud al-Lujayn fi Bayan Huquq al-Zawjayn* (Cairo: al-Matba'a al-Wahbiyya, 1878).

3. Nadia Sonneveld, *Khul' Divorce in Egypt: Public Debates, Judicial Practices, and Everyday Life* (Cairo: American University in Cairo Press, 2012), 17–34.

4. Al-'Idwi, *Ahkam 'Uqud al-Nikah*, 185; Muhammad Amin b. 'Umar, known as Ibn 'Abidin, *Radd al-Muhtar 'ala al-Durr al Mukhtar Sharh Tanwir al-Absar*, 3rd ed., vol. 2 (Bulaq: n.p., 1905–08), 269.

5. Kecia Ali, *Marriage and Slavery in Early Islam* (Cambridge, MA: Harvard University Press, 2010), 134; Ibn 'Abidin, *Radd al-Muhtar*, vol. 2, 325, 265; al-'Idwi, *Ahkam 'Uqud al-Nikah*, 178, 184.

6. On stipulations, see Nelly Hanna, "Marriage among Merchant Families in Seventeenth-Century Cairo," in *Women, the Family, and Divorce Laws in Islamic History*, ed. Amira El Azhary Sonbol (Syracuse: Syracuse University Press, 1996), 150, 152–53; and Ahmad b. 'Umar al-Dayrabi, *Ghayat al-Maqsud li-Man Yata'ati al-'Uqud* (Cairo: Matba'a al-Wahbiyya, 1880), 51. On conditional divorce, see Judith Tucker, *In the House of the Law: Gender and Islamic Law in Ottoman Syria and Palestine* (Berkeley: University of California Press, 1998), 103–5. On delegated divorce, see Fareeha Khan, "Tafwid al-Talaq: Transferring the Right of Divorce to the Wife," *The Muslim World* 99, no. 3 (2009): 503–505; and Ibn 'Abidin, *Radd al-Muhtar*, vol. 2, 494–505.

7. On Islamic legal pluralism and venue shopping, see Ido Shahar, "Legal Pluralism and the Study of the Shari'a Courts," *Islamic Law and Society* 15, no. 1 (2008): 112–41; and James E. Baldwin, *Islamic Law and Empire in Ottoman Cairo* (Edinburgh: Edinburgh University Press, 2017), 72–98.

8. On women's divorce for cause and *khul'*, see Judith Tucker, *Women, Family, and Gender in Islamic Law* (Cambridge: Cambridge University Press, 2008), 92–100; Tucker, *In the House of the Law*, 83; and Baldwin, *Islamic Law and Empire*, 85–88.

9. 'Abd al-Majid 'Ali, *Matla' al-Badrayn*, 14.

10. Kenneth M. Cuno, "Divorce and the Fate of the Family in Modern Egypt," in *Family in the Middle East: Ideational Change in Egypt, Iran, and Tunisia*, ed. Kathryn Yount and Hoda Rashad (New York: Routledge, 2008), 201. The crude divorce rate in the United States peaked in the 1990s at 4.6, but in conditions of greater longevity.

11. Rifa'a Rafi'i al-Tahtawi, *Al-Murshid al-Amin li-l-Banat wa-l-Banin*, ed. 'Imad Abu Ghazi (Cairo: al-Majlis al-A'la li-l-Thaqafa, 2002), 62–64.

12. 'Ali Mubarak, "'*Alam al-Din*," in *Ali Mubarak al-A'mal al-Kamila*, ed. Muhammad 'Imara, vol. 1 (Beirut: al-Mu'assasa al-'Arabiyya li-l-Dirasat wa-l-Nashr, 1979), 345–67; Gilbert Delanoue, *Moralistes et politiques musulmans dans l'Égypte du XIXe siècle (1798–1882)*, vol. 2 (Cairo: Institut Français d'Archéologie Orientale, 1982), 546.

13. Nikkie Keddie, *Ad-Din "Al-Afghani": A Political Biography* (Berkeley: University of California Press, 1972), 110–11; Muhammad 'Abduh, "al-Tarbiya," address given in 1900, in *al-A'mal al-Kamila li-l-Imam Muhammad 'Abduh*, ed. Muhammad 'Imara, vol. 3 (Beirut: al-Mu'assasa al-'Arabiyya li-l-Dirasat wa-l-Nashr, 1972), 170.

14. 'Abduh, *al-A'mal al-Kamila*, vol. 2, 88–92, 655–58, vol. 5, 170.

15. 'A'isha al-Taymur, *Mir'at al-Ta'ammul fi al-Umur*, 2nd ed. (Cairo: Women and Memory Forum, 2002), 34. For discussion, see Kenneth M. Cuno, *Modernizing Marriage: Family, Ideology, and Law in Nineteenth- and Early Twentieth-Century Egypt* (Syracuse: Syracuse University Press, 2015), 118–19; and Mervat F. Hatem, *Literature, Gender, and Nation-Building in Nineteenth-Century Egypt: The Life and Works of Aisha Taymur* (New York: Palgrave Macmillan, 2011), 116, 118.

16. Zaynab Fawwaz, *al-Rasa'il al-Zaynabiyya* (Cairo: al-Matba'a al-Mutawassita, 1905), 202. See also Marilyn Booth, *The Career and Communities of Zaynab Fawwaz: Feminist Thinking in Fin-de-siècle Egypt* (Oxford: Oxford University Press, 2021).

17. Bahithat al-Badiya, *al-Nisa'iyyat: Majmu'at Maqalat Nushirat fi al-Jarida fi Mawdu' al-Mar'a al-Misriyya* (Cairo: Matba'at al-Jarida, 1910), 4, 24, 26.

18. Zaynab Fawwaz, "Fair and Equal Treatment," in *Opening the Gates: An Anthology of Arab Feminist Writing*, ed. Margot Badran and Miriam Cooke, 2nd ed. (Bloomington: Indiana University Press, 2004), 223–25; Bahithat al-Badiya, "The Evils of Men. Tyranny," *Opening the Gates*, 228–31.

19. An earlier generation of scholars tended to ignore women's participation in these discussions. See Beth Baron, *The Women's Awakening in Egypt: Culture, Society, and the Press* (New Haven, CT: Yale University Press, 1994), especially 4–6.

20. Muhammad 'Imara, ed., *Qasim Amin: al-A'mal al-Kamila* (Cairo: Dar al-Shuruq, 1989), 330, 342–45, 347–48, 350, 352–55, 361–62.

21. Bahithat al-Badiya, "A Lecture in the Club of the Umma Party (1909)," *Opening the Gates*, 232. On the debate, see, e.g., Marilyn Booth, "Woman in Islam: Men and the 'Women's press' in Turn-of-the-20th-Century Egypt," *International Journal of Middle East Studies* 33, no. 2 (2001): 177–79; and Beth Baron "Unveiling in Early Twentieth Century Egypt: Practical and Symbolic Considerations," *Middle Eastern Studies* 25, no. 3 (1989): 370–86.

22. Among the intellectuals discussed above, only 'A'isha al-Taymur and Zaynab Fawwaz were not literate in French.

23. Kenneth M. Cuno, "Ambiguous Modernization: The Transition to Monogamy in the Khedival House of Egypt," in *Family History in the Middle East: Household, Property, and Gender*, ed. Beshara Doumani (Albany: State University of New York Press, 2003), 247–70.

24. On enslaved women as substitutes for wives, see Terence Walz, "Sudanese, Habasha, Takarna, and Barabira: Trans-Saharan Africans in Cairo as Shown in the 1848 Census," in *Race and Slavery in the Middle East: Histories of Trans-Saharan Africans in 19th-Century Egypt, Sudan, and the Ottoman Mediterranean*, ed. Terence Walz and Kenneth M. Cuno (Cairo: American University in Cairo Press, 2010), 56, 65–66. On the slave trade, see Walz and Cuno, "Introduction," *Race and Slavery*, 10–12.

25. The analysis is presented in Cuno, *Modernizing Marriage*, 70–72.

26. Ibid., 41–43.

27. Ibid., 64–67.

28. Sania Sharawi Lanfranchi, *Casting off the Veil: The Life of Huda Shaarawi, Egypt's First Feminist* (London: I. B. Tauris, 2012), 15–16; Huda Shaarawi, *Harem Years: The Memoirs of an Egyptian Feminist*, trans. and ed. Margot Badran (New York: Feminist Press, 1986), 18, 52–55.

29. Law No. 56 of 1923.

30. William Wendell Cleland, *The Population Problem in Egypt* (Lancaster, PA: n.p., 1936), 41–44; Philippe Fargues, "Terminating Marriage," in *The New Arab Family*, ed. Nicholas Hopkins (Cairo: American University in Cairo Press, 2001), 247–73.

31. Hanan Kholoussy, *For Better, For Worse: The Marriage Crisis That Made Modern Egypt* (Stanford, CA: Stanford University Press, 2010).

32. Arland Thornton, *Reading History Sideways: The Fallacy and Enduring Impact of the Developmental Paradigm on Family Life* (Chicago: University of Chicago Press, 2005), 21.

33. These laws were (1) La'ihat al-Qudat, 28 Rabi' II 1273 / 26 December 1856, in *Qamus al-Idara wa-l-Qada'*, Filib Jallad, vol. 4 (Alexandria, 1890–2), 129–32; (2) La'ihat al-Mahakim al-Shar'iyya, 9 Rajab 1297 / 17 June 1880, *Qamus*, vol. 4, 145–56; (3) La'ihat Tartib al-Mahakim al-Shar'iyya wa-l-Ijra'at al-Muta'alliqa biha, 27 May 1897, in *Majmu'at al-Awamir al-'Ulya wa-l-Dikritat al-Sadira fi Sanat 1897* (Bulaq: n.p., 1898), 155–75.

34. These changes and their effect are discussed in Kenneth M. Cuno, "Reorganization of the Sharia Courts of Egypt: How Legal Modernization Set Back Women's Rights in the

Nineteenth Century," in *Law and Legality in the Ottoman Empire and Republic of Turkey*, ed. Kent Schull, M. Safa Saraçoğlu, and Robert Zens (Bloomington: Indiana University Press, 2016), 92–107.

35. Muhmmad Qadri Pasha, *al-Ahkam al-Shar'iyya fi al-Ahwal al-Shakhsiyya* (Bulaq: al-Matba'a al-Amiriyya, 1875).

36. Cuno, *Modernizing Marriage*, 164–66.

37. Muhammad 'Abduh, *Taqrir Fadilat Mufti al-Diyar al-Misriyya al-Usthadh al-Shaykh Muhammad Abdu fi Islah al-Mahakim al-Shar'iyya* (Cairo: Matba'at al-Manar, 1900).

38. Abduh, *al-A'mal al-Kamila*, vol. 2, 657–58.

39. "Zawjat al-Mafqud bi-Hukm al-Shari'a al-Islamiyya al-Ghara," *al-Adab* 3:61, 16 February 1889, 201–2.

40. Abduh, *al-A'mal al-Kamila*, vol. 2, 654.

41. The text of the law and its explanatory memorandum are in Ibrahim Ahmad 'Abd Allah, *Majmu'at al-Awamir wa-l-Manshurat wa-l-Qawanin al-Muta'alliqa bi-La'ihat Tartib al-Mahakim al-Shar'iyya (al-Qanun Nimra 31 Sanat 1910) min Sanat 1910 ila Sanat 1926*, 2nd ed. (Tanta: al Matba'a al-Ahliyya al-Kubra, 1926), 166–79.

42. Muhammad Abu Zahra, *al-Ahwal al-Shakhsiyya: Qism al-Zawaj* (Cairo: n.p., 1950), 11; 'Abd Allah, *Majmu'at*, 188–89.

43. The text of the law and its explanatory memorandum appears in Ahmad Muhammad Ibrahim, *Majmu'a Qawanin al-Ahwal al-Shakhsiyya* (Alexandria: al-Dar al-Misriyya li-l-Tiba'a wa-l-Nashr, 1956?), 18–36.

44. Brinkley Messick, *The Calligraphic State: Textual Domination and History in a Muslim Society* (Berkeley: University of California Press, 1992), 61. In other colonial contexts, see M. B. Hooker, *Legal Pluralism: An Introduction to Colonial and Neo-colonial Laws* (Oxford: Oxford University Press, 1976), 94–100, 119–89; and Martin Chanock, *Law, Custom and Social Order: The Colonial Experience in Malawi and Zambia* (Cambridge: Cambridge University Press, 1985), 3–6.

45. Mohamed Afifi, "Reflections on the Personal Laws of Egyptian Copts," in *Women, the Family, and Divorce Laws in Islamic History*, ed. Amira El Azhary Sonbol (Syracuse, NY: Syracuse University Press, 1996), 203–4; Ron Shaham, "Communal Identity, Political Islam and Family Law: Copts and the Debate over the Grounds for Dissolution of Marriage in Twentieth-Century Egypt," *Islam and Christian-Muslim Relations* 21, no. 4 (2010): 410.

46. Afifi, "Reflections," 209; Shaham, "Communal Identity," 415; Ron Shaham, "Shopping for Legal Forums: Christians and Family Law in Modern Egypt," in *Dispensing Justice in Islam: Qadis and Their Judgements*, ed. Muhammad Khalid Masud, Rudolph Peters, and David Powers (Leiden: Brill, 2006), 463–64; Evelyn Baring, Earl of Cromer, *Abbas II* (London: MacMillan and Co., 1915), 72; James Harry Scott, *The Law Affecting Foreigners in Egypt. As the Result of the Capitulations, with an Account of Their Origin and Development* (Edinburgh: William Green and Sons, 1907), 266.

47. Magdi Guirguis and Nelly van Doorn-Harder, *The Emergence of the Modern Coptic Papacy: The Egyptian Church and Its Leadership from the Ottoman Period to the Present* (Cairo: American University in Cairo Press, 2011), 88–95; Vivian Ibrahim, *The Copts of Egypt: The Challenges of Modernisation and Identity* (London: I. B. Tauris, 2011), 34–37, 117–24.

48. Shaham, "Communal Identity," 411, 415.

49. The Karaite Jews accept only the authority of the Torah, not the oral law.

50. Gudrun Krämer, *The Jews in Modern Egypt, 1914–1952* (Seattle: University of Washington Press, 1989), 68–74; Ron Shaham, "Jews and the Shari'a Courts in Modern Egypt," *Studia Islamica* 82 (1995): 113–36.

51. Maurits S. Berger, "Secularizing Interreligious Law in Egypt," *Islamic Law and Society* 12, no. 3 (2005): 402.

52. Maurits S. Berger, "Public Policy and Islamic Law: The Modern *Dhimmi* in Contemporary Egyptian Family Law," *Islamic Law and Society* 8, no. 1 (2001): 94–95; Shaham, "Communal Identity," 410–12; Shaham, "Shopping for Legal Forums," 453.

53. Margot Badran, *Feminists, Islam, and Nation: Gender and the Making of Modern Egypt* (Princeton, NJ: Princeton University Press, 1995), 130; Fauzi M. Najjar, "Egypt's Laws of Personal Status," *Arab Studies Quarterly* 10, no. 3 (1988): 320.

54. Data compiled from decennial censuses and from the Central Agency for Public Mobilization and Statistics. Some estimates based on interpolation are necessary since polygyny has not been reported consistently.

55. Badran, *Feminists, Islam, and Nation*, 124–35; Margot Badran, "Competing Agenda: Feminists, Islam and the State in 19th and 20th Century Egypt," in *Women, Islam and the State*, ed. Deniz Kandiyoti (Philadelphia: Temple University Press, 1991), 208–10; Ellen Anne McLarney, *Soft Force: Women in Egypt's Islamic Awakening* (Princeton, NJ: Princeton University Press, 2015), 180–253 (reference to Rida, 236).

56. Laura Bier, *Revolutionary Womanhood: Feminisms, Modernists, and the State in Nasser's Egypt* (Stanford, CA: Stanford University Press, 2011), 110–11; Najjar, "Egypt's Laws of Personal Status," 319.

57. Bier, *Revolutionary Womanhood*, 112–13; Najjar, "Egypt's Laws of Personal Status," 320–22.

58. Cuno, *Modernizing Marriage*, 185 ff.; Bier, *Revolutionary Womanhood*, 113.

59. The provisions of Law No. 44 are presented in Najjar, "Egypt's Laws of Personal Status," 323–24; and Dawoud S. El Alami, "Law No. 100 of 1985 Amending Certain Provisions of Egypt's Personal Status Laws," *Islamic Law and Society* 1, no. 1 (1994): 117–29 (a translation of the nearly identical Law No. 100 of 1985).

60. Najjar, "Egypt's Laws of Personal Status," 324, 336; El Alami, "Law No. 100 of 1985," 116.

61. Najjar, "Egypt's Laws of Personal Status," 340–41; El Alami, "Law No. 100 of 1985," 117–19, 122.

62. Ron Shaham, "State, Feminists and Islamists—The Debate over Stipulations in Marriage Contracts in Egypt," *Bulletin of the School of Oriental and African Studies* 62, no. 3 (1999): 462–83; Diane Singerman, "Rewriting Divorce in Egypt: Reclaiming Islam, Legal Activism, and Coalition Politics," in *Remaking Muslim Politics: Pluralism, Contestation, Democratization*, ed. Robert W. Hefner (Princeton, NJ: Princeton University Press, 2005), 171–74.

63. Cuno, "Divorce and the Fate of the Family," 197.

64. Nathalie Bernard-Maugiron and Baudouin Dupret, "From Jihan to Susanne: Twenty Years of Personal Status Law in Egypt," *Recht van de Islam* 19 (2002): 15.

65. Mulki al-Sharmani, *Gender Justice and Legal Reform in Egypt: Negotiating Muslim Family Law* (Cairo: American University in Cairo Press, 2017), 6.

66. Law No. 12 of 1996 Promulgating the Child Law Amended by Law No. 126 of 2008, https://www.refworld.org/docid/5a4cb6064.html.

67. Mulki al-Sharmani, "Reforming Egyptian Family Laws: The Debate about a New Substantive Code," in *Feminist Activism, Women's Rights, and Legal Reform*, ed. Mulki al-Sharmani (London: Zed Books, 2013), 73–100.

68. Mariz Tadros, "Vicissitudes in the Entente between the Coptic Orthodox Church and the State in Egypt (1952–2007)," *International Journal of Middle East Studies* 41, no. 2 (2009): 269–87; Shaham, "Communal Identity," 412.

69. Nathalie Bernard-Maugiron, "Divorce and Remarriage of Orthodox Copts in Egypt: The 2008 State Council Ruling and the Amendment of the 1938 Personal Status Regulations," *Islamic Law and Society* 18, no. 3–4 (2011): 356–86.

70. Tadros, "Vicissitudes," 279; Bernard-Maugiron, "Divorce and Remarriage," 382.

71. See, e.g., Diane Singerman and Barbara Ibrahim, "The Costs of Marriage in Egypt: A Hidden Dimension in the New Arab Demography," in *The New Arab Family*, ed. Nicholas S. Hopkins, *Cairo Papers in Social Science* 24, nos. 1–2 (2001): 80–116. Among many journalistic accounts, see Khaled Diab, "All Tied Up in Knots," *The Guardian*, 13 December 2008, https://www.theguardian.com/commentisfree/2008/dec/13/egypt-middleeast; and Mohamed el-Shamma, "High Marriage Costs Cause Slump in Egyptian Weddings," *Arab News*, 14 July 2019, https://www.arabnews.com/node/1525181/middle-east.

72. Rania Salem, "Imagined Crises: Assessing Evidence of Delayed Marriage and Never-Marriage in Contemporary Egypt," in *Domestic Tensions, National Anxieties: Global Perspectives on Marriage, Crisis, and Nation*, ed. Kristin Celello and Hanan Kholoussy (Oxford: Oxford University Press, 2016), 246–48.

73. Rania Salem, "Changes in the Institution of Marriage in Egypt from 1998 to 2012," in *The Egyptian Labor Market in an Era of Revolution*, ed. Ragui Assaad and Caroline Krafft (Oxford: Oxford University Press, 2015), 179.

74. Tahira Yaqoob, "I Want to Get Married: Ghada Abdel Aal," *The National*, 4 June 2011, https://www.thenational.ae/arts-culture/books/i-want-to-get-married-ghada-abdel-aal-1.404934; Hadeel al-Salchi, "In a TV Comedy, Egyptian Women Gain a Voice," *The Associated Press*, 4 October 2010, https://www.dailynewsegypt.com/2010/10/10/in-a-tv-comedy-egyptian-women-gain-a-voice/. On delayed marriage, see Magued Osman and Laila S. Shahd, "Age-Discrepant Marriage in Egypt," in *The New Arab Family*, 50–61; and Salem, "Imagined Crises," 237.

75. Yolande Knell, "The Perils of Young Egyptians' Secret Marriages," BBC News, 19 January 2010, http://news.bbc.co.uk/2/hi/middle_east/8466188.stm.

76. Frances S. Hasso, *Consuming Desires: Family Crisis and the State in the Middle East* (Stanford, CA: Stanford University Press, 2011), 1–2.

77. Sharon Otterman, "Paternity Trial Shocks Egyptians / Court Rules against Famous Actor, Siding with Mother, Child," *SFGate*, 6 August 2006, https://www.sfgate.com/news/article/Paternity-trial-shocks-Egyptians-Court-rules-2491546.php.

78. Mahmoud El Gaafari, "Expert: A Divorce Occurs in Egypt Every 6 Mins," *Al-Masry al-Yaum*, 18 April 2010, https://www.egyptindependent.com/expert-divorce-occurs-egypt-every-6-mins/.

79. Cuno, "Divorce and the Fate of the Family," 197–202.

80. Lolwa Reda, "On Marriage and Divorce in Egypt," *Egypt Today*, 28 February 2019, accessed 25 August 2023, https://www.egypttoday.com/Article/6/66379/On-Marriage-and-Divorce-in-Egypt.

81. Statista, "Divorce Rate in the United States from 1990 to 2021," accessed June 2020, https://www.statista.com/statistics/195955/divorce-rate-in-the-united-states-since-1990/.

82. See Monika Lindbekk, "The Enforcement of Personal Status Law by Egyptian Courts," in *Adjudicating Family Law in Muslim Courts*, ed. Elisa Giunchi (London: Routledge, 2013), 88–89; and Salem, "Imagined Crises," 235.

Bibliography

Badran, Margot. *Feminists, Islam, and Nation: Gender and the Making of Modern Egypt.* Princeton, NJ: Princeton University Press, 1995.

Baron, Beth. *The Women's Awakening in Egypt: Culture, Society, and the Press.* New Haven, CT: Yale University Press, 1994.

Bernard-Maugiron, Nathalie. "Divorce and Remarriage of Orthodox Copts in Egypt: The 2008 State Council Ruling and the Amendment of the 1938 Personal Status Regulations," *Islamic Law and Society* 18, nos. 3–4 (2011): 356–86.

Bier, Laura. *Revolutionary Womanhood: Feminisms, Modernists, and the State in Nasser's Egypt.* Stanford, CA: Stanford University Press, 2011.

Booth, Marilyn. *The Career and Communities of Zaynab Fawwaz: Feminist Thinking in Fin-de-siècle Egypt.* Oxford: Oxford University Press, 2021.

Cuno, Kenneth M. *Modernizing Marriage: Family, Ideology, and Law in Nineteenth- and Early Twentieth-Century Egypt.* Syracuse, NY: Syracuse University Press, 2015.

Hasso, Frances S. *Consuming Desires: Family Crisis and the State in the Middle East.* Stanford, CA: Stanford University Press, 2011.

Hopkins, Nicholas S., ed. *The New Arab Family.* Cairo: American University in Cairo Press, 2001.

Kholoussy, Hanan. *For Better, For Worse: The Marriage Crisis That Made Modern Egypt.* Stanford, CA: Stanford University Press, 2010.

McLarney, Ellen Anne. *Soft Force: Women in Egypt's Islamic Awakening.* Princeton, NJ: Princeton University Press, 2015.

Salem, Rania. "Changes in the Institution of Marriage in Egypt from 1998 to 2012." In *The Egyptian Labor Market in an Era of Revolution*, edited by Ragui Assaad and Caroline Krafft, 162–81. Oxford: Oxford University Press, 2015.

Salem, Rania. "Imagined Crises: Assessing Evidence of Delayed Marriage and Never-Marriage in Contemporary Egypt." In *Domestic Tensions, National Anxieties: Global Perspectives on Marriage, Crisis, and Nation*, edited by Kristin Celello and Hanan Kholoussy, 231–54. Oxford: Oxford University Press, 2016.

Shaham, Ron. "Communal Identity, Political Islam and Family Law: Copts and the Debate over the Grounds for Dissolution of Marriage in Twentieth-Century Egypt." *Islam and Christian-Muslim Relations* 21, no. 4 (2010): 409–22.

Shaham, Ron. "Jews and the Shariʿa Courts in Modern Egypt." *Studia Islamica* 82 (1995): 113–36.

Shaham, Ron. "Shopping for Legal Forums: Christians and Family Law in Modern Egypt." In *Dispensing Justice in Islam: Qadis and Their Judgements*, edited by Muhammad Khalid Masud, Rudolph Peters, and David Powers, 451–72. Leiden: Brill, 2006.

Al-Sharmani, Mulki. *Gender Justice and Legal Reform in Egypt: Negotiating Muslim Family Law.* Cairo: American University in Cairo Press, 2017.

Singerman, Diane. "Rewriting Divorce in Egypt: Reclaiming Islam, Legal Activism, and Coalition Politics." In *Remaking Muslim Politics: Pluralism, Contestation, Democratization*, edited by Robert W. Hefner, 161–88. Princeton, NJ: Princeton University Press, 2005.

Sonbol, Amira El Azhary, ed. *Women, the Family, and Divorce Laws in Islamic History.* Syracuse, NY: Syracuse University Press, 1996.

Sonneveld, Nadia. *Khulʿ Divorce in Egypt: Public Debates, Judicial Practices, and Everyday Life.* Cairo: American University in Cairo Press, 2012.

Tucker, Judith. *Women, Family, and Gender in Islamic Law.* Cambridge: Cambridge University Press, 2008.

CHAPTER 14

REFASHIONING THE SHARIʿA COURTS IN THE SEMI-COLONIAL PERIOD

HANAN KHOLOUSSY

In his political treatise *Modern Egypt*, Lord Cromer, the British agent and consul-general in Egypt from 1883 to 1907, explained why his colonial administration did not attempt to reform or "Anglicize" the Islamic legal system in Egypt, despite the Brits' frequent criticisms of the Islamic (shariʿa) courts, after their disastrous efforts to reform the Islamic legal system in colonial India.[1] Cromer explained, "If they [the Islamic courts] are ever to be improved, the movement in favour of reform must come from within. It must be initiated by the Egyptians themselves. Any serious attempt to impose reforms by pressure from without would be extremely impolitic, and more, over, would probably result in failure."[2] The hesitancy of British officials to intervene in the Egyptian shariʿa legal system was also related to their unusual and awkward relationship to their semi-colonial Egyptian protectorate, where they officially claimed to leave domestic matters to the Egyptians during their imperial presence in Egypt from 1882 to 1956. While the British encouraged legal reform, the Egyptian administration restructured its Islamic legal system of its own accord, drafting, debating, and passing Islamic laws on religious endowments and issues of personal status (marriage, divorce, child custody, and inheritance) without any interference from the British.

Simultaneously, however, the Egyptian nationalists who advocated and sought Islamic legal reform had internalized many of the colonial assumptions and attitudes about the so-called backwardness of the shariʿa courts, which had monopolized Egypt's legal system during the period of direct Ottoman rule from 1517 until the late nineteenth century. As a result, the Egyptian administration reduced the jurisdiction of these courts to issues of the family, while simultaneously enlarging the state's control over this supposedly "private" domain that had often escaped the gaze of the state in earlier periods. The larger process in which the Egyptian administration revamped the Egyptian Islamic legal system, introduced Western laws and new legal systems, and privatized religious law was part and parcel of a larger westernizing reform movement that was partly responding to colonialism, even if it was undertaken by Egyptian nationalists.[3]

The Egyptian court registers of the revamped Islamic legal system from its waves of reform between 1897 and 1931[4] were unearthed by the staff of the Egyptian National Archives (ENA) during the summer of 2002, when staff members became aware of the research interests of the author, and therefore had not yet been cataloged. An overview of these court registers can open pathways to better understand and situate the completely reorganized and revamped—albeit more bureaucratized and hierarchical—Islamic courts in semi-colonial Egypt.[5] Colonial officials, Egyptian nationalists, and scholars either criticized or downplayed the significance of these shari'a court reforms. However, the sources show that they resulted in a comprehensive transformation that centralized, formalized, and enlarged the "public" role that these courts played in the "private" lives of Egyptians. Using shari'a records as a source for both legal and social history helps to place the court records in the larger context of national debates in the press. Scholars of the courts must transcend the theoretical and methodological divide between academic works that rely primarily on periodicals, and hence marginalize the illiterate masses, and those that make use of court records and rarely situate their litigants and personnel beyond the courtroom walls. By merging court records with press (and other historical) sources, it is possible to produce nuanced conceptualizations of early twentieth-century Egyptian history and demonstrate both discrepancies and convergences between legal practices and social perceptions of various institutions like marriage and the family, on the one hand, and the law, the courts, and the state, on the other hand.

THE CASE FOR SHARI'A COURT CASES

In his study of the German family, David Sabean astutely notes that "If we want to understand the moral and social relationships which bound together and divided houses and families, we have to examine in detail the tactical language, spatial interaction, and practical everyday exchanges."[6] Sabean emphasizes the importance of using court records to offer "an overview of the configuration of disputes, from which we tease an account of the claims, obligations, and expectations couples negotiated before the courts."[7] Steve Stern and Hendrik Hartog also employ court records to demonstrate how couples devised inventive solutions to intimate disputes in eighteenth-century and nineteenth-century Mexico and America, respectively. They argue that the most profound insights into marriage can be gained by examining the margins of marital life, that is, when a husband and wife are in court.[8] The early twentieth-century shari'a court registers, in particular, provide exceptionally rich insights into how Egyptian men and women viewed marriage and their related rights and duties.

These registers contain a wide variety of testimonies by plaintiffs, defendants, witnesses, and court inspectors, in addition to the verdicts and judicial opinions of judges. Handwritten court registers in their original form, as well as legal petitions and appeals, often record the direct voices of litigants, revealing perceptions and details that can rarely be found elsewhere in the historical record. As invaluable as these sources are, however, scholars now recognize that court records should not be treated as unfiltered mirrors of social reality and must be read critically and cautiously.[9] They do not capture empirical realities any more than other sources do and must be subject to the same rigorous interrogation and careful analysis. Yet they do provide some insight into litigants' and judges' perceptions of marriage and the family. Those who brought divorce cases and custody battles to court did so because they had certain perceptions about their duties and rights in marriage and divorce.

Although shari'a court transcripts do not divulge how women and men learned about their legal rights and duties or how to navigate the system, these cases indicate that knowledge of Islamic law was not determined by the social class, education level, or gender of the litigant. The fact that thousands of both urban and rural Egyptians of all classes frequented the shari'a courts to record marriage contracts, file for divorce, and claim custody rights implies that most Egyptians were at least partially aware of their rights in marriage and divorce, unlike today, where Egyptians rely extensively on lawyers to inform them of their rights and represent them in court. Because the courts charged minimal costs for their various services, litigants from all financial backgrounds could afford to access the courts, and impoverished litigants were eligible for exemption from court fees.[10] The standard fee for a marital legal decision in the cases reviewed was five piasters (one-twentieth of one Egyptian pound), which was set by the 1880 code.[11] While certain scholars who have not worked with shari'a court records argue that upper-class Egyptian men and women did not frequent the courts,[12] scholars of the nineteenth-century Egyptian courts have reached a consensus that rural and urban men and women of all classes did so.[13] Because early twentieth-century legislation mandated the registration of marriages and divorces, elite and non-elite Egyptians alike were forced to resort to the courts even more than their predecessors.[14] As a result, these early twentieth-century shari'a court records invite scholars to compare and contrast how different social classes understood and utilized the newly transformed courts and their laws.

Cases from the shari'a courts paint a very different picture of the early twentieth-century Islamic legal system than what colonial officials, nationalists, and scholars have portrayed. They reveal the improvisations of many couples and judges as well as their creative responses to the changing circumstances of early twentieth-century Egyptian life. Contrary to the portrayals of a static legal system, litigants employed a variety of strategies to manipulate the courts to their advantage. While nationalists and reformers conceptualized middle-class notions of legal rights and duties in the press, Egyptians of all classes understood and exercised these rights and duties in very different ways in the courtrooms. When husbands or wives divorced, when wives tried to force absent husbands to provide alimony, or when couples wrestled for custody over children, many turned to the legal system for redress. When Egyptians petitioned judges to challenge apparently fixed doctrinal understandings, they did so because they viewed the law as a crucial and flexible sociopolitical resource. As in the preceding centuries, husbands' and wives' extensive use of these courts suggests that shari'a law was hardly seen as a last resort and that Egyptians of all classes were aware of the legal and socially acceptable options available to them.[15]

THE REFORM OF THE LEGAL SYSTEM

Until the nineteenth century, Egyptian Muslims took a variety of civil, criminal, administrative, and personal status cases to the shari'a courts. Christians and Jews had their own religious court systems, but they also frequented the Islamic courts when a case involved Muslims or when the Islamic legal system provided them with more rights than their own systems did. During the nineteenth century, various nonreligious court systems emerged, which gradually assumed jurisdiction over all civil and criminal cases and eventually reduced the power and authority of the Islamic courts.[16] These courts, such as the Mixed Courts, the Judicial Council, and the Native (later to be renamed National) Courts, applied more "secular" laws, often inspired by European civil codes.[17] By the onset of the British occupation in 1882, the jurisdiction of the Islamic courts had been limited mostly to issues of religious endowments and personal status. Even before the British officially arrived, the Egyptian Ministry of Justice had contracted Muhammad Pasha Qadri to codify a Hanafi Code of Personal Status Law. Though the new law was published in 1875, its first code passed in 1880, formalizing the procedures and limiting the jurisdiction of the Islamic courts.[18] The 1880 code was merely the first of several codes passed. Later ones, passed in 1897, 1909–10, 1923, and 1931, regulated court operations, procedures, and personnel.[19]

The 1897, 1923, and 1931 codes also dealt with the registration and documentation of marriage contracts, the minimum age for brides and grooms, and the documentary evidence necessary for certain divorce disputes to be heard in court.[20] These laws formally expanded the encroaching role of the state into the lives of its subjects. Before a wife or husband could file a case, she or he had to show the court a registered marriage contract. This contract had to have been recorded at the hands of a government marriage officiate, who was required to confirm that the couple met the state's minimum requirements of age (eighteen for men and sixteen for women) after a 1923 law, which was further ratified in a 1931 law. By requiring registered marriage contracts before a wife's or husband's case could be heard in court, the state was assuring its regulation of the contraction of its subjects' marriages, potential disputes, and possible divorces. As legal historian Judith E. Tucker explains, "The advantages of such registration included the establishment of a permanent written record of the marriage agreement. To register your marriage in court was to place marriage and its consequent rights and obligations squarely under the jurisdiction of the Islamic court, in anticipation of the court's playing a role in any later disputes concerning marriage arrangements."[21] As Tucker points out, registering a marriage was a way to strengthen and substantiate subsequent claims or complaints.

THE REORGANIZATION OF THE COURTS

The 1897 Code of the Organization and Procedure for Islamic Courts reorganized the Islamic courts into a clear hierarchy of lower-level and appellate courts: Mahakim Juz'iyya (Courts of Summary Justice); Mahakim Ibtida'iyya (Courts of First Instance); and, in Cairo, the Mahkama 'Ulya (Supreme Court).[22] These courts existed until 1955, when President Gamal Abdel Nasser officially abolished them and transferred their jurisdiction to the postcolonial state's civil courts.[23] During the early twentieth century, Egypt was divided into thirty-six provincial court districts, each headed by an Islamic Court of First Instance, and major Egyptian cities could have several subdistricts. Cairo, for example, had nineteen subdistricts, each with its own Islamic Court of Summary Justice.[24] Cases brought to the Islamic Court of Summary Justice were adjudicated by one judge, whose authority to deliver final decisions was restricted by the suit's subject matter and financial value. His ruling could be appealed in the Islamic Court of First Instance, where three judges arbitrated the cases. Their decisions, in turn, could be appealed in the Islamic Supreme Court of Cairo, which was ruled by three judges.[25]

Litigants filed three different types of cases in the Cairo Islamic Court of First Instance: al-Ahkam al-Juz'iyya (summary verdicts), whose ledgers from 1898 to 1928 are available in the ENA; al-Ahkam al-Isti'nafiyya (appellate verdicts), available from 1914 to 1948; and al-Ahkam al-Habsiyya (detention verdicts), available from 1911 to 1928. All three registers contain marriage agreements, divorce settlements, child custody and support cases, obedience suits, spousal support agreements, inheritance disputes, and divorce alimony cases.

Because these uncatalogued documents had not yet been indexed at the time of the writing of this chapter, the numbering and date systems that the court's early twentieth-century scribes used for these registers are useful to follow when citing these court records in scholarship or locating them in the archives. It appears that the ENA staff had begun an incomplete project of numbering the registers because some registers list a new given number in addition to the original one. If another cataloging system is developed in the future, it might be more judicious to follow the original register number because it will be more beneficial for researchers than an interim or incomplete one. As an additional reference to cite and locate cases, it is always useful to include the date on which the cases were first opened because this date is invariably mentioned on the first line of the case transcript. Court transcripts provide the date according to both the Western and Islamic calendars.[26]

The first set of registers that contains summary verdicts encompasses cases that were usually tried for the first time. Consequently, they hold more detailed transcripts that contain a wide variety of testimonies by plaintiffs, defendants, and witnesses. This register consists of 324 separate ledgers, each containing a few hundred cases, spanning from January 1898 to January 1928. The first register naturally dates from the inception of the newly organized court system, but the reason why ledgers after 1928 ceased to exist remains unclear. Perhaps the archival staff has not yet unearthed them. In the years I surveyed (1898, 1906, 1914, and 1922), women opened cases much more frequently than men, most probably because the former were far more financially dependent and held fewer legal rights in marriage and divorce than the latter. For example, women sued their husbands and ex-husbands for financial support, divorce rights, and child custody nearly nine times more often than men filed child custody cases or obedience orders (*bayt al-ta'a*) against their wives and ex-wives.

The second set of registers holds the appellate verdicts, which were usually shorter and less detailed than summary verdicts because the typical appellate verdict was the result of an appeal seeking to overturn a summary verdict, to which the transcript referred by case number and date without recounting the details of the original case. Consequently, the appellate cases were more formulaic and rarely contained the first-hand personal testimonies of litigants and witnesses that the original summary cases had. As such, I sampled the years that immediately followed the original years I surveyed in the summary verdict register in an attempt to trace an appellate case to its original summary case. For example, I skimmed the names of the legal parties and original summary case numbers in the margins of the 1915 appellate verdict ledgers to match some appellate cases to the original cases I had already sampled in the 1914 summary verdict ledgers. In doing so, I was able to locate the original case, with its rich details and first-hand testimonies, in order to compensate for the lack of minutiae in its subsequent formulaic and abbreviated appellate case. However, what the appellate cases do offer the scholar that the summary verdicts do not are the individual opinions of the judges, especially when they overturned the original verdict, and the laws on which they based their decisions. The appellate verdict register consists of 231 separate ledgers, each containing a few hundred cases—sometimes several hundred cases—spanning from November 1914 to November 1948. The logic behind the dates of the first and last ledger in this registry is unclear, but the serial numbers that the original court personnel (not the archive staff) assigned to its registry indicate that this registry is complete.

The third and final set of court registers includes the detention verdicts. These cases were filed by plaintiffs who sought imprisonment for defendants who refused to obey previous summary verdicts and/or appellate verdicts that ordered them to pay financial compensation. The 1875 Personal Status Code—the unofficial law of state that was never promulgated—stipulated that if a financially competent husband repeatedly refused to support his wife despite one or more previous court orders, his wife could request that a judge imprison him for up to thirty days.[27] The state, however, did not make this principle mandatory until it issued Law No. 31 of 1910, which established separate detention courts within the Courts of First Instance where such cases were tried.[28] Not surprisingly, these cases are almost entirely woman-initiated. They mostly consist of women demanding that their husbands or ex-husbands serve time, but the occasional case of a woman taking her husband's guarantor or her father to court for lack of financial support can be found as well. These cases are often formulaic, but the testimonies provide exceptional insight into men's excuses for not fulfilling their Islamic obligations in marriage and divorce. Like the appellate verdicts, these summaries shed light on various women's understanding and employment of Islamic law as a crucial sociolegal tool of enforcement. Consequently, I followed the same sampling method as I did with the appellate registers. For example, I surveyed cases in 1923 to search for parties' names and summary verdict case numbers in the margins that I had gathered from the 1922 summary verdict registry. I did so to trace detention cases to their original ones to obtain a thorough understanding of the case from its inception to its conclusion. The detention verdict register contains sixty-one separate ledgers, each with a few hundred cases, spanning from April 1911 to October 1923. The first ledger naturally dates to the establishment of these courts, but the reason for the date of the last ledger is not known. As with the other two registers, the serial numbers that the court staff allotted its ledgers were followed and indicate that the register is complete.

COURT PERSONNEL

The 1880 code detailed the selection and appointment of judges, lawyers, marriage notaries, scribes, and inspectors.[29] All court personnel were adult male government employees appointed, promoted, transferred, retired, and paid a fixed salary by the Egyptian administration. The court judges obviously underwent the most training: they were drawn from the ranks of jurist-theologians of Islam, religious scholars who were trained in Islamic law at religious schools throughout Egypt, such as al-Azhar University.[30] From the establishment of a training school for shari'a judges (as well as court clerks and lawyers) in 1907 until its closing in 1923 (and again between 1927 and 1929 when it briefly reopened), many judges, clerks, and lawyers were educated in a professional institution that prepared them for the newly organized shari'a court system.[31]

Like their predecessors in the shari'a courts of the Ottoman period, few litigants in the early twentieth century hired professional lawyers. Lawyers more often represented a litigant who did not appear in court. For example, when a litigant did not appear in court or send a deputy, the court appointed a lawyer on his or her behalf. However, by the second decade of the twentieth century, and especially after Law No. 15 of 1916 organized the shari'a lawyers into a professional bar and expanded their rights and duties, most litigants hired lawyers.[32] The cost of contracting a shari'a lawyer was affordable. As a result, men and women from various socioeconomic backgrounds increasingly employed them throughout the twentieth century.[33] Additionally, a court-appointed lawyer was obliged to represent a client for free if the latter could not afford the lawyer's fees.[34]

Despite the personal affiliation of the litigants, the 1880 code instructed shari'a judges to implement the Hanafi school of law—one of the four Sunni Islamic legal schools of thought—which was the official school of the Ottoman Empire.[35] During the Ottoman period, most Muslims in Lower Egypt adhered to the Shafi'i school of law, while most in Upper Egypt followed the Maliki legal school.[36] In contrast to their twentieth-century successors, Egyptian shari'a judges of the Ottoman era were free to choose and implement principles from any of the four legal schools in their judicial decisions, even after the 1880 code was passed. Because Qadri's 1875 Hanafi Code of Personal Status Law was never officially promulgated, it was not binding for the Egyptian shariʿa courts. It did, however, serve as the unofficial law of state until 1920. In that year, Law No. 25 of 1920 codified a new set of personal status laws nationwide based on a strict state-sponsored hegemonic interpretation of shariʿa personal status laws. After the passing of this law in 1920, judges—who were official government employees of a much more watchful and intrusive modern Egyptian nation-state—were no longer permitted to independently choose minority opinions or implement alternative interpretations from the other schools of law.[37]

PERSONAL STATUS LAWS

Although Egyptian legislative reformers such as Ahmad Muhammad Shakir, Muhammad ʿAbduh, and Qasim Amin had made several attempts to "modernize" Islamic personal status laws in the 1890s, the 1875 Personal Status Code was not amended until 1920 and again in 1929 when major personal status laws affecting marriage and divorce were formally promulgated.[38] Law No. 25 of 1920 officially provided women with three grounds for judicial divorce, while men's unilateral and unfettered access to divorce was slightly curtailed by Law No. 25 of 1929. These two laws, which I have discussed extensively elsewhere,[39] departed from Hanafi legislation by drawing on the more liberal Maliki and Shafiʿi schools of Islamic law.[40] They deviated from Hanafi doctrine either by adopting elements from the other schools of law in an eclectic manner (*takhayyur*) or by combining elements from various schools (*talfiq*).[41] These two laws dominated the personal lives of Egyptians during the remainder of the twentieth century, with legislation remaining virtually unchanged until Law No. 1 of 2000, aside from a 1979 presidential decree offering women minor gains in divorce rights that would be revoked a few years later.[42]

Although several legal and women's scholars have described the laws of marriage and divorce in modern Egypt, none—to my knowledge—has been able to ascertain the effects of the reformed personal status laws in the courtrooms because the early twentieth-century shariʿa court records were previously unavailable.[43] Now that the ENA staff has unearthed these records, scholars can and should examine how these new laws were interpreted by shariʿa court judges, translated into practice in the courtrooms, and understood by litigants. Sampling cases before and after major years of marital legal reform enables an evaluation of these laws' effects in the courts. For example, in my own research, I made a special effort to locate cases in the 1922 summary verdict ledgers that referred to Law No. 25 of 1920 to compare them with similar cases in 1914. I did so to detect how judges and litigants used the law and to examine how its interpretation and application reflected changes in legal practices. Similarly, I reviewed the appellate verdict ledgers in 1923 and 1930 to locate cases that were appealed based on Law No. 25 of 1920 and 1929, respectively, for the same reasons.[44] Because the articles of these two personal status laws were often vaguely worded, court judges were often the only ones who held the power to interpret them and issue rulings based on them. The shariʿa court records from the 1920s onward thus provide glimpses of how judges construed these new laws and how their applications of the law affected the men and women who frequented the courts. Focusing on those men and women who raised marital disputes in court sheds light on how they understood marriage, divorce, the family, the revamped legal system, and the larger society, as well as their rights and obligations.

THE CASE FOR MARRYING SOURCES

In order to better comprehend the litigants, personnel, and issues at hand, shariʿa court records must be situated in their larger social, political, and economic setting beyond the courtroom walls (and the National Archives that currently house them). These cases did not occur in a vacuum, cut off from the rest of the burgeoning nation that was fighting a nationalist struggle for complete political and economic independence from British colonial rule. They were adjudicated by judges who returned home every afternoon and read the daily newspapers that were waging press debates about the struggle for independence; the new Egyptian woman and her influx into the so-called public spheres of school, university, and the workforce; the marriage crisis that turned men off of marriage because they were petrified by these new women, the skyrocketing divorce rate, and the responsibilities of marriage; and the role Islamic law should play, if any, in a newly emerging Egyptian state that many were hoping would become more secular with independence.[45] These cases were filed by men and women struggling to make ends meet during a period of European economic exploitation that was peppered with periods of inflation, low salaries, unemployment problems, wartime famines and shortages, and economic depression.

As we read these shariʿa court records, we should inquire how litigants' perceptions of their legal rights and duties to their families and nations compared to those espoused by the middle class in the press or how the various economic crises of early twentieth-century Egypt affected the financial claims of wives and pecuniary responsibilities of husbands. For answers to such questions, court cases must be read in conjunction with press sources. Many other questions can be asked and answered if read with other historical sources such as diaries, census registers, parliamentary debates, and the court records of the other legal systems in semi-colonial Egypt, to name a few.

It is time to bridge the theoretical and methodological divide between academic works that rely primarily on periodicals and those that make use of court records. Scholars of twentieth-century Egypt who have relied largely on the press to examine elite articulations of nationalism, feminism, and the family understandably cannot address how financially destitute and politically disenfranchised non-elites, who constituted most of the Egyptian population, participated in the nationalist and feminist struggles against colonialism. Likewise, scholars of the Ottoman-era courts in Egypt, who obviously did not have a flourishing press to consult before its emergence in the 1870s, rarely situate their litigants and personnel beyond the courtroom walls. Merging the two sources provides a more telling story of marriage and the nation in early twentieth-century Egypt. By combining both sets of sources, future studies can produce nuanced understandings of the ideas *and* practices of various processes and phenomena in early twentieth-century Egyptian history.

CONCLUSION

While the shari'a records of the Ottoman Egyptian courts have been studied extensively by scholars, those of the early twentieth century were only recently unearthed by the staff of the ENA and, thus, have been virtually untapped by scholars. These legal registers merit future studies of all kinds, perhaps most significantly because of the wave of legal reforms that transformed the shari'a legal system between 1897 and 1931. Colonial administrators, Egyptian reformers, and contemporary researchers have either disparaged or ignored the significance and success of these extensive shari'a reforms. However, the sources show that they resulted in a completely reorganized and more bureaucratized and hierarchical legal system than earlier ones, enlarging and formalizing the "public" state-sponsored role of these courts in the "personal" lives of most Egyptian men and women. These largely overlooked reforms not only constituted a major rupture in court practices and procedures but also assigned the state an unprecedented role in monitoring Egyptian women and men, drastically changing the very nature and role of the shari'a courts in semi-colonial Egypt.

These changes resulted in a three-tiered court system, each with its own set of rules, to which more and more Egyptians were forced to resort in order to solve their personal affairs. The new system devised legal regulations and procedures that governed each aspect of the courts and monitored every move of the litigants who had to maneuver these courts. It also sponsored a nationwide codification of the state's monolithic and hegemonic interpretation of shari'a personal status law and created a professionalized and differently educated cadre of judges, lawyers, scribes, and inspectors, all assisting the state to scrutinize and control the litigants, to name a few of the changes. While they still offer rare firsthand glimpses of this period in Egyptian history, the court records generated by these early twentieth-century reforms are unfortunately more formulaic than their predecessors in the Ottoman period. The state's bureaucracy simplified and shortened the transcription and filing of court cases with codes, formulas, and rules that reduced the scribe's need to capture every detail of the case and its litigants and catch every word of their various testimonies.

Simultaneously, however, if these shari'a court cases, along with their litigants, judges, scribes, inspectors, and other personnel, are situated both inside and outside the courtroom and read in conjunction with other historical sources, scholars can attempt to better comprehend much of the historical transformations of early twentieth-century

Egypt. Future scholarship can help uncover how the state and these courts assumed a more significant role in the lives of men and women who married, divorced, and wrestled over child custody before the courts, as well as the roles of the scribes, judges, ushers, and lawyers who worked in the courts. Undoubtedly, these court records can be used to study an array of phenomena, processes, and practices in early twentieth-century Egypt.

NOTES

1. Nathan Brown, *The Rule of Law in the Arab World: Courts in Egypt and the Gulf* (Cambridge: Cambridge University Press, 1997), 38–39.
2. Evelyn Baring Cromer, *Modern Egypt*, vol. 2 (London: MacMillan and Co., 1908), 515.
3. See Talal Asad, *Formations of the Secular: Christianity, Islam, Modernity* (Stanford, CA: Stanford University Press, 2003), 205–56.
4. It should be noted that Ron Shaham has written an extensive study on this same legal system of early twentieth-century Egypt. However, he relies on legal periodicals and not the original court cases housed in the Egyptian National Archives (ENA), which probably were not available at the time of his research, to uncover the masked assumptions of the Islamic legal system as well as the role of judges in personal status decisions. Unfortunately, the final summaries presented in these legal periodicals, which are housed in the Egyptian National Library (ENL), among many other libraries throughout the world, are written in an abbreviated style that does not reveal fully reveal the socioeconomic background of the case, firsthand testimonies of the litigants, or other telling details. Shaham's methodological approach and sources ultimately do not explain how Egyptian litigants understood marriage or their marital rights and duties because he focuses on the judges' understanding and use of the law. At the same time, however, the incredibly useful foundation his work established tremendously facilitated my own research in the ENA and enabled me to navigate the original uncatalogued court records better. See Ron Shaham, *Family and the Courts in Modern Egypt: A Study Based on Decisions by the Shari'a Courts, 1900–1955* (Leiden: Brill, 1997).
5. For an interesting overview of researching in the archives, see Lucia Carminati, "Dead Ends In and Out of the Archive: An Ethnography of Dar al-Watha'iq al-Qawmiyya, the Egyptian National Archive," *Rethinking History: The Journal of Theory and Practice* 23, no. 1 (2019): 34–51.
6. David Warren Sabean, *Property, Production, and Family in Neckarhausen, 1700–1870* (Cambridge: Cambridge University Press, 1990), 30.
7. Ibid., 37.
8. See Hendrik Hartog, *Man and Wife in America: A History* (Cambridge: Harvard University Press, 2000); and Steve J. Stern, *The Secret History of Gender: Women, Men, and Power in Late Colonial Mexico* (Chapel Hill: University of North Carolina Press, 1995).
9. Iris Agmon, *Family and Court: Legal Culture and Modernity in Late Ottoman Palestine* (Syracuse, NY: Syracuse University Press, 2006), 41–46; Leslie Peirce, *Morality Tales: Law and Gender in the Ottoman Court of Aintab* (Berkeley: University of California Press, 2003), 8–9; Dror Ze'evi, "The Use of Ottoman Shari'a Court Records as a Source for Middle Eastern Social History: A Reappraisal," *Islamic Law and Society* 5, no. 1 (1998): 35–56.

10. Section 16 in *La'ihat al-Wukala' amama al-Mahakim al-Shar'iyya* (Cairo: al-Matba'a al-Mawsu'a, 1900), 8.

11. Section 68 in *Ta'rifat al-Rusum al-Muqarrara bi-l-Mahakim al-Shar'iyya* (Cairo: Matba'at Bulaq, 1886), 8. This fee is also usually noted in the margins or at the end of the case transcripts in the ledgers of the early twentieth century.

12. Margot Badran, *Feminists, Islam, and Nation: Gender and the Making of Modern Egypt* (Princeton, NJ: Princeton University Press, 1995), 127; Enid Hill, *Mahkama! Studies in the Egyptian Legal System* (London: Ithaca Press, 1979), 92.

13. See, e.g., Byron Cannon, *Politics of Law and the Courts in Nineteenth-Century Egypt* (Salt Lake City: University of Utah Press, 1988); Cuno, *The Pasha's Peasants*; Khaled Fahmy and Rudolph Peters, "The Legal History of Ottoman Egypt," *Islamic Law and Society* 6, no. 2 (1999): 129–35; Amira El Azhary Sonbol, ed., *Women, the Family, and Divorce Laws in Islamic History* (Syracuse, NY: Syracuse University Press, 1996), 248; Ehud Toledano, *State and Society in Mid-nineteenth-century Egypt* (New York: Cambridge University Press, 1990); and Tucker, *Women in Nineteenth-Century Egypt*.

14. Although one's class is an ambiguous and evolving category that cannot always be clearly labeled, the social and financial background of the litigants in these records can be ascertained through their professions, honorary titles, and the monetary amounts mentioned in their suits.

15. For an extensive study on how Egyptian couples of all classes understood and exercised their marriage and divorce rights vis-à-vis the portrayals and practices of marriage by middle-class writers in the press, see Hanan Kholoussy, *For Better, For Worse: The Marriage Crisis That Made Modern Egypt* (Stanford, CA: Stanford University Press, 2010).

16. Fahmy and Peters, "The Legal History of Ottoman Egypt," 131–34.

17. Nathan Brown, "Shari'a and State in the Modern Middle East," *International Journal of Middle East Studies* 29, no. 3 (1997): 360.

18. Muhammad Pasha Qadri, *Kitab al-Ahkam al-Shar'iyya fi al-Ahwal al-Shakhsiyya 'ala Madhhab al-Imam Abi Hanifa al-Nu'man* (Cairo: Ministry of Justice, 1875). For an English translation of this book, see Qadri, *Code of Mohammedan Personal Law According to the Hanafite School*, trans. Wasey Sterry and N. Abcarius (London: Spottiswoode & Co., Ltd., 1914).

19. James N. D. Anderson, "Law Reform in Egypt: 1850–1950," in *Political and Social Change in Modern Egypt*, ed. P. M. Holt (London: Oxford University Press, 1968), 222; Shaham, *Family and the Courts in Modern Egypt*, 10–12. For the actual codes, see, respectively, *La'ihat al-Mahakim al-Shar'iyya bi-l-Aqtar al-Misriyya* (Cairo: al-Matba'a al-Miriyya, 1880); and *La'ihat Tartib al-Mahakim al-Shar'iyya wa-l-Ijra'at al-Muta'alliqa bi-ha* (Cairo: Matba'a al-Miriyya, 1897).

20. Anderson, "Law Reform in Egypt," 225; John L. Esposito, *Women in Muslim Family Law*, 2nd ed. (Syracuse, NY: Syracuse University Press, 2001), 51–52.

21. Judith E. Tucker, *In the House of the Law: Gender and Islamic Law in Ottoman Syria and Palestine* (Berkeley: University of California Press, 1998), 72.

22. Section 1 in *La'ihat Tartib al-Mahakim al-Shar'iyya*, 1. While the 1897 code refers to the first two courts with different names, the actual registers in the archives as well as legal journals used these names. See also Shaham, *Family and the Courts in Modern Egypt*, 12.

23. Anderson, "Law Reform in Egypt," 222; Shaham, *Family and the Courts in Modern Egypt*, 11–12. Although part of the Ottoman Empire until 1914, Egypt did not follow the Islamic legal reforms in other Ottoman provinces. For an overview of the Islamic personal status

reforms undertaken by the Ottoman Empire, see Judith E. Tucker, "Revisiting Reform: Women and the Ottoman Law of Family Rights, 1917," *Arab Studies Journal* 4, no. 2 (1996): 4–17. For an extensive study of the sociolegal reforms and their effects on family cases adjudicated in Ottoman Palestine, see Agmon, *Family and Court*.

24. Tucker, *Women in Nineteenth-Century Egypt*, 10–12.

25. Shaham, *Family and the Courts in Modern Egypt*, 12. For brevity and clarity, I prefer to use only the Western date. Because the pages of these early twentieth-century shari'a registers are not always numbered, I do not cite page numbers for the case transcripts as scholars of other legal records do. Although each case contained a consecutive serial number and a court case number, I cite only the consecutive serial number so that cases can be easily located.

26. For specific examples of my own method for citing these court records, see Kholoussy, *For Better, For Worse*.

27. Section 176 in Qadri, *Kitab al-Ahkam al-Shar'iyya*, 46.

28. Shaham, *Family and the Courts in Modern Egypt*, 71–72; "Ta'limat al-Habs," *al-Muhamma al-Shar'iyya* 2, no. 8 (1931): 763–65; "Tanzim al-Mahakim al-Shar'iyya: al-Habs fi Nafaqat al-Zawjiyya," *al-Ahram* 36, no. 10035, 17 March 1911, 1.

29. See *La'ihat al-Mahakim al-Shar'iyya*.

30. Tucker, *Women in Nineteenth-Century Egypt*, 10–12.

31. Shaham, *Family and the Courts in Modern Egypt*, 15; Farhat J. Ziadeh, *Lawyers, the Rule of Law and Liberalism in Modern Egypt* (Stanford, CA: Hoover Institution, 1968), 56–57.

32. Shaham, *Family and the Courts in Modern Egypt*, 15; Ziadeh, *Lawyers, the Rule of Law*, 57–58.

33. On the qualifications and regulations of shari'a lawyers, see *La'ihat al-Wukala' amama al-Mahakim al-Shar'iyya*.

34. Ibid., section 16, 8.

35. Shaham, *Family and the Courts in Modern Egypt*, 13.

36. Ibid., 12.

37. Amira El Azhary Sonbol, "Adults and Minors in Ottoman Shari'a Courts and Modern Law," in *Women, the Family, and Divorce Laws*, 248.

38. Proposals to reform shari'a divorce laws were made in the 1890s by Ahmad Muhammad Shakir, Muhammad 'Abduh, and Qasim Amin. See Ahmad Muhammad Shakir, *Nizam al-Talaq fi al-Islam* (Cairo: Dar al-Tab'a al-Qawmiyya, 1936), 9–11; Muhammad 'Imara, *al-Islam wa-l-Mar'a fi Ra'i al-Imam Muhammad 'Abduh* (Cairo: Dar al-Hilal, 1979), 25–31, 78–95; and Qasim Amin, *The Liberation of Women and The New Woman*, trans. Samiha Sidhom Peterson (Cairo: American University in Cairo Press, 2000), 99.

39. Hanan Kholoussy, "The Nationalization of Marriage in Monarchical Egypt," in *Re-envisioning Egypt, 1919–1952*, ed. Arthur Goldschmidt Jr., Amy J. Johnson, and Barak Salmoni (Cairo: American University in Cairo Press, 2005), 317–50.

40. James N. D. Anderson, "Recent Developments in Shari'a Law V," *Muslim World* 41, no. 4 (1951), 278–88; Esposito, *Women in Muslim Family Law*, 51.

41. Shaham, *Family and the Courts in Modern Egypt*, 14.

42. Mervat Hatem, "The Enduring Alliance of Nationalism and Patriarchy in Muslim Personal Status Laws: The Case of Modern Egypt," *Feminist Issues* 6, no. 1 (1986): 19.

43. James N. D. Anderson, *Islamic Law in the Modern World* (New York: New York University Press, 1959); Anderson, "Law Reform in Egypt," 209–30; Anderson, "The Problem of Divorce in the Shari'a Law of Islam: Measures of Reform in Modern Egypt," *Royal Central*

Asian Society Journal 37 (1950): 169–85; Anderson, "Recent Developments in Shariʿa Law II: Matters of Competence, Organization and Procedure," *The Muslim World* 40, no. 1 (1950): 34–48; Anderson, "Recent Developments in Shariʿa Law III," *The Muslim World* 41, no. 2 (1951): 113–26; Anderson, "Recent Developments in Shariʿa Law IV," *The Muslim World* 41, no. 3 (1951): 186–98; Anderson, "Recent Developments in Shariʿa Law V," *The Muslim World* 41, no. 4 (1951): 271–88; Anderson, "The Role of Personal Status in Social Development in Islamic Countries," *Comparative Studies in Society and History* 13, no. 1 (1971): 16–31; Badran, *Feminists, Islam, and Nation*, 124–41; Beth Baron, "The Making and Breaking of Marital Bonds in Modern Egypt," in *Women in Middle Eastern History: Shifting Boundaries in Sex and Gender*, ed. Nikki R. Keddie and Beth Baron (New Haven, CT: Yale University Press, 1991), 275–91; Noel J. Coulson, *A History of Islamic Law* (Edinburgh: Edinburgh University Press, 1964); Esposito, *Women in Muslim Family Law*, 47–126; Hatem, "The Enduring Alliance of Nationalism," 19–43; Amira El Azhary Sonbol, "Introduction," in *Women, the Family, and Divorce Laws*, 1–20.

44. See Kholoussy, *For Better, For Worse*, chapter 4.

45. For analyses of these various press debates, see, e.g., Badran, *Feminists, Islam, and Nation*; Beth Baron, *The Women's Awakening in Egypt: Culture, Society, and the Press* (New Haven, CT: Yale University Press, 1994), 7–8; Baron, *Egypt as a Woman: Nationalism, Gender, and Politics* (Berkeley: University of California Press, 2005); Marilyn Booth, *May Her Likes Be Multiplied: Biography and Gender Politics in Egypt* (Berkeley: University of California Press, 2001); Israel Gershoni and James P. Jankowski, *Egypt, Islam, and the Arabs: The Search for Egyptian Nationhood, 1900–1930* (New York: Oxford University Press, 1986); Israel Gershoni and James P. Jankowski, *Redefining the Egyptian Nation, 1930–1945* (New York: Cambridge University Press, 1995); and Kholoussy, *For Better, For Worse*.

BIBLIOGRAPHY

Anderson, James N. D. *Islamic Law in the Modern World*. New York: New York University Press, 1959.

Anderson, James N. D. "Law Reform in Egypt: 1850–1950." In *Political and Social Change in Modern Egypt*, edited by P. M. Holt, 209–30. London: Oxford University Press, 1968.

Anderson, James N. D. "The Problem of Divorce in the Shariʿa Law of Islam: Measures of Reform in Modern Egypt." *Journal of the Royal Central Asian Society* 37 (1950): 169–85.

Anderson, James N. D. "Recent Developments in Shariʿa Law III." *Muslim World* 41, no. 2 (1951): 113–26.

Anderson, James N. D. "Recent Developments in Shariʿa Law IV." *Muslim World* 41, no. 3 (1951): 186–98.

Anderson, James N. D. "Recent Developments in Shariʿa Law V." *Muslim World* 41, no. 4 (1951): 271–88.

Brown, Nathan. "Shariʿa and State in the Modern Middle East." *International Journal of Middle East Studies* 29, no. 3 (1997): 359–76.

Cannon, Byron. *Politics of Law and the Courts in Nineteenth-Century Egypt*. Salt Lake City: University of Utah Press, 1988.

Fahmy, Khaled, and Rudolph Peters. "The Legal History of Ottoman Egypt." *Islamic Law and Society* 6, no. 2 (1999): 129–35.

Goldschmidt Jr., Arthur, Amy J. Johnson, and Barak Salmoni, eds. *Re-Envisioning Egypt, 1919–1952*. Cairo: American University in Cairo Press, 2005.

Hatem, Mervat. "The Enduring Alliance of Nationalism and Patriarchy in Muslim Personal Status Laws: The Serial Case of Modern Egypt." *Feminist Issues* 6, no. 1 (1986): 19–43.

Hill, Enid. *Mahkama! Studies in the Egyptian Legal System, Court and Crimes, Law and Society*. London: Ithaca Press, 1979.

Kholoussy, Hanan. *For Better, For Worse: The Marriage Crisis That Made Modern Egypt*. Stanford: Stanford University Press, 2010.

Safran, Nadav. "The Abolition of the Shar'ia Courts in Egypt." *Muslim World* 48, no. 1 (1958): 20–28.

Shaham, Ron. *Family and the Courts in Modern Egypt: A Study Based on Decisions by the Shari'a Courts, 1900–1955*. Leiden: Brill, 1997.

Sonbol, Amira El Azhary, ed. *Women, the Family, and Divorce Laws in Islamic History*. Syracuse, NY: Syracuse University Press, 1996.

Tucker, Judith E. *Women in Nineteenth-Century Egypt*. Cambridge: Cambridge University Press, 1985.

Ze'evi, Dror. "The Use of Ottoman Shari'a Court Records as a Source for Middle Eastern Social History: A Reappraisal." *Islamic Law and Society* 5, no. 1 (1998): 35–56.

Ziadeh, Farhat J. *Lawyers, The Rule of Law and Liberalism in Modern Egypt*. Stanford: Hoover Institution, 1968.

CHAPTER 15

··

FROM THE COMMON GOOD
TO PUBLIC INTEREST

··

JEFFREY CULANG

IN 1890, a Syrian Catholic writer residing in Egypt named Habib Faris introduced his newly published translation of a European text titled *Les crimes rituels des Juifs* by "affirming publicly . . . the single purpose of the appearance of this book is to bring to light truths before the eyes not of a nation or government only but of all without respect to national or doctrinal difference or to class or rank distinction."[1] Faris had provided the first Arabic translation of this French work, which had only recently been published in France. The original work gathered, in encyclopedic fashion, the incidents of blood libel (*al-dhaba'ih al-bashariyya* or *tuhmat al-dam*) claimed to have occurred in both the East and the West. These included the recent alleged slaughter in Damascus of a six-year-old boy at the hands of a group of Jews said to have drained his blood to mix it in the dough they used to make ritual bread (matzoh) for the Jewish holiday of Passover. As Faris explained, "we clutched our hands on the only copy of this book in the world and decided to translate it into the Arabic language." What called him to this task was less an age-old fanaticism toward Jews, which many associated with the blood libel accusation, than a desire to serve the interests of a modern public. "If there was discovered among the religious groups [*tawa'if*] and nations [*umam*] residing in the Ottoman Empire an evil commanding the elimination or incineration of [justice]," Faris explained, "in this glorious age, we must bring it to light in any way possible."[2] In Faris's view, it was Jews, or certain among them, who still clung to old traditions.

About a decade later, in 1902, an actual blood libel accusation was made in Port Said, Egypt. The blood libel charge had a long history in Christian Europe, but this incident was the most recent in a string of such charges in the Ottoman Empire that began only in the early nineteenth century. The accused, a twenty-six-year-old Jewish man named Hayyim Daud Kahana, was convicted in court and then acquitted in appeal, largely thanks to the skilled defense of his lawyer, the prominent local Jewish reformer from Egypt's Karaite community, Murad Faraj.[3] During and after the affair, Faraj countered the charge against Kahana and denounced the blood libel in the press. Like Faris, he sought to reach a broad audience and invoked a new age of enlightenment and justice. Yet Faraj was developing a more inclusive approach to Egypt's plural condition. He came to see Egypt's diverse communities as bound together by a shared notion of the common good (*al-maslaha al-'amma, al-nafi' al-'amm*, among other terms), which demanded both moral improvement and avoidance of moral injury.

Faraj was one of many intellectuals in colonial Egypt to participate in the secularization of a long-standing notion of the common good before its gradual displacement by the modern idea of public interest (also *al-maslaha al-'amma*).[4] Although these two concepts share a phrase in Arabic and are both concerned with managing collective life, they carry very different meanings. Within the Islamic tradition, the common good is a legal concept intended to sustain a moral community through the bottom-up cultivation of virtuous subjects who look out for one another. Focused on the individual embedded within a community, it encourages acts that produce benefit (*manfa'a*) and discourages those that produce injury (*mafsada*), the twin aims of the Islamic duty *al-amr bi-l ma'ruf wa-l-nahi 'an al-munkar* (commanding right and forbidding wrong).[5]

Public interest, by contrast, is a modern legal concept generally concerned with satisfying an aggregate of the selfish interests of individuals who comprise a presumed public of citizens—the national body.[6] In place of a fluid relationship between community and subject, public interest presumes a sharp distinction between public and private, even as it is an aggregate of private interests that constitutes the nation's public interest. Moreover, within the private realm, it enacts a hierarchy of interests. Whereas the shared private interests of the majority comprise the national will, those of minorities come to be viewed as suspicious and even threatening. For this reason, public interest is never far from security. It can be seen as part of what Michel Foucault, in his discussion of biopolitics, referred to as the modern state's apparatus of security, the purpose of which is to maintain the equilibrium of the whole less through top-down regulation than through laissez-faire. Foucault viewed freedom as a core feature of security, which involved intervention only to root out internal dangers.[7] As a calculation of the greatest good, public interest often authorizes judicial or executive power to act extrajudicially to meet such dangers, including minority (private) interests.[8]

Historicizing the transition from the common good to public interest is, therefore, a window onto conceptions of subject, community, and nation as well as the relationships between them. For the case of Egypt, a focus on Egyptian Jews is logical for two reasons. First, during the colonial period, Jews were the second-largest non-Muslim religious group numerically after the Copts, and unlike the Copts, who were widely viewed to be an essential element of the nation (if often excluded internally), Jews were eventually excluded under the guise of national security. Second, and related, by the time Egypt approached sovereignty in 1936–37, and especially over the ensuing three decades, Jews were increasingly identified as one of the main threats to public interest due to the perception that their loyalty was to foreign capital and foreign powers rather than the Egyptian nation.[9]

Such an analysis can be pursued using state-produced legal texts and periodicals, the archives of the Alliance Israélite Universelle (AIU), and the fractured textual record of a dislocated and scattered Jewish community whose origin country prevents access to its remaining records there.[10] While communal archives and records are typically used to explore the social history of various religious communities in Egypt and their place in modern Egyptian society, they can also be used to examine broader societal transformations and their effects on how these communities related to each other and to the state.[11] In other words, as the state archive in Egypt is becoming increasingly inaccessible, historians can pose new questions of communal archives and records that transcend a narrow communal framework for understanding these communities' histories. In this way, "minority" histories can enable new ways of understanding more "central" stories.

Contained in the archives and records pertaining to Egyptian Jews is a set of texts and related accusations often bundled together under the umbrella of antisemitism. These texts include translations of Western European works on the blood libel, which represent the tail end of an old form of anti-Jewish Christian polemics, and the paradigmatic anti-Semitic work, the fictitious *The Protocols of the Elders of Zion*. Their appearance in Egypt and in Arabic for the first time coincided with and inspired, in the former case, a string of public accusations between the 1870s and 1920s that Jews murdered Christians for ritual purposes, and in the latter case, the claim that Jews sought to take over the main organs of state to channel them toward their own interests (*maslaha*) and achieve world domination. Amid a broad corpus of translations integral to local efforts at moral, legal, social, and political reform in colonial Egypt, this set of texts conveys translation's role in projects of violence, both physical and otherwise.

Blood libel accusations, almost unheard of in the Ottoman world prior to European imperial intervention and the expansion of Christian missions in the nineteenth century, and almost exclusively leveled by Christians, contended that Jews, allegedly guided by Talmudic prescriptions, sought to drink Christian blood or to siphon it to make Passover matzoh. Writers such as Faris defended such charges on the profane level, in the name of enlightenment, truth, and progress. Spurious and damaging as these accusations and insinuations were, they tended to be local rather than global in scope and were directed at specific Jews rather than imputing essential characteristics to Jews in general. Such distinctions would be lost on the radical translators and proponents of *The Protocols* during the 1940s and 1950s.

Due to their peculiar and incendiary nature, blood libel accusations attracted scrutiny and sometimes scorn in Egypt. Murad Faraj, the prominent Jewish reformer who defended Kahana against the blood libel accusation, countered them vociferously in both the courtroom and the press. To do so, Faraj expounded and modeled an unfolding vision of the common good premised not on top-down intervention, as with public interest, but on the bottom-up cultivation of virtues, especially sincerity (*ikhlas*). This form of edification (*al-tahdhib*) started with the individual and extended to the community and the broader collective. Faraj's approach to the common good intersected with the thought of other participants in the *nahda*, some of whom addressed the ritual murder charge directly.

Faraj's vision of the social runs counter to the two poles of modern Jewish politics, Zionism and assimilationism, both of which share a "fear of admitting that there are and always have been divergent interests between Jews and segments of the people among whom they live."[12] It therefore invites reflection on both Jewishness and its relation to ethics and politics as well as plurality as a problem of governance in the nation-state. Faraj's approach to Jewishness and plurality was ultimately jettisoned by the translation of public interest, which contributed to transforming the local Jew in Egypt (al-isra'ili) into an abstract Jew (al-yahudi) whose interests were deemed suspicious and threatening.[13] As in modern Europe, the abstraction of Jews—their transformation into a symbol—contributed to their exclusion from the nation-state.[14] Antisemitism, rather than being endemic to Egypt as an Arab or Islamic society, was a newly available European ideology that offered an idiom through which this exclusion could be expressed.

Tracing this process—the emergence of public/private interest and the exclusion of certain private interests—as it unfolded in Egypt reveals its connection to the rise of the nation-state but also to the problem of colonial rule and, in the case of Jews, Zionist ascendency in Palestine. The transition from the common good to public interest initiated structures, categories, and rationalities during the liberal period that would prove critical to acts of exclusion after the overthrow of the monarchy and establishment of a republic in 1952.

THE BLOOD LIBEL AND COLONIAL LAW

Habib Faris's decision to translate an antisemitic French text into Arabic was perhaps not as serendipitous as he suggests. His recognition of the book and interest in it were likely conditioned by the news he had recently heard of the blood libel accusation in Damascus. Even before he began curiously flipping through the pages of Les crimes rituels des Juifs, he had likely known that the 1890 affair was only the latest such case to have occurred within his Ottoman orbit—the most well-known being the Damascus Affair of 1840, which was an early instance of European Christian anti-Judaism being encoded into local inter-communal politics and vernaculars. The first ritual murder accusation in Egypt occurred in 1870. An elderly Jewish man was arrested in Alexandria, and rumors spread, particularly within the Maltese community, that he had intended to kill a young Christian boy and use his blood to make matzoh. In response, the Jewish community appealed to the then British consul general.[15] This was followed by another accusation in Damanhur in 1878 involving an Italian child, and then another in Alexandria in 1881 involving a young Greek boy, both activating responses from local police, state authorities, and foreign consulates.[16] In 1882, a Greek woman in Port Said witnessed her daughter wander into the home of an "Ottoman Jewish family" (perhaps Sephardic) and the door shut behind her. The mother notified passersby, and riots broke out among "Greeks and Arabs." The father of the house, an elderly man, was allegedly dragged from his home and trampled to death. Sixty Jews in Port Said, who were "citizens of various countries," signed a petition addressed to Khedive 'Abbas Hilmi and British Consul General Lord Cromer in which they demanded, among other concerns, that the consul general ensure those responsible be punished.[17]

Then, in 1902, an Italian family in Port Said accused Hayyim Kahana of the attempted kidnapping and ritual murder of their young daughter. In contrast to the prior cases, however, the Jewish community involved in this one appealed not to Lord Cromer, who was still Egypt's consul general, but to an emerging star of Egypt's legal profession, Murad Faraj. The case conveys the reality that by the turn of the twentieth century, many Jews had been absorbed into Egypt's nascent National Courts system and, by extension, into Egypt as a polity in formation under colonial rule.[18] Murad Faraj, in his role as a legal expert, was critical to this process.

Born in Egypt in 1866, Murad Faraj lived a life that spanned ninety years, during which his natal Ottoman province became British-occupied territory, a British protectorate, and finally a semi-sovereign and—just before his death in 1956—a sovereign nation-state. Faraj's intellectual and professional trajectory bears the marks of Egypt's shifting cultural, political, and social terrain. Having graduated from the Khedival Law School in 1889—the first Jew to do so since the institution's establishment in 1868—he served as a lawyer in the National Court of Appeals and wrote a series of manuals on Egyptian law.[19] Faraj was thus the product of a key colonial legal institution and in the state's employ, producing and disseminating legal knowledge. In fact, after gaining fame as a lawyer, he worked directly for Khedive 'Abbas Hilmi as a legal advisor. By the early 1900s, Faraj had been drawn to the linguistic, literary, and cultural revival of the *nahda* and, in its spirit, established the Karaite reform journal *al-Tahdhib* (Edification). Faraj was a *dayan* (judge) on the Karaite *bayt din* (court) in Cairo and helped codify Egyptian Jewry's personal status laws as part of the overall secularization of law in Egypt.[20] By 1908, he began to advocate patriotic ideals and constitutionalism in the Egyptian nationalist journals *al-Jarida* (The Newspaper) and *al-Mu'ayyad* (The Strengthened), considering himself part of an emerging Egyptian nation bound together by a shared sense of the common good.[21]

After World War I, Faraj encountered the growing acceptance of a powerful European discourse coupling Jewishness with nationality, which raised suspicion about the loyalty of Jews to the emerging Egyptian nation-state and, therefore, its public interest. In contrast, Faraj saw Egypt's Jews as a constituent group (*ta'ifa*) within the Egyptian nation. In the 1920s and 1930s, he sought to bring Karaites and Rabbanites together and highlight commonalities between Hebrew and Arabic, and Jews' place within Arab and Islamic culture and history.[22] He also may have been a member of Egypt's prestigious Arabic Language Academy.[23] In the 1940s and 1950s, Faraj witnessed his long-term projects become increasingly foreclosed due to contingent circumstances and events in Egypt, in Palestine/Israel, and globally. Faraj died several years after the Free Officers' Revolt of 1952 that ended the monarchy. He was largely forgotten thereafter, fitting into neither the logic nor the telos of Arab and Egyptian nationalism and Zionism.

Faraj approached adulthood at the time of Egypt's colonization. In 1882, Britain established control over Egypt militarily. One year later, the legal colonization of Egypt was underway, with British and Egyptian administrators and lawyers devising and implementing reforms to expand and empower positivist law, a codified set of abstract rules with no necessary relationship to morality that applied to all cases publicly and equally.[24] The spread of positivist law vis-à-vis the newly established National Courts confined the shari'a and the *milli* (non-Muslim) legal systems to the private domain (i.e., family law), transforming their content and, arguably, their conceptions of morality.[25]

Detaching subjects from these legal structures and subjecting them to colonial law also meant refashioning their historical memories and temporal sensibilities to produce loyalty to the state over their religious community. The ideology of legal reform presupposed a past characterized by chaos and despotism and a civilized present that progressed toward a future of justice and "rule of law" (always in the offing).[26] Established soon after the National Courts, the Khedival Law School, in which Faraj was trained, produced the first generation of lawyers, who, equipped with fluency in the national codes, filled the National Courts. Embodiments of a new kind of legal expertise, these lawyers competed for authority with legal practitioners of displaced traditions.[27] It is no wonder that many of Egypt's future nationalist leaders, including Mustafa Kamil and Sa'd Zaghlul, were among those to attend the Khedival Law School.

Three of Murad Faraj's works published between 1893 and 1901, or between his last days in law school and the establishment of his communal journal *al-Tahdhib*, illustrate his entanglement with colonial law—an entanglement that his Christian and Muslim colleagues shared. His works were part of a massive corpus of typeset and easily reproducible legal manuals published from 1883 onward. In their structure and language, and in their endless repetition, they helped produce the authority of positivist law, which they pitted against "atavistic" and "barbaric" legal frameworks of the past.[28]

The three works—*Risala fi Sharh al-Amwal 'ala al-Qanun al-Madani al-Ahli* (Commentary on Property in National Civil Law, 1893), *Kitab al-Majmu' fi Sharh al-Shuru' 'ala al-Qanun al-Misri al-Ahli* (Collected Work on Explaining the Inception of Egyptian National Law, 1894), and *Da'awa Wada' al-Yad* (Possessory Actions, 1901)—deal with various aspects of Egyptian law and engage with a legal corpus.[29] The first two, as Faraj points out, are based upon the works of jurists and legal theorists—most of them French—to whom he had been exposed in law school. In the earlier work, Faraj explains that he "drew upon some of the most well-known French commentators." The book, he goes on, "will be succeeded, God willing, by the publication of many other theses prepared on various topics of law."[30] For Faraj, Egyptian law is an open field of knowledge in need of explication. In his third book, published eight years after the first one, he suggests that a tradition of positivist law in Egypt had formed, and now he engages not foreign works alone but also texts by jurists from Egypt's National and Mixed Courts.[31] Revealing his attachment to Egyptian law and to an emerging Egyptian nation, Faraj refers to "our national law" when providing a genealogy of possessory actions (a proceeding to recover lost property).[32]

Faraj also contributed to consolidating a singular and unified legal system in Egypt under the control of the modern state. On their introduction in 1883, Egypt's National Courts claimed jurisdiction over all commercial and criminal cases from the shari'a and *milli* courts.[33] In the early twentieth century, Egyptian nationalists saw the National Courts as a medium through which to forge a sovereign and unified Egypt. This involved abolishing the Mixed Courts (and the Capitulations), which were obstacles to Egyptian sovereignty and, for some, integrating the hitherto autonomous "religious" courts into the National Courts. The shari'a and *milli* courts survived until 1955, three years after the 1952 Free Officers' Revolt (though communal personal status codes were integrated into Egyptian law), but heated debates continued throughout the first half of the twentieth century over whether to regulate or abrogate them. Legal thinkers, intellectuals, and the state, which authorized itself to approve non-Muslim communal codes, developed a keen interest in personal status law.

In this context, Faraj helped to found and participated in the Karaite communal council established in 1901, a main purpose of which was to organize and manage the community's personal status affairs.[34] In 1912, he translated Rabbi Mas'ud Hay Bin Shim'un's compilation of the Rabbanites' personal status codes from Hebrew into Arabic.[35] In 1917, Faraj translated and commented upon personal status statutes in Elijah Bashyatchi's fifteenth- and sixteenth-century codification of Karaite law, *Aderet Eliyahu* (The Mantle of Elijah).[36] After the passing of the 1923 Egyptian Constitution, as personal status law was again a focal point of debate, the Karaite rabbi Ibrahim Kuhayn commissioned Faraj to codify the Karaites' laws.[37] The manuscript he produced could not be approved by the communal council due to some community members' opposition to his reformist rendering of statutes on lineage and intermarriage between Jews of different sects. However, in 1935, the council reached out to Faraj after Egypt's Ministry of Justice requested the community's still unpublished codes. Faraj provided a copy, which was eventually approved by both the council and the Egyptian state.[38] In this way, Faraj played an important role in the legal formation of the modern Egyptian nation-state. We will now explore Faraj's location within both Jewish tradition and Egypt's secularizing society through a dramatic court case from the early twentieth century.

A RITUAL MURDER ACCUSATION

In December 1902, as Faraj was working on editing his communal reform journal, *al-Tahdhib*, in Cairo, he learned of the indictment of Hayyim Daud Kahana—a young Rabbanite Jew who was originally from Safed but resided in Port Said, where he sold wares on boats passing through the Suez Canal—for attempted kidnapping. The family of a six-year-old Italian Catholic girl named Pépina Papassi had accused Kahana of trying to abduct her from the family home in order to use her blood to make Passover matzoh. According to the ruling of the Zaqaziq National Court where the case was assigned, on the afternoon of 2 October 1901, Kahana had appeared at the apartment of the child in the European district. He was already familiar with her due to his frequent visits to the shop of a Jewish watchmaker named Pinhas Albert, which neighbored her father's own shop. At the time of Kahana's arrival, Pépina was playing on the outside steps with other children her age. According to the indictment, he approached the girl and attempted to lure her to his home by offering her sweets. Falling for the ruse, the girl began descending the stairwell toward him when a certain dame Marula, the family's Greek servant (*khadima*) who lived in the same building and had been observing the scene from behind the front door window, opened the door abruptly and called the girl's name. Frightened, Kahana quickly fled.[39] Marula then related details of the incident to the girl's mother, who screamed in horror.[40]

On 31 October, the Port Said Parquet, in the presence of the Italian consul, recorded depositions from Pépina and Marula, as well as the *bawab* (doorman), 'Abduh Sulayman, who confirmed their accounts. On this basis, the Parquet "recommended" to the Zaqaziq court that it convict the accused based on articles of the Egyptian Penal Code covering attempted kidnapping. The Baghdad-born Jew Samuel Somekh, founder of an AIU school in Alexandria, was following the events closely and kept the AIU abreast of developments. According to Somekh, amid the affair, Cairo's chief rabbi had left for vacation in Lebanon—an act that angered Somekh.[41] In the rabbi's absence, the community's leaders, wishing to provide succor, sent Kahana to a son of the influential Mosseri family. The son could do no more than provide a lawyer, whom Somekh accused of neglecting the case.[42]

The court was supposed to convene a criminal hearing that November, but it was ultimately delayed until September of 1902. When the hearing date arrived, the judges, 'Abd al-Shahid and Muhammad Zaki, heard the testimony of the girl, her father, the servant, and the *bawab*. They also heard the testimony of the watchmaker Pinhas Albert, though discounted his statements on the premise that he would naturally defend his co-religionist. The judges reasoned that because Kahana had persisted in offering Pépina sweets, he had a premeditated plan, and because he had her descend the stairwell, he intended to take her with him and perhaps kill her for her blood. Only causes "independent of his will," namely Marula, prevented him from carrying out the act. The court declared Kahana guilty of attempted kidnapping, sentencing him to one year of hard labor and charging him for the cost of the court proceeding.[43] Somekh attributed the verdict to foreign European pressure on the court.[44] Though an innocent person would have found the sentence harsh, the court seemed to be taking a middle position by not charging Kahana with the steeper charge of attempted murder.

Stunned by the ruling, Somekh decided to contact Murad Faraj, the well-known Karaite lawyer. Faraj took the case and, the next day, brought it to the National Court of Appeals in Cairo, where he was confident he could win an acquittal "so long as foreign pressure did not weigh on [the judge's] judgment."[45] His confidence signifies, on the one hand, his familiarity with and investment in the National Courts—an institution critical to his vision of Egypt's future—and on the other, his trust in relationships he had forged with fellow *nahda* reformers in Egypt. Faraj had surely been aware that it was the influential Muslim social reformer Qasim Amin who headed (*ra'is*) the appeals court in

Cairo. The two had likely met at the Khedival Law School, from which they graduated at roughly the same time; in any case, they were aware of each other's writings and saw each other as partners in reform toward the common good in Egypt.[46] On 15 December 1902, only three months after the initial verdict, Qasim Amin and two judges, including eventual prime minister (from 1924 to 1926) Ahmad Ziwar, would hear Faraj's defense of Kahana.

During the hearing, Faraj dismantled the testimony of the three witnesses by exposing gaps in their stories. How was it, he asked, that on witnessing the incident, Marula could call out indignantly to the *bawab*, as he had testified, that "a Jew was trying to take the girl," when she had only had a quick look at him and could not have determined his identity (*jinsiyyatuh*)? Likewise, how could the servant of a neighbor of the Papassi family, who had just witnessed the incident and rushed to the father's store, have told Mr. Papassi, as the latter testified, that "a Jew wanted to take your daughter," when he did not know this man, no less his religion (*dinuh*)? And how could the governess claim that Kahana was foolish enough to return to the scene of the incident the next day and to ask her whether there was an Italian (*rumiyya*) woman living in the house with young children, thus implying that he had sought the blood of Christians and especially Italians? It was this latter allegation that most offended Faraj, and the governess had supported it in her initial testimony in Zaqaziq by pointing out that Kahana had married the rabbi's daughter, suggesting he was pious and that it is "a custom of Jews to take a Christian girl every year."[47] Thus, much of Faraj's defense of Kahana in appeal was to explain Judaism, the content of its sacred books, and the meaning of moral Jewish subjecthood within the space of a secular Egyptian court that, it turns out, was receptive to his message.

Indeed, the court's judgment—signed by Qasim Amin himself—reflects Amin's sympathy for Faraj's reasoning and argumentation. To begin with, it found inadmissible the accounts of all witness testimony other than that of the *bawab*, the girl, and the governess. It also readmitted the testimony of the watchmaker Pinhas. The ruling concluded that the *bawab* had been playing backgammon nearby the family home and was unaware that anything was happening until Péppina's mother screamed and he went to the house. The mother had raised her voice only when the governess had told her what happened to her daughter, by which time Kahana had long left. In other words, the *bawab*'s testimony that he encountered Kahana on the stairs was inconceivable. Turning to Marula, the court, echoing Faraj's logic, concluded that her testimony was not dependable because the glimpse she had of Kahana was insufficient for her to commit his features to memory and recognize him. And the six-year-old girl was probably seen to have been unduly influenced by her family and the servant.

Attempting to reconstruct the likely course of events, the court suggested that a man other than Kahana had approached the girl to abduct her. The *bawab*, wanting to absolve himself of responsibility for not being on guard at the time, and influenced by the ideas and opinions of the Papassi household (Marula in particular) and the neighbors, declared that the person was a Jew who sought to kill her as part of a "religious ceremony [*hafla diniyya*], as is rumored about the Jews." Then the *bawab* "went on his way searching for a Jew, encountered the accused, and identified him." According to

Somekh, Kahana had been eating lunch at a local Jewish establishment when he was unexpectedly confronted by the *bawab* and two police officers and taken to the Papassi's property.[48] The court determined that when the *bawab* showed Kahana to Marula, "she thought that this is who she saw and she must have been influenced by the words of the *bawab* and was sure that he truly saw the accused just as the *bawab* had been influenced by her words, and it would not be surprising if this mutual influence happened without knowledge . . . and with good intentions." On this basis, the court acquitted Kahana and ordered the state to reimburse his legal fees.[49] Faraj praised the decision, stating, "we can almost imagine a definitive general ruling against the lie of the [blood] accusation as should come from people of infallible and elevated minds, whose existence protects the human being, and this [ruling] is fair enough and satisfactory in our view."[50]

Despite Faraj's optimism, three months later, another ritual murder accusation was leveled against a local Jew[51]—this one leading to violence. In response, Faraj presented further critique of the blood libel accusation in his journal. What he could not have known is that this would be the last major accusation of this kind in Egypt's history, though the charge continued to echo through the years.[52] Through the establishment of a new secular legal regime, the colonial state stopped the flow of blood—both imagined and real—associated with ritual murder accusations. But as we will see, this same regime would enable new and more pernicious danger to Egyptian Jews in the decades ahead via the secular notion of public interest. Rather than an old form of anti-Judaism, that danger would take the form of modern antisemitism.

DEFENDING THE COMMON GOOD

Farag began to see the blood libel accusation as a "contagion" that had spread from "ancestors to descendants" and that suddenly had become so widespread that even Jews had begun to wonder whether they were true.[53] Though conflicted about whether to address this contagion in writing,[54] Faraj penned a series of editorials in his journal *al-Tahdhib* rejecting the blood libel and defending Jewish tradition. Observing that it was almost always Greeks who leveled such accusations, Faraj called them the "most hateful" because they "think they are the intended target in particular and that their blood is more suitable for the Jews than the blood of other Christians." He attributed this hatred to an old form of Christian anti-Judaism. On the most general level, "it is sufficient for me to say one word by way of an answer to the first reason [for the accusation], which is that the Jews did not say that the messiah came . . . and that they are still not Christian."[55] It was also believed that Jews had been the ones to kill Christ. As for the accusation itself, Faraj protested that "there is nothing uglier, more abominable, more repugnant, farther from reason, the imagination, and humanity generally than what has been said [about our tradition]."[56]

As a corrective, Farag, writing from within his tradition, tried to educate his readers about Jewish law and practice. In one article, for instance, he contended that anyone who committed such a heinous act could not have been a Jew, for "if they were Jews, they would follow their Torah, pray to God for it, pray to our Master Moses who descended from heaven with the revelation in his hand . . . celebrate the holidays, circumcise, purify, marry . . . divorce . . . and other things, and in it [the Torah] killing and bloodshed is absolutely forbidden." He went on to explain that the Torah is the mother of the Christian Bible, and according to the Bible, one should not even kill a mosquito, no less a child. Faraj also clarified Jewish legal proscriptions around the consumption of blood and slaughter of animals, revealing the accusation to have no basis in Jewish law or custom.[57] Yet in countering the rumors, Faraj also sought to make the point that it was not just Jews who were their victims; the blood libel accusation caused damage to the moral society—characterized by enlightenment, decency, and refinement—that he and other reformers were working so hard to create and sustain.

Some of these reformers joined him in publicly rejecting the blood accusation. The journal *al-Hilal* (The Crescent), edited by the reformer and intellectual Jurji Zaydan, had a history of denouncing it in its pages, with an editorial on the subject appearing in 1895 and another in 1896. Soon after the 1902–03 accusations, *al-Hilal* published a question and answer on the subject. In a letter to the editor, an individual from Alexandria by the name of Salim Effendi As'ad—perhaps a penname of the editor—asked, "The chatter has increased lately on the issue of the Greek child whom a Jewish man was accused of kidnapping, and I heard some say that the Jews kidnap Christian children and withdraw their blood in order to use it in bread for a religious purpose, so what do you say?" The editor sought to dispel such rumors: "It is not appropriate for us when we are in the age of enlightenment to believe something like this accusation. [This is] not because the Jews do not kill anyone, for they do so just like people from other [religious] groups [*tawa'if*]. They kill a Christian or Muslim child just like some Christians and Muslims do, whether on purpose or out of ignorance or for other reasons that propel people to commit crimes."

What Zaydan rejected was not the premise that Jews can commit murder but that "Jews carry out that act as a religious injunction recorded in their books or spread among them through indoctrination." He suggested that, instead of textual or doctrinal injunctions, the blood libel accusation could be attributed to the writings of Jews who converted to Christianity and, wanting to ingratiate themselves among their new co-religionists and take revenge on their old tradition, invented scandalous stories. The effect of these stories, he suggested, was aggravated by people's tendency to believe oddities and to gossip, made worse by "remaining grudges from the dark ages and ignorance that does not befit folks of this age."[58]

Al-Hilal's dismantlement of the blood libel accusation caused some readers to respond with disapproval and accuse the journal of apology, propelling Zaydan to take up the issue again. In a 1905 editorial titled "al-Talmud wa-tarjamatuh ila al-'arabiyya" (The Talmud and Its Translation into Arabic) that again responded to a question from the same Salim Effendi As'ad, the journal, observing that over the past ten years there had been much chatter about "blood atrocities" (*al-faza'i' al-damawiyya*) attributed to the Jews and their attempts to hide their textual or doctrinal basis, reiterated its earlier position. But it also went further: "It came to our mind . . . to translate the Talmud into Arabic and abridge it, and its pages [would take up] not less than one thousand pages [published] in sections in *al-Hilal*." The project was still on hold when Zaydan met in the home of one of Egypt's rabbis with the Moroccan Jewish author Shim'un Moyal. The latter was in Egypt with his wife, Esther al-Azhari Moyal, herself an author and editor of the women's journal *al-'A'ila* (The Family), studying medicine.[59] In the rabbi's book collection, Zaydan noticed a copy of the Talmud in Hebrew. Reminded of his translation project, he mentioned the idea to Moyal and proposed pursuing it together.

Moyal eventually accepted the invitation and involved the rabbi as well. However, several days later, Moyal informed Zaydan that he and the rabbi preferred to translate a complete rather than abridged Talmud, with side-by-side Arabic translation and Hebrew original. Zaydan was hardly disappointed, for "our original goal [was] the appearance of this book in Arabic after the Arabs remained ignorant of it for 1,300 years."[60] The rabbi later backed out entirely for undisclosed reasons. However, Moyal had his translation published in Palestine in 1909, making it accessible to a public of modern subjects who he felt would read it and find it edifying.[61] Zaydan's idea to publish the first Arabic Talmud to counter blood libel rumors had come to fruition and contrasts sharply with the impetus behind later translations of the Talmud into Arabic.

Underlying Faraj's critique of the blood libel accusation, his reform project generally, and other reformers' defense of Jews was an intersecting notion of the common good (*al-maslaha al-'amma*) taking shape under modern conditions. Conceived as the goal of the Islamic duty *al-amr bi-l ma'ruf wa-l-nahi 'an al-munkar* (commanding right and forbidding wrong), the common good is a central concept within Islamic law that is intended to promote social welfare and the moral community. The eleventh- and twelfth-century scholar Abu Hamid al-Ghazali was among the first to articulate juristic methods to determine *maslaha*, which were refuted and elaborated upon over the centuries.[62] For the most part, these methods did not involve recourse to the revealed texts. Faced with cases having no clear solution within the textual tradition, jurists instead drew on local custom and knowledge as well as elaborated forms of legal reasoning (e.g., *qiyas*, or analogy) to make rulings that had a high probability of being sound and at the very least met the five so-called universals of the shari'a: protection of life, mind, religion, family/community, and property.[63] Jurists, therefore, had tremendous authority to interpret what was a flexible and adaptable moral law, and as products of the communities they served, they were well positioned to protect and preserve the interests of the people, to whom they saw themselves beholden.[64]

With the rise of the modern state, Muslim reformers found *maslaha* to be an especially handy tool. In her analysis of the modern reformer Muhammad 'Abduh, Samira Haj has shown how 'Abduh, embedded within the Islamic tradition rather than liberalism, sought to promote a modern Muslim subject "capable of being incorporated into the fabric of modern structures of power and governance" but also, through ritual and disciplinary practices, "fundamentally moral with a concern for the public good."[65] In this spirit, 'Abduh sought to extend the individual obligation (*fard 'ayn*) to determine the common good—previously the domain of jurists—to every educated member of the community, a possibility made available by the spread of modern education. The notion of the common good that he advanced was fundamentally different from utilitarian public interest, which he rejected.[66] This latter notion is centered on self-possessing individuals rather than the human as a moral subject within a community, and the formation of national sensibilities rather than the cultivation of a moral collective. The extension of *fard 'ayn*, Haj points out, was "meant to promote and benefit the community as a collective, rather than advance the selfish interests of its individual members. . . . As members of the community," she goes on, "individuals are accountable not only to themselves for their beliefs and actions . . . [but also] to others, while . . . putting others' beliefs and actions into question."[67]

In his journal, published in 1902–03, Faraj does not invoke *maslaha* per se, but his notion of reform was similarly centered on the construction of moral subjects, in his case Jewish, toward achieving a moral community and a broader moral collective to which he and other Jews felt connected. Some of Faraj's articles published half a decade later do engage directly with *maslaha*. For example, in a 1908 essay titled "Harb al-watan" (The Nation's Struggle), written amid a Copt–Muslim sectarian crisis, Faraj describes the common good of the Egyptian nation as the prevention of moral injury (*al-idha' al-ma'nawi*) toward a sound national collective. Concerned about relations among Egypt's religious groups, he advocates acts of sincerity (*ikhlas*) that will prevent or alleviate hard feelings.[68] In 1909, in response to growing sectarian division and nationalist activity, Consul General Eldon Gorst reinstated the 1881 Press Law restricting freedom of the press. In response, Faraj wrote a series of articles evaluating the role of the journalist and journalism in society. In one article titled "Fi al-Hurriyya ma hiyya" (On Defining Freedom), Faraj articulates a notion of freedom that is bound to the moral subject as part of a community rather than to the self-owning individual: "the human's freedom is confined if the diamond of excellent morals, upright conduct, and general rights, or mutual rights, are confined . . . [this] damages the prisoner and others aside from him."[69] In other words, individual freedom absent moral commitment endangered the subject and community. The role of the journalist was to cultivate virtue by speaking truth with equanimity or, in other words, by focusing on the "common good of the country" (*al-maslaha al-'amma li-l-balad*).[70]

In contrast to the process of abstraction that we will encounter, Faraj's politics were local and intimate. Addressing a public in Egypt, he advocated unifying the national spirit (*nafs*) through "public morality" (*al-adab al-'amma*), which depended on sincerity, or continuously identifying and resolving "unfavorable mutual feelings."[71] Drawing on his own experiences to convey his point, Faraj described the many occasions when a Muslim would greet him in public with the common Islamic salutation *al-salam 'alaykum* (peace be upon you) only to stop mid-utterance on realizing that Faraj was a Jew and switch to the more distant "good afternoon" (*naharak sa'id*).[72] Similarly, he described how whereas the Muslim press would note the passing of a Muslim with the prefix *al-marhum* (the late, denoting mercy and expressing grief), it would note the passing of a non-Muslim with the less elegant *al-mu'sif* (the regrettable).[73] Such distinctions, he asserted, while often premised on doctrine, violated religion because they caused humiliation and pain (*idha'*), whereas religion "preserves its strength in noninjury ['*adam idha'*] to others," exemplified for him by the Qur'anic injunction "there is no compulsion in religion" (*la ikrah fi al-din*). Citing post-1908 Ottoman society as a paragon of sincerity between religious groups, with a broad commitment to public morals, Faraj contended that Egypt ought to develop (*tataqaddam*) along similar lines. While "nothing is greater than people from all religions and doctrines coming together in friendship to become Egyptians in the true national sense of the word," he remarked, "nothing hurts more than moral injury."[74]

PUBLIC INTEREST AND ANTISEMITISM

As Faraj and others worked to realize the common good, another approach to collective life was being effectuated in Egypt. In 1883, Egypt's first Penal Code, based on the French Penal Code of 1810, was issued in parallel to the founding of the National Courts. It represented a significant transition point from a flexible, predominantly oral, and bottom-up legal culture prior to the mid-nineteenth century to a rigid, textual, and disciplinary one. By expanding and refining criminal law, it contributed to the establishment of legal personhood in Egypt, presuming a self-governing autonomous subject who was distinct in some respects but, before the law, fundamentally the same as other subjects.[75] The code remained in place until 1904, when it was replaced with a new iteration that introduced several modifications, including the abolishment of forms of punishment such as life imprisonment.[76]

The most important change in terms of the topic at hand was the introduction of public interest as a branch of criminal law (*qanun al-'uqubat*). Closely tied to security, public interest law was divided between offenses and crimes harmful to the security of the state from outside and those harmful to the security of the government from inside (*al-jinayat wa-l-junh al-mudarra bi-amn al-hukuma*). The law authorized the state to determine what constituted harm to its security.[77] Through the new code, public interest came to be associated with loyalty to the nation-state, while its opposite, *al-maslaha al-khassa* (private interest), became suspicious. This arrangement persisted in the subsequent Penal Code of 1937 and would remain consistent throughout Egypt's twentieth-century legal reform.[78] In sum, whereas the Islamic concept of the common good, uncodified and open, was intended to cultivate practices generative of a moral society from the bottom up, public interest, set down in law, was intended to regulate the population from the top down. Whereas the former presumed no division between public and private, the latter was yet another component to that divide's realization, with the private realm subject to suspicion for the threat it posed to public interest.

The establishment of this legal scaffolding of the nation-state over the first half of the twentieth century, coupled with new grammars of nationality and citizenship as well as the ascendency of Zionism in Palestine, all of which were forces beyond the control of Egyptian Jewry, contributed to transforming *isra'ilis* into undifferentiated universal Jews (*yahud*) and local Jewish *ta'ifas* into a homogenous enemy nation.[79] In contrast to Faraj's vision of the relationship between Jewish reform and the moral society in Egypt, Jewishness became a private interest that, especially after the 1948 war, was presumed threatening to public interest and the nation's security. Antisemitism, a modern European ideology that spread to Egypt during the 1930s but had limited currency among, and in fact was routinely denounced by, Egyptian intellectuals,[80] furnished an idiom through which this particular "threat" could be and increasingly was described. To understand how, we will turn to the first complete translation in Egypt of the paradigmatic antisemitic text, the falsified *The Protocols of the Elders of Zion*.

The first translation of *The Protocols of the Elders of Zion* as a published volume in Arabic was Taymur Muhammad Khalifat al-Tunsi's 1951 *al-Khatar al-Yahudi: Brutukulat Hukama' Sahyun* (The Jewish Peril: Protocols of the Elders of Zion).[81] The translator, al-Tunsi, was a disciple of the eminent Egyptian intellectual 'Abbas Mahmud al-'Aqqad, who embraced his translation project.[82] In addition to this work, al-Tunsi composed books on philosophy and language, poetry, and short stories. He sustained an interest in Jews and Judaism, especially the Talmud, throughout his intellectual career. His focus on the Talmud as a driver of nefarious Jewish acts reflected the enduring effects of the Christian anti-Jewish translation described earlier, though viewed in a wholly different context and serviced toward different ends.

The story of al-Tunsi's translation of *The Protocols*, as told by al-Tunsi himself in his introduction to the work, is one of an Egyptian Muslim lay scholar of Judaism refashioning an antisemitic idiom that had traveled to Egypt via pathways of British colonization. As the category of "the Jew" (*al-isra'ili*) was transforming from a marker of communal identification (*al-ta'ifa al-isra'iliyya*) into a homogenizing national identification (*al-yahud* or *al-sahyuniyyun*, the latter of which means "Zionists" but has come to be used by some Egyptians to refer to Jews generally), al-Tunsi and other Egyptian intellectuals, needing to frame and explain a new enemy, found and adapted a European discourse on Jews steeped in Christian eschatology but undoubtedly the product of processes of modernization across nineteenth-century Europe. Whereas it was largely Greek Orthodox Christians who had made blood libel accusations, this new, secular discourse was available to both Christian and Muslim Egyptians.

Al-Tunsi describes the origins of *The Protocols* and how it arrived in Egypt. Originally published in Russian, the work was translated into English by a Russian journalist named Victor Marsden on the heels of the 1917 Russian Revolution. This timing is no coincidence: that revolution was widely attributed in England to Jewish machinations and inspired frenzied belief in an international Jewish conspiracy to control the world. In 1920, the Britons, an English nationalist antisemitic group that had stirred this fervor and supported the creation of a national homeland for Jews, largely to rid England of its Jewish minority, published Marsden's text, which became the standard English-language version.[83] Copies of a subsequent edition of the work published in 1921 made their way to Cairo, likely in the hands of colonial officials.[84] Because India was a main target of Bolshevik propaganda, which encouraged Indians to rise up against British colonial rule, many British politicians, journalists, and officials came to believe that a network of Jewish plotters was actively seeking to dismantle the British Empire. Thus, *The Protocols*, newly available in English, proved a popular read among British colonial officials, including in Egypt. For example, Zionist leader Chaim Weitzmann, who spent time in Egypt during World War I, reports that Wyndham Deedes, a Christian Zionist who served as brigadier general in Cairo during the war and later chief secretary of the high commissioner in Palestine, showed him a copy of the text and told him it was a common sight among British personnel in Egypt.[85]

Yet *The Protocols* did not appear in Arabic translation in Egypt until 1951, decades after the first copies had arrived in the country. According to al-Tunsi, who was writing in the early 1950s, copies of the English version at the time were "few, nay rare, nay rarer than rare." Al-Tunsi's clichéd remark is contradicted, however, by Abbas al-ʿAqqad's comments in his acknowledgment of the publication of the translation. Al-ʿAqqad reported seeing three copies with his own eyes. The first he borrowed from "one of our military officers who pursue rare books on topics of war and strategies of invasion and conquest and the like." The second he bought secondhand and all cut up (*marjuʿ wa-maqtuʿ*), the seller having no knowledge of its title, no less its meaning. He claims the copy was stolen from him, along with other books and papers, by employees in the National Library. The third, a copy of the 1921 Marsden version inscribed with the word *souveni* [sic] (gift), he found among the items left behind (*mukhallifat*) by a prominent doctor (*tabib kabir*).[86] Clearly, old copies of the text, brought to Egypt initially by British officials, were lying around among Egypt's elite, but they were in neglect, perhaps neither interesting nor useful to their owners. According to al-Tunsi, initial interest in Egypt in translating *The Protocols* into Arabic dates to 1947, which coincides with the announcement of the UN Partition Plan for Palestine.[87] Al-Tunsi himself translated portions of the text for the newspaper *al-Risala* (The Message) in 1949 and 1950 and for the newspaper *Manbar al-Sharq* (Pulpit of the East) in 1950 and 1951.[88] Later in 1951, al-Tunsi's book, "the first complete, trustworthy Arabic translation" of the original, as he described it, was published, and over the next decade three editions would follow.[89]

The majority of al-Tunsi's text is a translation of an English translation of a Russian antisemitic text. In this respect alone, it is ripe for analysis. Here I will only briefly address the portion of the text that diverges from and frames the project of translation, al-Tunsi's introduction. In somewhat generic terms, al-Tunsi describes the alleged danger of *The Protocols*, the elements of the "Zionist plot," the meetings of the elders, the protocols that emerged from them, the story of how they spread, and Jewish attempts to prevent that spread—some of which we have already covered. More importantly for our purposes is the section where al-Tunsi, writing as an Egyptian Arab for an Arab audience, defines "the Jew" (*al-yahudi*), explains the danger he poses, and appeals to readers to respond to this threat. In contrast to the texts discussed earlier, including those that adapted Christian anti-Judaism, al-Tunsi describes "the Jew" in abstract and essentialist terms: "The Jew [*al-yahudi*] is a Jew before everything else, regardless of his nationality or whether he adopted certain creeds or principles on the surface."[90] Unified and homogenized, "he" is now also gendered male. For al-Tunsi, what distinguishes this figure more than any doctrinal commitment is an exclusive claim to chosen status and superiority. On this basis, he argues that Jews invariably pursue Jewish interests (al-maslaha al-yahudiyya) exclusively rather than the interests of society (al-maslaha al-'amma) or humanity (al-insaniyya). Thus, in the national context, Jews necessarily lack the characteristic of loyalty to the nation essential to membership in the national body. As al-Tunsi puts it, "he [the Jew] may adopt any nationality and will even serve the nation but only as long as doing so is in Jewish interests [al-maslaha al-yahudiyya]. Otherwise, the Jew will revert to some other nationality." In the global context, Jews prioritize their interests above the universal ideals of brotherhood, freedom, and equality, which they actively seek to sabotage. In both cases, "Jewish interests," or minority private interests, are cast as suspicious and a threat to public interest.

But al-Tunsi did not stop there. Blurring the presumed moral decline of the Arab nation with Jewish presence, he went on to represent Jews as a "parasitic element" that consumes the body of the Arab nation from within. "The disease does not kill the strong body but weakens it," he argued. "I advise [Arabs] to realize the danger they are living in," he continued, "[and] to remove the danger from themselves before the passing of time."[91] In contrast to the local isra'ili, some of whom were said to be capable of wicked deeds, the Jew in general (al-yahudi) had become the "evil principle of history," to use Arendt's phrasing.[92] This embodiment of the private interest needed to be excluded for the nation's survival.

Conclusion

Part of the legal and political lexical substructure of the nation-state, public interest is seemingly everywhere and nowhere. No complete history of it can be written, especially not on the basis of state archives alone. Instead, public interest is best accessed from both the center and the margins, simultaneously and symbiotically. In addition to analyzing public interest's translation into Egyptian law, this chapter therefore turned to the archive of Egyptian Jewry, which hitherto has principally been used to understand the social and political life of this complex and diverse community. Tracing public interest in this way opened the door to the attendant—and contingent—translation of antisemitism as part of the process of abstracting this particular presumed minority.

If the translation of anti-Judaism was largely limited to Christians, the translation of antisemitism, made available by pathways of British colonization and inseparable from the emergence of Zionism and Zionist/Israeli politics, was a more general phenomenon. Once war broke out in 1948, it proved a powerful tool for transforming local Jews into an abstract Jew whose private interests, already deemed suspicious, could be seen to conflict with the public interest of the Egyptian nation. Secular and profane public interest, intended to police sites of disloyalty to the nation, authorized the state to exclude such identifiable private interests, as it would, tragically, over the subsequent two decades.

NOTES

1. Habib Faris, *al-Dhaba'ih al-Bashariyya al-Talmudiyya* (Cairo: Kutub Qawmiyya, 1962 [1890]), 9–10. Emerging from a series of articles published in the journal *al-Mahrusa* (The Protected), the book was originally published as *Surakh al-Bari' fi Buq al-Hurriyya wa-l-Dhaba'ih al-Talmudiyya* and was republished by al-Matba'a al-Jami'a in 1891. In the new version, Faris included an additional introduction by 'Abd al-'Ati Jalal and edits that responded to critics, some of whom were likely from Egypt's Jewish communities.

2. Ibid.

3. Karaites are a minority within Judaism that, unlike the majority Rabbinates, rejects the authority of the oral law—the Talmud and later rabbinic works—relying solely on the Hebrew Bible. In Egypt, Karaites were an Arabic-speaking autochthonous community claiming ancient presence, whereas much of the larger and more diverse Sephardic community had arrived in Egypt from the eighteenth century. On Karaites in Egypt, see Joel Beinin, *The Dispersion of Egyptian Jewry: Culture, Politics, and the Formation of a Modern Diaspora* (Cairo: American University in Cairo Press, 1998).

4. On the common good (referred to as "public interest") in terms of professional journalism, see Dyala Hamza, "From *Ilm* to *Sihafa* or the Politics of the Public Interest (*maslaha*): Muhammad Rashid Rida and his journal *al-Manar* (1898–1935)," in *The Making of the Arab Intellectual: Empire, Public Sphere and the Colonial Coordinates of Selfhood*, ed. Dyala Hamzah (London: Routledge, 2013), 90–127. Public interest has received scant attention among historians of Egypt and the Middle East.

5. For a general definition of *maslaha*, see M. Khadduri, "Maslaha," in *Encyclopaedia of Islam*, 2nd edition, ed. P. Bearman et al., accessed 10 November 2017, http://dx.doi.org.ezproxy. gc.cuny.edu/10.1163/1573-3912_islam_SIM_5019.

6. This is true of both the liberal utilitarian and republican conceptions, for example, even as these are often considered opposite. For a clear overview, see Élisabeth Zoller, *Introduction to Public Law: A Comparative Study* (Leiden, Netherlands: Martinus Nijhoff Publishers, 2008), especially 11–15.

7. Michel Foucault, *"Society Must Be Defended": Lectures at the Collège de France 1975–1976*, ed. Mauro Bertani and Alessandro Fontana, trans. David Macey (New York: Picador, 2003), 247–49.

8. On the minority as a category in the Ottoman Empire and Egypt, see Aron Rodrigue, "Reflections on Millets and Minorities: Ottoman Legacies," in *Turkey between Nationalism and Globalization*, ed. Riva Kastoryano (New York: Routledge, 2013), 36–46; and Saba Mahmood, "Religious Freedom, the Minority Question, and Geopolitics in the Middle East," *Comparative Studies in Society and History* 54 (2012): 418–46.

9. On foreign minorities and compradors in Egypt, see Robert Vitalis, *When Capitalists Collide: Business Conflict and the End of Empire in Egypt* (Berkeley: University of California Press, 1995).

10. On the history of Egyptian Jews, see Shimon Shamir, ed., *The Jews of Egypt: A Mediterranean Society in Modern Times* (Boulder, CO: Westview Press, 1987); Gudrun Krämer, *The Jews in Modern Egypt, 1914–1952* (Seattle: University of Washington Press, 1989); Beinin, *The Dispersion of Egyptian Jewry*; and Dario Miccoli, *Histories of the Jews of Egypt: An Imagined Bourgeoisie, 1880s–1950s* (New York: Routledge, 2015).

11. On the AIU, see André Kaspi, ed., *Histoire de l'Alliance israélite universelle de 1860 à nos jours* (Paris: Armand Colin, 2010). For a recent history of Egyptian Jews that draws on the AIU archives, see Miccoli, *Histories of the Jews of Egypt*.

12. Hannah Arendt, *The Jewish Writings*, ed. Jerome Kohn and Ron H. Feldman (New York: Schocken Books, 2007), 51.

13. Ironically, in contemporary Egyptian discourse, the term *al-Isra'ili*, as in a citizen of the State of Israel, is often used to signify *al-Yahudi* and vice versa. In many cases, the two are considered equivalent, though this is subject to debate.

14. Arendt, *The Jewish Writings*, 62–65.

15. The event was described by British officials in Egypt. Reprinted in Jacob M. Landau, *Middle Eastern Themes: Papers in History and Politics* (Oxon, UK: Routledge, 1973), 105.

16. On these cases, see Archives of the Alliance Israélite Universelle (AIU), Égypte I C 01; and AIU Égypte I C 03.

17. Landau, *Middle Eastern Themes*, 105.

18. The Arabic phrase for these courts is *al-mahakim al-ahliyya*, which is often translated as "National Courts." The British referred to these courts as "native" or "indigenous" courts.

19. A list of graduates categorized by religion is printed in *al-Mu'tamar al-Misri al-Awwal: Majmu'a A'mal al-Mu'tamar al-Misri al-Awwal al-Mun'aqid bi-Hiliubulis (min Dawahi al-Qahira)* (Cairo: al-Matba'a al-Amiriyya bi-Misr, 1911), 12. Faraj appears to have been the only Jewish (*isra'ili*) graduate until 1912.

20. On *al-Tahdhib*, see Lital Levy, "Edification between Sect and Nation: Murad Farag and *al-Tahdhib*, 1901–1903," in *Intellectuals and Civil Society in the Middle East: Liberalism, Modernity and Politics Discourse*, ed. Mohammed A. Bamyeh (London: I. B.Tauris, 2012).

21. Some or all of his articles in these two journals were later published as a collection entitled *Maqalat Murad* (Murad's Oeuvre) (Cairo: Matba'at Kuhayn wa-Ibrahim Ruzintal, 1912).

22. See Murad Faraj, *Multaqa al-Lughatayn al-'Ibriyya wa-l-'Arabiyya* (Cairo: al-Matba'a al-Rahmaniyya, 1930–37); and Faraj, *al-Shu'ara' al-Yahud al-'Arab* (Cairo: al-Matba'a al-Rahmaniyya, 1929).

23. Sasson Somekh, "Participation of Egyptian Jews in Modern Arabic Culture, and the Case of Murad Faraj," in *The Jews of Egypt: A Mediterranean Society in Modern Times*, ed. Shimon Shamir (Boulder, CO: Westview Press, 1987), 138. Somekh was unable to confirm this. See page 140, note 37.

24. Samera Esmeir, *Juridical Humanity: A Colonial History* (Stanford, CA: Stanford University Press, 2012), chapter 1; Talal Asad, "Thinking about Law, Morality, and Religion in the Story of Egyptian Modernization," *Journal of Interdisciplinary Study of Monotheistic Religions* 1 (2006): 13.

25. Asad, "Thinking about Law."

26. Esmeir, *Juridical Humanity*, 21–23.

27. See Amr Shalakany, "'I Heard It All Before': Egyptian Tales of Law and Development," *Third World Quarterly* 27 (2006): 833–53.

28. On the relationship between such manuals and authority, see Esmeir, *Juridical Humanity*, part 1.

29. Murad Faraj, *Risala fi Sharh al-Amwal 'ala al-Qanun al-Madani al-Ahli* (Cairo: Matba'at al-Mahrusa, 1893); Faraj, *Kitab al-Majmu' fi Sharh al-Shuru' 'ala al-Qanun al-Misri al-Ahli* (Cairo: Matba'a al-Mahrusa, 1894); Faraj, *Da'awa Wada' al-Yad* (Cairo: Matba'at al-Ma'arif, 1901).

30. Faraj, *Risala fi Sharh al-Amwal*, 2. The "commentators," Boudreit (?), Désiré Dalloz, and Jean Charles Florent Demolomb, were nineteenth-century French jurists whose works were part of the curriculum at the Khedival Law School.

31. Established in 1875, the Mixed Courts had jurisdiction over cases involving foreign nationals or a foreign national and an Ottoman or local subject.

32. Faraj, *Da'awa Wada' al-Yad*, 2.

33. On the transformation of *shari'a* during this period, see Talal Asad, *Formations of the Secular: Christianity, Islam, Modernity* (Stanford, CA: Stanford University Press, 2003), chapter 7.

34. *Murad Faraj: Bi-Munasibat Dhikra Murur Khamsin 'Aman 'ala Wifatihi* (n.p.: Albert Gamil and Historical Society of Jews from Egypt, 2007). See also Jacob M. Landau, *Jews in Nineteenth-Century Egypt* (New York: New York University Press, 1969).

35. See Mas'ud Hay Bin Shim'un, *Kitab al-Ahwal al-Shar'iyya fi al-Ahwal al-Shakhsiyya li-l-Isra'iliyin* (Cairo: Matba'at Kuhayn wa-Ruzintal, 1912).

36. Murad Faraj, *Shi'ar al-Khidr: Adoret Eliyahu, Statut Personnel Israelite Caraite* (Cairo: n.p., 1917).

37. The work, eventually published in 1935, was titled *al-Ahkam al-Shar'iyya fi al-Ahwal al-Shakhsiyya li-l-Isra'iliyin al-Qara'in* (Personal Status Legal Statutes of Karaite Jews). Apparently, an attempt had already been made to compile the codes in Hebrew. See Mourad El-Kodsi, *The Karaite Jews of Egypt, 1862–1986* (n.p.: n.p., 2006), 77.

38. See *Murad Faraj: Bi-Munasibat Dhikra Murur Khamsin 'Aman 'ala Wifatihi*.

39. AIU, Égypte XE 182, "Acte d'accusation"; AIU, Égypte XE 182, "Jugement du Tribunal indigène de Zaqaziq."

40. *Al-Tahdhib*, "Hadithat Bur Sa'id – Tuhmat al-Dam – Tab i'a," 31 December 1902.

41. Somekh tended to be critical of Rabbanite Jews in Egypt and of Egyptian Jewry in general; his judgment of the chief rabbi should be viewed with this in mind. Elizabeth Antébi, "Somekh, Samuel," *Encyclopedia of Jews in the Islamic World*, ed. Norman A. Stillman, Brill Online, 2014, accessed 4 December 2014, http://www.paulyonl ine.brill.nl/entries/encyclopedia-of-jews-in-the-islamic-world/somekh-samuel-SIM_0020480.

42. AIU, Égypt, X.E.182.e., "S. Somekh to the President of the AIU in Paris," 17 October 1902, reprinted in *Murad Faraj: Bi-Munasibat Dhikra Murur Khamsin 'Aman 'ala Wafatihi* and in El-Kodsi, *The Karaite Jews*, 281–82.

43. AIU, Égypte XE 182, "Jugement du Tribunal indigène de Zaqaziq."

44. AIU, Égypt, XE 182, "Une accusation du sang á Port Saïd."

45. AIU, Égypt, X.E.182.e., "S. Somekh to the President of the AIU in Paris," 17 October 1902.

46. Thus, for example, after Amin's death in 1908, Faraj wrote a powerful eulogy mourning the loss of this national hero. *Diwan Murad*, 182–84. Connections of this kind between reformers from different religions were ubiquitous in Egypt during this period.

47. *Al-Tahdhib*, "Hadithat Bur Sa'id," 31 December 1902.

48. AIU, Égypte XE 182, "Une accusation du sang á Port Saïd."

49. Ibid., Faraj reproduced the Court of Appeals' decision in *al-Tahdhib*. See also *Murad Faraj: Bi-Munasibat Dhikra Murur Khamsin 'Aman 'ala Wifatihi*. For the French translation, see AIU, Égypte XE 182, "Jugement de la Cour d'Appel indigène du Caire."

50. *Al-Tahdhib*, "Hadithat Bur Sa'id," 31 December 1902.

51. *Bulletin l'Alliance israélite universelle*, no. 28, 1903, 162–64.

52. The insinuation that Jews drink blood or use it to make matzoh did resurface, but it does not seem to have been directed at an individual, except for a 1908 incident that proved relatively minor. On this, see *Journal du Caire*, 2 and 3 April 1908. For invocations of the blood libel, see, e.g., the 1925 case of a teacher at Saint Catherine's College in Alexandria described in *l'Égypte Nouvelle*, 16 May 1925.

53. *Al-Tahdhib*, "Tuhmat al-Dam—Bur Sa'id—2," 3 April 1903.

54. *Al-Tahdhib*, "Tuhmat al-Dam," 6 February 1902.

55. *Al-Tahdhib*, "Tuhmat al-Dam—Bur Sa'id—2," 3 April 1903.

56. *Al-Tahdhib*, "Tuhmat al-Dam—Tabi'a," 26 February 1902.

57. Ibid. On slaughter, see *al-Tahdhib*, "Tuhmat al-Dam—Tabi'a," 6 March 1902.

58. *Al-Hilal*, vol. 11, 15 April 1903, 435–36.

59. On Esther Moyal, see Beth Baron, *The Women's Awakening in Egypt: Culture, Society, and the Press* (New Haven, CT: Yale University Press, 1994), 20–22; and Lital Levy, "Partitioned Pasts: Arab Jewish Intellectuals and the Case of Esther Azhari Moyal (1873–1948)," in *The Making of the Arab Intellectual: Empire, Public Sphere and the Colonial Coordinates of Selfhood* (New York: Routledge, 2012), 128–63.

60. *Al-Hilal*, vol. 13, 1 February 1905, 303–5.

61. Yusuf Muyyal Shim'un, trans., *al-Talmud: Aslu wa-Tasalsulu wa-Adabu* (Cairo: Maktabat al-'Arab, 1909). For more on this project of translation and its ritual murder accusation context, see Jonathan Gribetz, "An Arabic-Zionist Talmud: Shimon Moyal's At-Talmud," *Jewish Social Studies* 17 (2010): 1–30.

62. Wael B. Hallaq, *A History of Islamic Legal Theories: An Introduction to Sunni usul al-fiqh* (Cambridge: Cambridge University Press, 1997), 88–90.

63. Wael B. Hallaq, *An Introduction to Islamic Law* (Cambridge: Cambridge University Press, 2009), 22–27.

64. Wael B. Hallaq, *The Impossible State: Islam, Politics, and Modernity's Moral Predicament* (New York: Columbia University Press, 2013), 52.

65. Samira Haj, *Reconfiguring Islamic Tradition: Reform, Rationality, and Modernity* (Stanford: Stanford University Press, 2008), 110.

66. Ibid., 125.

67. Ibid., 138.

68. I have accessed a reprinted version of the essay from a collection of Faraj's writings that was published four years after the essay's original publication date. Murad Faraj, *Maqalat Murad* (Cairo: Matba'at Ibrahim Ruzintal, 1912), 200–223.

69. Murad Faraj, "Fi al-Huriyya Ma Hiyya," in *Maqalat Murad* (Cairo: Matba'at Ruzintal, 1912), 249–51.

70. Faraj, "al-Quwwa fawq al-Hurriyya," 247–49.

71. Faraj, "Harb al-Watan," in *Maqalat Murad*, 202, 219.

72. Ibid., 207.

73. Ibid., 216.

74. Ibid., 204–5.

75. Samah Selim, "Fiction and Colonial Identities: Arsène Lupin in Arabic," *Middle Eastern Literatures* 13 (2010): 191–210.

76. For discussion, see Esmier, *Juridical Humanity*, 39–41.

77. *Qanun al-'Uqubat al-Ahli al-Misri* (Cairo: al-Matba'a al-Sharqiyya, 1904).

78. *Qanun al-'Uqubat al-Misri: al-Sadir bi-l-Qanun Raqm 58 li-Sanat 1937* (Cairo: Maktabat al-Nahda al-Misriyya, 1939).

79. The Arabic word *al-yahudi* and its plural, *al-yahud*, had long been used in Egypt and beyond, of course. In the early twentieth century, they were simply less common than *al-isra'ili* (plural *al-isra'iliyyun*) and *al-ta'ifa al-isra'iliyya*, likely due to norms around nomenclature established during the Ottoman period and connected to Ottoman modes of governance. By the mid-twentieth century, however, the terms had absorbed an element of abstraction that did not exist before.

80. Israel Gershoni and James Jankowski, *Confronting Fascism in Egypt: Dictatorship versus Democracy in the 1930s* (Stanford, CA: Stanford University Press, 2009), chapter 4.

81. Taymur Muhammad Khalifat al-Tunsi, *al-Khatar al-Yahudi: Brutukulat Hukama' Sahyun* (Cairo: Matba'at al-Kitab al-'Arabi, 1951).

82. See 'Abbas Mahmud al-'Aqqad, "Introduction," in *al-Khatar al-Yahudi: Brutukulat Hukama' Sahyun*, Muhammad Khalifat al-Tunsi, 4th ed. (Cairo: al-Kitab al-'Arabi, 1961).

83. Sergei Nilus, *The Protocols of the Elders of Zion*, trans. Victor Marsden (London: Britons Publishing Society, 1923).

84. Al-Tunsi claims that this was the fifth edition. He likely meant that it was the fifth edition in general of *The Protocols* in English, as Marsden was in fact the second translator of this text, after George Shanks, who is said to have distanced himself from the work. See Colin Holmes, *Anti-Semitism in British Society, 1876–1939* (New York: Routledge, 2016 [1979]), 147–48, 280n72.

85. Chaim Weitzmann, *Trial and Error: The Autobiography of Chaim Weizmann* (New York: Harper & Brothers, 2015 [1949]), 218.

86. 'Abbas Mahmud al-'Aqqad, "Taqdir Brutukulat Hukama' Sahyun," *al-Asas*, 23 November 1951. See also al-Tunsi, *al-Khatar al-Yahudi*, 12.

87. Al-Tunsi reports that the Egyptian daily *al-Asas* (The Foundation) commissioned one of its editors, Anis Mansur, to carry out the task, but he declined for fear of the potential consequences. Al-Tunsi, *al-Khatar al-Yahudi*, 12–13. Beyond Egypt, the first partial translation of *The Protocols* into Arabic appeared in 1925. Perhaps unsurprisingly, it was published in Palestine. See al-Khuri Antun Yamin, *al-Mu'amira al-Yahudiyya 'ala al-Shu'ub: al-Muqarrarat al-Sahyuniyya wa-Madabit al-Jalasat al-Sirriyya li-Hukama' Isra'il* (n.p.: n.p., 1925).

88. See *al-Risala* nos. 856 and 858–59, 1949; *al-Risala,* no. 862, 1950; and *Manbar al-Sharq,* nos. 616–53, 24 November 1950–10 August 1951.

89. I have accessed the first and last edition, cited previously.

90. Al-Tunsi, *al-Khatar al-Yahudi*, 35.

91. Ibid., 23.

92. Arendt, *The Jewish Writings*, 64.

BIBLIOGRAPHY

Arendt, Hannah. *The Jewish Writings*. Edited by Jerome Kohn and Ron H. Feldman. New York: Schocken Books, 2007.

Asad, Talal. *Formations of the Secular: Christianity, Islam, Modernity*. Stanford, CA: Stanford University Press, 2003.

Asad, Talal. "Thinking about Law, Morality, and Religion in the Story of Egyptian Modernization." *Journal of the Interdisciplinary Study of Monotheistic Religions* 1 (2006): 13–24.

Beinin, Joel. *The Dispersion of Egyptian Jewry: Culture, Politics, and the Formation of a Modern Diaspora*. Cairo: American University in Cairo Press, 1998.

Esmeir, Samera. *Juridical Humanity: A Colonial History*. Stanford, CA: Stanford University Press, 2012.

Gershoni, Israel, and James Jankowski. *Confronting Fascism in Egypt: Dictatorship versus Democracy in the 1930s*. Stanford, CA: Stanford University Press, 2009.

Haj, Samira. *Reconfiguring Islamic Tradition: Reform, Rationality, and Modernity*. Stanford, CA: Stanford University Press, 2008.

Hallaq, Wael B. *The Impossible State: Islam, Politics, and Modernity's Moral Predicament*. New York: Columbia University Press, 2013.

Hamzah, Dyala, "From *'Ilm to Sihafa* or the Politics of the Public Interest (*maslaha*): Muhammad Rashid Rida and His Journal *al-Manar*, 1898–1935." In *The Making of the Arab Intellectual: Empire, Public Sphere and the Colonial Coordinates of Selfhood*, edited by Dyala Hamzah, 90–127. London: Routledge, 2013.

Krämer, Gudrun. *The Jews in Modern Egypt, 1914–1952*. Seattle: University of Washington Press, 1989.

Levy, Lital. "Edification between Sect and Nation: Murad Farag and *al-Tahdhib*, 1901–1903." In *Intellectuals and Civil Society in the Middle East: Liberalism, Modernity and Politics Discourse*, edited by Mohammed A. Bamyeh, 57–78. London: I. B. Tauris, 2012.

Mahmood, Saba. *Religious Difference in a Secular Age: A Minority Report*. Princeton, NJ: Princeton University Press, 2016.

PART IV

TEXTUAL, PERFORMATIVE, AND VISUAL CULTURE

CHAPTER 16

EGYPT'S STATE PERIODICAL AS A TOOL OF GOVERNANCE, 1828–39

KATHRYN A. SCHWARTZ

A small broadsheet of text emerged multiple times from the press of the "Possessor of Noble Triumphs" (*sahib al-fatuhat al-saniyya*) in Bulaq, Cairo, on 3 December 1828, just six years after the first book was printed there. At the top of the page rests an urn overflowing with leafy blossoms, reputed to be cotton bolls, presiding above a stylized calligraphic header proclaiming "*al-Waqa'i' al-Misriyya*." The text's deliberate presentation, along with its assertive issue "number 1" written in the upper left corner, suggests that it was one of the author's triumphs and that it was here to stay. The two columns of writing that fill the page clarify who this man was, how we might translate the title of his document into English, and its purpose, with Ottoman Turkish on the right-hand side and its Arabic translation on the left.[1] The press belonged to the viceroy, or *wali*, of Egypt, Mehmed 'Ali, also known as the Benefactor, who founded a new, modern government in the Ottoman province between 1805 and 1848.[2] The "well-known" title he bestowed on the document could be understood as some combination of "Egyptian Happenings" and "Egyptian Developments." And he mandated that its aim was to do nothing less than "to compile ongoing matters from the society of Adam's tribe (*ijtima' jins bani adam*), and to record in a paper (*sahifa*) this world (*al-'alam*) comprising their unions and movements, and their abodes, dealings, and relationships (*mu'asharatihim*)."[3]

But *al-Waqa'i' al-Misriyya* did more than chronicle events. This chapter considers the purpose of *al-Waqa'i' al-Misriyya* as a tool for state-building, one that Mehmed 'Ali initiated to circulate his developing government's messages and decisions for a very specific community in formation, namely the officials who served it. The paper was to connect and organize these officials so that they could reform Egypt and its subjects according to Mehmed 'Ali's vision.[4] Though its task to relate what we might now call foreign and local news helped to secure its reputation as "the oldest Arab newspaper," a point so firmly established that it reaches us via the very entry for the word *waqi'a*, or "event," in the premiere modern Arabic–English dictionary, the paper defies this label during its early years.[5] Its stated objective, emphasizing the prescriptive attainment of a restricted set of readers, offers a different explanation. Reports of the world at large in *al-Waqa'i' al-Misriyya* would focus "attention and reflection on applying, perfecting, ascertaining, and growing familiar with general hard work (*al-ghaira al-'umumiyya*), causing those who read it to benefit from being informed about the present and about times past (*al-zaman*)." Word of the government's precise dealings would be responsible "for attaining ease and comfort (*al-rafahiyya*) and avoiding whatever it is that causes harm and suffering, especially in Cairo (*misr*), which is indeed the template (*al-asas*) for properly arranging towns (*al-buldan*) and regulating the well-being (*raha*) of their people." And by spreading such information, the paper "would bring about the benefits that are the Benefactor's goal, directing the actions of the eminences who are in charge (*al-ma'murin*) and the rest of the noble and lauded arbiters (*hukkam*) in applying orders and requirements."[6]

Al-Waqa'i' al-Misriyya was thus a government mechanism for guiding the work of its agents, who, growing in number by the year and radiating out from Cairo, were expected to use its contents to help bring order to all of Egypt and its general population. The paper's entries were selected and edited for publication not to offer comprehensive records for any specific office or unfolding event or to spread propaganda only but to convey all that was deemed worthwhile for the government's personnel to know about its affairs and interests. The paper, therefore, forms a curated trove of information, discussions, decisions, aims, accounts, and raw data from sources ranging from government bodies to European newspapers. Reports of the good and the bad and boasts of the government's marvel-worthy feats run alongside complaints about its failed endeavors, its own limitations and frequent lack of supplies, and the inadequacies of its representatives and the population they ruled over.

The impact of *al-Waqa'i' al-Misriyya* on Egypt's state and society is difficult to ascertain. Though it was not a confidential publication, there is no evidence to suggest that ordinary subjects had access to it during its early years, and while its circulation was significant for the time, it was not exceedingly high. The paper is reported to have been printed in runs of six hundred copies between 1828 and the 1840s, though it is more likely to have numbered in the low thousands.[7] Moreover, its actual consumption by its target audience was surely limited. Even if it arrived regularly to government personnel in far-flung places, many of the men who were expected to read it could not do so if others did not read it aloud to them, either because they were Europeans who did not read Eastern languages or because they were only just learning to read in any language, as is made clear by the paper's frequent reports on the problem of illiteracy among soldiers and functionaries.[8]

Still, within Middle Eastern historiography, references to *al-Waqa'i' al-Misriyya* across its long and enduring life span make it out to be a milestone along the region's march toward modernity. They imply that the paper had a consistently receptive readership and that it played a major role in shaping intellectual, cultural, and societal developments into the twentieth century. Hence a popular textbook on the history of the modern Middle East concludes that the establishment of this "first Arabic-language newspaper" had an outsized impact on Egypt's development."[9] The Egyptian state itself has stoked the legend of *al-Waqa'i' al-Misriyya* as a consequential modernizing force while laying claim to creating it for that purpose from at least 1942. That year, the state press at Bulaq published the most concerted scholarly treatment of the paper to date in honor of King Farouk I (r. 1936–52). Written by Ibrahim 'Abduh (1913–86) on the basis of his master's thesis for King Fu'ad I University's Faculty of Literature, where he had trained under the pioneering Egyptian historian Shafiq Ghurbal (1894–1961), the work examines progress-driven social reform via primary sources by researching the origins of Egypt's press.[10] 'Abduh combed through state archives and libraries, including those of 'Abdin Palace, the Citadel's Dar al-Mahfuzat, and Dar al-Kutub, to construct an indispensable, albeit patriotic, history of the paper from the years spanning 1828 to 1942. His book opens by proclaiming that "every civilized nation was wont to found an official paper, since civilization is characterized by the value and extent of its press (*al-sihafa*); and so was the case in Egypt."[11] More recently, under Husni Mubarak's (r. 1981–2011) presidency, the republican government reasserted this vision after the 2002 inauguration of the Bibliotheca Alexandrina. The library now holds a Bulaq Press Museum where *al-Waqa'i' al-Misriyya*'s first issue is displayed in a vitrine.[12]

Such claims of *al-Waqa'i' al-Misriyya*'s import to the history of modern Egypt and the Middle East take its impact on society as a given by explicitly or implicitly situating the paper within the history of printing and applying to it the conceptual importance assigned to Western textual genres and paradigms for print media's mass consumption. In this regard, it is no accident that *al-Waqa'i' al-Misriyya* has had an enduring relevance to studies of the Arabic press, the Arab cultural awakening (*al-nahda*), the rise of Egyptian politics, and Arabic print technology.[13] This observation is not intended to suggest that the history of printing is irrelevant to the paper's story. Rather, it calls attention to two consequences of narratively centering *al-Waqa'i' al-Misriyya* in the realm of print history. First, it minimalizes attention to the foundational reason for the establishment of the paper in the first place, that is, to enable Mehmed 'Ali's attempt to transform Egypt via state-building. Second, it flirts with the notion that the paper was an agent of change rather than a tool that its founder wielded to promote change. Taking these latter perspectives seriously requires relocating the paper historiographically from the sphere of media studies to that of state formation. This shift allows us to look beyond the still unsatisfying matter of ascertaining the extent of the paper's consumption and toward the more tractable nature of its production and what its intended audience was expected to take away from it.

Therefore, the first six hundred or so issues of *al-Waqa'i' al-Misriyya* shed light on the image and operations of Mehmed 'Ali's new polity, showing how the government presented itself to its growing ranks and allowing us to imagine what these men— women were not given positions of power within the growing state—might have learned from this novel corpus. The decision to focus on the period 1828–39 is based on the availability of the paper for consultation because systematic, though still incomplete, holdings at the Bibliothèque nationale de France (BnF) only seem to be available for the earliest years of the paper.[14] Although material realities determine the endpoint of the years under study, the period nevertheless covers the first decade of the text's publication and the high watermark of Mehmed 'Ali's challenge to the Ottoman Empire, of which he was nominally a mere vassal.[15]

The issues under consideration are important to modern Egyptian history not only because of their purported impact then but also because they document the embryonic development of the Egyptian state, which blossomed under the Khedivate during the late 1860s and survives in some form until today.[16] Leading scholars have studied its nature as an autocratic bureaucracy, an instantiation of European colonial power, and, most recently, an entity that touched the very bodies of Egyptian subjects who could reach out to the government in turn.[17] While *al-Waqa'i' al-Misriyya* supports all three of these foundational views, it aligns most closely with the first and third interpretations in stressing Mehmed 'Ali's polity as an entity unto itself. The developments it chronicles may indeed be taken to represent the spread of colonizing influences: the attempt to fashion a dependent bureaucracy from men of different backgrounds; the creation of a disciplinary state that sought to be all-knowing and reach out to the population one by one; and the need to rely upon trade with the West and keep up with Western advances. But these moves were also consistent with the Egyptian-Ottoman-Islamic context behind Mehmed 'Ali's precarious though transformational rule during an era of increasing global European might that witnessed the universal evolution of governance. That is, they were endemic to this place and time when the spread of European colonial power was but one key historical force at play. Moreover, as Khaled Fahmy points out, Egypt was not India and cannot be taken as an archetype for the spread of a particular type of Western political order.[18]

Al-Waqa'i' al-Misriyya asserts this distinctiveness through its very purpose: facilitating the realization of Mehmed 'Ali's vision for his polity. Moving select information of concern to the government to, from, and between its widespread operatives served his desire "to arrange the conditions of the villages" so that they would be like the cities, and especially Cairo, "by making them orderly and straightening out the affairs (*tamhidiha wa-i'tidal umur*) of their people and paving the way for them."[19] Doing so would not transform Egypt into Europe. Rather, it would make Egypt Europe's peer and ultimately reclaim what is suggested was Egypt's former greatness.

Al-Waqa'i' al-Misriyya was launched as a tool of statecraft to realize this goal in two ways. First, the paper served as a medium through which officials were kept informed of the government's perspective so that they could, by being privy to it, extend its work across the land. Second, the paper was meant to convey to these officials the government's expectations of them so that they could fulfill them and become one corps in the process. These points are established through representative entries in the paper, which abetted the attainment of Mehmed 'Ali's aim and reflect on the new vantage point that they opened up to his servants who were charged with bringing it to fruition. In the absence of scholars' regular and unfettered access to Egyptian state archives, the entries across *al-Waqa'i' al-Misriyya*'s pages also serve as an intriguing alternative resource.

A New Medium and New Content for a New Target Audience

From the Egyptian government's perspective, gathering information from many sources to publish for the benefit of its personnel marked a turning point in how it disseminated word of its dealings. Before the founding of *al-Waqa'i' al-Misriyya*, and at least into the mid-1830s, daily briefings from the administration had been limited to one hundred of its most powerful servants in the viceregal household, who received a lithographed journal (*jurnal*) containing summary reports from government councils, along with Mehmed 'Ali's responses to them.[20] *Al-Waqa'i' al-Misriyya* would similarly publish selections from the proceedings of Mehmed 'Ali's Department of the Interior (al-Diwan al-Khidiwi), which administered both the province and its administration, the Council of Cairo (Majlis Misr), the Military Council (Diwan al-Jihadiyya), and the Viceregal Council (Majlis al-Mashura or Majlis al-'Umumi).[21] But unlike the *jurnal*, *al-Waqa'i' al-Misriyya* would be printed typographically, include mention of foreign and local occurrences, and be circulated "publicly" (*'umumiyyatan*), as the first issue tells us.[22] The paper, therefore, represented a novel platform and source for various types of information previously unavailable in part or sum to many.

The audience that it endeavored to generate was also new. Rather than a "public" writ large, this audience comprised the expanded group of Turkish, Arab, and European functionaries whom Mehmed 'Ali had strung together to serve his reorganization of the province, not to mention those who worked alongside them or stood on the cusp of joining their ranks. Officeholders high and low, judges, doctors, teachers, technicians, soldiers, notables, and students formed the paper's target readership.[23] They did not share the same ethnicity, station, worldview, expertise, educational attainment, or language. However, they were now being forged into a bureaucratic class, which *al-Waqa'i' al-Misriyya* worked to facilitate, literally and rhetorically, by putting them on the same page.[24] The paper reached them wherever they were based, mapping onto the geography of Egypt's territorial holdings, places of engagement, and loci of interest. With other official documents, it circulated throughout Egypt and into the lands of Sudan, Palestine, Syria, the Hijaz, and Crete, in the hands of administrators, military commanders, and naval officers. It also traveled via post to Europe, as evidenced by the remnants of a "PURIFIÉ LAZARET MARSEILLE" fumigation stamp on one copy of an issue and a red wax seal on another.[25] Most of its recipients had no choice but to receive it. From May 1829, anyone earning more than one thousand piastres from the government was forced to purchase an annual subscription for just over seventy-seven piastres by way of a deduction from their salary. Soldiers and students of Mehmed 'Ali's new schools making less than that basic income, however, received their issues freely.[26]

The paper was to spread word of the government's dealings, "such that it becomes apparent to those in charge (*'ind al-ma'murin*) what is of benefit and harm so that they can adopt the beneficial from that which we disseminate, and steer clear of that which will lead to detriment."[27] This point about Egypt being on the up and up manifests itself immediately through the iconography of the paper's logo. After issue 18, it evolves from the urn of cotton signifying Mehmed 'Ali's state-building project (Fig. 16.1) to a more technically and symbolically ambitious pyramid. Featuring stone details and the title of the

FIG. 16.1 The initial logo of *al-Waqa'i' al-Misriyya* in 1828 was the urn of cotton, a symbol of the cash crop at the center of Mehmed 'Ali's state-building project. *Al-Waqa'i' al-Misriyya* no. 3, Salkh Jumada al-Akhir 1244, 1. Bibliothèque Nationale de France.

paper on its façade, and rising dynamically from the sands with cotton plants at its edges, the pyramid upstages a palm tree at its left and a rising sun emerging from its right side (Fig. 16.2).[28] The palm likely represents the Hijaz, which Egypt administered from 1818 to 1845, and the sun the Ottoman Empire. From issue 32, a stoneless pyramid likewise

FIG. 16.2 A new logo that appeared in issues 18–31 (April–May 1829) placed a pyramid with cotton plants in the foreground and a palm tree and the sun in the background, symbols for Egypt, Egypt-ruled Hijaz, and the Ottoman Empire, respectively. *Al-Waqa'i' al-Misriyya* no. 18, 8 Shawwal 1244, 1. Bibliothèque Nationale de France.

stripped of its cotton plants takes hold in front of a palm and sun, whose places are now switched (Fig. 16.3).[29] The message that officials were seemingly to take away from these icons, which is rather modestly made, given that they take up about one-eighth of the page, is that the new government rendered Egypt the epicenter of an anciently rooted

FIG. 16.3 Starting with issue 32 (May 1829), the components of the previous logo were reimagined and rearranged (now a pyramid with no cotton) to reflect the centrality of Egypt with its ancient rootedness to Islamic and Ottoman revival. *Al-Waqa'i' al-Misriyya* no. 32, 27 Dhu al-Qa'da 1244, 1. Bibliothèque Nationale de France.

yet Islamic-Ottoman revival of economic and imperial magnitude that bestowed greatness upon them by extension, since they were now part of this epic project.

Although *al-Waqa'i' al-Misriyya* was first published by the Bulaq Press in 1828, in
1833 it received a designated press of its own in the Citadel, which served as the seat of
Mehmed 'Ali's government.[30] Its issues appeared roughly every two weeks until around
1833, when they shifted to a more reliable interval of publication, every other day.[31] The
paper usually consisted of one large sheet folded in half, creating four pages of reading
material, with each page containing two columns, of which Ottoman Turkish takes pride
of place on the right. The printed nature of the page makes the document conspicuous
and attention-grabbing in the context of manuscript culture, as does its commanding
14.6- by 8.7-inch size. Nonetheless, the restrained layout of the text, inspired from
proclamations made by the French army nearly three decades beforehand, suggests a
utilitarian purpose.[32] Separating aesthetic intention from technical limitations is difficult when it comes to textual material from this era, for printing was new, exceptional,
and, in the case of Egypt, informed by examples from European print cultures. However,
one gets the sense that the publication's substantive role and mandated consumption
liberated it from the burden of trying to capture people's attention through its materiality alone, for, in theory, those who received it had no choice but to read it, although
they may have wanted to for the novel vantage points it provided. Appreciating days
for their "atmospheric measure" (*mizan hawa'i*) or temperature achieved in Cairo at
each of the five prayer times, for example, began to be possible from May 1829.[33] These
measurements were not prospective but rather pertained to time passed since the last
issue. Surely this was the result of what was then scientifically possible, but it is indicative of *al-Waqa'i' al-Misriyya*'s purpose in chronicling for its audience what had recently
been obtained and decided.

Reading the paper demanded doing so from start to finish. Entries defy any fixed
order across issues, and they are not arranged according to set categories. They tend to
flow in order of importance within each installment, from greatest to least, posing perhaps one way for readers to get around the fact that the earliest papers do not support
skimming. Blank spaces separate block paragraphs until headlines begin to appear inter-
mittently from issue 15. These headlines do not attract the eye from afar but, rather, appear modestly centered atop paragraphs in the same font as the rest of the text. Up close,
their wording does not pull the reader in either, disguising almost all the substance that
the following sentences hold in favor of indicating their source of origin. The earliest
headline in the BnF collection, for example, is "Mentioned in the Speech Delivered by
the Lord Chancellor to the Members of the Council Called Chambre des Communes."[34]
After a few exceptional issues in January 1830, in which headlines universally refer to
their provenances even more vaguely, with captions such as "Translation of a French
Gazette," headlines stabilize around identifying the government body that generated
the content underneath them and the nature of this material, such as "Notification
from the Viceregal Council" (*khabar majlis al-mashura*) or the more reliably reported
"Happenings from the Viceregal Council" (*hawadith majlis al-mashura*).[35]

These entries can appear in repetition one after the other, giving readers the sense
that they sat in the audience of a given body or, at least, had access to its registers. For

example, one issue posts "Hearings from the Viceregal Council" three times on the same page, offering a summary of a different hearing for each.[36] As with scribes' handwritten records for such sessions, readers of the paper are given the date of their occurrence, a brief overview of the protagonists involved, a summary of what motivated them to write to or appear before the body in question, and the resolution. Outcomes could be left open-ended, such as when the Department of the Interior found that the hour was getting late as it interrogated three men in the coffee business who were implicated in a theft. The department therefore decided to throw the men in jail overnight before interrogating them again the following day, ultimately determining to send them to a shari'a judge (*hakim al-shar'*) because the matter pertained to theft, the purview of Islamic law.[37] No other mention of this case, or its resolution, seems to appear in other issues. Indeed, developments from shari'a courts are not recorded in *al-Waqa'i' al-Misriyya*, suggesting that the bodies the paper covered represent the government's real and imagined reach during this period and its unstated boundaries by extension.

Privately paid-for advertisements are absent from the paper, presumably because of its official nature and its secured system for funding. But issues could offer content that resembled government marketing for particular products by notifying officials of surpluses and reallocations, presumably to encourage them to be provident and inform them of available resources. Hence, *al-Waqa'i' al-Misriyya* carried word of the guild supervisor of Cairo's alert to the government that honey from the sugar storehouse amounting to 6,000 *qantar*, or more than 600,000 pounds, would soon go bad, most of which the Department of the Interior then ordered for distribution among the oil vendors of Cairo.[38] The beginning of an issue from July 1831 even reported that "a Frankish man (*rajul ifranji*) named Luis Kurduluski," who surely possessed high-level government connections, "has just now come to Cairo and brought with him medical items (*mufradat tibbiyya*) and various chemicals (*ajza'*) from which people will derive many uses and great benefits, especially women for whom there are goods concerning hair."[39] But entries like this one were exceptional, and they were included in the paper less to sell goods than to speak to the wonders that the government could attract to Egypt.

Indeed, the corpus is striking for how certain it is of itself and the government's mission, more so given the infancy of both. It is self-referential from the start, citing back issues and interchangeably calling itself a "paper" (*sahifa* and *jarida*), as distinct from the Arabic cognate for "gazette" (*kazata*), which it reserved for references to Western newspapers from places such as France, Malta, Italy, and even America.[40] Its confident tone derived from its task to inspire readers to carry out their duties with a unity of purpose and from its closeness to Mehmed 'Ali. His name frequently appears by way of orders taken down and related by others, and 'Abduh's archival work shows that Mehmed 'Ali also took an active role in evaluating *al-Waqa'i' al-Misriyya*'s issues, even looking them over before they were put into print.[41] The paper's lead staff, Sami Effendi and later Darwish Ahmad Effendi in the Ottoman section, and al-Khawaja Nasrallah followed by al-Sayyid Shihab al-Din Muhammad ibn Isma'il in the Arabic section, may therefore be thought of as amanuenses-cum-editors.[42] We know of their names not from any fixed attribution feature within the publication itself but from details that make their way into the paragraphs of some issues. Hence, we also read an apology issued by the "corrector" (*taslih*) of books at Bulaq, Sa'id Effendi, who got into trouble when Mehmed 'Ali discovered that a handful of misspelled words had appeared in the paper after passing the corrector by because of his old age.[43] The words on *al-Waqa'i' al-Misriyya*'s pages needed to be related precisely because they came from the government, not from those who prepared them.

Uniting the Functionaries of a Transformational State in Formation

Mehmed 'Ali gained control of Egypt after Ottoman governors and Mamluk emirs divided its rule for centuries, and after the French army shook up this modus vivendi during its failed occupation of 1798–1801, which had attempted to render Egypt a colony.[44] To defend his seat against threats from Istanbul and European capitals, he took up an ambitious policy of defensive modernization, establishing an army in the mid-1810s that would run according to European military arts.[45] He manned it first with slaves and then forced conscripts. Indeed, his rule depended on coercion generally. Its funding was sourced from a monopoly that he imposed upon cultivators around the trade of Jumel cotton, as proceeds were put toward founding factories for the army's supply and the schools and hospitals that supported the training and health of its soldiers.[46] They were also put toward developing Egypt's infrastructure by way of canals, aqueducts, roads, and other public works projects that relied on his subjects' corvée labor. To manage these vast and varied efforts, which together contributed to Mehmed 'Ali's goal of making Egypt self-sustainable, worthy of its heritage, and a force to be reckoned with on the world stage, he began building a bureaucracy centered around him at its helm. *Al-Waqa'i' al-Misriyya* bolstered the work of this reforming body by consolidating it in one place, physically and narratively on the page, and by signaling to the men who were to read it what was expected of them as a group.

If Mehmed 'Ali's functionaries did read the paper, they would have been made privy to a range of information that they did not previously have access to, and they would have been inserted into the total orbit of the new government. The paper was the one place where the emerging polity came together for all its officials to see. Entries differed widely in their content, substantive heft, and length, yet each reinforced the aspirational magnitude of Mehmed 'Ali's vision. A short report from April 1829 about the invention of gas lighting in England illustrates this point. It relates that when Mehmed 'Ali learned that the English had devised this innovation fourteen years earlier, "at low-cost, which could be used widely, and which the French also used," he wanted to be certain that it worked. He therefore commanded that the necessary equipment be imported to Egypt for an engineer and several English workers to test in six rooms of his Shubra palace.

When Mehmed ʿAli approached the large pool beneath the palace at sunset, the illumination "delighted him enormously and he became very happy from it, and it was clear to those who were with him that his shock would be the talk of all his land." The paper appends a note to this report, perhaps dictated by Mehmed ʿAli himself, that draws out its significance in the context of his rule. It explains that "the intention of his highness the Benefactor, may his glory continue eternally, is for the people of Egypt to be masters of knowledge and possessors of industries (*arbab al-maʿarif wa-ashab sanaʾiʿ*) like the people of Europe, and towards this end he has spent uncountable sums" to bring experts to the province "to put before the students and to command that they teach them. This will greatly benefit them and organize their situations, which is clearly the first of his priorities, as is [demonstrated by] this light especially which no one has ever before seen the likes of in the Islamic lands." Whoever reflected upon this light was therefore to "know that it would not be except for the favor of their Highness and his beneficence towards the Muslim people that they could see industries such as this marvel, which no longer remains concealed from them."[47]

"Organizing" people's "situations" was the explanation that Mehmed ʿAli's government gave for what it set out to do, and *al-Waqaʾiʿ al-Misriyya* itself represented another marvel fostered by the government to lift the province and its population. More than impressing those who received copies of it with the polity's capability, ambition, and reach, it served as a tool for state-building. That is because it did not merely demonstrate the transformation that Mehmed ʿAli had planned but also helped its facilitation by conveying its necessity and what it entailed for functionaries tasked with its implementation. The contents of the paper opened up two possibilities to them. On the one hand, they were made privy to the government's regard for its own interests and concerns. On the other hand, they were exposed to the government's expectations of them so they could fulfill them as one harmonious body.

As for the first of these possibilities, the paper oriented functionaries toward putting the government of Mehmed ʿAli's creation at the center of their conception of the world. Readers were to see its disparate activities and concerns as falling under a common banner and to appreciate its milestones as preeminent above all else. To achieve this effect, the paper abounded with references to occasions and considerations that mattered to the life of this government, including the movements and activities of its key figures, with one notable example being the special issue that was devoted entirely to Mehmed ʿAli's 1839 "honor to the lands of Sudan" through his official visit to a region occupied by Egypt from 1821; the need for palaces to be constructed for him in seaside areas for "his implementation of authority" (*maslaha*); military ceremonies conducted in the presence of his son Ibrahim (1789–1848); the acquisition of horses from Egypt, Syria, and neighboring lands for the army; the death of important government personnel and the sadness felt by all upon the passing of Mehmed ʿAli's daughter, presumably Tawhida Hanim or Khadija Nazli Hanim; a destructive fire in the Bulaq arsenal; and the contents of a thank-you letter from Mehmed ʿAli to the French scholar Edme-François Jomard (1777–1862), composed in gratitude for his services in educating Egyptians and sent along with the gift of a box of snuff (*ʿulbat nashuq*).[48]

Al-Waqa'i' al-Misriyya collapsed all of Egypt into Mehmed 'Ali's Cairo-based government through its title, encouraging readers to view them as synonymous and take a province-level perspective on developments. Accounts of foreign occurrences that made their way into the paper reinforced this conflation. Rather than representing all mankind, as claimed in the first issue, *al-Waqa'i' al-Misriyya* most regularly reported on events in the Mediterranean region and the Ottoman and Russian empires. That is, it gestured out toward the geopolitics that Mehmed 'Ali's Egypt was impacted by and those that it pursued. Announcements of political alliances and battles, in addition to translated speeches made by foreign rulers and noteworthy happenings, filled its pages and advanced the interpretation that the province and its ruler were emerging powers because their names appeared alongside these other touchstones of authority. When functionaries read in an issue from 1829, for example, of the death of Pope Leo XII (1760–1829), they could appreciate that Mehmed 'Ali was, at some level, on a par with him and that his passing held implications for Egypt's relationship to Catholic countries in Europe and Catholic communities in the Ottoman Empire.[49] When they also read in that same issue that France intended to deploy fifty-five thousand soldiers to Algeria as part of its ongoing dispute with the Ottoman vassal in power there, they could recall that Mehmed 'Ali had deployed the Egyptian navy to fight the Greek rebellion on behalf of the sultan in the previous years.[50]

Beyond causing functionaries to orient themselves around the polity and the province, the paper enabled them to see what it set out to do. They could learn to appreciate, for example, the development of Egypt's political economy, as *al-Waqa'i' al-Misriyya*'s special issue 17 makes clear. Running twelve pages in length, it marks the longest issue stored in the BnF collection. The reason for this only becomes clear on the fifth page, where a seemingly verbatim transcription begins of the proceedings of a special general assembly (*majlis 'umumi*) held to discuss the topic of building up the province.[51] Ibrahim presided over this session in which the participating figures ranged from the treasurer (*daftardar*) to district chiefs (*kashifun*) to the superintendent of the military (*nazir al-jihadiyya*), and even named European advisers.[52] His preeminence emerges through him having the last word in each of the assembly's pursuant debates. In one, its members wished to determine how to increase Egypt's cotton output. They considered the amount of cotton that farmers produced, connecting this to land-plot distributions, the timing of when the crops were planted and watered so "cotton plants would not become weak and the fruit yellow," and even the construction of bridges, canals, and water wheels.[53] These latter works would facilitate the irrigation of the crop and its transport. The assembly considered what each of these initiatives entailed, while also discussing whether developing the lands would lead to the "comfort of all the people and their prosperity (*numuwihim*)."[54] Officials who read this issue could thus begin to appreciate how different arms of the government's works relied on one another.

A key trend that the paper highlighted for these officials was that the government was extending its initiatives out from the army and into other domains. Those who read *al-Waqa'i' al-Misriyya*'s eighth issue, for example, were informed that Mehmed 'Ali's investment in a new system of medicine originated to safeguard the military. The opening page explains that he strived in every regard to "raise up (*ta'mir*) the Egyptian administrative districts and restore (*islah*) their lands and fields" to benefit everyone under his rule, be they big or small in standing. For that reason, he founded the military troops (*al-'asakir al-jihadiyya*). But then, "he saw that they must be protected against circulating (*al-'arida*) diseases and that there are not at this time doctors (*atibba'*) who are experts (*rasikhun*)." Therefore, "it came to his generous mind to establish hospitals (*bimaristanat*) in appropriate places and to bring in doctors proficient in the science of the pulse (*'ilm al-nabd*) from European countries so that if one of the troops falls ill, he will be treated and the disease will be prevented from spreading . . . such that the people of Egypt will be double what they are now."[55] One such hospital was in Abu Za'bal, where the military was headquartered. It would accommodate "more than 1,500 sick" and train as doctors "one hundred students from the sons of Egypt."[56] Over time, this arrangement evolved even further. What began as a means of supporting the army directly, and ordinary people only secondarily insofar as they would not be exposed to diseases from soldiers, was made to benefit the study of medicine in Egypt and the Cairene public. The paper proclaimed in 1838 that Mehmed 'Ali ordered a change to the arrangement of hospitals. Abu Za'bal would now become a school, and the hospital (*isbitaliya*) at Azbakiyya would no longer serve soldiers but "be the preserve of the people (*ahl al-balad*)."[57]

Officials were to appreciate the government's expansion into society. One way came via its establishment of individual links to its subjects. Nearly the whole of issue 77, for example, is devoted to the regime of the "stamped permit" (*tadhkira makhtuma*), or government-issued identification document, which was originally mandated for its personnel only. The system was found to be so effective and widely beneficial that the government now promulgated "a new arrangement" over twenty-one sections in which functionaries would see these permits dispensed to every person in the land.[58] Another way that officials could appreciate the extension of the government's reach into society came via its efforts to support public hygiene. It used *al-Waqa'i' al-Misriyya* to announce that it was widening streets, supplying people with drinking water, and taking precautions in 1831 against "the plague that has appeared in these parts."[59]

Yet another way appeared through the government's takeover of domains that were traditionally not its own. This takeover may be seen through its assumption of the prerogative to make judgments against subjects who threatened public order, a responsibility that had long belonged to the office of the *muhtasib*, or Islamic marketplace inspector.[60] It was now being subsumed under the government's new institutions, as various reports that the paper published from the Council of Cairo and the Department of the Interior show. In 1832, readers learned of two thieves who had "created a seal like the seal of the Sharif 'Umar Agha, president of the merchants, using it to take dirhams from some people." Only one of the two was apprehended after this episode of counterfeiting. The council, which received the case from the Department of the Interior, determined that although his crime was punishable by death, he would receive in the department "250 lashes to set him straight (*ta'diban lahu*), and then be expelled from this land (*balad*)."[61] Yet another hearing, this time on the threat posed by men who harassed women in the street, reached the department by way of the deputy to the head policeman. It involved a woman named Fatima and a water carrier from the Citadel named Ahmad after a fight broke out between them. Fatima, when asked to explain herself, reported: "I sell bread and this Ahmad here, every day, dares to put his hands on me (*yutilu yadahu 'alay*). Today when I came to the Citadel . . . he saw me and sprayed me with water, which is when the fight broke out." The Department then asked Ahmad for his version of what happened. He said that he was spraying the ground with water where Fatima was sitting and that he warned her as he approached her. But she did not get out of his way, "so I got her clothes wet with water, and what she said is not true." The Department favored Fatima's word over Ahmad's, for "some of those present" at the hearing "believed the speech of the woman, and said the man was causing harm (*yasna'u al-adha*) to pedestrians in the street, so he was hit, let go, and sent on his way."[62]

Apart from providing officials with the possibility of seeing the government from afar and from within as it encouraged them to do, the paper engendered another possibility: that they appreciate their functional role within this system. In the first place, it signaled to them how valuable they were to its operations. This was true of workers generally, as readers discovered through entries concerning those whom the government had forced into labor, such as lists of statistics that included headcounts on the progress of a canal being dug at the hands of 43,755 "people who worked on the operation," decisions to exploit the manpower of subjects who came under the government's control (such as dwellers of the poorhouse in Bulaq, who were to be clothed, fed, and trained to staff workshops and factories in what the paper said was an effort to help advance them and local manufactories) and even hearings at the Department of the Interior of those who abandoned their posts.[63] An issue from 1832, for example, reported to readers that "a man named Mansur from among the watchmen (*min al-baltajiyya*)" of Cairo had alerted the police that he apprehended "a resident of Suq al-Silah named Muhammad who was dressing in women's clothing (*wa-huwa mutazi bi-ziyy al-nisa'*)." Muhammad disguised himself to escape his job in the government's saddle workshop, which paid him only six loaves of bread daily. The department commanded that he be returned there instead of punishing him, presumably because its need for his exertions was so great.[64]

But since *al-Waqa'i' al-Misriyya* did not expressly target the government's manual laborers who were referenced in the previous examples, focusing instead on its learned or would-be learned officials whom it leaned upon to direct them, the paper stressed to this elite group that their indispensability depended upon the ability to communicate adequately. Sometimes the linguistic limitations of government personnel were emphasized to them, as when they encountered reports such as one about a tax collector sent to the island of Crete who could not do his job because he did not speak the "foreign" languages of the people there, "did not understand a thing," feared that inconsistencies would surface in his records, and so asked to be moved elsewhere.[65] More often, the paper underscored the government's need for their proficiency in literacy through announcements from various departments concerning the demand for workers who could read and write properly or through model requests that literate functionaries put forward to take up new roles, such as one that students of Qasr al-ʿAyni raised for jobs at the Bulaq Press because they found themselves without work upon graduating despite "knowing how to read and write."[66] The paper supported the take-away of these reports all the more given that officials' very consumption of it encouraged greater proficiency in reading Ottoman Turkish and Arabic.

The readers of al-Waqaʾiʿ al-Misriyya were thus made to understand that basic training was key for anyone whom this reforming government put to work, whether they were to spend their days in its factories or its offices. But in their case, learning to read and write was only a means to reaching more specialized ends. Hence, they came across announcements pertaining to the 150 copies of a surgical textbook in the possession of the printing press, which "needed to be distributed . . . to the students so that they can read [it]," or the government's accounts of its struggles to impart technical knowledge to students during these early years.[67] There was word of a European chemist by the name of Juani Rafaʾili who received a six-year contract to convert deposits from the government's saltpeter reservoir to an enzyme, al-khamir, for the purpose of generating more of it, but especially "to teach his craft such that his assistants become skilled in it."[68] There were also announcements of new pa-perwork regimes to be learned, as when the paper reported, in July 1829, that Copts would no longer be asked to record Egypt's budget according to their centuries-honed shorthand, unique unto them. Henceforth, the system would be designed by "some Europeans skilled in arranging account books and in the art of accounting (fann al-hisab), since their method was in sync with the mood of the time (muwafiqan li-mizaj al-waqt) and printed" to be read by those in charge.[69]

Likewise emphasized to functionaries were the rewards that awaited them for their good performance and the sense that their poor performance would not go unnoticed. Acknowledgments of promotions, raises, and retirements dot the pages of the paper, presumably to celebrate their recipients and announce the new status to those who worked alongside them while motivating all to seek higher stations.[70] These entries conveyed the constancy and largesse of Mehmed ʿAli's government, which especially favored its most meritorious and valued workers who could receive special support for their work. The paper mentioned in one of its issues, for example, that the gov-ernment was providing a donkey to a certain Shaykh Mustafa so that he could more easily reach Bulaq to correct a text on veterinary medicine.[71] Cutting the other way, the paper published discussions of functionaries' malfeasance, such as the question of whether the son of a government tax collector, himself employed in secretarial work, had stolen from the government or was simply ignorant of notation standards and how to ultimately detect and manage the root cause of his transgression.[72] It also published complaints that various offices of the government levied against one another, such as that of a military teacher who noted that "the students of the Giza office have until now not received any part of the Qanunnama" just five days after the paper announced that this Arabic book of law codes "comprising the arrangement of the necessary war offices for the citadels and barracks (qashlat)" would be printed in one thousand copies.[73] The government presumably published such accounts to inform functionaries of noteworthy hiccups, but also to pressure individuals and bodies that erred or delayed in their work to do better.

Announcements like that on the *Qanunnama*, furthermore, gave officials instruction on how to govern. In general, these announcements could offer them insight into the structure and appearance of various bodies through explanations that delineated their organization and the appointments made to them. An 1829 report even waded into bureaucratic sartorial requirements while nodding to the Porte's supremacy by publicizing the change of its dress code to an embroidered tarbush and a white broadcloth cloak (*harwani*) with decorative threading around the neck.[74] But more specifically, such announcements directed functionaries toward the procedures and codes that they were to put to use, including expectations that were projected to make department heads "suitable for work" (*dusturan li-l-'amal*), new categories for supporting agricultural production that they were to deploy, and commands for local administrators to implement to "develop towns and to start giving comfort to the poor."[75] Only rarely did the paper publish the substance of regulations in full, tending instead to note that they were issued and to what and whom they pertained. Thus, again returning to the *Qanunnama*, came word in an issue from February 1830 that the Viceregal Council determined "to arrange the law codes comprising details of sowing the land, statements (*bayan*) on how to administer (*ru'ya*) governmental departments (*al-masalih al-miriyya*), and the civil code (*al-siyasa al-madaniyya*)." The codes would "inform all the department heads, district chiefs and managers, heads of subdistricts, administrators of towns and their shaykhs and tax collectors." Those who were to carry them out learned that they could soon expect them, as they were to be "organized, printed in Turkish and Arabic, and spread."[76]

As these announcements suggest, functionaries were encouraged to equate excelling with the proper implementation of their assignments in a government system that self-consciously endeavored to instill order in its personnel. Still, the paper offered them information that likely gave them some latitude in their work by anticipating trends. One example of this came in the form of the economic content it included, which was rife. Sometimes it came overtly in numeric form, as in issue 133, which provided a list of recently imported and exported goods from Alexandria, such as sugar, coffee, and paper, alongside their quantities.[77] But for the most part, it came in statements within, for example, announcements concerning boats that had docked on Egypt's shores, including one from France "with 170 prisoners from male and female Muslims of Morea" and another "from America after fifty-five days [at sea] containing sugar and goods."[78] The points of origin of these boats are given, along with their stops, the length of time they spent en route, a rough description of their holdings and value, and even the names of their backers. Readers encountered mention of boats reaching Egypt at Mehmed 'Ali's own expense alongside "an English boat at the expense of its captain" and frequent reference to a European man, al-Khawaja Danstasi, who must have been a major player on the scene of Austrian imports to Alexandria.[79] Through such information, readers could perhaps gain a sense of what might happen to the prices of particular commodities in their local markets or, even better, frame their requests for the government's distribution of goods to the outfits under their watch.

Altogether then, *al-Waqa'i' al-Misriyya* worked to unite the functionaries of a transformational state that, according to its own statements, set out to put Egypt at the vanguard of global power. It made them see the world according to the government's perspective, and it exposed them to what the government expected them to know. Bit by bit, functionaries were informed of what mattered and what could be done, how things fit together, issues to be on the lookout for, which bodies covered proceedings on certain topics, how matters passed between administrative divisions, where jurisdiction ultimately belonged, and the types of judgments that could be pronounced. The paper treated readers as one audience, and therefore one whole, which ruled in superiority over the general population according to the longstanding Ottoman view that society was composed of shepherds and their flock, despite the vast differences in these shepherds' backgrounds, postings, and career trajectories that would endure for decades.[80] It thus made for a state-building tool, where readers discovered that they could serve Mehmed 'Ali's government by reaching into all manner of affairs so that it not be "held back in anything (*kul shay'*) required for the life of Egypt."[81]

CONCLUSION

Al-Waqa'i' al-Misriyya endures as a product of the state. Today it circulates as an appendix to the government's bulletin, publicizing decisions of offices such as those of the prime minister, along with other ministries and governorships, as the history section of the web page for the al-Amiriyya state press, from which it is printed, relates.[82]

But while government workers continue to form a key audience for *al-Waqa'i' al-Misriyya*, another audience exists alongside them: the public. The expansion of the paper's hoped for readership beyond the confines of the government's functionaries to include all Egyptians was not a twenty-first-century phenomenon. In fact, it emerged sometime during the rule of Mehmed 'Ali's grandson and fourth successor, Isma'il (r. 1863–79), as a means of extending the reach of the government's message. The shift was made explicit after the 1861 shutdown of the Bulaq Press following problems with the press's management and output.[83] Since production for the paper had returned to Bulaq in 1845, its publication was paused too until Isma'il's predecessor, Sa'id (r. 1854–1863), gifted the press in 1862 to the director of the government's steamships on the Red Sea, 'Abd al-Rahman Rushdi Bey. Rushdi Bey was tasked with maintaining the press's government functions and was granted permission to publish *al-Waqa'i' al-Misriyya* at his own expense.[84] Just ten days after Sa'id died, Rushdi Bey requested of Isma'il's superintendent of the exchequer (*nazir al-maliyya*) that he be allowed to enlist the paper's old government employees to fill the contents of its pages once more.[85] The affirmative decree that the superintendent issued in response is notable for its unselfconscious emphasis on connecting *al-Waqa'i' al-Misriyya* to the Egyptian public. He writes that the government had thought it best that the paper, instead of "announcing its matters to the world (*li-l-'alam*) by way of its servants (*mustakhdimiha*)," now outsource this work to an editor from beyond the government's immediate payroll to reach both "the population and the government" (*al-ahali wa-l-hukuma*).[86]

The opening up of the government's paper to a wider reading public, so different from Mehmed 'Ali's time, caused a change in its contents. It began to disseminate excerpted works of literature, for example. But more important than changes to the paper's contents was the new functional role it took on in aspiring to shape public opinion.[87] This development did not merely lay the groundwork for the later vernacular press. It also engendered new forms of discourse and sociability, which, moving out from the bureaucratic public sphere that the paper first tried to foster among functionaries to a more society-wide public sphere, would come to inform the development of Egyptians' collective camaraderie and national identity, and the categories of citizens who would ultimately deliver it.[88] Crucially, though, the move to expand *al-Waqa'i' al-Misriyya*'s audience to Egypt's general population, the dynamics the paper inspired, and even the short-lived rise of the right to produce it "privately" never excised the state from the paper.[89] It was started as a tool of government and remained so despite its wider mandate, its changing contents, the short pause in its production, and its passage to privately funded, though not completely unaffiliated, ownership, before moving back into the government's possession, where it has stayed since 1880.[90]

Despite *al-Waqa'i' al-Misriyya*'s original and persistent embeddedness within the Egyptian state, the material form that the paper takes as a periodical has, since at least the late 1890s, allowed scholars to approach it as a journalistic pursuit.[91] The Beirut-born bibliophile Filib di Tarrazi (1865–1956), for example, labeled *al-Waqa'i' al-Misriyya* in his pioneering 1913 *History of the Arabic Press* as "the leader (*al-shaykha*) of all Arabic newspapers active in the East and West," by which he meant it was both the first of its kind and the source of inspiration for the press.[92] Many others have continued to conceive of the paper in this vein since then, classifying it in their research alongside "newspapers and magazines" such as the *Times* of London and *Revue des Deux Mondes* of Paris, using it as a log for public events instead of a source for changing projections of official power, or not relying upon it all despite taking up research agendas that excavate the early development and evolution of the Egyptian state and the ideas that it fostered.[93]

The physicality of the paper has perhaps prevailed all the more over the primacy of its nature due to its historical dependence on the labor of key *nahdawi* intellectuals such as Ahmad Faris al-Shidyaq, Rifa'a Rafi' al-Tahtawi, and Muhammad 'Abduh, all of whom hold standing in the history of the press for their respective roles in the periodicals *al-Jawa'ib* (Responses), *Rawdat al-Madaris* (Garden of the Schools), and *al-Manar* (The Lighthouse). But these men were not freelance intellectuals; they worked for the Egyptian government at least for a time, and they recognized how journalism functioned in the Western tradition. As early as 1834, for example, al-Tahtawi noted, after serving as the religious leader of Mehmed 'Ali's 1826 student mission to Paris, that French freedom of expression made it so that "people learn everything that goes on in the mind of their fellow man." Connecting this insight to "daily papers," he explained that the ideas within them were "issued by both important and insignificant people, since even a lowly person may think of something that does not come to the mind of important people," and that they were then spread among "the notables and the common people."[94] *Al-Waqa'i' al-Misriyya*, which al-Tahtawi edited upon his return to Egypt, was also supposed to be socially beneficial. But its original purpose was to organize people's situations, not by promoting ideas that percolated across society to all but rather by disseminating its top-down contents to those directed to transform the physical world and the lives of those living in it. More than a product of the media, it was a product of the state.

Egyptian scholars active through the mid-twentieth century maintained an awareness of *al-Waqa'i' al-Misriyya*'s role as a reflection of state power, perhaps because they lived and labored under the rule of Mehmed 'Ali's descendants. They cited it at length to give definitive portrayals of official events and proceedings, as the son of the Shaykh of al-Azhar Mahmud al-Biblawi did when describing the festivities surrounding the decision of Isma'il's son Tawfiq (r. 1879–92) to transfer the relics of the Prophet from 'Abdin Palace to al-Husayn mosque in his 1906–07 history of the latter.[95] More creatively, they mined *al-Waqa'i' al-Misriyya*'s contents to chart the development of major state institutions, even treating the corpus as a state archive on a par with internal government papers in the case of the educator and scholar Amin Sami's (1857–1941) compendium of government documents, *Taqwim al-Nil* (Chronology of the Nile).[96]

When the paper is viewed through the lens of the state, its contents show themselves to be a crucial, unique, and broadly applicable working government archive. This is especially true of the issues published before the paper was intended for public viewing. The archive of *al-Waqa'i' al-Misriyya* is crucial because scholars' access to books and records held in the government's care has been restricted steadily over the past several decades, with the Revolution of 2011 marking a particularly severe turning point after which most researchers have been blocked from studying this material.[97] The archive is unique because it was selected and edited for publication on a continuum, thereby signaling what the government found to be extraordinarily worthwhile for dissemination on a rolling basis. Simultaneously, its entries have not been culled or re-curated as they might have been upon entering a government archival office, making it likely that the paper contains information and portrayals that no longer exist elsewhere. Lastly, the archive is broadly applicable because it was meant to be fully accessible within the government's circle. It was not intended for the eyes of researchers or those of high functionaries or particular councils alone but rather for those of the government's officials at the moment it was produced, who were expected to absorb Mehmed 'Ali's vision for Egypt's transformation so that they could enact it. The issues of *al-Waqa'i' al-Misriyya*'s early years, therefore, offer the opportunity to understand this emerging community, the initiatives and wider project with which it was tasked, and the self-reported nature of the government in formation that it ultimately served. Those of its later years, though intended for public consumption, offer many of the same possibilities.

NOTES

1. This chapter focuses on the Arabic content instead of its Ottoman Turkish equivalent.
2. For the biography of Mehmed 'Ali, see Khaled Fahmy, *Mehmed Ali: From Ottoman Governor to Ruler of Egypt* (Oxford: Oneworld, 2009). For a close study of the life span of this government, see F. Robert Hunter, *Egypt under the Khedives 1805–1879: From Household Government to Modern Bureaucracy* (Pittsburgh: University of Pittsburgh Press, 1984).
3. *Al-Waqa'i' al-Misriyya* (*WM*) no. 1, 25 Jumada al-Awwal 1244, 1.
4. In his book on the Arabic press of the Middle East, Ami Ayalon rightly stresses this functional nature of the paper, explaining that "it did not aim to entertain. Rather, it was conceived as a serviceable tool in the governmental machinery of the efficiency-hungry pasha." But Ayalon's aim is to situate the paper in the history of the press, causing him to consider its "limitations" compared to the Western press instead of charting the early history of the paper according to its own terms. He also appears to rely on other sources for reports on the paper instead of the corpus itself. Ami Ayalon, *The Press in the Arab Middle East: A History* (New York: Oxford University Press, 1995), 15–19, 248.
5. Hans Wehr and J. Milton Cowan, ed., *A Dictionary of Modern Written Arabic (Arabic–English)* (Ithaca, NY: Spoken Language Services, 1994), 1277.
6. *WM* no. 1, 25 Jumada al-Awwal 1244, 1.
7. Ayalon, *The Press in the Arab Middle East*, 148. I arrive at the estimate of the low thousands by relying upon the record of *WM* budget for 1845–46, which shows that its production costs exceeded its revenue by only one purse and 109 piastres. Abu al-Futuh Radwan, *Tarikh Matba'at Bulaq wa-Lamha fi Tarikh al-Tiba'a fi Buldan al-Sharq al-Awsat* (Cairo: al-Matba'a al-Amiriyya, 1953), 274–75. Assuming that the paper's revenue of 155 purses and 70 piastres came from the high-level officials who were mandated to purchase it at the cost of 77 piastres and that one purse was equal to 500 piastres, the paper would have had just over one thousand paying subscribers that year. Meanwhile, several hundred, if not several thousand, more copies of the paper were likely to have been printed, given that the government distributed copies of it freely to officials who earned less than 1,000 piastres, and given that the costs of printing and paper that year amounted to 49 purses and 235 piastres, exclusive of the salaries of the paper's staff of five. For reference, had this sum been applied to paper alone, it would have amounted to approximately 989 reams to make nearly 100,000 copies of *WM*, assuming that one ream cost 25 piastres and amounted to 100 sheets of generously sized paper, when reams usually made for 500 sheets. Terrence Walz, "The Paper Trade of Egypt and the Sudan in the Eighteenth and Nineteenth Centuries and Its Re-export to the *Bilad as-Sudan*," in *The Trans-Saharan Book Trade: Manuscript Culture, Arabic Literacy and Intellectual History in Muslim Africa*, ed. Graziano Krätli and Ghislaine Lydon (Leiden, Netherlands: Brill, 2011), 96.
8. See, e.g., *WM* no. 285, 26 Muharram 1247; and *WM* no. 291, 16 Safar 1247, 1.
9. William L. Cleveland and Martin Bunton, *A History of the Modern Middle East*, 5th ed. (Philadelphia: Westview Press, 2013), 62.
10. For more on the Egyptian historical profession in the twentieth century and the institutions created to support it, see Yoav Di-Capua, *Gatekeepers of the Arab Past: Historians and History Writing in Twentieth-Century Egypt* (Berkeley: University of California Press, 2009). For a biography of 'Abduh and a discussion of the evolution of his politics before and after the 1952 Revolution, see J. J. G. Jansen, "Ibrahim Abduh (b. 1913):

His Autobiographies and His Political Polemical Writings," *Bibliotheca Orientalis* 37, nos. 3/4 (1980): 128–32.

11. Ibrahim 'Abduh, *Tarikh al-Waqa'i' al-Misriyya, 1828–1942* (Cairo: al-Matba'a al-Amiriyya, 1942), f, h.

12. For more on this museum, see Ahmed Mansour, "The Bulaq Press Museum at the Bibliotheca Alexandrina," in *Historical Aspects of Printing and Publishing in Languages of the Middle East*, ed. Geoffrey Roper (Boston: Brill, 2014), 287–315.

13. See, e.g., Filib Di Tarrazi, *Tarikh al-Sihafa al-'Arabiyya: Yahtawi 'ala Akhbar Kul Jarida wa-Majalla 'Arabiyya Zaharat fi al-'Alam Sharqan wa-Gharban ma'a Rusum Ashabiha wa-l-Muharririn fiha wa-Tarajim Mashahirihim* (Beirut: al-Matba'a al-Adabiyya, 1913–33); Ayalon, *The Press in the Arab Middle East*, 13–20; Dyala Hamzah, "Foundations of Religious Reform (Islah) and Cultural Revival (Nahda)," in *The Oxford Handbook of Contemporary Middle Eastern and North African History*, ed. Amal Ghazal and Jens Hanssen (New York: Oxford University Press, 2021), 46; Alexander Schölch, *Egypt for the Egyptians!: The Socio-political Crisis in Egypt, 1878–1882* (London: Ithaca Press for the Middle East Centre, St. Antony's College, Oxford, 1981); and Titus Nemeth, *Arabic Type-Making in the Machine Age: The Influence of Technology on the Form of Arabic Type, 1908–1993* (Leiden: Brill, 2017), 28–31.

14. The BnF claims not to have information on this corpus's origins or how it reached its holdings beyond the facts that it entered its collection after a 2004 donation and that it moved to its rare books department upon transfer from another department (Private Correspondence, 9 October 2019). The corpus could have eventually made its way to the library after being collated by a Frenchman on Mehmed 'Ali's payroll or by a member of one of his student missions to Paris. For more on the student missions, see Rifa'a Rafi' al-Tahtawi, *An Imam in Paris: Account of a Stay in France by an Egyptian Cleric (1826–1831)*, trans. Daniel Newman (London: Saqi, 2011), 15–28.

15. To my knowledge, this is the most complete set of the early years of the paper that is available for physical consultation. While there are lacunae in the BnF collection and the publication of the paper did not follow one fixed schedule for publication over the years, it does appear to have come out without interruption during this era. For example, issues from 1835 in the BnF collection refute Ayalon's claim that "between May 1834 and March 1836, no issue of the paper was published," Ayalon, *The Press in the Arab Middle East*, 16.

16. Adam Mestyan, *Arab Patriots: The Ideology and Culture of Power in Late Ottoman Egypt* (Princeton, NJ: Princeton University Press, 2017); Roger Owen, *State, Power and Politics in the Making of the Modern Middle East* (New York: Routledge, 2006); Khaled Fahmy, *All the Pasha's Men: Mehmed 'Ali, His Army and the Making of Modern Egypt* (New York: Cambridge University Press, 1997).

17. Hunter, *Egypt under the Khedives*; Timothy Mitchell, *Colonising Egypt* (Berkeley: University of California Press, 1991); Khaled Fahmy, *In Quest of Justice: Islamic Law and Forensic Medicine in Modern Egypt* (Oakland: University of California Press, 2018).

18. Fahmy, *In Quest of Justice*, 21.

19. *WM* no. 1, 25 Jumada al-Awwal 1244, 1.

20. There are no known copies of *Jurnal al-Khidiwi*. 'Abduh, *Tarikh al-Waqa'i' al-Misriyya*, 9–12; Hunter, *Egypt under the Khedives*, 86.

21. See, e.g., *WM* no. 343, 21 Sha'ban 1247, 1; *WM* no. 285, 26 Muharram 1247, 1; *WM* no. 346, 28 Sha'ban 1247, 1; and *WM* no. 58, 29 Rabi' al-Awwal 1245, 1. For an overview of the

relationship between, and purview of, these bodies, see Hunter, *Egypt under the Khedives*, 17–22. Which of them *al-Waqa'i' al-Misriyya* was to include reports from appears to have evolved over time. For example, the proceedings from the Viceregal Council, meeting at the palace of Mehmed 'Ali's son Ibrahim, were announced for consistent inclusion in the paper from issue 54; *WM* no. 54, 24 Rabi' al-Awwal 1245, 1.

22. *WM* no. 1: 25 Jumada al-Awwal, 1244, 1.

23. 'Abduh, *Tarikh al-Waqa'i' al-Misriyya*, 15–22.

24. For an account of the groups that formed the elite and their interests and influence under Mehmed 'Ali through 1874, see Hunter, *Egypt under the Khedives*, 80–122. For a focus on the Ottoman-Egyptian elite with an emphasis on the Ottoman historical context from 1841 to 1863, see Ehud R. Toledano, *State and Society in Mid-Nineteenth-Century Egypt* (New York: Cambridge University Press, 1990).

25. *WM* no. 607, 16 Jumada al-Awwal 1252, 1; and *WM* no. 614, 6 Shawwal 1253, 1.

26. 'Abduh, *Tarikh al-Waqa'i' al-Misriyya*, 15–22; for reference, a salary of one thousand piastres was about half of that due to artisans working in the government's factories into the 1830s, who officially earned eight piastres per day, Judith Tucker, *Women in Nineteenth-Century Egypt* (New York: Cambridge University Press), 76.

27. *WM* no. 1, 25 Jumada al-Awwal 1244, 1.

28. *WM* no. 18, 8 Shawwal 1244, 1.

29. *WM* no. 32, 27 Dhu al-Qa'da 1244, 1.

30. 'Abduh, *Tarikh al-Waqa'i' al-Misriyya*, 36. The first Citadel printing I could find in the BnF collection is *WM* no. 283, 22 Muharram 1247, 1. Printing at the Citadel continued until 1845, when the publication returned to the press at Bulaq, 'Abduh, *Tarikh al-Waqa'i' al-Misriyya*, 36.

31. Issue 341 appears to mark the break after which issues appear every other day, a move delayed because the press in the Citadel required replacing its outdated typefaces with new ones from the press at Bulaq, *WM* no. 341, 16 Sha'ban 1247. An English report from 1838 notes that the paper, "consisting principally of official documents," had "no fixed day or time of publication," John Bowring, *Report on Egypt and Candia: Addressed to the Right Hon. Lord Viscount Palmerston, Her Majesty's Principal Secretary of State for Foreign Affairs, &c. &c. &c.* (London: Printed by W. Clowes and Sons for Her Majesty's Stationery Office, 1840), 144.

32. Kathryn A. Schwartz, "Meaningful Mediums: A Material and Intellectual History of Manuscript and Print Production in Nineteenth-Century Ottoman Cairo" (PhD diss., Harvard University, 2015), 163–64.

33. *WM* no. 33, 3 Dhu al-Qa'da 1244, 1.

34. *WM* no. 15, 17 Ramadan 1244, 3.

35. *WM* no. 113, 28 Sha'ban 1245, 1; *WM* no. 124, 21 Ramadan 1245, 1.

36. *WM* no. 124, 21 Ramadan 1245, 1.

37. *WM* no. 312, 26 Jumada al-Awwal 1247, 3.

38. *WM* no. 13, 10 Ramadan 1244, 4.

39. *WM* no. 283, 22 Muharram 1247, 1.

40. *WM* no. 9, 20 Sha'ban 1244, 2; *WM* no. 1, 25 Jumada al-Awwal 1244, 1; *WM* no. 54, 24 Rabi' al-Awwal 1245, 1; *WM* no. 125, 22 Ramadan 1245, 3. The word *jurnal* appears in reference to individual documents transferred from the Department of the Interior to other government bodies. See, e.g., *WM* no. 303, 6 Jumada al-Awwal 1247, 1.

41. 'Abduh, *Tarikh al-Waqa'i' al-Misriyya*, 27–28; Radwan, *Tarikh Matba'at Bulaq*, 104–06, 271.

42. 'Abduh, *Tarikh al-Waqa'i' al-Misriyya*, 32–34.

43. *WM* no. 34, 2 Dhu al-Hijja 1244, 1.

44. For a history of the French invasion of Egypt, see Juan Cole, *Napoleon's Egypt: Invading the Middle East* (New York: Palgrave Macmillan, 2008).

45. First coined in the 1980s by the German historian Hans-Ulrich Wehler (1913–2014), *defensive modernization* describes programs of reform wherein local authorities implement foreign innovations to protect themselves from threats posed by foreign powers that boast such advantages already; Hans-Ulrich Wehler, *Deutsche gesellschaftsgeschichte* (Munich: Beck, 1987). See also Fahmy, *All the Pasha's Men*; and Emad Ahmad Helal, "Muhammad Ali's First Army: The Experiment in Building an Entirely Slave Army," in *Race and Slavery in the Middle East: Histories of Trans-Saharan Africans in Nineteenth-Century Egypt, Sudan, and the Ottoman Mediterranean*, ed. Terence Walz and Kenneth M. Cuno (New York: American University in Cairo Press, 2010), 17–42, 20–25.

46. Roger Owen, *Cotton and the Egyptian Economy, 1820–1914: A Study in Trade and Development* (Oxford: Clarendon Press, 1964).

47. *WM* no. 19, 13 Shawwal 1244, 3.

48. *WM* no. 618, 6 Safar 1255, 1–4. This issue is distinctive for its exclusive focus on this journey and for being printed in Arabic only; *WM* no. 3, Jumada al-Akhir 1244, 2–3, 4; 'Abduh, *Tarikh al-Waqa'i' al-Misriyya*, 40; *WM* no. 42, 27 Muharram 1245, 1–2; *WM* no. 590, Rabi' al-Thani 1251, 1.

49. *WM* no. 17, 28 Ramadan 1244, 4.

50. Ibid., 3.

51. Ibid., 7.

52. Ibid., 5–6.

53. Ibid.

54. Ibid., 6–7.

55. *WM* no. 8, 14 Sha'ban 1244, 1–2.

56. Ibid.

57. *WM* no. 614, 6 Shawwal 1253, 1.

58. *WM* no. 77, 5 Jumada al-Awwal 1245, 1–3.

59. *WM* no. 587, Rabi' al-Awwal 1251, 1–2; *WM* no. 303, 2 Jumada al-Awwal 1247, 1.

60. Enjoining the good and forbidding the bad nevertheless remained policy-based (*siyasa*), Kristen Stilt, *Islamic Law in Action: Authority, Discretion, and Everyday Experiences in Mamluk Egypt* (Oxford: Oxford University Press, 2011); Fahmy, *In Quest of Justice*, 179–225.

61. *WM* no. 303, 6 Jumada al-Awwal 1247, 1.

62. *WM* no. 313, 28 Jumada al-Awwal 1247, 2.

63. *WM* no. 283, 22 Muharram 1247, 4; *WM* no. 17, 28 Ramadan 1244, 1.

64. *WM* no. 298, 6 Rabi' al-Awwal 1247, 4.

65. *WM* no. 347, Salkh Sha'ban 1247, 1.

66. Ibid., 2; *WM* no. 536, 28 Safar al-Khayr 1249, 2; *WM* no. 537, 3 Rabi' al-Awwal 1249, 1.

67. *WM* no. 533, 16 Safar 1249, 1; *WM* no. 593, 2 Jumada al-Awwal 1251, 4.

68. *WM* no. 17, 28 Ramadan 1244, 3.

69. *WM* no. 41, 23 Muharram 1245, 2.

70. *WM* no. 49, 8 Rabi' al-Awwal 1245, 1; *WM* no. 327, 7 Rajab 1247, 4; *WM* no. 587, 22 Rabi' al-Awwal 1251, 4; *WM* no. 589, Salkh Rabi' al-Awwal 1251, 2.

71. *WM* no. 522, 12 Muharram 1249, 4.

72. *WM* no. 17, 28 Ramadan 1244, 10–11.

73. *WM* no. 546, 8 Rabi' al-Akhir 1249, 4; *WM* no. 545, 3 Rabi' al-Akhir 1249, 2.

74. *WM* no. 24, Ghurrat Dhu al-Qa'da 1244, 1.

75. *WM* no. 29, 17 Dhu al-Qa'da 1244, 2-4; *WM* no. 3, Salkh Jumada al-Akhir 1244, 1.

76. *WM* no. 113, 28 Sha'ban 1245, 4.

77. *WM* no. 133, 18 Shawwal 1245, 4.

78. *WM* no. 6, 4 Sha'ban 1244, 4; *WM* no. 591, 13 Rabi' al-Thani 1251, 2.

79. *WM* no. 17, 28 Ramadan 1244, 3-4.

80. For a description of the alienation of French government servants from ordinary people in particular, see Afaf Lutfi al-Sayyid Marsot, "What Price Reform?," in *La France et l'Égypte: à l'époque des vice-rois 1805–1882*, ed. Daniel Panzac and André Raymond (Cairo: Institut Français d'Archéologie Orientale, 2002), 3–11. For an account of the socio-political crisis that broke out in Egypt from 1878 to 1882 on account of tensions among classes within the government-military complex spreading out into society, see Schölch, *Egypt for the Egyptians!*.

81. *WM* no. 605, 6 Rabi' al-Akhir 1252, 1.

82. "Idarat al-Jarida al-Rasmiyya," al-Matabi' al-Amiriyya, accessed 21 August 2019, https://web.archive.org/web/20181003220940/http://alamiria.com:80/a/main_page/history.htm.

83. Amin Sami, *Taqwim al-Nil wa-Asma' man Tawallu Amr Misr wa-Muddat Hukmahum 'alayha wa-Mulahazat Tarikhiyya 'an Ahwal al-Khilafa al-'Amma wa-Shu'un Misr al-Khasa 'an al-Mudda al-Munhasira bayna al-Sana al-Ula wa-Sanat 1333 al-Hijriyya, (622–1915 Miladiyya)* vol. 3, part 1 (Cairo: al-Matba'a al-Amiriyya, 1915–36), 356–57.

84. 'Abduh, *Tarikh al-Waqa'i' al-Misriyya*, 36; for further details, see Radwan, *Tarikh Matba'at Bulaq*, 17–86.

85. Sami, *Taqwim al-Nil wa-Asma'*, vol. 3, part 2, 454.

86. Ibid., for subsequent correspondence between Rushdi Bey and the government with a similar emphasis on the public, see 'Abduh, *Tarikh al-Waqa'i' al-Misriyya*, 90–95.

87. 'Abduh, *Tarikh al-Waqa'i' al-Misriyya*, 90–122.

88. For the development of public opinion in the Ottoman bureaucratic sphere, see Murat R. Şiviloğlu, *The Emergence of Public Opinion: State and Society in the Late Ottoman Empire* (New York: Cambridge University Press, 2018), 72–109. For the development of collective camaraderie and national discourse in the vernacular press between the 1870s and the 1910s, see Ziad Fahmy, *Ordinary Egyptians: Creating the Modern Nation through Popular Culture* (Stanford, CA: Stanford University Press, 2011). For the rise of new categories of belonging in Egyptian politics and society, see Beth Baron, *The Women's Awakening in Egypt* (New Haven, CT: Yale University Press, 1994); Marilyn Booth, *May Her Likes Be Multiplied: Biography and Gender Politics in Egypt* (Berkeley: University of California Press, 2001); Lisa Pollard, *Nurturing the Nation: The Family Politics of Modernizing, Colonizing, and Liberating Egypt, 1805–1923* (Berkeley: University of California Press, 2005); and Lucie Ryzova, *The Age of the Effendiyya: Passages to Modernity in National-Colonial Egypt* (New York: Oxford University Press, 2014).

89. Sami, *Taqwim al-Nil wa-Asma'*, vol. 3, part 2, 454. Misunderstanding Rushdi Bey's relationship to Bulaq, the nature of how the paper's former workers would be paid, and the dating of this chain of events, Mitchell makes this point about the continued presence of the state despite the paper's privatization with some degree of surprise when he notes that "this decision marked an alteration in technique, not a relinquishing of [the government's] control," Mitchell, *Colonising Egypt*, 90–92.

90. The press and paper remained in private ownership throughout Isma'il's rule, though he returned them to the direct management of the viceregal fold in 1865 by forcibly repurchasing them from Rushdi Bey in the name of his familial holdings, rather than the Egyptian government, where they returned under Tawfiq; Radwan, *Tarikh Matba'at Bulaq*, 175–86, 206.

91. Martin Hartmann, *The Arabic Press of Egypt* (London: Luzac & Co., 1899), 2–3.

92. Filib di Tarrazi, *Tarikh al-Sihafa al-'Arabiyya*, vol. 3 (Beirut: al-Matba'a al-'Arabiyya, 1913), 162; for Tarrazi's somewhat unreliable history of the paper, see ibid., vol. 1, 49–50.

93. Toledano, *State and Society*, 302–03. Other studies that list *WM* as a general periodical include Schölch, *Egypt for the Egyptians!*, 3, though he notes of this "official gazette" that "the press of that time is anyway less important for its daily news than as a vehicle for the propagation of political and social ideas"; Ayalon, *The Press in the Arab Middle East*, 277; Fahmy, *Ordinary Egyptians*, 222–23; Mestyan, *Arab Patriots*, 318. For examples of studies that do not rely upon its contents, see Di-Capua, *Gatekeepers of the Arab Past*; Fahmy, *All the Pasha's Men*; Fahmy, *In Quest of Justice*; Albert Hourani, *Arabic Thought in the Liberal Age, 1798–1939* (New York: Cambridge University Press, 1983); and Mitchell, *Colonising Egypt*. One study that does categorize the paper as an official archive is Hunter, *Egypt under the Khedives*, 267.

94. Al-Tahtawi, *An Imam in Paris*, 208–9.

95. Mahmud al-Biblawi, *al-Tarikh al-Husayni* (Cairo: Matba'at al-Taqaddum, 1906), 39–41.

96. Sami, *Taqwim al-Nil wa-Asma'*. For examples of the former, refer to 'Abduh's use of the paper to track government positions in his history of *WM*, which he cites under "Articles in Newspapers and Magazines," and Radwan's reliance upon it as a trove of "Official Documents" to flesh out the history of the press at Bulaq; 'Abduh, *Tarikh al-Waqa'i' al-Misriyya*, 135; Radwan, *Tarikh Matba'at Bulaq*, 504.

97. Jan Just Witkam, "Manuscripts and Manuscripts," *Manuscripts of the Middle East* 2 (1987): 111–15; Hussein Omar, "Who Should Save Egypt's Archives?," *Al Jazeera*, 25 January 2012, accessed 27 December 2020, https://www.aljazeera.com/opinions/2012/1/25/who-should-save-egypts-archives; Khaled Fahmy, "Who Is Afraid of the National Archives?" *Ahram Online*, 16 June 2013, accessed 27 December 2020, https://english.ahram.org.eg/NewsC ontentP/4/74092/Opinion/Who-is-afraid-of-the-National-Archives.aspx; Khaled Fahmy, "The Crisis of the Humanities in Egypt," *Comparative Studies of South Asia, Africa and the Middle East* 37, no. 1 (2017): 142–48.

BIBLIOGRAPHY

'Abduh, Ibrahim. *Tarikh al-Waqa'i' al-Misriyya, 1828–1942*. Cairo: al-Matba'a al-Amiriyya, 1942.

Ayalon, Ami. *The Press in the Arab Middle East: A History*. New York: Oxford University Press, 1995.

Di-Capua, Yoav. *Gatekeepers of the Arab Past: Historians and History Writing in Twentieth Century Egypt*. Berkeley: University of California Press, 2009.

Di Tarrazi, Filib. *Tarikh al-Sihafa al-'Arabiyya: Yahtawi 'ala Akhbar Kul Jarida wa-Majalla 'Arabiyya Zaharat fi al-'Alam Sharqan wa-Gharban ma'a Rusum Ashabiha wa-l Muharririn fi-ha wa-Tarajim Mashahirihim*. Beirut: al-Matba'a al-Adabiyya, 1913–33.

Fahmy, Khaled. *All the Pasha's Men: Mehmed 'Ali, His Army and the Making of Modern Egypt*. New York: Cambridge University Press, 1997.

Fahmy, Khaled. *In Quest of Justice: Islamic Law and Forensic Medicine in Modern Egypt*. Oakland: University of California Press, 2018.

Fahmy, Khaled. *Mehmed Ali: From Ottoman Governor to Ruler of Egypt*. Oxford: Oneworld, 2009.

Fahmy, Ziad. *Ordinary Egyptians: Creating the Modern Nation through Popular Culture*. Stanford, CA: Stanford University Press, 2011.

Hunter, F. Robert. *Egypt under the Khedives, 1805–1879: From Household Government to Modern Bureaucracy*. Pittsburgh: University of Pittsburgh Press, 1984.

Mestyan, Adam. *Arab Patriots: The Ideology and Culture of Power in Late Ottoman Egypt*. Princeton, NJ: Princeton University Press, 2017.

Mitchell, Timothy. *Colonising Egypt*. Berkeley: University of California Press, 1991.

Ryzova, Lucie. *The Age of the Efendiyya: Passages to Modernity in National-Colonial Egypt*. New York: Oxford University Press, 2014.

Sadgrove, Philip Charles. "The Development of the Arabic Periodical Press and Its Role in the Literary Life of Egypt (1798–1882)." PhD diss. University of Edinburgh, 1983.

Şiviloğlu, Murat R. *The Emergence of Public Opinion: State and Society in the Late Ottoman Empire*. New York: Cambridge University Press, 2018.

CHAPTER 17

··

RETHINKING LITERACY
DURING THE *NAHDA*

The Many Lives of Texts

··

HODA A. YOUSEF

DOES literacy matter to the history of modern Egypt? The implicit answer in many of our historical narratives is yes. The spread of literacy and education is nearly synonymous with the many changes of the modern period. Historians often cite education and a new literary culture as catalysts for the *nahda*, or the Arabic cultural renaissance, which fostered a revival of Arabic literature and translations and provided a new impetus for political and social engagement. The classic historical telling of the *nahda* goes something like this: over the course of the nineteenth century, a new class of literate and educated Arabs from Greater Syria and Egypt was exposed, through modern schooling, to new ideas from Europe.[1] Once "awakened," these educated elites began a wholesale reappraisal of Arab society and culture. They rediscovered the high traditions of old and melded them with modern notions of nationalism, community, religion, women's rights, and science. While these elite groups represented a minority of the population, a burgeoning ecosystem of books, pamphlets, journals, and newspapers allowed their ideas to circulate and, in turn, transform the landscape of social practices, political movements, and subjectivities locally and, eventually, in the region as a whole. The centrality of the written word to this story is compelling; it appeals to our cultural predispositions, as moderns and academics, to see literacy as inherently transformative for individuals and, by extension, entire communities. It is also unsurprising that the written texts historians often rely on can color so much of what we tend to "see" in the past.

Of course, this story leaves out, among other things, the vast majorities in these societies who were not considered conventionally literate and who did not attend the new and very limited elite educational institutions. Can one speak of a renaissance in the modern era and a wholesale transformation of society if only a tiny fraction of people participated? Historians, aware of this conundrum, have worked to widen our vision of reform and reformers beyond simply the formally educated male elite. As a result, recent scholarship has explored the wider array of social classes and groups who have participated in the changes of this period—some of which were driven by individuals who would not have been considered literate, let alone "modernly" educated.[2] And, in a parallel fashion, nontextual sources have provided new "archives" for researchers to explore the histories of communities and moments that were historically less visible.[3]

Yet there is still much we can learn from our textual history. One productive avenue of research is to apply methodological approaches from the growing field of literacy studies to reassess who used texts and why. Rather than assuming literacy (and the literate) to be a fixed category, we can view literacy as a set of practices—some oral, some written—that can be pursued by anyone, regardless of their personal ability to read or write. Similarly, textual sources can be approached not as fixed texts but rather as one locale of a larger network of textual interactions used by large swathes of Egyptian society. More broadly, we can examine the diverse ways texts were deployed by the literate and illiterate alike to interact with the world around them. By expanding how we view literacy and textual interactions, we can paint a fuller picture of how ordinary people engaged with the intellectual and cultural debates of their time.

Handwritten petitions are one of many types of texts and literacy practices that historians can use to tease out the multiple valences of everyday textual interactions. In the context of the later *nahda* era—a period of reform and intellectual reassessment that spanned the end of the nineteenth and beginning of the twentieth centuries—petitions serve as a useful intermediary between the formal writings expounded upon by educated elites and the everyday concerns and literary practices of most Egyptians. Through a careful examination of these petitions, historians can trace how a confluence of textual exchanges served to move particular ideas through the social milieu of the time and allowed individuals to engage with larger public discourses even if they were not literate. This is the central advantage of expanding our view of literacy and its attendant practices: it allows us to explore how Egyptians of various educational backgrounds used both new and old textual practices to engage with the world around them. We can begin to trace how the written word, in its many forms, contributed to social change well beyond the most educated of society.

RECASTING THE ROLE OF EDUCATION AND LITERACY

Before delving into literacy practices associated with petitions, it is important to recognize the implications of the deep academic interest in education and literacy and how this interest has imposed a particular logic and locale for narratives about historical change in the modern period. Studies of the Middle East, starting in the 1950s, framed mass education systems and literacy as hallmarks of modernization and an essential precursor to entering the civilized world.[4] In these studies, the scope and impact of European influence served as a crucial benchmark for advancement, and the new European-modeled schools and the elites they produced reflected how far a society had progressed. For these early researchers, modern education—however defined—was the formative project of the modern Middle East. It is only recently that scholars have turned a critical eye toward the role of modern education in Middle Eastern societies, rebutting the strict dichotomies of secular versus religious and modern versus traditional schooling and rethinking the impact of education on society, religion, and colonial and postcolonial politics.[5]

Meanwhile, anthropologists, sociologists, and historians studying literacy across the globe have proposed new approaches to literacy studies.[6] Proponents of the ideological or new literacy studies model explicitly reject the idea of a global oral/written divide that separated cultures and their historical development across time.[7] In its place, scholars such as Brian Street, Harvey Graff, and others propose that literacy practices have always been historically bound and "inextricably linked to cultural power structures in society."[8] In this alternative framework, the idea of a universally defined literacy fractures into literacies built around "the idea that reading, writing, and meaning are always situated within specific social practices within specific Discourses."[9] Put differently, various kinds of literacies (in the plural) are studied in their original contexts, without assuming that literacy is a sort of neutral technology that, when applied to various societies, produces fixed and expected results.[10] Literacies are not simply qualifiable skills but rather are embedded sociocultural practices that allow us to contextualize literacy attainment in ways that are attentive to particular historical moments.

A potential strength of the new literacy studies approach is its emphasis on the multivalences and flexibility of literacy practices. Textual practices can be defined broadly to include hearing, seeing, reading, and writing. They can be transmitted in primarily oral or written form and can occur in formal or informal settings, such as schools, coffeehouses, or the theater stage.[11] Likewise, examining various layers of literacies has added nuance to heated debates about the impact of printing and print culture on the modern Middle East.[12] In the process, researchers have become more adept at examining how printing practices overlapped with older scribal and oral traditions and how these new materials were used in practice (and not simply in theory) by individuals and communities.[13] By looking at literacies in historical context, historians can study how broad segments of society engage with one another using texts in their myriad forms. Official institutions and particular technologies matter less than the spaces (and individuals) in between.

Historians have a deep stake in these examinations. With this approach, literacy practices move beyond what literacy should theoretically be or do for a society and on to the more pressing question of how literacies were actually used.[14] Recent studies demonstrate how studying the mechanics of literacy can produce insights that push the envelope of typical "educational history" in and beyond Egypt. Writing about the early modern period, Nelly Hanna and Dana Sajdi provide rich explorations of the literary lives of Egyptian and Syrian Ottomans who were not part of the traditionally literate religious elites.[15] Anthropologists such as Dale Eickelman and Helen Boyle, as well as developmental psychologist Daniel Wagner, explore education and literacy in Morocco, providing a unique perspective on how Qur'anic literacy and religious education continue to influence national educational models.[16] Brinkley Messick examines oral and written transmission, the importance of the scribal tradition, and the inherent differences between "open" legal texts and codified systems of law in modern Yemen.[17] Literacies and their many practices were central to historical shifts that occurred over the course of the nineteenth century and well into the twentieth century, including political and religious movements that saw literacy as a central tenet of reform, the creation and dissemination of what became "modern standard Arabic," and the effects of modernity on the use of Arabic and its role in Arab identity.[18] Similarly, beyond the Arabic-speaking Middle East, additional work has been produced on education, reading publics, the use of print, and associated practices in Qajar/Pahlavi Iran and the late Ottoman Empire.[19]

Meanwhile, historians have begun to unpack the methodologically thorny question of how texts were received and consumed by readers—and the larger circle of nonreaders who were invariably connected to them—in various settings and communities throughout the region.[20] For example, Marwa Elshakry's work extends the notion of readership to include the translations, layered discourses, and interpretations that are invariably part of texts as they moved through intellectual communities throughout the Middle East.[21] The "intellectual ecology" of translations in and out of Arabic is also garnering much-needed attention.[22] By expanding the scope of what literacy is and what it was used for, historians would, as Ziad Fahmy suggests, be "making room for the aural and oral alongside the visual and, in the process, providing a more comprehensive explanation for how individuals and communities process cultural information."[23] It is increasingly possible to trace the ways in which diverse and divergent literacies can be used by a variety of people for very different ends.

However, in the context of a period as transformative as the *nahda*, questions about the mechanics of literacy practices remain. How was the massive output of textual materials produced by elites understood and used by others in society? We have a sense that this literary material was "heard" (quite literally, if a newspaper was read aloud) by a wider community. Yet to what end and to what effect? Were the major intellectual debates that inspired educated elites also of interest to a wider, largely nonliterate, public? If so, how would we know? Did this wider community ever "speak back"?

One approach is to combine what we know about literacies with what Francis Cody calls the "circulatory process" of textual interactions in public spaces.[24] In this light, we can begin to examine how a spectrum of literacy practices allows ideas to enter into diverse public conversations, irrespective of whether the actors involved fulfill certain criteria—for example, a shared sense of literacy, social class, gender, or locale. Tracing the ways texts and ideas move through these shared communal spaces can provide a sort of "social history of ideas," to borrow Robert Darnton's phrase, in the context of modern public life.[25] In this way, we can center textual interactions—that is, moments when texts become a part of the socio-textual practices of individuals of varying literacy abilities within a community. After all, texts that may have originated among the literate elite could have second, third, or fourth lives—each time resurfacing with a new audience or use for literate, semiliterate, or illiterate people. In this framework, the physical texts themselves are not incidental; rather, they become important touchstones for various actors seeking to influence and insert themselves into these discussions— again, irrespective of their actual ability to read and write. Simply put, an individual's use and reuse of a text—either physically or discursively—becomes important because it represents their way of accessing this realm of communal interaction. In turn, these often-marginalized historical actors can be written back into the story of the mass-mediated subjectivity that makes publics so important to the modern world.[26]

THE MANY LIVES OF TEXTS

Egypt during the early part of the twentieth century can serve as an instructive setting in which to trace what we may call the "many lives of texts." By any measure, these decades saw a dramatic increase in the number and circulation of books, dailies, weeklies, and specialized journals of all sorts.[27] And yet textual practices were by no means limited to the relatively small, formally literate public;[28] rather, Egyptians disseminated all sorts of information throughout nonliterate and literate communities. For instance, we know from anecdotal reports that newspapers were often read aloud in public and were subject to communal debates.[29] Additionally, a single copy of a newspaper may have been read, returned, resold, and read again. At the same time, used-book markets and discarded texts were part of a secondhand economy that continues to be used by historians to this day.[30] Journals, once read for their timely information, could be bound and preserved and eventually make their way into library collections.[31] Textual materials could thus serve many audiences well beyond their initial consumer.

In addition to these many printed materials—which were usually created by the already highly educated—historians have sought out sources that emerged from more humble strata of society: personal notes, diaries, transactional documents, handwritten petitions, and the like. Using these less formal texts, we can continue to move beyond classic Habermasian "public spheres" made up of literate individuals to include communities who participated in public discussions even without any formal ability to read.[32]

Petitions are a unique source and nexus of literacies at the turn of the twentieth century.[33] Petitioning has a long and storied history in Egypt and beyond; seeking favor from the powerful is an age-old human practice. In tandem with the growth of the administrative apparatus of the state over the nineteenth century, an enormous number of petitions to Egyptian khedives and various ministries were preserved by the state and are now available in the Egyptian National Archives (Dar al-Watha'iq al-Qawmiyya [DWQ]).[34] Many of these petitions exist only as summaries produced by government officials who received them and noted what action was to be taken, if any.[35] However, the

'Abidin collection in the Egyptian National Archives includes both intake summaries organized by date and well over a thousand folders with original petitions organized by topic.[36] These original petitions mostly span the 1890s through the 1930s, although exceptions exist throughout.

The materiality of these extant petitions from the turn of the century mirrors the changing literacy practices of this era. Many earlier petitions were stamped with the official seal of the petitioner, a practice that seems to have fallen out of favor in the early 1900s. During these same decades, petitioners added telegrams and increasingly elaborate printed petitions to their petitioning repertoire.[37] We can also trace the unevenness of petitioning as a social practice. Nonelite women tended to be active petitioners for charity and on behalf of their families.[38] But they were largely absent from the organized "group" petitions and printed petitions that proliferated in the 1910s and 1920s. We also see the occasional ephemera that accompanied petitions: calligraphy; photographs; book excerpts; clippings from newspapers; and official documentation of other sorts.[39] Petitioners took the technologies available to them (telegraph, printing, photograph) and the textual world around them (books, journals, newspapers, bureaucratic paperwork) and repurposed them for their needs: a request to the powers that be for a desired favor.

In addition to the textual world within which these petitions were created, one other resource was indispensable for their creation: an anonymous scribal intermediary.[40] Very few Egyptians were capable of composing and writing a formal letter during this period, and even if they could, many still deferred to those with more expertise. A scribe (*katib*) could be a professional, one of the many who offered services in public places throughout a community, or a friend or family member who happened to know how to write. In either case, these individuals mediated the circulation of petitioning texts in the space between the aural and the textual. Men, women, students, religious scholars, bureaucrats, and inhabitants of rural and urban centers throughout Egypt did not need to possess a particular level of literacy to participate in textual interactions; rather, they turned to these "readers" and "writers" for assistance.[41] In turn, scribes were an integral part of social life: they served as a communal resource for reading letters, crafting responses, recording court proceedings, drafting official documents, completing government forms, and even relaying propaganda during moments of political upheaval.[42] They also allowed communities to make their voices heard. It is common to find collective, village-wide petitions from rural communities seeking redress or resources from central authorities.[43] Many of these letters included pages with lists of signatures, stamps, or names—adding to the letter's length and (literal and symbolic) heft.

Scribes served as a sort of "technology" that allowed individuals across the literacy spectrum access to the textual world around them.[44] They provided individuals with an intermediate space in which the everyday (the oral, the colloquial, the parochial concerns) and the formal (the written, the *fusha* language, and the administrative) could be negotiated. Petitions are particularly interesting in this regard because, as John Chalcraft suggests, these pleas served as a "site of suture" between the individual and the institutions they were petitioning.[45] This negotiated stance is not only about power dynamics (between the requester and the one able to grant the request) but also about the language and discourses that are framed by the various literacy practices scribes facilitated.

Beyond the physical texts, the content and "recycling" of national discussions are additional ways petitions represented circulating, layered textual interactions. Petitions seeking educational opportunities are instructive in this regard. As one of the main tenets of *nahda* social reforms, lofty rhetoric on the merits of "modern" schooling was often echoed in petitions by parents and students trying to navigate the practicalities of obtaining such an education.[46] This interplay is an important reminder that *nahda* discourses did not exist apart from material consequences and power structures. As Stephen Sheehi notes, we should see "the dynamic semiotic register of *al-nahdah* as a site of production of knowledge and subjectivities but also as a mechanism for the social mediation of tensions, contradictions and residues of the past contained within the discourses of modernity, progress, nationalism and colonialism."[47] In using a *nahda* register, petitioners sought to be a part of these negotiations and, perhaps, tip the scales in their favor.

A survey of educational petitions from the early twentieth century shows sustained interest in the promise of education among parents and students petitioning for access to government schools. Unlike requests made during the early nineteenth century, these petitioners' pleas were often framed in the language of advancement and nationalistic duty.[48] It was common for petitioners to invoke the new interest in education and the term *nahda* itself, which implies reawakening, as a part of their requests. Some referenced the *nahda 'ilmiyya* directly, while others spoke more generally of this "age where the light of knowledge and understanding has been lit."[49] After all, in the words of one father, education served as the "basis for any resurgence (*nuhud*) or improvement."[50] Petitioners were also unabashed in framing education as a right (*haqq*) and necessity (*wajib*) that would propel them, and indeed the whole nation, forward.[51] It is worth noting that while some petitioners were themselves products of modern schooling, many more were not; the latter included widowers who were seeking tuition for a child, laborers hoping for a better future for their children, and students pursuing more prestigious educational paths beyond their local religious (*kuttab*) or elementary (*awwali*) schools.[52] Petition after petition commissioned by people outside of the educated elites of society reflected the same themes *nahda* thinkers were grappling with around issues of reform, education, and national advancement.[53]

In highlighting these specific discourses, their letters tapped into the very trenchant debates of the day—waged on the pages of newspapers, journals, books, and beyond. Were petitioners aware of this? Or did clever scribes include these appeals to make their clients more appealing to the (likely educated) audiences at hand? In the hands of a professional, the overall form of the petitions was often rote, starting with the obligatory praise of the ruler and ending with prayers and well wishes. However, what started as a formal presentation of so-and-so from such-and-such a place could become, in the body of the letter, quite personal and slip into more colloquial expressions.[54] A reader can "hear" the language of the petitioners, even as the scribe added a flourish here and more formal language there. Overall, these personal touches indicate that the intent of these letters—if not every word—likely reflected those of the person paying for the ink, paper, and scribal services, even as the expression of that intent was mediated by a "professional." Furthermore, if petitioners were unaware of the larger national issues when they first resolved to petition their case, they likely became well aware of them from scribes and other petitioners as they went through the process of drafting and sending letters, sometimes several times over the years, in the persistent pursuit of governmental assistance.[55] Assuming that most of these petitioners were not literate, it is worth noting that the simple act of commissioning a letter may itself have been an important means of accessing ideas circulating in the larger intellectual environment of the time.

One striking moment of convergence between *nahda* discourses on education and the literacy practices of petitioners surfaced with the 1914 ascension of Husayn Kamil (r. 1914–17) as the ruler of Egypt. Kamil's connections to the British protectorate were controversial for many reasons, and as such, his ascension became the focus of the national press. Seeking to shield Kamil against criticism, supporters emphasized his advocacy for education—a long-standing nationalist issue—as proof of his fitness to rule the Egyptian people.[56]

This press coverage of the new sultan of Egypt inspired countless responses from Egyptians wishing to capitalize on Kamil's supposed educational fervor. These petitions shed light on how the idea of the beneficent ruler (or at least one who wanted to be seen as such) was filtering through the public discussions of the time. In one case, a sixteen-year-old boy named al-Farid wrote a petition to Kamil in 1915 seeking help to attend one of the rather expensive government schools of the day. According to al-Farid's letter, "we read daily in the newspapers of the desire of Your Greatness to spread knowledge and encourage students and teachers. Your generosity has encouraged me to throw myself between your hands and to explain my state."[57] Several other petitioners mentioned topics that were noted in sympathetic press coverage: the sultan's former role as head of the Islamic Benevolence Society, particular schools he had visited or endowed, and his interest in free public education.[58] For example, one student composed his pleas in poetic verse, asserting his need for free education (*bi-l-majjan*) in order to achieve knowledge and understanding (*al-'ilm wa-l-'irfan*).[59] In another case, a father of four daughters proclaimed his delight upon "hearing"—though the press or discussions in his community, it is unclear—of the sultan's interest in girls' education and wished to enroll his daughters in a new girls' school set to open in Alexandria.[60] Farther from the major urban centers, a group of villagers in Faqus requested a new educational center in order to take advantage of this era of education, learning, and religious knowledge.[61] Although a man named Mansur Zaydan penned the letter, more than seventy additional individuals were listed—some with signatures and others with stamped seals—indicating the letter and its contents were a matter of wide discussion in the town (Fig. 17.1).

These petitions also portrayed the intersection of other types of textual practices Egyptians used to spread news and information of particular concern to them.[62] In one case, Ahmad Rushdi, from the city of Mansoura, sought to make the case for increased financial support for a school he ran.[63] In a fairly staid bureaucratic move, Rushdi included with his petition a copy of the original royal family's endowment for the school and explained that the endowment payments had not been received in nearly a year. However, Rushdi also enclosed an eye-catching flyer the school administration had

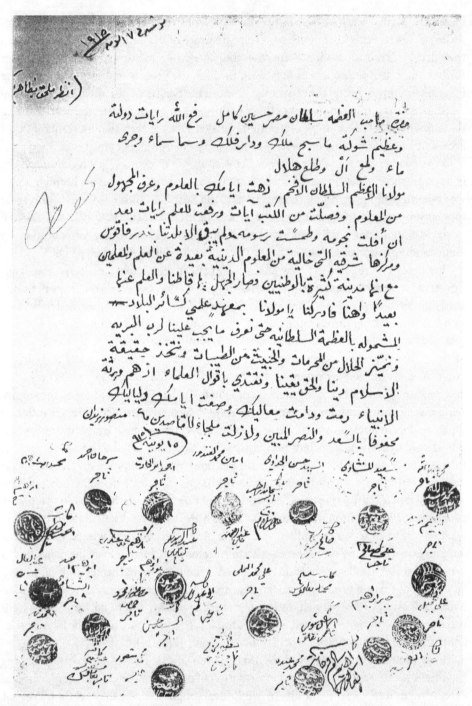

FIG. 17.1 The first page of a group petition from the villagers of Faqus requesting an educational center for their community. In total, the three-page petition included more than seventy signatures and stamps, indicating that the petition had been discussed widely in the community. DWQ, 'Abidin Collection, Box 483, Folder 7, 0069-009412, Mansur Zaydan et al. to Sultan, 15 June 1915.

FIG. 17.2 A printed flyer from a school in Mansoura announcing free tuition in the name of the Sultan. The flyer was included in the petition as evidence that the school was spreading the word about the educational opportunities it provided. DWQ, ʿAbidin Collection, Box 487, Folder 10, 0069-009560, Ahmad Rushdi to Sultan, 18 October 1916.

taken upon itself to print and distribute (Fig. 17.2); it lauded compulsory education and announced that the school would accept all students for free.[64] Rushdi noted how excited the people of his city were about these developments. The school expected a wave of applicants by the January 1917 deadline and was in dire need of past endowment payments and, ideally, increased support.

It is also notable that women, who were less likely than men to have formal literacy training, were active participants in literacy practices that involved the reuse of other texts and documents. In several cases, women appealing for governmental assistance included "supporting documents" to make their cases, indicating they had already submitted or circulated their requests among local authorities before turning to the state.[65] One of

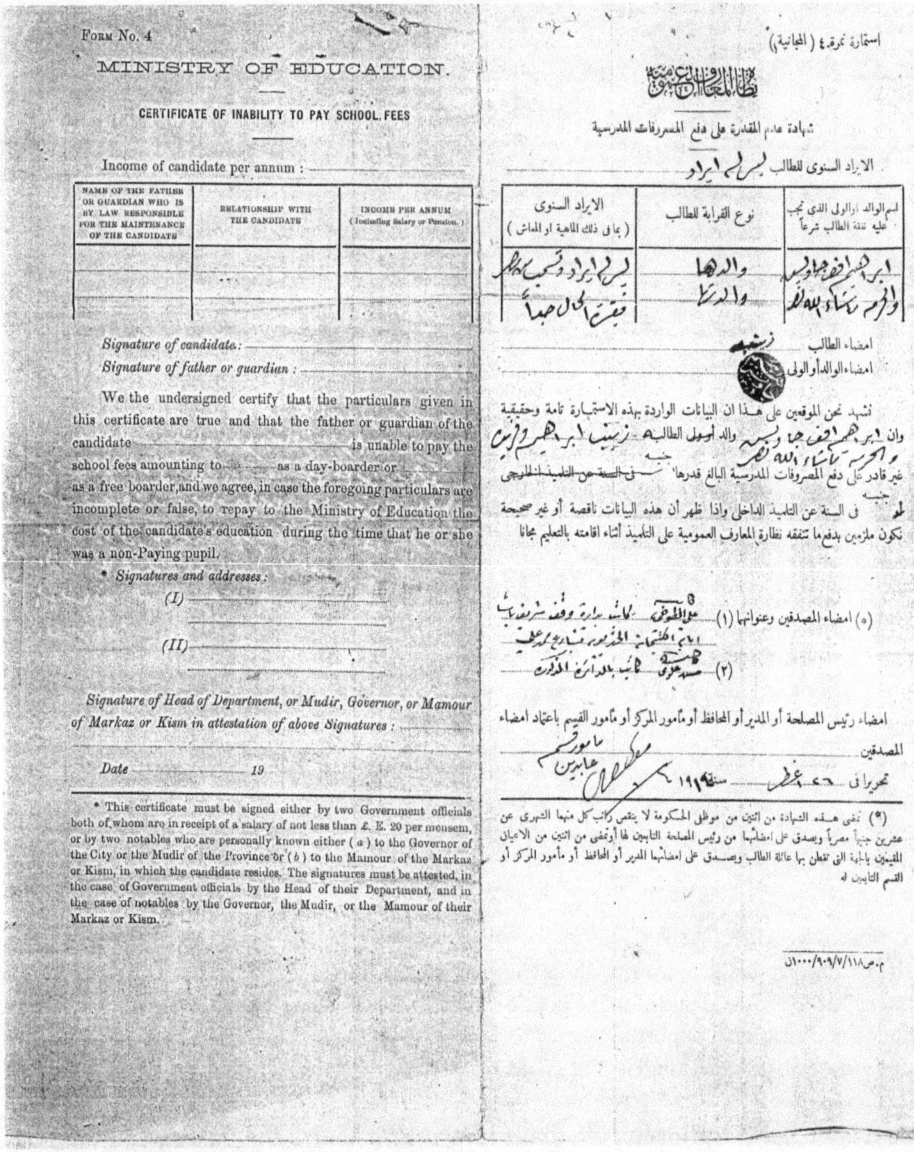

Form No. 4

MINISTRY OF EDUCATION.

CERTIFICATE OF INABILITY TO PAY SCHOOL FEES

Income of candidate per annum : ....

NAME OF THE FATHER OR GUARDIAN WHO IS BY LAW RESPONSIBLE FOR THE MAINTENANCE OF THE CANDIDATE	RELATIONSHIP WITH THE CANDIDATE	INCOME PER ANNUM (Including Salary or Pension.)

Signature of candidate: ....

Signature of father or guardian : ....

We the undersigned certify that the particulars given in this certificate are true and that the father or guardian of the candidate .... is unable to pay the school fees amounting to .... as a day-boarder or .... as a free boarder, and we agree, in case the foregoing particulars are incomplete or false, to repay to the Ministry of Education the cost of the candidate's education during the time that he or she was a non-Paying pupil.

* *Signatures and addresses :*

(I) ....

(II) ....

Signature of Head of Department, or Mudir, Governor, or Mamour of Markaz or Kism in attestation of above Signatures : ....

Date *19*

* This certificate must be signed either by two Government officials both of whom are in receipt of a salary of not less than £. E. 20 per mensem, or by two notables who are personally known either (*a*) to the Governor of the City or the Mudir of the Province or (*b*) to the Mamour of the Markaz or Kism, in which the candidate resides. The signatures must be attested, in the case of Government officials by the Head of their Department, and in the case of notables by the Governor, the Mudir, or the Mamour of their Markaz or Kism.

استمارة نمرة ٤ (المجانية)

نظارة المعارف العمومية

شهادة عدم المقدرة على دفع المصروفات المدرسية

الايراد السنوى للطالب ....

اسم الوالد اوالولى الذى تجب عليه نفقة الطالب شرعاً	نوع القرابة للطالب	الايراد السنوى (بما فى ذلك الماهية او المعاش)
	والدها	
	والدتها	

امضاء الطالب ....

امضاء الوالد أو الولى ....

نشهد نحن الموقعين على هذا ان البيانات الواردة بهذه الاستمارة تامة وحقيقية وان .... والد أو ولى الطالب .... غير قادر على دفع المصروفات المدرسية البالغ قدرها .... فى السنة عن التلميذ الخارجى .... فى السنة عن التلميذ الداخلى واذا ظهر أن هذه البيانات ناقصة أو غير صحيحة نكون ملزمين بدفع ما تنفقه نظارة المعارف العمومية على التلميذ أثناء اقامته بالتعليم مجانا

(*) امضاء المصدقين وعنوانهما (١) ....

(٢) ....

امضاء رئيس المصلحة أو المدير أو المحافظ أو مأمور المركز أو مأمور القسم باعتماد امضاء المصدقين ....

تحريرا فى .... سنة ١٩١

(*) تمضى هذه الشهادة من اثنين من موظفى الحكومة لا ينقص راتب كل منهما الشهرى عن عشرين جنيهاً مصرياً ويصدق على امضائهما من رئيس المصلحة التابعين لها أو تمضى من اثنين من الاعيان المقيمين بالجهة التى تقطن بها عائلة الطالب ويصدق على امضائهما المدير أو المحافظ أو مأمور المركز أو القسم التابعين له

م.ص ١١٨/٧/٩٠٩/١٠٠٠ ن

FIG. 17.3 A formal certificate of inability to pay school fees, which was used as a certificate of poverty (*shahadat faqr*). Like several petitions of this sort, the letter that accompanied this certificate was submitted by the mother of the student. DWQ, 'Abidin Collection, Box 483, Folder 7, 0069-009412, Ma Sha' Allah Nasr to Sultan, April 1915.

the most common of these documents was a certificate of poverty (*shahadat faqr*) that needed to be endorsed by local notables. For example, one such certificate from Asyut was signed by a group of seven religious figures who testified that Latifa bint Husayn was indeed a blind widow with four children and no source of income.[66] In another instructive case, an Egyptian woman named Jalila Jirjis Sa'd petitioned the central government several times between 1908 and 1913.[67] She, too, included a certificate of poverty with her initial request, but she also described accessing various administrative spaces—a local school and the magistrate's office—with her petitions and official documents in hand. Similar to other women claiming poverty, she was adept at using bureaucratic texts to gain access to governmental resources. It appears that women were frequent users of this means of persuading officials to address their concerns, as "early adopters" of the practice. After 1914, when certificates of poverty became required for scholarship enrollment in select government schools, these certificates appeared more regularly among both male and female petitioners (Fig. 17.3).[68]

The actual mechanics of how Egyptians, particularly from nonelite backgrounds, may have accessed communal public texts, such as newspapers or other forms of information, warrants further study. Likewise, it remains unclear how *nahda* discourses may have, in turn, been influenced and changed by these literacy practices. At the least, we can tell that, however information and documents were obtained, many textual sources served as a currency of trade for those who sought to advance their interests. Concerned students, parents, educators, and community members—irrespective of their literacy abilities—seeking to engage with their governments or communities used the textual world around them: individual letters, group petitions, poetry, proclamations, official documents, printed fliers, and the newspapers they either read or heard. As seen in the case of these petitioners, the circulatory process around textual practices mattered to those who may or may not have been able to read or write. Literacies begot literacies.

CONCLUSION

In historical treatments of modern Egypt, education and the educated often serve as the agents of change in the social, political, religious, and economic realms. However, new approaches to the idea of literacy, particularly in a region with historically low official literacy rates, provide a way to rethink the impact of reading and writing for nonelite segments of society. Historians are broadening the analytical lens to include a multitude of literacy practices and to expand our understanding of the influence of reading, writing, and textual materials for wider segments of the population. Rather than focusing on institutional or formal literacy, examining the impact of textual interactions and ideas on literate, semiliterate, and illiterate individuals ultimately provides a more holistic view of the changes associated with this period. In particular, exploring where these practices intersect with public debates and communal networks allows us to trace how texts and ideas moved through populations who were not among the already literate.

One word of caution for this type of research: just because something was published (by the elites who had control of these mediums) and *could* have spread to semiliterate and illiterate segments of Egyptian society through literacy practices does not mean that it *did*. It is not enough, for example, to know that elite men and women began writing about women's rights in the 1890s and that a debate ensued in the national press about the "woman question." Rather, an appreciation of literacy practices should evoke questions such as: How was this debate read, heard, and perhaps reappropriated by those beyond the formally educated? Where were the textual spaces that may (or may not) have allowed these ideas to reemerge and change as they moved through various communities? That is, what other lives did these elite texts have in the social and cultural milieus of ordinary Egyptians? The difficulty in tracing the actual arc of ideas through literacy practices suggests that future research will require a combination of mainstay sources (e.g., newspapers, journals, or literary tracts) with other less formal forms of writings (e.g., petitions, diaries, public speeches, oral or graphic sources, or reports of these practices).

This approach to examining various literacy practices can be helpful as we continue to examine the history of the Middle East during a period when more people became interested in social reforms, economic advancement, and political movements. The applications are myriad. For example, by tracing how ideas and perceptions of nationalism, religious ideologies, and gendered social roles intersected with public life, we can learn how these ideas were circulating in the literacy practices of nonelite communities. The very role of language itself was also a contested site as communities debated in which language, and in what form, their futures would be written, spoken, and read. When coupled with a sensitivity to the roles that women, working classes, and rural communities played in these practices, we gain new insight into how ideas filtered through society and were adapted creatively along the way. In other words, the literacy practices used throughout Egyptian society—and the debates they engendered—can be just as important as the other actors who fill our historical records.

NOTES

1. Albert Hourani, *Arabic Thought in the Liberal Age, 1798–1939* (Cambridge: Cambridge University Press, 1983); George Antonius, *The Arab Awakening: The Story of the Arab National Movement* (Beirut: Khayats, 1963).

2. See, e.g., Joel Beinin and Zachary Lockman, *Workers on the Nile: Nationalism, Communism, Islam, and the Egyptian Working Class, 1882–1954* (Princeton, NJ: Princeton University Press, 1987); Joel Beinin, *Workers and Peasants in the Modern Middle East* (Cambridge: Cambridge University Press, 2001); Nathan J. Brown, *Peasant Politics in Modern Egypt: The Struggle against the State* (New Haven, CT: Yale University Press, 1990); John T. Chalcraft, *The Striking Cabbies of Cairo and Other Stories: Crafts and Guilds in Egypt, 1863–1914* (Albany: State University of New York Press, 2004); Ziad Fahmy,

Ordinary Egyptians: Creating the Modern Nation through Popular Culture (Stanford, CA: Stanford University Press, 2011); and Michael Ezekiel Gasper, *The Power of Representation: Publics, Peasants, and Islam in Egypt* (Stanford, CA: Stanford University Press, 2009). While elite women of this period were often educated in various subjects, their education tended to be more informal and pursued outside of the elite governmental institutions of the day. Beth Baron, *The Women's Awakening in Egypt: Culture, Society, and the Press* (New Haven, CT: Yale University Press, 1994).

3. Ziad Fahmy, "An Earwitness to History: Street Hawkers and Their Calls in Early 20th-Century Egypt," *International Journal of Middle East Studies* 48, no. 1 (2016): 129–34; Andrew Simon, *Media of the Masses: Cassette Culture in Modern Egypt* (Stanford, CA: Stanford University Press, 2022); Stephen Sheehi, *The Arab Imago: A Social History of Portrait Photography, 1860–1910* (Princeton, NJ: Princeton University Press, 2016).

4. Daniel Lerner, *The Passing of Traditional Society: Modernizing the Middle East* (New York: Free Press, 1958); Manfred Halpern, *The Politics of Social Change in the Middle East and North Africa* (Princeton, NJ: Princeton University Press, 1963); James Heyworth-Dunne, *An Introduction to the History of Education in Modern Egypt* (London: Frank Cass, 1968); A. L. Tibawi, *Islamic Education: Its Traditions and Modernization into the Arab National Systems* (London: Luzac, 1972).

5. Benjamin C. Fortna, *Imperial Classroom: Islam, the State, and Education in the Late Ottoman Empire* (Oxford: Oxford University Press, 2002); Robert Hefner and Muhammad Qasim Zaman, eds., *Schooling Islam: The Culture and Politics of Modern Muslim Education* (Princeton, NJ: Princeton University Press, 2007); Sam Kaplan, *The Pedagogical State: Education and the Politics of National Culture in Post-1980 Turkey* (Stanford, CA: Stanford University Press, 2006); Timothy Mitchell, *Colonising Egypt* (Berkeley: University of California Press, 1988); Paul Sedra, *From Mission to Modernity: Evangelicals, Reformers and Education in Nineteenth-Century Egypt* (London: I. B. Tauris, 2011); Selçuk Somel, *The Modernization of Public Education in the Ottoman Empire, 1839–1908: Islamization, Autocracy, and Discipline* (Leiden, Netherlands: Brill, 2001); Gregory Starrett, *Putting Islam to Work: Education, Politics, and Religious Transformation in Egypt* (Berkeley: University of California Press, 1998).

6. For an application of these approaches to the Islamic world, see Nelly Hanna, "Literacy and the 'Great Divide' in the Islamic World, 1300–1800," *Journal of Global History* 2, no. 2 (2007): 175–93.

7. For a good overview of these debates, see Joyce Coleman, *Public Reading and the Reading Public in Late Medieval England and France* (Cambridge: Cambridge University Press, 1996), 1–33. See also Jack Goody, ed., *Literacy in Traditional Societies* (Cambridge: Cambridge University Press, 1968); Jack Goody and Ian Watt, "The Consequences of Literacy," *Comparative Studies in Society and History* 5, no. 3 (1963): 304–45; Marshall McLuhan, *The Gutenberg Galaxy: The Making of Typographic Man* (Toronto: University of Toronto Press, 1962); and Walter Ong, *Orality and Literacy: The Technologizing of the Word* (London: Methuen, 1982).

8. Brian Street, *Cross-Cultural Approaches to Literacy* (Cambridge: Cambridge University Press, 1993), 7. See also James Paul Gee, *Social Linguistics and Literacies: Ideology in Discourses*, 4th ed. (New York: Routledge, 2011); Jack Goody, *The Power of the Written Tradition* (Washington, DC: Smithsonian Institution Press, 2000); Harvey J. Graff, *The Literacy Myth: Literacy and Social Structure in the Nineteenth-Century City* (New York: Academic Press, 1979); and Brian Street, *Social Literacies: Critical Approaches to Literacy in Development, Ethnography and Education* (London: Longman, 1995).

9. James Paul Gee, "The New Literacy Studies: From 'Socially Situated' to the Work of the Social," in *Situated Literacies: Reading and Writing in Context*, ed. David Barton, Mary Hamilton, and Roz Ivanič (London: Routledge, 2000), 189.

10. See, e.g., David Barton and Mary Hamilton, *Local Literacies: Reading and Writing in One Community* (London: Routledge, 1998); James Collins and Richard Blot, *Literacy and Literacies: Texts, Power, and Identity* (New York: Cambridge University Press, 2003); and David Vincent, *The Rise of Mass Literacy: Reading and Writing in Modern Europe* (Cambridge: Polity, 2000).

11. For examples of non-institutional settings, see Ilham Khuri-Makdisi, *The Eastern Mediterranean and the Making of Global Radicalism, 1860–1914* (Berkeley: University of California Press, 2010); and Carmen M. K. Gitre, *Acting Egyptian: Theater, Identity, and Political Culture in Cairo, 1869–1930* (Austin: University of Texas Press, 2019).

12. For an overview of the debate, see Kathryn A. Schwartz, "Book History, Print, and the Middle East," *History Compass* 15 (2017): 3–5.

13. See, e.g., Dana Sajdi, "Print and Its Discontents: A Case for Pre-print Journalism and Other Sundry Print Matters," *The Translator* 15, no. 1 (2009): 105–38. Dyala Hamzah has also commented on the fluidity of print and scribal practices, "Introduction," in *The Making of the Arab Intellectual: Empire, Public Sphere and the Colonial Coordinates of Selfhood*, ed. Dyala Hamzah (New York: Routledge, 2013), 1.

14. As Harvey Graff notes, "literacy is a historical variable, and it is historically variable." Harvey J. Graff, "The Shock of the 'New' (Histories): Social Science Histories and Historical Literacies," *Social Science History* 25, no. 4 (2001): 510. This acknowledgment of the variability of literacies is perhaps even more crucial in areas with lower rates of official literacy through much of the modern period. Historians of African societies have also grappled with studying communities with low official literacy. See Derek R. Peterson, Emma Hunter, and Stephanie Newell, eds., *African Print Cultures: Newspapers and Their Publics in the Twentieth Century* (Ann Arbor: University of Michigan Press, 2016); and Karin Barber, ed., *Africa's Hidden Histories: Everyday Literacy and Making the Self* (Bloomington: Indiana University Press, 2006).

15. Nelly Hanna, *In Praise of Books: A Cultural History of Cairo's Middle Class, Sixteenth to the Eighteenth Century* (Syracuse, NY: Syracuse University Press, 2003); Dana Sajdi, *The Barber of Damascus: Nouveau Literacy in the Eighteenth-Century Ottoman Levant* (Stanford, CA: Stanford University Press, 2013). Nelly Hanna also makes an explicit application of this new literacy studies model in her article "Literacy and the 'Great Divide.'" For studies that explore earlier periods, see Michael Chamberlain, *Knowledge and Social Practice in Medieval Damascus, 1190–1350* (Cambridge: Cambridge University Press, 1994); Timothy J. Fitzgerald, "Reaching the Flocks: Literacy and the Mass Reception of Ottoman Law in the Sixteenth-Century Arab World," *Journal of the Ottoman and Turkish Studies Association* 2, no. 1 (2015): 5–20; Konrad Hirschler, *The Written Word in the Medieval Arabic Lands: A Social and Cultural History of Reading Practices* (Edinburgh, UK: Edinburgh University Press, 2012); Gregor Schoeler, *The Genesis of Literature in Islam: From the Aural to the Read*, trans. Shawkat M. Toorawa, rev. ed (Edinburgh, UK: Edinburgh University Press, 2009); and Muhsin J. al-Musawi, *The Medieval Islamic Republic of Letters: Arabic Knowledge Construction* (Notre Dame, IN: University of Notre Dame Press, 2015).

16. Dale F. Eickelman, *Knowledge and Power in Morocco: The Education of a Twentieth-Century Notable* (Princeton, NJ: Princeton University Press, 1985); Helen N. Boyle,

Quranic Schooling (London: Routledge, 2004); Boyle, "Memorization and Learning in Islamic Schools," *Comparative Education Review* 50, no. 3 (2006): 478–95; Daniel Wagner, *Literacy, Culture, and Development: Becoming Literate in Morocco* (Cambridge: Cambridge University Press, 1993).

17. Brinkley Messick, *The Calligraphic State: Textual Domination and History in a Muslim Society* (Berkeley: University of California Press, 1993).

18. Nermeen Mouftah, "Building Life: Faith, Literacy Development and Muslim Citizenship in Revolutionary Egypt" (PhD diss., Toronto, University of Toronto, 2014); Samah Selim, *Popular Fiction, Translation and the Nahda in Egypt* (New York: Palgrave Macmillan, 2019); Stephen Sheehi, *Foundations of Modern Arab Identity* (Gainesville: University Press of Florida, 2004); Yasir Suleiman, *The Arabic Language and National Identity: A Study in Ideology* (Washington, DC: Georgetown University Press, 2003); Hoda A. Yousef, *Composing Egypt: Reading, Writing, and the Emergence of a Modern Nation, 1870–1930* (Stanford, CA: Stanford University Press, 2016).

19. Fortna, *Imperial Classroom*; Fortna, *Learning to Read in the Late Ottoman Empire and the Early Turkish Republic* (New York: Palgrave Macmillan, 2011); François Georgeon, "Lire et écrire à la fin de l'Empire ottoman: quelques remarques introductives," *Revue du monde musulman et de la Méditerranée* 75–76, no. 1 (1995): 169–79; Afshin Marashi, "Print Culture and Its Publics: A Social History of Bookstores in Tehran, 1900–1950," *International Journal of Middle East Studies* 47, no. 1 (2015): 89–108; Negin Nabavi, "Readership, the Press and the Public Sphere in the First Constitutional Era," in *Iran's Constitutional Revolution: Popular Politics, Cultural Transformations and Transnational Connections*, ed. H. E Chehabi and Vanessa Martin (London: I. B. Tauris, 2010); Johann Strauss, "Who Read What in the Ottoman Empire (19th–20th Centuries)?," *Middle Eastern Literatures* 6, no. 1 (2003): 39–76; Farzin Vejdani, *Making History in Iran: Education, Nationalism, and Print Culture* (Stanford, CA: Stanford University Press, 2015).

20. Ami Ayalon, *Reading Palestine: Printing and Literacy, 1900–1948* (Austin: University of Texas Press, 2004); Ayalon, *The Arabic Print Revolution: Cultural Production and Mass Readership* (Cambridge: Cambridge University Press, 2016), chapters 5 and 6; Beth Baron, "Readers and the Women's Press in Egypt," *Poetics Today* 15, no. 2 (1994): 217–40; Fruma Zachs and Sharon Halevi, "From Difaʻ al-Nisaʼ to Masʼalat al-Nisaʼ in Greater Syria: Readers and Writers Debate Women and Their Rights, 1858–1900," *International Journal of Middle East Studies* 41, no. 4 (2009): 615–33.

21. Marwa Elshakry, *Reading Darwin in Arabic, 1860–1950* (Chicago: University of Chicago Press, 2013).

22. I am borrowing this phrase from Ilham Khuri-Makdisi's delivered remarks at the Middle East Studies Association meeting: "The Nahda, Translation Movements between Ottoman Turkish and Arabic, and Bilingualism 1860–1914" (16 November 2019). For other work on translation, see Marilyn Booth, ed., *Migrating Texts: Circulating Translations around the Eastern Mediterranean* (Edinburgh, UK: Edinburgh University Press, 2019); Marilyn Booth and Claire Savina, eds., *Ottoman Translation: Circulating Texts from Bombay to Paris* (Edinburgh, UK: Edinburgh University Press, 2022); Marwa Elsharky, "Knowledge in Motion: The Cultural Politics of Modern Science Translations in Arabic," *Isis* 99, no. 4 (2008): 701–30; Shaden M. Tageldin, *Disarming Words: Empire and the Seductions of Translation in Egypt* (Berkeley: University of California Press, 2011); and Selim, *Popular Fiction*.

23. Fahmy, *Ordinary Egyptians*, 15.

24. Francis Cody, "Publics and Politics," *Annual Review of Anthropology* 40, no. 1 (2011): 37–52.

25. Robert Darnton, "In Search of the Enlightenment: Recent Attempts to Create a Social History of Ideas," *The Journal of Modern History* 43, no. 1 (1971): 113. See also Darrin M. McMahon, "The Return of the History of Ideas?," in *Rethinking Modern European Intellectual History*, ed. Darrin M. McMahon and Samuel Moyn (Oxford: Oxford University Press, 2014).

26. Benedict Anderson, *Imagined Communities: Reflections on the Origin and Spread of Nationalism*, rev. ed. (London: Verso, 1991).

27. Ami Ayalon, *The Press in the Arab Middle East: A History* (New York: Oxford University Press, 1995), 198; 'Aida Nusayr, *al-Kutub al-'Arabiyya Allati Nushirat fi Misr Bayna 'Amay 1900–1925* (Cairo: Qism al-Nashr bi-l-Jami'a al-Amrikiyya bi-l-Qahira, 1983).

28. It is difficult to get an accurate picture of how many people were formally literate due to inconsistencies in how census officials measured literacy. But as an indication of the change over time, official literacy rates provide one snapshot. The census reported that only 7.3% of Egyptians over the age of ten were literate in 1907. The official number rose to 8.8% a decade later and by 1927 reached 14.1% of the population. The official literacy rate for women over ten years old was 1.4% in 1907 and only reached 4.4% by 1927. UNESCO, "Progress of Literacy in Various Countries: A Preliminary Statistical Study of Available Census Data since 1900" (Paris: United Nations Educational, Scientific and Cultural Organization, 1953), 83–86.

29. Ayalon, *The Press in the Arab Middle East*, 156–59; Juan R. I. Cole, *Colonialism and Revolution in the Middle East: Social and Cultural Origins of Egypt's 'Urabi Movement* (Cairo: American University in Cairo Press, 1999), 115, 131; Fahmy, *Ordinary Egyptians*, 33–34, 153–58.

30. Lucie Ryzova, *The Age of the Efendiyya: Passages to Modernity in National-Colonial Egypt* (Oxford: Oxford University Press, 2014), 29–31.

31. Baron, "Readers and the Women's Press in Egypt," 226.

32. Nancy Fraser, *Unruly Practices: Power, Discourse, and Gender in Contemporary Social Theory* (Minneapolis: University of Minnesota Press, 1989); Fraser, "Rethinking the Public Sphere: A Contribution to the Critique of Actually Existing Democracy," *Social Text* 25/26 (1990): 56–80; Michael Warner, *Publics and Counterpublics* (New York: Zone Books, 2002).

33. Studies that have used petitions from this period of Egyptian history include Chalcraft, *Striking Cabbies*; Chalcraft, "Engaging the State: Peasants and Petitions in Egypt on the Eve of Colonial Rule," *International Journal of Middle East Studies* 37, no. 3 (2005): 303–25; Chalcraft, "Counterhegemonic Effects: Weighing, Measuring, Petitions and Bureaucracy in Nineteenth-Century Egypt," in *Counterhegemony in the Colony and Postcolony*, ed. John T. Chalcraft and Yaseen Noorani (Basingstoke: Palgrave Macmillan, 2007), 179–203; Mine Ener, *Managing Egypt's Poor and the Politics of Benevolence, 1800–1952* (Princeton, NJ: Princeton University Press, 2003); Emad Ahmad Helal, "al-'Arduhal Sawt al-Fellah al-Muhtaj," in *al-Rafd wa-l-Ihtijaj fi al-Mujtama' al-Misri fi al-'Asr al-'Uthmani*, ed. Nasir Ibrahim (Cairo: al-Jam'iyya al-Misriyya li-l-Dirasat al-Tarikhiyya, 2004); Helal, "Al-'Arduhal: Masdar Majhul li-Dirasat Tarikh Misr fi al-Qarn al-Tasi' 'Ashar," *Al-Ruzname* 2 (2004): 303–37; and Hoda A. Yousef, "Losing the Future? Constructing Educational Need in Egypt, 1820s to 1920s," *History of Education* 46, no. 5 (2017): 561–77.

34. Emad Helal, who has written about these petitions and first introduced me to them, estimates that more than a million petitions are in the archives. Helal, "Al-'Arduhal: Masdar Majhul," 307–9.

35. For example, petition summaries from 1820 to 1823 have been published in Muhammad Sabir 'Arab, Ahmad Zakariyya al-Shalaq, and Nasir 'Abd Allah 'Uthman, eds., *al-Sulta wa-'Arduhalat al-Mazlumin: Min 'Asr Muhammad 'Ali, 1820–1823* (Cairo: Matba'at Dar al-Kutub wa-l-Watha'iq al-Qawmiyya, 2009).

36. In the old, non-electronic system, a large group of original petitions from roughly the 1890s to the 1930s was organized by topic in boxes in the 'Abidin collection. Most boxes were listed with the title "Iltimasat" and then a thematic topic (e.g., charity, hajj, Azhar, education). However, the new electronic system instituted in the last decade uses call numbers for individual folders. The longest "run" of folders containing original petitions that I came across was 0069-007455 to 0069-009979, representing a little over 1,000 folders, with each folder containing anywhere from one to fifty petitions. Olga Verlato kindly conducted electronic searches of the terms *iltimasat* and *'arduhallat* and found another 800 folders scattered throughout the collection, which suggests that there are many more documents related to these petitions in the 'Abidin collection. Beyond the 'Abidin collection, it is possible to find original petitions stored with the ministry that oversaw the resolution.

37. For more on the use and evolution of petitions (printed and otherwise) as part of broader public appeals, see Yousef, *Composing Egypt*, chapter 4.

38. See, e.g., Yuval Ben-Bassat, *Petitioning the Sultan: Protests and Justice in Late Ottoman Palestine* (London: I. B. Tauris, 2013), 52; Ener, *Managing Egypt's Poor*, 67–69; and Hoda A. Yousef, "Pleading for a Place in Modern Egypt: Negotiating Poverty and Patriarchy, 1908–1913," *British Journal of Middle Eastern Studies* 47, no. 2 (2020): 302–19.

39. DWQ, 'Abidin Collection, Box 655, Folder 13, 0069-014326, Fransis Mikha'il to Sultan, January 1915; DWQ, 'Abidin Collection, Box 476, Folder 3, 0069-009149, Talaba Jami' al-Azhar to Khedive, 4 November 1908.

40. Unfortunately, there is no definitive way to identify which petitions were written by scribes and which were not. However, we do know that scribes were a regular part of administrative life (indeed, to this day many government offices have "writers" outside ready to assist individuals filling out forms, etc.). The fact that most petitions followed the templates outlined in scribal manuals, started with a third-person introduction to the petitioner, and were written in a hurried and fluid script suggests that many were indeed products of a professional writer. Only occasionally did petitioners mention explicitly that they wrote the letter by their own hand.

41. For a thorough examination of petitioning practices during this era, see Ben-Bassat, *Petitioning the Sultan*.

42. For example, at one point during the 1919 Egyptian uprising against the British, colonial intelligence officers were concerned about how their propaganda would be read by rural, mostly illiterate communities and the possibility that the "official" message might be subverted by unscrupulous locals. However, British officers soon found that "in every little village there is a scribe . . . who will certainly be made to give an accurate reading" and concluded that leaflets sent out to rural communities were highly effective for this reason. The National Archives, London, Kew (TNA), Foreign Office (FO) 141/781/8915, "Verbal Propaganda," Major S. Delmé-Radcliffe, 28 April 1919. Also cited in Yousef, *Composing Egypt*, 125–26.

43. The 'Abidin collection in the DWQ includes several boxes of group petitions from rural communities, government employees, students, Azharis, etc., e.g., Boxes 407–408 (0069-007859 to 0069-007873) and 482 (0069-009364 to 0069-009379). In addition, group

petitions can be found intermixed within other petitions in thematic folders. In a different context, Doumani has explored the petitions of Palestinian peasants: Beshara Doumani, *Rediscovering Palestine: Merchants and Peasants in Jabal Nablus, 1700–1900* (Berkeley: University of California Press, 1995), chapter 4.

44. Yousef, *Composing Egypt*, 104–8.

45. Chalcraft, "Counterhegemonic Effects," 200.

46. Many excellent monographs explore the role of schooling during this period: Mitchell, *Colonising Egypt*; Lisa Pollard, *Nurturing the Nation: The Family Politics of Modernizing, Colonizing and Liberating Egypt* (Berkeley: University of California Press, 2005); Mona L. Russell, *Creating the New Egyptian Woman: Consumerism, Education, and National Identity, 1863–1922* (New York: Palgrave Macmillan, 2004); and Sedra, *From Mission to Modernity*.

47. Stephen Sheehi, "Towards a Critical Theory of Al-Nahdah: Epistemology, Ideology and Capital," *Journal of Arabic Literature* 43, nos. 2/3 (2012): 294.

48. Yousef, "Losing the Future?"

49. DWQ, 'Abidin Collection, Box 487, Folder 18, 0069-009568, Muhammad Ahmad al-Shayyal, 1 August 1922; DWQ, 'Abidin Collection, Box 483, Folder 2, 0069-009408, Mustafa 'Id to Khedive, May 1906; DWQ, 'Abidin Collection, Box 487, Folder 19, 0069-009569, Muhammad Husayn Kashif to King, 15 August 1923.

50. DWQ, 'Abidin Collection, Box 476, Folder 9, 0069-009155, 'Abd Allah al-Mughira to Sultan, 22 May 1915.

51. For example, DWQ, 'Abidin Collection, Box 487, Folder 11, 0069-009561, Abu al-'Ati to Sultan, 19 May 1917; DWQ, 'Abidin Collection, Box 482, Folder 6, 0069-009369, Muhammad Hanafi to Sultan, 27 January 1915; and DWQ, 'Abidin Collection, Box 490, Folder 7, 0069-009600, Mahmud Mustafa al-Maghribi, 1 April 1917.

52. For particularly vivid examples of a widower, a laborer, and a *kuttab* student, see DWQ, 'Abidin Collection, Box 487, Folder 18, 0069-009568, Zanuba bint Ghanim to King, 8 August 1922; DWQ, 'Abidin Collection, Box 487, Folder 9, 0069-009559, al-Farid to Sultan, 23 April 1915; and DWQ, 'Abidin Collection, Box 487, Folder 10, 0069-009560, al-Sayyid 'Abd al-Khaliq Ahmad to Sultan, 28 June 1916.

53. Yousef, "Losing the Future?," 569–76.

54. For example, using colloquial pleas such as *abus al-jazma bita'tak* (I will kiss your shoes) or *i'mal ma'ruf* (do me a favor/kindness), DWQ, 'Abidin Collection, Box 487, Folder 5, 0069-009555, Jalila Jirjis to Khedive, 29 March 1911.

55. In examples too numerous to cite here, petitioners mentioned their repeated attempts to garner attention by sending letters to various authorities. Indeed, several distinct attempts are sometimes preserved in the same folder or box in the DWQ.

56. Arthur Goldschmidt, *Biographical Dictionary of Modern Egypt* (Boulder, CO: Lynne Rienner Publishers, 2000), 83.

57. DWQ, 'Abidin Collection, Box 487, Folder 9, 0069-009559, al-Farid to Sultan, 23 April 1915. In another example, a student mentioned that he read about tuition increases in the newspaper, DWQ, 'Abidin Collection, Box 483, Folder 9, 0069-009415, Muhammad Mustafa al-Hawari to Sultan, 12 August 1916.

58. DWQ, 'Abidin Collection, Box 490, Folder 6, 0069-009599, 'Ali Muhammad Yusuf to Sultan, 24 September 1916; DWQ, 'Abidin Collection, Box 483, Folder 7, 0069-009412, 'Abd al-Fattah al-Sayyid to Sultan, 9 March 1915; DWQ, 'Abidin Collection, Box 483, Folder 7, 0069-009412, 'Abd al-Hakim Kamal to Sultan, 16 August 1914; DWQ, 'Abidin Collection,

Box 483, Folder 7, 0069-009412, Ahmad Badawi to Sultan, 10 March 1915; DWQ, 'Abidin Collection, Box 487, Folder 10, 0069-009560, Ibrahim Muhammad al-Hadidi to Sultan, 29 August 1916; and DWQ, Abidin Collection, Box 487, Folder 9, 0069-009559, 'Isa 'Abduh Barakat to Sultan, 6 August 1915,

59. DWQ, 'Abidin Collection, Box 490, Folder 7, 0069-009600, Sulayman Ahmad Abu Zayd to Sultan, 4 June 1917.

60. DWQ, 'Abidin Collection, Box 483, Folder 7, 0069-009412, Ahmad Badawi to Sultan, 10 March 1915. In another instance, a petitioner mentioned that from "time to time we hear and see of your pure help in raising the nation," DWQ, 'Abidin Collection, Box 487, Folder 10, 0069-009560, Mustafa Mushrif to Sultan, 18 July 1916. For the prevalence of reading newspapers aloud, see Ayalon, *The Press in the Arab Middle East*, 156–59; Cole, *Colonialism and Revolution in the Middle East*, 115, 131; and Fahmy, *Ordinary Egyptians*, 33–34, 153–58.

61. DWQ, 'Abidin Collection, Box 483, Folder 7, 0069-009412, Mansur Zaydan et al. to Sultan, 15 June 1915.

62. This aspect of using textual materials by nonliterate segments of Egyptian society was also on dramatic display during the 1919 revolution. See Fahmy, *Ordinary Egyptians*.

63. DWQ, 'Abidin Collection, Box 487, Folder 10, 0069-009560, Ahmad Rushdi to Sultan, 18 October 1916.

64. It seems that it was quite common for schools to advertise in various ways. Several of these pamphlets have made their way into the DWQ. For example, DWQ, 'Abidin Collection, Box 230, Folder 2, 0069-004462, *al-Kuliyya al-Ahliyya bi-Misr*.

65. See, e.g., DWQ, 'Abidin Collection, Box 377, Folder 7, 0069-007462, Wasf Nur to Khedive, January 1906; and DWQ, 'Abidin Collection, Box 487, Folder 3, 0069-009553, Jalila Jirjis Sa'd to Khedive, 23 January 1909.

66. DWQ, 'Abidin Collection, Box 377, Folder 7, 0069-009557, Latifa bint Husayn to Khedive, 2 January 1906.

67. DWQ, 'Abidin Collection, Box 487, Folder 3, 0069-009553, Jalila Jirjis Sa'd to Khedive, 23 January 1909; DWQ, 'Abidin Collection, Box 487, Folder 5, 0069-009555, Jalila Jirjis to Khedive, 29 March 1911; DWQ, 'Abidin Collection, Box 487, Folder 7, 0069-009557, Jalila Jirjis Sa'd to Khedive, 23 September 1913. For more details about her and her petitioning efforts, see Yousef, "Pleading for a Place in Modern Egypt."

68. For an example of the requirements for one primary school for boys, see DWQ, Majlis al-Wuzara', Nizarat al-Ma'arif, Box 23b, Folder 1, 075-045571, "Mudhakkira," 21 June 1914.

Bibliography

Ayalon, Ami. *The Arabic Print Revolution: Cultural Production and Mass Readership*. Cambridge: Cambridge University Press, 2016.

Barton, David, Mary Hamilton, and Roz Ivanič, eds. *Situated Literacies: Reading and Writing in Context*. London: Routledge, 2000.

Ben-Bassat, Yuval. *Petitioning the Sultan: Protests and Justice in Late Ottoman Palestine*. London: I. B. Tauris, 2013.

Chalcraft, John T. "Counterhegemonic Effects: Weighing, Measuring, Petitions and Bureaucracy in Nineteenth-Century Egypt." In *Counterhegemony in the Colony and Postcolony*, edited by John T. Chalcraft and Yaseen Noorani, 179–203. Basingstoke, UK: Palgrave Macmillan, 2007.

Chalcraft, John T. *The Striking Cabbies of Cairo and Other Stories: Crafts and Guilds in Egypt, 1863–1914*. Albany: State University of New York Press, 2004.

Cody, Francis. "Publics and Politics." *Annual Review of Anthropology* 40, no. 1 (2011): 37–52.

Collins, James, and Richard Blot. *Literacy and Literacies: Texts, Power, and Identity*. New York: Cambridge University Press, 2003.

Fahmy, Ziad. *Ordinary Egyptians: Creating the Modern Nation through Popular Culture*. Stanford, CA: Stanford University Press, 2011.

Goody, Jack. *The Power of the Written Tradition*. Washington, DC: Smithsonian Institution Press, 2000.

Graff, Harvey J. *The Literacy Myth: Literacy and Social Structure in the Nineteenth-Century City*. New York: Academic Press, 1979.

Graff, Harvey J. "The Shock of the 'New' (Histories): Social Science Histories and Historical Literacies." *Social Science History* 25, no. 4 (2001): 483–533.

Hanna, Nelly. "Literacy and the 'Great Divide' in the Islamic World, 1300–1800." *Journal of Global History* 2, no. 2 (2007): 175–93.

Helal, Emad Ahmad. "Al-'Arduhal: Masdar Majhul li-Dirasat Tarikh Misr fi al-Qarn al-Tasi' 'Ashar." *Al-Ruzname* 2 (2004): 303–37.

Pollard, Lisa. *Nurturing the Nation: The Family Politics of Modernizing, Colonizing and Liberating Egypt*. Berkeley: University of California Press, 2005.

Sajdi, Dana. "Print and Its Discontents: A Case for Pre-Print Journalism and Other Sundry Print Matters." *The Translator* 15, no. 1 (2009): 105–38.

Sedra, Paul. *From Mission to Modernity: Evangelicals, Reformers and Education in Nineteenth-Century Egypt*. London: I. B. Tauris, 2011.

Selim, Samah. *The Novel and the Rural Imaginary in Egypt, 1880–1985*. London: Routledge Curzon, 2004.

Street, Brian. *Cross-Cultural Approaches to Literacy*. Cambridge: Cambridge University Press, 1993.

Suleiman, Yasir. *The Arabic Language and National Identity: A Study in Ideology*. Washington, DC: Georgetown University Press, 2003.

Vincent, David. *The Rise of Mass Literacy: Reading and Writing in Modern Europe*. Cambridge: Polity, 2000.

Yousef, Hoda A. *Composing Egypt: Reading, Writing, and the Emergence of a Modern Nation, 1870–1930*. Stanford, CA: Stanford University Press, 2016.

CHAPTER 18

···

PHOTOGRAPHY, SELFHOOD, AND CULTURAL MODERNITY

···

LUCIE RYZOVA

SOMETIME in the mid-1890s, a young Alexandrian woman received a visit from the female relatives of a prospective groom. The women praised his qualities—all the while checking her appearance and demeanor—and handed her a tintype portrait of the young man. They apologized for the relatively meager dowry that he would be able to pay as a recent law school graduate whose career still lay ahead of him. The young lady was a descendant of a long lineage of prosperous Alexandrian seamen (*boghazi*) and had previously received marriage proposals from men of her own milieu. But this tintype photograph caught her attention. The young stranger, clad in formal attire (he wore a modern suit with a sash of office), was dressed unlike any other suitor she had encountered, and she understood the significance of his dress. He was a public prosecutor, and the sash signified authority and the promise of a distinguished public career. She had seen similarly clad men from her window on the city's main artery as they walked in and out of the viceregal palace. Though her family initially objected, her strong will eventually prevailed, and she went on to marry the gentleman in the photograph.[1]

This particular "photograph story" was told in Tawfiq al-Hakim's autobiography, *Sijn al-'Umr* (The Prison of Life), and described the marriage of his parents, but, crucially, it was just as likely to be extracted from any number of autobiographical narratives of his generation. Photography and the social practices surrounding its production, circulation, and consumption were primordial to the emergence in late nineteenth-century Egypt of a self that, as Timothy Mitchell put it, "comes to be understood as something fashioned by staging one's life as a story, in a continuous representation of oneself to oneself and to others."[2] Wherever photographic practices were to be found, photograph stories proliferated in line—both, as we shall see, were central to the Egyptian experience of modernity and should be at the heart of any critical historical retelling of it.

Photographs are ubiquitous. For well over one hundred years, analog photographs saturated the lives of most Egyptians: beginning from the late nineteenth century, when studio portraiture spread among the local middle strata, to about the end of the twentieth century, when their replacement by their even more ubiquitous digital avatars began. They take countless material forms: snaps of friends and family; framed portraits of deceased patriarchs or images of weddings or graduations adorning the walls of a living room; passport-size portraits of one's children or sweetheart carried around in a wallet; mug shot portraits on identity cards, school applications, or, indeed, police records; and countless instances of photographic remediations in public culture from newspapers, magazines, book covers, and foldout posters to advertising posters on lampposts and metro carriages—photographs are often simply too numerous to even grab our attention. They are the "visual dust" of the everyday.[3] Even if we limit ourselves to discussing personal photographs—thus leaving their institutional and scientific usages aside[4]—their sheer ubiquity represents a vast archive that increasingly demands our attention as historians.

Just as photographs confuse by their ubiquity, they seduce by their apparent transparency. As mechanical imprints of the "real," they give the impression of direct access to the past, to "historical truth"—or at least some parts of it. Their peculiar claim to realism rests on their status as mechanical traces of things or events that unquestionably "happened" because something or somebody certainly once stood in front of the camera.[5] At stake is their ontological status: What are they, really? Are they truthful representations of reality, reflecting how things or people in the past really looked? Or are they, rather, carefully (or even cunningly) composed performances with a hidden agenda? Are they media, artifacts of popular culture, or commodities? They are all these things, of course. Yet surely historians can do better than the largely illustrative purposes to which photographs have traditionally been put: as mere illustrations of events or people, or supporting arguments reached by other, textual means.[6] We would not be grossly mistaken if we started by approaching them as we do texts: hardly any of us would take any kind of text for a transparent truth. As Jennifer Tucker has remarked, photographs are neither more nor less transparent than other documentary sources, and the questions they pose reveal the potential and limits of all historical sources.[7] At the same time, there is no single recipe for how to read texts: our reading will naturally depend on the genre, purpose, and social context of any given text. Like texts, photographs communicate something. But what exactly do they say, how, and to whom? What are we *really* seeing when we look at any given photograph?

The analogy with texts is primarily intended to make photographs more user-friendly as historical sources but should not be limited to questions of syntax and language (in this case, a visual language). Photographs work like texts not only on the syntactic level, but also through their material being in the world, as socially embedded objects spread across multiple contexts and media.[8] Like texts, photographs are composed of utterances, particular forms of presentation of the self, but they also carry historically situated social expectations and enjoy specific properties and affordances as media. As with texts, therefore, our work should not end with the question of what a given text (or image) says. Rather, the question should be how they matter and how publics, power, selves, and relationships are constituted through the circulation of particular images—because the excitement and challenge inherent in working with photographs is that it is never just about the photographs alone. The most crucial historical questions that need answering are less about what is encoded in any single image and more about what kind of work—social, cultural, political—the photographs perform, and for whom. How exactly did they matter in their manifold incarnations as media, commodities, forms of inscription, or historically specific performances of selfhood? Rather than being stuck in any single image, we may venture outside of its frame and ask: What did going to the photographer mean? Why did vast numbers of Egyptians fancy, obsessively, snapping themselves posing in various settings? What kind of cultural work did photographs play as material objects that were displayed, exchanged, or, conversely, hidden from sight? How can we use photographs both critically and imaginatively?

These ways of mattering can be explored through what we may call "the local archive," meaning the corpus of photographs created, consumed, and circulated locally in Egypt from the late nineteenth century through the first half of the twentieth century. This is in contrast to the colonial archive, which has received disproportionate attention by earlier generations of scholars.[9] Well known for its overwhelmingly orientalist aesthetics, the colonial archive contains photographs produced locally but intended largely for consumption abroad and (unsurprisingly) located predominantly in private and institutional collections outside of Egypt.[10] Thus, the term *local archive* refers less to a specific location or archival institution(s)—the photographs discussed here are scattered across countless private and family collections in Egypt—than it does to a different field of power: photographs that Egyptians either commissioned or took of themselves as masters of their own representation.[11] This local archive has started receiving serious attention from scholars only since the 2000s.[12] But this archive, better known in Egypt as "local photographic heritage," has also been increasingly called upon, discovered, and reanimated especially online by a number of publics in Egypt for diverse purposes; it has also been an object of attention from local and regional collectors.[13] As such, it is not a static or "forgotten" archive awaiting our discovery; it has been alive and on the move, both physically and metaphorically, for the better part of two decades. Exploring how historians of Egypt may be able to make use of this local archive can expand the range of questions we have habitually been asking when we look at photographs, and in doing so, enrich our understanding of modern Egyptian history.

TOKENS OF URBAN MODERNITY

What was the point of the photograph in al-Hakim's autobiographical narrative? Certainly, it was not his father's dashing looks; good looks carried little weight in what was effectively a transaction between two families. Indeed, the bride's positive reaction is cast not in terms of the groom's likeness but in terms of his social status. The prospective groom was the son of an Azhar-educated village mayor, whose status as a rural notable was expressed through land ownership and the number of wives and children he had. His son, the groom on the tintype, was educated in Cairo's modern schools, epitomizing the rise of a local middle class (he was an effendi, a first-generation modern middle-class professional). The tintype photograph was used in this situation to impress the Alexandrian family of the bride, which perceived itself as more urbane. As a novelty, it was a token of urban sophistication deployed as a playing card intended to impress its recipient and increase the social capital of its holder in a high-stakes social setting. This is how photographs, in their various formats, were largely understood across the world after their commercial exploitation exploded in the middle decades of the nineteenth century.[14] As such, they were embedded less in the histories of technological transfer than they were in the spread of urban capitalism and class formation. Take what Egypt's diva Umm Kulthum had to say about her first visit to the studio as a child around World War I. As she was of very modest background, her recollection comes in the context of narrating the growing fame of her family's orchestra, when their fees were increasing to the point of their counting "as rich people" by the standards of their native village. "So my father decided we should try to behave like rich people. Rich people had photographs taken of their children, so why shouldn't he, Shaikh Ibrahim, have a portrait taken of his children?"[15]

The earliest photographic studios in Cairo and Alexandria opened their doors in the 1850s, though many appear to have been short-lived.[16] The next generation of studios that emerged in the 1880s produced some of the most famous and long-lasting names in the photography business in the region (Abdullah Frères, Sabunji, Lekejian, Sebah). These photographic establishments catered to two very different markets. One was the European market, comprising resident foreigners and tourists. Intended as souvenirs, their photographs included portraits of "local types," famously including scarcely clad women, archeological ruins, and landscapes. Some of these studios also carried a stock of "oriental" costumes, props, and backgrounds, giving their patrons the possibility of having themselves photographed as a Bedouin shaykh or an Arab warrior.[17] Tourists who came with preconceived ideas of "the East" could thus enact their oriental dreams in the studio, confirmed as "real" by the supreme authority of the camera.[18]

But many of these studios simultaneously catered to a wholly different market: wealthy local elites who came in to be photographed as proud and paying customers.[19] These elites included wide segments of the polite local society, composed of Turkish-speaking (but typically multilingual and cosmopolitan) Ottoman Egyptian elite, the more privileged among Coptic families, and the many locally established Levantine minorities. Through the second half of the nineteenth century, these elites developed the same photographic habits practiced by their European and American counterparts: exchanging photographs within their social circles, decorating the walls of their houses with enlarged and often heavily colored portraits, composing *carte-de-visite* portraits of their families and friends into albums, or indeed sporting albums of "famous personalities" of their time.[20] Some of the studios that sold souvenir photographs for the Western market also carried a stock of portraits of Ottoman princesses and dignitaries catering to this local clientele (Fig. 18.1).

FIG. 18.1 Late nineteenth-century Egyptian elite portraits. Author's collection.

This local market left its material traces in the archives of the descendants of elite Ottoman Egyptian families. One such collection belongs to a family whose men held high offices in the army and administration through the nineteenth and early twentieth centuries.[21] It contains more than two hundred photographs featuring portraits of men, women, and children (each of them alone or in small groups, though never within a nuclear family in this period), dating from the 1860s through the rest of the nineteenth century and executed in different formats. These portraits represent their subjects as the crème of Cairene society: ladies clad in Parisian fashions, gentlemen wearing smoking suits or ceremonial uniforms signifying their courtly functions. Some of these portraits were taken by the same studios well known to the canon of orientalist photography. Other studios amply represented in these local collections are barely known, suggesting that they placed their bets relatively early on the nascent local market for portraiture.[22] These two markets overlapped in the space of the studio, but there was little cultural blending; these publics represented two distinct communities of viewers who missed each other like ships in the night. As Stephen Sheehi convincingly argues, local visual production, rather than being an act of "speaking back" to the colonizer or being inspired by the colonial archive or orientalist aesthetics, was the product of genuinely local modernist impulses and dynamics.[23]

While there was clearly little resistance to photography as such in terms of religious doctrine (and whatever resistance there was appears marginal and short-lived), customary notions of gender were another matter.[24] Photographs spurred anxieties about exposure in a society in which understandings of gender, class, and respectability rested on the non-exposure of women to the eyes of undeserving strangers. Female seclusion was a powerful cultural ideal even if only practicable by a fraction of mostly urban women of middle- and upper-class status.[25] It was embedded within a broader "culture of covering" (*satr*), an understanding of the world in which much was to be gained from protecting (literally, shielding) all that was considered precious, beautiful, or a source of prosperity not only from the eyes of strangers but also from other invisible (otherworldly) forces of the universe.[26] Thus, while women do appear in the above-mentioned collections of nineteenth-century Ottoman Egyptian families, they do so much less than men and children.[27] This, however, was soon to change dramatically.

Soon after World War I, women's presence in public exploded, both physically in public spaces and as images in the mushrooming illustrated magazines and the cinema.[28] Up until the early years of the twentieth century, it was unthinkable for a groom to get a glimpse of his future bride, even in a photograph.[29] In 1915, Ahmad Amin's bride still did not feature in his "marriage portrait"; however, by the 1920s wedding photographs showing couples had become obligatory, including among local ("traditional") middle strata groups. While this process is often cast in teleological terms as "female liberation," the issue is, rather, one of a major transformation in local constructions of gender that was itself inextricable from significant changes in the role of visibility in social life. The sheer volume and ubiquity of new visual forms (photographs, newspapers, the cinema, advertising) worked to convey the message that to be modern, women had to be visible.

More research is needed to understand how exactly this happened, but photographs clearly played an important part in an emerging culture of display. With the arrival of the portable Kodak camera, photographic practices were not only democratized and domesticated but also substantially feminized. Certainly, secluded, or "harem," women posed for the camera, and their photographs circulated within small, carefully controlled circles long before they appeared in public culture (especially the press), exposed to the eyes of strangers. The point is not to say that photographic portraiture represented a key stage in women's liberation but that it played a crucial part in a major transformation in the understanding of the relationship between female visibility and notions of class and respectability. This process was further embedded in an underlying shift in sensory priorities, especially a new understanding of vision. From this perspective, everyday mundane practices of visual reproduction, such as print and photography, worked to normalize a new kind of eye understood as passive and purely optical. Notions of female respectability did not disappear, but they were transposed to other planes, toward other kinds of social performances. The issue of "veiling" (and the gradual reinscription of the veil with political significations as the twentieth century progressed) was largely born with modernity's insistence on female visibility and the simultaneous need to assert female respectability through other means, such as education, comportment, or "character."

SPACES OF THE MODERN

Photographs were signifiers of modernity as commodities whose presence in social relations played an important role in the construction of social status. From this perspective, they were not dissimilar from earlier status-making objects such as pocket-watches. But as particular forms of visual inscription, they were also fodder (enabling occasions) for the staging of a modern bourgeois self through the image. As Stephen Sheehi argues, the repetitive formalism of late nineteenth-century Egyptian and Lebanese portraiture was imbued with deeply local meanings that were intelligible within the framework of the Arab Renaissance, or *al-nahda*. The portraits of Arab literati and notables examined by Sheehi reflect quintessential values of modern Arab bourgeois selfhood, such as self-confidence, learnedness, moral propriety, culture (cultured-ness, or refinement, *al-taraqqi* as Egyptian sources often have it), and progress.[30] While it is not entirely clear what makes these virtues specifically Arab, Sheehi rightly insists that the sitters understood their modernity in strictly Ottoman and then Arab nationalist terms.

Indeed, there were many cases where photographs did the kind of ideological work described by Sheehi, though often reinforced by words. The vignettes of illustrious readers so often featured by illustrated magazines in the 1920s, extolling the virtues and achievements of their subjects, are a case in point (Fig. 18.2);[31] another is the frontispiece photographs increasingly featured in books in which the author gazes down on

FIG. 18.2 Vignettes of "illustrious readers" in illustrated magazines of the 1920s. *Al-Lata'if al-Musawwara*, 5 November 1923, 13.

the reader, literally embodying a modern textual authority forged by the luminaries of *nahdawi* letters and enabled by modern print culture. But it is equally possible that these photographs mobilized, or drew upon, an older pre-*nahda* understanding of texts through embodied authorial presence—presence previously enacted through sound and recitation, as well as embedded in the textual practice of *isnad*.[32] Certainly, photographic portraits, especially before their democratization when they were still a novelty and thus a rare and costly undertaking, were expected to convey an idealized likeness of the sitter and their moral qualities. But such qualities, while ideological for some, were probably more intelligible within local notions of *wiqar*, or gravitas, for many others (see, for instance, Fig. 18.1 again). As public forms of gendered self-presentation, the demands placed on early photographs were not entirely dissimilar to other instances of the public staging of respectable selfhood, whether in embodied terms through social encounters, writing, or oratory practices. Local modernity cannot be understood in purely ideological terms: photographs provide an opportunity to uncover precisely the kind of vernacular or popular meanings of modernity that remain obscured if we focus on learned intellectual production alone. The many ways people engaged with photographs as discussed throughout this chapter also suggest that photographs were quite a bit more agentive as historical actants than mere "imprints" or "reflections" of a preformed *nahdawi* subject.

The photographers' studio enabled, encouraged, and necessitated performances of the modern; in fact, the photograph itself was understood as the space of the modern. Take, for instance, the genre of wedding portraiture, which emerged among middle-class Muslim Egyptians in the 1920s. It is very likely that most of the seemingly modern bourgeois couples who posed together for their wedding portraits were the product of arranged marriages. Modern companionate couplehood, which became an increasingly normative form of framing matrimony in public culture during this period, is here literally enacted for the picture.[33] But the resulting image had tangible social effects. It allowed the couple to claim their modern middle-class status and urbanity by enacting an image of a "modern family." Rather than (a preformed) social identity being reflected in photographs, it was literally produced through them—as well as through their specific affordances as media objects. Understanding the social workings of photography in this way is consequential to scholarly, not least historical, questions of periodization and causation. As media (or as Latourian immutable mobiles: forms of inscription that circulate and carry their inscription across time and space), such photographs continued their cultural work across multiple social contexts when framed and displayed in homes or (as was then custom) exchanged or sent by post to friends, family, and colleagues.[34] These performances of selfhood or of social relationships (here, the modern companionate couple) were an important way through which modern subjects produced themselves. While often presented as an ideological commitment, modernity really is a performative position enacted through contextualized practices—whether in Egypt or anywhere else.[35] Indeed, the field of mass-mediated popular culture is where the categories of modernity and tradition were most saliently constituted in this period.[36] Photographs were part of these processes. Among the many everyday social practices that emerged in colonial Egypt and marked people as modern subjects, photographs were high on the list.[37] In other words, people made themselves into modern subjects through doing things with photographs, understood as the quintessential spaces of the modern. What was historically new, and analytically important, was the control over one's representation that photography as a technological-social practice (as Christopher Piney has it) now made possible. The camera became the perfect tool at the hands of many to realize their own versions of modernity, become in control of their representation, and project such a self-image (to make it work, to multiply its effects) across time and space.

It is, however, crucial to emphasize that this modernity never operated alone but rather gained meaning within a much broader social field. Modernity was an idiom meaningful only as far as it was deployed in specific social contexts, often in contrast to the idiom of "tradition" or "local authenticity." Take, for instance, the displayed wedding portrait, dating to the 1920s (Fig. 18.3). This couple's appearance is the product of a carefully staged performance; photographic portraiture was rarely about individual selves or "true likeness" but rather about performing social roles.[38] The groom's outfit, and its style and material, points to his wealth and social status, but one understood in deeply local terms; clearly, he comes from a notable family engaged in a traditional occupation or trade. The bride's wedding gown, by contrast, is executed in the latest fashion, as featured on the pages of illustrated magazines and available for purchase in Cairo's grand department stores. This image poses two different but simultaneous claims on social identity, using the registers of a local "traditional" (or "authentic") social role as well as a "modern" urbane one. The groom's local credentials (expressed by his dress) address his primary audience: his extended family and peers. While the bridal gown is a token of urban sophistication here—just as the tinplate photograph was in al-Hakim's story—it is worth noting how "modernity" is gendered female and enacted by a commodity, the "modern dress," but also how the woman herself becomes a commodity in this schema, along with the photograph. The key point is that these two registers were neither contradictory nor exclusive; they were complementary. Real social capital lay in being able to command both codes, but equally important was knowing the appropriate context in which to perform them. The photographic act was a suitable context for the enactment, display, and circulation of their social claims. It would have been unthinkable in this period for the bride to be seen wearing such an immodest outfit in any other context but the photograph.[39]

At the same time, this simultaneous use of the idioms of modernity and authenticity is often less visible in photographs (indeed, photographs such as this one are fairly rare), for these were semiotically understood as the exclusive space of the modern; it is, however, typically evident in the context. The decision of al-Hakim's father, or more likely his womenfolk, to use a photograph in the matchmaking process gave him a comparable advantage over his competitors, who, while richer, came across as less attuned to the times. The basic fact remains, however, that he only gained access to her by contacting her through his female relatives, mobilizing local codes of propriety and respectability. By contrast, when the Paris-educated Ahmad Shafiq insisted on seeing his prospective

FIG. 18.3 Wedding photograph, Anon, Alexandria, 1920s. This portrait uses sartorial markers of "tradition/authenticity" and "modernity" simultaneously. Author's collection.

bride, at least in a photograph, he encountered major resistance.[40] The photograph-wielding "modern groom" in both al-Hakim's case and Ahmad Amin's case (in the next section) never saw their brides before the night of the consummation of the marriage. Sometimes this modernity was deeply internalized, such as in the case of Ahmad Amin, for whom all knowledge resided in English books, an intellectual move common to his generation, for whom customary forms of knowledge and experience were rendered null and void. At other times, this modernity was performed or asserted through the picture (or a range of other well-defined objects, practices, or performances) where it would enhance the subject's social capital. This modernity was, however, always complemented by, or embedded in, a simultaneous claim to authenticity. We should never imagine these (modern) subjects as drawing a definitive boundary between themselves and their unmodern past. This performative capacity to claim both codes—to be both modern and yet authentic—is not some botched transition to modernity; it is an intentional articulation of a local modernity.[41]

Cultivating Modern Selfhood

When Ahmad Amin, a modernist intellectual and prolific writer, completed his degree at the School for Shari'a Judges, the time had come for him to marry. While he had been part of a circle of young reformist intellectuals who criticized what they perceived as antiquated social customs and championed women's unveiling, the fact remained that a young middle-class man in the 1910s had little opportunity to meet women of similar social stature outside his circle of relatives. Amin thus resorted to the established method of asking friends to recommend marriageable girls and sending his womenfolk around, eventually relying on his mother's choice. In many other respects, however, Amin's approach to marriage was a deeply modern affair. In the four months that separated the signing of the marriage contract and its actual consummation (time spent by the bride's family in preparing the trousseau), Amin busied himself with his own version of preparation for his upcoming role as a husband and the head of a family. He bought books on marriage, family, and childcare in an English bookshop in Cairo, which he studied carefully, acquainting himself with the latest theoretical foundations of a happy home.

A few days after the marriage took place, Amin visited a photographic studio to produce a "memorial picture" of himself (not yet of the couple on the day of the nuptials—such a convention would only emerge in the next decade). On the back of the photograph, he wrote a long text, cited in his autobiography. It begins as follows:

> This is my picture taken on Friday, April 7, 1916, four days after my marriage contract, and my age is twenty-nine years and six months. I have taken books as my distinguishing mark in the picture, and so the photographer placed books of his in front of me. In my left hand I held *Primer of Philosophy*, most of which I had translated into Arabic and almost finished. I wanted the picture taken to be extremely simple. Thus

I did not affect anything, except that I chose to wear the suit I wore on the marriage day. Perhaps the motive behind this photograph was that I felt I was approaching a new life and a new phase. For I have finished the life of solitude and am approaching family life. I am convinced that this new environment will have a great influence on my soul, my body, and my mind.[42]

This epic caption continues with Amin's self-searching reflection on his own character and its formative moments: a childhood and youth that knew no innocent entertainment, joy, or love, a result of his serious upbringing (associated, as was common in this genre of texts, with his father's strict and joyless Azhari culture[43]) and the ways in which this character had been changing in recent years by virtue of the books he had read and people he had encountered. It ends on strikingly practical terms: "I am now an instructor at the Judicial School. My salary is 1320 piasters per month. I have not become weary of teaching, and I still prefer it to judicature."[44]

What we have in Amin's caption above is neither a "text" nor just a "photograph," but a bundle of cultural practices and habits of mind of recent vintage, all of which produced modern selfhood: a visit to a photographer; a photographic object that prompts, inspires, or necessitates a particular kind of writing practice: a lengthy reflection on himself, including his career stage and salary, reading interests, mental states, and feelings. This photographic object was presumably carefully stored for decades before it was reactivated to play a part in a particular, equally new, genre of text: the autobiography. It prompts us to ask what paying attention to photographs in conjunction with texts reveals about the relationship between these novel practices of inscription and new forms of selfhood.

Personal photographic practices emerged in Egypt around the same time that writing practices (and, of course, reading practices) were undergoing important reconfiguration. Writing as such has a long history in Ottoman Egypt, but by the end of the nineteenth century, new writing practices emerged following the growth of commercial print culture.[45] These included new forms of self-writing: diaries, longer or shorter narrative journals, and, of course, letter-writing, which expanded significantly among middling groups with the growth of the postal service. These processes were also paralleled by the simultaneous expansion of the state bureaucracy, which instigated an expansion in popular petition-writing for justice and redress at the same time as it created its own forms of records, soon incorporating photographs into its fold as tools of order, classification, and documentation (Fig. 18.4).[46] All of these records are, in one way or another, traces of novel forms of inscription and, of course, of power. But leaving institutional contexts aside, the parallel emergence of distinctly modern writing practices and photography may just crystalize the connection between these practices and the cultural processes we call modernity. New forms of writing and personal photography became popular among the same middle-class publics who were themselves an emerging social

FIG. 18.4 In the early years of the twentieth century, photographs began to be used on ID documents. An identity card issued by the Ministry of Interior in 1912. Author's collection.

formation and who wielded these technologies of inscription, representation, and mediation, using them to literally constitute themselves as modern subjects and construct a new world around them.

Ahmad Amin was a case in point. His long caption (and his writing practices in general) had everything to do with how knowledge was constructed by his effendi peers.[47] His was a positivist and textual understanding of knowledge grounded in scientific rationalism, as also suggested in the way he prepared himself for marriage by studying books about it. Amin's autobiography is cast in terms of a lifelong search for knowledge, which was denied to him in his childhood, when his father, a religious scholar, decided to enroll Amin into the religious educational track (al-Azhar University) after having briefly put him into a modern school. The modern schooling experience largely contributed to the emergence of a new generation of "modern men" employed as bureaucrats or in new professions: doctors, lawyers, engineers, teachers, and journalists. Known as the effendis (*effendiyya*), they became the nucleus of a modern middle class, around which local modernity emerged in the early decades of the twentieth century.

Broadly speaking, the effendis perceived their society as sick ("backward") and in need of a cure, which evolved around notions of "order." Such order (standing for modernity, progress, or "civilization") was enacted through wide-ranging methods and projects that included the setting up of new schools to eradicate what they now saw as ignorance and superstition, the remaking of Egyptian cities, and various methods of personal and mental hygiene and forms of self-discipline.[48] This order became understood as that which is visible, as visibility became the principle of the physical ordering of things and people in space.[49] Scientific rationalism was the primary tool of this new relationship to the world—a world newly apprehended as a set of processes to be observed and described. While Amin was himself deprived of modern schooling due to his father's extensive piety, his lifelong struggle to acquire "modern knowledge" made him into an exemplary effendi.

It was not only his cultural and intellectual positions that made him into an effendi but also the way he used the pen—and the camera. Amin's autobiography takes a step back to subject his childhood environment to the dissecting eye of social analysis, classifying it into categories such as "economy" and "religion"—the latter, in his narrative, is mostly designated as delusion and superstition.[50] Like a camera, an autobiography examines the self as if it were another or presents a self-as-other. The status of photography as an "objective" representational practice nested perfectly with new notions of positivism, making the camera the perfect tool of observation, description, and classification.[51] But Amin's example (standing for many others among his generation) brings up two important points. First, the pen and the camera worked similarly by introducing distance between the subject and the object, the observer and the observed, realizing (or materializing) a desire for the disembodied and omniscient observer. Both the pen and the camera were understood as tools of "objective" representation that came to mediate between an observing self and the world. Indeed, as we saw, they were often used in tandem by order-desiring and science-worshipping men like Amin. Both were deployed to exorcise older forms of conceptualizing the real and normalizing new ones in their stead, based on the logic of objective, rational observation. Second, the world thus observed and examined was not only the external world, but equally often, the very observing self.

What we have here in Amin's case is a deeply modern piece of self-writing, a brief but concise examination of a "self," its intellectual formation, emotional disposition, and—crucially—the ways in which these have been changing over time. A prime example of new writing practices (Amin, like many of his first-generation effendi peers, was also an ardent diarist), this mini autobiography betrays a deeply modernist desire to record but also to objectify, exteriorize, and dissect one's own soul, personality, and character—in brief, to describe and order. Amin carefully notes what his current job is and how much he earns, what he reads in that particular year, and how much time had elapsed since he started learning English. This speaks volumes about his way of ordering or enframing the world in a rational and structured way, with almost photographic precision. The pen and the camera thus worked not only as tools of world-making, at this historical juncture, but also of self-making, what Michel Foucault had called technologies of modern selfhood.[52]

What other kind of work may the portrait be doing for Ahmad Amin? Amin's visit to the studio and the resulting photograph that he chose to adorn (or to "complete"?)

with a lengthy self-reflexive caption provided an avenue and a space for a contingent performance of his selfhood as autonomous (individuated) and singular. In the caption, Amin characterizes his life as one of "solitude," though he had lived his whole life with his parents and four siblings, and afterward with his wife.[53] His solitude is thus a state of mind, an intellectual (ontological) condition that he (and hundreds of his effendi peers) enacted through their texts, in which they distanced themselves from their backgrounds and families deemed unmodern.[54] Such novel practices of self-representation enabled rituals of modern selfhood to take place around them. The pen and the camera thus not only stood for the disembodied and omniscient observer, but they also realized a desire for a singular sovereign subject. Far from merely "reflecting" an already formed monadic modern Arab individual, new representational practices such as photographs and self-writing were the very mechanism of its making.[55] The modern individual literally emerges through precisely such practices of inscription and individuation. Put differently, an atomized, self-contained modern individual selfhood (whether Arab or any other) is produced, or produces itself, precisely through such contingent acts of self-presentation, using the twin technologies of the pen and the camera.[56]

Finally, such practices also worked to crystalize new linear notions of time. The photograph in Amin's story carries several temporalities: the time of visiting the studio (the moment of the photographic event); the time of marriage (four days before, as duly recorded) and fulfilled manhood; the time of writing the caption, when both the photograph and the marriage were already history; an extended past of a "sad childhood"; and an anticipated future that such a record implies and makes possible, which eventually materialized as the time of activating the photograph in Amin's autobiography. With the popularization of photography, when photographs became multiple and serial, it became necessary to inscribe time on their versos. Captions saying "me at the age of twelve" or "after my Secondary Exam" become common, inscribed either on the back of photographs or as ordering markers inside albums. Here, modern selfhoods literally historicize themselves. What the proliferation of photographic practices effected here was to force a particular register of time onto photographs, time understood as a linear progression with a clear and orderly definition of past, present, and future "documented" beyond doubt and leaving no space for imaginative (and necessarily more fluid) recollection. Such seemingly inconspicuous practices of inscription thus worked to entrench and normalize distinctly modern forms of temporality inserted into the flow of the everyday. Diaries were, of course, meant to do exactly that; this is another example of the parallel work of photography and writing as modern forms of inscription.[57] The modern self was thus a self that must represent itself in order to be, as well as a self that constructs its own temporality cast in linear and progressive terms.

Spaces of Modern Magic

In the early decades of the twentieth century, photographic studios mushroomed across Egyptian cities; their services became increasingly affordable to individuals and families with middling incomes.[58] Ambulant photographers now toured the provinces offering their services, especially during seasonal holidays; high schools had their own photography clubs; and several publications dedicated to amateur photography emerged.[59] In the 1920s, the portable Kodak camera became broadly advertised to Egyptians on middling incomes.

New kinds of leisure activities, especially outings in public parks or on beaches or riverbanks, became unthinkable without the camera's presence, which often inspired such outings in the first place (Figs. 18.5A–18.5D). Generations of youths dreamt of having a camera, and many of them did. Once one had a camera, one had to use it.[60] In the interwar period, novel photographic genres and industries emerged that bear witness to entirely new forms of urban experience: a new quality of the urban space as "public," where anonymity and display emerged as pleasurable and desirable. Here, specific parts of large cities became performance stages where pleasure and social distinction were to be gained from seeing and being seen. With the simultaneous emergence of new forms of public visual culture, such as the cinema and illustrated magazines, visibility emerged as the key preoccupation of modern forms of social life.

As middle-class publics became accustomed to having their portraits taken at somewhat regular intervals, new demands were placed on photographs. The camera became a tool of aspirational self-making. Photographic studios functioned, often literally, as performance stages where sitters could, and did, put on the public persona they wanted to project to a given audience in order to achieve particular social effects. The nature of these performances varied according to the intended audience or purpose (the highly choreographed wedding picture was one example) and the sitter's class position, which was largely the measure of not just their wealth but also their exposure to modern urban culture. Those not accustomed to the camera, or for whom one picture was all there was to be had, posed in solemn poses in their finest attire, enacting much desired but hard to access social roles. Others, especially those more familiar with the medium, used the camera as a space of experimentation, enacting multiple, playful, and sometimes transgressive versions of a self.

For women, such desired but hard-to-access social roles often pivoted on modern urban womanhood. As historians of modern Egypt have amply demonstrated, much cultural labor went into "remaking women" and creating the "new Egyptian woman."[61] In everyday practice, the key marker of such modern urban womanhood was the modern dress, which contrasted sharply with the *galabiyya* broad robe worn by local

FIGS. 18.5(a), 18.5(b), 18.5(c), & 18.5(d) Outdoor photography becomes an obligatory element of public leisure outings. Author's collection, 023; 012; 08; 026.

FIGS. 18.5(a), 18.5(b), 18.5(c), & 18.5(d) Continued.

women. (The 1920s, it ought to be stressed, saw a revolution in women's apparel glob-ally, not only in Egypt.) In the early 2000s, I carried out an oral history interview with a lady who grew up in the 1930s as a merchant's daughter in the city of Banha. Her family was locally prominent, but from the perspective of metropolitan culture, it was considered provincial. Like many women in her milieu, she longed to wear a modern dress, for modern dresses were the craze of the town (worn only by locally resident foreign minorities and women from families of local pashas, or absentee landlords), and they differed substantially from the broad-cut *galabiyya* robe that local women normally wore. She had a modern dress made by a local Levantine dressmaker, Umm Michel, and wore it only a handful of times when attending a wedding or a social occasion at the house of a local pasha. But she also wore it for a photograph taken by a local studio in Banha, accessorized with a feathery shawl reminiscent of Parisian elegance. In the studio, she magically transformed herself into the woman of her dreams and aspirations, enacting her desired self as a sophisticated modern urban lady, even holding a pen and paper (in a letter-writing pose), though she "could not quite" read and write.

Many photographs survive in the local archive featuring women of middling backgrounds putting their modern dress on for the first time in front of the camera (Fig. 18.6). As the wrinkles on the fabric suggest, these dresses were often kept folded and only worn in the studio; in many cases, the same "modern dress" was shared by several related women, each of them taking their turn to wear it for the camera. Other images show clear attempts to enact the look of a cinema star or advertising poster girl. Low-end ambulant photographers offered a hastily painted background and paper flower props to suggest bourgeois urbanity, just as many women with few literacy skills opted to pose with a book or magazine to conjure sophisticated urban womanhood. Young men, in turn, often had themselves photographed as athletes, dandies (often smoking a cigarette), or in the style of the cinema star Rudolph Valentino.[62]

FIG. 18.6 Women in wrinkled dresses, posing like poster girls or as if in advertising pictures. Author's collection.

Despite sometimes arresting details (the wrinkles on the dress, the occasional amulet or *khulkhal*, an ankle bracelet worn with a modern dress), the bulk of the local archive of personal portraiture remains intensely mimetic. These photographs emulate something, though most often they tend to copy each other. A defined range of poses endlessly repeats itself while apparently mimicking Western norms of composition, styles, and interiors. Candid snapshots taken with home-owned Kodaks then often sought to reproduce poses learned in the studio or observed on advertising posters or on the pages of illustrated magazines featuring cinema stars. The assumption remains that the imitation of what is a priori recognized as "Western" forms and fashions signifies the lack of authenticity and "localness." But we need to take this obvious desire for sameness seriously not only because it is a symptom of global capitalist modernity—which cannot be reduced to unidirectional cultural transfer, "copying," or "adoption" but is rather a process that was both unevenly structured and genuinely globally autogenetic—but also because such mimetic acts were socially productive in and of themselves. Stylistic emulation was exactly the point of studio portraiture. Studios, as we saw earlier, were spaces of the modern: they were where idioms of "modernity" and urban sophistication were to be enacted. The sitters went into the studio not because they wanted to capture their everyday self, but to look like somebody else.

Emulation is the basic principle, or building block, of human interaction. Everybody emulates something or somebody. It is whom we emulate that changes historically and contextually. Historically speaking, most local societies emulate within the parameters of a local repertoire of symbolic codes (or social roles): one's peers, parents, and social seniors. What changes, fundamentally, with the arrival of modernity as globally (or translocally) mediated flows of cultural or symbolic forms are the models that people emulate.[63] These images (and the social practices that produced them) betray a broader desire to forge a novel personhood, which dovetails with some of the core desires wrought by modernity, notably the possibility and imperative of social mobility, the desire to "become another." As the canon of modernist Egyptian literature never failed to emphasize in this period (think of Najib Mahfuz's *Palace Walk* and *Cairo Modern* or Latifa al-Zayyat's *The Open Door*), remaining or becoming just like one's father or mother now represented assured social death.[64] Departing from one's place of origin and assuming new social roles become socially imperative; hence the emergence of a modern middle class, the *effendiyya*, and the "modern woman." These images not only make these underlying social desires visible to us today, but they actively cultivated them and realized them. We need to understand mimesis (imitation) not as a lack, a shortcoming (perhaps a legacy of an art-historical obsession with originality?), but as social empowerment. From this perspective, we can understand photographic portraiture not as a poor imitation of foreign models or ideological imprints of modern forms of rationality or colonial culture but rather as a form of modern magic whereby re-enacting the original (or whatever counts as the model) works to assume its powers. The camera literally conjured up wonders; it realized dreams and materialized desires.

The spread of candid portraiture with the portable Kodak camera, and generally the proliferation of photographic opportunities (due to their affordability and disposability), opened further avenues for experimentation. Comfortably bourgeois women who did not need to assert their urbanity "for the picture" then playfully enacted different versions of their modern femininity, donning a variety of costumes for the camera (Fig. 18.7).[65] A stock of oriental costumes that upscale studios had carried for the tourists since the late nineteenth century became a veritable fad among the Egyptian and Lebanese bourgeoisie following the spread of Hollywood fashion in the 1920s. It was not uncommon to pose semi-nude, reclining on a sofa and holding a cigarette, enacting a femme fatale image of the silver screen. Using the portable Kodak camera, young ladies of leisure transgressed social boundaries in the privacy of their homes, donning men's costumes, often snatched from their brothers' wardrobes. At a time when young women were bombarded with novel demands placed on them in public culture and intellectual discourse, they used the camera to playfully experiment with the boundaries that publicly defined them as "good girls."

Such photographs were then composed into personal albums, shared, and circulated within small circles of friends. Such self-focused peer albums were common among middle-class urban youth in the middle decades of the twentieth century. While strongly gendered, they present a world of peer sociability and leisure marked by the exclusion of the family and social seniors. If, for Ahmad Amin, practicing self-narration worked to contingently individuate the writing subject and momentarily realize a desire for an atomized individuality, then these albums worked in a similar way. Together with the practices that preceded and followed them (from the moments of fun caught in the photographs to the moments of composing and then circulating the albums), peer albums created pockets of autonomy. They were spaces where young middle-class-aspiring people enacted and realized themselves as autonomous individuals, though more often than not within small peer groups, thus contingently breaking some forms of attachment (the family) and creating others in their place. Such practices are also, in many ways, the historical precursors of many contemporary social media practices that work as zones for the performance and curation of selfhood, from Facebook to Snapchat.[66] Such contingent realizations of autonomous forms of selfhood nested within broader patriarchal structures is precisely what characterized local modernity.

Egypt's local photographic archive clearly suggests that modern forms of selfhood and social identity were inseparable from and dependent on new representational practices. Such modern selfhood was a project forged through sustained exposure to mass-mediated popular culture, which introduced new forms of experience; but importantly, it was a project that afforded agency in the form of various acts of self-mediation. Taken together, the photographs discussed in this chapter speak to an emergent self that obsessively represents itself, a self that must be photographed or written about in order to be, a self that exteriorizes, objectifies, and looks on itself as if it were another. All of these processes and connections can be readily gleaned from the local archive but remain poorly understood.

FIG. 18.7 Girls of leisure experimenting with the camera, donning a variety of costumes. Author's collection.

NOTES

1. Tawfiq al-Hakim, *Sijn al-'Umr* (Cairo: Maktabat al-Adab, 1964), 23–25; English translation by Pierre Cachia, *The Prison of Life* (Cairo: American University in Cairo Press, 1992), 14–15.
2. Timothy Mitchell, "The Stage of Modernity," in *Questions of Modernity*, ed. Timothy Mitchell (Minneapolis: University of Minnesota Press, 2000), 21.
3. This formulation is inspired by Elizabeth Edwards, *Photographs and the Practice of History* (London: Bloomsbury Publishing, 2022).
4. These have only begun receiving scholarly attention in the region. See, e.g., Zeynep Devrim Gürsel, "Thinking with X-rays: Investigating the Politics of Visibility through the Ottoman Sultan Abdülhamid's Photography Collection," *Visual Anthropology* 29, no. 3 (2016): 229–42; "A Picture of Health: The Search for a Genre to Visualize Care in Late Ottoman Istanbul," *Grey Room* 72 (2018): 36–67; Ahmet A. Ersoy, "Ottomans and the Kodak Galaxy: Archiving Everyday Life and Historical Space in Ottoman Illustrated Journals," *History of Photography* 40, no. 3 (2016): 330–57; and Tamara Maatouk, "'On the Look-Out' for the Peculiar: Photography's Application to Medicine in Colonial Egypt" (paper presented at the "Medicine in the Middle East: Doctors, Bodies, Body Parts" Workshop, Middle East and Middle Eastern American Center, The Graduate Center, CUNY, 15 May 2020).
5. This claim on truth is the cornerstone of Western theories of photography deriving from Roland Barthes, *Camera Lucida*, trans. Richard Howard (New York: Farrar, Straus, and Giroux, Inc., 1981). For a good synthesis, see Margaret Olin, "Touching Photographs," *Representations* 80, no. 1 (2002): 99–118.
6. As pointed out by Carlo Ginsburg, *Clues, Myths and the Historical Method* (Baltimore: Johns Hopkins University Press, 1989), 35; and Peter Burke, *Eyewitnessing: The Use of Images as Historical Evidence* (Ithaca, NY: Cornell University Press, 2001), 10.
7. Jennifer Tucker, "Entwined Practices: Engagements with Photography in Historical Enquiry," *History and Theory* 48, no. 4 (2009): 5.
8. For an overview of the vast literature on material approaches to photographs, see Elizabeth Edwards, "Objects of Affect: Photography Beyond the Image," *Annual Review of Anthropology* 41 (2012): 221–34.
9. A selection includes Carney Gavin, *The Image of the East: Nineteenth-Century Near Eastern Photographs by Bonfils from the Collections of the Harvard Semitic Museum* (Chicago: University of Chicago Press, 1982); Engin Çizgen, *Photography in the Ottoman Empire, 1839–1919* (Istanbul: Haset Kitabevi, 1987); Nissan Perez, *Focus East: Early Photography in the Near East 1839–1885* (New York: Harry N. Abrams, Inc., 1988); Colin Osman, *Egypt: Caught in Time* (Reading: Garnet Publishing, 1997); Engin Özendes, *Abdullah Fréres: Ottoman Court Photographers* (Istanbul: Yapi Kredi Yayinlari, 1998); Engin Özendes, *From Sébah and Joaillier to Photo Sebah: Orientalism in Photography* (Istanbul: Yapi Kredi Yayinlari, 1999); and Ken Jacobson, *Odalisques and Arabesques: Orientalist Photography 1839–1925* (London: Bernard Quaritch Ltd., 2007). For a critical assessment, see Malek Alloula, *The Colonial Harem*, trans. Myrna Godzich and Wlad Godzich (Minneapolis: University of Minnesota Press, 1986); and Ali Behdad and Luke Gartlan, eds., *Photography's Orientalism: New Essays on Colonial Representation* (Los Angeles: Getty Publications, 2013).

10. For works questioning the limits of orientalist aesthetics, see Michelle Woodward, "Between Orientalist Clichés or Images of Modernization," *History of Photography* 23, no. 4 (2003): 363–74; and Behdad and Gartlan, *Photography's Orientalism*.

11. The expression "field of power" belongs to Suren Lalvani, *Photography, Vision, and the Production of Modern Bodies* (New York: State University of New York Press, 1996), 60. He builds on John Tagg's classic work on photographs and power, *The Burden of Representation: Essays on Photographies and Histories* (Minneapolis: University of Minnesota Press, 1988).

12. Sarah Graham-Brown, *The Portrayal of Women in Photography of the Middle East 1860–1950* (New York: Columbia University Press, 1988), was a pioneer. Beth Baron, *Egypt as a Woman: Nationalism, Gender and Politics* (Berkeley: University of California Press, 2005); Maria Golia, *Photography and Egypt* (London: Reaktion Books, 2009); Stephen Sheehi, *The Arab Imago: A Social History of Arab Photography, 1860–1910* (Princeton, NJ: Princeton University Press, 2016).

13. Lucie Ryzova, "Mourning the Archive: Middle Eastern Photographic Heritage between Neoliberalism and Digital Reproduction," *Comparative Studies in Society and History* 56, no. 4 (2014): 1037–61; Ryzova, "Nostalgia for the Modern: Archive Fever in Egypt in the Age of Post-Photography," in *Photo Archives and the Idea of Nation*, ed. Costanza Caraffa and Tiziana Serena (Berlin: Walter de Gruyter, 2015). For Egyptian initiatives, see Glimpses into Egyptian Middle Class Families, https://www.middleclassegypt.com.

14. Elizabeth Ann McCauley, *A. A. E. Disderi and the Carte de Visite Portrait Photograph* (New Haven, CT: Yale University Press, 1985).

15. Graham-Brown, *The Portrayal of Women*, 58.

16. The first documented photographic studio in Cairo is that of Antonio Schranz, which by 1850 was selling photographic prints as souvenirs to European tourists. Jacobson, *Odalisques and Arabesques*, 33; Golia, *Photography and Egypt*, 20.

17. Ozendes, *From Sébah and Joaillier to Photo Sebah*, 166; Osman, *Egypt: Caught in Time*, 45; Jacobson, *Odalisques and Arabesques*, 53; Wendy Shaw, *Possessor and Possessed: Museums, Archaeology, and the Visualisation of History in the Late Ottoman Empire* (Berkeley: University of California Press, 2003), 140.

18. On preconceived ideas, see Derek Gregory, "Performing Cairo: Orientalism and the City of Arabian Nights," in *Making Cairo Medieval*, ed. Nezar Alsayad et al. (Lanham, MD: Lexington Books, 2005); and On Barak, *On Time: Technology and Temporality in Modern Egypt* (Berkeley: University of California Press, 2013), especially 35–37.

19. As in other parts of the Ottoman Empire; Ozendes, *From Sébah & Joaillier to Photo Sebah*; Issam Nassar, "Familial Snapshots: Representing Palestine in the Work of the First Local Photographers," *History & Memory* 18, no. 2 (2006): 139–55.

20. Golia, *Photography and Egypt*, 67–68; Sheehi, *The Arab Imago*, 56–57, 74; Ozendes, *From Sébah and Joaillier to Photo Sebah*, 166. For a contemporary testimony on the cartemania at the khedival court, see Ellen Chenelle, *Recollections of an Egyptian Princess by Her English Governess* (Edinburgh: William Blackwood and Sons, 1893), 233–34. In the early 1900s, middle-class conduct manuals for girls began instructing their readers on how to decorate their homes with pictures; Beth Baron, *Egypt as a Woman*, 88; Lisa Pollard, *Nurturing the Nation: The Family Politics of Modernizing, Colonizing, and Liberating Egypt, 1805–1923* (Berkeley: University of California Press, 2005), 127.

21. Collection of Mahmud Sabit in Cairo, and interviews carried out by the author in 2011–12.
22. These included Desire, Heyman, Schier, and Schoefft.
23. Sheehi, *The Arab Imago.*
24. This feeble resistance to photography was due to its being consistently presented as a scientific process; Sheehi, *The Arab Imago,* 80–81, chapter 4. Rif'at al-Imam, *'Asr al-Sura fi al-Misr al-Haditha* (Cairo: al-Hay'a al-Misriyya al-'Amma li-l-Kitab, 2010), 52–54; Baron, *Egypt as a Woman,* 84; and Leor Halevi, *Modern Things on Trial* (New York: Columbia University Press, 2019) discuss religious opinions (*fatwas*) in favor of the many civic advantages of photography.
25. The issue was different among peasant and working women; Judith Tucker, *Women in Nineteenth Century Egypt* (Cambridge: Cambridge University Press, 1985).
26. See al-Sayyid al-Aswad, "Thaqafat al-Satr wa-Dalalatiha al-Ramziyya fi al-Haya' al-Sha'biyya al-'Arabiyya," *al-Ma'thurat al-Sha'biyya,* July 2004, 7–28.
27. While working in this collection, I was told a family anecdote of a great-grandfather who allegedly divorced his wife, a princess daughter of Khedive Isma'il, because she had herself photographed. Mahmud Sabit, interview by the author, 2011.
28. The process was more complex than can be developed here: specific 1920s magazines are indeed awash with images of women, but these are actresses, dancers, and foreign models, not actual middle-class Egyptian women. The commodification of female bodies in public culture thus preceded the normalization of images of "respectable" Egyptian women by about a decade. See Lucie Ryzova, "'I Am a Whore but I Will Be a Good Mother': On the Producing and Consumption of the Female Body in Modern Egypt," *Arab Studies Journal* 12/13 (2004/2005): 80–122. On women in public spaces, see Beth Baron, "Unveiling in Early Twentieth Century Egypt: Practical and Symbolic Considerations," *Middle Eastern Studies* 25, no. 3 (1989): 370–86.
29. Ahmad Shafiq Pasha, *Mudhakirati fi Nisf al-Qarn* (Cairo: al-Hay'a al-Misriyya al-'Amma li-l-Kitab, 1999 [1934]); Ibrahim al-Hilbawi, *Mudhakirat* (Cairo: al-Hay'a al-Misriyya al-'Amma li-l-Kitab, 1995); Muhammad 'Ali 'Alluba, *Mudhakirat Ijtima'iyya wa-Siyasiyya* (Cairo: al-Hay'a al-Misriyya al-'Amma li-l-Kitab, 1983).
30. Stephen Sheehi, "A Social History of Early Arab Photography or a Prolegomenon to an Archaeology of the Lebanese Imago," *International Journal of Middle East Studies* 39, no. 2 (2007): 178.
31. Discussed in Lucie Ryzova, *The Age of the Efendiyya: Passages to Modernity in National-Colonial Egypt* (Oxford: Oxford University Press, 2014), 46–48; and Baron, *Egypt as a Woman,* 93.
32. On notions of authorial presence, see Brinkley Messick, *The Calligraphic State: Textual Domination and History in an Islamic Society* (Berkeley: University of California Press, 1996), especially chapter 11; Messick, "Written Identities: Legal Subjects in an Islamic State," *History of Religions* 38, no. 1 (1998): 21–52; and Abdelfattah Killito, *The Author and His Doubles: Essays on Classical Arabic Culture,* trans. Michael Cooperson (Syracuse, NY: Syracuse University Press, 2001).
33. For the idiom of the modern companionate couple, see Kenneth Cuno, *Modernizing Marriage: Family, Ideology and Law in Nineteenth and Early Twentieth Century Egypt* (Syracuse, NY: Syracuse University Press, 2015); Hanan Kholoussy, *For Better, For Worse: The Marriage Crisis that Made Modern Egypt* (Stanford, CA: Stanford University Press, 2010); and Beth Baron, "The Making and Breaking of Marital Bonds in Modern Egypt,"

in *Women in Middle Eastern History: Shifting Boundaries in Sex and Gender*, ed. Nikki R. Keddie and Beth Baron (Yale University Press, 1991), 275–91.

34. These forms of exchange, or social lives of photographs, are amply demonstrated through their material qualities as enlarged and framed objects, and in many cases also by captions dedicated to friends, family, and colleagues (for men at this period). On "immutable mobiles," see Bruno Latour, "Visualization and Cognition: Drawing Things Together," in *Knowledge and Society Studies in the Sociology of Culture Past and Present*, ed. H. Kuklick (Greenwich, CT: Jai Press, 1986), 1–40.

35. My argument resonates with Timothy Mitchell's idea of "staging" in "The Stage of Modernity."

36. Walter Armbrust, *Mass Culture and Modernism in Egypt* (Cambridge: Cambridge University Press, 1996).

37. On modernity as a social position enacted through manifold acts of socialization and consumption, see Keith David Watenpaugh, *Being Modern in the Middle East: Revolution, Nationalism, Colonialism, and the Arab Middle Class* (Princeton, NJ: Princeton University Press, 2006); Nancy Reynolds, *A City Consumed: Urban Commerce, the Cairo Fire, and the Politics of Decolonization in Egypt* (Stanford, CA: Stanford University Press, 2012); and Wilson Chacko Jacob, *Working Out Egypt: Effendi Masculinity and Subject Formation in Colonial Modernity, 1870–1940* (Durham, NC: Duke University Press, 2011).

38. Pierre Bourdieu, *Photography: A Middlebrow Art* (Oxford: Blackwell Publishers Ltd., 1990); Elizabeth Edwards, "Little Theatres of Self, Thinking about the Social," in *We Are the People: Postcard from the Collection of Tom Phillips*, ed. James Fenton et al. (London: National Portrait Gallery Publications, 2004).

39. Similar examples include photographs of women lounging or reclining on sofas and/or holding a cigarette, which were similarly unthinkable in a social context involving strange men, but permissible, and often de rigueur, in the space of the photograph. For more, see Lucie Ryzova, *Camera Time* (forthcoming).

40. Ahmad Shafiq, *Mudhakirati fi Nisf al-Qarn*, 501.

41. For an extended discussion, see Ryzova, *The Age of the Efendiyya*.

42. Ahmad Amin, *My Life*, trans. Issa Boullata (Leiden, Netherlands: E. J. Brill, 1978), 122–23, Arabic original *Hayati* (Cairo: n.p., 1950), 130–31.

43. Other examples in Ryzova, *The Age of the Efendiyya*, 38–40, 56–58.

44. Amin, *My Life*, 122–23.

45. Hoda Yousef, *Composing Egypt: Reading, Writing, and the Emergence of a Modern Nation 1870–1930* (Stanford, CA: Stanford University Press, 2016); Lucie Ryzova, "'My Notepad Is My Friend': Efendis and the Act of Writing in Modern Egypt," *The Maghrib Review* 32, no. 4 (2007): 323–48.

46. For the increase in petition writing, see John Chalcraft, "Engaging the State: Peasants and Petitions in Egypt on the Eve of Colonial Rule," *International Journal of Middle East Studies* 37, no. 3 (2005): 303–25; for institutional uses of ID photographs, see Golia, *Photography and Egypt*, 78 and footnote 29; and Francesca Biancani, *Sex Work in Colonial Cairo: Women, Modernity and the Global Economy* (London: Bloomsbury Publishing, 2018), 54.

47. For the broader context, see Omnia El Shakry, *The Great Social Laboratory: Subjects of Knowledge in Colonial and Postcolonial Egypt* (Stanford, CA: Stanford University Press,

2007); El Shakry, *The Arabic Freud: Psychoanalysis and Islam in Modern Egypt* (Princeton, NJ: Princeton University Press, 2020); Marwa Elshakry, *Reading Darwin in Arabic, 1860–1950* (Chicago: University of Chicago Press, 2013); and Daniel Stolz, *The Lighthouse and the Observatory: Islam, Science and Empire in Late Ottoman Egypt* (Cambridge: Cambridge University Press, 2018).

48. Michael Gasper, *The Power of Representation: Publics, Peasants, and Islam* (Stanford, CA: Stanford University Press, 2009); Pollard, *Nurturing Egypt*; Zachary Lockman, "Imagining the Working Class: Culture, Nationalism, and Class Formation in Egypt, 1899–1914," *Poetics Today* 15, no. 2 (1994): 157–90.

49. Timothy Mitchell, *Colonising Egypt* (Berkeley: University of California Press, 1988); Stolz, *The Lighthouse and the Observatory*, 196–97. For the broader context, see Scott McQuire, *Visions of Modernity: Representation, Memory, Time and Space in the Age of the Camera* (London: Sage Publications Ltd., 1998); and David Martin, *Curious Visions of Modernity: Enchantment, Magic and the Sacred* (Cambridge, MA: MIT Press, 2011).

50. Amin, *My Life*, especially chapters 6 and 7; Ryzova, *The Age of Efendiyya*, 146–51.

51. As described in the local context in Stephen Sheehi, *The Arab Imago*; see also John Tagg, *The Burden of Representation: Essays on Photographies and Histories* (Minneapolis: University of Minnesota Press, 1988); Lalvani, *Photography, Vision, and the Production of Modern Bodies*; and Jennifer Tucker, *Nature Exposed: Photography as Eyewitness in Victorian Science* (Baltimore: Johns Hopkins University Press, 2005).

52. Michel Foucault, *Technologies of the Self: A Seminar with Michel Foucault*, ed. Luther H. Martin et al. (Amherst: University of Massachusetts Press, 1988).

53. When Amin actually found himself truly "alone," this left a strong negative mark on him, as he did not fail to mention decades later in his autobiography, Amin, *My Life*, 51.

54. Ryzova, *The Age of the Efendiyya*, chapter 4; see also Gasper, *The Power of Representation*; and Yoav Di-Capua, "The Professional Worldview of the Effendi Historian," *History Compass* 7, no. 1 (2009): 306–28.

55. "Reflected" is the key argument in Sheehi's book *The Arab Imago*.

56. This comes at a time when such forms of singular or individual selfhood become celebrated intellectually in scientific theory and psychology and when new notions of individual personhood become the basis of new legal codes and enacted politically through ideals of representative government.

57. On diary practices, see Ryzova, "'My Notepad Is My Friend'"; and Yousef, *Composing Egypt*.

58. Golia, *Photography and Egypt*, 56 onward for a discussion of the business side of these local studios.

59. Discussed extensively in al-Imam, *'Asr al-Sura*.

60. As Bourdieu famously observed, "nothing *may* be photographed apart that which *must* be photographed," Bourdieu, *A Middlebrow Art*, 24.

61. Mona Russell, *Creating the New Woman: Consumerism, Education, and National Identity, 1863–1922* (New York: Palgrave Macmillan, 2004); Baron, *Egypt as a Woman*; Lila Abu Lughod, ed., *Remaking Women: Feminism and Modernity in the Middle East* (Princeton, NJ: Princeton University Press, 1998); Pollard, *Nurturing the Nation*.

62. 'Abd al-Hamid Gawda al-Sahhar, *Hayati* (Cairo: al-Hay'a al-Misriyya al-'Amma li-l-Kitab, n.d.), 123.

63. John B. Thompson, *The Media and Modernity: A Social Theory of the Media* (Stanford, CA: Stanford University Press, 1995).

64. Also here, however, it remains crucial to maintain a claim on authenticity through ethical virtues; it is never about completely rejecting the mother or father—it works the same way as I just described above.

65. For these costume sessions, see Yasmine Nachabe Taan, *Reading Marie al-Khazen's Photographs: Gender, Photography, Mandate Lebanon* (London: Bloomsbury Publishing, 2020); and Ryzova, "Boys, Girls, and Kodaks: Peer Albums and Middle-Class Personhood in Mid-Twentieth-Century Egypt," *Middle East Journal of Culture and Communication* 8 (2015): 215–55.

66. Just as the genealogy of blogging extends to the self-writing practices of the early generations of effendi youth; Teresa Pepe, "Public and Private Diaries: The Ancestral Genres of the Blog in Egypt," *Middle East Journal of Culture and Communication* 14, nos. 2–3 (2021). But we need to consider both representational practices, visual and textual, together.

Bibliography

Armbrust, Walter. *Mass Culture and Modernism in Egypt*. Cambridge: Cambridge University Press, 1996.

Behdad, Ali, and Luke Gartlan, eds. *Photography's Orientalism: New Essays on Colonial Representation*. Los Angeles: Getty Publications, 2013.

Bourdieu, Pierre. *Photography: A Middlebrow Art*. Oxford: Blackwell, 1990.

Edwards, Elizabeth. "Objects of Affect: Photography beyond the Image." *Annual Review of Anthropology* 41 (2012): 221–34.

Foucault, Michel. *Technologies of the Self: A Seminar with Michel Foucault*. Edited by Luther H. Martin et al. Amherst: University of Massachusetts Press, 1988.

Golia, Maria. *Photography and Egypt*. London: Reaktion Books, 2009.

Graham-Brown, Sarah. *The Portrayal of Women in Photography of the Middle East 1860–1950*. New York: Columbia University Press, 1988.

Lalvani, Suren. *Photography, Vision, and the Production of Modern Bodies*. New York: State University of New York Press, 1996.

Latour, Bruno. "Visualization and Cognition: Drawing Things Together." In *Knowledge and Society Studies in the Sociology of Culture Past and Present*, edited by H. Kuklick, 1–40. Greenwich, CT: Jai Press, 1986.

McQuire, Scott. *Visions of Modernity: Representation, Memory, Time and Space in the Age of the Camera*. London: Sage, 1998.

Mitchell, Timothy. *Colonising Egypt*. Berkeley: University of California Press, 1988.

Ryzova, Lucie. *The Age of the Efendiyya: Passages to Modernity in National-Colonial Egypt*. Oxford: Oxford University Press, 2014.

Ryzova, Lucie. "Boys, Girls, and Kodaks: Peer Albums and Middle-Class Personhood in Mid-Twentieth-Century Egypt." *Middle East Journal of Culture and Communication* 8 (2015): 215–55.

El Shakry, Omnia. *The Great Social Laboratory: Subjects of Knowledge in Colonial and Postcolonial Egypt*. Stanford, CA: Stanford University Press, 2007.

Sheehi, Stephen. *The Arab Imago: A Social History of Arab Photography, 1860–1910*. Princeton, NJ: Princeton University Press, 2016.

Stolz, Daniel. *The Lighthouse and the Observatory: Islam, Science and Empire in Late Ottoman Egypt*. Cambridge: Cambridge University Press, 2018.

Tagg, John. *The Burden of Representation: Essays on Photographies and Histories*. Minneapolis: University of Minnesota Press, 1988.

Thompson, John B. *The Media and Modernity: A Social Theory of the Media*. Stanford, CA: Stanford University Press, 1995.

Watenpaugh, Keith David. *Being Modern in the Middle East: Revolution, Nationalism, Colonialism, and the Arab Middle Class*. Princeton, NJ: Princeton University Press, 2006.

Yousef, Hoda. *Composing Egypt: Reading, Writing, and the Emergence of a Modern Nation 1870–1930*. Stanford, CA: Stanford University Press, 2016.

CHAPTER 19

··

TAKING COMEDY SERIOUSLY

Theater in the 1920s

··

CARMEN GITRE

It was March 1920 in Cairo's roaring theater district, the Azbakiyya. At the Casino de Paris, the play *al-'Ashara al-Tayyiba* (The Ten of Diamonds) premiered.[1] Performed by Najib al-Rihani's beloved comedic theater troupe and "Egyptianized" by respected theater critic Muhammad Taymur, the four-act play was set in the Mamluk era of Egyptian history, a period when slave-soldiers governed the region. In a story reminiscent of the *Arabian Nights*, an insatiable Mamluk overlord marries women from local villages and sentences them to death when he tires of their company. His servant, Huzunbul, locates the women for him, but unwilling to carry out their death sentences, he secretly drugs and hides the condemned women instead of killing them. When the Mamluk determines his next victim to be the daughter of the local ruling pasha, Huzunbul can take no more. At a climactic moment, he humiliates the Mamluk overlord by revealing his secret and presenting the women he has protected to the local pasha. Huzunbul's refusal to murder the women and his unveiling of the Mamluk's cruelty ultimately leads to the overlord's downfall. Freed from his oppression and depredations, the country is restored to its rightful ruler, an Egyptian peasant prince.[2]

The story was not all death and humiliation, however. After all, this was a comedy or, as advertised, an "opera-comique."[3] So, for example, instead of a straight response when the pasha inquires about news from the Ministry of Justice, the chief clerk replies as follows:

> There is a wealth of news concerning your ministry, O Highness. To begin with, I personally have been stricken by spasms in my large intestine, the deputy-minister suffers from internal pains of the brain, the secretary suffers from an inflammation of the heart, while the chief has been ailing with an abscess in the liver.
> Pasha: But what about the ministry? Chief Clerk: Stricken by an internal disorder of all its parts.

He continues: There is much news concerning the ministry, O Highness. Firstly, a report has been issued to the effect that all accused persons must suffer imprisonment without trial. Secondly, it has been decided that the term "lawyer" be wiped out of legal terminology. Thirdly, a law has been passed that no judge is eligible for appointment unless he be deaf, dumb, and blind.[4]

Al-'Ashara al-Tayyiba was Mamluk oppression served up with a dose of wordplay and a touch of absurd wit. Inspired by a French folk tale–turned-play called *Barbe Bleu* (Bluebeard), the noted writer, poet, and critic Muhammad Taymur transformed the plot and details to fit an Egyptian context.[5] It was his attempt to put into practice what he had been writing about for years: the need to elevate comedy—indeed, all theater—by cultivating the audience's minds (*'aql*) rather than lazily appealing to their emotions and base instincts. Taymur worried that if audiences did not have the discernment and taste to demand "artistic" works, and troupes merely responded to audience desires, it would be impossible to improve the quality of theater. After all, troupes were commercially inclined to perform what pleased audiences, regardless of artistic value.[6] A contemporary put a fine point on it: "commercial theaters," he wrote, "exploit people's sensual desires by transforming theatres into places resembling brothels."[7] Changes, Taymur felt, had to be made.

Al-'Ashara al-Tayyiba had the makings of a successful show. The comedy featured catchy songs and popular performers of the era. In fact, its production team involved a veritable who's who of artists and performers. The celebrated Sayyid Darwish composed the play's music, the talented lyricist Badi' Khayri wrote the songs, and 'Aziz 'Id, a popular actor and director, produced the play. It debuted in the Azbakiyya district in the center of downtown Cairo, an area bustling with cafes, theaters, and cabarets where popular vaudeville shows and melodramas were performed nightly.[8] But something went terribly wrong. Instead of heaping on praise and adulation, critics pounded the show, and riots occurred during performances.[9] It closed after just one month, and Rihani, who lost his financial investment in the play, faced death threats for producing it. What caused such mayhem?

To better understand the politics of theater, its study must be grounded in its specific context, and the specific case of *Al-'Ashara al-Tayyiba*'s production is illuminating. In the late nineteenth-century writings of cultural and political leaders in Egypt, we see the influence of the *nahda*, a cultural movement that spanned roughly from the mid-nineteenth century through World War II, corresponding chronologically with "the region's integration into the imperial system and the capitalist world market, when new social and political movements, literacies, technologies, cultural forms and economic institutions and practices transformed the region."[10] But the *nahda* was as much a discourse as a time period. It promulgated a narrative of progress that located its origins in Europe and would end "in utopias of sovereignty (the authentic or liberal self, the nation-state, the *umma*).[11] In other words, the *nahda* focused on a developmental teleology that would unfold in the Arab world, leading to sovereignty and some sort of authenticity. As Samah Selim writes, "in turn-of-the-century Egypt, reformist intellectuals conceived of modern narrative in political and didactic terms. By educating and improving the collective character of the Egyptians, it would prepare them for citizenship in the modern nation-state." Simultaneously, the same intellectuals, who generally "shared a highly ambivalent attitude toward the Egyptian masses, urban and rural—understood popular narrativity as the antithesis of modern narrative."[12] For them, old forms of storytelling reinforced things like sloth, vice, superstition, and gullibility. "Artistic" theater could help usher in an era of progress, government, and authenticity, whereas "unartistic" (*la fanni*), or popular, theater simply diverted audiences without any greater benefit or function and signaled the poor state of Egyptian culture.

Elites developed these ideas in a context of anxiety over changing norms and identities. In the late nineteenth century, Egyptian elites included *a'yan* (rural, land-owning, Egyptian-born notables) and *dhawat* (aristocracy, persons of high state rank, and urban notables). They were marked by wealth, descent, and lifestyle, including the cultivation of "good taste" and visibility. Before the British occupation, elites considered their modernity to be tied up in global developments and considered themselves "equal players on a global stage."[13] Though *dhawat* and *a'yan* differed in terms of "ethnicity, wealth, seniority of public office, and residence (urban versus rural)" throughout much of the nineteenth century, by the last quarter "the lines between *dhawat* and *a'yan* blurred as Turks and rural notables intermarried, and *a'yan*—enriched by increased involvement in global markets and cotton cultivation—moved to cities to pursue political interests, enjoy urban life, and offer their children a better education."[14] People like Taymur were referred to as *ibn al-dhawat*, the offspring of this mix of *a'yan* and *dhawat*, a new Turko-Egyptian upper class.

Urbanization presented new challenges. In the 1870s and 1880s, nightlife in places such as Azbakiyya served up alcohol, gambling, and prostitution. According to contemporaries, "these activities destroyed men's rationality and made them lose their control over emotions."[15] In response to the argument by British colonial powers that such weaknesses within the Egyptian population justified occupation, Egyptian elites pointed out that the British occupation created, or at least exacerbated, these problems. Thus, control over emotion and rationality had to be addressed if the country was to "progress." When theater was unrestrained and driven by audiences' desires, the consequences were cheap entertainment and a rowdy populace, the opposite of a disciplined and rational citizenry and a threat to the social order that elites hoped to maintain.

While many of these concerns focused on the effects of theater on men, concerns about emotional control, bad taste, and the seductions of vice necessarily implicated the changing position of women—in society, on stage, and in audiences—as well. In the late nineteenth century, concerns over female segregation, education, marriage, and divorce burst into public debate. The rise of a new professional class, rapid urbanization, changing demographic distribution, British occupation, and a host of other factors meant tremendous social flux that found expression in the "woman question." As Marilyn Booth explains, the status of women "was a symbolically powerful articulation of issues of regeneration and community identity, of the localization of European cultures, of individual and national economic empowerment"[16] At once, women were symbols of both a modern and an authentic Egypt. How might they be both? The potential contradictions inherent in such a characterization reached far beyond debates within elite society to affect the lives of urban, middle-class, working, and rural women. For women across class and space, the landscapes of desire and opportunity were changing.

Taking theater, comedy, and popular culture seriously allows a fuller, richer understanding of dynamics of power—the ways it works, contradicts, dissolves, bullies, violates, and succumbs to other forces in society. The proscenium stage was a uniquely important forum for interpellating a particular kind of modern Egyptian—a class-driven conception of a male, rational, disciplined, educated, moral individual who came together with others like him to create a unified, cohesive society. Whereas women were symbols of the modern nation, their brothers, husbands, fathers, and sons labored to make Egypt modern. For both men and women, spending one's leisure time in the theater was considered edifying because plays could teach moral lessons and love of country.

Taymur sought to teach through drama and humor. Blaming popular comedians for cheapening Egyptian taste through silly and unedifying entertainments, he hoped to elevate comedy to serve as an appealing conduit to illuminate individual and societal flaws and demonstrate the imperative to fix them. Leisure could be simultaneously a source of enjoyment and refinement. And by using an elevated form of humor, Taymur hoped to appeal to audiences' higher capacities of beauty, morality, and reason.

Taymur's humor was different from the provocative and physical slapstick of popular revues and vaudeville favored by Cairene audiences of the time. Indeed, two of the most popular comedy troupes were those of Najib al-Rihani and 'Ali al-Kassar. Their audiences were a mix of the elite, middle classes, and the greater general ('amma) populace, who all enjoyed entertainment at the Egyptianna and the Majestique, Rihani's and Kassar's theaters, respectively. Their plays did not make sense temporally (particularly in terms of cause and effect) or homogenize representations of an ideal modern Egyptian. But their revues and vaudeville united people in laughter, empathy, and mockery, drawing from old, familiar forms and providing audiences an escape from the rules and restrictions of life. Their comedy was unifying and potent, as their characters tricked and defied abusive authority, mocked those in power, promoted patriotic, anti-imperialist sentiments, and delivered their own "alternative moral and ethical vision of the promise of the Egyptian nation."[17]

The cabarets and music halls of the 1910s and 1920s offered other diversions. There, predominantly male audiences were in thrall to female performers who danced and sang about topics ranging from love and material pleasure to abusive spouses and hypocritical religious men.[18] These working women did not fit the ideal of mothers of the nation, and the devotion some female performers garnered frightened those who saw them as seducers posing a threat to an ordered society.[19]

If, as Nicholas Holm claims, humor can be interpreted "as one of the major aesthetic nexuses where the distribution of the nonsensical is expressed, negotiated and fought over," then comedy was not simply a sideshow but rather was and is bound up with systems of power.[20] It was itself a domain of political contestation. What might the consequences be of poking fun and provoking laughter at the issues, ideas, and social norms that those in power considered sober matters? To navigate this domain, playwrights and anyone involved in theater production had to control the message. Though Taymur did not explicitly claim to have a political agenda, his narrative of what an independent Egypt should look like in its cultural and aesthetic sensibilities cast elites as Egypt's indisputable arbiters.

Nation, class, gender, and humor intertwined in complex ways in the immediate aftermath of the British occupation. I argue that Taymur and other cultural elites considered the theater a forum for cultivating a particular kind of Egyptian society, one that was modern but also upheld hierarchies of power with male elites at the top. Theater was one component of a larger, internal civilizing mission meant to raise and educate those members of society considered in need of edification—namely, the rising professional class, urban workers, and women. Taymur's concern with the stage and its function in Egyptian society was to use it as a mirror, a place to cultivate the audience's good taste and to heighten the aesthetic quality of production so that the whole of Egyptian society might benefit and bear the fruits of this unique leisure space. Like the European civilizing missions of the previous century, Egypt's political and intellectual elites sought to educate and uplift, but would not go so far as to challenge social hierarchies that kept *ibn al-dhawat* as powerbrokers despite the rise of a new professional class of effendis and an increasing number of women who sought greater access to the public sphere.[21]

Nonetheless, Taymur's dissemination of the message did not mean that audiences accepted it as intended. Instead of responding positively to *al-'Ashara al-Tayyiba*, audiences and critics ignored the play's message about resisting oppression and objected to what they saw as significant problems. Many Egyptian theatergoers were deeply offended by the kissing and affection they witnessed on stage, which they considered too vivid, threatening standards of decency. They also detested the humiliating representation of their ancestors. Meanwhile, many cultural critics, Taymur's peers, complained that portraying Mamluks as depraved and brutal made British imperialists, from whom Egyptians were actively trying to free themselves, appear rather benign by comparison, thereby weakening Egyptians' justification for political independence.

"Both Entertainment and Education"

Ahmad Kamal al-Hilli's review of *al-'Ashara al-Tayyiba* appeared in the daily journal *al-Ahram* on 10 April 1920. He had been reluctant to see the play due to its overwhelmingly bad reviews, but a friend convinced him to attend. What he experienced was quite different from the play described in the reviews. In fact, he started to think that perhaps one of *al-Ahram*'s chief critics was determined to make the play look bad. As he saw it, the play effectively "describes the total oppression of the psyche and the indiscretions taking place with beautiful women in luxurious palaces," not merely to titillate but to teach a lesson. "Anyone who sees it benefits from the fruit of the delicate young mind [that created it]," he effused. The music, instruments, and costuming were admirable and the actors masterful, "as if each actor was born to play their role." He conceded that the play likely was more meaningful for literary audiences than the general public, who experienced it as mere entertainment. Overall, however, it was "both entertainment and education."[22]

In the context of political upheaval and social dislocation after World War I, messages about unity, modernity, and nationalism spread via cultural arbiters, a mix of traditional elites and a rising professional class of effendis, who sought to educate the broader populace on how to be modern Egyptians. Taymur was one of them. A dramatist and journalist born in Cairo to a well-positioned literary family of Kurdish-Circassian origin, Taymur pushed for an Egyptian realist theater to help cultivate modern sensibilities and identity. From a very young age, he learned and recited poetry, and by age ten he was writing his own poems, articles, and plays that he performed at home. Perhaps this was unsurprising as his father, Ahmad Taymur Pasha, was a renowned Arabic scholar, and his aunt, ʿA'isha al-Taymuriyya, was a famous poet and novelist and one of the earliest women in modern Arabic literature.[23] His younger brother, Mahmud, would become a leading novelist and dramatist in the Arab world.[24]

As a young man, in 1911, Taymur traveled to Berlin to study medicine for a short time before changing plans and moving to France to study law. Much of his time, however, he spent reading Guy de Maupassant and Émile Zola, and he reportedly attended the theater almost every night.[25] His three years in Paris were formative, shaping his thoughts on freedom, democracy, equality, education, and criticism and inspiring him to re-evaluate Egyptian culture with new eyes.[26] Taymur was visiting Egypt when World War I broke out, and, unable to return to France, he turned to playwriting and acting, wrote poems for the reformist journal *al-Sufur* (The Unveiling), and published theater criticism in the journal *al-Manbar* (The Tribune). He also wrote short stories under a pseudonym. He played the lead in Ibrahim Ramzi's play ʿIza Bint al-Khalifa ('Iza, the Daughter of the Caliph) and worked in Sultan Kamil's palace until a new sultan, Fu'ad I, replaced him.

Taymur married his cousin, Rashida Rashid, in 1918, the same year the Rushdi acting troupe performed Taymur's first play, *al-ʿUsfur fi al-Qafas* (The Bird in the Cage). The story follows a young man born of a well-to-do family who shuns the restrictions of his privileged life to marry a nurse and live a life of poverty and freedom.[27] It was a direct critique of the strict parenting in elite families that Taymur considered cruel and stifling. The miserly, wealthy father, al-ʿUsfur, spent money to impress others but not feed or clothe his family. His greedy immorality sent his son into the arms of their Syrian maid, a clear transgression of social boundaries.[28] Though he originally wrote the play in formal Arabic, Taymur made the language colloquial so it was more realistic and accessible. It was an unusual decision at the time, as colloquial was typically associated with comedy rather than drama, which was believed to demand the gravitas of formal Arabic. Though it debuted to some success, it quickly lost popularity. His brother blamed "new actors" who "devalued and degraded the play," "the negligence and ignorance of the managers, and the tendency of the Egyptian public" toward cheaper entertainments.[29] Disappointed with the commercial failure of his attempt to create quality theater in a world dominated by cheap revues, farces, and melodramas, Taymur published a series of critical articles before turning to playwriting again.[30] Some of the comedians he criticized by name were at the height of their glory, including al-Kassar and al-Rihani. Al-Kassar played a recurring character named 'Uthman al-Basit, who described himself as "half-Nubian, half-Sudanese, and all Egyptian."[31] Rihani had his own recurring character, a foolish but witty street-smart, womanizing fellow named Kishkish Bey.

Hoping to draw an audience with a more humorous work that demonstrated how comedy might be successful without the use of popular comedies' outrageous devices, Taymur wrote the play *'Abd al-Sattar Effendi*, again in colloquial Arabic. The social comedy centered on the life and problems of a middle-class Egyptian family dominated by a loud, greedy wife and spoiled son.[32] This play, too, was unsuccessful in attracting crowds. Literary critic M. M. Badawi explained that it failed precisely "because of the absence of singing and sexual titillation."[33]

Dejected, Taymur turned away from playwriting again to edit the journal *al-Sufur*.[34] During this period Taymur co-founded a literary circle with Ahmad Khayri al-Sa'id that would come to be known as the Modern School (al-Madrasa al-Haditha).[35] The group promoted the development of an Egyptian artistic theater that would replace foreign adaptations with locally relevant themes and issues. This emphasis on topical literature was known as *adab qawmi*, a literary movement that championed the Egyptianization of literature and *al-waqi'iyya al-misriyya*, or Egyptian realism.

The "realist movement" became especially important in Egyptian theater between 1916 and 1923, when the literary sections of journals, including *al-Manbar*, *al-Sufur*, and *al-Tamthil* (Acting), called for literature to better express and reflect life.[36] These concerns were not new. From the nineteenth century, intellectuals feared that fiction peddled fantasies contributing to "backwardness" in society and might have harmful moral effects on "impressionable youth." By the early twentieth century, reformist intellectuals framed their concerns in political and didactic terms. For them, it was imperative to educate the broad population to prepare them for citizenship in the modern nation-state. Characterizing popular storytelling of epics and folk tales and the superstitions they incorporated as the "antithesis of modern narrative," they critiqued "the former as both a cause and a symptom of the corrupt state of the masses."[37]

The concerns intellectuals raised about the popular novel might just as well encapsulate the critique of comic theater. Comedy, in particular, borrowed old, recurring stock characters and themes even as it incorporated elements of European theater production. It was the mixing of European adaptations, contemporary themes, and older performative practices, tropes, and character types that made modern Arabic theater. Popular literature and comic theater were both faulted for their hyperbolic characters who had little to no interiority, excessive drama and titillation, vulgar language, and use of nonsensical, nonlinear time. Proponents of a national literature emphasized the need for the setting, characters, and stories to be truly Egyptian and for time to be represented as progressive and teleological.[38] Such concerns dovetailed with assumptions about what it meant to be modern: autonomous and rational, self-liberated from tradition and superstition, and in control of one's emotions.[39]

Taymur classified good, realistic theater as "artistic" theater, and al-Hilli's review of *al-'Ashara al-Tayyiba* echoed nearly point-by-point what Taymur had delineated were the essential components of "artistic" theater in Egypt. The playwright had a duty to use theater to educate (*tarbiyya*) while entertaining his audience—he was to create a work of *adab* (literature) that shaped a people of *adab* (decency). There were five principles of artful performance, Taymur argued. Plays needed to feature complex, developed characters who reflected local Egyptian color instead of the superficial characterizations on most comedic stages.[40] Accurate portrayals of local dress, music, ritual, and other traditions mattered, and plays needed to maintain the audience's interest. A performance might, for example, have characters speak in the relatable colloquial Arabic instead of the formal *fusha* (the descendent of classical Arabic).[41] Furthermore, the playwright should follow his natural bent, whether it is comedy or drama, as should actors and singers who, he lamented, sometimes take roles unsuited to their nature or physical appearance.[42] "Let us remember," he warned, "that freedom does not allow people to knock on the door of chaos."[43] Overall, Taymur argued, "We should . . . produce for the public plays which present current issues in order that it may derive useful lessons from them."[44]

By 1920, Taymur decided to involve himself with the very people he had criticized, in hopes of guiding them toward a new type of theater. In his brother's telling, Taymur "lowered himself" to Rihani's level to engage in comic theater with the aim of elevating it.[45] His brother found this admirable, and he claimed that Rihani learned something from Taymur in creating *al-'Ashara al-Tayyiba*.[46] Curiously, Rihani's memoirs say nothing of Taymur's role in the play.[47]

Historian Eve Troutt Powell describes Taymur as someone grappling with a complex identity who looked back at France "with a mournful nostalgia."[48] In Egypt, he "looked to fill the cultural gaps he experienced in what had once been the familiar setting of Cairo."[49] To his mind, this was not a political project but an aesthetic and social one that was heavily shaped by his class background and the access he had to the wider world. Taymur emphasized the unique contribution that Egyptians could make to the arts. Indeed, he saw Egyptians' experiences as essential in forging a uniquely Egyptian theater. Although aesthetic beauty was universal, it was locally rooted.

Yet Taymur's focus on aesthetics without acknowledgment of the current political climate posed a considerable problem. Playwright and critic Ibrahim Ramzi made this clear in his negative review of *al-'Ashara al-Tayyiba*. As someone who subscribed to many of the same ideals about quality plays that Taymur did, he was disappointed that he could not write a favorable review of a play that was "created by a graduate of the [School of] Fine Arts" because he could not ignore an overwhelming problem.[50] Taymur presented the Mamluks in a terrible light.[51] This issue superseded all else, as Ramzi largely ignored the quality of acting and writing to hone in on what he saw as a grave misrepresentation of Egypt's past. He acknowledged that the characters were well developed and that the language painstakingly depicted the dialects of Egyptian peasants, urban Cairenes, and Mamluks. But critiquing the former Mamluk leaders of Egypt, particularly in the fraught political moment of the postwar period, went too far. "Look at Europe at the same time," he urged. "Was there any justice or mercy there? After all, why did the French Revolution happen? . . . Turks were much better than their equals in Europe."[52] Why, Ramzi wondered, would Taymur castigate the Mamluks when he was of Turkish ancestry himself? Ramzi was furious at the gift the play handed to the British, who in early 1920 remained in Egypt, resisting nationalists' attempts to negotiate independence. Consider, he suggested, "how our enemies benefit? This is a lie for the British to use against us."[53]

Taymur may have been disconnected from political dynamics, but his concerns were very much about power and maintaining the parameters of an ordered society in a period of "transition from a colonial, late Ottoman community dominated by light-skinned landowners of Turkish and Caucasian ancestry to a postcolonial, indigenous Egyptian nationalism."[54] In his plays, all was well when elites properly fulfilled their roles at the top of the hierarchy. Household hierarchies mirrored those in broader society, and male heads were to lead with strength and generosity. When hierarchies were disrupted, order and boundaries between classes and people collapsed and individuals more easily succumbed to the seductions of drugs, alcohol, and women. Undoubtedly, beneath the challenging questions he put to his audience about changing social morals, Taymur's underlying question was "which class of Egyptians would lead Egypt into modernity"?[55]

The question of leadership was pressing in the aftermath of the British occupation and Ottoman collapse after World War I. In 1919, Egyptian protests peaked as men and women of diverse classes and faiths flooded the streets to call for independence from the British. As historian John Chalcraft explains, "the clubs, learned societies, charities, and leagues of the pre-1914 reformers were replaced with parties, unions, syndicates and mass societies. These were new forms of mass mobilization" uniting highly diverse constituencies in the face of a shared enemy.[56] Those ties persisted only so long as the shared enemy remained. Differences between constituencies became more evident in the aftermath of 1919 as the process of developing a new state system and national politics led to "contentious mobilization"—that is, debates within and between groups. The leadership that emerged was the one that told the story of 1919 and independence, a story that diminished or altogether wrote out differences to create an image of an ethnically and culturally homogenous society that erased Egypt's historically polyglot composition.[57]

Popular theater promoted this idea of unity, but without erasing difference. In the Rihani troupe's performance of the comic play *Diqqat al-Mu'allim*, for example, a chorus cheerfully concludes the show singing, "We vow, Muslims, Christians, and Jews will not separate!"[58] Calling on Egyptians to unite as one people did not require that they relinquish their individual identities. Indeed, the scope of theatrical experiences Cairenes might enjoy catered to an array of Egyptians' experiences, humor, knowledge, and history. The incorporation of slapstick and physical humor drew from a long and vast history of street theater in the Arab world. A recurring theme anchored nationalism and identity in the dignity and authenticity of the *ibn/bint al-balad* and not in Egypt's non-sensical elites. The message was clear: though the arrogant *ibn al-dhawat* led Egypt politically, it was *ibn* or *bint al-balad*, capacious terms for those considered to be the "true" sons and daughters of Egypt, who were the most authentic Egyptians. Ironically, the popular comedians whom Taymur accused of creating cheap, undignified, "unartistic" theater successfully created their own version of the authentic Egyptian theater that he yearned for.[59]

ENDANGERING DECENCY

The anticolonial uprising in Egypt in 1919 was not the culmination of social flux and Egyptian struggles for independence, freedom, and justice, but rather their beginning. Following 1919, demands for social change increased, and the theater became a space to debate, mirror, and disseminate some of those conflicting depictions of authentic heritage and modern identities. The dynamic period created unique contradictions for women. In the lifetime of 'A'isha Taymur, Taymur's aunt, elite society was multilingual, and elite women were often wives, mothers, and managers of large households.[60] By the late nineteenth century, however, census figures and court registers document decreasing polygamy rates, increasing marriage age for men and women, and a decrease in joint households. A new family ideology celebrated the conjugal family as the foundation of modern society. Similar trends appear to have cut across class and the rural–urban divide, albeit at different rates.[61] Although emancipation of women was considered a measure of the nation's modernity, the notion of woman as a "signifier of (a threatened) collective identity" persisted.[62] Intellectuals argued that a stable family was a primary site for educated mothers to raise patriotic subjects. Considering women "mothers of the nation" turned them into symbols of authenticity and unified identity, limiting the parameters of the freedoms women sought.[63] At the same time, women's political involvement in the 1919 uprising and the Egyptian Feminist Union in 1923, increased opportunities for higher education, and urbanization and the anonymity it allowed all contributed to the rise of the "new woman," with her "masculine" fashion choices and liberated style.[64] Historian Juan Cole has concluded that changes in women's lives did not apply evenly across class and region. Whereas elites might be willing to negotiate some of the women's petitions, "for the men of the new lower middle class, even . . . limited women's emancipation threatened to increase competition for scarce professional positions, to deny them a traditional source of status as guardians of family honor, and to impose upon them values associated with their European competitors and oppressors."[65]

As women entered the public sphere for work and pleasure, they increasingly participated in the theatrical world as actors and audience members. In the nineteenth century, female actors had been few, mostly from the Levant and primarily Jewish and Christian. Theater audiences, as well, were predominantly male. In the 1870s, women who attended shows were in the minority and usually sat in segregated spaces with some sort of netting in front of them to veil their identities, mimicking the "seclusion" of more elite households. By the 1920s, however, women were more prominent on stage and in audiences. In the words of musicians Billy Brooks and George Duncan, "now you cannot find half a dozen theatres in Egypt with harem boxes or anything stretched across boxes. Women now go to all places of amusement unattended and mingle with the men."[66]

Increasingly, theaters featured women-only matinees for those "who either did not want to watch a play with men in the audience or were worried about their reputation being harmed if they were seen at such a performance."[67] The famed comic actress and singer Badi'a Masabni was the first to offer this option in her cabaret. An anonymous woman writer for *al-Masrah* (Theater) reported on her experience: "Finally, there was a chance to watch a cabaret show in a roomful of women without a man in sight." She enjoyed the singing, dancing, and outfits, and only complained that the seating "physically enshrined a dangerously 'aristocratic' ethos." Noting a cordoned off area reserved for important women, she commented that "that kind of discrimination and social segregation did not seem right to her."[68]

Generally, however, theaters were spaces for the mixing of classes, religions, and nationalities. Dance halls and cabarets, in particular, boasted a primarily male clientele. Secret police records name military officers and upper-class patrons with pasha and bey as titles who attended these shows alongside effendis, village *'umda*s, and British military stationed in Cairo.[69] The diverse audiences that actors, singers, composers, and writers reached were not limited to those who paid for tickets to see them. They included people beyond the walls of the theater who heard recordings of plays and enjoyed mimics who imitated the leading actors and singers of the day.[70]

Dance halls and cabarets were certainly not part of Taymur's vision for artistic theater. Taymur elaborated in his writings on the genres he considered "unartistic." Melodrama and Grand Guignol were two categories that existed solely to shock and disturb, with no analysis of individuals or connection to reality.[71] The comic but more morally threatening equivalent of melodrama for Taymur was vaudeville. Aside from unbelievable stories, its authors filled each "play with lewd jokes, embarrassing situations, and surprises one after another to affect audiences."[72] In Taymur's reading, they involved neither character analysis nor local color, and they threatened behavior and decency.[73] Scenes that involved confrontations between a cheating character's girlfriend and wife or between a father and his son's girlfriend were not realistic or believable (*ghayr ma'qula*), but they made people laugh. Audiences, he argued, could not learn anything useful from the poor behavior exhibited on stage. Revues were no better, consisting "of a few songs sung on the stage, accompanied by scenes or sketches unrelated to the songs, with an admixture of crude jokes and immoral situations."[74] The obscene and shameful scenarios presented onstage were, he contended, "dangerous to decency and to morals, ethics, manners (*akhlaq*)."[75]

Yet some thought it was Taymur's work that endangered decency. On 19 March 1920, a reviewer in *al-Ahram* detailed his experience going to see *al-'Ashara al-Tayyiba* with a friend.[76] He began with the end. "The writers of the play," he wrote, "let down the people who were expecting . . . new ideas, good advice, and some wisdom." The beginning of the play did not bode well. "Two lovers appeared on stage and exchanged expressions of love. What is worse, one kissed her beloved on the cheek, and he held her close to his body in front of all the spectators, [including] the ladies and misses who blushed with modesty and embarrassment. The outrageous act defied respect for the sanctity of their women and girls, so they [men] protested and demanded the play be stopped . . . some cursed at the actors and writers. They were disgusted." The writer turned to a gentleman sitting beside him, ʿAbd al-Rahman Effendi Rushdi, and asked him what he thought of the play from an artistic point of view. Rushdi responded that the audience should wait until the end of the play before they judged it. He then turned and said as much to the rowdy audience: "the author has a point of view, the actor has a point of view, and the spectator has a point of view, but the spectator should not interrupt the playwright's production nor the actor as he performs." Perhaps, he suggested, there was a reason why the lovers kissed that would become apparent during the play. Rushdi's words seemed to have worked for a time. The writer records, "the fiery revolts calmed down, and we awaited what came next." But a subsequent scene stirred the audience again. When the Mamluk overlord arrived in Egypt, his boat docked on the river's shore, and an Egyptian entourage bent down in front of his majesty. He walked across their backs as if they were a bridge, then sat on one of his attendants as if he was a chair. "This agitated the people greatly," the writer reported, and "one of the Europeans said to me, 'if this is what the Turks did to you, then why don't you yield to the rule of the British now? They do not mock you like animals, nor do they whip you like these tyrants did with your fathers before.'" The people in the theater roared and cursed the playwrights. This time, Rushdi effendi concurred with their judgment. "We must bring him [the playwright] back to his senses. Let us calm down and go see something else." "The ending," the writer summed up, "did not make up for the beginning."[77]

The enraged men in the audience were furious at the embarrassment, nonsense, and bad example that *al-ʿAshara al-Tayyiba* foisted on their wives, daughters, and sisters. Taymur's efforts to teach lessons from history by depicting Turks in a negative light were not well received in the fraught political moment in which Egyptians found themselves, and representing the humiliation of their ancestors was too much to bear. For Taymur, however, what appeared on his stage was not a grotesque exaggeration or titillation but a representation of reality. In an article he wrote articulating theater's ideal characteristics, he warned against using irrelevant, absurd, melodramatic, or sexually titillating scenes or characters to lure audiences who "want to waste time." Women, for example, should not appear on stage "half-naked . . . if that is not essential to the story."[78]

However, who determined what was essential to the story was up for debate, as the reviews of *al-ʿAshara al-Tayyiba* made clear. Taymur's critics' responses were nonsensical to him and his brother Mahmud, who defended the play vigorously. The play, according to Mahmud, did not attain the success it deserved.[79] In his estimation, those who spoke ill of his brother's play failed to appreciate the effort and contribution it made to elevating Egyptian theater.[80] Mahmud's praise neatly followed Taymur's five-part prescription for "artistic" theater. For one, he argued, the play represented the

Mamluks realistically with strong local color and lively characters. It was funny but used elevated, appropriate language. Though originally a French play, his brother's skill in Egyptianizing it and making the topic so fitting was laudable.[81] Taymur's aim, according to Mahmud, was to reveal Egypt's current condition, to represent Mamluk oppression, and to demonstrate the consequences of that oppression.[82] He emphasized his brother's idealistic vision and ignored the heart of the issues critics raised, namely the tone-deafness of the play to the political moment and concerns about scandalizing audiences by representing vice and sexuality on stage.

Incorporating "local color" on stage required one to strike a balance between entertaining without overly exciting the audience. If the project was creating a self-disciplined, moral, educated, masculine ideal, there would always be debate about policing the limits of what could be presented on stage and how a didactic moment could be taken the wrong way to teach vice over good behavior. Ideally, the aim was to elevate and educate but stop short of upending the status quo by valorizing "realities" that were not considered admirable. At stake was the question of whose reality might be acknowledged and represented.

Conclusion

A tension permeated Muhammad Taymur's attempt to develop a realistic, artistic Egyptian theater. Taymur worked hard to indigenize plays by avoiding wholesale incorporation of European comedy and drama and, instead, creating complex characters coping with pressing local situations. He sought to create an art form on par with the rest of the world, to make entertainment an enjoyable means for self-improvement and a source of education for both the mind and the heart.

His concerns, however, did not always align with those of his audiences. In critiquing popular comedy for its irrationality, he missed its patriotic role in moving everyday people to celebrate their distinctive, human frailties and contributions to the nation. Audiences may well have enjoyed moral theater, but the range of what they enjoyed was so much broader. Lurid romances, silly songs, and vulgar arguments may not have been the "Egyptian" theater Taymur envisioned, but it may well have been part of the audiences' realities—or escape from reality. To laugh at such things could be a form of catharsis, a relief from the stressors of the day.

In this light, perhaps the failure of al-'Ashara al-Tayyiba is less surprising. The intent behind it was disconnected from many of its audiences' interests and concerns. In grounding his moralizing in the story of an oppressive Mamluk history, Taymur revealed, at most, a disregard for, and at least, a lack of engagement with or comprehension of the stakes of the political moment. Representing vice on the proscenium stage risked offense instead of education. Perhaps most glaringly, in insisting on "elevating" the comedy of beloved actors such as Najib al-Rihani and 'Ali al-Kassar, he and his peers neglected to understand the reason for which they were loved. The "unartistic" theater of Rihani and Kassar unambiguously and unapologetically incorporated patriotic themes and songs throughout their performances. Elevating the essential goodness of the *ibn* and *bint al-balad* was meaningful and empowering to those who witnessed it. While Taymur tried to create identifiable figures whose faults needed correction, Rihani, Kassar, and other popular comedians created identifiable figures who were beloved—not despite, but because of their weaknesses, foibles, surprising insights, self-deprecation, and honest commentary on life. Their troupes livened audiences' spirits with clever wordplay, catchy songs, and a host of characters representing different classes, ethnicities, and religions that mirrored their neighbors and friends. In those theaters, the only nonsense was elites attempting to usurp the claim to authentic Egyptianness of the *ibn* and *bint al-balad*, the true heirs of Egypt, the salt of the earth.

NOTES

1. "Al-'Ashara al-Tayyiba," *al-Ahram*, 19 March 1920, reproduced in Usama Abu Talib, *al-Masrah al-Misri* (Cairo: Dar al-Za'im li-l-Tiba'a al-Haditha, 2002), 334.
2. Nabil Raghib, *Muhammad Taymur* (Cairo: al-Hay'a al-Misriyya al-'Amma li-l-Kitab, 2005), 120–22.
3. Lila Nessim Abou Seif, "Theater of Najib al-Rihani: The Development of Comedy in Modern Egypt" (PhD diss., University of Illinois, 1969), 87.
4. Quoted in ibid., 89.
5. Mahmud Taymur, "Muhammad Taymur Hayatuhu wa-A'maluhu," *Mu'allafat Muhammad Taymur: Wamid al-Ruh*, vol. 1 (Cairo: al-Hay'a al-Misriyya al-'Amma li-l-Kitab, 1971), 39.
6. Muhammad Taymur, "al-Tamthil al-Fanni wa-la-Fanni," *Mu'allafat Muhammad Taymur Hayatuna al-Tamthiliyya*, vol. 2 (Cairo: al-Hay'a al-Misriyya al-'Amma li-l-Kitab, 1973), 96.
7. Quoted in Amr Zakaria Abd Allah, "The Theory of Theatre for Egyptian Nationalists in the First Quarter of the Twentieth Century," *Qaderni di Studi Arabi* 4 (2009): 194.
8. Raphael Cormack, *Midnight in Cairo: The Divas of Egypt's Roaring '20s* (London: W. W. Norton & Company, 2021).
9. Abou Seif, "Theater of Najib al-Rihani," 90; Taymur, "Muhammad Taymur," 38.
10. Sameh Selim, *Popular Fiction, Translation, and the Nahda in Egypt* (Cham, Switzerland: Palgrave McMillan, 2019), 3.
11. Ibid.
12. Ibid., 37–38.
13. Carmen M. K. Gitre, *Acting Egyptian: Theater, Identity, and Political Culture in Cairo, 1869–1930* (Austin: University of Texas Press, 2019), 20.
14. Ibid., 31.
15. Quoted in Joseph Ben Prestel, *Emotional Cities: Debates on Urban Change in Berlin and Cairo, 1860–1910* (New York: Oxford University Press, 2017), 16.
16. Marilyn Booth, *May Her Likes Be Multiplied: Biography and Gender Politics in Egypt* (Berkeley: University of California Press, 2001), xxi.
17. Quoted in Carmen Gitre, "Nonsense and Morality: Interwar Egypt and the Comedy of Najib al-Rihani," *Arab Studies Journal* 28, no. 1 (2020): 12.
18. Gitre, *Acting Egyptian*, 111.
19. Ibid., 112.

20. Nicholas Holm, "The Distribution of the Nonsensical and the Political Aesthetics of Humour," *Transformations* 19 (2011): 1–12.

21. This was not solely a concern of cultural elites. Hoda Yousef describes the writings of religious conservatives who cautioned that in the context of repeated challenges to what they saw as the "natural social order," change must be applied with "caution and conservatism." Hoda A. Yousef, *Composing Egypt: Reading, Writing, and the Emergence of a Modern Nation, 1870–1930* (Stanford, CA: Stanford University Press, 2016), 66.

22. Ahmad Kamil al-Hilli, "al-'Ashara al-Tayyiba," *al-Ahram*, 10 April 1920, reproduced in Abu Talib, *al-Masrah al-Misri*, 347.

23. See Mervat Hatem, *Literature, Gender, and Nation-Building in Nineteenth-Century Egypt: The Life and Works of 'A'isha Taymur* (London: Palgrave Macmillan, 2011). 'A'isha was born in 1840 to a freed Circassian slave mother. Her paternal grandparents were Kurdish and Turkish.

24. M. M. Badawi, *Early Arabic Drama* (Cambridge: Cambridge University Press, 1988), 101.

25. Zaki Tulaymat, "Tamhin," *Mu'allafat*, vol. 2, 17, 20.

26. Taymur, "Muhammad Taymur," 31–32.

27. E. C. M. De Moor, "Muhammed Taymur," in *Encyclopedia of Arabic Literature*, vol. 2, ed. Julie Scott Meisami and Paul Starkey (London: Routledge, 1998), 762–63.

28. Muhammad Taymur, *al-'Usfur fi al-Qafas* (Cairo: Markaz al-Ta'lif wa-l-Tarjama, n.d.).

29. Taymur, "Muhammad Taymur," 35–36.

30. Badawi, *Early Arabic Drama*, 102.

31. Eve M. Troutt Powell, "Burnt-Cork Nationalism: Race and Identity in the Theater of 'Ali al-Kassar," in *Colors of Enchantment: Theater, Dance, Music and the Visual Arts of the Middle East*, ed. Sherifa Zuhur (Cairo: American University in Cairo Press, 2001), 28.

32. Though the father's authority was diminished in a household whose hierarchy collapsed under the weight of individuals not knowing their place, Powell notes that their Black slave, Khalifa, served as "the barometer of morality in this household," maintaining the ideal of the father-centered family that Taymur supported. Eve M. Troutt Powell, *A Different Shade of Colonialism: Egypt, Great Britain, and the Mastery of the Sudan* (Berkeley: University of California Press, 2003), 204.

33. Badawi, *Early Arabic Drama*, 102.

34. In that time, he published the "amusing, as well as instructive series of articles on contemporary Egyptian dramatists in the form of mock trials which take place within the framework of a dream." The panel are Racine, Corneille, Moliere, Goethe, and Edmond Rostand, presided over by Shakespeare. Contemporary writers, including himself, were called to trial.

35. Badawi, *Early Arabic Drama*, 104.

36. Abd Allah, "The Theory of Theatre," 193.

37. Selim, *Popular Fiction*, 37–38.

38. Ibid., 40.

39. Yoav di-Capua, "Nahda: The Arab Project of Enlightenment," in *The Cambridge Companion to Modern Arab Culture*, ed. Dwight F. Reynolds (Cambridge: Cambridge University Press, 2015), 72. See also Wilson Chako Jacob, *Working Out Egypt: Effendi Masculinity and Subject Formation in Colonial Modernity, 1870–1940* (Durham, NC: Duke University Press, 2011); and Prestel, *Emotional Cities*.

40. Taymur, "al-Tamthil al-Fanni," 88.

41. Ibid., 95.

42. Ibid., 89.

43. Ibid., 93.

44. Ibid., 95.

45. Taymur, "Muhammad Taymur," 38.

46. Abou Seif says that Rihani hired Taymur, but Rihani's autobiography fails to mention Taymur's name entirely in recounting his experience performing the play. Najib al-Rihani, *Kish Kish Bey: Mudhakkirat Majhula* (Cairo: Manshurat Battana, 2017), 88–89.

47. Najib al-Rihani, *Mudhakkirat Najib al-Rihani: Za'im al-Masrah al-Fukahi* (Cairo: al-Mutahida li-l-Tiba'a wa-l-Nashr, 2000), 30–31.

48. Powell, *A Different Shade*, 196.

49. Ibid.

50. Ibrahim Ramzi, "Hawla al-Tamthil al-Hizli," *Mu'allafat*, vol. 2, 281.

51. Ibid.

52. Ibid.

53. Ibid., 282. He was not the only one concerned, as seen in the previously discussed *al-Ahram* review.

54. Alex Dika Seggerman, *Modernism on the Nile: Art in Egypt between the Islamic and the Contemporary* (Chapel Hill: University of North Carolina Press, 2019), 139.

55. Powell, *A Different Shade*, 197.

56. John Chalcraft, *Popular Politics in the Making of the Modern Middle East* (Cambridge: Cambridge University Press, 2016), 200.

57. Selim, *Popular Fiction*, 5.

58. Najib Effendi al-Rihani, Badi' Khayri, and Husayn Effendi Shafiq, *Diqqat al-Mu'allim* (Cairo: Maktabat wa-Matba'at al-Wahida al-Wataniyya, 1921).

59. Muhammad Taymur, "al-Rihani," *Mu'allafat*, vol. 2, 152–54.

60. Mervat F. Hatem, "The 1919 Revolution and Nationalist Constructions of the Lives and Works of Pioneering Women Writers," in *Re-Envisioning Egypt, 1919–1952*, ed. Arthur Goldschmidt, Amy J. Johnson, and Barak A. Salmoni (Cairo: American University in Cairo Press, 2005), 398–423, 418.

61. Kenneth M. Cuno, *Modernizing Marriage: Family, Ideology, and Law in Nineteenth- and Early Twentieth-Century Egypt* (Syracuse, NY: Syracuse University Press, 2015), 62–66, 71.

62. Booth, *May Her Likes Be Multiplied*, xxv.

63. For more on this, see Margot Badran, *Feminists, Islam, and Nation: Gender and the Making of Modern Egypt* (Princeton, NJ: Princeton University Press, 1995); Beth Baron, *Egypt as a Woman: Nationalism, Gender, and Politics* (Berkeley: University of California Press, 2005); and Lisa Pollard, *Nurturing the Nation: The Family Politics of Modernizing, Colonizing, and Liberating Egypt* (Berkeley: University of California Press, 2005).

64. Cormack, *Midnight in Cairo*, 119.

65. Juan Cole, "Feminism, Class, and Islam in Turn-of-the-Century Egypt," *International Journal of Middle East Studies* 13, no. 4 (1981): 387–407, 405.

66. *Chicago Defender*, 20 January 1923, 13, reproduced in Cormack, *Midnight in Cairo*, 118.

67. Cormack, *Midnight in Cairo*, 270–71.

68. *Al-Masrah*, 6 December 1926, 13, reproduced in Cormack, *Midnight in Cairo*, 271.

69. Cormack, *Midnight in Cairo*, 43.

70. Ziad Fahmy, *Ordinary Egyptians: Creating the Modern Nation through Popular Culture* (Stanford, CA: Stanford University Press, 2011), 38, 117.

71. Taymur, "al-Tamthil al-Fanni," 93–94.

72. Ibid., 94.
73. Ibid.
74. Badawi, *Early Arabic Drama*, 103.
75. Taymur, "al-Tamthil al-Fanni," 95.
76. "Al-'Ashara al-Tayyiba," *Al-Ahram*, 19 March 1920, reproduced in *al-Masrah al-Misri* (Cairo: Dar al-Za'im li-l-Tiba'a al-Haditha, 2002), 333–34.
77. Ibid.
78. Taymur, "al-Tamthil al-Fanni," 89.
79. Taymur, "Muhammad Taymur," 38.
80. Ibid.
81. Ibid., 39.
82. Ibid.

BIBLIOGRAPHY

Amin, D. *Alfred Farag and Egyptian Theater: The Poetics of Disguise, with Four Short Plays and a Monologue*. Syracuse, NY: Syracuse University Press, 2008.

Badawi, M. M. *Early Arabic Drama*. Cambridge, UK: Cambridge University Press, 1988.

Baron, Beth. *Egypt as a Woman: Nationalism, Gender and Politics*. Berkeley: University of California Press, 2005.

Booth, Marilyn. *May Her Likes Be Multiplied: Biography and Gender Politics in Egypt*. Berkeley: University of California Press, 2001.

Cormack, Raphael. *Midnight in Cairo: The Divas of Egypt's Roaring '20s*. London: W. W. Norton & Company, 2021.

Danielson, Virginia. *The Voice of Egypt: Umm Kulthum, Arabic Song, and Egyptian Society in the Twentieth Century*. Chicago: University of Chicago Press, 2008.

Fahmy, Ziad. *Ordinary Egyptians: Creating the Modern Nation through Popular Culture*. Stanford, CA: Stanford University Press, 2011.

Gitre, Carmen M. K. *Acting Egyptian: Theater, Identity, and Political Culture in Cairo, 1869–1930*. Austin: University of Texas Press, 2019.

Jacob, Wilson Chako. *Working Out Egypt: Effendi Masculinity and Subject Formation in Colonial Modernity, 1870–1940*. Durham, NC: Duke University Press, 2011.

Landau, Jacob. *Studies in the Arab Theater and Cinema*. Philadelphia: University of Pennsylvania Press, 1958.

Litvin, Margaret. *Hamlet's Arab Journey: Shakespeare's Prince and Nasser's Ghost*. Princeton, NJ: Princeton University Press, 2011.

Pahwa, Sonali. *Theaters of Citizenship: Aesthetics and Politics of Avant-Garde Performance in Egypt*. Evanston, IL: Northwestern University Press, 2020.

Powell, Eve Troutt. *A Different Shade of Colonialism: Egypt, Great Britain, and the Mastery of the Sudan*. Berkeley: University of California Press, 2003.

Ryzova, Lucie. *The Age of the Efendiyya: Passages to Modernity in National-Colonial Egypt*. Oxford: Oxford University Press, 2014.

Sadgrove, Philip. *The Egyptian Theatre in the Nineteenth Century: 1799–1882*. Berkshire: Ithaca Press, 2007.

Selim, Sameh. *Popular Fiction, Translation, and the Nahda in Egypt*. Cham, Switzerland: Palgrave Macmillan, 2019.

Taylor, Diana. *The Archive and the Repertoire: Performing Cultural Memory in the Americas.* Durham, NC: Duke University Press, 2003.

Taymur, Muhammad. *Mu'allafat Muhammad Taymur: Wamid al-Ruh,* 2 vols. Cairo: al-Hay'a al-Misriyya al-'Amma li-l-Kitab, 1971–73.

Yousef, Hoda A. *Composing Egypt: Reading, Writing, and the Emergence of a Modern Nation, 1870–1930.* Stanford, CA: Stanford University Press, 2016.

Zuhur, Sherifa, ed. *Colors of Enchantment: Theater, Dance, Music and the Visual Arts of the Middle East.* Cairo: American University in Cairo Press, 2001.

CHAPTER 20

···

HOLLYWOOD ON THE NILE
Cinema and Revolution

···

JOEL GORDON

THE year 1952 marks a political transition in Egypt's history, a coup d'état by a secret organization of self-styled "Free Officers" (al-Dubat al-Ahrar), young nationalists disaffected with a decaying parliamentary order. They interceded, so they asserted, to restore clean politics and hand power to civilian age-mates of like mind. Six months after seizing power, the junta rebranded itself the Revolutionary Command Council, abolished all political parties, and declared a three-year transition period to civilian rule. By 1955, any thoughts of returning to the barracks had been buried. Gamal Abdel Nasser, the Free Officers' leader, had been elected president, the first of three successive single-rule parties had been established, and political opponents had been defeated, and in some instances, jailed. The social revolution that became known as Nasserism entailed national independence, nonalignment, Arab socialism, the nationalization of key industries, universal education, and public funding for the arts.[1]

Nasser ruled formally for sixteen years (1954–70). His successor, Anwar al-Sadat (1970–81), redressed the disastrous defeat of June 1967, regarded by Nasser as *al-naksa* (the setback), in October 1973, then set about to restore a strong private sector through a program of economic liberalization known as *al-infitah* (the opening). Al-Sadat initiated halting steps toward multiparty democracy, ended Egypt's state of war with Israel in 1979, and promoted a civic turn toward public religion. Radical forces, encouraged by his patronage yet disappointed by his peace initiative, assassinated him in October 1981 on the anniversary of his 1973 attack on Israel. Husni Mubarak (1981–2011), al-Sadat's vice president, initially allowed for more open civic discourse, including the certification of independent opposition parties, but ultimately quashed democratic aspirations and, in his later years, oversaw an increasingly draconian state that appeared to be the legal fiefdom of his family. The January 2011 "revolution" upended the Mubarak family, and Egypt experienced its first truly free elections since 1950. In 2013, however, the army, cheered on by many who had stood against the system in 2010–11, deposed

Muhammad Mursi (2012–13) and reinstituted authoritarian rule arguably more oppressive than at any point in modern Egyptian political history.[2]

The praetorian state, rooted in a military–industrial complex initiated under Nasser, though without the forward-looking emphasis on social justice, strains to regain the pride rooted in Egypt's former political and cultural dominance of the region. The year 1952 thus marks a significant embarkation point in Egyptian history. The film industry is one of many aspects of Egyptian cultural history that might be viewed against this backdrop.

HOLLYWOOD ON THE NILE

Egypt has long been the center of film production in the Arabic-speaking world.[3] The first studio was constructed in Alexandria in 1907; by the mid-1920s, the coastal city had become a film hub, funded primarily by foreign capital and supervised by foreign-born artists or members of Egypt's foreign-origin minority communities. What constituted an Egyptian "national" cinema in such a fluid "Levantine" cultural milieu remains a contested question.[4] By the early 1930s, the film moguls began to relocate to Cairo, though several early hits were filmed entirely or partly abroad. Studio Misr, financed by the prominent national capitalist Tal'at Harb, opened in 1935. Fully outfitted with state-of-the-art equipment for filming and editing, it set standards for a local industry that, by the mid-1940s, numbered some twenty-four production companies. Between 1939 and 1944, Egyptian studios produced 106 films per year.[5] It was to Egypt that aspiring actors, actresses, and singers migrated from both east and west, and it was here where they were embraced and, arguably, Egyptianized. Farid al-Atrash, a child of Syrian Druze nobility, whose mother fled with her children to Egypt after World War I, became the great musical leading man of the 1940s and 1950s, while his sister Amal morphed into the indomitable singer Asmahan but died tragically in 1944. In a musical magic carpet tour of the Arab world, Farid changed costumes and professed beguilement by the local beauties, but in the end, he donned the garb of an Egyptian fellah and proclaimed how good it was to be "home." Cairene Arabic, stylized by the first generation of actors in talking pictures, became the lingua franca of Arab cinema, with recognizable dialects for rural, nomadic, and different urban classes. Some actors who settled in Egypt accentuated their foreign enunciation to play a variety of local minority characters.[6]

The industry adopted the studio model that had emerged in the United States, England, India, and elsewhere. Primary and secondary stars played to character, often shooting multiple films at once. Directors took their lead from powerful producers, even as the best developed a signature style. Scriptwriters, including major literary figures, churned out dialogue, while composers added theme and incidental music. Early on, the biggest stars were singers—Umm Kulthum, Layla Murad, Muhammad 'Abd al-Wahhab, Farid al-Atrash, and Asmahan—who, as in Hollywood, acted and sang on-screen. Comic stars—Najib al-Rihani, 'Ali al-Kassar, and Chalom—many of whom got their start in popular theater troupes, also headlined popular productions.[7] Most films featured musical numbers, songs, and/or dance, often in a cabaret or theater setting. The label "Hollywood on the Nile," however apt in many respects, became for most critics a derogatory designation, particularly those who focused on independent and, since the 1960s, Third (or Third World) cinema of "liberation." Until recent decades, even cultural historians ignored the industry, except for a very few who sought those rare films (from their perspective) that dealt directly with politics or social reform and those that appeared to look most like foreign (either Afro-Asian or European) products, even if they made little impact at home or in the wider Arab world.[8]

Censorship, overseen by the Egyptian state with British overlords heavily involved, played an important role in defining—and delimiting—popular cultural expression. In 1947, the government promulgated a stringent code that divided some sixty prohibitions into two broad categories: social mores and state security. The first category included depictions or references to overt sexuality, social and sexual immorality, and anything defaming religion. The second forbade any expressions of nationalist sentiment, social reform, or politics in general. With the monarchy facing a growing call for "social justice," censors outlawed potentially damning depictions of rural or urban poverty and the mobilization of workers or peasants. Class status, even the desire for upward mobility, was a dominant melodramatic theme, so long as it did not cross over censorial boundaries to call for social leveling.[9]

The Egyptian film industry began to boom after World War II, driven by an influx of capital and greater spending power of consumers. Between 1945 and 1952, Egyptian film production jumped to around fifty films per year. Although most films followed convention, venturesome artists began to push at censorial restrictions as the country plunged into a paroxysm of political violence—anticolonial and, eventually, antimonarchical—that set the stage for the Free Officers' coup. An aggressive, socially conscious cinema was germinating. Kamal al-Tilmissani's controversial *al-Suq al-Sawda'* (Black Market, 1945), although heavily redacted by the censors, confronted dislocations of the postwar economy. In *Ibn al-Nil* (Nile Boy, 1951), the second film by Youssef Chahine, a rural migrant to the city is nearly swallowed by urban corruption. *Usta Hasan* (Boss Hasan, 1952), an early film by Salah Abu Sayf, depicted stark economic differences between working-class and elite neighborhoods and championed honest labor over ill-gotten wealth (Fig. 20.1). Ahmad Badrakhan, a major director, filmed *Mustafa Kamil* (1951), a biopic of the early nationalist firebrand, but it remained closeted until after the Free Officers' coup.[10]

REVOLUTIONARY MELODRAMA

With the onset of the Free Officers' rule, censorship shifted to a new Ministry of National Guidance, and many barriers to depicting social ills and promoting social reform vanished almost overnight. The cinema of the Nasser era was the product of a military coup d'état turned revolution that initiated a new social ethos at home and

FIG. 20.1 Newsprint film advertisement for *Usta Hassan* (1952). Author's collection.

promoted decolonization and national liberation struggles throughout the "Third World." This emergent revolutionary ethos allowed for, in fact sparked, filmmakers (and other creative artists) to engage issues that had been taboo under a British-dominated constitutional monarchy; the most creative of them produced a stunning new synthesis of commercial films with a strong social grounding. This new-found artistic freedom coincided with the emergence of a new generation of directors, actors, scenarists, lyricists, and composers who came to define what is still recalled as a golden age of Egyptian and, by extension, Arab cinema.

I have designated this synthesis "revolutionary melodrama" as a way of addressing those critics, referred to above, who dismissed the Egyptian film industry as mere entertainment, lacking political or activist social impact and, worst of all, failing to produce meaningful art or artists. Instead, the discourse of films across the board—social drama, romance, comedy, and, of course, musicals—began to shift precipitately by the mid-1950s as the self-proclaimed revolutionary regime consolidated its power, put in place a new constitution, and increasingly turned its gaze outward, toward Nasser's "three circles": Arab, African, and Islamic.[11]

Several dramatic shifts can be noted from the earliest days of the Free Officers' rule. Romance became more clearly identified with toppling class barriers. Prerevolutionary films had dangled the prospect but often relied upon plot contrivances to skirt dangerous turf: the peasant girl in love with the pasha's son turns out to be an aristocratic foundling (there are important exceptions, but often the lower-class lover was a female in love with an upper-class male). Suddenly, the lower-class lover, often now a male—a phone repairman as played by actor/director Anwar Wagdi in the comic musical romance *Bint al-Akabir* (Daughter of Nobility, 1954) (Fig. 20.2), the rural overseer's educated son in the searing Chahine drama *Sira' fi al-Wadi* (Blazing Sun, 1954)—could dream of marriage to the landowner's granddaughter or daughter.[12]

Romance became a rejuvenated genre, fueled by greater social interaction between young men and women farther from their parents' protective gaze. The potboiler novels

FIG. 20.2 Still from *Layla Bint al-Akabir* (1954) starring (l–r) Anwar Wajdi as the phone repairman and Zaki Rustum and Sulayman Najib as the pashas. Author's collection.

and short stories penned by Ihsan 'Abd al-Quddus—with his world of illicit affairs, premarital sexual encounters, female Oedipal fantasies, and beach trysts—made their way to the big screen. In cinematic translation, the explicit often became implicit and the endings were often rewritten to allot punishment and/or restore a degree of normative social mores. But the films still packed their punch, and audiences, expecting a conventional ending, learned to read past them. The "bad girl" characters—victims of parental and social orthodoxy such as Nadya in *La Anam* (Sleepless, Salah Abu Sayf, 1957) and Maddy in *al-Nadara al-Sawda'* (The Dark Glasses, Hussam al-Din Mustafa, 1963), 'Aliya in *Ayna 'Umri* (Where Is My Life, 'Atif Salim, 1956), and elusive first love Samiha in *al-Wisada al-Khaliya* (The Empty Pillow, Salah Abu Sayf, 1957)—were played by the leading starlets of the day: Faten Hamama, Nadya Lutfi, Magda al-Sabahi, and Lubna 'Abd al-'Aziz, respectively. The young, aspiring middle-class men seeking true love were played by new male idols whose stars rose with the new era: Omar Sharif, Shukri Sarhan, Ahmad Mazhar, Rushdi Abaza, and *al-'Andalib al-Asmar* (the Brown Nightingale), 'Abd al-Halim Hafiz (Fig. 20.3).[13]

More directly, social films encompassed key elements of melodrama while boldly staking new claims to social relevance. Fellahin and migrant workers were helpless victims of tyrannical feudal lords in *Sira' fi al-Wadi, al-Haram* (The Sin, Henri Barakat, 1965), and *al-Ard* (Egyptian Earth, Youssef Chahine, 1970). But longshoremen and railroad coolies stood up against corrupt guild bosses in *Sira' fi al-Mina* (Dark

FIG. 20.3 'Abd al-Halim Hafiz with frequent co-star and rumored love interest Su'ad Husni. Author's collection.

Waters, 1956) and *Bab al-Hadid* (Cairo Station, 1958), both directed by Chahine. Crime thrillers, such as Abu Sayf's *al-Wahsh* (The Monster, 1954) and Salim's *Ja'aluni Mujriman* (They Made Me a Criminal, 1954) and *Ihna al-Talamidha* (We the Students, 1959), explored social bases for delinquency. A powerful adaptation of Taha Husayn's *Du'a' al-Karawan* (The Call of the Curlew, Henri Barakat, 1959) condemned honor killing and scandalized viewers by promoting women's revenge. Another adaptation, this time of Latifa al-Zayyat's feminist novel *al-Bab al-Maftuh* (The Open Door, 1963), also directed by Barakat, trumpeted the heroine's cry that a "girl is just like a boy!" The promotion of women as equal partners in the professional labor force was promoted comically in such films as *Li-l-Rijal Faqat* (For Men Only, Mahmud Dhu al-Fiqar, 1964) and *Imrati Mudir 'Amm* (My Wife Is General Director, Fatin 'Abd al-Wahab, 1966). The anticolonial struggle, before and after 1952 (Husayn Sidqi's *Yasqut al-Isti'mar* / Down with Colonialism, 1952; Ahmad Badrakhan's *Allah Ma'ana* / God Is on Our Side, 1955; and 'Izz al-Din Dhu al-Fiqar's *Port Said*, 1956) could now be filmed, and historical dramas (*al-Nasir Salah al-Din* / Saladin the Victorious, Youssef Chahine, 1963) carried clear contemporary allusions. Military officers became heroic protagonists. The epic of the revolution, broadcast annually on 23 July with the advent of television in the early 1960s, was *Rudd Qalbi* (Return My Heart, 'Izz al-Din Dhu al-Fiqar, 1957), the story of a peasant boy who joins the army, helps make a revolution, and returns to the estate to reclaim the heart of the ex-lord's daughter.[14]

Prominent directors, masters of the studio system who put their own imprimatur on their films and who came of age during the early Nasser years, were Salah Abu Sayf (realism), Henri Barakat (social melodrama), and Kamal al-Shaykh (suspense). Each of these three directors made numerous films, all featuring major stars and many of which today are considered masterworks. Alongside them, and equally renowned, were Youssef Chahine and Tawfiq Salih. Chahine would become the most widely known director outside Egypt, celebrated, although often incorrectly, as the most European of Egypt's directors. Salih made only five films in Egypt during the Nasser years (he later made several films in Syria and Iraq), garnering a reputation as a difficult but brilliant director. Shadi 'Abd al-Salam, an art director with Hollywood experience (he worked on the 1963 *Cleopatra*), directed only one full-length feature film. His highly stylized tale of an Egyptian archaeologist working to uncover a smuggling ring in Upper Egypt, *al-Mumya'* (The Mummy, also known in English as Night of Counting the Years), completed in 1968 but released only in 1975, mystified audiences but has been recognized as a treasure. Other directors, purveyors of more classic entertainment, such as Fatin 'Abd al-Wahhab, 'Atif Salim, Hussam al-Din Mustafa, and Hasan al-Imam, deserve credit for producing delightful comedies, crime dramas, romances, and musicals, many of which spoke to changing social mores and reflect the self-confidence of a newly independent, proudly revolutionary state.

Debates persist over state moves to nationalize the film industry in 1957, part of a wider effort to boost state funding for the arts. This process commenced with the foundation of the General Egyptian Organization for Cinema, Radio, and Television, which went through a variety of incarnations (eventually becoming the Egyptian General

Film Organization [EGFO] in 1963), and the Higher Cinema Institute in 1959. As with other industries, nationalization was never total. Private funding for films was allowed, but by 1964, producers had to rent government-owned facilities. The calls were for Egypt to train its own new cohorts of filmmakers, who would look beyond profit margins, take greater artistic risks, challenge genre conventions, and adapt more important literary fiction works while seeking wider Arab audiences and international recognition. The first film institute graduates began work by the late 1960s, but well-established directors continued to dominate the industry. Of all films shot between 1963 and 1971 (153 features), 30% came from the public sector. If the call for fewer but better movies did not exactly resonate, even at the highest levels (two ministers of culture, Tharwat 'Ukasha and 'Abd al-Qadir Hatim, took opposing views), several films that failed to attract large audiences, even though they featured celebrated stars and were shot by major directors, are now considered classics. Even members of the arts community found themselves on opposing sides. Future Nobel Laureate Naguib Mahfouz served as both director of the Cinema Institute and chief censor, while acclaimed director Salah Abu Sayf, as head of the production sector, championed the mission. Leading directors Henri Barakat and Youssef Chahine, as well as the superstar actress Faten Hamama, took their talents to Lebanon for several years to avoid state supervision, rebelling against what future chief censor Durriya Sharaf al-Din would term *sinima al-khawf* (cinema of fear).[15] Those tensions lingered long after the dismantling of the EGFO under Anwar al-Sadat.[16]

The spread of cinemas to provinces and villages accelerated during this period, creating a truly national audience. Plans to create a theater for every ten thousand people did not materialize; by the late 1960s, officials recorded a dip from 350 to 240 working cinemas and bemoaned the deterioration of equipment in older venues. Still, rural and working-class patrons bought affordable tickets and flocked to action films and popular romances (even if they rejected more artistic ventures). Farid Shawqi (Fig. 20.4), *wahsh al-shasha* (the screen monster), multitalented but applauded for his heroics, reigned as *malik al-tirsu* (king of the cheap seats).[17]

The fallout of the stunning defeat of June 1967 at the hands of the Israelis led the regime to loosen censorial restrictions, particularly relating to the treatment of contemporary social and political ills. During this phase, dubbed *al-daw' al-akhdar* (the green light) and lasting from roughly 1967 to 1969, what Sharaf al-Din has called *sinima al-hazima* (cinema of the defeat), numerous films that once might have never been allowed to screen drew wide audiences at cinemas, perhaps a determined move to allow a degree of public criticism, mollify dissenters, and reassert the revolution as a project that might be renewed. Nasser personally approved some of these films and delegated al-Sadat to deliver official acceptance. Arguably, the most important was *Miramar* (Kamal al-Shaykh, 1968), adapted from a Naguib Mahfouz novella in which the lead character, played by the iconic industry pioneer, Yusuf Wahbi, defends the old regime, while others, all residents of an Alexandrian pensione, criticize a public sector that spawns opportunism. Other films depicted sympathetic old-regime figures or symbolically challenged authoritarianism.[18]

FIG. 20.4 Poster for the 1953 Farid Shawqi film *Hamidu*. Author's collection.

A risqué adaptation of an Ihsan 'Abd al-Quddus short story, *Abi Fawq al-Shajara* (Father Is Up a Tree, Husayn Kamal, 1969), the last film of 'Abd al-Halim Hafiz, played at theaters for a year, drawing repeat viewers endeavoring to count the reputed hundred kisses between the star and his two female leads, the prudish girl-friend, reticent to spend time alone with him during a summer beach holiday, and the prostitute with whom he takes up. The blockbuster captured Egypt's swinging 1960s.[19] Yet for many, the father's drink-induced descent into adultery while searching the bars for his wayward son represented the leader's shaky stewardship of the nation.[20]

Nasser died—a sudden and unexpected event for a public that had been shielded from his precarious health—in September 1970. He was succeeded by al-Sadat, whom he had appointed vice president shortly before his death. Al-Sadat fooled the leading members of the inner circle of the Arab Socialist Union, the single ruling party, who, envisioning him as their puppet, approved his constitutional ascendancy. In May 1971, he purged the notorious *marakiz al-quwwa* (centers of power) and asserted his control over the state.

Al-Sadat tolerated a relatively open public criticism of both the Nasser era and Nasser's shortcomings, errors, and abuses. The movie that most encapsulated this critique and the attendant artistic opportunities was *al-Karnak* (Café Karnak, 'Ali Badrakhan, 1976), an adaptation of a powerful novella by Naguib Mahfouz. The story covers the cavalier imprisonment and torture of a group of students, all patriotic Nasserist youth, who are accused of conspiring against the state, first as communists, then as Muslim Brothers. The rape of Zaynab, the lead female character, played by the 1960s screen sweetheart Su'ad Husni, pushed filmic depictions of sexual violence to new heights, shocking audiences. A series of related films that followed, all depicting Nasser-era police brutality, became known as *al-karnakiyya* (Karnak films). Still, *al-Karnak* followed the old dictum of Egyptian cinema—broken only rarely—to provide a happy ending and let audiences leave the theater satisfied that their money had been well spent. The novel ends on a somber note: the chief of state security, personally responsible for the abuse of the young people, himself purged, intrudes upon the students' space in the café that gives the story its name. In the film, however, redemption follows as Zaynab and her broken lover, Isma'il (Nur al-Sharif), are reunited at the front during the 1973 October War.[21]

The Nasser era would, on occasion, be reprised in films, but Nasser-era cinema came to a close as al-Sadat took Egypt in new directions after the war. The cinema of the 1950s and 1960s remains the epitome of Egyptian film production in popular and critical memory, what I have termed "nostalgia in black and white" because only a few films during this era were shot in color.[22] Allusions to this era are frequent in films to this day—titles, stars, and especially songs—most often those by 'Abd al-Halim Hafiz. Such allusions continue to reinforce a nostalgia for an era of postcolonial optimism rooted in national and regional importance and visions of a more equitable, fair society with upward mobility opportunities that do not require clambering over others. And they have reverberated at times throughout Arab cinema at large, long after the Egyptian studios lost their domineering cultural grip on the Arabic-speaking world.

Intermission

In many respects, the films of the 1970s look much like those of the preceding decade. Social dramas and adaptations of major works by Egypt's literary giants continued to define quality cinema, while the majority of films repeated safe genre conventions. The great directors of the Nasser era continued to work, though, with the exception of Youssef Chahine, the best of their work had been completed. The same could be said for the great young stars, male and female, of the 1950s and 1960s, most of whom now transitioned into supporting roles or nonromantic leads. Their places were taken by a new cohort: Mirvat Amin, Najla' Fathi, Husayn Fahmi, Nur al-Sharif, and the new comic king, 'Adil Imam. Al-Sadat's government determined to dismantle the social welfare state and reinvigorate the private sector. In 1973, the state shut down the EGFO. Still, a strong crop of new directors who had studied under the state sector aegis would emerge in the 1980s and help refashion a new social realism. In the interim, the industry flagged.

The primary visual marker of Egyptian cinema of the 1970s is the shift to color. In prior decades, as far back as the late 1940s, color had been used for select spectacles, guaranteed blockbusters. In Egyptian collective memory, the golden age of black and white films was over. Musicals faded away by the end of the 1970s and have resurfaced only sparingly in subsequent years. The last great musical, *Khalli Balak min Zuzu* (Watch Out for Zuzu, Hasan al-Imam, 1972), starring Su'ad Husni as a belly dancer's daughter trying to hide her identity from fellow Cairo University students, explored lingering class barriers and resilient cultural prejudices while nodding comically to the rise of neoconservative piety among the youth.

Two directors exemplify countervailing trends. Youssef Chahine produced his second masterpiece, *al-Ard* (his first was *Bab al-Hadid*), adapted from a popular novel about the last days of feudalism, under the auspices of the EGFO. In succeeding decades, his films became more eccentric and personal. Foreign funding led to local charges that his films were somehow less Egyptian, while foreign critics championed him as the exception to "Hollywood on the Nile." A star outside of Egypt, he received mixed reviews at home. By the mid-1980s, he opened his own theater in downtown Cairo. His *Iskandariyya . . . lay?* (Alexandria . . . Why? 1979), a paean to the cosmopolitan hometown of his childhood, depicts his own aspiration to pursue an acting career.[23] Husayn Kamal, a rising star of public sector artistry, moved in the opposite direction, proclaiming a desire to please audiences, if not critics. He broke through with *Abi Fawq al-Shajara* and then directed a series of films that conveyed social messages but did so in ways that ensured commercial success. *Tharthara Fawq al-Nil* (Chatter on the Nile, 1971), based on a Naguib Mahfouz novella, depicted late-Nasser social malaise as embodied by rampant drinking and drugging by young professionals on a Nile houseboat. *Imbaraturiyyat Mim* (M Empire, 1972) disguised national politics, especially youthful impatience, in light-hearted family drama. And *Ihna Bitu' al-Utubis* (We Are the Bus People, 1980) looked back to Nasser-era empty dreams—and police brutality—albeit in a sardonic, comic mode. Kamal, for many the exemplar of someone who had succumbed to the lure of commercialism, retorted boldly that he preferred filling theater seats to winning critical acclaim.[24]

Egypt's redemptive victory in the 1973 war was chronicled in one major film, *al-Rasasa La Tazal fi Jaybi* (The Bullet Is Still in My Pocket, Hussam al-Din Mustafa, 1974), in which the protagonist, shamed by the 1967 defeat, returns a hero. Youssef Chahine's *al-'Usfur* (The Sparrow, 1972), released a year before the October War, examined the internal decay that produced the *naksa* but without carrying the story beyond Nasser's resignation on 8 June 1967 and the surge of popular support for his retraction. Al-Sadat's agenda to liberalize personal status laws—known as "Jihan's laws" after his wife, who took the lead on them—received a boost from a searing drama, *Uridu Hallan* (I Want a Solution, Sa'id Marzuq, 1975), starring former heartthrobs Faten Hamama and Rushdi Abaza as an estranged couple. The costs of al-Sadat's unchecked economic "open door" became focal points as his popularity faded. The sense of social dislocation was treated most vividly in comic caricature by 'Adil Imam, Egypt's emergent everyman, who in a series of films (Ahmad Fu'ad's *Rajab Fawq Safih Sakhin* / Ragab on a Hot Tin Roof, 1979; Henri Barakat's *Sha'ban Taht al-Sifr* / Sha'ban below Zero, 1980) rose from rags to vulgar riches, only to fall again. Such films have been read as cynical contemporary recasting of the more optimistic films of the mid-twentieth century that played as political violence and social strife escalated during al-Sadat's last years.[25]

The revised 1971 censorship code allowed more forthright depictions of drug and alcohol consumption as long as such activities remained socially deviant. Missing throughout the decade (and well into the decades beyond) was any honest depiction of the social cleavages that increasingly fractured Egyptian society: the growing divide between the rich and the very poor, the rise of religious self-identification and political extremism, and the sectarian violence that characterized al-Sadat's final years. The Muslim Brotherhood, which had produced a new generation of social activists, some hyper-radicalized, others more determinedly working to transform civil society, was treated as a historical artifact at best. Serious strands of religious, social, and political activism remained taboo.

New Social Realism

Shifting national politics allowed for the emergence of socially conscious films that thematically mirrored the Nasser era while opening cinematic artistry. Assuming the presidency in the wake of al-Sadat's assassination and an aborted Islamist insurrection, Husni Mubarak endeavored initially to defuse escalating social unrest by allowing true opposition parties (not "platforms" within the ruling party, as al-Sadat had envisioned) to contest elections and publish their own largely unregulated newspapers. The omnipresent official state narrative dating back to the anticolonial struggle and, especially, the origins of the Nasserist Free Officers' coup d'état crumbled, and a truly multivocal civil society began to take root.

Part of this social discussion included a harsh critique of al-Sadat's liberalization and the disillusion engendered by the false hopes of Egypt's October 1973 victory. Egypt seemed awash in conspicuous wealth, much of it ill-gotten—its urban streets choked by an explosion of private automobiles competing for space with a decrepit and crowded public transportation system, and its villages empty of young and middle-aged men, many of whom had migrated to neighboring oil-rich Arab countries in search of work. Popular social dramas played an important part in furthering this momentum, at least for a time. These films, artistic or purely commercial, evoked a bitter sense that the country had been reoccupied by old feudal elites and, worse, a nouveau riche criminal class that was poisoning the country from above and below, not only in government offices and corporate boardrooms, but also at the neighborhood and, worst of all, family level.[26]

A cohort of young directors, trained under the auspices of the Higher Institute for Cinema, took their cameras into city streets and village lanes to author a striking corpus of films that were celebrated as a new social realism (the designation seems to have been coined by film critic Samir Farid). 'Atif al-Tayyib's *Sawaq al-Utubis* (The Bus Driver, 1983) remains the prototype. It is the story of an October War veteran (Nur al-Sharif, Egypt's new everyman in serious film) driving a decrepit, overcrowded city bus plagued by pickpockets and moonlighting as a taxi driver at night (using his friend's car) to make ends meet. All the while, his family, many involved in smuggling luxury items such as alcohol, cigarettes, and electronics in the new free-trade zone of Port Said, seek to sell off his father's lumber business. Al-Tayyib died prematurely in 1995; his fellow directors—Muhammad Khan, Khayri Bishara, Daud 'Abd al-Sayyid, and 'Ali 'Abd al-Khaliq primarily—created a string of powerful, successful social dramas, many of them original screenplays, featuring working-class heroes and antiheroes well into the 1990s. Ahmad Zaki personified the underclass protagonist, quick to use his hands and guile to play—and often beat—the system, although in some memorable roles, he was ultimately defeated by it. In the mid-1990s, the hairstyle he wore in Bishara's *Kaburya* (The Crab, 1990) became a fad for young men and teenage boys (Fig. 20.5). Zaki had far duskier features than any prior screen star (many of whom had darkened their skin in such roles), contributing to the new realism of Egyptian films.[27]

The 1980s sparked a lively debate about the state of culture as social critics bemoaned the death of high art and the rise of lowbrow, *habitt* (vulgar) production and public taste.[28] The raucous, at times raunchy, comedies of 'Adil Imam encapsulated the debate, clouding the discourse through the celebration of vulgar popular artists such as the singer Ahmad 'Adawiyya, even as they appeared to be criticizing social and economic trends. In many films of the 1990s, Egypt's loss of its moral compass would be signaled by a fleeting portrait, in an office or home, of Nasser, or the strains of a socialist anthem or torch song by 'Abd al-Halim Hafiz, the last great crooner (Muhammad 'Abd al-Wahhab lived on but had ceased to record), who died in 1977 at age 47. In a flashback opening to Muhammad Khan's *Zawjat Rajul Muhim* (Wife of an Important Man, 1987), a teenage girl in school uniform slips into a matinee seat to watch 'Abd al-Halim sing to Magda—it is halfway through the film—in a 1957 melodrama. The song follows her throughout her unhappy marriage to a police officer (Ahmad Zaki), who is rising in the ranks of state security, and up until her ultimate murder at his hands.[29]

FIG. 20.5 Ahmad Zaki from a lobby card for *Kaburya* (1990). Author's collection.

CRISIS

By the second decade of Mubarak's rule, any hopes for true democratization had vanished. The state continued to control film production through censorship, but social malaise and an upturn in political violence forced the authorities to take note. Two films from the early and mid-1990s stand out as significant markers of this effort to confront the growing prevalence of religious extremism. Sharif 'Arafa's *al-Irhab wa-l-Kabab* (Terrorism and Kebab, 1992) is an uproarious yet ultimately moving comedy about a middle-class engineer, played by 'Adil Imam, interminably petitioning to have his children moved to a neighborhood school. Outraged at his endless wasted hours in the Mujama', the gargantuan downtown Cairo structure that houses multiple government offices, he loses his temper, inadvertently disarms a security guard, and takes the twelve-story structure, as well as all who cannot escape, hostage. Gathering allies—a military orderly, an undercover agent posing as a shoeshine, a high-class escort, and a young man bent on suicide to avoid an arranged marriage—he defends the building from assault and, asked finally for his demands, orders grilled meat, an unthinkable delicacy for many, hostages and captors alike. That act, plus a passionate speech in which he explains his frustrations, wins him the support of even his most antagonistic hostage—a government official who avoids work with ostentatious public prayer—allowing him, in the end, to slip away with the crowd. Nadir Jalal's *al-Irhabi* (The Terrorist, 1994), described aptly by Walter Armbrust as a "conversion narrative," is a bald, sociologically problematic caricature of a radical jihadi assassin, also played by Imam, who, taking refuge with an upper-class suburban nationalist and fiercely secular family, comes to see the error of his ways, only to fall victim to the bullets of police and Islamist gunmen alike.[30]

Both films may be characterized as "dramas of nationhood"—a phrase coined by Lila Abu-Lughod to describe television serials of the era. Her pointed critique at the unwillingness of state cultural doyens, products of the secular intelligentsia, to honestly engage the prevalent culture wars, instead parodying all expression of religion beyond personal piety as aberrant, strikes just as squarely at the film industry. Abu-Lughod's focus on television in the 1990s is pointed as well because during this decade, the film industry began to slide in terms of production and box office receipts, and talk of a crisis began to proliferate.[31]

By the late 1990s, the National Feature Film Festival, founded in 1990 to help the ailing industry (the name was formalized in 1995), screened virtually every film produced in a given year—twenty-one in 1998, eighteen the following year. Film critics at times scorned what they watched but recognized that they could not judge hypothetical productions. Rising costs effectively proscribed production of low-budget films—a positive development, said some critics, with regard to cheap action films. Simultaneously, creative young directors struggled to gain financial backing, often waiting years between films. When they succeeded in finishing a movie, they often found it difficult to book theaters, particularly during peak seasons—the two Eids—when a shrinking number of bankable film stars, such as 'Adil Imam, ageless screen vamp Nadya al-Jindi, and belly dance queen Fifi Abdou, commandeered major cinemas; even those in relative proximity to each other showed the same films (Fig. 20.6).

Ticket prices rose precipitately, depleting working- and lower-middle-class audiences or consigning them to run-down neighborhood theaters showing decaying copies of old films and catering primarily to young men.[32] The family outing at the movies became an ever-distant memory. Television, a repository at the time of a great deal of creative energy and the preferred venue for many leading stars, especially but not limited to those entering midcareer roles, was partly to blame. Television had already been viewed as a threat in the mid-1960s, after its establishment, with viewers forgoing theaters and awaiting home broadcast.[33] Now the availability of home video options—a global phenomenon at the time—offered new alternative viewing to the cinema, including foreign productions, pirated or legal. There would be a price to pay: much of Egypt's film archive was purchased by private entrepreneurs. At home, the Subki family, their fortune rooted in a successful butchering business, moved into home video production. More controversially, Saudi and other Arab Gulf–based financiers bought rights to a substantial percentage of the film corpus, holding authority over what would be released, first on video and later on satellite television, and increasingly moving into production of new films.

FIG. 20.6 Nadya al-Jindi Ramadan feature *Muhima fi Tal Abib* (1992) in the downtown Karim Theater. Photo by author.

Egyptian filmmakers complained of rigid conservative reins, commercial rather than state censorship.

Seeking to boost filmmaking via new state-of-the art studios and compete with a growing regional market, the state invested $300 million in a new Media Production City on the edge of Cairo, based near the growing 6th of October satellite city. The most successful inauguration of the new facility was the release of a historical film on the 1956 Suez Crisis, *Nasser 56* (Muhammad Fadil, 1996). Originally conceived as a short TV drama, the project grew into a full-fledged feature film produced—a risky venture to be sure—in black and white. Featuring Ahmad Zaki as Nasser, the film broke long-standing taboos on depicting recent political figures and broke box office records when released on the fortieth anniversary of the Suez Crisis. The rave reception to previews, however, caused state officials to pause initially. In addition to boosting the industry, the film was promoted as a tool to remind Egyptians of a moment when they stood arm-in-arm, in contrast to the internecine violence that again plagued the country. However, authorities felt that the depiction of Nasser as charismatic and incorruptible, a man of modest appetite and taste, reflected poorly on Mubarak. For nearly a year, the film sat unreleased despite advertisements on placards throughout Cairo and broadcast commercials on state television.[34]

The crisis in the film industry persisted into the next decade. Digital technology had not yet been introduced in Egypt to the extent that Egyptian directors could market movies (or television dramas) able to compete visually with foreign products. The old cinemas fell into disrepair; moviegoers who could afford to attend foreign features and films featuring local favorites gravitated to newer, smaller theaters in five-star hotels and, gradually, new shopping malls. A 1997 law ruled that cinema companies must be involved in all aspects of film production, including distribution. At times, government officials and industry representatives seemed to be working at cross-purposes. An effort to limit foreign film imports to 300 per year, capping the number of copies of each film at five, irked representatives of those who had invested in new theaters, who complained that the scant number of Egyptian films produced annually strangled their profits and argued, therefore, for a cap of eight copies of 360 films. They also complained about rules mandating that theaters show only Egyptian films during both Eid holidays and that, year-round, Egyptian films must screen at home prior to release abroad. The latter, they argued, only served to encourage piracy. Anecdotes abounded about filmmakers and stars seeing their work on foreign satellite channels prior to official release in Egypt. This attitude represented a reversal from the late 1980s, when the same Cinema Industry Chamber pressed for strict limits on Hindi-language/Bollywood films: five films per year with a six-week screening limit and reciprocal arrangement for the export of five Egyptian films annually.

Nonetheless, creative directors persisted in pushing the boundaries of public expectations and censorial prerogative. Usama Fawzi's *Jannat al-Shayatin* (Fallen Angels Paradise, 1999), adapted from a short story by Jorge Amado, is a case in point (Fig. 20.7). When a mysterious denizen of Cairo's cemetery drug dens dies, his much younger friends steal his body from his respectable family and take his corpse on a last joy ride.

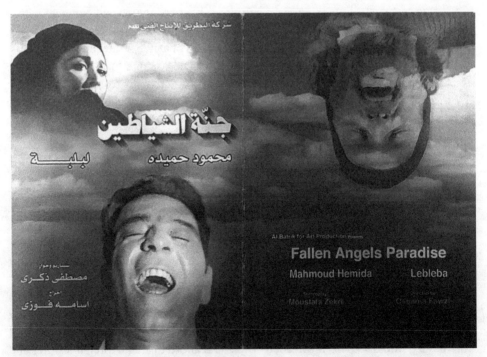

FIG. 20.7 Promotional brochure for the premiere of *Jannat al-Shayatin* (1999). Author's collection.

Fawzi's film, in which Mahmud Himayda plays the deceased hero, left the crowd at the premiere (which I attended) speechless; Fawzi's subsequent films, noted in the next section, challenged conservative religious sensibilities.

BEFORE THE FLOOD

By the early 2000s, Husni Mubarak had positioned himself globally as a crucial figure in the US-led "War on Terror" and at home as the last bastion against a potential Islamist deluge. The upsurge of social protest that suddenly unseated Mubarak in late 2010 and early 2011 caught old-regime officials—and many Egypt watchers—by surprise, but in retrospect, without predetermining the course of events, it is not difficult to chart warning signs, or at least significant socio-cultural moments, during the preceding decade. From the standpoint of the film world, there are markers of social malaise, escalating outrage, and a seeming drift toward chaos. Mubarak's last decade may be remembered as a period, not unlike the years before 1952, in which new directors such as 'Amr Salama, Ahmad 'Abd Allah, Muhammad Diyab, Kamla Abu Dhikri, and Khalid Yusuf, and film stars such as Khaled Abol Naga, Amr Waked, Minna Shalabi, Nelly Karim, Ahmad al-Fishawi, and Khalid Salih emerged to push the boundaries of what was socially and politically acceptable. Such films, however, remained a minority, even as total offerings increased slightly. But the push and tug with foreign interests grew more intense as Syrian, and later Turkish, television serials dominated viewer attention.[35] Another round of protectionism, this time initiated by the chairman of the actors' union, sought to limit screen appearances by non-Egyptian Arab actors. A compromise measure exempted those foreign actors deemed to have compiled a record of merit.

Youssef Chahine's 2007 drama *Hiyya Fawda* (Chaos, It's Chaos, or All is Chaos), which focuses on the tyrannical behavior of a local police precinct officer, seemed prescient. Chahine's opening scene incorporates real footage of a demonstration inspired by Kifaya (Enough), a broad-based, cross-sectarian movement that decried the persistence of Mubarak's martial rule and feared the ascendancy of his son Jamal. Demonstrators are hauled into the precinct, where they are physically abused and confined in a secret basement dungeon. The police officer stalks and then kidnaps a young schoolteacher who resists his attentions. In the end, the neighborhood awakens to storm the police station and liberate the prisoners. Sardonically optimistic, and with allusions to his 1958 masterpiece, *Bab al-Hadid*, this film would be Chahine's swan song, as he outlasted all of his contemporaries, working nearly up to the January 2011 "revolution."[36]

Other serious filmmakers addressed a changing social landscape. Khalid Yusuf, Chahine's latest understudy (he had directed much of *Hiyya Fawda* due to Chahine's illness), directed two epic working-class sagas—*Hina Maysara* (When Things Work Out, 2007) and *Dukkan Shahata* (Shahata's Grocery, 2008)—in which family and neighborhood conflict signify the nation. Kamla Abu Dhikri's *Wahid-Sifr* (One-Zero, 2009) is a panoramic view of life struggles that culminates with momentary civic unity around

Egypt's 2008 Africa Cup championship victory over Cameroon. Social constraints of gender received stark attention as well. Majdi Ahmad 'Ali's *Asrar al-Banat* (Girls' Secrets, 2002) is a sensitive treatment of an unmarried middle-class teen whose pregnancy throws her family into chaos. Yusri Nasr Allah's *Ihki ya Shahrazad* (Scherezade, Tell Me a Story, 2009) focuses on a television talk show host who gives voice to her female guests. In Muhammad Diyab's *678* (2010), a young working woman harassed daily on a city bus (#678) starts to carry a penknife and surreptitiously attacks her gropers. Two summer films about the romantic trials and tribulations of young professionals caught between family obligations and pressures of modern marriage became surprise sensations, if lighter in tone: Tariq al-'Aryan's *al-Sulum wa-l-Tha'ban* (Snakes and Ladders, 2001) and Hani Khalifa's *Sahar al-Layali* (Sleepless Nights, 2003). The latter signifies a rare case of a director daring to depict personal expressions of piety, such as the hijab, as normative rather than extreme behavior.

Eventually, the film world could not ignore the religious, social, political, and cultural landscape that had come to define—or at least contest—Egyptian identity. The filmic gaze still represented a secular perspective, but the caricatures of religious extremism or the essentialism reflected in more serious works such as 'Atif Hitata's *Abwab Mughlaqa* (Closed Doors, 1999) or Youssef Chahine's *al-Masir* (Destiny, 1997) gave way to more honest, sophisticated treatments. A surprise summer hit, Muhammad Mustafa's *Awqat Faragh* (Leisure Time, 2006), featuring a cast of relatively unknown young actors, depicted a group of well-off college students torn between rampant materialism—defined for the boys by alcohol, drugs, and casual sex—and a new religious soundscape. This is not the hectoring preaching of the mosque but a modern call, emanating from media-savvy lay video-Internet-satellite televangelists, for "clean" living that did not proscribe song, dance, movies, premarital mixed company, or even dating. For women, this means proper Islamic dress, and one of them vacillates throughout, appearing at times in a fashionable hijab, and at other times head uncovered, hair teased out, and in more revealing clothing. The film was written and directed by rookies, age-mates of their scripted characters. If they ultimately reject the televangelists' call, they leave their male protagonists literally hanging, stuck on a stalled amusement park ride, calling into the void for help. Usama Fawzi's *Bi-l-Alwan al-Tabi'iyya* (In Natural Colors, 2009), the story of art students at Cairo University, recognizes the religious contingent, an important cohort in the college, foregrounding the tensions inspired by the new religious mediascape. Such films did not promote a religious agenda but depicted an Egypt that finally looked like itself, come what may.[37]

Sectarian tensions that had punctuated al-Sadat's last years continued to smolder, at times erupting into violence. Films caricaturing Islamist violence depicted Coptic Christian victims, sometimes, as in *al-Irhabi*, seeking balance by including extremists among the minority. In general, the depiction of Coptic Christians, even by Coptic filmmakers, raised hackles from clerics and lay community leaders sensitive to negative imaging. Usama Fawzi's depiction of a religiously conservative father in *Bahibb al-Sima* (I Love Cinema, 2004) prompted a lawsuit; a subplot about a Coptic woman seeking a divorce, prohibited by the faith, in *Wahid-Sifr* drew similar outcry. Comedy at times provided an acceptable outlet if the underlying theme was national unity, the depictions of extremism were balanced, and the story did not stray into matters of doctrine. In the popular *Hasan wa-Murqus* (Hasan and Marcus, Rami Imam, 2008), 'Adil Imam and Omar Sharif seek state-sponsored protection from Coptic and Muslim extremists respectively by switching religious identities. The film title references the 1954 classic comedy (directed by Fu'ad al-Jazayirli) based on a stage play, *Hasan wa-Murqus wa-Kuhayn* (Hasan, Marcus, and Cohen), in which a trio of unscrupulous businessmen—Muslim, Christian, and Jew—conspire to undermine a romance that threatens to upset their financial ties. In the "remake," Hasan and Marcus reminisce about better days when Egyptians celebrated sectarian and multicultural diversity, not least in their films, however rife with caricature.[38] Yet 'Amr Salama's tale of a Christian boy posing as a Muslim in a primary school to avoid social ostracizing, *Law Mu'akhdha* (Excuse My French, 2014), was rejected numerous times by censors and only screened after the toppling of Mubarak.

Critics lauded films that pushed back against constraints imposed by conservative backers and challenged audiences to think. Though three Egyptian films screened at the Venice Film Festival in 2009, the biggest hits continued to be youth-oriented comedies and Taiwanese- or Hollywood-inspired action films. Muhammad Sa'd's personification of the crass, mentally slow Upper Egyptian stoner in the *al-Limbi* films (2002, 2003, and 2010) made him the leading screen comic of the decade. Ahmad al-Saqqa emerged as the hero combatting foreign agents and mafia lords, surrounded by a new crop of secondary actors. Muhammad Ramadan reprised the role of the repentant neighborhood *baltaji* (thug) who battles corrupt politicians and their minions.[39]

The biggest hit of the decade and perhaps most impactful film was a star-studded adaptation of *'Imarat Ya'qubian* (The Yacoubian Building, Marwan Hamid, 2006), the bestselling novel by Alaa Al Aswany, featuring 'Adil Imam as a romantic ex-pasha still living in the family flat in a decaying downtown building. Like the novel, the film fused social criticism—class boundaries, state torture, sexual harassment, and high-level corruption—and a dose of pre-Nasserist cosmopolitan nostalgia with potboiler melodrama and a rare open depiction of homosexuality. As with other media, the red line that could not be crossed was criticism of the president or his family. A character in the novel and film was widely understood to be a Mubarak son, but so long as that remained speculation, it was allowed.

AFTER THE FLOOD

In the decade following the deposition of Husni Mubarak and beyond, Egyptian film production has ranged from the predictable to the remarkable. The number of films released per year remains low. Comedies and action dramas reign supreme, perhaps accentuated at times by a heightened patriotism that can border on the ethnocentric. In *Jahim fi al-Hind* (Indian Inferno, 2016), a summer adventure caper, a military music ensemble, recruited mistakenly but still led by a crack commando, parachute into India to rescue a kidnapped diplomat, achieving what the Indians cannot and managing to reinforce every age-old stereotype of those who "speak Hindi"—that is, those who are incomprehensible, exotic, childlike, and in need of guidance.[40]

At the same time, numerous films have presented aspects of the revolutionary turbulence with a marked honesty and even endeavored, against many prevailing trends, to address political and cultural divisions that rent the popular upsurge of 2010–11. This includes films produced during the troubled year of rule by Muhammad Mursi, Egypt's first freely elected leader since 1950, who was toppled by the army in 2013 with the support of many secularists who, two years earlier, had stood against Mubarak's authoritarian rule.

Ibrahim al-Batut's *al-Shita illi Fat* (Winter of Discontent, 2012) looks back to the torture regime of the late Mubarak years while referencing a present in which revolutionary potential seems poised to succeed. The protagonist, an Internet hacktivist who has suffered at the hands of the state, sits in virtual self-imposed house arrest in his apartment, peering out from his balcony as the cacophony of street protests resounds in the background. Muhammad Diyab's *Ishtibak* (Clash, 2016), set during the demonstrations surrounding the June 2013 military coup, is filmed almost entirely from the inside of a police truck in which a group of citizens—some active demonstrators, some ideologically motivated, others drawn into the fray by the excitement of events—are thrown together and left to fend for themselves and sort out their relationships, despite many belonging to antagonistic camps. 'Amr Salama's *Shaykh Jackson* (2017) tells the story, in flashback and present tense, of Khalid, a middle-aged imam who has a crisis of conscience, in part prompted by the news of the death of Michael Jackson, his childhood idol. Dangling stereotypes and teasing viewer expectations—and recreating "Thriller" and other Jackson music videos—the film rejects traditional secular tropes about religious adherents. Khalid suffers illusions and nightmares but never succumbs to mania or, more tellingly, rejects his calling, even as he channels his idol via a dance rendition that neither expels his demons nor reinforces his calling.[41] Ahmad 'Abd Allah's *Layl/Kharij* (Exterior/Night 2018), the story of three people thrown together in a taxi for a night of revel and trouble, even offers a constrained optimistic end, with one character's successful plea to the police officials who arrest them for disturbing the peace that all Egyptians are caught in a vicious cycle of oppression.[42]

The film and televisual landscape has changed dramatically over the last decade. Hollywood films, especially the latest superhero sagas and serialized action films, remain dominant. The paucity of local products to screen at brand new, state-of-the-art multiplex cinemas has led theater owners to press for revisitation of the informal ban on Bollywood films, in place since the late 1980s, with all the attendant risks of bringing in a far superior product, at least in terms of pyrotechnics, digital animation, and extravagant song and dance spectacles. In 2013, Egyptian theaters screened films by three of Bollywood's leading figures: Shah Rukh Khan (*Chennai Express*), Hrithik Roshan (*Krrish 3*), and Aamir Khan (*Dhoom 3*). Without attending theaters, Egyptians can watch nonstop Bollywood on cable television, in addition to Indian, Brazilian, and, especially,

Turkish television serials (*musalsalat*, singular *musalsal*). Ramadan remains largely the turf of national productions, but many eyes and ears are turned outward during the rest of the year. The surge of post-Ramadan Eid blockbuster films has been pallid in recent years: few offerings with little allure. Egypt, once the draw for Arabs (and others) to Hollywood on the Nile (the great Omar Sharif being the exceptional export to global cinema), can now boast multiple stars abroad who are either Egyptian-born or born to Egyptian parents: Rami Malek (*Bohemian Rhapsody*, 2018), Meena Massoud (*Aladdin*, 2019), Khalid Abdalla (*The Kite Runner*, 2007), Amr Waked (*Lucy*, 2014), Yassmine al-Massri (*Quantico*, 2015–17), Omar Metwally (*The Affair*, 2015–18), Khaled Abol Naga (*The Tyrant*, 2016), and Ramy Youssef (*Ramy*, 2019–).

In popular memory and popular criticism, the films of the 1950s and 1960s remain the benchmark for evaluating everything that has followed.[43] The ranks of these masters, the filmmakers and their stars, have depleted, but their films—and not only the good ones—are still widely available on television and the Internet (as DVDs vanish from most markets). Much of Egypt's early film heritage has been lost to negligence and reckless profiteering (here Egypt is not alone), and too much remains only on low-quality videotape. But Rotana, the Saudi-owned company that purchased the largest private collection of Egyptian films, has restored some 250 movies.[44] Existing physical film archives and libraries in the region still suffer from poor storage conditions, meager budgets, and fortress mentalities. But attitudes are shifting, and the preservation and digitization of film memorabilia—hand-drawn posters, lobby cards, press kits, and stills—have become a serious venture for local and foreign archivists and librarians. Cairo bookstores carry comprehensive encyclopedias of films, filmmakers, and actors, the type of published material that in the past too often gathered dust in the offices of the Cairo Film Festival or Film Institute. Film scholarship, long confined to the margins of academic discourse, has become a lively field of study. Especially in recent years, state bureaucrats and media figures, overly focused on regulating patriotic sentiment, remain hesitant to promote movies that they fear will reflect poorly on the nation, failing to recognize that the best of these works speak to a long tradition of creative artistry that has exerted profound influence on the Arab world.[45]

Notes

1. Joel Gordon, *Nasser: Hero of the Arab Nation* (Oxford, UK: Oneworld, 2006).
2. Dalia Fahmy and Daanish Faruqi, eds., *Egypt and the Contradictions of Liberalism: Illiberal Intelligentsia and the Failure of Egyptian Democracy* (Oxford: Oneworld, 2017).
3. Pioneering works include Jacob Landau, *Studies in the Arab Theater and Cinema* (Philadelphia: University of Pennsylvania, 1958; New York: Routledge, 2016); Galal El Charkawi, "History of the U.A.R. Cinema: 1896–1962," in *The Cinema in the Arab Countries*, ed. Georges Sadoul (Beirut: Interarab Centre of Cinema and Television, 1966), 69–97; Magda Wassef, ed., *Égypte: 100 ans de cinéma* (Paris: Institut du Monde Arabe, 1994); and Viola Shafik, *Popular Egyptian Cinema: Gender, Class, and Nation* (Cairo: American University in Cairo Press, 2007). Two of the earliest academic articles on Egyptian cinema,

both pioneering, if limited in their focus on overtly political films, are Raymond William Baker, "Egypt in Shadows: Films and the Political Order," *American Behavioral Scientist* 17, no. 3 (1974): 393–423; and Jane Gaffney, "The Egyptian Cinema: Industry and Art in a Changing Society," *Arab Studies Quarterly* 9, no. 1 (Winter 1987): 53–75.

4. Deborah A. Starr, *Togo Mizrahi and the Making of Egyptian Cinema* (Berkeley: University of California Press, 2020) is a welcome corrective to the traditional narrative.

5. Landau, *Studies*, 157–60; Kamal Ramzi, "Des pionnières qui ont enrichi le cinéma égyptien," in *Égypte: 100 ans de cinéma*, 74–83; Ahmed al-Hadari, "Les Studios Misr," in *Égypte: 100 ans de cinéma*, 86–97.

6. Farid el-Mazzawi, "The U.A.R. Cinema and Its Relations with Television," in *The Cinema in the Arab Countries*, 213; Joel Gordon, "River Blindness: Black and White Identity in Early Nasserist Cinema," in *Narrating the Nile: Politics, Cultures, Identities*, ed. Israel Gershoni and Meir Hatina (Boulder, CO: Lynne Rienner 2008), 137–39.

7. Deborah Starr, "Masquerede and the Performance of National Imaginaries: Levantine Ethics, Aesthetics, and Identities in Egyptian Cinema," *Journal of Levantine Studies* 1, no. 2 (2011): 31–57.

8. Teshome H. Gabriel, *Third Cinema in the Third World: The Aesthetics of Liberation* (Ann Arbor, MI: UMI Research Press, 1982), 122.

9. The code was rewritten in 1955; now censors could ban films for poor artistic quality. It was rewritten again in 1976. Samir Farid, "La censure mode d'emploi," in *Égypte: 100 ans de cinéma*, 102–17; Mustafa Darwish, "al-Riqaba wa-l-Sinima al-Ukhra: Shahadat Raqib," in "Cinematics: Toward the New and the Alternative," special issue, *Alif: Journal of Comparative Poetics* 15 (1995): 91–98; El Charkawy, "History," 93–94.

10. El Charkawi, "History," 87–92. For the Kamil biopic, see Joel Gordon, "Film, Fame and Public Memory: Egyptian Biopics from *Mustafa Kamil* to *Nasser 56*," *International Journal of Middle East Studies* 31, no. 1 (1999): 61–79.

11. Joel Gordon, *Revolutionary Melodrama: Popular Film and Civic Identity in Nasser's Egypt* (Chicago: Middle East Documentation Center, 2002).

12. Joel Gordon, "Class-Crossed Lovers: Popular Film and Social Change in Nasser's Egypt," *Quarterly Review of Film and Video* 18, no. 4 (2001): 385–96.

13. Gordon, *Revolutionary Melodrama*, 133–62.

14. Ibid., 64–81, 115–16, 148–56, 172–78.

15. Durriya Sharaf al-Din, *al-Siyasa wa-l-Sinima fi Misr 1961–81* (Cairo: Dar al-Shuruq, 1992), 35.

16. Ali Abou Chadi, "Le secteur public 1963–1972: esquisse d'analyse economique et artistique," in *Égypte: 100 ans de cinéma*, 118–23; Salah Abu Sayf, "The Cinema and State Enterprise in the U.A.R.," in *The Cinema in the Arab Countries*, 195–99.

17. Munir Abdel Wahab, "The Industry in the U.A.R. 1964–1965," in *The Cinema in the Arab Countries*, 168–70; Walter Armbrust, "Farid Shauqi: Tough Guy, Family Man, Cinema Star," in *Imagined Masculinities: Male Identity and Culture in the Middle East*, ed. Mai Ghassoub and Emma Sinclair-Webb (London: Saqi, 2000), 199–206.

18. Gordon, *Revolutionary Melodrama*, 205–32; Sharaf al-Din, *al-Siyasa wa-l-Sinima*, 115–28.

19. Ifdal Elsaket, "Counting Kisses at the Movies: The Screen Kiss and the Cinematic Experience in Egypt," *International Journal of Middle East Studies* 55, no. 2 (2023): 211–37.

20. Joel Gordon, "The Slaps Felt around the Arab World: Family and National Melodrama in Two Nasser-era Musicals," *International Journal of Middle East Studies* 39, no. 2 (2007): 209–28.

21. Gordon, *Revolutionary Melodrama*, 232–41.

22. Ibid., 244–77.

23. Ibrahim Fawal, *Youssef Chahine* (London: British Film Institute, 2001). For a fresh take on Chahine's immediate post-1967 output, see Tamara Maatouk, "On the Heels of 1967: Chahine, Cinema, and the Emotional Response(s) to the Defeat," *International Journal of Middle East Studies* 55, no. 1 (2023): 25–42.

24. Gordon, *Revolutionary Melodrama*, 126–28.

25. Walter Armbrust, "The National Vernacular: Folklore and Egyptian Popular Culture," *Michigan Quarterly Review* 31, no. 4 (1992): 25–42.

26. Lizbeth Malkmus, "The 'New' Egyptian Cinema: Adapting Genre Conventions to a Changing Society," *Cineaste* 16, no. 3 (1988): 30–33.

27. For earlier racially charged depictions in Egyptian pop culture, see Eve Troutt Powell, "Burnt-Cork Nationalism: Race and Identity in the Theater of 'Ali al-Kassar," in *Colors of Enchantment: Theater, Dance, Music and the Visual Arts in Egypt*, ed. Sherifa Zuhur (Cairo: American University in Cairo Press, 2001), 13–26; and Joel Gordon, "River Blindness: Black and White Identity in Early Nasserist Cinema," in *Narrating the Nile*, 137–56.

28. Walter Armbrust, *Mass Culture and Modernism in Egypt* (Cambridge, UK: Cambridge University Press, 1996).

29. Joel Gordon, "The Nightingale and the Ra'is: 'Abd al-Halim Hafiz and Nasserist Longings," in *Rethinking Nationalism: Revolution and Historical Memory in Modern Egypt*, ed. Elie Podeh and Onn Winckler (Tallahassee: Florida University Press, 2004), 307–23.

30. Gordon, *Revolutionary Melodrama*, 267–71; Walter Armbrust, "Islamists in Egyptian Cinema," *American Anthropological Review* 104, no. 3 (2002): 922–31; Raymond Baker, "Combative Cultural Politics: Film Art and Political Spaces in Egypt," in "Cinematics: Toward the New and the Alternative," special issue, *Alif: Journal of Comparative Poetics* 15 (1995): 6–38.

31. Lila Abu-Lughod, *Dramas of Nationhood: The Politics of Television in Egypt* (Chicago: University of Chicago Press, 2004).

32. Walter Armbrust, "When the Lights Go Down in Cairo: Cinema as Secular Ritual," *Visual Anthropology* 10, no. 2–4 (1998): 413–42.

33. El-Mazzawi, "U.A.R. Cinema," 209–14.

34. Joel Gordon, "Nasser 56/Cairo 96: Reimaging Egypt's Lost Community," in *Mass Mediations: New Approaches to Popular Culture in the Middle East and Beyond*, ed. Walter Armbrust (Berkeley: University of California Press, 2000), 161–81.

35. For the impact of television dramas, see "Televisual and Cinematic Narratives of the Middle East," *Review of Middle East Studies,* roundtable 52, no. 1 (2018): 66–146.

36. Joel Gordon, "Chahine, *Chaos* and Cinema: A Revolutionary Coda," *Bustan: The Middle East Book Review* 4, no. 2 (2013): 99–112.

37. Joel Gordon, "Piety, Youth and Egyptian Cinema: Still Seeking Islamic Space," in *Islamism and Cultural Expression in the Arab World*, ed. Abir Hamdar and Lindsey Moore (Abingdon, UK: Routledge, 2015), 103–20.

38. The absence of Cohen—explicit in the title for those with a sense of pop culture history—underscores the gradual departure of Egypt's "foreign" minorities as the country nationalized in the late 1950s and 1960s and as the conflict with Israel intensified. See Joel Gordon, "*Hasan and Marika*: Screen Shots from a Vanishing Egypt," *Journal of Levantine Studies* 7, no. 1 (2017): 35–56.

39. Frances Hasso, "'I Have Ambition': Muhammad Ramadan's Proletarian Masculinities in Postrevolution Egyptian Cinema," *International Journal of Middle East Studies* 52, no. 2 (2020): 197–214.

40. Joel Gordon, "The Indian Other as Alternate Oriental" (unpublished paper).
41. Joel Gordon, review of *Eshtibak* [*Clash*], by Mohamed Diyab, *Journal of Islamic and Muslim Studies* 3, no. 1 (2018): 95–99; Gordon, review of *Sheikh Jackson*, by 'Amr Salama, *Journal of Islamic and Muslim Studies* 4, no. 2 (2019): 110–13.
42. Heba Abdelfattah Arafa, review of *Exterior/Night/Layl Kharji* [*Khargi*], by Ahmad Abd Allah, *Journal of Islamic and Muslim Studies* 5, no. 1 (2020): 122–30.
43. When the arts magazine *al-Funun* (May–June 1984) asked Egyptian critics to rank the top ten Egyptian films in 1984, nine of ten films came from these two decades. None preceded 1952, and only 'Atif al-Tayyib's *Sawaq al-Utubis* (1983) came afterward. Recent lists posted on the Internet by film buffs still weigh heavily in this direction.
44. Yasmin Desouki, "A Map of Love and Loss" and Rotana Advertorial, "Diamonds in the Dust: Shedding Light on Rotana's Film Restoration Project," *Rawi: Egypt's Heritage Review* 9 (2018): 72–77, 78–79.
45. For example, see Sameh Fathy, *Classic Egyptian Movies: 101 Must-See Films* (Cairo: American University in Cairo Press, 2018); Rawi, *Egypt's Heritage Review*; Mona al-Bindari, Mahmud Qasim, and Ya'qub Wahbi, *Mawsu'at al-Aflam al-'Arabiyya* (Cairo: Bayt al-Ma'rifa, 1984); and Mahmud Qasim, *al-Film al-Siyasi fi Misr* (Cairo: al-Hay'a al-Misriyya al-'Amma li-l-Kitab, 2012).

BIBLIOGRAPHY

Abdelfattah, Heba Arafa. *Filming Modernity and Islam in Colonial Egypt*. Edinburgh: Edinburgh University Press, 2023.

Armbrust, Walter. *Mass Culture and Modernism in Egypt*. Cambridge, UK: Cambridge University Press, 1996.

Al-Bindari, Muna, Mahmud Qasim, and Ya'qub Wahba. *Mawsu'at al-Aflam al 'Arabiyya*. Cairo: Bayt al-Ma'rifa, 1994.

El Khashab, Chihab. *Making Film in Egypt: How Labor, Technology and Mediation Shape the Industry*. Cairo: American University in Cairo Press, 2021.

El-Shamaa, Magdy Mounir. *The National Imaginarium: A History of Egyptian Filmmaking*. Cairo: American University in Cairo Press, 2021.

Fathy, Sameh. *Classic Egyptian Movies: 100 Must-See Films*. Cairo: American University in Cairo Press, 2018.

Ghazal, Ahmed. *Egyptian Cinema and the 2011 Revolution: Film Production and Representing Dissent*. London: I. B. Taurus, 2020.

Gordon, Joel. *Revolutionary Melodrama: Popular Film and Civic Identity in Nasser's Egypt*. Chicago: Middle East Documentation Center, 2002.

Hammad, Hanan. *Unknown Past: Layla Murad, the Jewish Muslim Star of Egypt*. Stanford, CA: Stanford University Press, 2020.

Khouri, Malek. *The Arab National Project in Youssef Chahine's Cinema*. Cairo: American University in Cairo Press, 2010.

Qasim, Mahmud. *Mawsu'at al-Mumathil al-'Arabi*. Cairo: Delta li-l-Nashr wa-l-Tawzi', 2017.

Shafik, Viola. *Popular Egyptian Cinema: Gender, Class, Nation*. Cairo: American University in Cairo Press, 2007.

Starr, Deborah. *Togo Mizrahi and the Making of Egyptian Cinema*. Berkeley: University of California Press, 2020.

Wassef, Magda, ed. *Égypte: 100 ans de cinéma*. Paris: Institut du Monde Arabe, 1995.

PART V

STATE, POLITICS, AND INTELLECTUALS

CHAPTER 21

....

ENCOUNTERS WITH
MODERNITY

Egyptian Politics in the Nineteenth Century

....

JAMES WHIDDEN

EGYPTIAN historical writing from the late nineteenth century normally dated the origin of the modern state in Egypt to Napoleon's expedition in July 1798, followed by the rise of Muhammad 'Ali al-Kabir ("The Great," r. 1805–48). Royalist ideologues and historians underlined the liberal character of Muhammad 'Ali's rule, referring to him as an "Enlightened Despot" or, as he called himself, the "Benefactor," with a clear sense that he ruled in the public interest and fought wars to win Egypt's independence from "Turkish" overlordship. Even after the fall of the monarchy in 1952 and the creation of a republican government, many historians continued to uncritically identify Muhammad 'Ali as the founder of the Egyptian nation-state.[1] Conventionally, these events were seen to have brought about a rupture with the Ottoman imperial past and opened a pathway for Egypt's future as a modern nation-state. This view has been described as the "teleology of the state," the idea that the realization of Egyptian sovereignty as a nation-state was inevitable and the central drama of Egyptian history. That teleology has been questioned by revisionist histories that point to a regional system of inter-Ottoman household politics in an era of Ottoman legal and governmental "reordering" (*tanzimat*), or the "new order" (*nizam jadid*). Egypt led in the innovation of methods of governance and social management and the representations of power in law and institutions, with the intent of the Muhammad 'Ali's dynasty in that era to increase its patrimonial powers, excluding the indigenous population, within an Ottoman imperial context. However, the methods used in the process of building state structures, such as European-type administrative law codes and pedagogy, transformed politics by inducing a "subjectivity" amongst a "public" that was manifested in oppositional political movements in the last quarter of the century.

EGYPT IN THE INTERNATIONAL SYSTEM

Egypt was not a sovereign state until the twentieth century. Uniquely in the Ottoman Empire, it was one administrative unit under an Ottoman governor (Turkish *vali* or Arabic *wali*, and khedive after 1863) and the richest of the provinces beyond the Anatolian and European heartland. Ottomans had been frustrated by their governors having to contend with the powerful factions of a mamluk military aristocracy, organized into households, that jockeyed for power through the control of tax fiefdoms (*iltizams*), the holder of which was known as a *multazim*. When Napoleon invaded Egypt in 1798, the government was in the hands of a mamluk faction, not the Ottoman governor, and Napoleon attempted to represent himself variously as a liberator of the people of Egypt and a restorer of Ottoman order. The Ottoman government re-established its authority through its alliance with the British in an international force sent to evict the French. An officer in that force, Muhammad 'Ali, sidelined his Ottoman superiors, and the sultan recognized his governorship in 1805. He then massacred the mamluk aristocracy in 1811, monopolizing violence and initiating sovereign state formation.

The causes of the subsequent expansion of Egypt's power in the region have been disputed. Some have emphasized the economic motives: a revival of Egypt's merchant and entrepreneurial classes resulted in a demand for new markets and resources.[2] Politico-cultural forces have also been considered: the Egyptian campaigns of conquest in Arabia, Sudan, and Syria were an attempt to build an Arab kingdom, a revival of Arab greatness, and the founding of an Egyptian empire.[3] Yet the *vali* went to great lengths to bow to the Ottoman sultan's authority. His campaigns in the Hijaz and Greece followed imperial directives. Indeed, Sultan Mahmud II tested his governor's loyalty with reckless directives to fight in Morea when Muhammad 'Ali advised negotiating a truce with the Greeks. Previously undefeated, Muhammad 'Ali's army suffered a setback in Greece that Muhammad 'Ali blamed solely on the Ottoman court; in recompense, he invaded the Ottoman province of Syria in 1831.[4]

The Syrian war was an intra-Ottoman conflict, not an attempt to reset the international system. In fidelity with the nationalist school, some historians suggest the British involved themselves in this war to bring Egypt into its free trade sphere, aborting the first industrial development project outside Europe.[5] However, the British Foreign Secretary, Lord Palmerston, avoided involvement in the struggle until the complete rout of the Ottoman army in 1839. Palmerston was unmoved to respond to the appeals of the Ottoman sultan in 1833 and was only forced to act after 1839, when the threat posed by Muhammad 'Ali's forces to the Ottoman capital in Istanbul played into the hands of the Russians. And so began the British doctrine of protecting the "integrity" of the Ottoman Empire. That doctrine probably came as no surprise to Muhammad 'Ali, who was a keen observer of European balance of power politics. Therefore, when the campaign commander, his son and heir, Ibrahim, begged to capitalize on the defeat of the Ottoman forces with a march on Istanbul, his father demurred. The ruler had always been aware of the need to placate the British. Nor was tying Egypt to the 1838 commercial treaty with Britain as disastrous to Egyptian autonomy and development as it has been described. In the first half of the nineteenth century, the Egyptian economy was designed less to keep European imports out and more to ensure that all profits went into the state treasury to finance the military machine, the prime instrument of Muhammad 'Ali's foreign policy. The 1841 international settlement of the Syrian war realized that aim: Lord Palmerston insisted that the sultan recognize Muhammad 'Ali's claim to an independent patrimony within the Ottoman Empire.

Foreign policy was dynastically driven. Egypt was Ottoman in political culture, it was staffed by Ottoman officers and officials, and its first language was Ottoman Turkish, with the Egyptian Arabic-speaking soldiers and officials taking the lower positions in the hierarchy. The higher positions were held by members of the Muhammad 'Ali household: the ruler's sons, grandsons, nephews, and former slaves (*mamluks*), all of whom commanded an immense network of clients in administration, industry, and agricultural estates. The ruler's domain was a "patrimonial state," with the land belonging to the dynast and its wars fought in the name of the ruler, not "Egypt" or the "Egyptians." These observations suggest the continuity of Ottoman identity in Egypt's ruling group. As Khaled Fahmy has argued, the origins of Egyptian national identity are to be found not in the revolt of Muhammad 'Ali and Ibrahim against Ottoman overlords, but in the resentments occasioned by the recruitment of Arabic-speaking Egyptians into state service under the abusive and cruel command of the Ottoman Egyptian elite. However, these resentments were not manifested until the 1870s.[6]

Politics in the mid-nineteenth century remained court politics. Briefly preceded by Ibrahim in 1848, Muhammad 'Ali's grandson 'Abbas (r. 1848–54) acceded to power late that year. Harried by Ibrahim's household, 'Abbas sought legitimacy through the Ottoman connection while also resisting imperial interference in the Ottoman Egyptian administration. 'Abbas defended his dynastic base by refusing to apply Ottoman reform law (*tanzimat*) because it would have superseded the Egyptian reformed law codes that had already established the supremacy of the new order (*nizam jadid*) over religious (*shari'a*) and customary (*'urfi*) codes.[7] Yet unlike his predecessors, 'Abbas's investiture as *vali* took place in Istanbul, according to Ottoman custom and ritual, including religious symbolism, to legitimate his rule within an Ottoman context.

As was usually the case, the accession of a new ruler was a critical moment in dynastic government. 'Abbas was tested by Sultan Abdulmaçit and the household of Ibrahim. There was an ideological dimension to this contest, as most of Ibrahim's family was associated with Muhammad 'Ali's reformist agenda and a state administration that included many Europeans. Observers portrayed 'Abbas's regime as divided between the pro-European "reformist party" and a "reactionary party" led by 'Abbas. Revisionists have suggested that far from being reactionary, 'Abbas turned to the Ottoman court to counter his rivals and build up a household with new personnel loyal to him. Solidarity with the Ottoman elite in Istanbul served to break the influence of the European consuls.

For this, he earned the enmity of European observers, establishing the legend of his support for a "fanatical party" that undid the process of modern nation-state building begun by his grandfather. This interpretation found its way into the nationalist school of history.[8]

However, the context in which 'Abbas operated was much more complex. An imperial diaspora enabled the recruitment of new state servants in Istanbul, either Ottoman officials or mamluks, to serve 'Abbas. Meanwhile, these recruits were indigenized, indoctrinated to serve "Pasha and Country," according to a cultural code that conceived Egypt as a royal domain belonging to the Ottoman Egyptian elite. 'Abbas entrenched the division of Egyptian political society between "Turk" and "fellah," Ottoman Egyptian and Arabic-speaking Egyptian, yet his reforms also launched the revival of an indigenous notability. He pursued a policy of allotting state lands to loyal household members, which enabled long-term landholding, and re-established religious endowments terminated by his forbear. Private property and the endowments provided autonomy for a re-emerging class of notables, a middle stratum conversant in Ottoman and indigenous cultures.[9]

The concept of diaspora is one way to appreciate Egypt's place in the international and imperial systems.[10] Among the indigenous Egyptian, Ottoman, and European residents, identities were malleable, as analysis of Ottoman Egyptian court records and European consular records indicates.[11] The growing European colonies, with their distinct law codes applied in consular courts, alongside the Mixed Courts from 1876, imparted immense power to the consular agents and enabled the growth of the sovereign power of the European colonies. Egypt came to be regarded by Europeans as an international society. Legal and geographical studies have shown that Egypt was conceived as an extension of Europe, with its historical sites of sacred memory incorporated into a European narrative and a Christian landscape.[12] Europeans and Ottoman subjects shifted their legal status based on circumstance, which was characteristic of residents of Alexandria, most obviously among Christian and Jewish residents.[13] In this sense, Egypt already had a colonial geography and a French imperial presence, after the restoration of the pro-European party at the Egyptian court during the reign of Sa'id (r. 1854–63). Previously, the balance of power had belonged to the ruler, not the consuls.[14]

Even with these international incursions, Egypt remained a regional power until the 1870s, extending direct rule over Sudan and retaining a sphere of influence in the Hijaz. An Egyptian naval presence in the Red Sea symbolized Egypt's regional dominance through the reign of Isma'il (r. 1863–79). The French did not join the European concert that forced Muhammad 'Ali's withdrawal from Syria in 1841 but did check a diplomatic alliance between the Bey of Tunis and 'Abbas in 1849. French imperial power in the region was obvious during another power struggle in the Egyptian palace when 'Abbas's son Ilhami sued Sa'id over his inheritance. Ilhami borrowed from European financial markets on the collateral of that inheritance, and consequently, upon Ilhami's early death, the responsibility for his debts fell on Sa'id. Borrowing on European credit to pay off those debts began a cycle of state indebtedness to European financiers, sponsored by the European consuls, that culminated in the British military occupation of 1882.[15]

As economic historians have shown, the initiators of this cycle were not the French or British governments but the lending houses of Paris and London and their agents in Alexandria and Cairo. The vectors moving these processes were diasporas of financiers and merchants, including Ottoman Egyptians, Europeans, and the "Levantines," those Ottoman groups, normally resident in the Ottoman Empire, with political, cultural, or economic connections to Europe. The triumph of international finance and the European colonies was symbolized by the appearance of Empress Eugenie, who represented France, at the opening of the Suez Canal in 1869. The Suez Canal Company, with offices in Paris, seemed to suggest that Egypt was an extension of France, but this was illusory because by a simple stock purchase on the international markets in 1875, the British government of Benjamin Disraeli became the controlling shareholder in the company. The Dual Control, a debt commission set up subsequently, included French and British officers. The intersection of one international diaspora (the financial) with British, French, and Ottoman imperial networks led to an international political crisis between 1876 and 1882.[16]

The cause of the British occupation was, ostensibly, to quell a military revolt against the legitimate authority of the Ottoman Egyptian ruler. The idea that the war minister in the national government of 1881–82, Ahmad 'Urabi, sought a military dictatorship was a myth propagated by the European consuls that also found its way into the historiography. But republican era (post-1952) histories interpreted the crisis, or "revolution," as a dynamic relationship between the initially reformist "agricultural bourgeoisie" and "petty-bourgeois" revolutionaries.[17] Revolutionaries like 'Urabi were associated with the rural and urban notables or the "three strata": rich fellahin, urban guilds, and intelligentsia.[18]

Revolutionary political activism affected the established international pact between the Ottoman Egyptian ruler, the Ottoman sultan, and European consuls. That pact had been established with the European intervention in 1841 and reasserted with the Debt Commission of 1876. The revolution threatened those international conventions. Therefore, it has figured prominently in British imperial studies of informal empire, wherein a British "free trade" policy was premised on collaborating Ottoman Egyptian elites. In this interpretation, the British empire of free trade generated an agricultural bourgeoisie.[19] Revisionist economic historians argue, however, that rather than "free trade," the colonial consuls established mercantilist-type controls over custom duties and enhanced the legal privileges of the foreigners at the expense of the Egyptian landholders, large and small.[20]

The growth of colonial power was an unexpected consequence of reforms initially designed to ensure dynastic stability in line with customary Ottoman Egyptian practice: dispersing land grants to Ottoman recruits and local magnates to foster allegiance to the dynasty.[21] Muhammad 'Ali tried to avoid the emergence of households with independent power in the land, but his heirs regarded their domain lands as symbolic of their status. 'Abbas alienated Ibrahim's line and extended patronage in the form of landed estates to a new generation of royal clients, broadening the dynastic circle even as he altered the terms of land ownership to increase the tax (tithe, such as the 'ushur) and enabled proprietorship. Sa'id also made new grants of land known as *kharajiyya* to create large tax-producing estates on lands previously worked communally by the fellahin under the *shaykh al-balad* (a communal leader). Sa'id's land law of 1858 allowed male heirs to inherit *kharaji* and *'ushuri* land grants. The Ottoman Egyptian elite expanded, and the dynast secured clients, including indigenous Egyptians. Yet the rise of a rural notability led to peripheral members of the Ottoman Egyptian elite gaining a stake in dynastic or, in some interpretations, "national" politics. The power of this notability was not critical until state bankruptcy in 1876, when the ruler was deprived of his sources of patronage and household politics lost its rationale.

The place of the notables in Ottoman politics was memorably discussed by Albert Hourani.[22] Previous to the building of the modern military and other state departments, politics in Egypt had been controlled by the Ottoman governors through the notables, the Arabic-speaking Muslim urban elite of merchants and 'ulama' and rural elite of *multazims*, mostly mamluks and their local agent, the *shaykh al-balad*. Muhammad 'Ali eliminated these groups or placed them under strict supervision to stifle any possible opposition. However, land and tax reforms and the modernizing policies of Isma'il resulted in the re-emergence of the notability as a political factor, as represented in the composition of the Chamber of Deputies (*majlis shura al-nuwab*), formed in 1866.[23] After 1876, the notables lined up behind those in the court inspired by the Ottoman constitutionalists in Istanbul seeking to limit the sultan's powers. When the court politicians (Ottoman Egyptian "haute bourgeoisie") split with the notables and intelligentsia (petty-bourgeois revolutionaries), the latter sought to put the state on a new footing with the creation of an emergency commoner (*'urfi*) majlis in 1882. The consuls mobilized against the revolutionaries, legitimizing their position by underlining the threat posed to the legitimate authority of the ruler, Khedive Tawfiq (r. 1879–92), whose accession followed the deposition of Isma'il. Some observers at the time credited these European interventions to the interests of the financial houses of London and Paris. However, that the French withdrew their ships while the British remained to bomb Alexandria suggests the government of William Gladstone was also moved by the significance of the Suez Canal in the international system.[24]

The British military invasion of 1882 restored the Muhammad 'Ali dynasty, and Egypt remained technically a province of the Ottoman Empire. The British in Egypt legitimized the occupation by pointing to financial reform and technical development, particularly irrigation, including a cadastral survey that made the landholding system more legible. The survey increased the scope of foreign investment and the incorporation of even the small landholders in the market economy. British colonial agents imagined that improved material conditions would depoliticize the majority rural population.[25] However, the combination of intrusive state infrastructure and the fluctuations of a market economy enhanced the interests of small farmers in state policy.[26] Thus, British policy had the effect of uniting the rural and urban notables. The urban notables, particularly those seeking posts in the administration, were aggrieved at the neutralizing of the majlis, reorganized as a general assembly, and the appointment of British advisers to all the ministries.

However, colonial studies underline that nationalism was an incomplete process in the late nineteenth century; for instance, biographical studies of exemplary effendi "nationalists" indicate that most belonged to the Ottoman diaspora and were socialized in Ottoman Egyptian culture.[27] Mustafa Kamil and Ahmad Lutfi al-Sayyid represent the shift from an Ottoman to a more exclusively Egyptian identity. However, even these effendis do not fit a common mold: Lutfi al-Sayyid, a colonial liberal, accepted the premises of the colonial "civilizing mission" and thus tutelage within the British Empire; Kamil, the ideologue of a new generation of effendi nationalists, lobbied for Egyptian national independence in the Ottoman court and the French salons.

Underlining the complexities of Egyptian identity, the politicians in the general assembly protested when the British negotiated an international demarcation line that meant Istanbul had to concede the Sinai Peninsula to Egypt in 1906. The territorial concession was interpreted by nationalists as a British, not Egyptian, gain, at the cost of the Ottoman sultan-caliph. On the western border, the Ottomans and the British found common cause in avoiding any demarcation that might have meant recognizing an independent state in Egypt.[28] These negotiations and disputes suggest that the nation as a territorial entity remained amorphous. The persistent Ottoman affiliation also meant that the centuries-old Ottoman Capitulations still determined the status of European residents in Egypt. Meanwhile, the British system of finance and trade meant that Egypt was as much a part of the British Empire as Australia and Canada.[29] France recognized this situation in the Entente Cordiale of 1904.

REPRESENTATIONS OF POWER

Timothy Mitchell's seminal study of modernizing or, as he said, "colonizing" Egypt begins in Paris at the world exhibition of 1889, where Egyptians appeared as artifacts in an exhibition. Egyptian visitors who happened upon the exhibition were consciously aware of their objectivity in this display of world cultures. The exhibition underlined the alienation of the subject from the object—the Egyptian visitors were conscious that they were not the objects represented in the Oriental display at the exhibition but that observers viewed them as an object in a display. In general terms, the exhibition represented how the modern (colonial) state made "society" the object of its reforms. Mitchell then turns to the object of Muhammad 'Ali's reformist projects in Egypt: the fellahin transformed into regimented soldiers, industrious workers led by European technicians and those Egyptians who had been sent to Europe to learn its techniques. The Ottoman Egyptian state was "civilizing" according to the methods of the European colonial state: Muhammad 'Ali tore down the old status hierarchies and ripped the fellahin from their villages, ordering the social units into new ranks, with the modern legal codes creating a politics (*siyasa*) in the sense of the state managing society. Egyptians, who had been accustomed to the social assemblages of family, clan, village, and mosque, had to reorient themselves to a state that represented its power in impersonal, rational terms, and found its political legitimacy in its claim to represent "an effect of order and an effect of truth."[30]

The symbolic power of the Muhammad 'Ali state was in the very human material it had mustered, the troops who formed its armies. Thus, in a portrayal of the war in Syria, the Egyptian peasant army stands in lines marshaled into formations, with uniform dress and guns raised in unison, under the choreographed orders of the commanders. The troops fire into a disordered Ottoman cavalry.[31] The image recalled Antoine Jean Gros's painting of Napoleon's troops at the Battle of the Pyramids by effecting the same division between modern order and disorder. As Mitchell said, this was not a distinction between the modern and the past; instead, modernity relied on this effect of order against disorder to represent its power. Nationalist histories published from the 1930s onward celebrated this march of Egypt toward statehood and the "modern."[32] The cruel punishments meted out to the fellahin were represented not as the whim of the despot but the requirements of a state at war, with regulations and punishments regularized and universalized—even the Ottoman Egyptian officer corps came under these state provisions. When the necessity to wage war ended, the regime was "liberalized"; thus, the severe methods of punishment observed at the height of the Syrian war were reformed in 1836 to ensure the welfare of the fellahin.[33]

Military methods provided the blueprints for state policies. These blueprints were evident in the "model villages" set up on royal estates from the 1840s. Trained in military cultures, the Ottoman Egyptian elite subjected the fellahin on their estates to severe discipline, justified in state manuals and regulations as necessary to increase taxes and productivity. The model village represented the organization of an industrious modern state, its objectivism, and its impersonal and rational character. The ideologues of Muhammad 'Ali's court, and later the nationalist historians, represented these measures as designed for the welfare—the social improvement—of the fellahin. More critical studies, like those of 'Ali Barakat, described the new order as regulated despotism, as opposed to earlier forms of unregulated despotism.[34] Studies in this vein have likened state policies, including the model villages, to the pacification of a conquered people. The expansion of the school system universalized this kind of discipline, subjecting the general population to a new regime that maximized production, taxes, and profits, while also transforming the "subjectivity" of its object, the fellahin.

Mitchell explored the state regulations, the blueprints of state building, while other scholars investigated the ruling group behind these policies. The Egyptian royal palaces constructed in the mid-nineteenth century reflect a political elite modeled after the imperial style of the Ottoman palaces on the Bosphorus: the palace at 'Abbasiyya on Cairo's eastern edge had three wings: one for the harem, another for a school for the education of household members, including mamluks, and the third for an administrative wing, with offices for the ministers of state and technical advisers, including Europeans. Without rejecting the modern methods of his predecessors, 'Abbas made the royal palaces symbolic of the ruling group.[35] The royal household was a model for elite society, including members of the rural notability who were absorbed into the elite. Two of the leading political theorists of the nineteenth century, 'Ali Mubarak and Rifa'a al-Tahtawi, were from that category. Mubarak adapted a literary format practiced for centuries, the biographical dictionary, to document the accomplishments of the dynasty in his *al-Khitat al-Tawfiqiyya* (Tawfiq's New Plans), a biographical and geographical survey. Al-Tahtawi, on the other hand, employed modern European political theories, vocabularies, and models but adapted to defend autocracy. He referred to Montesquieu's separation of powers; yet, as a monarchist, he represented the ruler as combining in his person executive, legislative, and judicial powers.[36]

Banished to the remote Sudan during the middle years of the century, al-Tahtawi was afterward employed by Isma'il in the new Bureau of Schools alongside Ibrahim Adham, where they devised a state-wide schooling system that represented the social order in a hierarchy of preparatory, primary, and secondary schools. The size of each class of students diminished as one climbed the hierarchy, indicating the construction of an educated landholding elite, dominating yet civilizing the agricultural masses. During Isma'il's reign, the new palace at 'Abdin was built in the heart of the new or "European" Cairo. Western designs in clothing, furnishings, and palaces, as well as the lifestyle of the royal family, provided a bourgeois model for the elites. These models proliferated in the upper-class suburbs of Cairo and Alexandria, where single-family villas marked a departure from the great households and political confederacies of Ottoman Egyptian court politics.[37]

In the second half of the nineteenth century, the gradual abolition of slavery contributed to the breakdown of large Ottoman Egyptian households. State centralization also had the effect of eliminating the independent power of rival households. In their place, the reformist legislators and educators identified the virtues of the bourgeois family and women's role in fostering a national or public sphere. Women, as nurturers of the "new generation," were regarded as the key instrument, or object, of a social transformation designed to capture the minds of the entire population. The "new woman" would engender a new family, fitted to bourgeois culture, with its logic premised on the idea of both increased productivity and consumerism. By the end of the century, civilizing nationalists, led by Qasim Amin, grasped onto the status of women and the structure or moral order of the family as a measure of modernity and nationhood. The honor of women or the family came to represent national honor. This gendering of politics also emphasized the male effendi as the heroic leader of this transformation. The society upon which the effendi acted, on its behalf or for its education, was often represented as a fellahin girl, indicating the division of society between these ideal types, effendi and fellah. The ideal was that the effendi civilizers would transform the fellahin culture through modern educational methods, which had the effect of separating the new elite from society, not unlike colonial representations of the advanced nations to the "backward," where the imagery was similarly gendered. Nevertheless, the ideal was to bring effendi and fellah together in a single whole, realizing national strength and advancement.[38]

These developments carried dangerous implications for women seeking to emancipate their roles on an equal basis with men because of the religious implications of these discussions of national identity. In Orientalist explorations of these themes, Islamic law was critiqued as the cause of women's degraded status. By the end of the century, the emancipation of women as represented by de-veiling was interpreted by some as an affront to morality, forcing women to accommodate "tradition" in their emancipation by wearing the hijab.[39] The effendi was similarly compromised, his modernity a sign of his alienation from society, as represented by the fez and modern suit, as opposed to the authenticity of the fellah dressed in *jallabiyya*. This dichotomy between ideal types of Egyptians was commonplace by the end of the century and came to symbolize a political struggle over social values in national politics. The hegemony of *effendiyya* nationalism produced its opponents, the "traditionalists," who turned back modern "temporality" to Islamic, Ottoman, or patrimonial symbols, sometimes expressed in counter-texts.[40]

The biographical dictionaries published from the latter half of the century into the twentieth seemed "traditional." They had been used by Islamic scholars over the centuries; however, their purpose was to represent the modern state in moral terms and the elite as representative of society in accord with patrimonial politics.[41] The patrimony of the ruler was represented as the state itself, referring to the Ottoman ideology of the elite (*khassa*) as guardians of the subjects (*ra'iya*) or the public (*'amma*). While *'amma* had come to be associated with notions of the "public," the traditionalists sought to bring back the idea of the elite as benefactors and patrons of multiple communities, Muslim and Christian, urban guilds, and the fellahin, as a prescription for political order in a period of disorienting change. Indeed, the image of the agricultural "commoner" obedient to the lords (*dhawat*) of the Ottoman Egyptian elite was a metaphor for hierarchical social relations according to Ottoman "tradition." Behind the new legal codes, schools, and political assemblies was a ruling group, which the biographical dictionaries documented, placing the ruler at the apex of a political society organized by family connection, attachment, and service to the dynasty.

In the last quarter of the century, a sort of silence was observed between those writing in Arabic in traditional formats and the satirists, dramatists, novelists, and ideologues of effendi nationalism.[42] Among historians of nationalism, it is conventional to associate the *effendiyya*, those trained in modern schools or at least familiar with ideas emanating from Europe, as the originators of the nation-state idea.[43] This interpretation has been revised by studies that underline the diversity of identities in Egypt in the nineteenth century, those that regard nationalism not as the diffusion of ideas in the hands of an enlightened elite but as changes wrought upon the "subjectivity" of Egyptians by modern state formation and colonial economies.[44] Through the recruitment and employment of ordinary Egyptians in state enterprises at an unprecedented level, the consciousness of indigenous Egyptians was transformed. They were schooled or disciplined in the "truths" of the nation, and dress and fashion were symbolic of new identities. Peasant garb was removed when they entered administrative roles. Individuals had to situate themselves in a new representational order, one where deciding to wear the signs of the effendi, fez and suit instead of turban and *jallabiyya*, or to wear the hijab or veil, was a political decision. As early as the Syrian campaign, Ibrahim noted that a peasant removed from his village and subject to the army's discipline, its standardized regulations, refused to accept the arbitrary commands of his Turkish-speaking superiors. That consciousness or "subjectivity" spread from the military conscripts to other sectors of society, from state actors to nonstate actors.[45]

NONSTATE ACTORS

The modern state represented its power by maintaining inequalities between Ottoman Egyptians and the Arabic-speaking Egyptian majority, emphasizing the state's power over society. Yet power was also to be negotiated with nonstate actors: households, descent groups, and religious networks and constituencies. In this sense, the study of politics involves a different set of rules, beyond the legal codes and symbolism of the modern state and the elites, involving those of lower-class or marginal groups.

Defining the boundaries of the state, and therefore state and nonstate actors, is not necessarily straightforward. Historically, the state relied on the autonomy of social networks to provide basic services. In Cairo, the destitute resorted to the beneficence of the religious networks housed in the mosque complexes of al-Azhar or al-Husayn. In the provinces, as Judith Tucker has observed, the state could extract resources and labor from the fellahin because households provided all the basic needs of the population: subsistence farming; shelter; care for the young, the old, and the sick; and basic "social regulation."[46] The intrusive character of the modern state meant that it was situated in spheres of authority that overlapped with existing social authorities. The shaykh, a term designating the head of the village community, urban neighborhood, guild, or Sufi brotherhood, was exemplary of this role. Normally it is argued that these social authorities came under state control in the nineteenth century. The heads of the villages and neighborhoods acted as state servants, conducting census surveys for tax collection, levying the corvée, and conscripting for the military. But the shaykhs could open or close their communities to the state, impose regulations, and carry petitions to rulers—in short, they could act as leaders of social protest.

The ambitious state projects of Muhammad ʿAli or Ismaʿil exaggerate the state's power and its capacity to manage society. Before 1848, village revolts against conscription and tax collection constituted a kind of primary resistance to the state, but secondary forms of resistance involved negotiations and accommodations with the ruling elite.[47] Studies of *siyasa,* or administrative court records, demonstrate that ordinary subjects appealed to the apparent universalism of the modern legal codes to protect their "rights" against the power of state officials, as represented by the great Ottoman Egyptian households. This meant conflict between the Arabic-speaking Egyptians (*ibn al-balad* or fellah) and the Ottoman Egyptian elites (pasha, bey, or, as a collective, *dhawat*). In cases where the application of modern legal codes was intrusive or wielded by the elites for self-interest, complainants turned to the *siyasa* courts. The creation of the modern criminal code and a new police service might have provided an enhanced mechanism of state control, but it also represented the principle of universal justice and due process. The resort to law by subjects revealed the way the representational effect of the modern codes created competing authorities: the rising fortunes of the educated technicians, like those of the police, staffed by Arabic-speaking Egyptians, offered a means for lower orders to protest elite demands by an appeal to legality.[48] In his discussion of medical reform, Khaled Fahmy regards medical professionals as offering mechanisms for lower-class Egyptians to seek social justice through the new legal codes on autopsy and burial, which again placed the lower-level officials in the position of representing the people against the power of the Ottoman Egyptian elite. *Siyasa* regulations were a leveler, applied and interpreted differently by different spheres of authority: elite, middle-level technicians from the modern schools, and the 'ulama', with the latter two categories sometimes acting as popular representatives.[49]

These changes resulted in diverse interpretations of the legal codes and an increasing consciousness of the political implications of the new laws. Particularly, the private property law of 1858 and the abolition of the corvée in the 1860s provided new incentives for nonstate actors to involve themselves in politics. Workers, particularly those involved in transportation services in Alexandria, where European merchants had transformed the market, contravened old guild customs and took competitive bids on their labor. Guild masters and state authorities attempted to control wages through old guild mechanisms against individualist claims to sell labor freely. In some cases, however, guild masters represented these new claims by attempting to assert the guild's right to sell its services to competing bidders on the market rather than bowing to state directives. Likewise, because private ownership of land and the development of wage labor or sharecropping on the Ottoman Egyptian estates had a negative impact on the small landholding fellahin, peasants turned to the cotton market to raise profits. Resentment against the elite monopoly of land and labor resulted in petitions and encroachments on the royal estates. These examples suggest a desire to renegotiate the "social contract" during a period of rapid economic and demographic change. The evidence suggests that sometimes the shaykhs manipulated the new economy for personal profit, often in alliance with Ottoman Egyptian elites, but the shaykhs could also represent the interests of their constituents and seek a renegotiation of state–society relations.[50] These examples indicate that the notables, shaykhs of guilds and village communities, were not overawed by the power of the state. Because the state depended upon community leaders for essential services, the social leadership was semi-autonomous and representative.[51]

In the 1870s, state debt, overtaxation, penury, and the starvation of thousands in the summer of 1878 pushed the shaykhs, urban and rural, toward identification with the lower orders against the Ottoman Egyptian elite. Studies have applied the insights of social historians to illustrate the workings of the social contract or "moral economy" of Egyptian social relations.[52] Thus, the Ottoman concept of the sultan as the shepherd of his flock, or the circle of equity, that had legitimized rule when it was just or moral could also serve as a justification for revolt when it was not. Timothy Mitchell's insight with regards to Muhammad al-Muwaylihi's work *Eight Words* (1880) suggests that interpretations that emphasize the proliferation of liberal ideas through concepts like citizenship, rights, and liberty miss the point that the main reference was to the circle of equity principle, that is to say, the mutual obligations of the ruling group and subject population. Similarly, historians in Egypt writing biographical dictionaries spoke of the revival of the role of the notables, *a'yan* and *'ulama'*, as leaders of the community in critical moments. The community was conceived as a hierarchy in which the notables invoked the obligation of the ruler and the elites to govern for the common good. In these interpretations, the notables were leaders of their communities, the "people," rather than state agents. This interpretation found its way into the nationalist histories of the liberal and republican eras.[53]

These studies emphasized the overlapping spheres of authority of the state and social corporations, like village and guild. To some degree, the revolutionary years of the 1870s and 1880s indicate continuity with the court politics of the middle years, with branches of the royal household attempting to bring about regime change by patronizing political "societies," or salons, and employing discourses on constitutionalism that were then current in Istanbul. On the other hand, the period suggests a break with court politics and the introduction of new groups in politics, often associated with the emergence or revival of civil society organizations. From the middle years of the century, the reformist royal households used charitable organizations to legitimate their authority, building hospitals, dispensaries, orphanages, schools, and other service "societies." In doing so, the dynasty created competing authorities, offering new opportunities to nonstate actors. The formation of something like a civil society intersected with the appearance of the notables or middle stratum as autonomous social actors in the second half of the century, evident in the formation of various *jam'iyyat*, or "societies," whether charitable, literary, scientific, mystic, or political. The *jam'iyyat* took inspiration from old institutions, like the guilds or religious fraternities, but reoriented toward new memberships and clienteles. These societies were not conceived as Ottoman, imperial, or state enterprises. Al-Jam'iyya al-Khayriyya al-Islamiyya (Muslim Benevolent Society) and other societies from the 1870s offered various services for the lower classes as well as political forums for critiques of despotic government and European interventions, like the Debt Commission. Although founded on regional, neighborhood, religious, or other networks, the societies provided the organizational capacity, or "resource mobilization," for political opposition, as evident in the "movement" that led to the deposition of Isma'il in 1879 and the revolution of 1881–82. The societies continued to flourish after the British military occupation, with the ruling household, as well as leading politicians like Sa'd Zaghlul and Mustafa Kamil, enabling societies of various types that advocated on behalf of the "people" or "nation." In fact, these concepts were adopted as the labels for the two prominent political parties that emerged at the end of the century, the *umma* (people) and *watani* (national) parties. These oppositional political groups (after 1907, political parties) were pivotal in producing revolutionary and nationalist critiques of colonial rule.

Like the societies, the revival of print media began with the accession of Isma'il to power in 1863. Initially under state management, by the 1870s a private press had formed and served the evolving sense of a "public" sphere of political activity, as represented primarily by the rural notables, urban guilds, and merchants. Each group had by then invested in an economy loosened from state management through private property holdings and wage labor markets. This autonomy was threatened by the excessive taxes of post–debt crisis Egypt. It was to this "public" that the ideologues and activists of the societies and the press appealed as consumers of their words, images, and texts.

The power of societies and the press, however informal, was substantial because public advocacy brought about a change of policy and personnel, memorably in the 1879 deposition of Isma'il and the accession of Tawfiq. That the latter failed to bring about a change of policy led to the parliament of 1881–82. It was a parliament of rural and urban notables; even its most prominent Ottoman Egyptian politician and great landlord, Muhammad Sultan, had his origins in the rural notability. The clash between the Ottoman Egyptian elite and the popular representatives had an impact on nonstate actors, integrating various social groups into politics. The formation of the revolutionary "crowd," evident in protests and demonstrations in cities and the provinces, involved nonstate social networks: guilds, professional associations, societies, neighborhood leaders (*futuwwa*), and their constituencies.[54]

Popular politics resulted in new political idioms, evident in revolutionary documents that indicate the influence of Islamic ideology during the 'Urabi-led campaign, such as the petitions sent by guild shaykhs to the Ministry of Interior in the late 1870s asserting the obligations of the ruler to his subjects.[55] There were also popular (*baladi*) expressions of dissent in colloquial Arabic, particularly in musical and theatrical performance, that appealed to the ordinary residents of Cairo. This "nativist" language was also appropriated by the cultural leadership, creating a colloquial style that emphasized a local or "national" identification with politics.[56] This strand of revolutionary activism was influenced by European, Armenian, and various Levantine groups resident in Egypt—which were particularly open to the political radicalism of southern Europe—and was disseminated in the press, *jam'iyyat*, and nonstate schools.[57]

The British intervention of 1882 resulted in the constitutional reform ("Organic law") of 1883, after which European colonies formed a kind of senate that checked Egyptian administrative initiatives through their powers in the Mixed Courts and consular courts. The 1895 administrative reorganization also increased the power of the executive branch under British advisers. Therefore, informal societies and the press remained important oppositional tools. Mustafa Kamil deployed each for the reformation of cultural attitudes from the 1890s. His work involved the publication of articles in *Majallat al-Madrasa* (School Journal), and afterward *al-Liwa'* (The Standard), and the mobilization of activist cadres, evident in the student strikes of 1906, a rehearsal for the sort of political mobilization that marked the first stages of the 1919 Revolution.[58]

Conclusion

Egyptian politics was transformed by an experiment in state-building drawing on models imported from Europe. The consequence was a new patrimony with Cairo as its center. Muhammad 'Ali secured the dynasty in relation to the Ottomans and Europeans and deepened its ability to mobilize resources for the military through the export of commodities and the building of the necessary infrastructure.

In the first half of the nineteenth century, the new order (*nizam jadid*) and its method, *siyasa*, seemed to act upon the inert body of Egyptian society. Perhaps this image captures the shock of the new and the difficulty for society to respond and make or stake its claims upon the state. Certain social groups did so in autochthonous revolt; others engaged in negotiations with the new state regulations and their agents, the effendi administrators, and the Ottoman Egyptian elite. These elite groups expanded and integrated in the course of the nineteenth century, resulting in the formation of a political society conscious of its place in a public sphere. A combination of these responses and developments took complex form in the revolution of 1881–82 because the popular movement dovetailed with the constitutionalists in Istanbul and their satellites in Cairo. The revolution indicated that the state was not so powerful and that social groups and institutions had adapted to modern forms of political management. This "national" challenge to the "dual elite," dynastic and colonial, was subsequently associated with the *effendiyya*, a "class" emerging from the last quarter of the nineteenth century. It was this class that, through its cultural works, particularly historical and political writings, framed a "temporality" in which the nineteenth century was a precursor to national emancipation in the twentieth. This historical framework is problematic because it was premised on conformity to modernity and the nation, an attitude never entertained by Muhammad 'Ali and his heirs, nor even by some of the more exemplary effendi nationalists in the late nineteenth century.[59]

NOTES

1. A critical study of the historical literature in this vein can be found in Kenneth Cuno, *The Pasha's Peasants: Land, Society, and Economy in Lower Egypt, 1740–1858* (New York: Cambridge University Press, 1992).
2. Fred Lawson, *The Social Origins of Egyptian Expansionism during the Muhammad 'Ali Period* (New York: Columbia University Press, 1992).
3. Gabriel Piterberg, "The Tropes of Stagnation and Awakening in Nationalist Historical Consciousness: The Egyptian Case," in *Rethinking Nationalism in the Arab Middle East*, ed. James Jankowski and Israel Gershoni (New York: Columbia University Press, 1997).
4. Khaled Fahmy, *All the Pasha's Men: Mehmed Ali, His Army, and the Making of Modern Egypt* (New York: Cambridge University Press, 1997).
5. Afaf Lutfi al-Sayyid Marsot, *Egypt in the Reign of Muhammad 'Ali* (New York: Cambridge University Press, 1984).
6. Fahmy, *All the Pasha's Men*, 268–77.
7. Rudolph Peters, "State, Law, and Society in Nineteenth-Century Egypt," *Die Welt des Islams* 39, no. 3 (1999): 267–72.
8. Ehud Toledano, *State and Society in Mid-Nineteenth-Century Egypt* (Cambridge: Cambridge University Press, 1990), 125, 135–39, claims the demon image was jointly a product of the French colony and Ibrahim's household within the Muhammad 'Ali dynasty and their allies in Istanbul and Paris.

9. F. Robert Hunter, *Egypt under the Khedives, 1805–1879: From Household Government to Bureaucracy* (Pittsburgh: Pittsburgh University Press, 1984).

10. Anthony Gorman and Sossie Kasbarian, eds., *Diasporas of the Modern Middle East: Contextualising Communities* (Edinburgh: University of Edinburgh Press, 2015); Mary Louise Pratt, *Imperial Eyes: Travel Writing and Transculturation* (New York: Routledge, 1992); Sami Zubaida, "Cosmopolitanism in the Middle East," *Amsterdam Middle East Papers* 12 (1997): 1–21; David Lambert and Alan Lester, eds., *Colonial Lives across the British Empire: Imperial Careering in the Long Nineteenth Century* (Cambridge: Cambridge University Press, 2006).

11. Will Hanley, *Identifying with Nationality: Europeans, Ottomans, and Egyptians in Alexandria* (New York: Columbia University Press, 2017); Shana Minkin, *Imperial Bodies: Empire and Death in Alexandria, Egypt* (Stanford, CA: Stanford University Press, 2020).

12. Edward Said, *Orientalism* (New York: Routledge, 1978); Derek Gregory, "Performing Cairo: Orientalism and the City of the Arabian Nights," in *Making Cairo Medieval*, ed. Nezar Al-Sayyad, Irene A. Bierman, and Nasser Rabbat (Lanham, MD: Lexington Books, 2005).

13. Shane Minkin, "Documenting Death: Inquests, Governance, and Belonging in 1890s Alexandria," in *The Long 1890s in Egypt: Colonial Quiescence and Resistance*, ed. Marilyn Booth and Anthony Gorman (Edinburgh: Edinburgh Press, 2014), 31–56.

14. Michael Reimer, *Colonial Bridgehead: Government and Society in Alexandria, 1807–1882* (Cairo: American University in Cairo Press, 1997).

15. David Landes, *Bankers and Pashas: International Finance and Economic Imperialism in Egypt* (Cambridge, MA: Harvard University Press, 1958).

16. Roger Owen, *Cotton and the Egyptian Economy: A Study in Trade and Development* (Oxford: Clarendon Press, 1969).

17. Latifah Muhammad Salim, *al-Quwa al-Ijtimaʿiyya fi al-Thawra al-ʿUrabiyya* (Cairo: al-Hayʾa al-Misriyya al-ʿAmma li-l-Kitab, 1981); ʿAbd al-ʿAzim al-Ramadan, *Tatawwur al-Haraka al-Wataniyya fi Misr*, 2 vols. (Cairo: al-Hayʾa al-Misriyya al-ʿAmma li-l-Kitab, 1998).

18. Juan Cole, *Colonialism and Revolution in the Middle East: Social and Cultural Origins of Egypt's ʿUrabi Movement* (Princeton, NJ: Princeton University Press, 1993).

19. Ronald Robinson, "The Non-European Foundations of European Imperialism: Sketch for a Theory of Collaboration," in *Studies in the Theory of Imperialism*, ed. Roger Owen and Robert Sutcliffe (London: Longman, 1972). See a critical reappraisal of the view that the term *free trade* is applicable to the situation in A. G. Hopkins, "The Victorians and Africa: A Reconsideration of the Occupation of Egypt, 1882," *Journal of African History* 27, no. 2 (1986): 363–91.

20. For a study critical of the republican-era histories and their description of social relations as feudal, see Raouf Abbas and Assem El-Dessouky, *The Large Landowning Class and the Peasantry in Egypt, 1837–1952* (Cairo: Dar Qiba li-l-Nashr wa-l-Tawziʿ, 1998; Syracuse: Syracuse University Press, 2011), who point to the mutually beneficial relationship foreign financiers and industrialists had with the large landowning class, to the cost of the fellahin, or smallholders.

21. Gabriel Baer, *The History of Landownership in Modern Egypt, 1800–1950* (London: Oxford University Press, 1962); Baer, *Studies in the Social History of Modern Egypt* (Chicago: University of Chicago Press, 1969).

22. Albert Hourani, "Ottoman Reform and the Politics of the Notables," in *Beginnings of Modernization in the Middle East: The Nineteenth Century*, ed. William Polk and Richard Chambers (Chicago: University of Chicago Press, 1968).

23. Jacob Landau, *Parliaments and Parties in Egypt* (Tel Aviv: Israel Publishing House, 1953).

24. Roger Owen, "Egypt and Europe: From French Expedition to British Occupation," in *Studies in the Theory of Imperialism*. Contemporary opinion critical of the convergence of bondholders with government officials and agents is represented by Wilfred Scawen Blunt, *The Secret History of the English Occupation of Egypt: Being a Personal Account of Events* (New York: Alfred A. Knopf, 1922).

25. Roger Owen, *Lord Cromer, Victorian Imperialist, Edwardian Proconsul* (Oxford: Oxford University Press, 2004).

26. Aaron Jakes, "The Scales of Public Utility: Agricultural Roads and State Space in the Era of the British Occupation," in *The Long 1890s in Egypt*, 57–86.

27. Ehud Toledano, "Muhammad Farid: Between Nationalism and the Egyptian-Ottoman Diaspora," in *Diasporas of the Modern Middle East*, 70–102.

28. Matthew Ellis, *Desert Borderland: The Making of Modern Egypt and Libya* (Stanford, CA: Stanford University Press, 2018).

29. Roger Owen and Şevket Pamuk, *A History of Middle East Economics in the Twentieth Century* (Cambridge, MA: Harvard University Press, 1999), 4.

30. Timothy Mitchell, *Colonising Egypt* (Cambridge: Cambridge University Press, 1988), 32.

31. Fahmy, *All the Pashas Men*, 152.

32. The nationalist school, royalist and republican, similarly viewed Muhammad 'Ali as the founder of the Egyptian nation. The royalist nationalist school is represented by Hanotaux Gabriel, *Histoire de la nation Égyptienne*, 7 vols. (Paris: Ouvrages publie sous les auspices et la haute patronage de sa majesté Fouad I, Roi de l'Égypte, 1930–37); the republican nationalist school is represented by 'Abd al-Rahman al-Rafi'i, *'Asr Muhammad 'Ali* (Cairo: Mataba'at al-Fikra, 1930).

33. The point was made by a royalist historian, Diaeddine Saleh, *Les Pouvoirs du Roi dans la Constitution Égyptienne* (Paris: Libraire Générale de Droit et le Jurisprudence, 1939). It was also the opinion of the European colonies resident in Egypt during the era of Muhammad 'Ali; see Edward William Lane, *The Manners and Customs of the Modern Egyptians* (London: Society for the Diffusion of Useful Knowledge, 1836; The Hague: East-West Publications, 1978), 115, 195, 562, nn. 10 and 11.

34. 'Ali Barakat, *Tatawwur al-Milkiyya al-Zira'iyya al-Kabira fi Misr, 1813–1914* (Cairo: Dar al-Thaqafa al-Jadida, 1977).

35. Nihal Tamraz, *Nineteenth-Century Cairene Houses and Palaces* (Cairo: American University in Cairo Press, 1998).

36. Ellen A. McLarney, "Freedom, Justice, and the Power of *Adab*," *International Journal of Middle East Studies* 48, no. 1 (2016): 25–46.

37. Mona Russell, *Creating the New Egyptian Woman: Consumerism, Education, and the National Identity* (New York: Palgrave, 2004).

38. Michael Gasper, *The Power of Representation: Publics, Peasants, and Islam in Egypt* (Stanford, CA: Stanford University Press, 2009).

39. Beth Baron, *Egypt as a Woman: Nationalism, Gender, and Politics* (Berkeley, CA: University of California Press, 2007), 58–63.

40. James Whidden, "Zaki Fahmi's *Safwat al-'Asr*: A Description of the Egyptian Elite and an Islamic Prescription for the Political Order," *The Journal of North African Studies* 2, no. 2 (1997): 68–82.

41. Ali Mubarak, *Al-Khitat al-Tawfiqiyya al-Jadida* (Cairo: n.p., 1886–89); Butrus al-Bustani, *Da'irat al-Ma'arif* (Cairo: n.p., 1900); Ilyas Zakhura, *Mir'at al-'Asr* (Cairo: n.p., 1897–1916); Zaki Fahmi, *Safwat al-'Asr* (Cairo: Maktaba al-Nahda al-Misriyya, 1926); Ahmad Taymur, *Tarajim A'yan* (Cairo: 'Abd al-Hamid Ahmad Hanafi, 1940).

42. Toledano, *State and Society*, 31–32, notes that indigenous historical writing in the late nineteenth century seemed unaware of the European narratives on Egypt that would come to influence the nationalist writings in Arabic in the twentieth century.

43. Toledano, *State and Society*, 87; Leila Ahmed, *Women and Gender in Islam* (New Haven, CT: Yale University Press, 1992).

44. Lisa Pollard, *Nurturing the Nation: The Family Politics of Modernizing, Colonizing and Liberating Egypt, 1805–1923* (Berkeley: University of California Press, 2005).

45. On the significance of peasant dress, see 'Ali Mubarak, as cited by Baer, *Social History*, 37; Toledano, *State and Society*, 160–63; and Wilson Chacko Jacob, *Working Out Egypt: Effendi Masculinity and Subject Formation in Colonial Modernity, 1870–1940* (Durham, NC: Duke University Press, 2011), 195–98.

46. Judith Tucker, *Women in Nineteenth-Century Egypt* (New York: Cambridge University Press, 1985), 42.

47. Zeinab Abul-Magd, "Rebellion in the Time of Cholera: Failed Empire, Unfinished Nation in Egypt, 1840–1920," *Journal of World History* 21, no. 4 (2010): 691–719.

48. Khaled Fahmy, "The Police and the People in Nineteenth-Century Egypt," *Die Welt des Islams* 39, no. 3 (1999): 340–77; Toledano, *State and Society*, 177.

49. Khaled Fahmy, "The Anatomy of Justice: Forensic Medicine and Criminal Law in Nineteenth-Century Egypt," *Islamic Law and Society* 6, no. 2 (1999): 224–71.

50. Cole, *Colonialism and Revolution*, 74, for "social contract" and, 64–71, for examples of activism in the guilds and "social conflict" in the villages.

51. The issue of the autonomy of the guild shaykhs can be followed in Gabriel Baer, *Egyptian Guilds in Modern Times* (Jerusalem: Israel Oriental Society, 1964); André Raymond, *Artisans et commerçants au Caire au XVIII siècle* (Damascus: Institut Français de Damas, 1973); and Gabriel Baer, "Ottoman Guilds: A Reassessment," in *Social and Economic History of Turkey*, ed. Osman Okyar and Halil Inalcik (Ankara: Hacettepe University, 1980).

52. Nathan J. Brown, *Peasant Politics in Modern Egypt: The Struggle against the State* (New Haven, CT: Yale University Press, 1990), 183–93, argues that the rural notables, the shaykhs, could be the leaders of revolutionary activism.

53. Afaf Lutfi al-Sayyid Marsot, *A Short History of Modern Egypt* (Cambridge: Cambridge University Press, 1984). Representatives of the "new history" include Muhammad Sabry, *L'Empire égyptien sous Ismail* (Paris: Paul Geuthner, 1933); and 'Abd al-Rahman al-Rafi'i, *al-Thawra al-'Urabiyya* (Cairo: Maktaba al-Nahda al-Misriyya, 1939). The republican school is represented by Rif'at al-Sa'id, *al-Asas al-Ijtima'i fi al-Thawra al-'Urabiyya* (Cairo: Dar al-Kitab al-'Arabi, 1967).

54. The autonomy of lower-class revolutionary activism is underlined by 'Ali Barakat, *Tatawwur al-Milkiyya al-Zira'iyya*.

55. Cole, *Colonialism and Revolution*, 94; indebted to Eric Hobsbaum, *Primitive Rebels: Studies in Archaic Forms of Social Movement in the 19th and 20th Centuries* (London: Norton, 1959); E. P. Thompson, *The Making of the English Working Class* (New York: Vintage, 1963); and George Rudé, *The Crowd in History: A Study of Popular Disturbances in France and England, 1730–1848* (New York: John Wiley, 1964).

56. Ziad Fahmy, *Ordinary Egyptians: Creating the Modern Nation through Popular Culture* (Stanford, CA: Stanford University Press, 2011).

57. Ilham Khuri-Makdisi, *The Eastern Mediterranean and the Making of Global Radicalism, 1860–1914* (Berkeley: University of California Press, 2010). The term *nativist* was applied by Cole, *Colonialism and Revolution*, 94.

58. 'Abd al-Rahman al-Rafi'i, *Mustafa Kamil Ba'ith al-Haraka al-Wataniyya* (Cairo: Maktaba al-Nahda al-Misriyya, 1939), 199, 251.

59. Marilyn Booth, "Wayward Subjects and Negotiated Disciplines: Body Politics and the Boundaries of Egyptian Nationhood," *International Journal of Middle East Studies* 45, no. 2 (2013): 353–74.

BIBLIOGRAPHY

Abbas, Raouf, and Assem El-Dessouky. *The Large Landowning Class and the Peasantry in Egypt, 1837–1952*. Syracuse, NY: Syracuse University Press, 2011.

Baer, Gabriel. *Studies in the Social History of Modern Egypt*. Chicago: University of Chicago Press, 1969.

Baron, Beth. *Egypt as a Woman: Nationalism, Gender, and Politics*. Berkeley: University of California Press, 2007.

Booth, Marilyn, and Anthony Gorman, eds. *The Long 1890s in Egypt: Colonial Quiescence, Subterranean Resistance*. Edinburgh: Edinburgh University Press, 2014.

Cole, Juan. *Colonialism and Revolution in the Middle East: Social and Cultural Origins of Egypt's 'Urabi Movement*. Princeton, NJ: Princeton University Press, 1993.

Cuno, Kenneth. *The Pasha's Peasants: Land, Society, and Economy in Lower Egypt, 1740– 1858*. New York: Cambridge University Press, 1992.

Daly, M. W., ed. *The Cambridge History of Egypt*. Vol. 2, *Modern Egypt, from 1517 to the End of the Twentieth Century*. Cambridge: Cambridge University Press, 1998.

Fahmy, Khaled. *All the Pasha's Men: Mehmed Ali, His Army, and the Making of Modern Egypt*. New York: Cambridge University Press, 1997.

Groupe de Recherches et d'Études sur le Proche-Orient. *L'Égypte au XIXe Siècle*. Paris: Éditions du Centre National de la Recherche Scientifiques, 1982.

Holt, P. M. *Egypt and the Fertile Crescent, 1516–1922, A Political History*. Ithaca, NY: Cornell University Press, 1966.

Hunter, F. Robert. *Egypt under the Khedives, 1805–1879: From Household Government to Bureaucracy*. Pittsburgh: Pittsburgh University Press, 1984.

Mitchell, Timothy. *Colonising Egypt*. Cambridge: Cambridge University Press, 1988.

Owen, Roger. *The Middle East in the World Economy*. London: Methuen, 1981.

Pollard, Lisa. *Nurturing the Nation: The Family Politics of Modernizing, Colonizing and Liberating Egypt, 1805–1923*. Berkeley: University of California Press, 2005.

Russell, Mona. *Creating the New Egyptian Woman: Consumerism, Education, and the National Identity*. New York: Palgrave, 2004.

Al-Sayyid Marsot, Afaf Lutfi. *Egypt in the Reign of Muhammad 'Ali*. New York: Cambridge University Press, 1984.

Toledano, Ehud. *State and Society in Mid-Nineteenth-Century Egypt*. New York: Cambridge University Press, 1990,

Tucker, Judith. *Women in Nineteenth-Century Egypt*. New York: Cambridge University Press, 1985.

CHAPTER 22

....

LOCAL ENLIGHTENMENT IN THE COLONIAL PERIOD

Ahmad Lutfi al-Sayyid in Perspective

....

ISRAEL GERSHONI

AHMAD Lutfi al-Sayyid was among modern Egypt's most influential public intellectuals. A true Renaissance man, he was a lawyer, a journalist, an editor, a philosopher, an educator, a translator, a university rector, a politician, and a cabinet minister. Lutfi al-Sayyid left an indelible impact on twentieth-century Egyptian intellectual, academic, cultural, and political life, ripe for study by Egyptian and Western scholars of the Middle East. However, the historiography on his life and work is largely outdated; the last serious study on the subject is more than fifty years old.[1] In many respects, Lutfi al-Sayyid has been left by the wayside, at least within Middle Eastern studies.

Lutfi al-Sayyid's thought is therefore in need of reappraisal. Within his vast oeuvre, penned during his tenure as editor of *al-Jarida*, three main discursive formations stand out: his perspectives on Enlightenment and "civilization," his understanding of nationalism, and his attitude toward colonialism. Through an analysis of each theme, commonly held historiographical narratives about Lutfi al-Sayyid can be problematized, deconstructed, and refreshed. Whereas most research is narrowly focused on Lutfi al-Sayyid as a nationalist thinker, he is better thought of as a producer of Enlightenment, a project he aimed to transmit and domesticate within the local Egyptian environment. Lutfi al-Sayyid's liberal nationalist outlook was, in fact, but one aspect of his broader Enlightenment project. Moreover, in contrast to the perspective that he was a collaborator with the British occupation, which assumes that he was an Anglophile, Lutfi al-Sayyid thoroughly understood the coercive essence of British imperialism and virulently opposed it, seeking to bring about Egypt's liberation and independence.

LUTFI AL-SAYYID'S LIFE

Lutfi al-Sayyid was born on 15 January 1872 to a landowning family in the village of Barqayn, located in the district of Sinbillawayn in the Daqahliyya province, where his father was the village shaykh (*'umda*). He studied in the local village *kuttab* (Qur'anic school), then at the government elementary school in Mansoura (1882–85), and subsequently at the khedival secondary school in Cairo (1885–89). Lutfi al-Sayyid's father wanted his talented son to study at the prestigious al-Azhar Islamic religious college; however, at the suggestion of a family friend, Lutfi al-Sayyid was sent to the khedival school of law in Cairo (1889–94). After graduating, he was appointed by the Ministry of Justice of the Egyptian-British colonial government to the post of deputy public prosecutor in Bani Suwayf, then in al-Fayum, and finally in Mit Ghamr, and was promoted in 1896 to head prosecutor in al-Minya.

Simultaneously, he took part in nationalist, anticolonial activities and joined the underground organization al-Hizb al-Watani (the Patriotic Party, later the Nationalist Party), which was supported by Khedive 'Abbas Hilmi II. At the behest of the khedive, Lutfi al-Sayyid was sent to study in Geneva to gain Swiss citizenship. Once he returned, he would establish and edit a national newspaper that opposed the British occupation, though the newspaper was protected from prosecution by the Capitulations under the Press Law of 1881, thanks to his newly gained foreign citizenship. However, while in Geneva, Lutfi al-Sayyid met Muhammad 'Abduh, the Islamic reformist and modernist, and Qasim Amin, the feminist thinker, and under their influence he began to distance himself from the autocratic khedive and embrace a more liberal reformist worldview. Upon his return to Egypt, he continued for a short time as a public prosecutor until his alienation from the Egyptian-British colonial regime spurred him to quit in 1905 and seek a new channel for expressing his oppositional views. He identified an outlet for his public engagement in September 1907 when a group of liberals, with the support of respected landowning notables, founded the political party Hizb al-Umma (Party of the Nation). The party was established as a moderate force against British colonialism, in opposition to both the khedive and Mustafa Kamil's Islamic Ottoman-oriented nationalism. Lutfi al-Sayyid was appointed secretary of the party and editor of its daily publication, *al-Jarida*, launched in March 1907, and emerged as the party's most prominent ideologue.

Al-Jarida operated under his leadership until 1915, when Britain's declaration of a protectorate over Egypt and the outbreak of World War I forced the daily to fold. Lutfi al-Sayyid had been appointed director of the National Library (Dar al-Kutub), a position he held until slightly after the end of the war. During this period, he began systematically translating the works of Aristotle, starting with *Nicomachean Ethics* (*'Ilm al-Akhlaq*, published in 1924). He later translated other central works of the Greek philosopher, chief among them *Politics* (*al-Siyasa*, published in 1947).

In the fall of 1918, Lutfi al-Sayyid was among the founders of the Wafd and a senior member of its high command. He took part in the Wafd's activities and in leading the 1919 Revolution in challenge to the British protectorate and in support of Egyptian self-determination. But conflict with the Wafd's authoritative leader, Sa'd Zaghlul, forced him and other activists to leave the Wafd and establish a new party, Hizb al-Ahrar al-Dusturiyyin (Liberal Constitutionalist Party), in 1922–23. Shortly thereafter, Lutfi al-Sayyid left party politics entirely for the life of a scholar and academic administrator. In 1925, he was appointed rector of the Egyptian University (Cairo University since 1952). As rector between 1925 and 1932 (with a short break to serve as minister of education) and then again between 1935 and 1941, Lutfi al-Sayyid was the driving force behind the university's growth, including the integration of female students. Between the two world wars and in the 1940s, he was asked numerous times to serve as a senior government minister. He served as minister of education in Muhammad Mahmud's first government (1928–29), as minister of state in Mahmud's second and third governments (1937–38), and as minister of foreign affairs under Isma'il Sidqi in 1946. In 1942, he became, for a limited time, a member of the senate. In 1940, he was appointed a member of the Arabic Language Academy, and, in 1944, he was elected to serve as its president, a role he held until his death.

Despite diverse academic, educational, and political activities spanning more than seven decades, Lutfi al-Sayyid's primary intellectual contribution was concentrated in a short, defined, and extremely productive period: early in his career as the founder and editor of the daily *al-Jarida* (1907–14). As editor, Lutfi al-Sayyid surrounded himself with a talented group of young Egyptian intellectuals and authors, male and female, whose careers began, with his encouragement, via the publication of their early works in *al-Jarida*. Lutfi al-Sayyid was their mentor. He was their model of a public intellectual, shaping their ideological and ethical world through his striking charisma. Many of them, in the interwar period and later in the 1940s–60s, went on to become some of the most creative and prominent producers and architects of print culture in Egypt and the Arab Middle East. Out of immense admiration, his disciples and followers bestowed upon Lutfi al-Sayyid the nickname "the teacher of the generation" (*ustadh al-jil*), a title that no one held before him or would hold after him. Lutfi al-Sayyid died on 5 March 1963.[2]

LUTFI AL-SAYYID'S TEACHINGS:
GENERAL BACKGROUND

As the prolific editor of *al-Jarida* between 1907 and 1915, Lutfi al-Sayyid contributed almost daily editorials, articles, essays, and reviews. Without a doubt, this was his finest hour as a public intellectual, fulfilling Antonio Gramsci's prototype of an "organic intellectual" or Edward Said's dictum "speaking truth to power."[3] Many of his articles included responses to current events, placing them in their philosophical, historical, or sociological contexts, and weaving politics into social, cultural, economic, gender, ethical, or aesthetic issues. His editorial pieces came together as an extensive corpus of hundreds of articles, essays, and responsa, characterized by his sharp and clairvoyant insights. In the 1930s and 1940s, hundreds of his articles on various topics from *al-Jarida* were compiled and republished, institutionalizing and canonizing his writings in twentieth-century Egyptian thought.

A substantial portion of his articles challenged Egypt's very foundation: Lutfi al-Sayyid composed in-depth criticisms of the political system, declaring its enslavement by unbridled autocratic and authoritarian forces. He indiscriminately critiqued the British colonial regime and the acquiescent Egyptian government led by Khedive 'Abbas Hilmi II and his Islamist Ottomanism. Lutfi al-Sayyid even went as far as skewering the leaders of his own political party, Hizb al-Umma, which represented the interests of the large landowners in Egypt. He demanded that Egypt's political system become a modern constitutional parliamentary democracy, based on the separation of powers, the rule of law, and general elections, in order to enable Egyptians to rule themselves, bringing their own interests and aspirations to fruition.

In Lutfi al-Sayyid's discussions of the relations between nation and class, he always put the nation first. Yet within conventional historiography, Lutfi al-Sayyid's corpus of thought was reduced to his material interest, driven by the class to which he belonged: the *a'yan*, or landowning notables. This prevailing argument further claims that his liberal weltanschauung (worldview) was cultivated to provide ideological legitimacy to this elitist stratum, from which Lutfi al-Sayyid and other members of Hizb al-Umma originated. The overall aim of this liberal ideology, as claimed by scholars, was to translate their socioeconomic power into political hegemony.[4] However, a more contextualized reading of Lutfi al-Sayyid's work clearly debunks this misleading material, classist explanation. First, there is absolutely no mention of classist motivation in any of his writing. Second, and more importantly, Lutfi al-Sayyid always discussed "the nation" in its entirety, using the term *umma* (nation) and sometimes *sha'b* (people) or *ahl misr* (inhabitants of Egypt). His nationalist message was never aimed at any specific class (*tabaqa*). Third, many of the young writers he mentored, such as Taha Husayn, 'Abbas Mahmud al-'Aqqad, or Malak Hifni Nasif, originated from the lower and middle classes, reflecting his prioritization of the nation as a whole rather than classist snobbery.

ENLIGHTENMENT: ASSIMILATION AND DOMESTICATION

Historians regard Lutfi al-Sayyid as the founder of Egyptian nationalism, positing that his life's work strove to shape a distinctive Egyptian territorial nationalism and a unique and localized national identity.[5] However, in many ways, this is a reductionist, misleading narrative that does little justice to Lutfi al-Sayyid's broader, multilayered worldview and is incorrect in the historical context in which he wrote and worked. From 1907 to 1915, his writing focused systematically on the Enlightenment and the need for its localization within the Egyptian landscape. Lutfi al-Sayyid seems to have been obsessed with assimilating Enlightenment principles, values, and practices into Egypt's sociopolitical fabric and cultural life to create tangible change. He consistently strove to shape an indigenous, homemade Egyptian Enlightenment as a model for the rest of the Arab Middle East. Hence, Lutfi al-Sayyid should not be seen primarily or only as a visionary of modern Egyptian nationalism, important as it is. Rather, he should be identified as the major agent in the creation of an Egyptian version of the Enlightenment, promoting and encouraging Egypt within the global context.

Lutfi's interaction with the European Enlightenment (*al-tanwir*) and "civilization" (in his words, *tamaddun, tamdin*) was not made from scratch. He was one *nahdawi* intellectual in a long chain of *nahdawis* (Enlightenment thinkers) dating back to the mid-nineteenth century who created a discursive context to compile and execute the Enlightenment project, which Lutfi al-Sayyid applied in his own Egyptian recitation. Throughout the late nineteenth century, particularly from 1870 to 1914 (the late *nahda* period), intellectuals and authors from the Ottoman Arab provinces confronted the European Enlightenment and proposed strategies for its propagation in their local environment. Prominent among these men and women were Ahmad Faris al-Shidyaq, Rifa'a Rafi' al-Tahtawi, Butrus and Sulayman al-Bustani, Ibrahim and Nassif al-Yaziji, Ya'qub Sanu', Jamal al-Din al-Afghani, Muhammad 'Abduh, 'Abd Allah al-Nadim, Farah Antun, Shibli Shumayyil, Zaynab Fawwaz, Jurji Zaydan, Rashid Rida, 'Abd al-Rahman al-Kawakibi, Esther Moyal, Labiba Hashim, and Mayy Ziyada as well as Lutfi al-Sayyid's close peers Qasim Amin, Ahmad Fathi Zaghlul, and Malak Hifni Nasif.[6] The modernist intellectual activities of the Young Ottoman movement in the 1860s and 1870s also contributed to reckoning with Enlightenment values promoted by Tanzimat (Ottoman-era government reforms) leaders and bureaucrats, especially from 1839 to 1876.[7] In Egypt itself, throughout the entire nineteenth century, Mehmet 'Ali and his heirs, the khedives, and Isma'il in particular persistently worked toward reform and modernization, creating an environment ripe for Lutfi al-Sayyid and *al-Jarida*'s ambitious undertakings.

Furthermore, under Lutfi al-Sayyid's leadership, *al-Jarida* infused the *nahdawi* scene with new energy, groundbreaking terminology, and a more systematic, aggressive effort to spur change by borrowing and transferring Enlightenment concepts, ideas, practices, and institutions to the local Egyptian environment. This process was accomplished mainly through disseminating knowledge: educating elite groups as well as broader sectors of society to accept these innovative, modern products. Simultaneously, Lutfi al-Sayyid identified archaic traditions, habits, ideas, and practices that needed to be changed or eliminated to pave the way for these new modern systems. In this pioneering enterprise, Lutfi al-Sayyid mobilized a broad effort to compose an authentic Egyptian Enlightenment with distinctive characteristics—later, during the interwar era, taken over and refined by his disciples, Taha Husayn, Muhammad

Husayn Haykal, 'Abbas Mahmud al-'Aqqad, Salama Musa, Ahmad Amin, Ibrahim 'Abd al-Qadir Mazini, Malak Hifni Nasif, Labiba Hashim, Mayy Ziyada, Nabawiyya Musa, and even younger thinkers such as Luwis 'Awad and A'isha 'Abd al-Rahman, known as Bint al-Shati'.[8]

Historically, Lutfi al-Sayyid stood apart in his rigorous, systematic, and comprehensive pattern of thinking, meticulously implementing this local Enlightenment project. The first step was methodological: he clarified for himself and explained to his readers the necessary procedures to appropriate and convert intellectual and material products from Europe to Egypt, particularly those from England and France, where he visited more than once. Lutfi al-Sayyid innovated his procedural approach: understanding the idea, preparing it anew, appropriating it, translating it, and adapting it to the unique local context through arduous domestication. He was entirely aware, perhaps even more than those before him, that it was infeasible to simply imitate a European concept or institution and integrate it, as is, into the local environment. He learned this lesson from the failures of the megalomaniacal undertakings executed by Khedive Isma'il to "simply" Westernize Egypt, which he strongly opposed. As a solution to this gaffe, he created the process of "Egyptianization" (*tamsir*): infusing European concepts, practices, and institutions with local Egyptian culture, norms, and values. The guiding principle was that products that could not be Egyptianized would be left by the wayside. Thus, in tens of articles, Lutfi al-Sayyid established that only through this creative, involved enterprise would it be possible to "enlighten" Egyptian society and bring it forth to the modern age.

The process of "Egyptianizing civilization" (*tamsir al-tamaddun*) involved reinterpreting ideas and terms from the nineteenth-century Enlightenment. For example, the concept of "progress" (*taqaddum*) must be value-based rather than technical, encompassing far more than technology and requiring an internalized "progressive consciousness" to integrate innovation into Egypt's frame of mind. Similarly, the concept of "nationalism" (*qawmiyya*) was to be reshaped and genuinely domesticated to match the diverse identities of the local Egyptian populace: it needed to be charged with indigenous motifs, symbols, memories, and practices. In this process of assimilating Enlightenment, the intellectual is an architect, building a "domestic" structure on "imported" scaffolding. The intellectual's work is not passive but creative, not mechanical but artistic, involving a strategic selection to market his products to target consumers. Thus, the integration and domestication process was an expansive, ambitious, detail-oriented project undertaken by Lutfi al-Sayyid and *al-Jarida* for the Egyptian community, Copts, Muslims, and Jews residing in the Nile Valley.[9]

Lutfi al-Sayyid's encounter with Enlightenment ideas and practices was mainly with seventeenth- and eighteenth-century European philosophers and their followers in the nineteenth century. He read and carefully absorbed the writings of John Locke, Charles Montesquieu, Jean-Jacques Rousseau, and Immanuel Kant, as well as those by Jeremy Bentham, Alexis de Tocqueville, John Stuart Mill, Leo Tolstoy, and most importantly, Herbert Spencer. Indeed, Spencer became a central intellectual figure whose diverse writings impacted Lutfi al-Sayyid, along with the later *nahda* discourse. Some of

Spencer's and other European Enlightenment thinkers' writing was already translated into Arabic, but Lutfi al-Sayyid read them in the original French or English. From these *luminaires*, Lutfi al-Sayyid realized that to be modern and enlightened, Egyptian society must accept the central ideas of individual and collective freedom, reason, rationalism, science, justice and equality, positivism, utilitarianism, evolutionism, modern technology, nationalism, feminism, civic rights, democracy, constitutionalism, parliamentarism, the new role of religion in secular life, and more. These Enlightenment ideas, values, and institutions had to be domesticated to spur a modern revolution in Egyptian culture, society, and politics. Like some of his *nahdawi* peers, Lutfi al-Sayyid assumed that there is only one way to reach modernity and civilization, grounded in the enlightened European model. The role of the non-European intellectual was to manufacture a homemade version of this global civilization—to be an emissary and advocate of this overarching, universal effort across the world, including Asia, Africa, and the Middle East.[10] Lutfi al-Sayyid and his colleagues represented what Sebastian Conrad later articulated: the idea that "'Enlightenment' cannot be understood as the sovereign and autonomous accomplishment of European intellectuals alone; it had many authors in many places."[11]

Three major principles were most important to Lutfi al-Sayyid: freedom (*al-hurriyya*), progress (*al-taqaddum, irtiqa', taraqqi*), and civilization/civilized (*tamaddun, mutamaddin*). Lutfi al-Sayyid hypothesized that freedom and progress would ipso facto bring about civilization (*tamaddun*). Once these three concepts were absorbed, the rest of the Enlightenment's ideas, norms, and practices would come to fruition. Hence, Lutfi al-Sayyid dedicated many essays to systematically examining the nature of freedom and progress, the two gateway concepts, and how these could be expressed and implemented across Egypt's public, initiating them as part of establishing indigenous civilization and eventually the wider scope of the Enlightenment.

For Lutfi al-Sayyid, freedom had to be expressed on both the individual and collective levels. He believed that freedom is realized through interconnected spheres: individual freedom, social freedom, and national freedom from foreign colonial occupation. On the individual level, Lutfi al-Sayyid followed in the footsteps of Enlightenment thinkers such as Locke and Rousseau, stating that freedom is inherently natural. For him, humans are born free, and external factors shackle them in oppression, negating their freedom; these shackles had to be broken and removed. Lutfi al-Sayyid established that just as "our existence is through nourishment by water and bread," so too is our existence intertwined with freedom: "if we demand [individual] freedom, we are not demanding anything special, but rather the requisite nutrition for our existence, for our lives."[12] Thus, Lutfi al-Sayyid's premise is that each step toward modern civilization must be based on the complete adoption of individual freedom as an integral part of human existence. Each man and woman must enjoy full freedom, as naturally guaranteed for them, just as nature satiates their hunger and thirst each day.[13]

FROM THE INDIVIDUAL TO SOCIETY

Following in the footsteps of Enlightenment thinkers, Lutfi al-Sayyid assumed that individual freedom is reliant on public freedom, or "civil freedom" (*hurriyya madaniyya*), which he considered the second sphere. The freedom of civil society, ranging from families to government, alongside "political freedom" (*al-hurriyya al-siyasiyya*) would forge the enlightened political system. In order to guarantee these collective freedoms, Lutfi al-Sayyid advocated for a social and political parliamentary order, a fully representative government, which would guarantee that "the nation is above the government" (*al-umma fawq al-hukuma*). In his opinion, the prerequisite to this outcome in Egypt was the elimination of absolutism, including Khedive 'Abbas Hilmi II's "personal rule," backed by traditional Ottoman autocracy and facilitated by British colonialism. He systematically criticized what he called absolutism and subjugation (*istibdad* and *isti'bad*), which had "enslaved" Egyptians for far too many generations. The shift away from the Egyptian-British-Ottoman authoritarian regime had to be gradual though decisive. Representative institutions and a social and political constitutional parliamentary government would allow the people of the nation to rule themselves, over themselves, and for themselves.[14]

In order to realize this vision for collective social freedom practically, Lutfi al-Sayyid called for a constitution (*dustur*) that would secure a version of John Stuart Mill's "representative government." In tens of articles, he explained that a constitution was essential for creating a liberated public sphere and a democratic government. Much of this perspective was inspired by the formation of the publicly elected Legislative Assembly (al-Jam'iyya al-Tashri'iyya) in 1913, which replaced the pseudo-representative nominated institutions installed by the British colonial system. Developing an open political arena that encouraged active parties and cultivated diverse public opinion through a free press would further empower the Legislative Assembly and simultaneously balance the khedivate's power. More specifically, his vision assumed that the constitution would bring about general elections for party representatives in a parliament with two houses, a house of representatives and a senate, in which the majority party would form a government. This new constitutional parliamentary system would secure the country's modernity and, with it, Enlightenment.

The third sphere of freedom is the national struggle to achieve Egyptian independence from British colonial rule. Challenging his contemporary nationalist rivals, led by Mustafa Kamil's heirs, Muhammad Farid and 'Abd al-'Aziz Jawish, Lutfi al-Sayyid believed that Egypt did not need to wait for liberation from colonialism in order to jumpstart the realization of its freedom. He believed that Egypt must strive to adopt freedom on the individual and collective levels immediately. Yet he also understood that bringing freedom to full fruition could only take place once British soldiers had left the Nile Valley and Egypt was an independent and sovereign nation-state. Independence had to be claimed by the nation's own hands, driving its swift transition toward modern progress and civilization.[15]

Lutfi al-Sayyid's second pillar for bringing enlightenment to Egypt was progress. First and foremost, progress was an intentional process, a revolution in the mind to internalize the belief in the ability of Egyptians to develop, ameliorate, and mature. For Lutfi al-Sayyid, as with other Enlightenment thinkers, particularly Spencer with his evolutionary theories, progress is an axiom anchored in nature. Human progress moves from a state of backwardness (*ta'akhkhur*) to a state of development and prosperity (*taqaddum*). It is deterministic, inexorable, and irreversible, driven by "the law of evolution," moving from the simple to the complex, from the plain to the sophisticated. Once Egyptians recognized they were already experiencing progress and believed in their ability to develop and advance, civilization (*tamaddun*) would be realized. This would trickle down from the intellectual and spiritual to the practical and material: a swift application to innovative science and technology; advanced transportation and communication; print culture; new industry and agriculture; modern education, rule of law, and modern culture, including burgeoning genres of literature, poetry, theater, music, aesthetics, fine art, sculpture, drawing, and architecture; a new system of ethics; and more. Thus, the "civilized Egyptian" (*mutamaddin*) would emerge, with Enlightenment values personified in Egypt's men and women.[16]

NATIONALISM: EGYPTIANIZING THE EGYPTIANS

It is commonly held that Lutfi al-Sayyid was the architect of modern Egyptian nationalism. However, his brand of nationalism must be understood as one component of his broader Enlightenment enterprise. He coined the term *Egyptianism* (*al-misriyya*) as key to "civilization" (*tamaddun*). Although Lutfi al-Sayyid was not the first to speak of a local Egyptian patriotism (on the level of homeland, *wataniyya*), he was the first to adopt and use the term *Egyptian nationalism* (*al-qawmiyya al-misriyya*), and he certainly institutionalized and conventionalized the idea of a unique Egyptian national identity. Earlier studies justifiably highlight that Lutfi al-Sayyid advocated for a liberal, inclusive, and pluralist nationalism, yet this liberal definition of the nation lacked grounding in his overarching Enlightenment ideas of freedom, progress, and civilization.

Moreover, these studies, which analyzed Lutfi al-Sayyid's Egyptian nationalist ideology, also argued that his liberalism included a pessimistic, biological, organic, and primordial component. They claimed that Lutfi al-Sayyid's concept of the Egyptian nation was imbued with ethnic, racial, and biological elements derived from two main sources: first, through his cult of land, the distinctive environment, with its unique topography, fauna, and flora of the Nile Valley, in which the nation resided and evolved; and second, his characterization of the Egyptian nation as a Pharaonic or neo-Pharaonic entity, galvanized from its ancient Egyptian roots. They characterized Lutfi al-Sayyid as a national ideologue who rediscovered and dogmatically reclaimed Egypt's Pharaonic essence, paying homage to the Egyptian Pharaonic Golden Age.[17]

However, a more accurate reading of Lutfi al-Sayyid's writing on nationalism disproves this ethno-symbolic Pharaonicism. Lutfi al-Sayyid insisted on placing freedom at the top of the hierarchy of values, inherently and vehemently negating an organic, deterministic, and historicist Egyptian nationalism. Lutfi al-Sayyid charged nationalism, first and foremost, as a modern unveiling of a new product, the summation of specific social, political, and economic conditions. The new educated elite that grew up in this modern urban context, with an extensive modern European education including proficiency in Western languages, modern science, and philosophy, and a commitment to transforming society toward modernity, was fertile for the seeds of nationalism. Lutfi al-Sayyid saw himself as a part of this modernist intelligentsia. As an educated and dedicated public intellectual, he tested the waters to create a new Egyptian national community and advocated for the residents of the Nile Valley to appropriate modernity in order to become a free, enlightened, and distinguished nation.

Furthermore, Lutfi al-Sayyid's relationship to the nation's past, and his attitude toward history more generally, was surprisingly limited and embarrassingly rudimentary. Lutfi al-Sayyid served more as a national sociologist and psychologist than as a historian. One of the motifs of his life was that "the world's present is better than the past, and the future will be better than the present."[18] He was far from an idealist romantic about the collective past of mythological history, worshipped by the community like a golden calf and yearning to return to the days of yore. He looked critically upon those in his community and demanded they recognize their "true" modern Egyptian identity and act upon it, now, for the betterment of tomorrow. As a result, Lutfi al-Sayyid never hesitated to condemn, sometimes brutally, his nation's flaws and weaknesses, aggressively exposing the outdated sources of its ills and demanding that it urgently overcome them to launch Egypt toward an inventive and inspired future.

Given that Lutfi al-Sayyid was a future-oriented thinker, it is not at all surprising that he addressed Egypt's Pharaonic history only twice in hundreds of articles in *al-Jarida*. In these two essays, he discusses this period in a shallow, cursory way. Lutfi al-Sayyid, who consistently learned any subject in detail, attended to Egypt's Pharaonic era without attempting to display proficiency, which is particularly striking considering the accessibility of Egyptological knowledge with the opening of Cairo's Egyptian Museum in 1902. It is crucial to note that in these two anomalous articles, Lutfi al-Sayyid took a clear pedagogical and utilitarian approach: he discussed the Egyptians' general ignorance of their past, the same obtuseness that prevented them from recognizing their true nationalist identity, and the same simplicity that Enlightenment philosophers blamed for pre-Enlightenment inferiority and backwardness. These two articles aimed to expose the public's lack of awareness and reclaim their ties with Egypt's past, just as Europeans related to Ancient Roman and Greek civilization. Revealing this ignorance was also intended to inspire self-confidence and empower Egyptians, shepherding them toward a promising new future. As Anthony Pagden correctly observes, Enlightenment thinkers did not "attempt to rescue some hallowed past" but looked forward, leveraging their "assault on the past in the name of the future."[19] Lutfi al-Sayyid similarly did not write about this matter in reverence of Egypt's Pharaonic past. Rather, it was a cautionary tale to criticize his compatriots for their shallow historical knowledge.

Another misleading historiographical narrative asserted that Lutfi al-Sayyid was obsessed with the Nile Valley as proof of the "natural" birthplace of the Egyptian nation. Lutfi al-Sayyid was far from a geographic or environmental determinist. He recognized the particular territorial framework in which the Egyptians resided but saw the borders of the Nile Land contextually, mainly as arbitrarily imposed guidelines dictated by imperialist muscle flexing. Instead, Lutfi al-Sayyid's reflections addressed the people, men and women, youth and elderly, of all religions, languages, and races, whom he characterized as Egyptians. For him, anyone who lived in the Nile region, by their own free choice, was equally Egyptian. It did not matter if they and their ancestors had lived there for hundreds or thousands of years, or just a few years; whether they were members of rural communities with deep roots, or members of urban communities who had just arrived from Europe, Africa, Asia, or the Middle East—all of them were Egyptians, members of a common Egyptian national community. This open and inclusive nationalism transcended tribal, religious, linguistic, ethnic, racial, or cultural attachments.

In other words, Lutfi al-Sayyid's Egyptian nationalism is connected to the country's territory but was not constructed based on the length of time therein. The only criteria for owning a common Egyptian national identity were the conscious decision and genuine desire to be Egyptian, to exist in Egypt, to take part in the collective Egyptian experience, to identify with both the good and the bad and the beautiful and the ugly within it, and to prefer it over any other communal identity. It was equally important that Egypt's sons and daughters choose to work to promote its interests and toil for its economic, cultural, and political prosperity. Thus, "Egyptianism" was, foremost, a utilitarian construct, defined as an identity framework for those who understood and saw their life in Egypt as providing them with material and spiritual benefits. In Lutfi al-Sayyid's eyes, Egyptians were those who subscribed to Egyptian identity and nationalist belonging; only this deliberate will and intention could construct the Egyptian nation (*al-umma al-misriyya*), Egyptian nationalism (*al-qawmiyya al-misriyya*), and Egyptianism (*al-misriyya*). Thus, Lutfi al-Sayyid's national outlook was liberal, pluralistic, and utilitarian, based on choice and freedom, and rooted in the awareness and desire of Egypt's residents to be members of a united Egyptian nation.[20] Lutfi al-Sayyid puts it as follows, using the third person:

> One of our prominent learned intellectuals was asked, who is Egyptian? He answered: the Egyptian is one who does not identify with a homeland (*watan*) other than Egypt. Someone who identifies himself with two homelands [or more] and resides in Egypt, but yet continues to have for himself another [external] homeland, to assure himself—it will be difficult to consider him Egyptian in the truest meaning of the word . . . our Egyptianism (*misriyyatuna*) demands that our motherland will be our exclusive *qibla* that has no alternative . . . [therefore] this current generation, or the current nation, must undertake the task of training the next generation in the

fortitude and [modern] development so that they can bring our national character (*sibghatuna al-qawmiyya*) to full fruition: Egypt for the Egyptians.[21]

In the opening sentence of his memoir, *Qissat Hayati* (The Story of My Life), Lutfi al-Sayyid modestly describes his national identity: "I was raised in an authentic Egyptian family that never attached itself to a homeland (*watan*) other than the Egyptian homeland (*al-watan al-misri*)[,] that never took pride other than in Egyptianism (*al-misriyya*), and that never belonged other than to Egypt (*misr*)."[22]

IMPERIALISM: THE BRITISH OCCUPATION

Much of the literature on Lutfi al-Sayyid barely deals with his position on empire and imperialism. Generally, scholars point to his "soft" attitude toward the continued British occupation of Egypt.[23] In comparison with Mustafa Kamil and the anticolonial rhetoric and activities of his al-Hizb al-Watani, Lutfi al-Sayyid and *al-Jarida* were seen as either indifferent to or active collaborators with the occupation. Lutfi al-Sayyid's famous article, "Lord Cromer before History," published in *al-Jarida* in April 1907, praised the British agent and consul-general's efforts and policies, further reinforcing these conclusions.[24] However, a closer reading of the article reveals Lutfi al-Sayyid's ability to reckon with the honest duality, acknowledging the material benefits of British presence in Egypt while also disapproving of Cromer's colonial behavior, which aimed to consolidate British control in the country.[25] In this endeavor, Lutfi al-Sayyid both viciously critiques Cromer's "political rule" and his colonial coercive policies and recognizes his accomplishments regarding the development of the Egyptian economy.

It would be a mistake to rely solely on one article to represent Lutfi al-Sayyid's attitude toward imperialism (*al-isti'mar*). Lutfi al-Sayyid's rejection of the British occupation (*ihtilal*) and support for liberation (*hurriyya*) and independence (*istiqlal*) were abundantly clear. His views were expressed in many articles in *al-Jarida*, later compiled in a special collection entitled *Safahat Matwiyya* (Occulted Pages, 1946), subtitled "The History of the Independence Movement in Egypt, March 1907 to March 1909: The Era of the Intellectual Revolution in National Politics." In these early essays, Lutfi al-Sayyid sharpened his perceptions of British imperialism and his strategies for liberating Egypt from its yoke. He resentfully expressed his disdain for British presence in Egypt, calling it a "conquest," "occupation," "imperialism," or "foreign rule" enforced brutally against the Egyptian people's will and right to self-determination. He insisted that Egypt was occupied (*muhtalla*) and that the colonial situation was unnatural and illegitimate.[26]

Lutfi al-Sayyid's ideas on Egypt's freedom and independence were anchored in Enlightenment weltanschauung. He believed that every nation had the right to self-determination, liberty, independence, and self-government, as well as the right to promote its own development, prosperity, and happiness. Lutfi al-Sayyid believed these rights were natural and no foreign power could rob Egypt or any other modern nation of them. For him, foreign occupation was diametrically opposite to Enlightenment values, the embodiment of injustice and deprivation of "civilization." Breaking the shackles of this foreign occupation to exercise freedom, independence, and sovereignty was an historical inevitability derived directly from the very nature of the Enlightenment project first created and experienced in Europe. Hence, in both theory and practice, Lutfi al-Sayyid in this period refused to cooperate with colonial authorities (unlike his associate Saʻd Zaghlul or prominent political figures such as Husayn Rushdi or ʻAdli Yakan). He had no illusions about the alienation, injustice, and lack of legitimacy of colonial rule. In all his writings and actions, Lutfi al-Sayyid saw himself as an Egyptian nationalist thinker associated with the Egyptian national liberation movement, drawing his ideas on anticolonialism directly from the Enlightenment.[27] In this sense, Lutfi al-Sayyid should be categorized as a colonial intellectual, without the title's negative connotation, as his project addressed colonial Enlightenment and colonial modernity.

Operationally, Lutfi al-Sayyid believed that only Egyptians, through self-reliance, could bring about "full liberation" and "complete independence" (istiqlal tamm) for their country. Only they could solve the "Egyptian Question" (al-masʾala al-misriyya) and emancipate Egypt without relying on external help in its struggle. In a May 1908 essay addressing the social and political climate under the British occupation, Lutfi stated, "I have no doubt that all the preparatory and training operations, which will eventually result in final [complete] independence, are only in the hands of the Egyptians and depend exclusively on their own efforts, while Europe or the Ottoman Empire does not have any part in it."[28]

Lutfi al-Sayyid challenged the two anticolonial strategies prominent in elite circles and on the street. He came out strongly against both the position of Khedive ʻAbbas Hilmi II and his "Ottomanist" allies as well as the naive Francophile positions of Mustafa Kamil and the Nationalist Party. He criticized the former's mistaken expectations that the Ottomans would facilitate Egyptian independence. The khedive advocated that because the Ottoman state was the de jure power (al-sulta al-sharʻiyya) in Egypt, it had the responsibility to overthrow the "temporary" British occupation. Lutfi al-Sayyid argued that even if the Ottoman Empire were to expel the British from Egypt, Egyptians would reclaim Egypt as their own, thereby precluding true independence. Lutfi al-Sayyid recognized this as delusional: the Ottomans would be easily defeated by superior British forces on land or at sea. Of course, this understanding was buttressed by Lutfi al-Sayyid's Egyptian-centric perspective, believing that Ottoman rule over Egypt was no less foreign or colonial than British rule.[29]

As for the Francophile positions, Lutfi al-Sayyid heavily disapproved of the assumption that France would come to Egypt's aid and liberate it from the British. Until 1904, Mustafa Kamil and his followers threw their support behind the French. They advocated this approach because France never accepted Britain's conquest of Egypt and because of the prevalence of anti-British sentiment and the networks of French right-wing nationalists that they could leverage. In 1904, the Entente Cordiale agreement between France and England was signed, dividing colonial lands in Africa between the two powers. Suddenly, the Nationalist Party's dreams were dashed. The French would no longer come to help the Egyptians. This development only reinforced Lutfi al-Sayyid's stance on the indispensability of self-reliance. In contrast, Kamil and his disciples responded by reasserting their Ottoman-based strategy for Egypt's liberation.[30]

Political realism was not the sole reason for this strategy of self-reliance; it was also rooted in national pride and the nation's self-confidence. Only Egypt and the Egyptian people could muster the energy and power to fight the British colonial occupation. Egypt, according to Lutfi al-Sayyid, did not need the illusory support of an external power to free it from colonial rule. Sanctifying the ideas of the "Egyptian nation," "Egyptian nationalism," and "Egyptianism," he was convinced that by transmitting this inclusive national consciousness to a broader sector of society and by popularizing the understanding that Egypt was arbitrarily occupied, the Egyptian people would rally around the causes of liberation and independence.[31]

Lutfi al-Sayyid's anticolonial agenda was aggressive and antagonistic despite his moderate and restrained language. He believed that the first step against British de facto rule (*al-sulta al-fi'liyya*) was accurately diagnosing the "enemy's" intentions and interests. Lutfi al-Sayyid explained that the occupation was a result of "imperialist interests" (*maslahat al-isti'mar*),[32] embodied by Lord Cromer in his racist, interest-oriented imperialism. After Cromer published his two-volume *Modern Egypt*, following his retirement in 1908,[33] Lutfi al-Sayyid called out Cromer's imperialist "white man's burden"–inspired policies, which aimed to justify British imperial interests in Egypt and subjugate its population to colonial exploitation, oppression, and political enslavement. Lutfi al-Sayyid was particularly incensed that Cromer undermined Egypt's right to self-determination and "self-rule." He highlighted Cromer's racist and orientalist arguments that Egypt was so backward it was incapable of self-government, thereby necessitating continued British rule. Per Lutfi al-Sayyid, arrogant, superior, and paternalistic Cromer could not fathom national resistance to this British occupation and denied the very existence of Egyptian nationalism, calling the national struggle insolent and ungrateful toward his "enlightened" colonial government. Thus, for Lutfi al-Sayyid, Cromer provided tangible evidence of the British intention to remain Egypt's rulers and deprive Egypt of any national rights.[34]

But Cromer's successor, Sir Eldon Gorst (r. 1907–11), was even worse for the Egyptian national movement and its aspirations, according to Lutfi al-Sayyid. The two consuls were different in their relationship to the khedivate, which, in Lutfi al-Sayyid's opinion, made Cromer look acceptable relative to his predecessor. Cromer brutally and systematically confronted 'Abbas Hilmi II from the moment the khedive ascended to power in 1892. He assertively undermined the young, inexperienced khedive's ambitions to reclaim Egyptian autonomy. The pitched battle between the sworn enemies created a cleavage in which Lutfi al-Sayyid and his political camp could maneuver themselves and expand their nationalist activity, both anti-khedive and anti-British. However, upon Gorst's appointment, the British agent and consul-general forged a political alliance with the khedive, which Lutfi al-Sayyid dubbed "the politics of agreement" (*siyasat al-wifaq*). In Lutfi al-Sayyid's eyes, this collusion between the "legal ruler" (the khedive) and the "de facto ruler" (the British) solidified the absolutism of colonialism, hindering any opportunity for activities promoting anticolonialism and, with it, Egyptian self-government (*al-hukm al-dhati*).[35]

Contrary to other strategies (especially those of Kamil and his successors, Farid and Jawish), Lutfi al-Sayyid insisted that Egypt did not have to wait for the complete "evacuation" (*jala'*) of the British to begin shaping Egypt's liberal political culture. He rejected the radical nationalist attitude that called for independence before sovereignty. Lutfi al-Sayyid saw the process of shaping a constitutionalist parliamentary government itself as an act of liberation. He called on the Egyptian intelligentsia to immediately establish a democratic parliamentary government, free itself from the grip of colonial rule, and demonstrate its maturity to itself and the British. This would invalidate Gorst and Cromer's position that Egypt "needed" to be occupied to maintain order. Thus, the focus of Lutfi al-Sayyid's anticolonial strategy was not contingent solely on street demonstrations, protests, and civil disobedience, but also on preparing the nation for its constitutional democratic future.[36]

However, at least until the outbreak of World War I, Lutfi al-Sayyid insisted that the national movement avoid violent means. He reiterated time and again that struggle must be based on moderate and tolerant measures (he used the words *salam*, *silm*, and *silmiyya*) "in civilized, peaceful ways."[37] On this account, scholarly works often tagged Lutfi al-Sayyid a collaborator; however, such a view does not present a full or nuanced picture of Lutfi al-Sayyid's perspective. As soon as the British imposed a protectorate (*al-himaya*) on the country in late 1914, accompanied by martial law and paralyzing censorship, Lutfi al-Sayyid's bitterness skyrocketed and his opinion about-faced. When the war ended in the autumn of 1918, and the British government still refused to remove the protectorate, Lutfi al-Sayyid and other Egyptian nationalist leaders admitted that "civilized means" were insufficient and no longer fitting. Lutfi al-Sayyid helped found the Wafd, which led the national popular revolution in the spring of 1919, and became one of its early leaders. After nearly four decades of British occupation and in light of its escalation to a protectorate, Lutfi al-Sayyid advocated more militant means, albeit alongside negotiation and reconciliation, to force the British from Egypt. In the end, it was the radical, nationalist fight against the British Empire that brought Egypt its long-awaited independence.[38]

CONCLUSION

Ahmad Lutfi al-Sayyid's intellectual influence on the younger producers of modern Arab culture in Egypt and the Arab Middle East was impressive. He curated a new model of public intellectual, serving as a mentor to many, shaping their conceptual and moral world. His impact lasted for decades, inspiring a whole generation of intellectuals: journalists, fiction writers, playwrights, and artists, who took a central role in the design, distribution, and reception of twentieth-century Egyptian Arab print culture. The most notable among them began writing for *al-Jarida* under his direction. After the journal folded, Lutfi al-Sayyid was seen as their guru, and from the 1920s onward was honorarily nicknamed the "teacher of the generation" (*ustadh al-jil*) or "philosopher of the generation" (*faylasuf al-jil*).

Lutfi al-Sayyid's philosophy was not without critics. His contemporaries, particularly the Nationalist Party's leaders and activists, al-Azhar's clerics, and the khedive's entourage, accused Lutfi al-Sayyid of anti-Islamism, anti-Ottomanism, appeasement of British colonial rule, and even collaboration with it. They provocatively declared that "the Egyptian self-reliance strategy" promoted by Lutfi al-Sayyid was nothing but a mirage and would not bring about Egyptian independence. These forces argued that Lutfi al-Sayyid was imposing an artificial European Enlightenment on the country as a "disgraceful imitation" that pandered to the West and its imperialism. They saw this Enlightenment as an alien and foreign power, destroying local traditions and culture and eroding Egypt's Islamic identity.[39]

Later, new critics emerged. Following the July 1952 Free Officers Revolution and the rise of Nasserist Pan-Arabism, spokespeople from the new republican regime accused Lutfi al-Sayyid of being a Pharaonicist and an anti-Arabist, underlining his rejection of Arab unity. They condemned him as an outmoded classist, an elitist liberal aristocrat whose bourgeoise philosophy only served the interests of the *bashawat*, the landed aristocracy under the monarchial, reactionary ancien régime. Further, they demonized him for abandoning the needs of broader sectors of society and culture.[40] Later on, Islamists, including the Muslim Brotherhood, disparaged him as the "Pharaonic prophet" who sought to rehabilitate Egypt's idolatrous past. Obviously, these perspectives were rooted in diverse ideological outlooks that coexisted in the twentieth-century Egyptian political scene.[41]

In the academic field, conventional studies were principally generous toward Lutfi al-Sayyid and *al-Jarida*, yet they simultaneously missed critical aspects of his weltanschauung. They incorrectly prioritized his nationalism over his Enlightenment and mistakenly categorized him as a collaborator with British colonialism. This invited further denigration of Lutfi al-Sayyid in later postcolonial interventions, perpetuating this mischaracterization. The postcolonial narrative asserted, without always directly naming Lutfi al-Sayyid, that this group of liberal intellectuals sometimes unintentionally propagated and therefore encouraged colonial discourse, providing it with legitimacy and further emboldening imperialism. These intellectuals were accused of "falling in love" with colonial cultural products and missing their inherent imperialism and oppression, which actually destroyed their own local culture. Captivated by imperialist Stockholm syndrome, they fell into the colonialist's trap, which disarmed their words and rendered them paralyzed to combat these coercive forces. This further isolated them, leaving them detached from reality, society, and their own people.[42]

Criticizing this postcolonial approach, Peter Hill recently called it "a tragic metanarrative" of the *nahda*. In his words, these postcolonial scholars wrongly assumed that "the Nahda was the moment when Arab intellectuals and elites capitulated to European ideas; they abandoned their own Arab and Islamic traditions, becoming conscious or unconscious agents of the Western project to colonise their countries."[43] More generally, dealing with liberal Indian intellectuals who faced similar dilemmas in their colonial setting, C. A. Bayly challenges "colonial modernity," emphasizing that this intellectual group "did not simply copy Western ideas from the texts they received through metropolitan sources. Instead, they cannibalised, reconstructed and re-authored those ideas, often using them in an intellectual assault on the policies, moral character and culture of their rulers . . . [they] believed that they could rewrite the liberal discourse so as to strip it of its coercive colonial features and re-empower it as an indigenous ideology, but one still pointing towards universal progress."[44] Lutfi al-Sayyid definitely fits into both Hill's critique and Bayly's reading of these liberal colonial intellectuals.

As this chapter tried to show, this postcolonial critique lacked context. It did not read Lutfi al-Sayyid's texts carefully enough and did not properly place his writing and its intended audience in its time and space. Moreover, it ignored Lutfi al-Sayyid's rich and consistent anticolonialist corpus of writing. Lutfi al-Sayyid's attack of Cromer and his white man's burden doctrine alone is sufficient to demonstrate his genuine awareness of the dangers of imperialism as well as his ongoing efforts to liberate Egypt and bring about its independence.

In sum, Ahmad Lutfi al-Sayyid played a major role in shaping Egyptian Arab modernism by strategically localizing Enlightenment ideas, values, and institutions for Egypt and, in many respects, for the rest of the Arab Middle East. This study attempted to reconstruct and reclaim this project, offering an essential revisionist reading. First, it centered Lutfi al-Sayyid's major intellectual project in domesticating and assimilating the Enlightenment in Egypt. Second, it emphasized the inclusive, liberal values that Lutfi al-Sayyid promoted within Egyptian nationalism through its natural continuation from the Enlightenment's weltanschauung. Finally, it debunked the misunderstanding of Lutfi al-Sayyid as a collaborator with British colonialism, clarifying his systematic oppositional activism to undermine imperialism and bring about Egyptian independence.

Notes

This research was generously supported by the Israel Science Foundation grant number 945/30. I would like to thank Molly Bernstein for her insightful comments and thorough edits on the chapter.

1. Charles Wendell, *The Evolution of the Egyptian National Image: From Its Origins to Ahmad Lutfi al-Sayyid* (Berkeley: University of California Press, 1972).
2. A major source for Ahmad Lutfi al-Sayyid's biography is his self-narrated memoir, *Qissat Hayati* (Cairo: Dar al-Hilal, 1962), hereafter *QH*. This autobiography was first published as a series of articles in *al-Musawwar*, during the summer and fall of 1950, entitled "Mudhakkirat Ustadh al-Jil Lutfi al-Sayyid Pasha." In order to reconstruct the life of Lutfi al-Sayyid, I also consulted the following works and sources: *al-Jarida*, 1907–15; Isma'il Sidqi, *Mudhakkirati* (Cairo: Maktabat Madbuli, 1950); Jacob M. Landau, *Parliaments and Parties in Egypt* (Tel Aviv: Israel Publishing House, 1953), 104–73; Muhammad Husayn Haykal, *Mudhakkirat fi al-Siyasa al-Misriyya*, vols. 1 and 2 (Cairo: Dar al-Ma'arif, 1951, 1953); 'Abd

al-Latif Hamza, *Adab al-Maqala al-Suhufiyya fi Misr*, 8 vols. (Cairo: Dar al-Fikr, 1950–56), vol. 6 in particular; Ahmad Lutfi al-Sayyid, *Mushkilat al-Huriyyat fi al-ʿAlam al-ʿArabi* (Beirut: n.p., 1959); J. M. Ahmed, *The Intellectual Origins of Egyptian Nationalism* (Oxford: Oxford University Press, 1960); Albert Hourani, *Arabic Thought in the Liberal Age, 1798–1939* (Oxford: Oxford University Press, 1962), 161–92; ʿAbd al-ʿAziz Fahmi, *Mudhakkirat*, ed. Tahir al-Tanahi (Cairo: Kitab al-Hilal, 1963); Husayn Fawzi al-Najjar, *Lutfi al-Sayyid wa-l-Shakhsiyya al-Misriyya* (Cairo: Maktabat al-Qahira al-Haditha, 1963); Muhafazat al-Daqhaliya, *Maharajan al-Dhikra al-Ula li-Wafat Ahmad Lutfi al-Sayyid: Ustadh al-Jil, 28–29 March 1964* (Cairo: Muhafazat al-Daqhiliyya, 1964); Husayn Fawzi al-Najjar, *Ahmad Lutfi al-Sayyid: Ustadh al-Jil* (Cairo: al-Muʾalifa al-Misriyya al-ʿAmma 1965); Afaf Lutfi al-Sayyid, *Egypt and Cromer: A Study in Anglo-Egyptian Relations* (London: John Murray, 1968); Arthur Goldschmidt, Jr., "The Egyptian Nationalist Party: 1892–1919," in *Political and Social Change in Modern Egypt*, ed. P. M Holt (New York: Oxford University Press, 1968), 308–33; P. J. Vatikiotis, *The Modern History of Egypt* (London: Weidenfeld and Nicholson, 1969), 214–35; Wendell, *The Evolution of the Egyptian National Image*; Walid Kazziha, "The Jaridah-Umma Group and Egyptian Politics," *Middle Eastern Studies* 13, no. 3 (1977): 373–85; Ahmad Zakariyya al-Shalaq, *Hizb al-Umma wa-Dawruha fi al-Siyasa al-Misriyya* (Cairo: Dar al-Maʿarif, 1979); Louis Awad, *The Literature of Ideas in Egypt*, part 1 (Atlanta: Scholars Press, 1986), 107–22; ʿAbd al-ʿAziz Sharaf, *Lutfi al-Sayyid: Faylasuf Ayqaza Ummatan* (Cairo: al-Hayʾa al-Misriyya al-ʿAmma li-l-Kitab, 2002); Kitab al-Thaqafa al-Jadida, *al-Jamiʿa al-Misriyya: Mukhtarat min Ahmad Lutfi al-Sayyid wa-Taha Husayn* (Cairo: al-Hayʾa al-ʿAmma li-Qusur al-Thaqafa, 2004); and Dar al-Kutub wa-l-Wathaʾiq al-Qawmiyya, *Turath Ahmad Lutfi al-Sayyid* (Cairo: Matbaʿat Dar al-Kutub wa-l-Wathaiq al-Qawmiyya, 2008), vols. 1 and 2. See also *QH*, 94–105, 145–57; and Dennis Patrick Walker, "Supra-Egyptian Islamic and Pan-Arab Identifies and Acculturated Muslim Egyptian Intellectuals, 1892–1952" (PhD diss., Australian National University, Melbourne, 1991), A283–348.

3. Antonio Gramsci, *Selections from the Prison Notebooks*, ed. and trans. Q. Hoare and G. Nowell Smith (New York: International Publishers, 1971); Edward Said, *Representations of the Intellectual* (New York: Pantheon Books, 1994).

4. See, e.g., Kazziha, "The Jaridah-Ummah Group." For a further critique of this conventional approach, see Israel Gershoni, *Enlightenment in Colonial Egypt: Modernity, Nationalism, Gender, and Colonialism in Ahmad Lutfi al-Sayyid's Teachings* (forthcoming).

5. See, e.g., Ahmed, *The Intellectual Origins of Egyptian Nationalism*; Wendell, *The Evolution of the Egyptian National Image*, 201–93; al-Najjar, *Lutfi al-Sayyid wa-l-Shakhsiyya al-Misriyya*; and Walker, "Supra-Egyptian Islamic and Pan-Arab Identities."

6. "Nahda studies" have been flourishing in recent years, in dozens of scholarly books and articles. For the most recent works, see, e.g., Stephen Sheehi, *Foundations of Modern Arab Identity* (Gainesville: University Press of Florida, 2004); Tarek El-Ariss, *Trials of Arab Modernity: Literary Affects and the New Political* (New York: Fordham University Press, 2013); Marwa Elshakry, *Reading Darwin in Arabic, 1860–1950* (Chicago: University of Chicago Press, 2013); Marilyn Booth and Anthony Gorman, eds., *The Long 1890s in Egypt: Colonial Quiescence, Subterranean Resistance* (Edinburgh: Edinburgh University Press, 2014); Adel Beshara, ed., *Butrus al-Bustani: Spirit of the Age* (Melbourne: Iphoenix Publishing, 2014); Ami Ayalon, *The Arabic Print Revolution: Cultural Production and Mass Readership* (Cambridge: Cambridge University Press, 2016); Wael Abu-ʿUksa, *Freedom in the Arab World: Concepts and Ideologies in Arabic Thought in the Nineteenth Century* (Cambridge: Cambridge University Press, 2016); Jens Hanssen and Max Weiss, eds., *Arabic*

Thought beyond the Liberal Age: Towards an Intellectual History of the Nahda (Cambridge: Cambridge University Press, 2016); Tarek El-Ariss, ed., *The Arab Renaissance: A Bilingual Anthology of the Nahda* (New York: Modern Language Association of America, 2018); Jens Hanssen and Max Weiss, eds., *Arabic Thought against the Authoritarian Age: Towards an Intellectual History of the Present* (Cambridge: Cambridge University Press, 2018); Peter Hill, *Utopia and Civilization in the Arab Nahda* (Cambridge: Cambridge University Press, 2020); and Jens Hanssen and Hicham Safieddine, eds., *The Clarion of Syria: A Patriot's Call against the Civil War of 1960: Butrus al-Bustani* (Berkeley: University of California Press, 2020). Gender studies focusing on women's *nahdawi* and post-*nahdawi* contributions and activities in Egypt and the Arab Middle East have also been flourishing in recent decades. See, e.g., Judith E. Tucker, *Women in Nineteenth Century Egypt* (Cambridge: Cambridge University Press, 1986); Leila Ahmad, *Women and Gender in Islam: Historical Roots of Modern Debate* (New Haven, CT: Yale University Press, 1992); Beth Baron, *The Women's Awakening in Egypt: Culture, Society, and the Press* (New Haven, CT: Yale University Press, 1994); Margot Badran, *Feminists, Islam, and the Nation: Gender and the Making of Modern Egypt* (Princeton, NJ: Princeton University Press, 1995); Lila Abu-Lughod, ed., *Remaking Women: Feminism and Modernity in the Middle East* (Princeton, NJ: Princeton University Press, 1998); Nadje Al-Ali, *Secularism, Gender, and the State in the Middle East: The Egyptian Women's Movement* (Cambridge: Cambridge University Press, 2000); Marilyn Booth, *May Her Likes Be Multiplied: Biography and Gender Politics in Egypt* (Berkeley: University of California Press, 2001); Mona Russell, *Creating the New Egyptian Woman: Consumerism, Education, and National Identity, 1863–1922* (New York: Palgrave Macmillan, 2004); Lisa Pollard, *Nurturing the Nation: The Family Politics of Modernizing, Colonizing, and Liberating Egypt, 1805–1923* (Berkeley: University of California Press, 2005); Arthur Goldschmidt, Amy J. Johnson, and Barak A. Salmoni, eds., *Re-Envisioning Egypt*, 1919–1952 (Cairo: American University in Cairo Press, 2005), Part 4 (chapters by Hanan Kholoussy, Nancy Gallagher, Shaun T. Lopez, and Mervat F. Hatem); Beth Baron, *Egypt as a Woman: Nationalism, Gender, and Politics* (Berkeley: University of California Press, 2005); Cathlyn Mariscotti, *Gender and Class in the Egyptian Women's Movement, 1925–1939* (Syracuse, NY: Syracuse University Press, 2008); Kenneth M. Cuno and Manisha Desai, eds., *Family, Gender, and Law in a Globalizing Middle East and South Asia* (Syracuse: Syracuse University Press, 2009); Hanan Kholoussy, *For Better, For Worse: The Marriage Crisis That Made Modern Egypt* (Stanford, CA: Stanford University Press, 2010); Liat Kozma, *Policing Egyptian Women: Sex, Law, and Medicine in Khedival Egypt* (Syracuse: Syracuse University Press, 2011); Wilson Chacko Jacob, *Working Out Egypt: Effendi Masculinity and Subject Formation in Colonial Modernity, 1870–1940* (Durham, NC: Duke University Press, 2011); Boutheina Khaldi, *Egypt Awakening in the Early Twentieth Century: Mayy Ziyadah's Intellectual Circles* (New York: Palgrave Macmillan, 2012); Hoda Elsadda, *Gender, Nation, and the Arabic Novel: Egypt, 1892–2008* (Edinburgh: Edinburgh University Press, 2012); Marilyn Booth, *Classes of Ladies of Cloistered Spaces: Writing Feminist History through Biography in Fin-de-siécle Egypt* (Edinburgh: Edinburgh University Press, 2015); Kenneth M. Cuno, *Modernizing Marriage: Family, Ideology, and Law in Nineteenth and Early Twentieth-Century Egypt* (Syracuse, NY: Syracuse University Press, 2015); Fruma Zachs and Sharon Halevi, *Gendering Culture in Greater Syria: Intellectuals and Ideology in the Late Ottoman Period* (London: I. B. Tauris, 2015); and Beth Baron, "Round Table: Gendering Middle East History," *International Journal of Middle East Studies* 48, no. 3 (2016): 551–69.

7. Serif Mardin, *The Genesis of Young Ottoman Thought: A Study in the Modernization of Turkish Political Ideas* (Princeton, NJ: Princeton University Press, 1962); Madeleine Elfenbein, "No Empire for Old Men: The Young Ottomans and the World, 1856–1878" (PhD diss., University of Chicago, 2017).

8. Lutfi al-Sayyid's autobiography, *QH*, 32–120, 131–81; for a broader examination of this, see Gershoni, *Enlightenment in Colonial Egypt*.

9. See, e.g., the following articles by Lutfi al-Sayyid: "Dahaya al-Abrar," *al-Jarida* (*JA*), 28 June 1908, in *al-Muntakhabat* (*MN*), ed. Isma'il Mazhar, vol. 1 (Cairo: Dar al-Nashar al-Hadith, 1937), 20–23; "al-Ra'i al-'Amm," *JA*, 11 July 1908, in *MN*, vol. 1, 28–32; "Shay' Akhir (Ma'alish)," *JA*, 3 August 1908, in *MN*, vol. 1, 37–41; "Quwat al-Ra'i al-'Amm," *JA*, 21 November 1908, in *MN*, vol. 1, 67–71; "Shay' fi al-Ta'lim," *JA*, 6 December 1908, in *MN*, vol. 1, 83–86; *JA*, 30 January 1909, in *MN*, vol. 1, 101–3; *JA*, 29 September 1909, in *MN*, vol. 1, 167–69; "'Ibadat al-Basala," *JA*, 8 February 1911, in *MN*, vol. 1, 217–21; *JA*, 26 February 1912, in *MN*, vol. 1, 276–79; "'Amaluna," *JA*, 2 March 1913, in *Ta'ammulat fi al-Falsafa wa-l-Adab wa-l-Siyasa wa-l-Ijtima'* (*TA*), ed. Isma'il Mazhar, 2nd ed. (Cairo: Matba'at al-Muqtataf wa-l-Muqattam, 1945), 75–79; "al-Taqlid," *JA*, 4 March 1913, in *TA*, 80–83; and Lutfi al-Sayyid's articles in *Mabadi' fi al-Siyasa wa-l-Adab wa-l-Ijtima'* (Cairo: Kitab al-Hilal, 1963), hereafter *MB*, 94–112, 210–21.

10. See, e.g., the following articles by Lutfi al-Sayyid: "al-Ra'i al-'Amm"; "Min Misr ila Baris," *JA*, 5 July 1909, in *MN*, vol. 1, 140–44; "Fi Baris," *JA*, 26 July 1909, in *MN*, vol. 1, 145–48; "Min Baris ila Lundra," *JA*, 3 August 1909, in *MN*, vol. 1, 149–53; "Fi Inkiltra," *JA*, 16 August 1909, in *MN*, vol. 1, 154–59; "Fi Inkiltra Aydan," *MN*, vol. 1, 160–63; and Lutfi al-Sayyid's articles in *MB*, 94–112, 210–21.

11. Sebastian Conrad, "Enlightenment in Global History: A Historiographical Critique," *American Historical Review* 117, no. 4 (2012): 1001, and more broadly, 999–1027.

12. Lutfi al-Sayyid, "al-Hurriyya," 19 December 1912, in *TA*, 59–64.

13. Ibid. See the following articles by Lutfi al-Sayyid: "al-Hurriyya al-Shakhsiyya," *JA*, 28 September 1913, in *TA*, 87–94; "Dahaya al-Abrar," *JA*, 28 July 1908, in *MN*, vol. 1, 20–23; "Inkar al-Dhat," *JA*, 12 January 1909, in *MN*, vol. 1, 93–96; "al-Istiqlal al-Dhati," *JA*, 30 January 1911, in *MN*, vol. 1, 201–03; "'Ibadat al-Basala"; "al-Shakhsiyya," *JA*, 24 December 1911, in *MN*, vol. 1, 259–61; "al-Hurriyya," *JA*, 1 May 1912, in *MN*, vol. 1, 296–98; Lutfi al-Sayyid's articles about "Freedoms" in *JA*, 17 December 1913–1 January 1914, in the section "Ila Nuwwab al-Umma," *MN*, ed. Isma'il Mazhar, vol. 2 (Cairo: Matba'at al-Muqtataf wa-l-Muqattam, 1945), 57–98; Lutfi al-Sayyid's articles in *JA* about "al- Hurriyya," *MB*, 132–46.

14. Lutfi al-Sayyid, "al-Hurriyya," 19 December 1912, in *TA*, 59–64; "al-Muwazzaf al-Misri," *JA*, 16 March 1909, in *MN*, vol. 1, 117–20; "Utlubu al-Hurriyya Utlubu al-Istiqlal," *JA*, 21 December 1909, in *MN*, vol. 1, 180–82; "'Ibadat al-Basala"; "Muwazzafuna," *JA*, 11 March 1912, in *MN*, vol. 1, 290–92; "al-Hurriyya"; "Hurriyyat al-Ra'i," *JA*, 16 May 1912, in *MN*, vol. 1, 299–302; Lutfi al-Sayyid's articles in *JA* about "al-Umma wa-l-Hukuma," collected and republished in *MB*, 28–62; "al-Hala al-Hadira," *JA*, 17 May 1908, in *Safahat Matwiyya* (*SM*), ed. Isma'il Mazhar (Cairo: Maktabat al-Nahda al-Misriyya, 1946), 7–24; and *MB*, 64–91.

15. Lutfi al-Sayyid, "Min Ajli Dhalika Natlubu al-Dustur," *JA*, 7 January 1914, in *TA*, 98–100; "Huquq al-Umma," 10 January 1914, in *TA*, 101–40; "al-Ra'i al-'Amm"; "Hudud al-Ta'a," *JA*, 3 November 1908, in *MN*, vol. 1, 53–56; "Inkar al-Dhat," *JA*, 12 January 1909, in *MN*, vol. 1, 93–96; "Ahmad 'Urabi," *JA*, 21 September 1911, in *MN*, vol. 1, 252–56; "Ghard al-Umma Huwa al-Istiqlal," *JA*, 2 September 1912, in *MN*, vol. 1, 313–18; and Lutfi al-Sayyid's articles about "Freedoms" as well as those in *JA* about "al-Ra'y al-'amm" in *MB*, 94–112.

16. "Al-Sharaf," *JA*, 9 May 1909, in *MN*, vol. 1, 135–36; "Ila al-Imam," *JA*, 12 December 1909, in *MN*, vol. 1, 177–79; "al-Thiqa," *JA*, 27 December 1910, in *MN*, vol. 1, 197–200; "al-Hubb wa-l-Sadaqa," *JA*, 31 January 1911, in *MN*, vol. 1, 204–8; "al-Tafaʾul bi-l-Khayr," *JA*, 1 February 1911, in *MN*, vol. 1, 209–12; *MB*, 186–90; Lutfi al-Sayyid's articles about the need to develop the Egyptian local, modern, and progressive industry in *JA*, 24 February 1912; *JA*, 26 February 1912; *JA*, 27 February 1912, in *MN*, vol. 1, 272–83; "Huriyyat al-Raʾi"; "Wasaʾil al-Istiqlal: al-Tarbiya wa-l-Taʿlim," *JA*, 5 September 1912, in *MN*, vol. 1, 329–32; "Fi Sabil al-Irtiqa," *JA*, 15 September 1912, in *TA*, 55–58; "Amaluna"; *MB*, 217–21; "al-Taqlid," *JA*, 4 March 1913, in *TA*, 80–83; and "Sirr Tatawwur al-Umam," *JA*, 7 April 1913, in *TA*, 84–86.

17. See, e.g., Hourani, *Arabic Thought in the Liberal Age*, 173, and more broadly, 170–81; al-Najjar, *Lutfi al-Sayyid wa-l-Shakhsiyya al-Misriyya*; Wendell, *The Evolution of the Egyptian National Image*, 266–76; Donald Malcom Reid, *Whose Pharaohs? Archaeology, Museums, and Egyptian National Identity from Napoleon to World War I* (Berkeley: University of California Press, 2002), 210–11, 288; Elliot Colla, *Conflicted Antiquities: Egyptology, Egyptomania, Egyptian Modernity* (Durham: Duke University Press, 2007), 142–55; and Walker, "Supra-Egyptian Islamic and Pan-Arab Identities," A283–298.

18. ʿAfaf Lutfi al-Sayyid, "Lutfi al-Sayyid al-Insan," *al-Hiwar* 4 (1963): 16–21.

19. "Al-Athar al-Qadima," *JA*, 8 December 1912, in *TA*, 17–21; *MB*, 205–09; "Athar al-Jamal wa-Jamal al-Athar," *JA*, 12 December 1912, in *TA*, 22–28; *MB*, 210–16; and Anthony Pagden, *The Enlightenment and Why It Still Matters* (New York: Random House, 2013), 14.

20. See Lutfi al-Sayyid's articles in *al-Jarida* as follows: "Sultat al-Umma," *JA*, 14 September 1912, in *TA*, 50–54; "Tadamununa," *JA*, 2 January 1913, in *TA*, 65–68; "Misriyyatuna," *JA*, 6 January 1913, in *TA*, 69–71; "al-Misriyya," *JA*, 16 January 1913, in *TA*, 72–74; "Huquq al-Umma," *JA*, 10 January 1914, in *TA*, 101–4; "ʿAlaykum Anfusakum," *JA*, 7 September 1909, in *MN*, vol. 1, 164–66; "al-Jamiʿa al-Misriyya," *JA*, 5 October 1909, in *MN*, vol. 1, 170–72; *JA*, 9 October 1909, in *MN*, vol. 1, 173; "al-Idtirab fi al-Raʾi al-ʿAmm," *JA*, 1 September 1912, in *MN*, vol. 1, 307–12; *MB*, 106–12; "Halatuna al-Siyasiyya," *JA*, 25 September 1913, in *MN*, vol. 2, 112–14; "Mushahadat bi-Sikulujiyya," *JA*, 2 February 1913, in *MN*, vol. 2, 115–20; "Taqdis al-Hukuma wa-Nafi al-Karama wa-l-Istiqlal," *JA*, 2 September 1908, in *MB*, 60–62; "Fa-li-Nafham al-Istiqlal," *JA*, 2 September 1912, *MB*, 123–29; "Amaluna"; and "Ila al-Fityan: al-Wataniyya," *JA*, 11 June 1914, in *MN*, vol. 2, 163–66.

21. "Al-Misriyya"; and "Amaluna."

22. *QH*, 18, and more broadly, 18–29, 42–47, 80–91, 129–43, 160–67, 172–81.

23. Z. M. Quraishi defines Lutfi al-Sayyid as "a moderate nationalist of *Hizb al-Umma* . . . and partially anglicized in his political attitude." *Liberal Nationalism in Egypt*, 217.

24. See, e.g., Wendell, *The Evolution of the Egyptian National Image*, 256–76, 295–301; Landau, *Parliaments and Parties in Egypt*, 104–40; Vatikiotis, *The Modern History of Egypt*, 214–35; Nadav Safran, *Egypt in Search of Political Community: An Analysis of the Intellectual and Political Evolution of Egypt, 1804–1952* (Cambridge, MA: Harvard University Press, 1961), 85–97; and Kazziha, "The Jaridah-Umma Group," 373–85. See also Zaheer Masood Quraishi, *Liberal Nationalism in Egypt: Rise and Fall of the Wafd Party* (Delhi: Kitab Mahal, 1968), 217–18; and Abdeslam M. Maghraoui, *Liberalism without Democracy: Nationhood and Citizenship in Egypt, 1922–1936* (Durham: Duke University Press, 2006), 70–73.

25. "Lurd Krumir imam al-Taʾrikh," *JA*, 13 April 1907, in *SM*, 69–74; *QH*, 52–61; *JA*, 5 May 1907, in *SM*, 80–95.

26. Ahmad Lutfi al-Sayyid, *Safahat Matwiyya: Min Ta'rikh al-Haraka al-Istiqlaliyya fi Misr min Mars 1907 ila Mars 1909, 'Asr al-Inqilab al-Fikri fi al-Siyasa al-Wataniyya* (Cairo: Maktabat al-Nahda al-Misriyya, 1946).

27. "Al-Hala al-Hadira"; Lutfi al-Sayyid's address in Alexandria, in *JA*, 23 August 1908, in *SM*, 25–38; and "Ghard al-Umma Huwa al-Istiqlal."

28. "Al-Hala al-Hadira," *SM*, 7, republished in *MB*, 64–91; "Nahnu wa-l-Istiqlal," *JA*, 8 April 1908, in *SM*, 121–25; "Ghard al-Umma Huwa al-Istiqlal"; "al-Tarbiyya wa-l-Ta'lim"; "Amaluna"; and "Huquq al-Umma." For a broader critical discussion of Lutfi al-Sayyid's articles about British colonial rule, 1882–1909, see *SM*, 161–227.

29. See articles in *JA*, 31 March 1907, in *SM*, 57–60; *JA*, 27 May 1907, in *SM*, 61–66; "'Alaykum Anfusaqum"; "al-Shakhsiyya," *JA*, 24 December 1911, in *MN*, vol. 1, 259–61; "al-Qalaq al-Fikri," *JA*, 31 August 1912, in *MN*, vol. 1, 303–06; "Ghard al-Umma Huwa al-Istiqlal"; and "Madhhabuna wa-Madhhabuhum," *JA*, 6 April 1907, in *MB*, 55–59.

30. "Ghard al-Umma Huwa al-Istiqlal"; "Muqaddima li-Wasa'il al-Islah," *JA*, 3 September 1912, in *MN*, vol. 1, 319–23.

31. "Al-Jami'a al-Misriyya," *JA*, 5 October 1909, in *MN*, vol. 1, 170–72; *JA*, 9 October 1909, in *MN*, vol. 1, 173; "Ghard al-Umma Huwa al-Istiqlal"; "Wasa'il al-Istiqlal," *JA*, 4 September 1912, in *MN*, vol. 1, 324–28; "Sultat al-Umma," *JA*, 14 September 1912, in *TA*, 50–54; "Misriyyatuna"; "al-Misriyya"; and "Huquq al-Umma."

32. See the many articles of Lutfi al-Sayyid in *JA*, 1907–9 that systematically criticized British colonial rule, 1882–1909, in *SM*, 137–277. See also "al-Ra'i al-'Amm"; "Utlubu al-Huriyya Utlubu al-Istiqlal"; and "al-Tarbiyya wa-l-Ta'lim."

33. The Earl of Cromer, *Modern Egypt*, vols. 1 and 2 (London: MacMillan and Co., 1908).

34. Lutfi al-Sayyid's harsh criticism of Cromer's colonial policies in Egypt began before Cromer's *Modern Egypt*. See, e.g., "Khawatir wa-Ara," *JA*, 16 April 1907, in *SM*, 75–76; "al-Mas'ala La al-Mu'nida," *JA*, 30 April 1907, in *SM*, 77–79; "Taqrir li-l-Lurd Krumir," *JA*, 7 May 1907, in *SM*, 96–101; and *QH*, 64–68. For Lutfi al-Sayyid's responses to Cromer's *Modern Egypt*, see "al-Inkliz fi Misr," *JA*, 14 April 1908, in *SM*, 106–12; "Hafat al-Jinna bi-l-Mukaraha," *JA*, 9 July 1908, in *MN*, vol. 1, 24–27; "Utlubu al-Huriyya Utlubu al-Istiqlal"; and "Muqaddima li-Wasa'il al-Islah."

35. Lutfi al-Sayyid's address in Hizb al-Umma's Club, *JA*, 2 January 1909, in *SM*, 39–56; "Nahnu wa-l-Istiqlal," *JA*, 8 April 1908, in *SM*, 121–25; "al-Ghard min Siyasat al-Wifaq," *JA*, 2 July 1908, in *SM*, 137–39; "Nata'ij Siyasat al-Wifaq," *JA*, 4 July 1908, in *SM*, 140–48; "Ansar al-Sultatayn," *JA*, 6 September 1908, in *SM*, 151–54; and "Hadith al-Sir Aldun Ghurst," *JA*, 29 December 1908, in *SM*, 155–60.

36. "Fi Sabil al-Hukm al-Dhati," *JA*, 15 September 1907, in *SM*, 113–14; "al-Hukm al-Dhati," *JA*, 16 September 1907, in *SM*, 115–17; *JA*, 17 September 1907, in *SM*, 118–20; "Nahnu wa-l-Istiqlal," *JA*, 9 April 1908, in *SM*, 126–29; *JA*, 11 April 1909, in *SM*, 130–34; "Nata'ij Ma bayna al-Siyasatayn," *JA*, 6 July 1908, in *SM*, 149–50; "Utlubu al-Huriyya Utlubu al-Istiqlal"; "al-Qalaq al-Fikri," *JA*, 31 August 1912, in *MN*, vol. 1, 303–06; "Muqaddima li-Wasa'il al-Islah"; and "Wasa'il al-Istiqlal."

37. "Ghard al-Umma Huwa al-Istiqlal"; and "Wasa'il al-Istiqlal."

38. *QH*, 80–91, 129–30, 132–43, 160–67, 172–81. See also "Halatuna al-Siyasiyya," *JA*, 25 September 1913, in *MN*, vol. 2, 112–14; and "Mushahadat bi-Sikulujiyya."

39. *QH*, 42–91; and al-Shalaq, *Hizb al-Umma*, throughout the book.

40. See, e.g., the series of obituaries by Luis 'Awad: "Ahmad Lutfi al-Sayyid," *al-Ahram*, 15 March 1963, 13; "al-Fatra al-Harija," *al-Ahram*, 22 March 1963, 11; and "Madinat Aristu," *al-Ahram*, 29 March 1963, 13.

41. Anwar al-Jundi, *Ukzubatan fi Ta'rikh al-Adab al-Hadith* (Cairo: Dar al-Ansar, 1972); Abu Islam Ahmad 'Abd Allah, *Anbiya' al-Fir'awniyya: Min Lutfi al-Sayyid ila Taha Husayn* (Cairo: Markaz al-Tanwir al-Islami, 2004).

42. See, e.g., Shaden M. Tagledin, *Disarming Words: Empire and the Seduction of Translation in Egypt* (Berkeley: University of California Press, 2011); and Ahmad, *Woman and Gender in Islam*. For a similar yet different approach, see Meghraoui, *Liberalism without Democracy*.

43. Peter Hill, *Utopia and Civilisation in the Arab Nahda*, 4.

44. C. A. Bayly, *Recovering Liberties: Indian Thought in the Age of Liberalism and Empire* (Cambridge: Cambridge University Press, 2012), 3–4.

BIBLIOGRAPHY

Abu-'Uksa, Wael. *Freedom in the Arab World: Concepts and Ideologies in Arabic Thought in the Nineteenth Century*. Cambridge: Cambridge University Press, 2016.

Ahmed, J. M. *The Intellectual Origins of Egyptian Nationalism*. Oxford: Oxford University Press, 1960.

Awad, Louis. *The Literature of Ideas in Egypt*. Part I. Atlanta: Scholars Press, 1986.

Ayalon, Ami. *The Arabic Print Revolution: Cultural Production and Mass Readership*. Cambridge: Cambridge University Press, 2016.

Ayalon, Ami. *The Press in the Arab Middle East: A History*. New York: Oxford University Press, 1995.

Baron, Beth. *The Women's Awakening in Egypt: Culture, Society, and the Press*. New Haven, CT: Yale University Press, 1994.

Booth, Marilyn, and Anthony Gorman, eds. *The Long 1890s in Egypt: Colonial Quiescence, Subterranean Resistance*. Edinburgh: Edinburgh University Press, 2014.

El-Ariss, Tarek. *Trials of Arab Modernity: Literary Affects and the New Political*. New York: Fordham University Press, 2013.

Elshakry, Marwa. *Reading Darwin in Arabic, 1860–1950*. Chicago: University of Chicago Press, 2013.

Goldschmidt, Jr., Arthur. "The Egyptian Nationalist Party: 1892–1919." In *Political and Social Change in Modern Egypt*. Edited by P. M Holt, 308–33. New York: Oxford University Press, 1968.

Hanssen, Jens and Max Weiss, eds. *Arabic Thought beyond the Liberal Age: Towards an Intellectual History of the Nahda*. Cambridge: Cambridge University Press, 2016.

Hill, Peter. *Utopia and Civilization in the Arab Nahda*. Cambridge: Cambridge University Press, 2020.

Hourani, Albert. *Arabic Thought in the Liberal Age, 1798–1939*. Oxford: Oxford University Press, 1962.

Jakes, Aaron. *Egypt's Occupation: Colonial Economism and the Crises of Capitalism*. Stanford, CA: Stanford University Press, 2020.

Landau, Jacob M. *Parliaments and Parties in Egypt*. Tel Aviv: Israel Publishing House, 1953.

Owen, Roger. *Lord Cromer: Victorian Imperialist, Edwardian Proconsul*. Oxford: Oxford University Press, 2004.

Al-Sayyid, Afaf Lutfi. *Egypt and Cromer: A Study in Anglo-Egyptian Relations*. London: John Murray, 1968.

Sheehi, Stephen. *Foundations of Modern Arab Identity*. Gainesville: University Press of Florida, 2004.

Vatikiotis, P. J. *The Modern History of Egypt*. London: Weidenfeld and Nicholson, 1969.

Wendell, Charles. *The Evolution of the Egyptian National Image: From Its Origins to Ahmad Lutfi al-Sayyid*. Berkeley: University of California Press, 1972.

CHAPTER 23

....

STATE, INTELLECTUALS, AND THE PAST

....

YOAV DI-CAPUA

In 1969, the accomplished Egyptian poet and literary critic Luwis 'Awad published a popular book titled *Tarikh al-Fikr al-Misri al-Hadith* (History of Modern Egyptian Thought). Conceived of in the context of the *naksa* (the setback), a time of cultural confusion and insecurity, the book was meant to orient the public by identifying and reaffirming a broad cultural denominator, or a nucleus, around which the political community could begin to rebuild itself. The publisher's (Dar al-Hilal) declared goal was to "conduct a search in the depths of Egyptian personality . . . so we can understand our present in terms of our past and thus comprehend our strengths and weaknesses in preparation for the struggles ahead."[1] Responding to the challenge, 'Awad decided that the best means for achieving this urgent goal was to account for modern Egyptian history in purely intellectual terms. He situated nationalist and revolutionary political thought at the heart of this investigation, depicting it as a transhistorical force, a *perpetuum mobile*, that is essentially Egyptian and, by its very nature, unstoppable. Though a good argument for its time, 'Awad knew all too well that he reduced the edifice of modern Egyptian thought to a simple form of nationalism. In fact, five years later, in 1974, he published another book that acknowledged this reduction and argued instead that Egyptian culture was situated at a critical juncture—read crisis—and that fresh thought was needed in order to avoid a total cultural meltdown.[2] He handed the baton to his young colleagues who were tired of bombastic nationalism, spoke openly about a politico-cultural crisis, and were ready to do something about it. For all 1970s culturally active generations, especially for the younger one, it was clear that a new kind of historical engagement with Egypt's past was desperately needed.

One of the intellectuals who answered the call was Ghali Shukri, a critical reader of Arab literature and 'Awad's protégé. In a little over a decade, Shukri published a staggering string of twenty books that collectively distilled a cluster of issues, concerns, and problems that he thought were characteristic of Egyptian and Arab thought. With time spent in prison—for no reason other than his thoughts—behind him, his thin yet powerful booklet *Min al-Arshif al-Sirri li-l-Thaqafa al-Misriyya* (From the Secret History of Egyptian Culture, 1975) exposed unknown scenes from the annals of the politics of knowledge and opened a much-needed discussion about the repressed problem of the relationship between intellectuals and the state.[3]

Though Egyptian state publications and media accounts continued to publish the narrow message of exceptional nationalism in the same old terms that 'Awad had briefly suggested (and almost immediately divested from), by the end of the 1970s, these terms were no longer relevant. Abandoning the certainty and sterility of such narratives and facing an avalanche of new Islamic publications, Shukri and a few others launched a revisionist line of inquiry with a critical agenda that was also relevant for much of the postcolonial era and even today. At the heart of this agenda was the uncompromising insistence of getting to know the past not through triumphant nationalist rendering or an Islamist promise of "return" to a golden age, but through free critical engagement.

Reviewing Egyptian thought in the second half of the twentieth century, one can easily catalog key concerns such as social justice and distribution of wealth, the ideal form of political community and the body of the state, the pursuit of political freedoms, the quest for cultural authenticity, the ideal relationship between self and society, the role of religion and the army in public life, and other derivative questions. Egyptian and foreign intellectuals have debated these issues continuously and repeatedly, and surely any comprehensive intellectual history of Egypt must explore this landscape in some depth. However, the telling experiences of 'Awad, Shukri, and others underscore several interrelated conditions that determine the possibility of thinking about such issues. For them, no sustainable, reliable, and effective social, political, or economic thought can emerge without the precondition of a critical engagement with the past. This chapter follows this line of argumentation and seeks to elucidate what is at stake when societies embrace a historical or unhistorical mode of thinking. By very broad definition, to think historically means to gain the ability to do the following: "conceptualizing, applying, analyzing, synthesizing, and/or evaluating information gathered from, or generated by, observation, experience, reflection, reasoning, or communication, as a guide to belief and action."[4] Given the right conditions, politically and otherwise, critical historical consciousness foregrounds general thought on the pressing issues of the day.

Though different from each other, 'Awad, Shukri, Islamist thinkers such as Yusuf al-Qaradawi, and, more recently, neo-*nahda* thinkers such as Jabir 'Asfur have reckoned with the same question: What is the desired Egyptian relationship to the past, and which habits of mind can sustain and develop this relationship? To answer this question is to decide on an entire set of derivative concerns regarding the community's general cultural orientation. There has been a long and contentious debate over critical historical consciousness. Post–World War II Egyptian thought responded to the legacy of colonial modernity and its material (extreme poverty) and ontological (inauthenticity, anxiety) implications. With no escape from the legacy of colonial modernity, since the 1940s, Egypt, as the rest of the Arab world and much of the Global South, was locked in a permanent state of decolonization.

This state of being has conditioned the rapport between intellectuals and the state. All Egyptian intellectuals were forced into a relationship with an authoritarian and often-times violent state whose attitude to culture and critical thinking remains paradoxical. Unable to generate its own independent thinking and sustain and develop the cultural sphere, the state is dependent on intellectuals whom it does not trust. Thus, the desired attitude toward the past is a function of this impossible relationship. Since the 1960s, Islamist thinkers such as al-Qaradawi have rejected critical historical consciousness altogether and engaged instead in a metaphysical and nonhistoricist approach to the past. This new mode of thinking became a mass phenomenon that promised to fix the problems of the present via the fiction of an instant "return" to a glorious Islamic past. During the 1990s, a renewed neoliberal engagement with the values and intellectual procedures of Arab Enlightenment, or the *nahda*, began pushing against this type of metaphysical thinking in a more systematic fashion.

The amorphous but foundational problem of collective attitude to the past ought to be considered against the broader context of existing Egyptian intellectual history in the second part of the twentieth century.[5] If we unpack this complex intellectual web without offering a specific set of arguments, it nonetheless appears that within the Egyptian political tradition, the collective right to the past emerges as nothing but a foundational human right. Though this right pertains to all practicing intellectuals, such as Suhayr al-Qalamawi, the most accomplished woman in Egyptian academia and state institutions of culture, those who argued over it publicly were men.

On Permanent Decolonization

Contrary to common wisdom, the defining factor that shaped post–World War II Egyptian thought was not a single political event like the Nasserist revolution or a set of contested ideologies such as socialism and Pan-Arabism. Rather, it was a condition with concrete material, political, and ontological aspects that all postcolonial Egyptian systems of governance and ideologies needed to reckon with and address. At its core lay a wretched material reality characterized by extreme poverty, low literacy rates, poor hygiene, low life expectancy, and the resulting stress on an already sensitive socioeconomic fabric. This reality limited human potential and condemned much of the citizenry to a life of sickness, abject misery, and an overall subhuman state of existence. Politically and economically disenfranchised, the people were robbed not only of basic human freedom but also of their very dignity.

But even classes that were better off economically, such as entire sectors of the *effendiya*, struggled. Like postcolonial subjects elsewhere, the Egyptian subject was not only profoundly unfree but also inauthentic and hence culturally disoriented. A function of unfreedom, the problem of *asala* (authenticity) is endemic to colonial modernity and its persistent efforts to transform its subjects into so-called civilized Europeans. As a result, Egyptians gradually lost the ability to think about their present in cultural means that stemmed from their own experience and that were organic and authentic to them. Instead, they began to consider their situation by resorting to European cultural means entirely external to their culture. Slowly losing the historicity of their present, Egyptians ran the risk of living in a state of cultural exile.

With time, this prevalent condition metamorphosed into a full-fledged epistemological crisis and a state of cultural schizophrenia in which public culture simultaneously pointed to two contradictory pasts and hence to two incompatible futures. For this reason, after World War II drew to a close and the era of decolonization began in earnest, the momentous question "Who and what should we be?" reverberated all over the Middle East and especially in Egypt. Responding to this reality, in 1946 the young philosopher 'Abd al-Rahman al-Badawi wrote the following:

> We, the Egyptian and Arab youth . . . are unable to bear our situation and surrender to our wretched fate. . . . We find ourselves in the same state of destruction of Eastern youth from India, Japan, and China. . . . In our minds we live the tribulations of European youth and we became spiritually preoccupied by them . . . [but when attached] to our own actual painful experiences, enormous charges of revolt, anxiety, spiritual confusion, and psychological disorder generated in us an exceptional sensitivity.[6]

Finding one's place in a world made by others for others was a challenge that hinged not only on establishing authenticity (*asala*), but also on claiming various forms of political, economic, and cultural sovereignty (*siyada*). These two aspects, authenticity and sovereignty, were the key to freedom (*hurriyya*). Defined as an ontological challenge, a problem of *being* or, for lack of better terminology, identity touched on these three interrelated sub-aspects of *asala*, *siyada*, and *hurriyya*. Being authentic and sovereign meant owning the ability for self-determination and hence for establishing one's world. In this constellation, authenticity and sovereignty functioned as preconditions for freedom, which, in turn, was dependent on sound material conditions. From the born-again Islamist Sayyid Qutb to his former liberal mentor Taha Husayn and many others, when Egyptian intellectuals of this era addressed the issue of freedom, they did so in terms of a conception of social justice whose explicit ontological outcome was life with dignity (*karama*).

Initially, the *nahda*, that is, the Arab project of Enlightenment, was supposed to address many of these issues. However, its cultural blueprint was heavily invested in colonial modernity and its problem of authenticity. Further complicating matters was that, as state-led projects, *nahda*-inspired societies failed to build robust institutions that would deliver social justice and political sustainability. For this reason, once the Free Officers, the secretive military political society that conspired to terminate the liberal order, took over, Egyptians did not fight to defend the *nahdawi* "Liberal Experiment" and its parliamentary politics. Yet some progress was made. By the 1950s, the Egyptian public as a whole had achieved a measure of conceptual clarity vis-à-vis this challenge and, thanks to early Nasserism, developed an entire political vocabulary and concrete policies and institutions to deal with it.

This newly acquired clarity is succinctly captured by Gamal Abdel Nasser's repeated promises for *'aysh, hurriyya, 'adala ijtima'iyya*, and *karama insaniyya* (bread, freedom, social justice, and human dignity). That, in a nutshell, is Egypt's longstanding postcolonial *problematique*—one that still animates present-day life. Nasserism was the most holistic and comprehensive effort to address this situation. In addition to a new economic and political philosophy, the Nasserist declared ambition involved no less than creating a new human subject (*al-insan al-jadid*). Bearing an entirely new consciousness, this new type of human being was supposed to be selfless, resolute, free, rational, and independent. In other words, he was a revolutionary man who symbolized the rebirth of the sovereign Arab nation as a whole and the resurrection of its masses. Assumed to be a man—a separate tradition of state feminism dealt with the construction of female subjectivity[7]—this project tragically collapsed with the *naksa*, which inflicted a painful psychic wound—a wound so profound that, according to exiled Syrian thinker Jurj Tarabishi, it called for urgent cultural attention.[8]

Alas, no comprehensive cultural response was dedicated to the issue. In fact, since the 1970s, the tendency of the state, its bureaucracy, and the political system as a whole was to reduce this complex postcolonial *problematique* to economic development. The domain of culture and the ambition to reconfigure Egyptian ontology was entirely appropriated by Islamist religiosity, with its version of a new subject/man (the born-again pious believer). Islamists, too, had a parallel effort to construct the ideal type of the Islamic woman with active participation from activist-intellectuals such as Kazim Safinaz and Zaynab al-Ghazali. Al-Ghazali was especially active in this regard and became a highly influential figure in the Muslim Brotherhood and beyond. As the founder of the independent Muslim Sisterhood, al-Ghazali had a lifelong engagement with female activism. She had strong ideas about the role of the new woman in contemporary Islam and, especially after her imprisonment and torture (1965–71), began publishing her thoughts more systematically.[9]

The quality and nature of the Islamic solution to the problem of being was, and continues to be, the subject of fierce public struggle and, therefore, a major intellectual preoccupation. Egyptian society has not yet found a consensual and successful way of dealing with established religion and its popular iterations. As the 2011 revolution and its slogan of *'aysh, hurriyya, karama insaniyya* made abundantly clear, six decades after achieving conceptual clarity with regard to the postcolonial challenge, Egypt is still struggling to meet the original goals of decolonization. In that sense, we can speak of a permanent, and perhaps even chronic, condition of decolonization whose implications form the basis for much of contemporary Arab and Egyptian thought.

Egypt was not unique in this regard. Taking a hard look at the complex issues associated with living in the contemporary world and considering them collectively, Moroccan philosopher Muhammad 'Abd al-Jabiri succinctly addressed this challenge. In his book *Ishkaliyat al-Fikr al-'Arabi al-Mu'asir* (The Problematique of Contemporary Arab Thought, 1989), al-Jabiri distilled a list of issues that all Arab societies, including Egypt, are forced to deal with and that call for a radical project of decolonization. These issues include cultural inauthenticity in the shape of alienation from Islamic heritage (*turath*), the inability to claim the past and make it meaningfully relevant in the present, the related difficulty of establishing critical historical consciousness on a mass scale and normalizing critical thinking, the need to rethink the institution of the Arab state entirely, and tension between the self and the "other" as a problem that not only affects minorities, marginalized classes, and women, but also other national groups and cultures.[10] With this in mind, the permanent state of decolonization refers to a continuous effort to come to terms with al-Jabiri's *problematique* or with what some scholars of the Global South call the "colonial present."[11] As al-Jabiri and others repeatedly noted, the success of decolonization hinges on the capacity for critical historical analysis as well as access to the past and work through it. For such capacity to emerge, intellectuals had to come to terms with the growing ambition of the state to organize and preside over the cultural sphere.

THE STATE CANNOT THINK!

Given that from the 1950s to the present, generation after generation of Egyptian and, more generally, Arab intellectuals landed in prison, our tendency to consider thought, and specifically historical inquiry, in separation from prison experience is problematic. The same is true with regard to the experience of intellectuals in exile. In fact, in both "prison thought" and "exile thought," we dwell very little on the main cause of these experiences: the relationship with the state. Indeed, "prison thought" and "exile thought" are only symptoms of this difficult relationship. Viewed from the standpoint of the sociology of knowledge, the radical separation of thought from the conditions of its creation blurs our ability to understand the meaning and function of ideas in society and, as a result, of society itself. Though we are still awaiting a comprehensive study of intellectuals, prison, exile, and thought, these issues cannot be considered solely in liberal moral terms as crude violations of individual freedom. A new form of intellectual history should include a full consideration of the authoritarian nature of the postcolonial state and its relationship to ideas and intellectuals as they have manifested from the 1950s to the present.

In postcolonial Egyptian history, the tension between intellectuals and the state, as well as that between intellectuals and authority (*al-muthaqafun wa-l-sulta*), is a harrowing and intimate issue that did not escape the attention of local intellectuals.[12] For the most part, their corpus of writing on this issue is interested in the specific power play between intellectuals and the state's function of political authority. With one pioneering exception, that of Richard Jacquemond, missing from this consideration are both the historicization and theorization of this relationship:[13] How did postcolonial intellectuals conceive of the state, and what were the long-term implications of this imagination? Sharing the public domain of culture with the state, what were their expectations for creative freedom, and what kind of partnership did they strike? What were the intellectual interests and needs of the state? Did intellectuals identify the state as a demystified product of history and, therefore, as a possible subject of critical inquiry? Was there a tradition of state critique? If so, who and what guided it? What did intellectuals make of the contradictory nature of the state, which, regardless of how it presented itself, was never a unified monolith but a cluster of fragmented institutions struggling internally as well as externally? Finally, given the ideological and political diversity of intellectuals, what modes of behavior did they develop vis-à-vis the state?

The vantage point for this much-needed consideration is that the postcolonial Egyptian (and Arab) state was not similar to the normative European state with which much of existing political philosophy, from British liberalism via Karl Marx to Giorgio Agamben, is preoccupied. The main difference stems from the fact that from the very beginning, the postcolonial state developed in opposition to an ideal European nation-state and was entrusted with the metaphysical mission of saving its citizens from colonialism and giving them freedom via a radical project of decolonization. In other words, though fascinated by the European nation-state model and seeking to emulate it, the "decolonizing state" was entrusted not only with the task of maintaining the political community and extending social justice by managing and improving daily life as all states do, but also, and perhaps primarily, with the metaphysical quest for freedom. This mission determined the role, function, and space of all forms of thought from pure philosophy and literature to political and economic thought.

Thus, as a very different entity than the highly theorized European nation-state, the "decolonizing state" and its relationship to thought, and specifically historical thought, should be understood in entirely different terms. Propelled by the true revolutionary properties of Nasserism, which were developed to the point of becoming a theology, the state became a force that manufactured its own truth and hence its own objectivity. With that (revolutionary) objectivity being the main source of its authority, the state intentionally blurred the distinction between the ideational and ideological framework of Nasserist nationalism and the actual institution of the state and its many levers of power. With nationalism and statism appearing to be the same, the state gradually developed a sacred aura as a mystical institution—and the only institution—that could potentially deliver society from the painful world of colonial subjugation to an era of freedom, dignity, and prosperity. The association between statism and nationalism, including the association between various ideologies and the state, further amplified the notion that the state's existence, its abstract rationality, and actions are objective and, as such, beyond any critical inquiry.

Suffocating critical inquiry and flagging it as a type of political opposition, intellectuals such as Anouar Abdel-Malek and dozens of others who engaged in critical thought during the 1950s and 1960s found themselves on a collision course with the objective status of the state. Though any healthy society depends on critical thought, by the mid-1960s the critical intellectual domain became antithetical to state and nation alike.[14] In reaction to this development, Egyptians, Iraqis, and Syrians moved to Beirut, where the state was relaxed—if not altogether absent—or even Paris.[15] In the course of his life, Ghali Shukri would work in both Beirut and Paris. Others, such as Yusuf al-Qaradawi, would find intellectual freedom in Qatar.

The normalization of the structural restriction on critical thought (by the early 1960s almost any form of critical thought was viewed by the state as political opposition) forced intellectuals to choose between voluntary exile and involuntary prison, thus associating critical spirit with the loss of freedom or the pain of an inauthentic life in exile. The degree to which the properties of thought itself internalized this link is still an open question. For its part, the state, too, was not as free to shape the world of ideas as it saw fit. By definition, *the state does not think*, does not generate critical meaning, and, therefore, is entirely dependent on the creativity and goodwill of others to do so. Literarily short of ideas, it was against this backdrop that in 1961 the state announced the first so-called crisis of the intellectuals. Since then, in all of its different iterations, the Egyptian state has continually suffered from a severe intellectual deficit to which it has responded with an active, and at times desperate, effort to co-opt, lure, and persuade intellectuals to join its ranks and make the state think again.[16]

The fact that, for much of the second half of the century, the state presided over nationalized institutions and the very infrastructure of public culture (theaters, universities, the publishing industry, cinema, music, and mass media) made resisting its call very difficult (perhaps the only cultural and political institution that was still outside the reach of the state was the neighborhood cafe and, later, Islamist institutions of the so-called parallel state, including the neighborhood mosque).[17] Indeed, until the 1980s, one can find a long list of critical intellectuals such as Lutfi al-Khuli and Mahmud Amin al-ʿAlim who, in a matter of days, moved from the prison cell to the editing room. Many of them believed that they could reform the state and correct its ways. Granted, their communist, Marxist, and socialist ideologies did not portray the state as an enemy but as an ideological vehicle whose errors should be rectified. However imperfect and un-ruly, it was still a trusted ally—the only ally. In fact, under Nasserism there was an en-tire intellectual ideology of alliance with the state known as *iltizam*, or commitment.[18] However, over time the heavy-handed policies of the Nasserite state and the demystifi-cation of the state following the *naksa* pushed a new generation of intellectuals (*jil al-sittinat*, or the generation of the sixties) to divest and dissociate from state and society alike. Others developed specific strategies, or even complete personalities or behavioral profiles, for dealing with state power, such as "the loyalist," "the rejectionist," "the critical dissident," "the opportunist," "the escapist," and so on.[19]

That arrangement with the state did not survive the *naksa*, which initiated a rupture between the civic aspects of nationalism and the defeated, and now demystified, polit-ical state. All of a sudden, the state and the nation were no longer one and the same.[20] With this functional separation of state power from the political community came the painful realization that the state is not the incarnation of liberation but simply a tool, a mere disenchanted instrument. Gone, too, was the objective nature of the revolu-tionary state and its claim for truth. Thereafter, the possibility of critical thought was briefly reopened, and its spectrum was considerably expanded. Though there is still much work to be done on the intellectual history of 1967, preliminary research suggests that the war ushered in a radical reconsideration of all aspects of public (and even pri-vate) life. From political philosophy to gender relationships, sexuality, the role of politics and religion, and the place of reason in human affairs, a new generation of disillusioned postrevolutionary thinkers began to tackle these concerns.[21]

It is still not entirely clear what happened to the relationship between intellectuals and the state during the post-ideological transition era of the 1970s. Clearly, in sharp opposition to Nasserism, few intellectuals believed in the basic righteousness of the present political project anymore. It also became more difficult to understand what the political project actually was. Thus, returning to run a journal right after serving time for dissent was no longer a viable path. Though we still need comprehensive research on the culture of the prison system, it appears as if the prison has changed, too, and was no longer a place where intellectuals could read, write, correspond, and debate, as was the case in some prisons during the 1960s. Increasingly, the prison became a place where non-Islamist intellectuals were tortured and sexually violated just like the Islamist enemies of Nasserism were. Whether it was under Anwar al-Sadat or Husni Mubarak, the emerging new state had acquired an entirely new configuration.

This "presidential security state" was characterized by Roger Owen as a personalized enterprise that was run by the presidential office, the presidential family, and a small group of advisers drawn from the military, the security services, and the business elite. These were further supported by a secondary tier of senior members of the bureaucracy, which reached deep into the civic sphere of education, the judiciary, and the media.[22] Perfected since the 1970s, "the presidential security state" still needed to fulfill all the long-overdue material and ontological tasks of decolonization, including the promise of freedom. It chose to do so not by crafting a unified cultural vision, a set of shared ideals, an ideology, and a definite sense of political community, but by focusing exclusively on "the economy." In doing so, it forfeited any metaphysical claim as a basis for shared communal life and left its citizens suspended in a perpetual present that lacked any collective vision.

A PEOPLE WITHOUT HISTORY?

In May 1996, veteran historian 'Abd al-'Azim Ramadan published an angry newspaper article in which he complained, not for the first time, that contemporary Egyptian history is falsified. The specifics of his case concerned the legacy of the 1967–70 war of attrition with Israel. While Ramadan saw the war as a continuation of the disastrous 1967 debacle and an utter failure, defenders of the Nasserist legacy sought to portray the thousand-day war as a success that led to the substantial achievement of the 1973 October War. Though accusations, arguments, counteraccusations, and more arguments abounded, none of the participating parties could back their claims with any meaningful documentation.[23] Simply put, because there was no archive to foreground any of the arguments, all that the participating parties could do was rehearse opinions and positions that relied, more than anything else, on personal memoirs. Known as *harb al-mudhakarat* (war of the memoirs), this episode extended not only to the war of attrition but to the entire Nasserist legacy, including the disastrous 1967 war and its aftermath. This historical saga comprised a series of circular and self-referential debates that repeated, ad nauseam, questions such as "1952: revolution or coup?" or "What did Nasser know about the state of the army?" Projecting their politics onto the past, the authors of these debates created an ecosystem of pseudohistory—the only history the state facilitates and supports, and the more, the better.[24]

Though often initiating these debates himself, Ramadan understood his professional predicament and knew fairly well that this was not the first time, nor would it be the last, that historians complained about a concentrated effort, by state actors and others, to falsify, forge, and fabricate Egyptian history. In fact, earlier efforts by members of the historical profession to persuade the state to make the records of the 1967 war available failed. Even the documents of the July Revolution, the most significant political movement in modern Egyptian history, went missing, including the documentation of some of its key projects, such as the construction of the Aswan Dam.[25]

One of the main factors that shaped the status of contemporary Egyptian society as one whose people surely have a rich past but who otherwise have hardly any history to show for it, especially not for the second half of the twentieth century, was the state. The most important cause for this grim reality is the effective actions of the state to erase its tracks. This habit started with the monarchy, accelerated with Nasserism, and intensified further with the death of Nasser in September 1970. Thereafter, al-Sadat led a wide-scale campaign of de-Nasserization whose thrust was to discredit Nasserism as a political institution and an identity via, among other actions, an attack on its history. As Ramadan noted, al-Sadat did so by eradicating historical records and resorting to pseudohistory in which historical veracity could not be established by anyone. Consequently, the Muslim Brotherhood, liberals, Marxists, Nasserists, and, of course, al-Sadat and Mubarak themselves cultivated their own sectarian history.

With no state archive to support a critical investigation of any meaningful episode in contemporary Egyptian history, be it the history of its wars, high politics, economic and agrarian policies, the business of the armed forces, the neoliberal history of privatization, or the war against Islamist groups and their communities, the public sphere was, and still is, flooded with educated and less educated guessing, second-guessing, circular arguments, self-referential ones, and endless memory wars. Though this crisis of historical representation exists in most postcolonial societies, it has Arab and Egyptian specificities.[26] In the words of al-Jabiri, "Arab cultural history, as we read it today in books . . . is a fragmentary history, the history of differences of opinions and not a history of constructing opinions."[27] This situation raises the question: What are the civic implications of public life with no meaningful access to the past?

The answer is a straightforward one: living without history, that is, in a state of exile or separation from one's past, constitutes a condition whose civic and political implications are twofold. First, a citizen who cannot reason historically about the business of his or her political community is not a participating and change-demanding citizen but rather a docile subject whose basic human dignity is at constant risk. Ultimately, living without critical historical consciousness leads to living without rights. This is why in the Egyptian context, the right to the past is nothing but a basic human right, something that any credible process of decolonization is required to ensure. Second, and of equal and related importance, is the fact that diminishing critical historical consciousness clears the ground for an ahistorical connection to an imagined, unadulterated, and "perfect" past. It is this kind of past and reasoning that Islamists of all stripes have cultivated. This problem will be addressed at greater length in the next section, in the discussion of *turath*.

However, although this temporal aspect of decolonization failed to materialize, and consequently successive generations were robbed of their right to the past and have suffered from being historically alienated from it, historians began to respond by establishing alternative archives. These archives rely on a critical method of reading open-source material such as the daily and periodic press. Though admittedly limited in scope, the idea of the alternative archive as an institution that supports critical historical consciousness is an important one.[28] In that context, it is perhaps telling that once the 2011 revolution was set in motion, activists became concerned that archive disease would result in the erasure and distortion of their sacrifices. For this reason, these revolutionary groups meticulously documented their actions, collected documents (including stolen state documents), and established alternative and open-access archives of the revolution, such as the "Tahrir Documents."[29] Further attention to this problem can be seen in the coverage of media platforms such as *Mada Masr*, which extended its interest to historical episodes such as the 1967 war.[30]

THE PERILS OF INSTANT AUTHENTICITY

But the authoritarian state, its problematic relation with intellectuals, and the self-destruction of historical records were only one complex aspect of the war against critical historical consciousness. In the 1970s, a new and much more dangerous threat emerged: that of instant ahistorical authenticity. With the *naksa*, anybody in the business of thinking had some serious intellectual work to do. In the case of Yusuf al-Qaradawi, an al-Azhar scholar who had moved to Qatar six years earlier, the critical ideas about Nasserism were already organized in his head, and some of them were ready for print. Like Ghali Shukri, following the war, al-Qaradawi immediately published a series of books that analyzed the defeat and proposed a solution. His first book, now largely forgotten, drew a line between the 1967 defeat and the Palestinian *nakba*, or catastrophe. The cause for both, according to al-Qaradawi, was the abandonment of faith.[31]

Next came more explicit explorations of this idea and talk about an exclusive "Islamic solution." Writing about *hatmiyat al-hal al-islami* (the predetermined necessity of the Islamic solution), al-Qaradawi borrowed the Marxist idea of predetermined necessity from his adversaries, who used it extensively to justify Arab socialism and other Marxism-related solutions. Like Marx, al-Qaradawi believed in predetermined sequences, except that in his work the generating impersonal actor was not material forces but an abstract entity called "Islam." Like the prevalent Marxist logic, he also argued for the scientific and objective nature of his analysis and, by implication, its inevitability. But he knew to keep it simple; he told his readers that Islam was the solution for everything.

Then he explained. He wrote that all imported ideologies such as liberalism, capitalism, and socialism failed miserably. He named all the great Arab projects that have failed, beginning with two defeats in Palestine and continuing with Arab unity. He ridiculed left-wing revolutionary radicalism as meaningless bombastic talk and an utter failure. He pointed out the absence of social justice, lack of development, and total want in political and personal freedoms. He then moved to a new sphere by arguing that the Muslim individual and the entire society that surrounded it were sick. Many symptoms came to mind: intellectual confusion and disorientation, immorality, rampant corruption, and social and familial disintegration.[32] This list was by no means new. In fact, it was a version of the exact list of concerns, goals, and objects, material as well as ontological, that constituted the core of the effort to decolonize Egypt since the late 1940s. The only difference was that, following Sayyid Qutb, al-Qaradawi announced the willingness of a newly invigorated Islam to assume the burden and responsibility. Al-Qaradawi then suggested to stop conducting all aspects of Arab and Egyptian life in imported European terms and return to authentic terms that were organic to Islam and its people. He concluded by saying that "this is the only solution that can save the *umma* and safeguard its existence."[33] Indeed, he was troubled by the challenges to Muslim existence and, just like the Nasserists before him, responded by calling for the making of a new type of human being.[34]

Al-Qaradawi was neither alone in his call to return to an unspecified form of Islam nor unique in terms of the nature of his call. As is commonly known, thousands of public figures divested from the Nasserist intellectual and cultural protocols and turned instead to find meaning in the *turath*, that is, in Islamic heritage. Thereafter, the *turath* emerged as the only authentic reservoir for Arab Islamic culture and an ultimate source for all forms of meaning. Any other cultural reference was vehemently rejected. Powered by the unstoppable force of "Petro-Islam" and the spread of a popular Islamic culture of preachers and cassette tapes, the association between *turath* and *asala* became firm as well as hegemonic.[35]

In response, hundreds of intellectuals from across the region joined the fray, and debates about the enormous field of *turath* proliferated. More than any other issue, the question of *turath*, defined as *the contemporary utility of the entire legacy of Islam*, forms the most intensive, passionate, and continuous debate in contemporary Arab thought. No other topic or ideology, not even Arab nationalism, has produced more conferences, seminars, articles, books, and exchanges. Forming the very core of the problem of *asala*, the question of *turath* and the attitude toward its past was understood to be the problem of all Muslims and Arabs (including Christian Arabs, who share the legacy of the ecumenical Christian-Islamic *nahda* as a joint project).[36]

Therefore, on account of this transregional debate, distilling the Egyptian contribution to *turath* is not only difficult but also unnecessary. However, it should be acknowledged that, as the country with the deepest roots in colonial modernity, Egypt was an important center of the debate and one where its most striking consequences were at play. In the 1970s, Egypt saw a shift toward religiosity and its well-known consequences, such as the rise of the "parallel state" of the Muslim Brotherhood, the overtaking of the public sphere, the politicization of faith, and eventually an unmistakable shift toward murderous forms of terrorism. But there was another, much less discussed consequence concerning the infrastructure of the mind: *the shift to metaphysical reasoning and ahistoric consciousness.*

Time and again, intellectuals expressed concern that the generational transition toward Islamism was destroying the ability to historicize the Islamic past and meaningfully connect it to the present. At stake was the ability of every participating citizen to think critically in a historical manner, that is, to be able to conceptualize, analyze, and synthesize the historical knowledge they gathered and apply it to everyday public life. It was understood that such a practice is sustained by crucial skills that form the backbone of any critical reasoning, such as clarity, accuracy, precision, consistency, relevance, sound evidence, depth, breadth, and fairness, to name a few.[37] With millions habituated to the idea that they can "flee" the present to the imagined domain of a pure Islamic past, home of the *turath*, the basic and quintessential modern mindset of historicism came under severe attack. This metaphysical escape was nothing but a form of mass dissociation from a difficult present—a dissociation so severe that it sacrificed being in the present for the solace of self-transcendence and the opportunity to be part of something eternal that, unlike Nasserism, cannot be defeated in war.

In her book on contemporary Arab thought, intellectual historian Elizabeth Suzanne Kassab covered at great length two decades of *turath* debates in which a diverse group of intellectuals pushed back against the fetishization of the *turath* and the inability to think about it critically. This corpus comprised thousands of articles and books that tackled issues and aspects related to law, theology, governance, freedom, minorities and nonbelievers, the status of women, cultural regeneration, and much more.[38] Kassab's research and that of Ahmad Agbaria on the same topic reveal that only a few scholars took issue with the core problem of ahistorical consciousness and drew on earlier post-1967 critiques by Moroccan philosopher Abdalla Laroui and others to point out this new danger. Among these intellectuals was the Syrian philosopher in exile Jurj Tarabishi. From his small apartment in Paris, he directed much of his critique at Egyptians. Versed in psychoanalysis, Tarabishi argued that the current reading of *turath* was nothing but a form of traumatic regression following the pain of the *naksa*. With the defeat of revolutionary Nasserism, the *turath* became a substitute framework (or a substitute cultural father figure) that, by way of magical thinking and the projection of collective wishes onto a vacuous temporal landscape, eliminated critical analysis of the past and the ability to utilize this reasoning in the present, politically and otherwise.[39] As Kassab points out, whether we accept this type of psychological reading or not, "the fact remains that most Arab critical thinkers agree that *turath* and the idea of authenticity associated with it are the last desperate resort for pride and hope after a century of disasters in the face of an unbearable present."[40]

Weighing in on the utility of *turath* in his major work about reason, Jabiri wrote:

> Indeed, cultural heritage (*turath*) constitutes the primary component of the inclina-
> tion toward unity among Arabs throughout all times, and it stimulates this tendency
> even more strongly in the present era. Despite this, it is essential to recognize that we
> have not yet been able to organize the relationship between the component parts of
> that traditional heritage on the one hand, and between tradition and ourselves on
> the other hand, in a way that would permit it to establish our Arab self-according to
> the requirements of our time . . . our cultural history demands to be rewritten and
> reconstructed.[41]

And so, in addition to the previously mentioned war on archives and historical infrastructure, a parallel destructive effort was unleashed against the modern mode of historical reasoning and the simple idea that understanding any present phenomenon
requires viewing it as part of a temporal process of causal and continuous development.
This difficulty to collectively organize the relationship to the past is also mirrored in the
relationship between intellectuals and the state. This latter relationship, which saw many
surprising twists and turns, the last of which happened during the 2013 counterrevolu-
tion, is worthy of significant scholarly attention.

ENLIGHTENMENT NOW!

With the decisive turn toward neoliberalism in the 1990s, when everything hinged on
economic performance, it became increasingly difficult for the state to mobilize political support. Instead, the state doubled down on ruling through exceptional emergency
laws. In place since the fall of Nasserism, but radically amplified since the 1980s, this
so-called state of exception was predicated on sheer power with no collective vision or
consensus. Kassab observes that "during those decades, Egyptian and Syrian societies
suffered the worsening impact of corrupt and autocratic regimes in almost every aspect
of life. All efforts at protest and change had failed, leaving people with a deep sense of
helplessness. State violence, repression, censorship, the absence of the rule of law, pau-
perization, and the collapse of the health and education services had traumatized these
countries and exhausted their people. Various sectors of society, including workers,
students, women, peasants, and intellectuals, had tried to oppose, resist, and reform
to no avail."[42] How did all of this shape the relationship between intellectuals and the
state? Notwithstanding the absence of scholarship on this issue, it appears that many
intellectuals dissociated from the state and began to develop a sustained critique of it in
the tradition of "epistemological and ethical anti-statism."[43] The entire field of human
rights activism that has developed since the 1990s should be understood as part of this
ethical shift. The fact that much of the funding that supported NGOs arrived from outside of Egypt surely awarded it a measure of independence. Drawing on small-scale ad

hoc politics, intellectuals took issue with the daily realities of the state of exception and the linkages it made between law and violence. Since the early 2000s, micro-activism in all areas of civic life, such as in the sphere of labor and legal justice, began to metamorphose into a full-scale struggle over the character of the state itself.[44] It, too, produced forms of thought designed to address the major issues at hand while bypassing the state.

Thus, divesting from the political imagination of the nation-state and its bookshelf of ready-made ideologies, intellectuals began exploring a new conceptual language that, though specifically Egyptian and hence authentic, did not fall into the trap of *turath*. Such was the case with the concept *'amara*, "a collective expressive force that is at once an aesthetic of resonance and an ethic of solidarity, offering visions of social cohesion that do not readily translate into the modes of knowledge production in discourses of power and their conceptual languages."[45] As a new form of critical practice, *'amara* is politically fresh as well as seasoned, established, familiar, and even old. Indeed, as a cultural practice, *'amara* "is specifically Egyptian, both in the use of the term and in the manner in which it is developed in particular social situations."[46] However, it was also part of a much more significant preoccupation with advancing a new kind of civic state (*al-dawla al-madaniyya*). In this configuration, a civic sphere would regulate both the role of religion and the army in the affairs of the state. Those who espoused checking the power of the state and reconfiguring it were relatively young, unestablished, and unknown. They had their moment in 2011, but the counterrevolutionary coup of 2013 practically eliminated the possibility that their abstract designs for a civic state would turn into a political reality.[47]

However, not everybody who sought to reinvigorate the tradition of *tanwir* (Enlightenment) also sought to bypass a state-sanctioned intellectual scene. Alongside these oppositional elements were established intellectuals, such as Murad Wahba and Jabir 'Asfur, who championed the cause of *tanwir* as a cultural response to escapist Islamist thinking and saw an alliance with the state's political establishment, and later even with the army, as a dire necessity. Supported by the neoliberal presidential security state and serving full terms in its institutions, these thinkers preached for the absolute authority of critical reasoning and have done everything in their capacity to develop and preserve the capacity for such reasoning.

In particular, they sought to promote sound historical consciousness as the only antidote for the Islamists' habit of metaphysical reasoning. Offering a clearer public alternative, they emphatically rejected and refuted the monopoly that Islamists had acquired over Islamic historical knowledge and over political and social interpretations of the present. They poured into this battle everything they had, publishing new series of subsidized books and amplifying their public profile by flooding the media with interviews, articles, and opinion pieces. Equally important, they sponsored high-profile public events that carried their message as a semi-official state ideology.[48]

In their effort to save and resurrect *nahdawi* culture, people like 'Asfur entirely overlooked the problematic nature of an intellectual alliance with the state. As one critic put it, "The reality is that, instead of being the progressive avant-garde calling upon the people to change, the secularized intelligentsia has only succeeded in becoming part and parcel of the institutions and instrumentalities of despotism."[49] Indeed, many members of this class, including academic scholars, would eventually support the army's counter-revolution of 2013, with all of its dreadful implications. Perhaps the most controversial case in this regard is that of Sharif Yunis, a venerable historian of Nasserism. Intimately aware of the historical role of the armed forces in politics and the many ways in which intellectuals were entangled with both the state and the army, Yunis nonetheless trusted the army to save culture from the clutches of the Islamists.[50] Alas, the result was the exact opposite of what he had hoped for: in 2017, a proposed legislation offered to criminalize the so-called humiliation of national symbols, thus significantly, if not mortally, limiting the ability to think and speak historically. Though Yunis argued that the law would "muzzle mouths more than it will free minds,"[51] it remains a direct result of the support that he and others extended to the coup. Indeed, the failed struggle for the civic state and the military coup that decided it entirely reconfigured the intellectual sphere and ushered in a new state effort to erase and distort the history of the revolution (and, in fact, all history), thus continuing the war against the past.

Conclusion

In 2019, film producer Hisham 'Abd al-Khaliq released the blockbuster war movie *al-Mamar* (The Crossing). Produced with the logistical and possibly financial help of the armed forces, the film tells the story of the miraculous resurrection of the army from the 1967 defeat and the war of attrition to the heroic 1973 crossing of the Suez Canal and the (partial) defeat of the Israeli army. In 129 minutes of saturated action and pathos, director Sharif 'Arafa presents a triumphant national history that has not much to do with historical reality but is a reminder of the power of mythical narration. If the Islamists practice mass dissociation from the present and its concrete difficulties via the imagination of a return to the days of Islamic glory, *al-Mamar* was an equally problematic response. Successful in the box office, *al-Mamar*, as well as its endorsement and celebration by the military-political elite and its docile servants, is a sad reminder of the ongoing failure to establish a new and critical relationship to the past. Moviegoers surely appreciated the muscles and pyrotechnic effects, but they might have been surprised to learn that state archives that account for this piece of military action do not appear to exist, and if they do exist, in some hidden vault, they cannot be accessed. In fact, there is no robust infrastructure—institutional, notional, or normative—to support historical inquiry into episodes such as the 1967 war.[52] At stake in this divestment is not simply an abstract past but the present dignity of Egyptian citizens.

More than six decades after intellectuals clarified the challenges of postcolonial life and the country embarked on the major Nasserist project of decolonization, the daily Egyptian struggle to be human and live with dignity continues to crash against the bankrupt order of an ossified state structure, with its hollowed institutions and self-serving elites. Perpetually seeking to constitute valuable life, this Sisyphean struggle could not progress without a historical process that is critical, accumulative, nuanced, mindful of difference, meaningful, and accessible. This, in and of itself, is nothing but a precondition for any progressive political change, which is precisely why it serves as a major site of struggle. Between state efforts to expunge the past and control the work of intellectuals on the one hand, and the destructive fetishization of *turath* on the other, the possibility of thinking historically on a mass scale is constantly being restricted, if not altogether blocked. Some extend this difficulty to the general crisis of the humanities in Egypt (and elsewhere) and to a mass public divestment from any critical reasoning and analytical skills.[53]

If these abstract terms of discussion are still difficult to grasp, one can consider some of its concrete manifestations, such as the promise of the 2011 revolution and its emphatic and violent subversion. It is no wonder that during the tumultuous years of 2011–13, activists paid close attention to contemporary history by desperately trying to document the revolution before it was overcome, erased, and suppressed. Against the familiar *problematique* of the relation between state, intellectuals, and the past that this chapter analyzes, the revolutionaries of the past decade posed a haunting question: Where did the revolutionary moment come from, did it have a history, and if so, what was it? Thus, we end where we began, with Luwis 'Awad's publisher, who, in response to the *naksa*, called to reengage the past.

Notes

1. Luwis 'Awad, *Tarikh al-Fikr al-Misri al-Hadith* (Cairo: Dar al-Hilal, 1969), back cover.
2. Luwis 'Awad, *Thaqafatuna fi Muftaraq al-Turuq* (Beirut: Dar al-Adab, 1974).
3. See, e.g., Ghali Shukri, *Min al-Arshif al-Sirri li-l-Thaqafa al-Misriyya* (Beirut: Dar al-Tali'a, 1975); Shukri, *al-Muthaqafun wa-l-Sulta fi Misr* (Cairo: Dar Akhbar al-Yawm, 1990); and Shukri, *al-Nahda wa-l-Suqut fi al-Fikr al-Misri al-Hadith* (Beirut: Dar al-Tali'a, 1978).
4. Michael Scriven and Richard Paul, "Critical Thinking as Defined by the National Council for Excellence in Critical Thinking, 1987," The Foundation for Critical Thinking, https://www.criticalthinking.org/pages/defining-critical-thinking/766.
5. As Egyptian intellectuals themselves frequently acknowledged, the idea of a body of Egyptian thought that is distinct and historically separated from its global, Arab, and Islamic environment and its transregional networks of intellectual exchange and collaboration is somewhat artificial. Indeed, many of the intellectual themes discussed here, such as the question of *turath*, are basically regional in nature, and others, such as the unease with the state of critical inquiry, characterize all postcolonial societies. However, at the same time, other intellectual threads such as the decades-long memory wars about the legacy and value of Nasserism are uniquely Egyptian.
6. 'Abd al-Rahman Badawi, *Humum al-Shabab* (Cairo: Maktabat al-Nahda al-Misriyya, 1946), 135.
7. Laura Bier, *Revolutionary Womanhood: Feminism, Modernity, and the State in Nasser's Egypt* (Stanford, CA: Stanford University Press, 2011).
8. Elizabeth Suzanne Kassab, *Contemporary Arab Thought: Cultural Critique in Comparative Perspective* (New York: Columbia University Press, 2010), 166–71.

9. Valerie Hoffman-Ladd, "Zaynab al-Ghazali," in *The Oxford Encyclopedia of the Modern Islamic World*, ed. John Esposito, vol. 2 (Oxford: Oxford University Press, 1995), 64–66. For a comprehensive view of the role of women in the newly made Islamic sphere, see Ellen McLarney, *Soft Force: Women in Egypt's Islamic Awakening* (Princeton, NJ: Princeton University Press, 2015).

10. Muhammad 'Abd al-Jabiri, *Ishkaliyat al-Fikr al-'Arabi al-Mu'asir* (Beirut: Markaz Dirasat al-Wahda al-'Arabiyya, 2010).

11. Graham Huggan, "Part Two: The Colonial Present," in *The Oxford Handbook of Postcolonial Studies*, ed. Graham Huggan (Oxford: Oxford University Press, 2013), 170–297.

12. See, e.g., Mustafa 'Abd al-Ghani, *al-Muthaqafun wa-'Abd al-Nasir* (Kuwait: Dar Su'ad al-Sabah, 1993); Salah 'Isa, *Muthaqafun wa-'Askar: Muraja'at wa-Tajarib wa-Shahadat 'an Halat al-Muthaqafin fi Zil Hukm 'Abd al-Nasir wa-l-Sadat* (Cairo: Madbuli, 1986); Muhammad Sabir 'Arab, *al-Mufakirun wa-l-Siyasa fi Misr al-Mu'asirah: Dirasa fi Mawaqif 'Abbas Mahmud al-'Aqqad al-Siyasiyya* (Cairo: al-Hay'a al-Misriyya al-'Amma li-l-Kitab, 1993); Mustafa 'Abd al-Ghani, *al-Shahadat al-Akhira: al-Muthaqafun wa-Thawrat Yulyu* (Cairo: Markaz al-Ahram li-l-Nashr wa-l-Tarjama wa-l-Tawzi', 2010); and *Mubarak wa-l-Muthaqafun* (Cairo: al-Hay'a al-Misriyya al-'Amma li-l-Kitab, 1993).

13. Richard Jacquemond, *Conscience of the Nation: Writers, State, and Society in Modern Egypt* (Cairo: American University in Cairo Press, 2008).

14. It is perhaps telling that the most creative critical thinking in the Arab world at the time was practiced by stateless Palestinians.

15. Robyn Creswell, *City of Beginnings: Poetic Modernism in Beirut* (Princeton, NJ: Princeton University Press, 2019).

16. See Muhammad Hasanayn Haykal, *Azmat al-Muthaqafin* (Cairo: Dar al-Udaba', 1961).

17. Jacquemond, *Conscience of the Nation*.

18. Yoav Di-Capua, *No Exit: Arab Existentialism, Jean-Paul Sartre and Decolonization* (Chicago: University of Chicago Press, 2018).

19. See, e.g., Samah Idriss, "Intellectuals and the Nasserite Authority in the Egyptian Novel" (PhD diss., Columbia University, 1991).

20. On the dynamics between intellectuals, the state, and "the people" during this era, see Ayman El-Desouky, *The Intellectual and the People in Egyptian Literature and Culture: Amara and the 2011 Revolution* (Basingstoke, UK: Palgrave Macmillan, 2014).

21. Elizabeth Suzanne Kassab, *Enlightenment on the Eve of Revolution: The Egyptian and Syrian Debates* (New York: Columbia University Press, 2019).

22. Roger Owen, *The Rise and Fall of Arab Presidents for Life* (Cambridge: Harvard University Press, 2014), 38.

23. 'Abd al-Azim Ramadan, *Harb al-Istinzaf fi Mahkamat al-Tarikh* (Cairo: al-Hay'a al-Misriyya al-'Amma li-l-Kitab, 1996), 31–41.

24. In a 2002 newspaper article, Yasir Tal'at coined the term *war of the memoirs*. For more on the absence of revolutionary documents, see Joyce van de Bildt-de Jong, "The Contested Memory of the 1952 Revolution in Egypt, 1970–2010" (PhD diss., Tel Aviv University, 2017), 236–84.

25. Khaled Fahmy, "Rubabikya: Ayna Watha'iq al-Thawra?," *Akhbar al-Adab*, 29 July 2012, https://www.masress.com/adab/4870.

26. Omnia El Shakry, "History without Documents: The Vexed Archives of Decolonization in the Middle East," *The American Historical Review* 120 (2015): 920–34.

27. Mohammed Abed al-Jabri, *The Formation of Arab Reason: Text, Tradition and the Construction of Modernity in the Arab World* (London: I. B. Tauris, 2011), 46.

28. El Shakry, "History without Documents," 920–34; Di-Capua, *No Exit*, 1–25.

29. Tahrir Documents, accessed 26 July 2019, https://www.tahrirdocuments.org/.

30. Osman El Sharnoubi, "Historiographical Frustrations: Writing the History of the 1967 Defeat," *Mada Masr*, 8 June 2017, https://madamasr.com/en/2017/06/08/feature/politics/historiographical-frustrations-writing-the-history-of-the-1967-defeat/.

31. Yusuf al-Qaradawi, *Dars al-Nakba: Li-Madha Inhazamna wa-Kayfa Nantasir* (Cairo: Maktabat Wahba, 1987).

32. Yusuf al-Qaradawi, *al-Hulul al-Mustawrada wa-Kayfa Janat 'ala Ummatina* (Cairo: Maktabat Wahba, 1977), 1–9, 249.

33. Ibid., 8.

34. Yusuf al-Qaradawi, *al-Hal al-Islami: Fardiya wa-Durura* (Cairo: Maktabat Wahba, 1977), 116–19.

35. See, e.g., Abdullah Al-Arian, *Answering the Call: Popular Islamic Activism in Sadat's Egypt* (Oxford: Oxford University Press, 2014); and Carrie Rosefsky Wickham, *Mobilizing Islam: Religion, Activism, and Political Change in Egypt* (New York: Columbia University Press, 2002). On the ecumenical Christian-Islamic *nahda*, see Ussama Makdisi, *Age of Coexistence: The Ecumenical Frame and the Making of the Modern Arab World* (Berkeley: University of California Press, 2019).

36. Michelle Browers, *Political Ideology in the Arab World: Accommodation and Transformation* (Cambridge: Cambridge University Press, 2010); Ahmad Agbaria, *Age of Authenticity: Arab Heritage and the Postcolonial Challenge* (New York: Columbia University Press, 2022).

37. "On the Concept and Definition of Critical Thinking," The Foundation for Critical Thinking, accessed 1 July 2021, https://www.criticalthinking.org/pages/index-of-articles/our-concept-and-definition-of-critical-thinking/411.

38. Kassab, *Contemporary Arab Thought*, 116–71.

39. Jurj Tarabishi, *al-Muthaqafun al-'Arab wa-l-Turath: al-Tahlil al-Nafsi li-'Isabin Jama'i* (London: Riyad al-Rayyis li-l-Kutub wa-l-Nashr, 1991). Agbaria, *Age of Authenticity*, 147–82.

40. Kassab, *Contemporary Arab Thought*, 169.

41. Abed al-Jabri, *The Formation of Arab Reason*, 46.

42. Kassab, *Enlightenment on the Eve of Revolution*, 1.

43. On the European version of these traditions, see Antonis Balasopoulos, "Intellectuals and the State: Complicities, Confrontations, Ruptures," *Occasion: Interdisciplinary Studies in the Humanities* 3 (2012): 1–34.

44. Asef Bayat, *Life as Politics: How Ordinary People Change the Middle East* (Stanford, CA: Stanford University Press, 2013).

45. El-Desouky, *The Intellectual and the People*, 12.

46. Ibid., 21.

47. Limor Lavie, *The Battle over a Civil State: Egypt's Road to June 30, 2013* (Albany: State University of New York, 2018).

48. Kassab, *Enlightenment on the Eve of the Revolution*, 1–79.

49. Khaled Abou El Fadl, "Egypt's Secularized Intelligentsia and the Guardians of Truth," in *Egypt and the Contradictions of Liberalism: Illiberal Intelligentsia and the Future of Egyptian Democracy*, ed. Dalia Fahmy and Daanish Faruqi (London: Oneworld Publications, 2017), 235–52.

50. For a roundup of the debate around Sharif Yunis, see Ahmad Nada, "Sharif Yunus . . . al-akhar," *al-Modon*, 7 March 2016, https://tinyurl.com/t29lpdb.

51. "'Tajrim Ihanat al-Rumuz' . . . Himaya li-l-Tarikh am Quyud 'ala Hurriyat al-Ta'bir?," *Bawabat al-Ahram*, 13 November 2017, http://gate.ahram.org.eg/News/1640546.aspx.

52. On the possible histories of the 1967 war, see El Sharnoubi, "Historiographical Frustrations," accessed 5 October 2019, https://www.madamasr.com/en/2017/06/08/feature/politics/histor iographical-frustrations-writing-the-history-of-the-1967-defeat/. See also a public lecture by Khaled Fahmy, "The Egyptian Army in the 1967 War," 6 May 2020, https://khaledfahmy.org/en/2020/05/10/the-egyptian-army-in-the-1967-war/.

53. Khaled Fahmy, "The Crisis of the Humanities in Egypt," *Comparative Studies of South Asia, Africa and the Middle East* 37 (2017): 142–48.

Bibliography

Abou El Fadl, Khaled. "Egypt's Secularized Intelligentsia and the Guardians of Truth." In *Egypt and the Contradictions of Liberalism: Illiberal Intelligentsia and the Future of Egyptian Democracy*, edited by Dalia Fahmy and Daanish Faruqi, 235–52. London: Oneworld Publications, 2017.

El-Desouky, Ayman. *The Intellectual and the People in Egyptian Literature and Culture: Amara and the 2011 Revolution*. Basingstoke, UK: Palgrave Macmillan, 2014.

Fahmy, Khaled. "The Crisis of the Humanities in Egypt." *Comparative Studies of South Asia, Africa and the Middle East* 37 (2017): 142–48.

Jacquemond, Richard. *Conscience of the Nation: Writers, State, and Society in Modern Egypt*. Cairo: American University in Cairo Press, 2008.

Kassab, Elizabeth Suzanne. *Contemporary Arab Thought: Cultural Critique in Comparative Perspective*. New York: Columbia University Press, 2010.

Kassab, Elizabeth Suzanne. *Enlightenment on the Eve of Revolution: The Egyptian and Syrian Debates*. New York: Columbia University Press, 2019.

Lavie, Limor. *The Battle over a Civil State: Egypt's Road to June 30, 2013*. Albany: State University of New York Press, 2018.

El Shakry, Omnia. "History without Documents: The Vexed Archives of Decolonization in the Middle East." *American Historical Review* 120 (2015): 920–34.

CHAPTER 24

....

THE ARMY, STATE, AND SOCIETY

....

ZEINAB ABUL-MAGD

SINCE the 1950s, the Egyptian military has established full or partial control over the state and the economy in Egypt and hegemonized everyday life in society. In Egypt's postcolonial history, the army has acted as the "guardian" of nation-building and posed as the "savior" from internal strife three times: in 1952, when a group of young officers ended the British occupation, deposed the monarchy, and subsequently established an independent republic; in 2011, when the armed forces took the side of mass protests to depose an autocratic president, himself an ex-general; and in 2013, when the army again backed protesting masses to overthrow an Islamist regime. In each case, saving the nation was inseparable from militarizing it, as ruling officers dominated the government and used that political power to amass economic privileges. Moreover, they established systems of deep surveillance over society, penetrated the daily lives of their civilian subjects, and deployed propaganda tactics to manipulate them, eventually achieving full supremacy over the country's political and economic milieus and successfully securitizing everyday life.

Since the 1950s, the Egyptian postcolonial state has been uninterruptedly (except for one brief year) ruled by ex-army officers who took off their uniforms and swept presidential elections. The first military president of the country, Gamal Abdel Nasser (r. 1954–70), developed a socialist system administered by fellow officers and ex-officers. This new ruling elite not only served as self-appointed managers of the state-owned enterprises but also created political institutions that assimilated Egyptian citizens across social strata into a complicated web of closely surveilled organizations. After a humiliating defeat by Israel in the 1967 war, these officers fell from grace and power. Under the second military president, Anwar al-Sadat (r. 1970–81), the army restored its reputation through a partial victory over Israel in the 1973 war. Nevertheless, al-Sadat pursued a demilitarization policy that marginalized the officers from the bureaucratic apparatus while reversing his predecessor's socialist policies and liberalizing Egypt's economy. The third military president, Husni Mubarak (r. 1981–2011), allowed the military to regain influence by appointing generals in top governmental positions and authorizing them to establish a vast business empire that capitalized on his neoliberal schemes. When mass uprisings deposed Mubarak in 2011, the military almost lost its privileges in both politics and business. However, it quickly adapted to fluid realities, weathered hard times, and returned to complete dominance in 2013. The fourth military president, Abdel Fattah El-Sisi (r. 2014–), has won two presidential elections so far. His reign is marked by a conspicuous expansion of the number of military bureaucrats and the monopolistic businesses of military entrepreneurs.[1]

While adapting to profound transformations over several decades, the officers heavily militarized the state and deeply securitized the daily life of the country's docile and rebellious citizens alike. Hardly challenged by repressed civilians, the military has successfully turned the urban and rural milieus into an ever-expanded military camp: sites of permanent armed presence, continuous gaze, and manipulation of families from all social backgrounds inside and outside their homes. For the past several decades, ex-officers have been routinely appointed heads of public sector companies that provide citizens with basic services, from water and sewerage, to transportation and road maintenance, to telephone lines and internet connections. The army bakes subsidized bread, builds affordable apartments, manages wedding halls, constructs football stadiums, and sells consumer goods of all kinds to subservient citizens. It has also monopolized mass media, from owning news channels to producing popular songs, movies, and TV shows that millions of citizens watch during prime time.[2]

SOCIALISM WITHOUT SOCIALISTS
(1950s–1960s)

In July 1952, Colonel Gamal Abdel Nasser and several other young officers embarked on a military coup that terminated British colonialism and forged the country's first republic. Calling themselves the "Free Officers," they soon turned the coup into a "social revolution" by applying economic reform policies that favored the lower and middle classes over the aristocratic elite of the colonial monarchy. From a humble social background and with leftist political inclinations, Nasser emerged as the charismatic hero of social justice in the liberated state and led a "revolution from above."[3] He introduced agrarian reform laws that distributed the fiefs of large landowners to small peasants, nationalized foreign capital, granted workers socioeconomic rights, extended women's political rights, and much more. Opting for an alliance with the Soviet Union against US imperial capitalism during the Cold War, Nasser transitioned the republic into full-fledged socialism by publishing a socialist National Charter and inaugurating the Arab Socialist Union (ASU) as a single ruling party in 1962. His ambitious project to forge a society based on social equality and state capitalism had one major problem: his fellow officers were in complete charge of the developmentalist government, and most of them were cultural and political conservatives who did not believe in socialism. Moreover, they created and stretched out civilian organizations to intensely securitize politics and society.[4]

Throughout the 1950s and 1960s, officers and ex-officers seized key government positions responsible for applying economic reforms and gradually formed a new elite of "military technocrats." First, in the early 1950s, the officers' Revolutionary Command Council (RCC) took over the cabinet and governmental authorities. Still in army uniform, the Free Officers became self-appointed prime ministers, ministers, administrators of nationalized foreign companies, editors-in-chief of nationalized newspapers, ambassadors abroad, and much more.[5] Though most of them were not qualified to undertake their civilian jobs, the military regime followed the golden rule of favoring the "people of trust" (*ahl al-thiqa*) over the "people of qualifications" (*ahl al-khibra*).[6] Later, many officers rushed to switch careers by studying technical fields such as engineering, physics, journalism, law, history, and political science and then using this specialized education to fill vital bureaucratic positions. As a result, a distinct social group of "military technocrats" who were both highly influential and wealthy took shape. By the early 1960s, ex-officers who had earned professional degrees grew in number and power to replace many civilians as upper-echelon administrators. In 1962, "underneath ministers and deputy ministers, there were about 5,766 bureaucratic positions, of which 3,714 were occupied by army officers (and police) in different ministries," according to a sociological survey.[7]

Nasser's officer regime was hardly composed of the coherent socialist ideologues whom he hoped would implement his socialist dream. In fact, he ended up creating a system of socialism without socialists—without an indoctrinated vanguard. Whereas Nasser had a lower-class background (he was the son of an Upper Egyptian postman) and his socioeconomic dream had leftist underpinnings, most of the other ruling officers came from more privileged families and ideologically leaned to the right. The leading officers were mostly sons of well-to-do urban and rural families and civil servants, and some had landowning and aristocratic backgrounds. For example, 'Abd al-Hakim 'Amir, Nasser's closest friend and his army's commander-in-chief, was the son of a large landowner who was also the village mayor. More importantly, the leading officers adopted various ideological stances that did not always match Nasser's. Many were attracted to the Muslim Brotherhood's religious dicta; some supported the liberal ideas of the pre-1952 ruling Wafd Party, whose leaders were mostly aristocratic landowners; and a few adopted Marxism.[8] Eminent economist Samir Amin, who was among the Marxists Nasser appointed to the government in positions as high as ministers or lead economic researchers, asserted that many of the ruling officers were "reactionaries, friends of capitalism, or conservatives."[9]

In the early 1960s, Nasser's state capitalism fundamentally benefited lower- and middle-class citizens throughout the country. Through centralized planning, the developmentalist government invested in an ambitious industrialization scheme that provided hundreds of thousands of workers and college graduates with jobs, and its agricultural expansion program provided small peasants with access to capital and subsidized technology. The secular welfare state provided the masses with subsidized education, healthcare, social housing, food, books, and more, and granted women full equality in education and work rights. However, the ruling officers used the ASU as an inflated, far-reaching, and repressive apparatus of surveillance and control over the same social groups that benefited from Nasser's development projects. The Free Officers controlled the ASU's supreme executive committee by excluding anybody outside their closed circle from serving on it. The ASU approved candidates for parliamentary elections and managed elections in every civil society organization. Moreover, it penetrated every trade union, agricultural cooperative, professional syndicate, and women's association in the country and placed every individual member of these entities under unescapable security surveillance.[10]

For example, the socialist laws granted industrial workers the right to share a percentage of the annual profits and be elected board members in their public sector factories (alongside technocratic managers), presenting them with opportunities for social mobility. However, these workers fully depended on the state for stable wages, social housing, and subsidized food and services.[11] The ASU co-opted the leaders of trade unions, which now had to work within the boundaries and securitized structure of the single ruling party. That party's statute stated plainly that these unions were to "implement the policy drawn up by the ASU."[12] The situation was not significantly different for peasants. The ASU controlled local village positions and agricultural cooperatives by recruiting from a favored class of richer farmers. Economist Mahmoud Abdel-Fadil reveals that agrarian reform—often applied by officers coming from landowning families—ended up benefiting mainly a group of medium-sized landlords rather than small farmers or landless seasonal laborers as Nasser originally planned. Abdel-Fadil asserts that the ASU selected a class of "agricultural capitalists" to take up most positions as village mayors and officials. It then mobilized them to dominate village cooperatives and, more importantly, approved their names for parliamentary elections.[13] Professional syndicates were likewise securitized under the control of the ASU. The party assimilated the syndicates of lawyers, journalists, doctors, engineers, teachers, cinema actors, stage actors, musicians, accountants, and so on, through different mechanisms, including the localized intelligence services extended by its loyal members. In the ASU's crackdown on syndicates after 1964, for instance, the party made sure that the syndicates' elected presidents and vice presidents were party loyalists.[14]

Through Nasser's program of "state feminism," lower- and middle-class women were fully integrated into the welfare state with unprecedented economic and political rights. They earned equal access to free education, government jobs, healthcare, and suffrage rights. In a secular, progressive state, the headscarf disappeared from the factory floor and workspaces, and women were free to use birth control, which the state encouraged in order to structure productive socialist families.[15] Mervat Hatem indicates that Nasser's "explicit commitment" to state feminism contributed to the regime's "political legitimacy . . . and progressive credentials," while the state utilized women as an additional large labor force in a centralized economy. Nonetheless, like workers and peasants, women were subjugated to the officers' conservative surveillance. The ASU assimilated women's associations into its labyrinthian apparatus and monopolized the public discourse on women's liberation.[16]

Propaganda was indispensable to military control during this period. The state owned all forms of media: newspapers, radio stations, television channels, and publishing houses. Movies and songs were produced to celebrate the heroism of fighting officers, and some ex-officers even turned into scriptwriters and filmmakers to contribute to the officers' good image. For example, the iconic singer and movie star 'Abd al-Halim Hafiz praised the nation's expanding factories and their dedicated laborers in many cheerful, highly motivating but state-produced songs. He especially sang for the workers of the Aswan High Dam, while the ASU suffocated workers in other locations through its intricate web of security agents.[17] Throughout the 1960s, the newly founded state-owned TV station screened the movie *Rudda Qalbi* (My Hurt Is Returned, 1957) on the anniversary of the 1952 revolution. The epic romance film narrated the story of 'Ali, a fictional Free Officer who was originally the son of a poor gardener and was in love with a princess whose feudal father shamefully rejected his marriage proposal before the revolution. After confiscating the landed properties of her father, 'Ali finally marries his childhood sweetheart. The movie was based on an epic two-part novel penned by an ex-officer, and its filmmaker was similarly an ex-officer—ironically, they both came from well-to-do families.[18]

The first military regime suffered a humiliating defeat in the 1967 war with Israel that resulted in Egypt losing the Sinai Peninsula to Israeli occupation. State-owned media dubbed this event the *naksa*, or setback. With the regime's socialist economy struggling to achieve its main goals and youth discontent against the brutal security grip of the ruling party and overall lack of political freedom increasing, widespread mass demonstrations organized mainly by workers and an emerging student movement broke out in 1968. When Nasser died suddenly in 1970, he was immediately succeeded by another Free Officer, al-Sadat. Although an ex-officer would continue to control the highest political authority in the county, the military institution did not maintain the same status during the following decade.

THE BIRTH OF MILITARY ENTREPRENEURS (1970s–1980s)

During the 1970s, the military fell from public grace and lost most of its political and economic might. However, this drained institution quickly adapted to new domestic realities and returned to political influence and social domination in the 1980s. Once he assumed the position of the second military president of the postcolonial republic, al-Sadat initiated radical steps to take the army out of politics, re-professionalize its officers, and fight a war to regain the lost land. After he engineered a partial victory in the 1973 war and eventually freed Sinai from Israeli occupation after several years, al-Sadat applied harsh policies to demilitarize the state, dismember the ASU, and reverse the country's economy from socialism back to pre-1952 liberalism. As the third military president, Mubarak expanded his predecessor's economic liberalization schemes, but he allowed the officers to restore their political influence, and they profitably positioned themselves in the open market economy that he promoted.

Al-Sadat started demilitarizing the state in 1971 through what he called the "Corrective Revolution" (*thawrat al-tashih*). He sent to jail many fellow ex-officers who were government officials, ASU leaders, chiefs of state security, and army officers in service.[19] He followed these measures by demilitarizing the cabinet and the bureaucratic apparatus. Robert Springborg asserts that under the new president "every time officers were retired [from the government], civilians occupied their positions." In al-Sadat's last cabinet, only two ministers came from the military. Furthermore, he drastically reduced the number of military governors of provinces, which declined from twenty-two (out of twenty-six total governors) in 1964 to only five in 1980.[20]

In 1974, a year after he declared victory in Sinai, al-Sadat gained enough political legitimacy and popularity to undo Nasser's socialism by liberalizing the economy through an "open door" policy known as *infitah*, which included reversing agrarian reform laws to the benefit of the old landowning bourgeoisie; privatizing the public sector by selling it to local and foreign capital; eradicating the political influence of agricultural cooperatives at the expense of small and medium peasants; and reducing food subsidies and state support for public services that benefited the lower classes. Moreover, he dismantled the single ruling party, dividing the ASU into various platforms, each with its own political stance. Al-Sadat's demilitarization, market liberalization, and eradication of the ASU's omnipotent power by no means meant that civil society was now free from the military president's tight and brutal control. On the contrary, the struggling masses were released from the harsh circuits of surveillance in the ASU and its repressive army officers to face other forms of oppression: crushing social disparities and poverty.[21]

When he encountered public unrest escalating to bread riots in reaction to his *infitah* reforms, al-Sadat opted to bring the army out of its barracks again to help restore social order. He had already switched Cold War alliances from the Soviets to the US soon after assuming power. After Egypt had experienced many years of a war economy with dire budgetary conditions, al-Sadat sought the help of Western institutions to rescue his friendly regime. Under pressure from the International Monetary Fund (IMF) and foreign banks to cut public expenditure, he began with the food subsidies that Nasser's regime extended to the middle and lower classes.[22] Instantly, violent protests broke out in January 1977. Al-Sadat had no choice but to ask the minister of war to deploy troops to the troubled urban areas in Cairo and elsewhere, but the officers were returned to their barracks immediately after completing the mission. Al-Sadat kept the state and the economy demilitarized until his assassination by an Islamist army officer in 1981.[23]

In the 1980s, after a brief period of marginalization, the army returned to dominance in public life—albeit with entirely new roles and tools. Under Mubarak, the military embarked on building an empire of business enterprises that granted it once again the ability to penetrate social realms and people's daily life. A former bomber pilot, Mubarak did not have to fight any major wars against the country's neighboring enemy after al-Sadat had already signed a peace treaty with Israel in 1979. Thus, on the eve of the 1980s, the Egyptian army almost lost its importance in society and was supposed to keep to its barracks. Nevertheless, it successfully managed to adapt to change and reposition itself within the shifting domestic conditions around it. The military created gigantic business entities that tapped into Mubarak's expanded *infitah* economy and a stretched consumer market of all social classes to profit and reinstate its tight grip on the everyday movements of civilians simultaneously. In fact, Mubarak allowed the officers to focus on economic activities based on the peace treaty with Israel, which enabled the army to create an economic organization with commercial firms in order to assimilate their idle energy in noncombat activities.[24]

Although Mubarak faced constant pressure from the US and the IMF to finish the job that al-Sadat had started and fully liberalize the economy, he resisted this pressure in an attempt to avoid triggering more bread riots. Thus, Mubarak continued to provide the masses with subsidized goods and services. Meanwhile, he allowed the *infitah*'s nouveau riche to multiply their fortunes through free international trade. Many social groups, including a new generation of army officers, indulged in postsocialist consumerism after long years of austerity. The military entrepreneurs took advantage of the existence of such an "ambivalent market"—neither socialist nor fully neoliberal—by acting as "parastatals" that took charge of large governmental duties for profit.[25] Officially part of the public sector that Mubarak inherited from Nasser, military firms built apartments for social housing, produced foodstuff, constructed bakeries for subsidized bread, renovated telephone lines, and made cheap clothes. Moreover, the military created its own business ventures in the form of car manufacturers, luxury real estate brands, American-style shopping malls, and lavish hospitals to cater to the newly rich.

These ventures were devised by one entrepreneurial mind and empire builder: Field Marshal Abu Ghazala, Mubarak's minister of defense and military production from 1981 until 1989. For this task, Abu Ghazala capitalized on the above-mentioned economic organization. Upon signing the peace accord with Israel, the Egyptian military created an entity called the National Service Projects Organization (NSPO), the purpose of which was to establish business enterprises for civilian production in order to redirect the efforts of officers and soldiers toward noncombatant activities. Presidential Decree No. 32 of 1979 established the NSPO as a corporation with its own legal personality, and its budget was to be independent from that of the Ministry of Defense (MoD).[26] Abu Ghazala used the NSPO and several other military corps to take charge of public projects in key sectors, such as construction and food security, in order to make millions of dollars of extrabudgetary profits every year.[27]

Initially, the NSPO focused heavily on food production through widespread land reclamation activities of tens of thousands of acres. Its Food Security Division grew into the "single largest agro-industrial organization in Egypt," as Springborg asserts.[28] Besides cultivating wheat for bread, the NSPO built numerous automated bakery plants for subsidized bread as well as sale outlets to help the state avoid shortage crises of this staple food item for the Egyptian lower and middle classes.[29] Based on its large farms, the NSPO built dairy plants, mechanical slaughterhouses, poultry farms, egg production units, fish farms, and frozen vegetable factories. Acting as superior parastatal, the Engineering Authority of the Armed Forces (EAAF) constructed roads, bridges, schools, middle- and low-income apartments, stadiums, airports, and water desalination plants. It also constructed expansive urban communities and suburbs in the outskirts of Cairo to cater to the growing upper classes. For the Ministry of Culture, the military engineers even constructed "cultural palaces" for public performances and art exhibitions designed after the reigning officer's own taste in art. The Signals Corps renewed the telephone infrastructure for the Ministry of Communication in various upper- and middle-class neighborhoods in the capital.[30]

The military entrepreneurs also attempted to tap into the upper- and middle-classes' rush to purchase cars in the ever-expanding city of Cairo in the 1980s. In the big capital's *infitah* society, owning a private vehicle grew into another mark of social mobility and prestige. During these years, social historian and economist Galal Amin was astounded by the number of private cars (*al-sayyarat al-khassa*) that suddenly flooded and overcrowded the already jammed streets of Cairo, speeding next to cheap and decaying public transportation inherited from socialist times. "Something happened that made private cars not only a means of transportation, but also a symbol of social mobility, and the inability to buy one became a sign of failure and a source of great frustration," Amin noted.[31] Taking advantage of such a consumerist trend, the Arab Organization for Industrialization (AOI), a military-run conglomerate for arms and civilian production, founded a car-making firm, Arab American Vehicles (AAV). Since then, AAV has been assembling cars for Western brands, such as the American Jeep Cherokee, the German Chrysler, and the French Peugeot, to sell to urban elites.[32]

Cheap or free labor was then, and still is, the most abundant resource in military enterprises through a constant flow of conscripted soldiers. Although the size of the armed forces after the peace treaty was reduced to between 300,000 and 450,000 personnel, this number was more than enough to be deployed in profit-making commissions. The year Abu Ghazala left his position, in 1989, around 550,000 men between the ages of 18 and 30 were drafted into the armed forces. The armed forces' firms used conscripts who were not "medically, culturally, technically, or psychologically fit [for combat duties]" in civilian projects.[33] For instance, bakeries for subsidized bread used illiterate soldiers recruited from villages. While constructing one of the automated bakery plants, the EAAF attached a five-story barracks serving as a dormitory for the soldiers working in it.[34] Today, compulsory conscription of male youth for a period of between one and three years, based on level of education, continues to be the primary source of free labor at old and new military businesses.

Thus, the military entrepreneurs practically inserted their businesses everywhere in the citizens' urban milieus, and their projects conspicuously penetrated the daily life of subordinated consumers. In order to justify activities irrelevant to defense, Abu Ghazala perpetuated propagandistic rhetoric about the dual goal of the army's self-sufficiency and assisting the state with its developmental plans. Each time Abu Ghazala launched a new project, he reiterated the same rhetoric emphasizing that such economic activities were for the armed forces' self-sufficiency as well as helping the government address pressing economic problems.[35]

During the same decade, the 1980s, officers understandably disappeared from media— both movies and TV shows—as sacred war heroes. In the wake of the 1973 war, numerous movies were produced to celebrate epically the heroism of the officers and poor soldiers who fought in the war and sacrificed their blood in Sinai. This filmmaking euphoria lasted for several years during the 1970s, but it faded in the 1980s when the image of officers engaged in combat activities became a distant memory. As the army became less occupied with war and more with profit-making projects, criticism of officers surfaced on some popular TV shows. The most popular dramatic series of the period, *Layali al-Hilmiyya* (Nights of al-Hilmiyya, whose first season was aired in 1987), depicted gradually failing and disgraced army officers. Among this show's many vivid characterizations of pashas, workers, belly dancers, student activists, and communists in colonial and postcolonial Cairo, army officer Mustafa Rif'at appeared as probably the dullest figure. He was originally a member of the 1952 revolutionary Free Officers and was appointed chairman of a complex of public sector factories and companies. An incompetent manager who was removed from the plant's administration in the 1967 crisis, Rif'at married a belly dancer to live off her fortune.[36]

The military did not launch counterpropaganda campaigns in reaction to this negative representation in a show produced and repeatedly screened by state-owned TV and watched by family members of all ages in every home. It probably counted on its ability to maneuver and monitor civilian families through other channels: producing staple food, constructing public buildings, and selling consumer goods. Military enterprises reached a new stage of colossal expansion, coupled with a steady return of the military to politics and surveilling the population's everyday life, from the 1990s onward.

NEOLIBERAL OFFICERS (1990S–2000S)

In the early 1990s, under Mubarak, the military embarked on yet another era of renewed political and economic dominance along with social hegemony in Egypt. Reversing al-Sadat's policy, Mubarak "remilitarized" the state by hiring large numbers of fellow generals in top administrative positions in the government. When he finally and fully transitioned the previously socialist economy to neoliberalism, the military took advantage once more of the new socioeconomic environment to further advance its economic interests over an open market. Thus, remilitarizing the Egyptian state went hand in hand with economic liberalization, and the growth of the officers' power was deeply engrained in Mubarak's infamously corrupt market. Society was then subjected to a new, distinct form of security state in which citizens' urban milieus and homes were intensely penetrated by military bureaucrats and entrepreneurs alike. Such intricate military presence in civilian life ensured the regime's ultimate surveillance over and repression of citizens in the middle and lower classes—or those who lost and suffered as a result of neoliberal measures.

At the level of military bureaucrats, Mubarak brought back the officers to control the government and its public service provisions after years of exclusion under al-Sadat. Many of the "heroes" of the 1973 war were now retired generals, and Mubarak gradually hired them in essential state positions. While Mubarak maintained a civilian face for the regime in Cairo by forming cabinets of technocrats, retired generals were the invisible de facto rulers of the country. Ex-generals ruled most of provincial Egypt by serving as local governors, heads of towns, and heads of neighborhoods. They also managed every sea, river, and land port and dominated government authorities that provided public transportation, from buses and ferryboats to airlines. Moreover, they took charge of state authorities that provided basic public services, from water, sewerage, and affordable housing to garbage collection and urban beautification. More importantly, ex-officers were hired as heads of numerous governmental bodies responsible for the main economic activities of the liberalized market. They ushered in the swift transition to the market economy by running critical administrative posts in control of foreign investment, allotting state land to private investors, adjusting exports and imports, chairing holding companies, and more.[37]

At the level of military business, the Egyptian army decided to convert significant parts of its defense industry to civilian production in the early 1990s. Egypt's numerous military factories at the Ministry of Military Production (MoMP) and the military-owned AOI, conglomerates established between the 1950s and 1980s, were now busily manufacturing civilian goods and competing in a globalized market. Military factories that had previously produced serious ordnance such as ammunition, missiles, aircraft, rockets, explosives, pistols, and armor were now utilizing their facilities and labor to produce consumer goods such as washing machines, fridges, TVs, kitchen stoves, kitchenware, fertilizers, pesticides, and drugs.[38] Defense conversion came with immediate legal advantages for military businesses, particularly in tax breaks, as Mubarak issued several laws that exempted converted military plants from various forms of domestic taxes in addition to tariffs and customs on imports and exports.[39]

Therefore, a new class of "neoliberal officers" was born in Egypt in the early 1990s and expanded vastly throughout the 2000s. Military entrepreneurs now produced almost everything in most sectors, from canned food to heavy tractors. Moreover, they presented almost all types of public services for profit: they opened wedding halls and lavish hotels, built sea ships, and ran river transport firms; they grabbed expansive pieces of public land from the state to construct toll highways and cultivate vast commercial farms; and they continued to heavily influence the daily life of the lower and middle classes by baking and selling subsidized bread, building affordable flats, trading in medicine, and sponsoring popular sports. While accumulating profits, the untaxed military businesses functioned above state auditing and public accountability and outrageously violated labor rights.[40]

Arguably, Mubarak's policy of hiring retired generals in bureaucratic positions and allowing military entrepreneurs to expand business activities was part of his strategy to "coup-proof" his regime.[41] Economic liberalization necessitated significant cuts in the state budget, as the IMF and other international institutions dictated, and Mubarak had to reduce public spending in many sectors, including the military. To avoid an officer mutiny as a result of budget reductions, the country's military president sought to appease the institution from which he had come and co-opted as many of its older leaders as possible by extending political and business privileges to them. This strategy became particularly important in the 2000s, when Mubarak was grooming his civilian son, Gamal, to inherit his presidential seat. This political succession plan was fundamentally problematic to the officers, who since 1952 had only been commanded by military presidents. Gamal took over his father's ruling party, the National Democratic Party (NDP), and major business tycoons in his clientelist circle dominated the parliamentary and cabinet seats and rapidly applied extreme neoliberal measures. In the face of Gamal's imposed changes, it was necessary for Mubarak to appease the old war heroes.[42]

During the 2000s and after Gamal's domineering presence in politics was established, almost 50% of Mubarak's provincial governors came from a military background. One of them was the governor of al-Gharbiyya province in the Delta, where the huge 2008 textile workers' strike took place in the city of Mahalla, but he lost his seat after the violent turmoil in the area. Some provincial governors were elevated to ministers of "local development" after leaving their posts, becoming the highest state officials taking charge of all provinces across the country. Within every ministry, ex-officers were appointed heads of numerous public authorities responsible for day-to-day management of the citizens' needs. For example, ex-generals controlled the National Authority of Potable Water and Sewage throughout the 2000s. Noticeably, the country suffered from a severe decline in the infrastructure of sanitation services, pollution of potable water, incomplete lines across the north and the south, and wasted public funds during the last decade of Mubarak's reign.[43]

The year 2000 was another moment of great transformation in Egyptian military business. Gamal Mubarak's neoliberal cabinet was executing a large-scale privatization scheme selling state-owned enterprises to local and foreign investors. Using their membership in the "privatization committee," the generals audaciously seized many public-sector factories and companies that were up for sale and transferred their ownership to the various military entities. For example, the AOI seized the only manufacturing plant of railway wagons in the country when it was privatized in 2004, thereby establishing a monopoly over this sector. In addition, the military invested in new ventures for heavy manufacturing, such as plants for shipbuilding, steel, and cement. The officers continued to keep their activities and profits clandestine without any level of public transparency. When Gamal reactivated the country's stock market and both private and public enterprises were listed on it, none of the military companies were registered.[44]

Mubarak appointed only one minister of defense throughout these two eventful decades: Field Marshal Muhammad Husayn Tantawi (who held office from 1991 to 2012). Tantawi also served as a member of Gamal's privatization committee. Every time Tantawi opened a new economic enterprise for the military, he reiterated the same rhetoric that his predecessor, Abu Ghazala, had produced: that its goal was to bolster the army's self-sufficiency and contribute to the country's economic development. Additionally, he emphasized the aim of defying monopolistic practices and helping with price control on the domestic market as military enterprises established their own monopolies and the prices of their products were equal to or sometimes higher than those of the private or public sector. For example, the NSPO's new cement production plant in the Sinai Peninsula, called al-'Arish li-l-Asmant and initiated in 2010, took advantage of the neoliberal construction boom in the country that catered to the rising upper classes, especially in areas such as the rapidly expanding suburbs of New Cairo. The NSPO partnered with a Chinese firm to provide technology for the plant, which had about eight hundred civilian workers. With fewer financial obligations to the state and to some of its labor force, the listed prices of al-'Arish often exceeded those of its competitors.[45]

Meanwhile, workers at military enterprises were confused about their status: they were not sure whether they were just skilled civilian laborers at state-owned plants or military personnel. When they accidently made technical mistakes or challenged their military administrators, they were arbitrarily sent to military trials. In August 2010, when workers at military Factory 99 (producing gas canisters for the civilian market) attempted to strike to protest poor safety measures at their work premises that had killed at least one worker and injured many others, they were accused of exposing "military secrets" and sent to a military court to be punished.[46] Generally, as opposed to both public and private sector labor enjoying the right to unionize, workers at military enterprises are prohibited from creating their own trade unions. For example, laborers at the military-owned Egyptian Company for Ship Repairs and Building in Alexandria were denied the right to organize themselves into a union in 2008. The nine hundred workers at this company, which had been annexed to the military's Maritime Industries and Services Organization a few years earlier, cried for help as the company used almost half of them as seasonal laborers and denied all of them the right to form any representative bodies to resolve their daily problems with an administration of officers.[47]

On the eve of the 2011 uprisings, ex-generals were evidently an integral part of Mubarak's authoritarian regime and major contributors to the infamous weaknesses of his socially troubled neoliberal economy. Such weaknesses included a severe decline in public services, business favoritism, corrupt cronyism, and deeply entrenched social disparities.[48] As neoliberal inequalities generated simmering discontent, the position of officers in bureaucratic or business posts reflected increasing securitization of urban realms and the regime's capabilities to contain potential public unrest. The army's surveilling outreach could not withstand the social storm when the situation exploded in 2011 with unprecedented mass uprisings, forcing Mubarak to abdicate. Ironically, the military abandoned the falling ex-military president and presented itself as the nation's savior from his corrupt regime and a neutral arbitrator among civilians in internal conflicts. Shortly afterward, deploying tanks and employing various means of propaganda, the officers not only succeeded in keeping their privileges intact but also embarked on another era of absolutist military control.

Saving the Nation (2011–23)

Between 2011 and 2013, the Egyptian military posed twice as the savior of the nation. It supported mass uprisings to overthrow two different regimes, Mubarak's and that of a group of Islamists, and subsequently emerged as the ultimate political and economic winner. On 25 January 2011, protests erupted in Cairo's Tahrir Square to demand that Mubarak step down. Army tanks surrounding the square claimed to back the eighteen-day sit-in until the autocrat was eventually ousted. Immediately afterward, the Supreme Council of Armed Forces (SCAF) offered its help to run the country for a transitional period of six months. Grateful for such favors, the Egyptian masses chanted "the army and the people are one hand" while state-owned media played the 1960s national songs of Nasser's revolutionary times. The army sought to revive its old image as the state's guardian at times of distress. SCAF stayed in power for an entire year and a half until it delivered authority to an elected president from the Muslim Brotherhood in June 2012. One year later, as this president drastically failed to revive the country's crumpling economy and public discontent escalated again, the military decided to overthrow him. Cheerfully expressing their appreciation, the celebrating masses filled Tahrir Square in the lead-up to the ouster of the Brotherhood, and they carried posters of Nasser and General 'Abd Fattah El-Sisi, the then-new minister of defense. The army's propaganda department, Idarat al-Shu'un al-Ma'nawiyya, funded the production of a song titled "Tislam al-Ayadi" (May These Hands Be Safe), greeting the soldiers' hands that rescued the nation and invoking the good memories of 1973 war heroism.[49]

Soon afterward, El-Sisi swept his first presidential election in 2014 to become the fourth military president of the postcolonial state. He promulgated a new constitution that placed the military above the elected parliament, the civilian judiciary, and the state accountability and auditing agencies. After winning a second presidential term in 2018, El-Sisi changed that constitution to legally permit himself to be re-elected and remain in office until at least 2030. In the previous eight years, El-Sisi has consolidated a new military regime that installed ex-officers as the inexperienced and arbitrary administrators of the state's bureaucratic apparatus, all the way from ministers and vice ministers to governors of provinces, heads of governmental authorities, and chairs of essential state-owned holding companies. El-Sisi has maintained Mubarak's liberalized economy but has devised a maximized hegemonic role for the military in his own version of an open market, which fundamentally hurt the lower and middle classes and further expanded the profits of military entrepreneurs. More importantly, the new military regime has invented new methods of securitizing and surveilling society that deploys, in addition to traditional media for propaganda, new information technology for cyber control.

At the governmental level, El-Sisi has overridden Mubarak's formal bureaucracy and informally rules through a set of loyal army officers and meek state officials. His civilian prime ministers are usually fearful and obedient figures, and he appoints ex-officers in the cabinet to occupy vital ministerial posts that directly impact the daily needs of all social strata, such as the minister of supply (responsible for subsidized food provisions) and the minister of transportation (responsible for public transit and relevant construction projects). He further increased the number of ex-military governors of provinces, and Cairo and Alexandria received their first ruling generals in decades. In 2016, his government acquired a large IMF loan that included strict terms of wide-scale economic liberalization, and the ruling officers applied related measures that have since rapidly eliminated state subsidies for bread, food, gas, electricity, water, healthcare, and education.[50]

Meanwhile, the economic hegemony of military business has been conspicuously increasing with overwhelming monopolies. Expanding old businesses and venturing into new sectors, military entrepreneurs penetrate into the civilian population's everyday life more than ever by controlling the production of the most vital goods or presenting essential services to civilians. The military continues to expand its agribusiness in land reclamation by adding hundreds of thousands of acres, in addition to continuing to manufacture cement and steel, constructing and managing luxury hotels, manufacturing and trading in pharmaceuticals, seizing fisheries, and enlarging gas station chains. The MoMP's pharmaceuticals firm controls supplies of drugs and baby formula to the Ministry of Health. The NSPO has seized thousands of miles along Egypt's northern shores for fishery investments. Under El-Sisi's version of neoliberalism, the military engineers' EAAF has grown into the sole monopolistic contractor for public construction projects. It has taken charge of El-Sisi's megaprojects such as the New Suez Canal and the New Administrative Capital, along with numerous airports, highways, bridges, roads, and public schools and hospitals.[51]

In contrast to Nasser's industrialization, as economist and former minister of supply Gouda Abdel-Khalek points out, El-Sisi's new officer regime has concentrated most of the government's investments in the construction sector and granted military contractors complete control over it. Gouda Abdel-Khalek insists that Egyptian society "won't eat or wear real estate . . . a sector that has been multiplied in a very short period."[52] The regime has advanced its own notions about the country's urban development that are largely inspired by the model of the oil-producing Gulf, heavily focusing on real estate projects as the main driver of the national economy. As a result, military engineers and bureaucrats are diligently gentrifying vital districts in Cairo. Many of Cairo's old slums ('ashwa'iyyat) have been recently evacuated, demolished, and replaced by upscale developments funded by Arabian Gulf investors. Most of these vacated slums existed in historic Cairo, Islamic areas suitable for touristic ventures, or near the Nile, where luxury apartment buildings and office buildings could be erected. The inhabitants of the old slums have been relocated to new apartment buildings constructed by military engineers in desert areas on the outskirts of Cairo. In these new neighborhoods, the displaced families are confined in ghetto-like communities that suffer from heavy securitization and a lack of jobs and basic services. Moreover, military contractors are busily building numerous bridges and toll highways running through the congested city in order to connect the newly developed urban areas and their elite residents to the regime's new capital city, which is similarly being lavishly constructed by military engineers to the north of Cairo.[53]

Military entrepreneurs have ventured into new business areas that specifically facilitate cyber-surveillance by deploying up-to-date information and communications technology. The military currently owns shares in or informally controls telecommunication firms providing land and wireless phone lines and internet services at a widely publicized level. Needless to say, this grants the military unlimited access to phone calls and social media activities.[54] El-Sisi has embarked on a "Digital Egypt" (Misr al-Raqamiyya) project to switch to providing state services electronically, and military bodies have taken charge of digitizing governmental data for all civilians. For example, the MoMP has started digitizing the records of the Ministry of Supply, responsible for providing lower- and middle-class citizens with subsidized food and issuing new smart cards that eligible families use to obtain their monthly rations at government outlets. Similarly, the MoMP has digitized records for the Ministry of Health and issued new medical insurance cards for the citizens who benefit from public health services at state-owned hospitals or pharmacies. The MoD takes care of saving and securing the electronic files of the new healthcare system.[55] Moreover, in order to contribute to digitizing the electricity services, the MoMP has just started a new production line for smart electricity meters to sell to the Ministry of Power—the sole provider of power services to all homes in the country.[56] This means that the MoMP and the MoD now have access to data on millions of civilians—in addition to basic info, such as date of birth and address, as well as a photo for facial recognition—about the food they eat, the drugs they take, and the energy they consume every month.

In order to control media for propaganda purposes, one military-controlled company has recently monopolized the production of TV shows and popular dramas.[57] Although this company (currently called Synergy) poses as a private business with a civilian chairman, it is no secret that it is owned and controlled by *jihat siyadiyya*—a term commonly used to refer to intelligence or security agencies closely connected to the president. Besides producing shows, the company undertakes censorship duties and crowds out politically problematic scriptwriters and filmmakers from the media market.[58] In the past two years, this company produced several epic dramatic series celebrating the heroism of army, police, and intelligence officers combating Islamist fundamentalism and terrorism in post-2011 Egypt. For instance, it funded and aired the following series, each with thirty episodes, aired during Ramadan's prime times: season one of *al-Ikhtiyar* (The Choice, 2020), about an army officer from an elite unit who heroically fought against ISIL in Sinai and was killed in action; season two of the same series, about state security police officers who made similar sacrifices in Cairo; and *Hajma Murtada* (A Counter-Attack, 2021), a narration of the patriotic adventures of general intelligence officers combating Egyptian human rights activists allegedly recruited by foreign intelligence agencies before and after the 2011 uprisings. In addition, the MoD still keeps its own sophisticated propaganda department with YouTube channels and social media pages that attract millions of loyal subscribers.[59]

Inevitably, with intensely direct encounters between ex-military bureaucrats or uniformed project managers on the one hand and repressed civilians on the other at almost all public sites daily, societal grievances against the ruling officers have grown, and the frequency of clashes with them have surged. One major incident of civilian–officer conflict involved both the minister of supply and the minister of military production. El-Sisi hired two ex-generals in a row as ministers of supply, who implemented his policy to substantially reduce food subsidies, while, as mentioned, the MoMP took charge of digitizing the lists of the beneficiaries of these subsidies and issuing them new smart cards. During the digitization process, the MoMP removed millions of names from the system, having rendered them unqualified to continue to receive government support. Subsequently, numerous bread riots erupted across the country in early 2017, while the ruling officers devalued the Egyptian pound and drastically increased gas, electricity, and water prices. As security forces dispersed the protests, social media activists called the events "the supply riots" (*intifadat al-tamwin*)—reminiscent of the 1977 violent bread riots against al-Sadat.[60] Protests erupted again for the same reason in late 2019, and El-Sisi salvaged the situation by bringing back around two million names of beneficiaries to the subsidies lists.

CONCLUSION

Since Egypt's independence from British colonialism and the creation of a republic in 1952, the postcolonial state has been uninterruptedly (except for one year) ruled by civilianized military presidents, ex-officers who took off their uniforms and won the most civilian votes in questionable elections. During these long decades, the Egyptian political and economic systems went through many fundamental transformations: from socialism in the 1960s, to *infitah* in the 1970s and 1980s, and finally to full-fledged neoliberalism from the 1990s until today. The military successfully adapted to such changes and repositioned itself within transitioning governments to always maintain a domineering status in the state and a privileged position within the economy. Under previous military presidents, through occupying key bureaucratic posts and managing public or military-owned business enterprises, officers and ex-officers had constantly penetrated into public spaces and the homes of civilian citizens to surveil their daily life movements and manipulate them by traditional means of propaganda.

After posing as the savior of the nation in the face of violent Islamists, the current military regime of El-Sisi has granted fellow generals maximized hegemony over the government, and these generals administer his socially resented version of a liberalized economy. Moreover, this regime deploys new technologies of information and communication to tap into the population's urban realms and private spaces for ultimate surveillance of rebellious and docile citizens alike. According to El-Sisi's constitution, he could remain in power until at least 2030. Unless another wave of mass uprising like that of 2011 takes place in the near future, Egypt's prospects of demilitarization seem limited.

NOTES

1. Zeinab Abul-Magd, *Militarizing the Nation: The Army, Business and Revolution in Egypt* (New York: Columbia University Press, 2017).

2. Ibid.

3. The phrase "revolution from above" was coined by sociologist Ellen Trimberger to describe the acts of Egyptian officers in the early 1950s. Ellen Kay Trimberger, *Revolution from Above: Military Bureaucrats and Development in Japan, Turkey, Egypt, and Peru* (New Brunswick, NJ: Transaction Books, 1978), 41–43.

4. Abul-Magd, *Militarizing the Nation*, 52–61.

5. Morroe Berger, *Military Elite and Social Change: Egypt since Napoleon* (Princeton, NJ: Princeton University, 1966), 21; Muhammad Naguib, *Kuntu Ra'isan li-Misr: Mudhakkirat Muhammad Najib* (Cairo: al-Maktab al-Masri al-Hadith, 1984), 156, 201–207.

6. Samir Amin Interview, Economic and Business History Research Center (EBHRC), American University in Cairo (AUC), Cairo, 20 April 2004 [audio recordings]. For a full list of prime ministers and ministers during this period, see Mahmud Zuhdi, *al-Wizarat al-Misriyya* (Cairo: Markaz Watha'iq wa-Tarikh Misr al-Mu'asir, 2008).

7. Ahmad 'Abd Allah, *al-Jaysh wa-l-Dimuqratiyya fi Misr* (Cairo: Dar Sina li-l-Nashr, 1990), 35. For tables of all names of military officials and ministers, see ibid., 40–50; and Mark Cooper, "The Demilitarization of Egyptian Cabinet," *International Journal of Middle Eastern Studies* 14 (May 1982): 208.

8. Anouar Abdel-Malek, *Egypt: Military Society; the Army Regime, the Left, and Social Change under* Nasser (New York: Random House, 1968), 44–45; Birlanti 'Abd al-Hamid, *al-Mushir wa-Ana* (Cairo: Maktabat Madbuli, 1992); Rashad Kamil, *Hayat al-Mushir 'Abd al-Hakim Amir* (Cairo: Dar al-Khayal, 2002).

9. Amin Interview, EBHRC, AUC, Cairo, 20 April 2004.

10. On the ASU's control over elected bodies, see Ali Ed-Dean Hillal Dessouki, "The Party as a Mass Political Organization in Egypt, 1952–1967, (PhD diss., McGill University, 1968), 152.

11. Mark Cooper, "State Capitalism, Class Structure, and Social Transformation in the Third World: The Case of Egypt," *International Journal of Middle East Studies* 15 (May 1983): 451–69.

12. Dessouki, "The Party as a Mass Political Organization," 157. See also Nazih Ayubi, *al-Dawla al-Markaziyya fi Misr* (Beirut: Markaz Dirasat al-Wahda al-'Arabiyya, 1989), 109–10.

13. Mahmoud Abdel-Fadil, *al-Tahawwulat al-Iqtisadiyya fi al-Rif al-Misri (1952–1970)* (Cairo: al-Hay'a al-Misriyya al-'Amma li-l-Kitab, 1978), 22–29, 46–47.

14. Robert Springborg, "Professional Syndicates in Egyptian Politics, 1952–1970," *International Journal of Middle East Studies* 9 (1978): 287.

15. Laura Bier, "The Family Is a Factory: Gender, Citizenship, and the Regulation of Reproduction in Post-War Egypt," *Feminist Studies* 36, no. 2 (2010): 404–32.

16. Mervat Hatem, "Economic and Political Liberation in Egypt and the Demise of State Feminism," *International Journal of Middle East Studies* 24, no. 2 (1992): 231–33.

17. For example, 'Abd al-Halim Hafiz's song "Hikayat Sha'b." For documentation of workers' life in the High Dam, see Sun' Allah Ibrahim, *Najmat Aghustus* (Cairo: Dar al-Thaqafa al-Jadida, 1974).

18. The novelist was Yusuf al-Siba'i, and the filmmaker was 'Izz al-Din Dhu al-Fuqqar. For more details on films and novels produced during the 1950s and 1960s for propaganda purposes, see Dalia Said Mostafa, *The Egyptian Military in Popular Culture: Context and*

Critique (London: Palgrave Macmillan, 2017); and Joel Gordon, *Revolutionary Melodrama: Popular Film and Civic Identity in Nasser's Egypt* (Chicago: Middle East Documentation Center, 2002).

19. 'Abd Allah Imam, *'Ali Sabri Yatadhakkar* (Cairo: Ruz al-Yusuf, 1987), 114, 120–21, 123–24.

20. Robert Springborg, "al-Ra'is wa-l-Mushir: al-'Alaqat al-Madaniyya al-'Askariyya fi Misr al-Yawm," in *al-Jaysh wa-l-Dimuqratiyya fi Misr*, 66.

21. Abul-Magd, *Militarizing the Nation*, 69–77.

22. Raymond Hinnebusch, *Egyptian Politics under Sadat: The Post-populist Development of an Authoritarian Modernizing State* (Cambridge: Cambridge University Press, 1985), 134–35.

23. *Al-Jumhuriyya*'s issues of 18–21 January 1977.

24. Abul-Magd, *Militarizing the Nation*, 93–104.

25. Zeinab Abul-Magd, "The General's Secret: Egypt's Ambivalent Market," *Sada*, Carnegie Endowment, 9 February 2012, https://carnegieendowment.org/sada/47137. For the definition of *parastatal*, see Kevan Harris, "The Rise of the Subcontractor State: Politics of Pseudo-Privatization in the Islamic Republic of Iran," *International Journal of Middle East Studies* 45 (2013): 45–70.

26. "Wazarat al-Difa' wa-l-Intaj al-Harbi, Qarar Raqm 65 li-Sanat 1979 bi-Sha'n al-Nizam al-Asasi li-Jihaz Mashru'at al-Khidma al-Wataniyya," *al-Waqa'i' al-Misriyya* 172, 25 July 1979.

27. Abul-Magd, *Militarizing the Nation*, 93–104.

28. Robert Springborg, *Mubarak's Egypt: Fragmentation of the Political Order* (London: Westview Press, 1989), 112–13.

29. *Al-Malaff al-Watha'iqi li-l-Mushir Muhammad 'Abd a-Halim Abu Ghazala* (Cairo: Markaz al-Ahram li-l-Tanzim wa-l-Mikrufilm, 1981–89), Part 2, 425, 434, 494.

30. For detailed examples, see ibid., 421–38, 456.

31. Galal Amin, *Madha Hadath li-l-Masriyyin: Tatawwur al-Mujtama' al-Misri fi Nisf Qarn, 1945–1995* (Cairo: al-Hay'a al-'Amma li-l-Kitab, 1999), 185–87.

32. "Arab American Vehicles Corporation," *Infocredit Group Business Information Reports-Egypt*, 2 June 2011, http://www.aav.com.eg/Pathtosuccess.html.

33. 'Abd Allah, *al-Jaysh wa-l-Dimuqratiyya fi Misr*, 97.

34. *Al-Malaff al-Watha'iqi li-l-Mushir*, Part 2, 434, 450.

35. See, e.g., *al-Malaff al-Watha'iqi li-l-Mushir*, Part 2, 426, 431, 494.

36. Script writers: Usama Anwar 'Ukasha, *Layali al-Hilmiyya* 1987 (first season), 1988 (second season), 1989 (third season), 1992 (fourth season), 1995 (fifth season); producer: state-owned Egyptian TV.

37. For detailed info from the military's official websites, local newspapers, and government documents, see Abul-Magd, *Militarizing the Nation*, 152–85.

38. For information on defense conversion, see ibid., 117–25.

39. For example, one law issued in 1991: "Qanun Raqm 11 li-Sanat 1991 bi-Isdar Qanun al-Dariba al-'Amma 'ala al-Mabi'at," *al-Jarida al-Rasmiyya*, no. 18 (Tabi' Alif), 2 May 1991.

40. For detailed information from the military's official websites, local newspapers, and government documents, see Abul-Magd, *Militarizing the Nation*, 112–51.

41. Holger Albrecht, "The Myth of Coup-Proofing: Risk and Instances of Military Coups d'Etat in the Middle East and North Africa, 1950–2013," *Armed Forces and Society* 41, no. 4 (August 2014): 1–29.

42. Abul-Magd, *Militarizing the Nation*, 152–85.

43. See, e.g., Muhammad al-'Issawi, "Infijar Mawasir al-Miyah wa-l-Sarf Yghriq Sibin al-Kum," *al-Ahram*, 13 December 2010; 'Abd al-Mun'im Hijazi, "Sami 'Imara . . . Muhandis Takhrib al-Munufiyya," *al-Wafd*, 8 April 2011; and 'Umar Shawki et. al, "Sarf Sihhi . . . Masdud," *al-Misa*, 1 November 2013.

44. For detailed information on acquired or new enterprises, see Abul-Magd, *Militarizing the Nation*, 126–36.

45. See, e.g., Dalia 'Uthman, "al-Mushir Yaftatih Masna' Asmant al-'Arish," *al-Masry al-Yawm*, 1 May 2012, https://www.almasryalyoum.com/news/details/1784430.

46. Egyptian Center for Social and Economic Rights, "al-Mudhakkira al-Ula al-Muqaddama min al-Markaz al-Masri fi Qadiyyat 'Ummal Hilwan," http://ecesr.org/?p=1018; "al-Mudhakkira al-Thaniyya al-Muqaddama min al-Markaz al-Masri fi Qadiyyat 'Ummal Hilwan," http://ecesr.org/?p=1014; "al-Mudhakkira al-Thalitha al-Muqaddama min al-Markaz al-Masri fi Qadiyyat 'Ummal Hilwan," http://ecesr.org/?p=1021, all accessed 1 June 2014; Dar al-Khadamat al-Niqabiyya, "Waqa'i' Muhakamat 'Ummal Masna' 99 al-Harbi," 22 August 2010, http://www.ctuws.com/?item=511.

47. "Istighatha min 'Ummal al-Sharika al-Misriyya li-Islah wa-Bina' al-Sufun bi-l-Iskandariya," *Tadamun Misr*, 23 July 2008, https://tadamonmasr.wordpress.com/2008/07/23/%D8%A7%D8%B3%D8%AA%D8%BA%D8%A7%D8%AB%D8%A9-%D9%85%D9%86-%D8%B9%D9%85%D8%A7%D9%84-%D8%A7%D9%84%D8%B4%D8%B1%D9%83%D8%A9-%D8%A7%D9%84%D9%85%D8%B5%D8%B1%D9%8A%D8%A9-%D9%84%D8%A5%D8%B5%D9%84/; "Ihdar Huquq 'Ummal al-Misriyya li-l-Sufun wa-l-Sijn al-'Askari li-l-Mu'tarid," *al-Badil*, 6 April 2015.

48. Bassam Haddad, Max Ajil, and Zeinab Abul-Magd, "State, Market, and Class: Egypt, Syria, and Tunisia," in *A Critical Political Economy of the Middle East and North Africa*, ed. Bassam Haddad and Sherene Seikaly (Stanford, CA: Stanford University Press, 2021), 46–67.

49. Mu'taz Nadi, "Bi-l-Video . . . Film al-Jaysh: 30 Yunyu laysa Inqilab wa-Mursi Inhaz li-l-Ikhwan," *al-Masry al-Yawm*, 14 July 2013; Bel Trew, "Welcome to the Department of Morale Affairs: Belly Dancers, Billboards, and Egypt's Military Propaganda Machine," *Foreign Policy*, 15 January 2013, https://foreignpolicy.com/2014/01/15/welcome-to-the-department-of-morale-affairs/.

50. Zeinab Abul-Magd, "Egypt's Revolt of the Poor," *Foreign Policy*, 31 March 2017, https://foreignpolicy.com/2017/03/31/egypts-coming-revolt-of-the-poor/; Abul-Magd, "The Egyptian Military's Economic Solution: Is It Working?," Italian Institute for International Political Studies, 15 March 2018, https://www.ispionline.it/en/pubblicazione/egyptian-militarys-economic-solution-it-working-19866.

51. See, e.g., Muhammad Hamam, "Hadhihi Hiya al-Qita'at al-Iqtisadiyya Allati Dakhalaha al-Jaysh fi 12 Shahr," *Mada Masr*, 3 September 2016, https://www.madamasr.com/ar/2016/09/03/feature/%D8%A7%D9%82%D8%AA%D8%B5%D8%A7%D8%AF/%D9%87%D8%B0%D9%87-%D9%87%D9%8A-%D8%A7%D9%84%D9%82%D8%B7%D8%A7%D8%B9%D8%A7%D8%AA-%D8%A7%D9%84%D8%A7%D9%82%D8%AA%20%D8%B5%D8%A7%D8%AF%D9%8A%D8%A9-%D8%A7%D9%84%D8%AA%D9%8A-%D8%AF%D8%AE%D9%84%D9%87%D8%A7/. For detailed data, see Yezid Sayigh, *Owners of the Republic: An Anatomy of Egypt's Military Economy* (Washington, DC: Carnegie Middle East Center, 2019).

52. Nisma Tallima, "Gouda Abdel-Khalek li-l-Ahali . . . ," *al-Ahali*, 8 January 2020.

53. Nisma Tallima, "al-Mudir al-Tanfidhi li-Sunduq Tatwir al-'Ashwa'iyyat al-Muhandis Khalid Siddiq . . . ," *al-Ahali*, 11 March 2020. For examples about displaced slums, see Zeinab Abul-Magd, "Diaries of a Surveilled Citizen after a Failed Revolution in Egypt," *International Journal of Middle East Studies* 53, no. 1 (2021): 145–54.

54. See, e.g., Wazarat al-Ittisalat, Bayan I'lami, "Waziray al-Intaj al-Harbi wa-l-Ittisalat Yabhathan al-Ta'awun fi Mashru'at al-Mujtama' al-Raqami," 26 June 2018; and Hossam Bahgat, "Tafasil Istihwaz al-Mukhabarat al-'Amma 'ala I'lam al-Misriyyin," *Mada Masr*, 20 December 2017, https://www.madamasr.com/ar/2017/12/20/feature/%D8% B3%D9%8A%D8%A7%D8%B3%D8%A9/%D8%AA%D9%81%D8%A7%D8%B5%D9 %8A%D9%84-%D8%A7%D8%B3%D8%AA%D8%AD%D9%88%D8%A7%D8%B0- %D8%A7%D9%84%D9%85%D8%AE%D8%A7%D8%A8%D8%B1%D8%A7%D8%AA- %D8%A7%D9%84%D8%B9%D8%A7%D9%85%D8%A9-%D8%B9%D9%84%D9%89//.

55. Muhammad Zayn, "Hiwar Ra'is 'Ma'lumat al-Intaj al-Harbi' Yakshif Aliyyat Hadhf Ghayr al-Mustahiqqin min al-Tamwin," *Akhbar al-Yawm*, 12 September 2019, https://akhbarelyom.com/news/newdetails/2911143/1/%D8%AD%D9%88%D8% A7%D8%B1--%D8%B1%D8%A6%D9%8A%D8%B3--%D9%85%D8%B9%D9%84%D9% 88%D9%85%D8%A7%D8%AA-%20%D8%A7%D9%84%D8%A5%D9%86%D8%AA%20 %D8%A7%D8%AC-%20%D8%A7%D9%84%D8%AD%D8%B1%D8%A8%D9 %8A--%D9%8A%D9%83%D8%B4%D9%81-%D8%A2%D9%84%D9%8A%D8%A9- %D8%AD%D8%B0%D9%81-%D8%BA%D9%8A%D8%B1-%D8%A7%D9%84%D9%85% D8%B3%D8%AA%D8%AD%D9%82%D9%8A%D9%86-%D9%85%D9%86-%D8%A7%D 9%84%D8%AA%D9%85%D9%88%D9%8A%D9%86-(%D9%81%D9%8A%D8%AF%D9% 8A%D9%88).

56. Hiba al-Sayyid, "al-Misriyya li-l-Ittisalat: I'timad Ta'yin Tariq al-Zahir Mumathil 'an al-Hukuma bi-Majlis al-Idara," *al-Yawm al-Sabi'*, 10 January 2019, https://www. youm7.com/story/2019/1/10/%D8%A7%D9%84%D9%85%D8%B5%D8%B1%D9 %8A%D8%A9-%D9%84%D9%84%D8%A7%D8%AA%D8%B5%D8%A7%D9%8 4%D8%A7%D8%AA-%D8%A7%D8%B9%D8%AA%D9%85%D8%A7%D8%AF- %D8%AA%D8%B9%D9%8A%D9%8A%D9%86-%D8%B7%D8%A7%D8%B1%D9%82- %D8%A7%D9%84%D8%B8%D8%A7%D9%87%D8%B1-%D9%85%D9%85%D8 %AB%D9%84%D8%A7%D9%8B-%D8%B9%D9%86-%D8%A7%D9%84%D8%A D%D9%83%D9%88%D9%85%D8%A9-%D8%A8%D9%85%D8%AC%D9%84%D 8%B3/4099387; Rahma Ramadan, "Iftitah Masna' Intaj al-'Addadat al-Dhakiyya," *al-Yawm al-Sabi'*, 31 October 2018, https://www.youm7.com/story/2018/10/31/%D8%A7% D9%81%D8%AA%D8%AA%D8%A7%D8%AD-%D9%85%D8%B5%D9%86%D8%B9- %D8%A5%D9%86%D8%AA%D8%A7%D8%AC-%D8%A7%D9%84%D8%B9%D8%AF% D8%A7%D8%AF%D8%A7%D8%AA-%D8%A7%D9%84%D8%B0%D9%83%D9%8A%D 8%A9-%D8%A8%D8%B7%D8%A7%D9%82%D8%A9-500-%D8%A3%D9%84%D9%81- %D8%B9%D8%AF%D8%A7%D8%AF-%D8%B3%D9%86%D9%88%D-9%8A%D8%A7/4013959.

57. Bahgat, "Tafasil Istihwaz al-Mukhabarat al-'Amma,"; "Falcon: Meet Egypt's Most Famous Security Company," *Egypt Independent*, 9 October 2014, https://egyptindependent.com/ falcon-meet-egypt-s-most-famous-security-company/; "Egypt's Most Famous Security Company 'Falcon' Seizes 'al-Hayah' Channel," *Egypt Independent*, 13 September 2017, https://egyptindependent.com/egypts-famous-security-company-falcon-seizes-al-hayah-channel/.

58. Nivin Yusuf, "Hal Bat al-Intaj al-Drami fi Misr Taht Saytarat al-Dawla," *BBC Arabic*, 6 May 2019, https://www.bbc.com/arabic/middleeast-48178108; Sara Ramadan, "Li-Man al-Ghalaba . . . Intaj al-Drama Bayna Ajhizat al-Mukhabarat wa-l-Qita' al-Khass," Mu'asassat Huriyyat al-Fikr wa-l-Ta'bir, Cairo, 23 December 2020, https://afteegypt.org/publicati ons_org/2020/09/23/20020-afteegypt.html.

59. See MoD's YouTube channel and Facebook page, accessed 30 December 2020, https://www. youtube.com/channel/UC5AvwPAoewLnAcNvCF8ZEhg, https://www.facebook.com/EgyA rmySpox.

60. "Muzaharat al-Khubz Tamtadd ila al-Qahira wa-l-Iskandariyya . . .," *Mada Masr*, 7 March 2017, https://www.madamasr.com/ar/2017/03/%2007/news/u/%D9%81%D9%8A-%D9%8A%D9%88%D9%85%D9%87%D8%A7-%D8%A7%D9%84%D8%AB%D8%A7%20 %D9%86%D9%8A-%20%D9%85%D8%B8%D8%A7%D9%87%D8%B 1%D8%A7%D8%AA-%D8%A7%D9%84%D8%AE%D8%A8%D8%B2- %D8%AA%D9%85%D8%AA%D8%AF-%D8%A5%D9%84%D9%89/.

BIBLIOGRAPHY

'Abd Allah, Ahmad. *Al-Jaysh wa-l-Dimuqratiyya fi Misr*. Cairo: Dar Sina li-l-Nashr, 1990.

Abdel-Fadil, Mahmoud, *al-Tahawwulat al-Iqtisadiyya fi al-Rif al-Misri (1952–1970)*. Cairo: al-Hay'a al-Misriyya al-'Amma li-l-Kitab, 1978.

Abdel-Malek, Anouar, *Egypt: Military Society; the Army Regime, the Left, and Social Change under Nasser*. New York: Random House, 1968.

Abul-Magd, Zeinab. "Diaries of a Surveilled Citizen after a Failed Revolution in Egypt." *International Journal of Middle East Studies* 53, no. 1 (2021): 145–54.

Abul-Magd, Zeinab. "Egypt's Revolt of the Poor." *Foreign Policy*, 31 March 2017, https://foreig npolicy.com/2017/03/31/egypts-coming-revolt-of-the-poor/.

Abul-Magd, Zeinab. "Fi al-Drama al-Misriyya . . . Dubbat al-Jaysh Laysu Abtal." *Al-Manassa*, 15 July 2017, https://almanassa.com/ar/story/4913.

Abul-Magd, Zeinab. *Militarizing the Nation: The Army, Business and Revolution in Egypt*. New York: Columbia University Press, 2017.

Albrecht, Holger. "The Myth of Coup-Proofing: Risk and Instances of Military Coups d'Etat in the Middle East and North Africa, 1950–2013." *Armed Forces and Society* 41, no. 4 (2014): 1–29.

Amin, Galal. *Madha Hadath li-l-Masriyyin: Tatawwur al-Mujtama' al-Misri fi Nisf Qarn, 1945–1995*. Cairo: al-Hay'a al-'Amma li-l-Kitab, 1999.

Ayubi, Nazih. *Al-Dawla al-Markaziyya fi Misr*. Beirut: Markaz Dirasat al-Wahda al-'Arabiyya, 1989.

Berger, Morroe. *Military Elite and Social Change: Egypt since Napoleon*. Princeton, NJ: Princeton University Press, 1966.

Gordon, Joel. *Revolutionary Melodrama: Popular Film and Civic Identity in Nasser's Egypt*. Chicago: Middle East Documentation Center, 2002.

Haddad, Bassam, Max Ajil, and Zeinab Abul-Magd. "State, Market, and Class: Egypt, Syria, and Tunisia." In *A Critical Political Economy of the Middle East and North Africa*, edited by Bassam Haddad and Sherene Seikaly, 46–67. Stanford, CA: Stanford University Press, 2021.

Al-Malaff al-Watha'iqi li-l-Mushir Muhammad 'Abd a-Halim Abu Ghazala. Cairo: Markaz al-Ahram li-l-Tanzim wa-l-Mikrufilm, 1981–89.

Mostafa, Dalia Said. *The Egyptian Military in Popular Culture: Context and Critique*. London: Palgrave Macmillan, 2017.

Naguib, Muhammad. *Kuntu Ra'isan li-Misr: Mudhakkirat Muhammad Najib*. Cairo: al-Maktab al-Masri al-Hadith, 1984.

Springborg, Robert. *Mubarak's Egypt: Fragmentation of the Political Order*. London: Westview Press, 1989.

Springborg, Robert. "Professional Syndicates in Egyptian Politics, 1952–1970." *International Journal of Middle East Studies* 9, no. 3 (1978): 275–95.

Trimberger, Ellen. *Revolution from Above: Military Bureaucrats and Development in Japan, Turkey, Egypt, and Peru*. New Brunswick, NJ: Transaction Books, 1978.

CHAPTER 25

ARCHIVES OF OUR DISCONTENT

Nationalism and Historiography after 2011

PASCALE GHAZALEH[1]

SINCE 2011, Egypt has undergone such profound changes that parts of the physical landscape are unrecognizable to visitors who have not seen the country since before the uprising. Politically, economically, and culturally, boundaries have shifted. The urban landscape has changed, sometimes dramatically: in downtown Cairo alone, new landmarks have sprung up, for example in Tahrir Square, now anchored by an obelisk that refers to a past far more ancient and pervasive than that of the uprising. Elements that were part of the background have taken center stage, while features Egyptians took for granted seem never to have existed. Despite these far-reaching transformations, of course, the past weighs heavy on the regime and the population alike, shaping horizons of possibility and limiting what may be articulated in word or deed. How, then, has history been imagined and produced in Egypt since 2011? How has the regime co-opted the past to project itself into the future? What alternative visions of the past exist, and how have they been articulated?

Since the 2011 Egyptian uprising, various (re)productions of the past have occurred. By examining how different groups and institutions perceive and present history, it becomes possible to see history as a site of contestation where rival imagined nations jostle for space. As the actor with a preponderance of material and symbolic resources, the regime is the most prolific producer of legitimizing narratives. To position itself as the rightful heir to a nation born of military triumph and successful mega projects, the regime must invent a genealogy connecting it to an ancient Egyptian past while emphasizing its modernity and referencing its piety. It has done so by deploying authority in three arenas simultaneously: the archives, the heritage industry, and the media. More importantly, the regime has sought to foreclose alternative narratives that could threaten its monopoly over history and posit itself as the only actor entitled to articulate truth about the past. The result of its interventions is the occultation of history as a public domain, on the one hand, and the transformation of the past into a commodity whose value is precisely equal to its ability to generate revenue, on the other.

As Achille Mbembe has suggested, "The relationship between the archive and the state . . . rests on a paradox. On the one hand, there is no state without archives—without its archives. On the other hand, the very existence of the archive constitutes a constant threat to the state. . . . The act that creates the state is an act of 'chronophagy.'"[2] Scholars who study the archive's conditions of production have shown that regimes everywhere engage in similar practices of categorizing and policing, as well as silencing, destroying, and repressing. In the Middle East, this is true of colonial and postcolonial regimes alike. Most recently, Rosie Bsheer has analyzed incisively how the Saudi regime has engaged in "archive wars" designed to bolster its legitimacy by selectively collecting and suppressing documents that told histories and suggested futures diverging from the official Saudi narrative. As Omnia El Shakry has pointed out, in other countries emerging from the colonial period "the archive has functioned as a dense locus of post-colonial power, and its impermeability has often masked the precise nature of the political and social debates that went into the consolidation of regimes in the aftermath of decolonization."[3]

Analyzing the case of Egypt since the 2011 uprising that toppled President Husni Mubarak and replaced him with a Muslim Brotherhood cadre, Muhammad Mursi, who was unseated in turn by a general, Abdel Fattah El-Sisi, conveys how a "chronophagous" regime reworks the past, producing history through archives, museums, textbooks, the media, and the built heritage, while bulldozing, closing, or burying pasts it deems unworthy of preservation. It also enables an exploration of the conditions of possibility that shape (paraphrasing Ann Stoler) what can be written, what warrants repetition, what competencies are rewarded in archival writing, what stories cannot be told, and what cannot be said.[4]

DANGEROUS SCHOLARS

Scholars in the humanities and social sciences are acutely aware of the power structures, political stakes, and mechanisms of repression that underlie the research process.[5] In the Middle East, as elsewhere, it has become common for writing about the research process to precede, and sometimes to replace, the research process itself, so fraught with risk has academic work become, whether in the field or in the archives. The archival turn in this region is inextricably associated with wider military and political conflicts in which archives serve as pawns or sacrifices. The disappearance of archives, whether through deliberate destruction, neglect, incorporation into commercial circuits, or the imposition of draconian security measures, shapes in turn the construction of certain narratives at the expense of others. The archival turn is not merely an intellectual movement or a methodological choice; it is becoming an inescapable condition of research.

Scholars in much of the region face acute, concrete obstacles when attempting to gain physical access to archives. Historians working on sites of recent or ongoing conflicts

(Syria, Iraq, Libya, and Yemen) face insurmountable difficulties in recovering historical documents. From where we stand today, it is entirely possible to see how the politics of destruction, dissimulation, and selective amnesia will limit how historians work in the future—what they are able to recover and how they are able to read it. Archives that have been looted and expatriated, even when they are accessible to researchers, are also afflicted by this violent rupture: the Ba'th Party papers, for example, were not so much made available for scholarly investigation as deployed to be used as evidence of Saddam Husayn's atrocities and thereby to justify US military intervention in Iraq.[6]

Even in countries not torn apart by war, research is fraught with real, immediate risks beyond the routine harassment, intimidation, or stonewalling that scholars have come to accept as the price for access to information. It is telling that the torture and murder of Giulio Regeni, an Italian student at Cambridge University who was writing his dissertation on independent trade unions in Egypt, were immediately incorporated into the spectrum of possible risks that academics must reckon with before embarking on research. The incident also canceled the margin of immunity that researchers from abroad had previously enjoyed.

Regeni's murder, however brutal and absurd, was the logical culmination of the "security mindset" that Khaled Fahmy has identified as pervading the Egyptian academic and scientific landscape since 2011. The struggle to control scholars and the narratives about Egypt they produce has been particularly acute since 2013 when Egypt's current president Abdel Fattah El-Sisi took power. Starting in 2014, state bodies and academic institutions (themselves often affiliated with the state) began imposing restrictions on travel for faculty and researchers. The prevailing atmosphere of xenophobia, furthermore, expanded the definition of "foreignness" to include Egyptian scholars living or studying abroad. Waleed Salem, for instance, an Egyptian PhD student at Washington University who was conducting research on the judiciary in Egypt, was detained while leaving the country, and the security forces withdrew his passport. After seven months of pretrial detention followed by fifteen months of precautionary measures, including the requirement that he check in at his district police station several times per week, he remained in limbo, unable to continue working on his dissertation or to leave the country.[7] Alia Mosallam, a historian based in Berlin, where she is working on a postdoctoral project on the 1919 Egyptian revolution, was detained on returning to Egypt, where she was visiting family, and questioned by state security for long hours before being released. Patrick Zaki, who was pursuing a postgraduate degree in women and gender studies at the University of Bologna, was detained on returning to Egypt in February 2020. He eventually received a presidential pardon in July 2023.

In July 2021, Egypt's minister of state for migration, Nabila Makram 'Abd al-Shahid, provided confirmation of official suspicion directed against Egyptian academics abroad, noting that her ministerial mandate included those studying outside Egypt. The ministry's goal, she said, was to "deepen the spirit of loyalty" and to create "a strong bond with their mother country" in order to defend them against violent extremists seeking to plant erroneous ideas in their minds. Interestingly, the minister said she had been misquoted as having described these students as "the greatest threat to Egypt" and claimed she had actually said they were the most exposed to threats of the sort she was describing.[8] This clarification notwithstanding, the charges leveled against academics are similar to those used to target political activists: publishing rumors that aim "to disturb social peace and sow chaos"; inciting protest; calling for the overthrow of the state; undermining social order and public safety via social media; and "incitement to commit violence and terrorist crimes."[9]

ABSENCES, INVENTED AND REAL

Threats to researchers constitute just one way that public access to information is regulated in Egypt and elsewhere in the region today. Others include closing off access to the archives, which in Egypt have been placed under the authority of the security apparatus since late 2013.[10] Shortly after Egypt's current president seized power, historians applying for permits to carry out research in the archives noticed that these permits were taking far longer to be processed than had previously been the case. Whereas the application process had previously taken weeks, now it took months or even years. In addition, many applications were now being rejected, even when the proposed research focused on seemingly tame topics such as eighteenth-century agrarian practices or early twentieth-century educational reforms. Informally, it was rumored that research proposals containing certain words (e.g., *land*, *class*, *state*, *border*) would be rejected out of hand. In addition to increased security measures, the first-line gatekeepers of the past—the staff of the reading rooms—became ever more diligent in ensuring that researchers viewed as a potential threat to national security would not have access to the records they sought.[11]

It has long been common knowledge among historians of Egypt that certain attitudes and topics are less likely than others to curry favor with staff members at the National Archives. Gender norms and national origin are two factors that play a part in determining whether a scholar will be able to access the materials they need for their research, even if they have overcome the initial hurdle of the permit. Anyone affiliated with an Israeli institution is likely to discover that none of the sources they wish to consult can be found. Women of any nationality will realize that modest dress and a deferential demeanor improve the chances that useful documents will suddenly materialize.

The archives housed in Dar al-Mahfuzat (which contains the documents produced by Egypt's civil courts, registers related to land administration during the Ottoman period, and birth and death certificates) at the Cairo Citadel are also guarded by a series of institutional and individual gatekeepers. Personal anecdotes abound: one man who sought a copy of his grandfather's birth certificate was told that none of the employees would enter the storerooms because they were full of rats; when he said he was willing to brave them, the employees informed him they had introduced snakes to get rid of the rats and that he may try again a few years hence. One scholar who did gain access to Dar al-Mahfuzat offered several tips to colleagues seeking to work on the material kept there:

permission must be sought from the Ministry of Finance; a security guard will follow the researcher everywhere and observe every note they take; and research is limited to three hours per day.

Still, the diligence of a few individuals, or the "security mindset" that informs the functioning of various government bodies—a mindset so widespread as to warrant the description of systematic or institutionalized (quite unlike the documents that it seeks to safeguard against the "wrong kinds" of questions)—cannot account for all that is missing from the potential archives. One young PhD student who was writing her dissertation on Muhammad 'Ali's military campaigns in the Hijaz found that every box of files she consulted contained, at most, one or two documents. Rumor had it that wealthy Saudis had bought most of that collection.[12] Whatever the motives prompting such purchases, the disappearance of original archival material is common, as is the circulation of documents and photographs in commercial networks.[13]

In the 1990s, Saudi purchasers were also interested in a newer archive: the negatives of classic Egyptian films. Two Saudi satellite television channels are now said to own most of these negatives, bought up, according to some in the Egyptian cinema industry, to compensate for the lack of an indigenous Saudi film archive ("The blunt comparison being between an indebted nation with so much historic accumulation that it's being sold or given away as gifts, and another that is rich enough not to care about historical capital, but is able to buy its way when needed").[14] Thus, despite the authorities' great care to police access to certain archives, the market for different types of historic artifacts remains vibrant, especially when such artifacts are not perceived as having any relevance to the image the regime wishes to project.

Maps as Menace

After 2013, the Egyptian state extended and strengthened its control over the archives, not merely as an attempt to control the historical narratives that could emerge from the records kept there, but also as an assertion of its exclusive right to own them and dispose of them as it sees fit. It did so by virtue of the status it claims as the guardian of national identity against attempts to besmirch it, whether by foreigners or disloyal citizens. This bid to limit access to the archives reached a paroxysm of intensity in 2016 when a territorial dispute revealed the contemporary geopolitical power that archives could have when left unguarded for even a moment.

The dispute concerned the Red Sea islands of Tiran and Sanafir, which the Egyptian government transferred to Saudi Arabia in 2016, claiming that the islands had always belonged to Saudi Arabia and that Egypt had only exercised custodianship over them on the Saudis' behalf. Tiran and Sanafir, while small and deserted, hold great strategic importance due to their position in the Strait of Tiran, the entry point to the Gulf of Aqaba. In return for Tiran and Sanafir, Egypt was supposed to receive twenty-two billion USD in oil and development aid from Saudi Arabia over the following five years.[15]

Widespread opposition to the deal developed: street protests broke out in April and May 2016, and the authorities arrested hundreds of activists. An agreement setting maritime boundaries in a way that attributed the islands to Saudi Arabia was nevertheless pushed through the courts and parliament and went into effect in June of the same year. This development only galvanized popular discontent, which spread among Egyptian citizens of all walks of life, from parliamentarians to amateur historians. Khalid 'Ali, a lawyer known for his defense of human rights and labor activists, filed a case against the government challenging the decision on the islands and posted a request for assistance on social media. In response, hundreds of people came forward to bring him historical maps, atlases, geographical surveys, textbooks, birth certificates, and other documents showing that Egypt had controlled the islands since at least 1906—in direct contradiction with El-Sisi's claims that Egypt had only administered the islands on Saudi Arabia's behalf since the 1950s.[16]

To the regime, the Tiran and Sanafir affair was a clear reminder of how dangerous historical documents could be to its popularity and its strategic deployment of history as a legitimating device. Suspicion toward scholars redoubled after 2017. Khaled Azab, a specialist in Islamic archaeology and the head of a prestigious project titled "Egypt's Memory" at the Bibliotheca Alexandrina, whose good standing with the authorities was enshrined in such accolades as the State Award for Excellence in the Social Sciences, which he received in 2016, was suddenly arrested at his home in April 2019. The charges against him ("spreading false news and misusing social media") seem to have been related to a post on his Facebook page regarding the theft and auction of a Mamluk-era Qur'an, but some speculated that his role in posting historical maps that showed Tiran and Sanafir on the Bibliotheca Alexandrina's website had been a more compelling motive for his arrest. The authorities' understanding of national security grew ever more amorphous and far-reaching; increasingly, those defined as threats to state security in the broadest and most vague sense were conflated with potential traitors of the nation, the disloyal citizens whose national identity had to be challenged not at the borders, but on the street or in government offices.

The vulnerability of state power accounts for part of the protective hysteria demonstrated by self-appointed gatekeepers of the past. More importantly, it is simply the right to scrutinize, assess, approve, or reject—the right to pass judgment on who may speak of the past and what questions they may ask—that the security institution claims. What is at stake, in other words, is the assertion of uncontested ownership of the past, a claim that includes the right to interrogate that past or, on the contrary, to let it languish, unexamined, for as long as its sentinels decide.

Building on the Past

In contrast to the recent past, Pharaonic history might be deemed a safe space, sufficiently distant in time to be relatively uncontroversial. Indeed, the state has appropriated its symbolism since the beginning of the twentieth century to emphasize the common ground shared by Christian and Muslim Egyptians. The mausoleum of Sa'd Zaghlul, a leader of the nationalist movement that after World War I sought independence from British occupation, is a textbook example of how Pharaonic revivalism served to illustrate the slogan "Religion is for God and the nation for all." Even at the time of Zaghlul's death in 1927, the style of the mausoleum was the subject of debate, with some public figures arguing for a neo-Pharaonic style of the 1920s, others for an Arabo-Islamic revival style, and still others for a Napoleonic style.[17] The proponents of neo-Pharaonism won out, and the tomb's structure and ornamentation are profoundly inspired by ancient Egypt. No sooner was it finished, though, than it became the site of another symbolic confrontation when Mahmud Sidqi, the royalist prime minister, placed twenty-four mummies from the Egyptian Museum next to the leader of the 1919 revolution in his final resting place. As Hussein Omar notes, "Piling the uninvited mummies alongside Zaghlul was Sidqi's way of arguing that the popular leader had been as much of a tyrant as the kings that preceded him."[18] Two years later, Sidqi resigned and the mummies were returned to the museum.

Gamal Abdel Nasser (r. 1954–70) is better known for nationalizing the Suez Canal and losing the 1967 war than for promoting Egypt's Pharaonic heritage, but it was during his time as president, in 1963, that the Mallawi Museum was created. Located near al-Minya, it seems to have been conceived as an initiative to bring history out of the capital and the ivory tower and into Upper Egypt, making it accessible to people who could not visit the Egyptian Museum. This project was in line with Nasser's more populist orientations and may be seen as a snub to the colonial and urban elitist genealogies of modern Egyptology.

Starting in the 1980s, ancient Egypt once again became fertile ground for the deployment of contending articulations of national identity, as evidenced by a renewed surge of awareness of Egyptology as a field from which Egyptians were largely excluded and growing demands for the repatriation of Egyptian antiquities from European museums, coupled with criticism of government officials who could not or would not prevent the widespread theft of and trade in artifacts.[19] At the same time, as archeologist Monica Hanna points out, the pharaohs remained synonymous with polytheism and despotism in some branches of religious discourse.[20] Despite his ambivalence toward ancient Egyptian heritage—which he downplayed to appease religious sensibilities, according to some analyses, or to express reverence for the kings of antiquity, according to others—Anwar al-Sadat (r. 1970–81) was assassinated by Islamist militants who marked the event by proclaiming, "We have killed Pharaoh."[21] Although Pharaonic iconography might thus be deemed too politicized to function as a universally palatable nationalist symbol, the Supreme Constitutional Court, which overlooks the Nile south of Cairo, was built in 2000 in a style that observers dubbed "Mickey Mouse Pharaonic"—a hulking take on a temple in reinforced concrete, with entrances "designed to allow complete separation between the different types of circulation (judges, public, VIPs, employees)."[22]

The current regime is strategic in its deployment of ancient Egyptian heritage. At times, it eschews neo-Pharaonism in favor of a Graeco-Roman aesthetic, as in the New al-'Alamayn City, a vast project along Egypt's Mediterranean coast.[23] At others, it combines Pharaonic symbolic references with Islamic motifs, as in the New Administrative Capital, where lotus-capped columns are surrounded by the ninety-nine names of God.[24]

While neo-Pharaonism may no longer serve as a leading architectural reference for government buildings, actual Pharaohs are important to the regime in spectacular assertions of legitimacy. The Pharaohs' Golden Parade was a televised spectacle widely hailed as a public relations success for the government and El-Sisi personally. In April 2021, twenty-two mummies traveled from the Egyptian Museum in Tahrir Square (the same square that was the symbolic epicenter of the 2011 uprising) to the new Museum of Egyptian Civilization in al-Fustat (a center of Egyptian Christian and Jewish houses of worship and cemeteries, as well as the site where 'Amr Ibn al-'As, the Muslim conqueror, built Egypt's first mosque in 642). Hussein Omar noted acerbically that the vehicles constructed to transport the mummies resembled not ancient chariots, as intended, but rather the armored vans "used to haul off political prisoners."[25]

Next, El-Sisi inaugurated Sphinx Avenue, connecting the temples of Karnak and Luxor. Excavation of the three-thousand-year-old avenue had begun under Mubarak—the inauguration was initially planned for 20 February 2011; however, by then, the president had stepped down.[26] Hundreds of buildings had already been demolished, and the project's estimated cost had reached over seven million USD when work was suspended. At the opening ceremony, which finally took place in November 2021, no one mentioned Mubarak. Like the mummies' parade, the event was a spectacle designed for a television audience and targeted mainly non-Egyptian viewers. A documentary screened during the event and titled *Luxor Secret* portrayed the town as a haven of tourist attractions and tolerance; the minister of culture singled out the General Intelligence Service for thanks in his speech.[27]

Ancient Egypt has served the regime in other ways since 2013. School textbooks, for example, establish a filiation with the past based on a selective reading of ancient Egyptian history; the national curriculum social studies textbook for fifth grade praises the stability, military strength, and territorial integrity achieved by rulers like Narmer and Thutmoses III, noting: "The Egyptian army through the ages was characterized by its adherence to moral values in dealing with civilians and civilian installations."[28]

Pharaonic artifacts and aesthetics constitute some of the most emblematic of the historical repertoires used to signify Egypt, but they are by no means the only ones. Regardless of whether they can name the builders of the Mamluk mausolea, Cairenes and Egyptians outside the capital are no doubt familiar with the image of a forest of minarets rising from the cemeteries. Second to Pharaonic structures and representations, Islamic architecture serves to identify Egypt to the outside world. Here, too, one finds conflicts over who has the right to speak of these structures, decide what they can and cannot represent, and dispose of them. Conservationist practices in Cairo are sites of intense contention because of the vast number of extant structures. Debates over such practices are eminently political because so many aspire to speak on behalf of heritage posited as mutually exclusive; as elsewhere, staking claim to the past means projecting one's vision into the future and establishing the authority to imbue space and built structure with legitimacy.

Thus, while the very concept of Islamic Cairo may be seen as a construct that initially gained currency through imperialist practices, its place in the shared imaginary of what constitutes Egypt, carved out and shaped during the twentieth century, is now established. Every Egyptian regime since the late 1970s has sought to assert its piety and dedication to upholding a socially conservative and morally rigid interpretation of Islam, and the current one is no exception. Yet the principle of state exigency trumping private property, on the one hand, and historical value, on the other, has rarely been asserted as openly as now. This architecture's current deterioration is common knowledge; equally well known are stories about the contracting companies, hastily repackaged as experts in historical architecture, bidding to capture lucrative deals in the growing restoration industry. After 2013, when large infrastructure projects began to impinge publicly on swathes of Cairo, displacing residents in the drive to widen highways, build bridges, and establish a new presidential capital, the regime demolished parts of the Cairo Necropolis. The families of those buried in the tombs targeted for removal, as well as historians and conservationists, expressed their outrage on social media and in articles and interviews. Yet, although the area is on UNESCO's World Heritage List, the Egyptian Supreme Council of Antiquities—while denying that any buildings of historical value were torn down—provided a spectacular example of closing the stable door after the horse's departure when it "created a committee to inspect the remains of the demolition to decide if any decorated or inscribed debris should be displayed in museums."[29]

The government gives itself the right to determine which parts of the built heritage are worthy of conservation and showcasing and which can or should be demolished for different reasons, whether profit, strategic considerations, or political purposes. The wholesale destruction of dwellings in the Maspero–Ramlat Bulaq area, perceived as a center of resistance during the 2011 uprising, can be seen as combining two of these exigencies: the neighborhood is now under development by a company belonging to the Sawiris family, whose financial clout has allowed it to carve out spheres of relative autonomy within the Egyptian real estate market. Maspero and Ramlat Bulaq (between the 26th of July Corridor and the 6th of October Bridge) house the Ministry of Foreign Affairs building and the Maspero radio and television building as well as a host of other commercial and government buildings; it is home to several Ottoman mosques and, until recently, was also the site of nineteenth-century buildings that combined European and Arab motifs in a manner characteristic of Khedive Isma'il's era. The neighborhood was home to a thriving secondhand clothing and textile market, small wood and iron workshops, and informal dwellings, built in the interstices of the original layout. Although the initial plan for redevelopment provided for the residents to be housed on-site, many of them accepted financial compensation and/or relocation to a closed neighborhood on the outskirts of the city.[30] Residential buildings have largely been razed; while the implementation of the development plan raised a host of issues, the one that gained the most sympathy from international journalists and urban intellectuals was the loss of an underappreciated architectural heritage, not the displacement of thousands of residents.[31]

Although preserving built heritage and respecting the rights of those who live in and around it are not necessarily contradictory, the conservation debate in contemporary Egypt tends to portray them as such. A small number of restoration experts and urbanists are working to protect the urban fabric and make community participation an integral part of work on monuments: Athar Lina (The Monument Is Ours), perhaps the most successful of these, has been building ties and organizing events in the Khalifa neighborhood for years while engaging in participatory restoration. The project now includes an annual invitation to tour al-Khalifa, with activities for children and awareness-raising events for residents and visitors. This is particularly rare in a city so divided that some university students, raised in upmarket compounds on the outskirts of Cairo, have only a vague idea of where or what downtown Cairo is; for them, the word *downtown* evokes not Tahrir Square but the name of a mall near the American University in Cairo's new campus.

Who owns the city, and who owns its past? These questions have different answers depending on whom one asks and when. In the late nineteenth century, the inhabitants of what came to be called Islamic Cairo saw the city as theirs; they owned or rented their living spaces and worked in the centers of production and commerce nearby. But it was during that time, after the 1867 Paris Exposition, that French specialists designated the area around the mosques of al-Azhar and al-Husayn as Islamic Cairo and earmarked it as worthy of conservation—from its inhabitants, if necessary. Cairenes soon became involved in the heritage industry, where historic preservation was the ostensible goal, but "medieval" Islamic Cairo was a project largely confined to European and local elites. Although it did not take the preferences of the area's residents into account, it affected their lives: "Displacement, relocation, and the reordering of social rituals and patterns were only some of the ramifications of the making of 'medieval' Islamic Cairo. The true actors and audiences of this new geography were scholars and professionals from such newly founded disciplines of the eighteenth and nineteenth centuries as Egyptology, archaeology, architecture, and urban planning. With rare exception, they lived outside the space of 'medieval Islamic Cairo,' either within other areas of Cairo, or in Europe."[32]

In the decade from 2011 to 2021, the situation in Islamic Cairo changed in many respects. For one thing, more than one hundred historic buildings in al-Darb al-Ahmar, the Cairo district where Mamluk and Ottoman architecture is concentrated, were torn down and replaced with high-rises after central authority collapsed in 2011.[33] A frenzy of demolition and construction occurred as soon as the authorities' attention was elsewhere; properties that were entangled in inheritance disputes or that were registered monuments were destroyed to make room for more profitable buildings. If one is interested in laying blame for this process, at least part of it should be placed at the doorstep of a conservation industry that continues to regard buildings as historically valuable only for the tourism revenues or restoration contracts they can generate. Intellectual elitism and economic neoliberalism together have placed the built heritage in an impossible situation—either it becomes part of a vast open-air museum, surrounded by empty space where people once lived and worked, or it must give way to more profitable ventures. Simultaneously, espousing the idea of heritage and its value has become an important marker of class distinction, as a plethora of Facebook pages dedicated to Egypt in "the good old days" indicates. While some of these pages embrace the image of a liberal, Europeanized Egypt—a country where the middle class could ascend into modernity unimpeded, where women wore miniskirts and couples frolicked on empty beaches—others are specialized in the types of photographs popularized by Swiss travelers Lehnert and Landrock and titled "Native Quarters" or "Arab Woman." Social media thus offers a space where self-identified archivists or guardians of the past may "negotiate ideal social imaginaries."[34]

CONTROVERSIAL COMMEMORATIONS

While monument making and nationalist spectacle have been carefully designed for mass consumption by passive spectators, and conservation has been a space largely reserved for elites, within Egypt or outside it, other ways of making history have been more open and accessible to a wider public. Commemorations of noteworthy events tend to receive media attention and encourage participation from historians— even those from the provinces, often marginalized in interactions with European and North American academia due to lack of funding, language barriers, or the encyclopedic, empiricist tendencies of history departments at Egyptian universities. Commemorations are also interesting because—unlike iconography and mass education, which are designed to generate consensus and are relatively durable features of the nationalist landscape—they are events into which it is necessary to pack sometimes-contradictory messages; they are also inherently fragile and often lack even a baseline agreement on what is being commemorated. The two hundredth anniversary of the end of the French Expedition to Egypt (1798–1801) was one such ambiguous commemoration. Calling it "l'année franco-égyptienne," "cultural institutions in France and Egypt planned a wide range of events—from academic conferences to book publications and gala exhibitions—to commemorate the special relationship or, as it was officially labeled, 'les horizons partagés,' that this colonial encounter engendered."[35]

Another controversial event is the 1919 revolution, which sought Egypt's emancipation from British colonial rule. Within Egypt, the revolution's legacy and meaning have been contentious topics, with two political parties, the New Wafd and the Nasserists, clashing at a conference held in 2009 to commemorate its ninetieth anniversary. When the Nasserists criticized the 1919 revolution for being bourgeois, the New Wafd asserted that the 1952 revolution was a military coup. Several senior Wafd members walked out in protest.[36] Jabir 'Asfur, the former minister of culture, wrote an article titled "1919, Ninety Years On: The Revolutionary and the Reformist,"[37] in which he extolled the separation of religious institutions from the state, a line in keeping with his secularist stance.[38]

Ten years later, the 1919 revolution's one hundredth anniversary provided the impetus for an outpouring of articles, videos, concerts, television shows, and conferences. The American University in Cairo marked the occasion with considerable pomp.[39] One main message was national unity, understood to mean harmony between Egypt's Muslim majority and Coptic minority, which faces institutional discrimination and (especially for poorer rural Copts) outbreaks of violent persecution. The image of a priest ascending the pulpit of al-Azhar to deliver a sermon, evoked in Naguib Mahfouz's *Palace Walk*, inspired some journalists in 2019 to write self-congratulatory articles[40]—none of which, naturally, mentioned the October 2011 Maspero massacre, in which twenty-four protestors, most of them Copts, were killed by security forces and the army after they had staged a peaceful sit-in.[41] Substantive discussion of 1919 and the changes that have come about since—the preponderance of the military in the country's political and economic landscape, sectarian tensions, the worsening plight of the working class, the fate of an increasingly desperate middle class, the dismal state of public education—was, in contrast, lacking, and 1919 was largely reduced to the celebration of national independence and religious harmony. Nor (unsurprisingly) did celebrations of the Wafd Party's role in the uprising, which hyped the affiliation of the New Wafd with Sa'd Zaghlul's party,[42] refer to the peasant and worker revolts that preceded 1919.[43] Commemorations of 1919, then, served to showcase a particular idea of Egypt in the first decades of the twentieth century: a nation of well-dressed and well-behaved revolutionaries, emancipated yet understated women (with Huda Sha'rawi as their genteel representative), a signal lack of class conflict, and harmony between crescent and cross.

While the armed forces did not take part in the 1919 commemorations—indeed, their silence on this front was testimony to their inability to affiliate themselves with (or co-opt) the values of the revolution—they did celebrate another event with considerable fanfare. On 11 November 2013, the Military Research Department of the Egyptian Armed Forces staged a grand event commemorating the ninety-ninth anniversary of the outbreak of World War I. The assistant to the minister of defense delivered a speech that highlighted "the heroic sacrifices of the Egyptian army in that war, and its magnificent deeds, which changed the course of military history, and which contributed to the upkeep of lofty principles of human civilization."[44]

What was odd, writes Khaled Fahmy, was that this was the first time anyone had mentioned the Egyptian Armed Forces participating in World War I. For ninety-nine years, the army had never staged any such commemoration, but then suddenly, in 2013, and for the following four years, the army staged huge celebrations, with a different major-general delivering the same speech, verbatim, each year. These commemorations of the Egyptian army's glorious achievements in World War I (involving between one hundred thousand and 1.5 million men, according to different accounts), Fahmy observed, were based on spurious claims made by a scuba diving enthusiast who had examined shipwrecks off Egypt's northern coast. Significantly, these claims, and the commemorations that were based on them, served to elide the factual participation in the war effort of a quarter million Egyptians, mostly peasants, who were drafted into the Labor Corps and sent to various fronts.[45] Fahmy concludes in indignation that "by relying on a charlatan, [the present Egyptian army] has convinced itself that the Egyptian Labor Force was composed of soldiers not of peasants, that this force was part of the Egyptian not the British army, and that the sacrifices endured during the war were endured by the military rather by the civilian population."[46]

While this is an extreme example of historical distortion and obfuscation, perhaps it also points to the military's need for genealogical legitimacy. By asserting (even fictitious) ties with past victories, it draws attention away from potential scrutiny of its present capabilities, or lack thereof, on the battlefield. Projecting an aura of battle-readiness is crucial to the military's image as a "factory of men," exacting yet benevolent with civilians and ruthless toward Egypt's "enemies." This may be why it marked the forty-eighth anniversary of the 1973 war by reopening the military museum at the Cairo Citadel. The museum, closed in 2011, was refurbished extensively and opened to the public on 6 October 2021; among other artifacts, it includes a collection of statues of "Egyptian kings who led military campaigns, such as Thutmose III," indicating that successful belligerence is a sufficient condition for inclusion.[47]

The event that undermines this aura is, of course, the 1967 war—a black hole of sorts in the collective psyche, inexplicable in its devastating finality.[48] Every part of the story seems to derive its absurdity from the founding paradox: a state run by military men, defeated before it had arrived on the battlefield. Indeed, narratives of the 1967 war often lead to a logical dead end—questions that cannot be answered, or can only be answered by reference to individual corruption, evil, or incompetence, rather than systemic dysfunction or structural breakdown. This is at least partly because, as Omnia El Shakry notes, "the archive has functioned as a dense locus of post-colonial power, and its impermeability has often masked the precise nature of the political and social debates that went into the consolidation of regimes in the aftermath of decolonization."[49]

Thus, the war was lost because a spy betrayed his country, or a president bluffed his way to the brink, or an inept commander decided to shut off the air defense systems—not because the economy was collapsing, education was abysmal, or the leadership had been pouring resources into its war against various potentially threatening social forces at home and in the region. Nasser resigned but was convinced to return, whether by popular acclaim or to assuage popular rage. Field Marshal 'Abd al-Hakim 'Amir committed suicide or was compelled to do so.

The military defeat thus became an analytical and historiographical failure: a way of explaining (away) all subsequent developments, from economic liberalization to the rise of Islamism, from political corruption to the bankruptcy of the left. Moral judgment, which we should understand as being exempt from the requirements of logic or rationality, has served to invoke and dismiss the least plausible moments in the war: the decision to disable the air defense system at the peak of hostile posturing; the withdrawal of UN troops from the Sinai buffer zone; the abandonment of troops in the desert. Emotion, serving here as the antithesis of politics, justified and precluded questioning about the aftermath. Political space continued to shrink, authoritarianism to flourish, and the military to consume ever more space "because of the *hazima* (defeat)."

Political histories of the war, while emphasizing the ruptures in the chain of command and the turning points induced by betrayal, present a succession of implausible premises with cataclysmic conclusions: sending troops to Yemen while escalating tension with Israel; switching off air defense systems on the eve of the war; issuing contradictory orders; leaving troops exposed in Sinai; or losing an entire air force within hours. Such narratives have had the effect of shutting down analysis or even comprehension of the war, even for those who participated in it, whether as soldiers or citizens. Pervasive despair precluded understanding or demands for real accountability.

In her memoirs, Arwa Salih reflects on the effect of the 1967 defeat on the student movement, whose activists had believed "that liberation from colonialism and Western imperialism went hand in hand with class struggle." The young leftists of Salih's generation had led the protests, she writes, "'in the name of an insurgent dream: to change the future of the nation, to save it.' But her generation became 'superfluous' before it could realize any of its dreams: 'Barely launched on its journey into politics, art and science, it was quashed along with the world it had attempted to bring into being.' It had grown 'suddenly old; its children became incomplete projects—a stillborn generation.'"[50] As Salih remembers it, then, the event of the military defeat, like a black hole, collapsed and subsumed personal experience. The student activists became "incomplete projects." As Manfred Sing has noted, even the new wave of social criticism that unfurled after the war, entailing public criticism of shortcomings in politics and society and theorizing the absence or failure of revolutionary mass movements, used terms such as *takhalluf* and *ta'akhkhur* to understand this absence rather than articulating alternatives.[51]

The idea that the defeat was also an individual personal experience of annihilation has been voiced most recently by Shakir Jarrar, one of the writers who contributed to a commemorative book published by *Mada Masr* for the fiftieth anniversary of the war. "Perhaps the worst thing about the June defeat," he writes, "is the way it made the defeat permanent and entrenched it, not as a military defeat in the context of a conflict against Israel—which, like all conflicts, would imply the possibility of winning one battle and losing another—nor as a defeat tied to the Arab leadership, but as the reflection of a distortion in our 'selves.'"[52]

Screening the Nation's Histories

In the absence of state archives that would allow historians to make sense of Egypt's history since 1952, El Shakry has suggested that we "look to the textured local debates, endogenous forces, and minor literatures" to better understand the struggles that mark an ongoing process of decolonization.[53] In many ways, the present is an ideal moment for this effort, as the El-Sisi regime endeavors daily to sanitize, censor, and repackage the past. While this process is underway, it remains possible to unpack some of its workings and perhaps even to hamper its attempt to foreclose not only alternative histories but also dissenting visions of the future.

The regime has been intensely preoccupied with the ways media can bolster its legiti-macy; El-Sisi is said to have admired Nasser's control of radio and television and to have made draconian oversight his goal, though in the age of digital media this seems like a Sisyphean task. Censoring, blocking websites, monitoring social media, and producing its own publicity and feature films are among the means adopted by the state in its attempts to achieve this end. Television is perhaps one of the easier media to control, notwithstanding the existence of multiple satellite channels, and is still one of the most important ways of making meaning about the past, especially in a country where literacy rates average 70%. Television series and historical fiction are both popular genres and effective means of establishing links with the past, whether to justify the present or celebrate it.

In the past decade or two alone, the television landscape has changed considerably. Lila Abu-Lughod's *Dramas of Nationhood* is perhaps the most recent major work in English to examine Egyptian television from an anthropologist's perspective, and its conclusions already seem dated.[54] One significant development is the media company "shopping spree" undertaken by Egypt's General Intelligence Service, which in 2017 be-came sole or part owner of several media groups.[55] By 2021, Synergy, a company owned by the intelligence service, was producing several of the television series that most Egyptians watch avidly during Ramadan. It was thus unsurprising that several of the Ramadan 2021 series glorified the police and the military, portraying them as working selflessly in the shadows to protect unsuspecting citizens from untold dangers. One popular show was *al-Ikhtiyar 2* (The Choice 2), which recounted the heroic exploits of police officers confronting terrorist plots in the aftermath of the 2013 Rab'a massacre (which the synopsis refers to as "breaking up the sit-in").[56] Another, *Hajma Murtadda* (Counterstrike), starring Hind Sabri and Ahmad 'Izz, followed well-dressed young in-telligence agents as they foiled multiple plots hatched on various fronts to destabilize Egypt before 2011. Reinforcing the message that research is inherently suspect, episode twenty-four showed the director of a research center hiring Hind Sabri for purposes later revealed as nefarious: to recruit and train enthusiastic young people who would take over after the region's regimes had been overthrown because they were "bad for business." The director revealed part of his treacherous hidden agenda in episode twenty-six, when he suggested to the students that Egypt's victory in the 1973 war was not as decisive as they had been led to believe.

In these and other series, the message delivered by Synergy-produced shows was that citizens could not know of the many dangers that face the security forces in their dif-ferent guises. These dangers are directed against the state, its loyal citizens, and the re-gime, a wise and benevolent power led by its sense of duty to punish the recalcitrant and reward its obedient children. This message was conveyed in blatant, even crude terms but couched in slick productions put together by advertising executives. In the Ramadan dramas, the recent past was repackaged to justify the regime's existence, nat-uralize the military's involvement in political life, celebrate the bravery and selfless-ness of the security forces, and identify the ruthless enemies of the nation (Islamists, Arabs—the accents in *Hajma Murtadda* suggest the characters are Syrian, Palestinian, or Qatari—and researchers).

Yet Egyptians are not passive consumers of slick regime propaganda. One Synergy-produced show halted production because the outcry the trailer triggered on social media could not be ignored. The series, titled *The King* and based on the Naguib Mahfouz novel *Kifah Tiba* (Thebes at War), portrayed Pharaoh Ahmose as a staunch and intrepid ruler and extolled his triumphs in defending Egypt against the Hyksos. When the trailer was released, however, the social media backlash was so virulent that production was paused just weeks before the series was to air while the director addressed historical inaccuracies. Among commentators' objections was that the star of the show, Amr Youssef, was seen as "foreign looking" because of his blond hair, light skin, and green eyes. Other historical inaccuracies included the actors' beards and mustaches as well as their costumes, which even Zahi Hawass, the "Indiana Jones of Egyptology," criticized as anachronistic.[57]

Apart from sometimes-virulent media criticism, popular responses to the state's uses of history have been limited. Perhaps this is because the onslaught of material and symbolic transformations has been overwhelming; contending with rapid erasures and the dissemination of new realities leaves little space for alternatives. The Tiran and Sanafir case stands out as one of the only times when a concerted, far-reaching popular alternative to the state's narrative was articulated effectively. Still, on social media and among young researchers, inside and outside academic settings, history is enormously popular. Military history buffs, amateur historians, alternative education associations, and young scholars are all working, explicitly or not, on the question of who owns the past. Their efforts sometimes garner audiences in the tens of thousands: one Facebook page devoted to the history of Ismailia, a city in the Suez Canal zone, has forty thousand followers. There are organizations devoted to documenting the history of cities and neighborhoods, serving as vehicles for the promotion of a community's noteworthy features but also as a means of unearthing and preserving a past that has been neglected, ignored, or silenced.[58]

There are other ways of contesting the state's claim to exclusive ownership of the past, arguably less legitimate than those just mentioned. Since 2011, archaeologists have noted a dramatic rise in the number of looting incidents, especially from sites in Middle Egypt, where residents are struggling to make a living in the absence of tourism. Clearly, looting cannot be included among the efforts to articulate alternative histories, but—at least in cases that do not involve the international antiquities mafia—it arguably constitutes the assertion of local rights of ownership over artifacts that would otherwise be displayed in the capital, viewed by elites, and used to generate revenue that will not benefit residents. The looters, after all, are following the same neoliberal logic as the state, which regards history as a commodity, extracted from its context and valued for its market price.

Conclusion

This contribution to the study of nationalism and historiography in contemporary Egypt does not claim to be exhaustive. It has suggested that public historiography in Egypt is beset with enormous tensions. These are due, at least partly, to the fact that the single most important development in Egypt since 1952 has been the army's rise to power and transformation into a major economic actor. This also happens to be a phenomenon that historians (and other scholars) cannot approach due to the closure of the archives and entire fields of investigation on the pretext of security imperatives.[59] Indeed, the armed forces seem to be pushing for the securitization of academic fields (like Ottoman history) that were not previously subject to such scrutiny.[60]

In the interplay of nationalism and historiography since 2013, the exclusion of certain social groups from the regime's answer to the question of "who owns the past?" has expanded in proportion to how recent that past is. The process of Saturn devouring his children gained such momentum that even the 30 June 2013 "coup-volution," in which El-Sisi seized power, was quickly excised from the textbook narrative of Egypt's modern history. In 2017, the Ministry of Education removed passages referring to both the 25 January 2011 uprising and the 30 June 2013 military coup from the high school history curriculum. A committee on educational reforms had recommended this expurgation. As ministry officials explained, topics related to the causes and results of the "revolution" of 30 June "may cause more troubles and problems both in schools and during setting exams." They added that "Documenting historical events needs at least 15 years." The 23 July 1952 Free Officers' revolution was thus the last political upheaval mentioned in the new history curriculum.[61]

Notes

1. I presented some of the ideas outlined here at the Forum Transregionale Studien (Berlin) in 2017–18, as a Georg Forster Fellow of the Alexander von Humboldt Foundation. This chapter is part of a wider project on property and citizenship, initiated through a grant from the Arab Council for Social Sciences in 2013 and further developed within the framework of a working group led by Simona Cerutti and Isabelle Grangaud at the École des Hautes Études en Sciences Sociales (Paris). Some paragraphs of this chapter appear in an account of my personal experience in the Egyptian National Archives; see Pascale Ghazaleh, "Past Imperfect, Future Tense: Writing People's Histories in the Middle East Today," *Perspectivia, Essays of the Forum Transregionale Studien* 5 (2019), https://www.perspectivia.net/receive/pnet_mods_00001161.
2. Achille Mbembe, "The Power of the Archive and Its Limits," in *Refiguring the Archive*, ed. Carolyn Hamilton et al. (Dordrecht, Netherlands: Kluwer Academic Publishers, 2002), 23.
3. Omnia El Shakry, "'History without Documents': The Vexed Archives of Decolonization in the Middle East," *The American Historical Review* 120, no. 3 (2015): 924.
4. Laura Ann Stoler, "Colonial Archives and the Arts of Governance: On the Content in the Form," *Archival Science* 2 (2002): 91.
5. See Lara Deeb and Jessica Winegar, *Anthropology's Politics: Disciplining the Middle East* (Stanford, CA: Stanford University Press, 2015).
6. Wisam H. Alshaibi, "Weaponizing Iraq's Archives," *Middle East Report* 291 (2019), https://merip.org/2019/09/weaponizing-iraqs-archives/.

7. "AFTE Calls on the Egyptian Government to Allow Researcher Waleed Salem to Travel after His Passport Was Withdrawn," Association of Freedom of Thought and Expression, 28 July 2020, https://afteegypt.org/en/advocacy-en/statements-en/2020/07/28/19768-afteegypt.html; and Evan Bush, "Egypt Releases UW Doctoral Student from Prison—but Uncertainty Remains amid Crackdown on Free Expression," *Seattle Times*, 22 December 2018, https://www.seattletimes.com/seattle-news/egypt-releases-uw-doctoral-student-from-prison-but-uncertainty-remains-amid-crackdown-on-free-expression/

8. "Wazirat al-Hijra: Abana'una bi-l-Kharij Akbar Shariha Mu'arada li-l-Khatar wa-Layssu Akhtar min al-Kharij," *al-Yawm al-Sabi'*, 3 July 2021, https://www.youm7.com/story/2021/7/13/5505388/أخطر-وليسوا-للخطر-معرضة-شريحة-أكبر-بالخارج-أبناؤنا-الهجرة-وزيرة.

9. "Campaigns: Free Patrick," Egyptian Initiative for Personal Rights, https://eipr.org/en/campaigns/free-patrick.

10. The precise nature of the body overseeing the archives is uncertain; researchers refer to it as *al-amn* but are unsure whether it is affiliated with national security (*mukhabarat*), general intelligence (*mabahith*), or the military. See Khaled Fahmy, "Ma'lumat Awwaliyya 'an Dar al Watha'iq al-Qawmiyya," 6 June 2015, khaledfahmy.org.

11. See, e.g., Lucia Carminati, "Dead Ends in and out of the Archive: An Ethnography of Dar al Watha'iq al Qawmiyya, the Egyptian National Archive," *Rethinking History* 23, no. 1 (2019): 34–51; and Chloe Bordewich, "I Am Still Not a Spy," 16 January 2017, https://chloebordewich.wordpress.com/2017/01/16/i-am-still-not-a-spy. I have written in some detail about my attempts to secure security clearance for research at the archives; see Ghazaleh, "Past Imperfect, Future Tense."

12. In *Archive Wars: The Politics of History in Saudi Arabia* (Stanford, CA: Stanford University Press, 2020), Rosie Bsheer traces the Saudi government's efforts to collect as much archival material as possible in order to present a sanitized and hegemonic vision of Saudi Arabian history.

13. See Lucie Ryzova, "Mourning the Archive: Middle Eastern Photographic Heritage between Neoliberalism and Digital Reproduction," *Comparative Studies in Society and History* 56, no. 4 (2014): 1027–61, on the quest for photographs. The increasing interest in original historical material is not incompatible with broad-based access. Digitization of private collections, while it entails acceptance that the original artifacts are no longer available to the public, can nevertheless make images and contents accessible.

14. Muhammad A. Jawad, email correspondence with the author, 22 October 2021. On the purchases, see Said Sadek, "Cairo as Global/Regional Cultural Capital?," in *Cairo Cosmopolitan: Politics, Culture, and Urban Space in the New Globalized Middle East*, ed. Diane Singerman and Paul Amar (Cairo: American University in Cairo Press, 2006): 71.

15. Karim Adel Kebeish, "Tiran & Sanafir: A Historical and Constitutional Argument Opposing the Territorial Cession of the Tiran and Sanafir Islands to Saudi Arabia," *Texas Law Review* 97, no. 4 (2019): 835–58.

16. Beesan Kassab and Jano Charbel, "Lawyers, MPs Say Tiran and Sanafir Are Egyptian," *Mada Masr*, 11 January 2017, https://madamasr.com/en/2017/01/11/feature/politics/lawyers-parliamentarians-say-tiran-and-sanafir-are-egyptian/.

17. Mohamed Elshahed, "The Tomb of Saad Zaghloul," Cairobserver, 30 March 2012, https://cairobserver.com/post/20143117045/the-tomb-of-saad-zaghloul#.YaKAwS_72L1.

18. Hussein A. H. Omar, "Mummies on Parade," *London Review of Books*, 6 April 2021, https://www.lrb.co.uk/blog/2021/april/pharaohs-on-parade.

19. See the text of Law No. 117 (1983), amended by Law No. 3 (2010) for an attempt to regulate smuggling of antiquities and to repatriate looted artifacts: https://en.unesco.org/sites/defa ult/files/egypt_law3_2010_entof.pdf.

20. Monica Hanna, "Documenting Looting Activities in Post-2011 Egypt," in *Countering Illicit Traffic in Cultural Goods: The Global Challenge of Protecting the World's Heritage*, ed. France Desmarais (Paris: ICOM, 2015): 47–63.

21. Michael Wood, "The Use of the Pharaonic Past in Modern Egyptian Nationalism," *Journal of the American Research Center in Egypt* 35 (1998): 186. Sadat had prohibited public viewing of the mummies in 1980, after the sight of Ramses II covered only by a thin cloth shocked him; Jeffrey Bartholet, "Forsaken Mummies to Be Housed in Digs Worthy of Ramses," *Chicago Tribune*, 5 November 1986, https://www.chicagotribune.com/news/ct-xpm-1986-11-05-8603230175-story.html.

22. "Egyptian Supreme Constitutional Court," Archnet, https://archnet.org/sites/5063/media_contents/46575. On the mausoleum of Ataturk, which serves many of the same purposes, see Christopher S. Wilson, "Representing National Identity and Memory in the Mausoleum of Mustafa Kemal Atatürk," *Journal of the Society of Architectural Historians* 68, no. 2 (2009): 224–53.

23. "In Pics: Sisi, Bin Zayed Tour New el-Alamein City," *Egypt Today*, 29 March 2019, https://www.egypttoday.com/Article/1/67610/In-Pics-Sisi-Bin-Zayed-tour-New-El-Alam ein-city.

24. I would like to thank filmmaker Muhammad A. Jawad for this reference and for pointing out the state's endeavors to override the negative autocratic connotations of the Pharaonic heritage through an "Islamopharaonic reconciliation." He notes the camera lingering on "al-Fattah" in the promotional video "Watch the New Administrative Capital Turn into a Green Paradise in Record Time," YouTube, 11 October 2021, https://www.youtube.com/watch?v=A2REFbrJ-i8. Private correspondence with the author, 22 October 2021.

25. Omar, "Pharaohs on Parade."

26. "Mubarak and Berlusconi to Inaugurate Luxor's Sphinx Avenue," *Egypt Independent*, 11 January 2011, https://egyptindependent.com/mubarak-and-berlusconi-inaugurate-lux ors-sphinx-avenue/.

27. Egyptian State Information Service, "The Opening Ceremony of the Sphinx Avenue in Luxor," 25 November 2021, https://sis.gov.eg/Story/160245/The-Rams-Road-Celebration-in-Luxor?lang=en-us.

28. *Al-Dirasat al-Ijtima'iyya. Watani Misr. Al-Ard wa-l-Hadara* (*Social Studies. Egypt, My Country. Land and Civilization*), fifth year primary, first term, 2022–23.

29. Pariesa Young, "Graves in Egypt Relocated and Demolished to Make Space for a Highway," *France 24*, 24 July 2020, https://observers.france24.com/en/20200724-graves-egypt-relocated-demolished-highway.

30. On Bulaq, see especially Nelly Hanna, *An Urban History of Bulaq in the Mamluk and Ottoman Periods*, Supplément aux Annales Islamologiques, No. 3 (Cairo: Institut Français d'Archéologie Orientale, 1983); for comments on the urban fabric and the disruption of urban life, see Mona Abaza, "Egyptianizing the American Dream: Nasr City's Shopping Malls, Public Order, and the Privatized Military," in *Cairo Cosmopolitan*, 200–202. Abaza notes that "The aggressive process of 'cleaning up' and consequently modernizing the area started late in the Sadat era (1970–81), when the government decided to relocate five thousand working-class families from Bulaq to the public-housing area of al-Zawya al-Hamra." For a critique of the plan, see "Cairo 2050," Cairo from Below: Information and Debate on

the Urban Future of Cairo, https://cairofrombelow.org/cairo2050/; for a thorough study of the area, see "al-Nashatat, al-Tahmish wa-'Alaqat al-Quwa fi Ramlat Bulaq: Sinaryyuhat al-Taghyyir al-'Umrani wa-l-Ijtima'i," 'Ashara Tuba, http://www.10tooba.org/en/wp-cont ent/uploads/2016/04/Transformation-of-Ramlet-Bulaq-2016.pdf; for an investigation of Asmarat, where residents were to be rehomed, see Mostafa Mohie, "Asmarat: The State's Model Housing for Former 'Slum' Residents," trans. Salma Khalifa, *Mada Masr*, 18 June 2018, https://www.madamasr.com/en/2018/06/18/feature/politics/asmarat-the-states-model-housing-for-former-slum-residents/.

31. Farid Farid, "'How Can a Proud Country Kill Its Heritage?' Cairo Calls Time on Oldest Watch Shop," *Guardian*, 7 August 2018, https://www.theguardian.com/cities/2018/aug/07/cairo-redevelopment-plan-calls-time-on-egypts-oldest-watch-shop.

32. Nezar Alsayyad et al., eds., *Making Cairo Medieval* (Lanham, MD: Lexington Books, 2005), 2.

33. Patrick Werr, "'Blindsided by the Beauty': Architects Struggle to Save Cairo's Historic Heart," Reuters, 11 September 2019, https://www.reuters.com/article/us-egypt-culture-idUSKCN1VW1K3.

34. Nermin Elsherif, "Sociotechnical Imaginaries of a Modern Past: Facebook as an Exhibition of Middle-class Subjects and their Narratives of *the Great Old Days*," unpublished presentation, EUME Summer Academy, American University in Beirut, August 2019; and Elsherif, "The City of al-Zaman al-Gamil: (A)political Nostalgia and the Imaginaries of an Ideal Nation," *Égypte: Monde arabe* 23 (2021): 1–18.

35. Elliott Colla, "Non, non! Si, si!: Commemorating the French Occupation of Egypt (1798–1801)," *Modern Language Notes* 118 (2003): 1043–69.

36. Giedre Sabaseviciute, "Re-creating the Past: The Manipulation of the Notion of Rupture in Egyptian Revolutions," *La Révolution française,* Rupture(s) en Révolution, 17 December 2011, http://journals.openedition.org/lrf/348.

37. Jabir 'Asfur, "Thawrat 1919 ba'd Tas'in 'Aman: al-Thawri wa-l-Islahi," *Shorouk News*, 21 May 2009, https://www.shorouknews.com/columns/view.aspx?cdate=21052009&id=40817 3bf-0e7a-4c4c-90c9-944ee82cd7ad.

38. Ashraf Khaled, "University Sacking Exposes Religious, Political Tensions," *University World News*, 12 May 2017, https://www.universityworldnews.com/post.php?story=201705 10115423262.

39. Nahla El Gendy, "Celebrating Egypt's 1919 Revolution," American University in Cairo, 11 March 2019, https://www.aucegypt.edu/news/celebrating-egypts-1919-revolution.

40. For example, Mahir Hasan, "100 Sana 'ala Thawrat 1919," *al-Masry al-Youm*, 8 March 2019, https://www.almasryalyoum.com/news/details/1376521.

41. Amr Khalifa, "Maspero: A Massacre Revisited," Tahrir Institute for Middle East Policy, 9 October 2014, https://timep.org/commentary/analysis/maspero-massacre-revisited/.

42. "Wafd Party Celebrates 100th Anniversary of Egypt's 1919 Revolution," *al-Masry al-Youm*, 10 March 2019, https://cloudflare.egyptindependent.com/wafd-party-celebrates-100th-anniversary-of-egypts-1919-revolutionwafd-party-celebrates-100th-anniversary-of-egy pts-1919-revolution/.

43. Alia Mosallam, "al-Wajh al-Akhar li-Thawrat 1919 al-Misriyya: Thawrat Fallahi al-Hamamiyya," Bidayyat 23/24 (2019), https://bidayatmag.com/node/1052.

44. Statement cited in Khaled Fahmy, "The Great Theft of History: The Egyptian Army in the First World War," Khaled Fahmy: Reflections on Egypt, the Middle East, and History,

11 November 2019, https://khaledfahmy.org/en/2019/11/11/the-great-theft-of-history-the-egyptian-army-in-the-first-world-war/.

45. Alia Mosallam, "Strikes, Riots and Laughter: Tracing a Geography of Resistance by Egyptian Workers in World War I," EUME Berliner Seminar, 5 December 2018, https://www.eume-berlin.de/en/events/calendar/details/strikes-riots-and-laughter-tracing-a-geography-of-resistance-by-egyptian-workers-in-world-war-i; and Kyle J. Anderson, "The Egyptian Labor Corps: Workers, Peasants, and the State in World War I," *International Journal of Middle East Studies* 49, no. 1 (2017): 5–24.

46. Fahmy, "The Great Theft of History."

47. "In Photos: Military Museum at Salaheddin Citadel Inaugurated in Celebration of October War Anniversary," *Ahram Online*, 12 October 2021, https://english.ahram.org.eg/News/426765.aspx.

48. I presented some of the ideas in the following paragraphs at the conference of the Arab Council on Social Sciences, Beirut, April 2019.

49. El Shakry, "History without Documents," 924.

50. Arwa Salih, *The Stillborn: Notebooks of a Woman from the Student-Movement Generation in Egypt*, trans. Samah Selim (Chicago: University of Chicago Press, 2018). See Ursula Lindsey, "Lessons of Defeat: Testimonies of the Arab Left," *The Point* 18, 14 January 2019, https://thepointmag.com/2019/politics/lessons-of-defeat-testimonies-of-the-arab-left?fbclid=IwAR1XEzRKH_R9Gkrzom2TXrXDU2aTB01JaheuUm_yId3SVzqvYSD3ieCzmW0.

51. Manfred Sing, "Arab Self-Criticism after 1967 Revisited: The Normative Turn in Marxist Thought and Its Heuristic Fallacies," *Arab Studies Journal* 25 (2017): 144–90.

52. Shakir Jarrar, "Hazimat Man? Naqd al-Manhaj al-Thaqafawi fi Tahlil Asbab Hazimat 1967," *Malaff 67: Khamsuna 'Aman 'ala Harb Huzayran 1967, Mada Masr* special dossier (June 2017): 14.

53. El Shakry, "History without Documents," 934.

54. Lila Abu-Lughod, *Dramas of Nationhood: The Politics of Television in Egypt* (Chicago: University of Chicago Press, 2004).

55. Hossam Bahgat, "Looking into the Latest Acquisition of Egyptian Media Companies by General Intelligence," *Mada Masr*, 21 December 2017, www.madamasr.com/en/2017/12/21/feature/politics/looking-into-the-latest-acquisition-of-egyptian-media-companies-by-general-intelligence/.

56. Part 2 was subtitled *Rijal al-Zull* (Shadow Men), https://elcinema.com/work/2064777/.

57. "'El-Malek' Series Resumes Filming Following Outcry," *Daily News Egypt*, 17 April 2021, https://dailynewsegypt.com/2021/04/17/el-malek-series-resumes-filming-following-outcry/.

58. "Ismailia History Unfolded," Facebook Group, https://www.facebook.com/groups/286802905054757/. The Canal cities are especially active in this regard: an association for documenting Ismailia's untold history also exists. See Shirin Shaltut, "al-Ismailia al-Maskut 'anha," *Gomhuria Online*, 21 February 2021, https://www.gomhuriaonline.com/Gomhuria/781800.html?fbclid=IwAR21CPSvolCmuTomjGYC8NN0Bh1H0Marzr-Tg018ddZGgEpEjGPLn5veSLM. I would like to thank Mohamed Yehia Kamel for these references and for conversations on alternative models of researching and teaching history.

59. See Zeinab Abul-Magd, *Militarizing the Nation: The Army, Business, and Revolution in Egypt* (New York: Columbia University Press, 2018).

60. See, e.g., Ghazaleh, "Past Imperfect, Future Tense."
61. "Educational Reforms Cuts Revolutionary Events," *Egypt Today*, 18 June 2017, https://www.egypttoday.com/Article/1/8050/Educational-reforms-cuts-revolutionary-events. See also M. Cherif Bassiouny, *Chronicles of the Egyptian Revolution and Its Aftermath, 2011–2016* (Cambridge: Cambridge University Press, 2017), 531–32.

BIBLIOGRAPHY

Bsheer, Rosie. *Archive Wars: The Politics of History in Saudi Arabia*. Stanford, CA: Stanford University Press, 2020.

Deeb, Lara, and Jessica Winegar. *Anthropology's Politics: Disciplining the Middle East*. Stanford, CA: Stanford University Press, 2015.

El Shakry, Omnia. "'History without Documents': The Vexed Archives of Decolonization in the Middle East." *The American Historical Review* 120, no. 3 (2015): 920–34.

Ibrahim, Mina. "SARD: The Story of a Research Center in Urban Cairo." In *Public Space, Public Sphere, and Publicness in the Middle East: Proceedings of the International Seminar*. Edited by Agnès Deboulet and Erina Iwasaki (Cairo: SIAS Working Paper Series 32, 2021), 31–38.

Mossallam, Alia. "History Workshops in Egypt: An Experiment in History Telling." *History Workshop Journal* 83, no. 1 (2017): 241–51.

Ryzova, Lucie. "Mourning the Archive: Middle Eastern Photographic Heritage between Neoliberalism and Digital Reproduction." *Comparative Studies in Society and History* 56, no. 4 (2014): 1027–61.

Seikaly, Sherene. "How I Met My Great-Grandfather: Archives and the Writing of History." *Comparative Studies of South Asia, Africa and the Middle East* 38, no. 1 (2018): 6–20.

Sleiman, Hana, and Kaoukab Chebaro. "Narrating Palestine: The Palestinian Oral History Archive Project." *Journal of Palestine Studies* 47, no. 2 (2018): 63–76.

INDEX

·······················

For the benefit of digital users, indexed terms that span two pages (e.g., 52–53) may, on occasion, appear on only one of those pages.

Figures are indicated by *f* following the page number